CW00589578

REFORMASI

REFORMASI

*The struggle for power in
post-Soeharto Indonesia*

Kevin O'Rourke

ALLEN&UNWIN

To the people of Indonesia

First published in 2002

Copyright © Kevin O'Rourke, 2002.

All rights reserved. No part of this book may be reproduced or transmitted in any form or by any means, electronic or mechanical, including photocopying, recording or by any information storage and retrieval system, without prior permission in writing from the publisher. The *Australian Copyright Act* 1968 (the Act) allows a maximum of one chapter or ten per cent of this book, whichever is the greater, to be photocopied by any educational institution for its educational purposes provided that the educational institution (or body that administers it) has given a remuneration notice to Copyright Agency Limited (CAL) under the Act.

Allen & Unwin
83 Alexander Street
Crows Nest NSW 2065
Phone: (61 2) 8425 0100
Fax: (61 2) 9906 2218
Email: info@allenandunwin.com
Web: www.allenandunwin.com

National Library of Australia
Cataloguing-in-Publication entry:

O'Rourke, Kevin, 1971– .
    Reformasi: the struggle for power in post-Soeharto Indonesia.

    Bibliography.
    Includes index.
    ISBN 1 86508 754 8.

    1. Indonesia – Politics and government – 1998– .
    2. Indonesia – Economic conditions – 1998– . I. Title.

320.9598

Set in 10/12 pt New Baskerville by Midland Typesetters, Maryborough
Printed by South Wind Production (Singapore) Private Limited

10 9 8 7 6 5 4 3 2 1

Contents

Preface   vii
Map of Indonesia   xi
Map of Jakarta   xii

PART I   HUBRIS OF THE ELITE
 1   Loomings   3
 2   Legacy   22
 3   Crisis of Confidence   38
 4   Predatory State   52
 5   Forcing Reform   74
 6   'Closer to God'   87
 7   Impeccably Amok   97
 8   Coup à la Java   118

PART II   TYRANNY OF THE ELITE
 9   Zing-a-Bust   139
10   Photocopying Soeharto   153
11   'Cruelism versus Cruelism'   166
12   'Stay Indoors'   174
13   Nail of the Universe   189
14   Oligarchy of the Party Bosses   197
15   Under-Democracy   213
16   'Slander is Worse than Murder'   238
17   Heroes of Integration   256

PART III   MELEE OF THE ELITE
18   Acrimony and Larceny   283
19   Guerilla Politics   297

20 Shock Therapy   323
21 East Timor Writ Large   340
22 'Raid Cendana'   359
23 State of Emergency   381
Epilogue   407

APPENDICES
Appendix I   Rupiah Exchange Rate   419
Appendix II   Short Biographies   420

Notes   430
Bibliography   468
Glossary   473
Notes on the text   478
Index   479

Preface

Reformasi relates Indonesia's political events from 1996 through 2001—a period marked by tumult, intrigue, tragedy and mystery.

The book is deliberately broad in scope, and it seeks to provide a 'holistic' account—that is, one that integrates subjects (such as banking, Islam and military history) that are too often considered in isolation. Because the events of the period lend themselves to a narrative format, the book proceeds chronologically. I have also sought to capture the drama of this period, but I have tried to avoid melodrama and 'craftsmanship'. I have therefore aspired to relating the events in a clear and credible style; the intention is to let the events and protagonists convey their own drama.

To support this narrative approach, I have emphasised careful research and annotation. This research effort would not have been possible without several factors: the preceding work of such authors as Adam Schwarz, Michael Vatikiotis, Hamish McDonald, Benedict Anderson, Howard Palfrey Jones and others; the liberalisation of the Indonesian press; and the Internet. The work of Indonesia's superb foreign press corps was particularly important, as was the Joyo News Service of the indefatigable Gordon Bishop.

The research for *Reformasi* builds upon my experience of writing the *Van Zorge Report*, a bi-weekly journal on Indonesian politics and economics. I performed this role from mid-1998 through early 2000, a period that coincided with much of the political tumult. During this time I conducted in-depth interviews with around 60 policy-makers, politicians, generals, Islamic leaders, academics, NGO figures, student activists and journalists. Sarwono Kusumaatmadja, Andi Mallarangeng and Azyumardi Azra were particularly helpful and enlightening; I refrain from naming a great many others because of the sensitive nature of this book, and the country's continued political uncertainty.

I certainly gained the most valuable insights from innumerable encounters with Indonesians from all walks of life. I first came to

Indonesia in 1990, and I have been living in Jakarta for seven years. Throughout this time I have been continuously amazed by the people of Indonesia. Ultimately, it is their graciousness—amid hardship—that inspired me to produce this book. *Reformasi* takes a hard look at Indonesian politics, but it does so in tribute to a wonderful people who, I believe, deserve better leadership.

Reformasi has been an entirely independent effort in that I've received no financial contributions or sponsorship of any sort. However, this book received a tremendous amount of support in terms of encouragement, advice, corrections and input. I am very fortunate indeed that such a large number of extraordinary people were eager to help. Rather than making a difficult effort to rank them in importance, this acknowledgements section will, like the book itself, follow chronologically.

My parents inspired my interest in both writing and government, and my brother Gerald first brought me to Indonesia at age 19. During my undergraduate studies at Harvard, Amir Soltani, Richard Patten and Don Johnston exerted strong influences on me. Jonathan Harris and Gene Galbraith first employed me in the securities industry in Jakarta, and Belinda Tan was an exceptional colleague and friend. And my experience of performing political risk analysis with Dennis Heffernan and James Van Zorge provided invaluable experience.

Gary Goodpaster convinced me to start this project, and important words of encouragement came from Mary Schwarz, Paul Wolfowitz and Adam Schwarz. Mark Hanusz's support was enthusiastic, astute and crucial. Peter Milne provided editing assistance, instructive ideas and myriad shows of support along the way. Christopher Lingle, John McBeth and John Haseman each provided generously of their time and patience to offer insights, corrections and instruction in their respective fields of expertise: economics, politics and military analysis.

Others who provided important input and encouragement include Chris Bendl, Michael Chambers, James Corcoran, Michael Horn, Kate Linebaugh, Rhea McGraw, David Roes, Frank Shea, John Su, Adnan Tan, Bjorn Thurmann, Roderick des Tombe, Fred Thomas and Edwin Wong. Dean Carignan performed a characteristically thorough and thoughtful critique of the text. My classmate Jean-Jacques Barrow lent his inimitable perspicacity. Arif Sani lent his graphic design expertise and I received help with photos from *Tempo*'s Pak Priatna, AFP's Carol Li, Kees Metselaar and the Gamma team. Other friends who have always been reliable are too numerous to mention, but they include Mike Graff, Peter Hogg, Quentin Jordan, Sean MaGuire, Dan Murphy, Jonathan Phillips and Sebastian Sharp. I am especially grateful to John O'Reilly, Arian Ardie and Christine Bader. From Allen & Unwin, Patrick Gallagher and Rebecca Kaiser have been enormously helpful and thoroughly professional throughout.

Having said all this, I alone am responsible for the misinterpretations,

inaccuracies and errors that no doubt exist within this text. I have refer-
enced the text with more than 1000 endnotes, but in many cases time
constraints prevented me from delving deeper and achieving greater
accuracy. I hope that some of the issues that I have been unable to fully
answer will eventually be resolved.

I have tried to delineate fact from supposition by consistently
denoting the latter as such. Nonetheless, I believe that perfect objectivity
is impossible to attain, and the interpretations and analysis in *Reformasi*
ultimately stem from my own sense of what can—and cannot—be reasonably deemed as 'fair'. I hope I have done justice to a story that richly
deserves just that.

A government post: that is everything and all things for one who is neither a farmer nor a tradesman. Wealth may vanish, families may disintegrate and reputations may fall, but the post must be secured. It is not just a livelihood—it's also prestige, righteousness, self-esteem and a way of life. People fight, pray, fast, slander, lie, work themselves to the bone and back-stab each other, all for the sake of a government post. One would sacrifice anything to obtain it—because with it, all can be restored.

—Pramoedya Ananta Toer, *Child of All Nations*

A corrupt regime has only one alternative: to stay in power.

—Siswono Yudohusodo

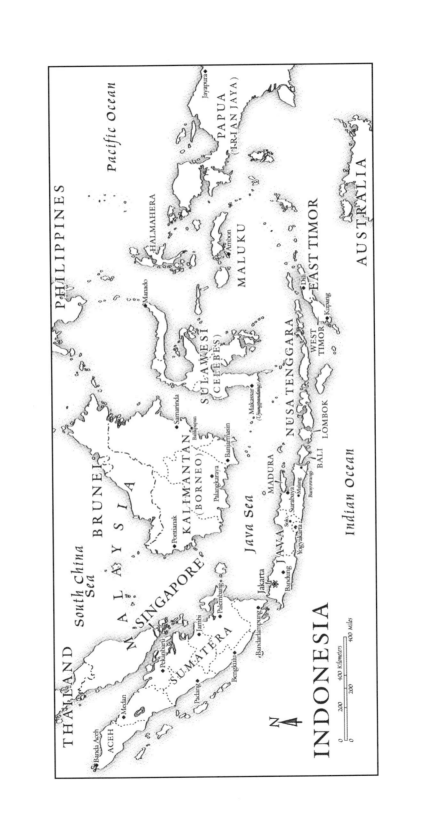

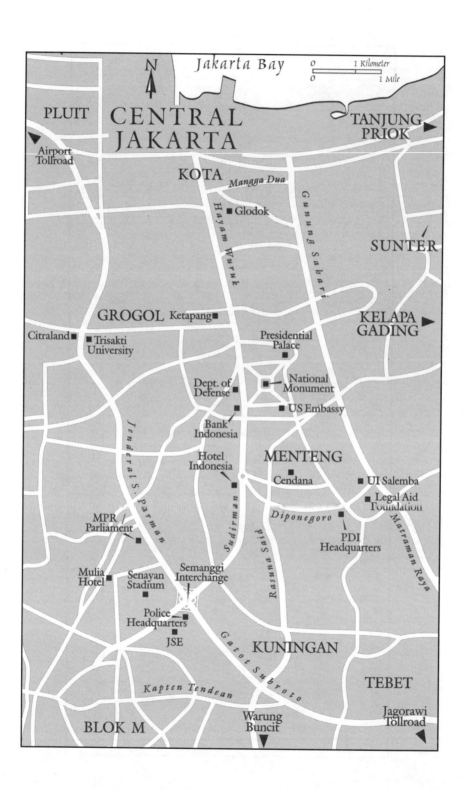

PART I

HUBRIS OF THE ELITE

1

LOOMINGS

'**R**aid PDI Headquarters.' That simple command, issued by President Soeharto to his security forces in July 1996, triggered the extraordinary political power struggle that would consume Indonesia for years to come.

The raid itself was a simple affair. Several hundred youths who were protesting Soeharto's rule had barricaded themselves inside a colonial-era mansion in central Jakarta. The building served as the headquarters for Indonesia's only credible opposition party, the Indonesian Democratic Party (PDI). Troops launched an attack at dawn on a Saturday, and by noon they controlled the premises. The event marked a strategic success for Soeharto: it sidelined his main rival, PDI chair Megawati Soekarno-putri, at a critical juncture. It did not, however, constitute a triumph.

The PDI Headquarters raid was not the first time that Soeharto's 'New Order' regime had cracked down on its opponents, but it was close to being the last. The blunt attack made the president appear cruel and desperate. It also dashed hopes for a peaceful political transition, by demonstrating that Soeharto, at age 75, was determined to cling to power by force. For more than 200 million Indonesians the ensuing political struggle would exact exceedingly high costs. The prize was paramount control over the most corrupt state in Asia—and the rules were non-existent.

After several years, and after the loss of thousands of lives, the forces of change would triumph and Indonesia would become the world's third largest democracy—or at least so it would appear. In fact, appearances can be misleading in Indonesia, and triumphs can prove ephemeral.

Soeharto was born to a family of impoverished petty aristocrats in rural Central Java, and at the age of seventeen he joined a local military unit under the supervision of the Dutch colonial authorities. It was the eve of World War II. After the invasion of the Netherlands East Indies in 1942,

Soeharto served in a similar unit under the Japanese occupiers. The Dutch sought to reclaim their huge colony after the war, but the nationalist leaders Soekarno and Mohammad Hatta declared Indonesia an independent republic. Among the few Indonesians with formal military training, Soeharto became an officer in the republic's hastily formed army—the ideal place for the savvy youth to realise his ambitions.

Although little more than a loosely organised network of volunteer militias, the army waged a determined guerilla campaign against Dutch forces for nearly five years. This helped win international recognition for the new republic, but Indonesia's leaders soon faced daunting challenges. Indonesia was blessed with natural resources but three centuries of colonial rule had left the population poor and undereducated. In a dazzlingly diverse archipelago, national unity was sorely lacking. And perhaps most significantly, the political institutions left over from the Dutch colonisers were designed, not to serve the interests of the people, but to uphold the authority of the rulers.

While the young Soeharto steadily rose through the ranks of the army, the political elite affirmed Soekarno, the country's most popular revolutionary, as Indonesia's first president. Although his economic ideas were based on a crude form of socialism, Soekarno's ardent nationalism and respect for pluralism helped unify the country. Meanwhile, he and Indonesia's other political leaders struggled to build a stable democracy.

The 1945 Constitution, which had been drafted under emergency conditions, was rife with vagaries. A more sophisticated Constitution was therefore introduced in 1950—but whereas the earlier version lacked checks on presidential authority, the second provided for a parliamentary system that proved chronically unstable. Soekarno was reduced to a figurehead, and parliamentary cabinets rose and fell in rapid succession. The country's first national election, in 1955, failed to bring stability: the vote was fragmented among nearly 30 parties, ranging from communist to Islamist, with socialists and nationalists in between. Two years later Soekarno finally intervened.

Siding with one faction of the military, the president imposed martial law and revived the 1945 Constitution. He used the euphemism 'Guided Democracy' to disguise his authoritarian rule. Genuine democracy would not return for more than 40 years.

Amid economic malaise, Soekarno survived through cunning tactics: he mesmerised the nation with his grandiloquence, distracted potential critics with adventurous foreign policy campaigns and encouraged political rivals to fight among themselves. He balanced his presidency between three political forces: military nationalists, Communists and, to a lesser extent, Islamic groups. This formula kept Soekarno in power for nine years, but corruption and economic neglect eventually took their toll. By late 1965 the currency was in free-fall and Indonesians struggled to cope with runaway inflation. Soekarno increasingly associated himself with the Communists, who whipping the political atmosphere into a frenzy. Meanwhile, the president's relations with the army suffered a corresponding decline.

In September 1965 Soekarno was led to believe that the anti-communist army leadership was poised to launch a coup d'état. He apparently gave his consent to a pre-emptive strike, dubbed the '30 September Movement'.[2] Two Soekarnoist army officers, Col. Abdul Latief and Lt Col. Untung, mustered several hundred soldiers from a variety of units, including the president's palace guard. Around 4 a.m. on 1 October, the soldiers raided the homes of seven generals. They abducted and killed six of the targets—the head of the army, his top four assistants and the military's chief prosecutor.

Controversy persists over who encouraged the attackers to act.[3] The standard version (encouraged by the New Order regime) has been that the Communist Party commissioned the murders. However, Latief, Untung and at least one other senior conspirator had previously served in the Central Java Garrison under the command of Maj. Gen. Soeharto. In 1965 Soeharto was based in Jakarta, commanding the army strategic reserve (Kostrad), the military's premier combat-ready force. As such, he was one of two generals with direct command over troops in the capital; the other was the Jakarta Garrison commander, Maj. Gen. Umar Wirahadikusumah. To have any chance of success, an attack against the army leadership in Jakarta would, presumably, have had to target these two—unless the attackers believed them to be partisans. Both were inexplicably spared.

Latief claimed that he had warned Soeharto about the abductions two days before they took place, and that the conspirators had been assured of the Kostrad commander's support.[4] But on the morning after the murders Soeharto acted swiftly and assertively. With assistance from Kostrad's intelligence officer, Ali Murtopo, Soeharto mobilised his forces and persuaded the conspirators' troops to surrender their weapons. When President Soekarno appointed a communist-leaning general to head the army, Soeharto objected and assumed the command himself. He denounced the 30 September Movement as a communist coup attempt and arrested the conspirators. Latief says that he felt betrayed.

A bloody, nationwide anti-communist pogrom ensued. Estimates of the death toll range from 80 000 to 500 000.[5] Another 500 000 confirmed or suspected communists were eventually jailed, including Col. Latief, who remained in prison for 33 years. And within a few months Soeharto had wrested control of the government away from the disgraced Soekarno. The New Order had been born.

Many viewed Soeharto's arrival as a blessing. He imposed order, rectified the economy and eradicated the threat of communism.

Indonesians craved stability, and therefore few complained when Soeharto's party, Golkar, won a landslide victory in the 1971 polls. And the ensuing oil boom, which brought unprecedented riches to Indonesia, also enabled Soeharto to consolidate his grip on power. It was not until the mid-1970s, therefore, that succession worries first began to arise.

Election outcomes were never in doubt: parliamentary polls were rigged to favour Soeharto's Golkar party, while presidential elections were dominated by Soeharto's handpicked loyalists in the 1000-member People's Consultative Assembly (MPR). Nonetheless, the build-up to a parliamentary election was always marked by abnormally high levels of political tension. Before each new presidential term the cagey but inscrutable Soeharto intimated that the upcoming term would be his last. But five years later he would invariably 'agree' to serve just one more term.[6] Meanwhile, his political longevity hinged on his ability to continue delivering macro-economic growth.

Soeharto portrayed himself as the country's saviour from communism and regional secessionism, but his most vaunted role was as the 'Father of Development'. In 1965 Indonesia was the poorest country in Asia, with an estimated 60 per cent of the population—or around 55 million people—living in poverty.[7] After Soeharto took over the following year, annual growth in Gross Domestic Product (GDP) exceeded 6 per cent in all but two of the next 30 years. By 1996 the poverty rate had been cut to 11 per cent, or 22 million people.[8] Impressive gains had been recorded in life expectancy, fertility, infant mortality and food self-sufficiency. Perhaps most impressive of all, Indonesia ranked among Asia's most attractive 'emerging tiger' economies—and among the world's most popular destinations for long-term investment. With land, labour and natural resources in abundance the outlook was bright for sustained growth. But despite these achievements there were reasons for dissatisfaction.

In the latter years of Soeharto's rule a host of ills came to the fore—such as income disparity, urban squalor, environmental degradation and neglect of human rights. At the root of these ills was Indonesia's most tenacious problem: corruption. Entire economic sectors were elaborately structured to funnel abnormal profits, or rents, to Soeharto's family, their inner circle of business partners (or 'cronies') and a select few leaders of the powerful military. Rather than serving the public, most functions of the state apparatus were concerned primarily with upholding these rent-seeking structures. Many poor Indonesians were growing gradually better off, but they also confronted mounting injustice in their daily lives.

Therefore, in early 1996, as Soeharto entered the penultimate year of his sixth presidential term, Indonesia's succession worries were at their highest point in three decades. And while the reasons for opposing Soeharto were stronger than ever, the president had grown out of touch with the population he governed: three out of five Indonesians were too young to have known any other president during their lifetime, and most were eager for change. In contrast, Indonesians young and old were turning their attention to a politician whose lineage had always captivated their imagination: Soekarno's daughter, Megawati Soekarnoputri.

A self-proclaimed 'Sybarite', Soekarno indulged his senses to excess. He used the former Dutch governor-general's residence, set in the foot-hills south of Jakarta, as his presidential palace. There Megawati was raised like a princess—but her luxurious lifestyle changed abruptly at the age of eighteen, when her father was deposed.

While her father remained under house arrest, Megawati tried twice to obtain an undergraduate degree but dropped out both times. Rather than pursuing a career, she chose to marry, but her first husband died in an aircraft crash and her second marriage was annulled. Her father died in 1970 and she finally married her third husband, Taufik Kiemas, three years later.[9]

Eschewing a professional career, Megawati focused on raising her three children. In the 1980s, however, her husband helped persuade her to enter politics. Megawati had accrued few official distinctions to her name, but her name alone was sufficient distinction for prominence in Indonesian politics. She followed the proud, albeit vague, tradition of her father: secular-nationalism.

Soekarno had founded the Indonesian Nationalist Party (PNI) in 1927, and youth militias had rallied around its symbol, a fattened bull, during the struggle for independence. PNI stood for prosperity, unity and plurality, but its prime motivating force was Soekarno's own charisma. After Soeharto's takeover, PNI was forced to merge with several smaller parties to create PDI. The party entered a long period of decline, eventu-ally becoming a token opposition party whose leaders willingly complied with Golkar and the military. But despite this ignominious role, Megawati joined PDI as a member of parliament in 1987.

The first few years of Megawati's political career were uneventful, but by the early 1990s a small clique within PDI was growing increasingly outspoken. Rallying around the party's relatively liberal-minded chair, Suryadi, PDI's 'reformists' waged an unusually aggressive campaign in the 1992 parliamentary elections.[10] At rallies across the country, they called for clean government, electoral reforms and presidential term limits. Most outlandishly, PDI demanded multiple candidates in the 1993 presidential election, to be held in the MPR (which consisted of all 500 parlia-mentarians, plus 500 appointed representatives). But in addition to the unusually daring platform, PDI's main draw was Soekarno's benevolent-looking daughter.

Exactly how much electoral support PDI mustered in the 1992

election remains uncertain: the elections were far from free or fair. The Golkar-controlled election authorities credited Golkar with 68 per cent of the national vote—a figure typical of the official results of past elections. The following year the MPR dutifully handed Soeharto his sixth presidential term. But while PDI's campaign looked like a failure on the surface, Suryadi's party had at least voiced criticism; at the time, this alone was an important achievement. And by eliciting a stern response from Soeharto, PDI set in motion a train of events that would shape the nature of Indonesian politics for years to come.

S oeharto's style of rule was apparently shaped by his upbringing. He was steeped in traditional Javanese values, which extol harmony and emphasise deference to elders. He was trained by the Dutch and Japanese militaries, which were naturally preoccupied with imposing security. And as an army officer, Soeharto joined or led campaigns to quell such threats as local uprisings, communist rebellions and regional secession movements. It seemed that a product of these cumulative experiences was a fixation on stability and order. Soeharto displayed little tolerance for dissent, and his inclination was to repress opposition before it could gain strength. Immediately after surpassing his re-election hurdle in 1993, this is precisely what he proceeded to do.

Over time, Soeharto had grown adept at defending his regime. He developed a host of instruments that he could use to punish his critics and opponents: among others, these included the police, the attorney general's office and the courts. But the most serious threats to the regime were dealt with by the military.

Despite a proud history, Indonesia's military gradually evolved into an instrument for upholding Soeharto's authority.[11] By the 1990s the military had become Indonesia's most powerful political institution by far. It played an overt political role that was rationalised through its so-called 'dual-function' doctrine. This maintained that the military was the protector of the nation, and was obliged to contribute its institutional resources to the nation's development. In fact, the military's dual function was an anachronism that had gone badly awry.

The military had been a politically motivated force from its inception. In the struggle against the Dutch the newly formed officer corps included substantial numbers of Javanese, *priyayi* aristocrats, through whom the Dutch had governed for over two centuries. Once independence had been won, the natural inclination of these *priyayi* was to carry on governing as they had before—but on their own behalf, rather than on behalf of the Dutch.

As the Communist Party gained strength in the late 1950s, anti-communist generals sought to counter the threat by seconding military personnel to civil service posts throughout the government bureaucracy.

President Soeharto, however, sustained this practice long after the threat of communism had receded. Rather than countering communism, the military was countering political opposition to Soeharto. By 1993, thousands of active and retired officers served at all levels of government, including several hundred generals in the cabinet, parliament, Supreme Court, Golkar, gubernatorial offices and state-owned enterprises.[12]

Even more important than the military's civil service role was its 'territorial system'—a force structure that made the Indonesian army look as if it was occupying its own country. The army maintained a physical presence at almost every administrative level of the state, from regional garrisons commanded by two-star generals to village-level posts manned by sergeants.[13] These 'territorial commanders' typically wielded paramount authority in their respective districts, and through them the military wielded the bulk of its political clout.

The priority attached to the military's overt political role was readily apparent from a glance at its command structure. The military's top post was the armed forces commander, a four-star officer who presided over the chiefs-of-staff of the four services (army, navy, air force and police). But reporting directly to the armed forces commander were two crucial three-star officers: the commander of the army strategic reserve (Kostrad); and the kaster, or chief-of-staff for territorial affairs.[14] While the command of Kostrad was purely a combat role, kaster was almost exclusively political. The kaster formulated the military's policies on 'socio-political' events and intervened, where necessary, to guide developments in Soeharto's favour.

The chief political instruments at the kaster's disposal were the military's powerful strategic intelligence agency (Bais) and the Special Forces. Bais had an extensive reach: it maintained a network of intelligence operatives attached to all but the lowest levels of the territorial system.[15] The agency focused on internal threats to the regime, such as political dissidents or regional secessionist movements. To carry out covert operations against these threats, Bais would typically work with the Special Forces, an elite commando outfit with special 'anti-terrorist' capabilities.

Soeharto therefore possessed formidable and well-honed instruments with which to confront challenges to his authority. Because numerous threats had been surpassed in the New Order's first 25 years, it seemed a relatively simple matter when Soeharto turned his attention to the nettlesome PDI in 1993. As he had done so often before, Soeharto summoned his armed forces chief, Gen Feisal Tanjung, and discussed what he wanted done.

After each presidential election Indonesia's three political parties installed new leaders in special party congresses. These were well-rehearsed affairs that were full of 'guidance' from above—particularly PDI's 1993 congress. When the party convened in mid-year to re-elect

Suryadi as chair, Tanjung intervened. His subordinates, including the kaster and various intelligence officers from Bais, approached individual PDI members and delivered tailored messages: Suryadi's supporters were issued threats, while his opponents were given inducements.[16] The process dragged on for several months, but PDI finally voted to oust Suryadi. In the process, however, Tanjung's men suffered a setback.

Either through a bargain or a blunder, the military allowed PDI's reformers to replace Suryadi with a potentially more potent leader: an offspring of Soekarno. But rather than the eldest son, Guntur, or the politically active daughter, Rachmawati, PDI settled on the more demure Megawati. But while she was deemed the least aggressive sibling, Megawati was still a threat to Soeharto—by virtue of her pedigree alone. In effect, the military's meddling had backfired.

With crucial support from a handful of reform-minded PDI colleagues, Megawati used her position as party chair to criticise the government and make strident calls for *'reformasi'*—i.e. political and economic reforms. Although the tightly controlled press rarely publicised her statements, Megawati's appeal nonetheless grew throughout 1994 and 1995—particularly on the island of Java, Indonesia's political heartland and home to 60 per cent of the national population. By early 1996 it was clear that PDI would make the following year's parliamentary election the most exciting contest in decades. As usual, PDI had no hope of securing a victory in the rigged polls, but Megawati's campaign appearances alone promised to generate a groundswell of anti-government sentiment.

Soeharto was in a difficult predicament. Letting Megawati campaign would be humiliating, but arresting the daughter of a national icon would be foolhardy. He therefore settled on a middle course: he would depose Megawati as PDI chair, just as he had done with Suryadi three years before. Megawati's term was not yet halfway completed, but it would not be the first time that Soeharto had illegally removed a critic from the political limelight. This time, however, the stakes were far higher than ever before.

Again Soeharto turned to Tanjung. At 57, the rotund, mustachioed general was already two years beyond mandatory retirement age, but Soeharto had retained him as armed forces commander in light of his able service. Tanjung had developed a wide-ranging reputation for greed and malice, but he was a ruthless hardliner who could read political trends with skill.

Having sidelined the officers responsible for the blunder three years before, Tanjung delegated this project to his new kaster and fellow hardliner, Lt Gen. Syarwan Hamid. A tough, chain-smoking Sumateran, Hamid was destined to crop up repeatedly over the next few years in a host of different roles. At the time, however, he was known primarily as the general who had recently jailed several labour leaders, while issuing stern warnings about the latent threat of a communist-inspired 'new left'.[17]

Hamid was stout and balding, though he compensated for a lack of martial bearing with skills as a cunning tactician. He put these skills to use in forming a plan to deal with Megawati.

Hamid perceived that a significant number of PDI delegates could be persuaded to do his bidding. Although the party leadership contained a number of dedicated reformists, PDI's rank-and-file was riddled with more pliable figures. But the key to Hamid's plan was his choice as Megawati's replacement. He realised that to insert a political unknown as party chair would only make the military's meddling all the more transparent. He therefore called on a figure who possessed considerable credibility as a reformer: Suryadi, the party chair whom the military had worked so hard to oust just three years before.[18]

Hamid told Suryadi that if he agreed to obey orders he would be allowed to return from forced retirement and reclaim his old post as party chair, usurping Megawati. Like many within his party, Suryadi proved willing to bend. Some also suspect that he was threatened into complying. In any event, on Hamid's instructions, Suryadi mustered a 'turncoat' faction within PDI. An extraordinary party congress was scheduled for June 1996.

Tanjung and Hamid chose to hold the congress in Medan, the principal city of their native Sumatera. Tanjung, in his youth, had reputedly worked for Medan's portside racketeers as a local hoodlum.[19] Such hoods were called '*preman*'—a word coined in early colonial times to refer to an ex-slave, or 'free man', who resorted to crime to survive.[20] As will be seen, *preman* still played prominent roles in Indonesia; Tanjung and Hamid were just a few of the military officers who made frequent use of *preman* gangs to carry out underhanded 'regime maintenance' chores. In Medan, Tanjung and Hamid would have few security concerns while they performed the most high-stakes 'regime maintenance' chore of their careers.

Breaking their usual habit of keeping a low profile, both generals appeared at the Medan congress and figured prominently in the proceedings. Megawati and her supporters were prohibited from attending the congress, which achieved a quorum only by including new members whose right to take part was dubious at best. In businesslike fashion the congress voted to cut short Megawati's term as party chair and reinsert Suryadi.[21] The procedures violated the party's articles of confederation, but Tanjung and other cabinet officials were on hand to endorse the decision.[22] Megawati was rendered powerless, while Soeharto achieved a long-awaited triumph—or so it seemed at the time.

It soon became clear that Megawati's ardent followers were unwilling to concede defeat. In particular, some 200 student activists refused to leave the premises of PDI's headquarters. The building they occupied was a large house situated on Jalan Diponegoro—a noisy but stately avenue on the edge of Jakarta's most prestigious residential neighbourhood, Menteng.[23] The students maintained a nonstop vigil in front of the building, denouncing the Medan congress and Suryadi's turncoat faction. Fearing retaliation from the authorities, Megawati urged the youths to abandon the headquarters and fight another day. Instead, their protest movement grew in size. Attracting a wide assortment of courageous government critics, the students erected a podium on the footpath where democracy activists delivered fiery speeches to the assembled crowd.

The gatherings on Jalan Diponegoro quickly grew to become the most strident, and embarrassing, protests in the history of Soeharto's rule. The protests also jeopardised the already dubious validity of the Medan congress: not until Suryadi physically occupied the headquarters building could he plausibly claim PDI's chair. But the students refused to leave. Police units sometimes dispersed the crowds on the street; the students would simply recede inside and re-emerge later.

Hamid urgently needed a solution. He met repeatedly with intelligence officials, particularly a young general who, as head of Bais's powerful Directorate A, was directly responsible for the president's physical and political security: Brig. Gen. Zacky Anwar Makarim.[24] Another one-star general involved in the planning was Brig. Gen. Susilo Bambang Yudhoyono.[25] Like Hamid, Makarim and Yudhoyono would play critical roles in the years to come. But in July 1996 the generals were faced with a thorny problem. They finally determined that to end the protests, install Suryadi and seal the results of the Medan congress, the students would have to be ousted by force.

Hamid's problem, however, was that a direct assault by security forces would be unseemly. Military rhetoric held that the security forces were the impartial guardians of the nation's interest. To be seen intervening in practical politics—or, worse still, taking sides in an internal squabble of an ostensibly independent opposition party—would make a mockery of the military's vaunted neutrality. Moreover, an overt military attack would only reinforce public sympathy for Megawati—at the expense of the military and Soeharto.

Hamid and Makarim therefore turned to a plan that was standard procedure in such situations: the use of *preman* in the place of regular troops.[26] By the 1990s it was common for military officers and entire units to provide 'backing', or protection, for illicit businesses run by mafia-style gangs.[27] The gangs would be allowed to smuggle, run casinos, manage brothels or deal drugs—and the military would receive a cut to complement its meagre budget or to simply enrich its top officers. When necessary, the military could also rely on these gangs to provide manpower for special jobs.

Indonesia's surplus of unskilled labour meant that gangsters could easily recruit hundreds of young thugs whenever the military wanted to avoid a direct clash with civilians. July 1996 was one of these instances. When it became clear that the pro-Megawati students were not going to be coaxed or cajoled into surrendering, Hamid decided to recruit *preman* and disguise them as angry partisans of Suryadi. Hamid therefore called on Yorrys Raweyai, arguably Indonesia's most prominent underworld figure.

Raweyai was a native of Indonesia's largest, most remote and most underdeveloped province: Irian Jaya, on the western half of the island of New Guinea. The 45-year-old Raweyai, who was of mixed Papuan and ethnic-Chinese descent, had distinguished himself by overseeing protection rackets and collecting debts for Irian Jaya's logging and mining interests, most of which involved Soeharto-family cronies.[28] By 1996 Raweyai had taken over operational control of Pemuda Pancasila (Pancasila Youth). Ostensibly the youth wing of Golkar—and ostensibly dedicated to upholding the state ideology, Pancasila—the organisation was widely viewed as a state-sanctioned crime syndicate.[29] In mid-July, Raweyai reportedly brought several dozen Pemuda Pancasila members to a field in Menteng, where they conducted a training drill under Hamid's supervision.[30]

Soon afterwards, Soeharto summoned senior military leaders to his residence on Jalan Cendana, on the opposite side of Menteng from Jalan Diponegoro. Attending the meeting were Tanjung, Hamid and at least six other senior generals.[31] Soeharto expressed his vexation with the incessant protests being staged on Jalan Diponegoro. According to three of those present, Soeharto issued an unmistakable order that the protests be put to a stop; Tanjung then formulated the detailed plan.[32]

Following the Cendana meeting, control over the operation was delegated to the Jakarta Garrison—the military command that co-ordinated security measures in the capital. Yudhoyono, the garrison's second-in-command, chaired a crucial planning session on 22 July. In attendance were Makarim, Suryadi aides from PDI and several garrison officers.[33] Immediately thereafter, Yudhoyono's subordinates began contacting *preman* bosses in the Jakarta area to recruit manpower.

As Raweyai later explained: 'I received a telephone call on 26 July from the intelligence staff of the Jakarta Garrison.'[34] He was instructed to supply around 100 *preman* for an operation that night. The staging ground was the Artha Graha office building, owned by a financier of the military. In addition to Raweyai's men, around 100 thugs from other gangs also arrived, plus more than 100 regular garrison troops dressed in plain clothes. In addition, six companies of police mobilised before dawn to place cordons across the streets surrounding PDI Headquarters.[35]

'Around 4 a.m. on 27 July,' said Raweyai, 'Pemuda Pancasila members were sent to the home of the women's affairs minister [next to PDI Headquarters on Jalan Diponegoro]. They were given red PDI shirts which they were forced to wear.'[36] This detail was meant to create the impression that the impending attack was strictly an internal party affair, conducted by supporters of Suryadi's faction.

Inside the headquarters building on Jalan Diponegoro, the pro-Megawati students braced for an attack. Their number had been reinforced to nearly 400. They had constructed barricades around the compound, but they were not optimistic about being able to withstand an assault. As dawn broke, the 'Suryadi supporters' began their attack.

The *preman* and soldiers started by hurling rocks, bricks and molotov cocktails, hoping to frighten the students into surrendering. When this failed, small groups of attackers clambered over the compound walls. The professional soldiers and street-hardened thugs should have overpowered the university students but, perhaps because they only launched piecemeal attacks, the attackers were kept at bay for over two hours. Finally the security forces abandoned the pretext of an internal PDI dispute and committed a company of baton-wielding riot police.[37] This turned the tide.

When the police poured into the compound, a portion of the students exited over the building's rear wall and were allowed to flee. The remainder stayed to fight, but the police, together with the 'Suryadi supporters', gained ground. One by one, room by room, the youths succumbed to kicks, blows and beatings from batons. Two were killed, 181 injured and 124 arrested.[38] By 9 a.m. the fighting at PDI Headquarters was over—but now an even bigger battle was brewing nearby.

Located just across the railroad tracks from Menteng, and less than a kilometre from PDI Headquarters, was a district of Jakarta known as Matraman. The area contained several poor, densely packed neighbourhoods called *kampung*, and as morning wore on, news of the nearby melee spread rapidly through the narrow alleyways and back streets. All morning, boys and young men poured out of the neighborhood to assemble on the wide boulevard of Jalan Matraman Raya. By midday the crowd numbered more than 10 000, and the youths surged up against the police barricades that blocked off Jalan Diponegoro.

Although a small detachment of police sought to disperse the youths, television cameras captured the cane-wielding officers retreating pell-mell amid a hail of rocks and stones. The burgeoning crowd quickly turned into a riotous mob—vandalising banks, showrooms and shop-houses. The rioters destroyed the local police station and set fire to a nearby bank, sending thick plumes of smoke high into the sky—which, in turn, attracted yet more youths from more distant *kampung*.

Better equipped police and military units finally arrived late in the afternoon. Using water cannons and tear gas, these units dispersed the crowd, but the most famous images of the riot were video footage of police and soldiers using canes to batter youths who were cowering on the ground. In the end, five people died and 149 were injured. Twenty-three went missing and were never found.[39]

The Matraman riot revealed that, behind its tranquil facade, Indonesian society harboured deepseated animosity toward the New Order regime. For Soeharto the Matraman unrest was the worst of his entire presidency—and it was also a harbinger of what lay ahead. At the time, however, Soeharto apparently overlooked the riot's significance and focused on the PDI raid, which he regarded as a success.

As Raweyai later noted, to have taken part in the raid was a source of distinction.[40] The key figures involved received prompt promotions: Makarim took command of Bais, Yudhoyono rose to major general and Raweyai was appointed to the MPR.[41] The commander of the Jakarta Garrison, Maj. Gen. Sutiyoso, soon obtained one of the government's most coveted posts: governor of Jakarta.

Soeharto's satisfaction was not without reason: with parliamentary elections just around the corner in June 1997, Megawati had been deprived of her political vehicle. And with his main source of political opposition neutralised, Soeharto could turn his attention to the only other figures who posed any real threat. These were Indonesia's two chief religious leaders: Abdurrahman Wahid and Amien Rais.

 In the 1920s, Hasyim Ashari propounded a religious doctrine that synthesised Java's indigenous mysticism with Middle Eastern Islam.[42] The doctrine itself was not new, but Ashari's contribution was to organise a network of *pesantren*, or traditional religious boarding schools that emphasised moral values. His movement quickly developed into a grassroots socio-religious organisation known as the Nahdlatul Ulama (NU), or 'Revival of the Religious Scholars'. Ashari's son, Wahid Hasyim, oversaw NU's expansion from its stronghold in East Java to other parts of the densely populated island. He became minister of religion in 1950, but three years later died in a car crash. His son, Abdurrahman Wahid, was thirteen years old at the time.

Reared in *pesantren*, Wahid pursued his higher education in the 1960s in Cairo and pre-Baath Iraq. He was always destined to play a prominent role within NU: familial ties figured prominently in NU's complex organisational hierarchy and Wahid's exalted lineage provided him, in effect, with royal status in NU circles. Upon his return to Indonesia in the early 1970s, Wahid studied and lectured in a host of *pesantren*. It was during this time that he refined the philosophy that would guide his later career: respect for religious pluralism.

Given that the Indonesian archipelago was arguably the world's most culturally diverse country, Wahid adamantly believed that tolerance of religious differences was essential for Indonesia's national unity. He applied this principle to NU: rather than an 'exclusive' institution that championed rigid dogma, Wahid wanted NU to be an 'inclusive' organisation that remained tolerant and openminded. This message resonated with the membership of NU—after all, NU professed a 'syncretic' Islam that incorporated elements of Javanese mysticism, as well as ancient Hindu and Buddhist traditions.[43] Given his pedigree and energetic campaigning, Wahid quickly emerged as NU's pre-eminent leader. In 1984, at age 44, he attained the organisation's top administrative post as NU chair, a position he would hold until 1999.

By the mid-1990s NU claimed nearly 40 million members.[44] Although this figure was exaggerated, NU was indisputably the largest Islamic organisation in Indonesia. And because Indonesia was the world's largest Muslim country, NU may also have been the world's largest Islamic group. Although Wahid generally refrained from taking an active role in politics, the sheer size of his organisation—and his revered status among NU's grassroots membership—made him a consequential political figure by default.

Wahid was not, however, without rivals. Despite NU's size, the bulk of its members were confined to rural Java. Elsewhere, in the cities and in the Outer Islands, the dominant organisation was Muhammadiyah.

Founded in 1912, Muhammadiyah mirrored Middle Eastern movements that sought to reconcile Islam with an increasingly modern and secular world. In religious terms, this involved the promotion of Middle Eastern orthodoxy in place of indigenous beliefs. In educational terms, Muhammadiyah emphasised the teaching of science and technology rather than liberal 'Western' philosophy.[45] And although Muhammadiyah disavowed any involvement in politics, the organisation was, in fact, intensely political.

Like NU, Muhammadiyah was large—by the mid-1990s it was claiming nearly 30 million members—but its political significance was due to more than size alone. It was the chief proponent of Islamic modernism, and the modernist movement had always harboured those who pursued expressly political goals. These goals varied widely. One general aim was to simply improve governance by contributing ethical values derived from Islam. Many modernists, including Muhammadiyah leaders, believed that this laudable goal could be achieved without offending nominal Muslims or religious minorities. Others, however, had more ambitious goals.

Some of the more ardent proponents of Islamic modernism rejected the separation of temporal and religious authority as illogical, and they therefore hoped to draw the two closer together. These 'political Islamists' varied widely. Some sought a limited Islamicisation of specific branches of the government, while others wanted a wholesale switch to a state based on Islamic law. Some sought to move swiftly—even militantly—while others pursued a gradual approach.

'Political Islam' was therefore a diffuse movement. It never appealed to more than a minority of modernists and it was never explicitly endorsed by Muhammadiyah. Nonetheless, it had affected national politics since the founding of the republic in the late 1940s. And by the latter stages of Soeharto's rule it was playing a particularly important role: it was the principal lever that Soeharto used to pry apart Indonesia's two largest Islamic organisations. This is because political Islam—and modernism in general—was regarded as an alarming threat by Abdurrahman Wahid.

Wahid's lifelong campaign to promote religious tolerance had an ironic flipside: he was extremely intolerant of one specific branch of modernism, political Islam. This intolerance was not without reason. As Wahid would point out, the more fanatic elements of political Islam had mounted armed insurrections in West Java in the 1950s and in Aceh in the present day. He harped on the threat that political Islam would alienate Indonesia's religious minorities. Although they formed no more than 15 per cent of the national population, some of these minorities were the dominant groups in certain far-flung regions of the archipelago; the advance of political Islam, Wahid argued, would exacerbate secessionist tendencies in these areas and thus jeopardise national unity.

Perhaps most importantly, there was the threat of demagoguery: like any ideological movement, political Islam harboured cynics who were ready to deliberately exploit religious sentiments to promote their own quest for power. In a country with a long history of authoritarian rule, there was ample reason to fear that what started out as a sincere ethical movement could be misappropriated and misused. But Wahid's vehement opposition to political Islam stemmed not only from his concerns for the nation—his institutional interests also played a part.

Wahid opposed not just political Islam but Islamic modernism as a whole, including Muhammadiyah. As something of a puritan reform movement, Muhammadiyah sought to 'rectify' indigenous beliefs that were at odds with Middle Eastern orthodoxy. Foremost among these were the mystic beliefs that were inextricably intertwined with NU's traditional brand of Javanese Islam. In doctrinal terms, Muhammadiyah challenged NU's core principles. And in more practical terms, it also encroached on NU's domain. Indonesia possessed a finite number of Muslims, and the two organisations competed aggressively at the margins to recruit new members. These considerations undoubtedly contributed to Wahid's unerring opposition to Islamic modernism and Muhammadiyah. And in the 1980s they also put him on common ground with an unlikely ally: Soeharto.

By the start of the 1980s the New Order had succeeded in regulating political discourse in virtually all facets of society, including schools, media organisations, civic associations and professional guilds. Indonesia's thoughtful and increasingly well-educated Muslim youths faced a dearth of credible institutions through which to channel their political interests. Many therefore turned to one of the last available refuges: the mosque. Precisely because he quashed dissent with such zeal, Soeharto created a political void in which political Islam was able to prosper.

Modernist-inspired mosque networks were soon blossoming throughout the country. In addition to sheltering free speech, these networks possessed formidable organisational capabilities such as community-based funding, hierarchies of command and sophisticated channels for communicating messages or ideas throughout the archipelago. Whereas the government was able to co-opt or coerce other organisations, mosque networks were more difficult to control. Nonetheless, Soeharto had paid close heed to the Islamic revolution that had swept through Iran.[46] Thwarting such a movement at home became the primary focus of his security apparatus, which was headed in the 1980s by Gen Benny Moerdani.

An expert in covert operations with a penchant for furtive tactics, Moerdani was also a devout Catholic with a deepseated aversion to Islam. Moerdani's intelligence operatives carried out a bloody purge of suspected political Islamists throughout the 1980s. This campaign won the army lasting enmity from a wide range of Muslims—including many within the armed forces itself.[47] But Moerdani's campaign worked at cross-purposes: while it frustrated efforts by Islamists to organise themselves, its heavy-handedness also hardened moderate attitudes and prompted many to turn more radical. Despite Moerdani's purge, therefore, political Islam grew inexorably.

By 1990 Soeharto realised that Moerdani's heavyhanded approach was backfiring. It was creating martyrs, radicalising the regime's Islamic critics and, perhaps most importantly, creating unhealthy fissures within the military. Abandoning the use of brute force, Soeharto switched to a tactic that had become a hallmark of his regime: co-optation. After nearly a decade of antagonising the leaders of political Islam, the president abruptly began currying their favour by offering sinecures, perks and power. The centrepiece of this strategy was the creation in December 1990 of the Association of Islamic Intellectuals, or Icmi (pronounced 'itch-mee').

A 'religious thinktank' designed to give modernist Islam a higher profile, the idea for Icmi came from a diverse group of influential Islamic thinkers. Lively debates ensued about whether the new body would help Indonesia's modernists influence the government, or vice versa.[48] Soeharto, for his part, clearly intended to keep Icmi subservient: he selected one his most loyal acolytes to head the high-profile organisation, the minister for research and technology, B.J. Habibie.

Soeharto's choice of Habibie was ironic—the German-trained engineer was hardly known for his Islamic credentials—but it was also politically expedient. Habibie had owed his rise largely to his sycophantic support for Soeharto, and if he was to advance farther he urgently needed to begin developing his own political vehicle. For their part, Icmi's founding intellectuals recognised that, for their organisation to survive, it needed the backing of someone close to Soeharto.[49] Icmi and Habibie were therefore well matched. Although Icmi itself was a relatively moderate organisation, the technology minister used it to make inroads to political Islam, which thus became Habibie's most important political vehicle. Although it would prove an exceedingly difficult vehicle to steer, it would take Habibie far.

The founding of Icmi also helped a number of other politicians. Among the most notable was a fiery young religion professor from the prestigious Gadjah Mada University, Amien Rais. Rais hailed from a middle class family in Yogyakarta, the epicentre of the Javanese heartland. The people of this region are renowned for their deference, refined manners and reverence for harmony—but Rais blatantly contradicted this typecast. He was blunt, caustic and unabashedly ambitious.

From an early age Rais devoted his energies to religious studies. Although he was an ardent proponent of modernist Islam, he attended university at the most famous Catholic institution in the United States, Notre Dame, and later obtained a doctorate in religion from the University of Chicago. But unlike some other Islamic scholars who studied abroad, Rais did not return to Indonesia with temperate views.

During his teaching career at Gadjah Mada, Rais stood out for the forcefulness with which he promoted Islamic modernism. His occasional anti-Christian and anti-Chinese remarks stirred controversy but they also helped him win a dedicated constituency within political Islam.[50] When Icmi was formed, Rais was among a number of Islamic politicians who recognised the organisation as an opportunity to elevate their public profile.

By playing along with Soeharto, Rais used his membership in Icmi as a national pulpit from which to promote Islamic modernism. By 1995, at age 51, he was rewarded with what was arguably the most influential position in the modernist community: chair of Muhammadiyah. In return for being part of Icmi and refraining from criticising Soeharto, he also won considerable state support for Muhammadiyah.[51] This also cemented his status as the foremost arch-rival of NU's chair, Abdurrahman Wahid.

Wahid and NU had remained aloof from national politics while Moerdani's pogrom was taking place in the 1980s. Although Wahid was not an avowed supporter of Soeharto, neither was he a notable critic. That changed abruptly with the introduction of Icmi in 1990. Having witnessed the relentless rise of Islamic modernism despite Moerdani's efforts to contain it, Wahid was alarmed to see Soeharto suddenly embrace modernist leaders and political Islamists.

Wahid warned the president that he was courting disaster and that the Islamists would come back to haunt him.[52] The unsolicited advice infuriated Soeharto, and with their relations souring, Wahid became more outspoken. In early 1991 he founded his own elite thinktank, dubbed Democracy Forum.[53] Relying on input from a clutch of intellectuals who were dedicated pro-democracy activists, Wahid issued brazen criticisms of Soeharto's government. He also worked closely with the reformist leaders of PDI.

Eventually Soeharto struck back: in 1994, as NU prepared to re-elect Wahid to his third term as the organisation's chair, the president's political fixers intervened in an effort to depose Wahid and promote a more obedient figure in his place. The effort nearly succeeded: Wahid won re-election by a very narrow margin. At the time, it seemed as if Soeharto had suffered another setback, just a year after Megawati had attained the chair of PDI. Together Wahid and Megawati continued to agitate against Soeharto. All that changed, however, with the 1996 PDI Headquarters raid.

Soeharto's decision to raid PDI Headquarters upset Indonesia's delicate political balance. For more than two decades the president had made intelligent use of PDI and its fellow faux-opposition party, the Islamic-oriented United Development Party (PPP). In the parliamentary elections held every five years, these parties absorbed anti-government votes without ever posing a real threat to the regime. As long as PDI and PPP retained any credibility as opposition parties, Soeharto could at least partially obfuscate the dictatorial nature of his rule. But when he forcibly usurped Megawati in 1996, Soeharto destroyed the last vestiges of PDI's independence.

PDI's erstwhile supporters reviled Megawati's usurper, Suryadi. It was clear that voters would abandon the party in the parliamentary elections to be held one year hence. But to abstain from voting was illegal, and therefore PDI's supporters had only one alternative for registering their opposition to Golkar: voting for PPP. This placed Abdurrahman Wahid in a quandary.

PPP had started out in the 1970s as a forced amalgamation of a wide array of Islamic parties, including NU, but in the mid-1980s Wahid had withdrawn his organisation's support. Since then the party had fallen under the sway of modernists and other figures from Icmi—most of whom were Wahid's traditional adversaries. And although PPP was far from being a genuine opposition party, the sidelining of PDI meant that PPP would receive a significant show of support in the upcoming election. Voters who wished to register their dissent with Soeharto had nowhere else to turn.

Even non-Muslim voters were prepared to join PPP rallies. The 1997 parliamentary election was therefore shaping up to be a bipolar contest between Golkar and PPP—and this forced Wahid to make an agonising decision.

Obliged to take a political stance, Wahid could support PPP against the Soeharto regime, support Golkar against the Islamic modernists, or try to remain neutral. In a decision that cast doubt on his commitment to democratic principles, Wahid abandoned his pro-democracy rhetoric and sided with Golkar. In East Java, where Wahid commanded vast legions of supporters, the enigmatic cleric climbed on to grandstands accompanied by Soeharto's eldest daughter, Siti Hardiyanti (Tutut) Rukmana, and army chief-of-staff Gen. Hartono, the military's foremost Golkar supporter. Wahid also became a member of the MPR, the handpicked body that convened every five years to re-elect Soeharto. Wahid's reformist allies from his Democracy Forum days could only look on with dismay.[54]

Wahid's endorsement for Golkar marked another coup for Soeharto. The outcome of the June 1997 parliamentary election came as no surprise—Golkar galloped to its sixth straight runaway victory. By side-lining Megawati and courting political Islam, Soeharto had cornered Wahid and forced him to capitulate. Despite mounting discontent among the people he governed, Soeharto had manipulated the nation's political elite with stunning success.

All that remained was for the country's highest law-making body, the MPR, to re-elect Soeharto to his seventh term as president when it convened in March 1998. Because the MPR's 1000 members consisted almost uniformly of Soeharto loyalists, there was little doubt that the assembly would re-elect the president, who was nearing his 77th birthday. The main topic of political speculation, therefore, was whom Soeharto would tap for the vice-presidency.

As Indonesia entered the last half of 1997, the economy continued to boom and Soeharto had masterfully consolidated his grip on politics—but the president still refused to anoint a clear successor. In the absence of an obvious transition plan, Soeharto's physical health became a foremost topic of concern. It was widely feared that his sudden demise would trigger a political crisis that would, in turn, damage the economy. In fact, the economic crisis came first.

2

LEGACY

Most economies sputter before they crash, but it was not so for Indonesia. In the first half of 1997 there were few macro-economic indicators that pointed to imminent recession, much less crisis. Gross domestic product (GDP) had expanded by 8 per cent in 1996 and it was on track to match that rate in 1997. Inflation was contained to single digits and real wages were rising. Export growth was healthy and the balance of payments seemed secure: compared with other countries in the region, Indonesia had one of the lowest current account deficits and highest ratios of international reserves to months of imports.[1]

Perhaps more important than Indonesia's headline indicators was a factor that could not be measured quantitatively, yet was palpable to all in the economy: confidence. Indonesia was the beneficiary of remark-ably positive business sentiment. Blessed with extraordinary natural resources and home to the world's fourth largest population, Indonesia was endowed with factors that could sustain growth well into the future. Perhaps most importantly, the Soeharto government had already been producing such rapid growth for the past three decades, almost without interruption.

Some investors were deterred by corruption and succession worries, but many others accepted these risks in light of what they saw as Indonesia's 'blue sky' potential. Each successive year of macroeconomic stability and high GDP growth attracted yet more interest from investors. Asia's four 'tiger' economies—Hong Kong, South Korea, Taiwan and Singapore—had already accomplished remarkable feats of rapid indus-trialisation. By the early 1990s global investors hoped to take part in the next 'growth miracle' in Southeast Asia's four 'tiger cubs': Malaysia, Thailand, the Philippines and Indonesia. Jakarta was now the scene of a vigorous investment boom.

Spearheading it was an array of multinational corporations (MNCs) eager to serve Indonesia's consumers or use its labour and resources.

Many were Japanese manufacturers that had been driven to relocate their operations by the strength of the yen in the 1980s. These MNCs brought an ideal type of investment for a developing country: foreign direct investment (FDI), or long-term, project-specific investment that was not likely to exit the country in the event of a downturn. FDI inflows promised to help sustain economic growth, boost efficiency and, with appropriate regulation, promote the transfer of skills and technology that Indonesia sorely needed. Between 1990 and 1997 Indonesia received around $25 billion in FDI, and in the latter two years of this period the country was Asia's second largest destination for FDI after China—surpassing other booming markets such as South Korea, Malaysia and Thailand.[2] (Unless otherwise indicated, dollar amounts referred to are in US dollars.)

The rate at which MNCs were investing in Indonesia provided one of the most persuasive reasons for banking on the country's long-term prospects—and this is precisely what a host of international commercial banks proceeded to do in the early 1990s, by lending aggressively to Indonesian corporations. Again the trend was spearheaded by Japanese institutions: mired in a stagnant domestic market and reeling from overseas losses, these banks were desperately trying to boost their short-term profitability. Southeast Asian markets such as Indonesia provided Japanese banks with opportunities to expand their loan books while earning far wider margins than they could achieve at home. European and US banks soon followed suit, fearful that their Japanese rivals would dominate what was seen as one of the world's fastest growing and most lucrative markets.

With many of the world's major commercial banks active in Jakarta, the path was blazed for another, more fickle, form of investment: portfolio funds. Encompassing a wide range of types (such as pension funds, mutual funds or hedge funds), portfolio funds emanated from the financial centres of Asia, Europe and the United States. Some portfolio fund managers had long-term horizons, but many were impatient—interested only in short-term returns in instruments that were easy to offload in a hurry, if necessary. These instruments included high-yielding rupiah deposits in Indonesian banks and, more notably, shares listed on the Jakarta Stock Exchange (JSE).

The JSE opened for business at a fortunate time: 1988, the start of a five-year period in which both US and Japanese interest rates were unusually low. Capital fled these markets to seek higher returns elsewhere—such as miniature stock markets in developing countries, places which were soon called, euphemistically, 'emerging markets'.[3] Latin America's emerging markets boomed first and Asian markets were quick to follow. In 1988 a mere $2.5 billion had flowed into Asian equity markets, but by 1993 (the boom year) this figure had reached $39 billion.[4]

The fledgling JSE was well positioned to enjoy the regional boom.

Emerging markets investors typically diversified their portfolios across many markets, to limit their losses from a crash or recession in any one place. The key, therefore, was to determine how much of the portfolio to invest in each market and which stocks to choose. A great many investors took their cues from benchmark indices such as those compiled by Morgan Stanley Capital International (MSCI). The MSCI Emerging Markets Index was based on a weighted basket of key stocks from key markets; by measuring the performance of their own portfolio against the performance of this neutral index, fund managers could determine whether they had 'outperformed' or 'underperformed' during any given period of time.

This benchmarking practice led to what was commonly called a 'herd mentality' among portfolio investors.[5] By 'mirroring' the index, or filling their own portfolios with the same proportion of the same stocks that made up the MSCI index, fund managers could ensure that their portfolios would not deviate significantly from the industry's benchmark. This, in turn, meant that their portfolios would not lose more money than the industry average—and therefore they themselves would not lose their jobs.

Thus when the JSE was included in the key MSCI Asia ex-Japan index in 1991, the tiny Indonesian market was destined to grow in pace with the global boom in portfolio investment that took place over the next decade. The size of the JSE, measured in terms of total market capitalisation, mushroomed from $2 billion in 1990 to $117 billion at its peak in July 1997. Over the same period the number of companies listed on the exchange rose from a mere 24 to 282; while the latter number was still tiny by developed-world standards, it included the bulk of Indonesia's private sector.[6]

By supplying Indonesian firms with equity capital, portfolio funds were instrumental in sustaining Indonesia's economic boom—but they also contributed mightily to its undoing. Against the backdrop of this avalanche of capital, Indonesia possessed a peculiar mix of circumstances and policies that formed a recipe for disaster.

Unlike many other developing countries Indonesia had maintained an open capital regime since 1971. The policy was designed to attract foreign investment by allowing international capital to flow in and out of the country unfettered. The policy was important as an expression of Soeharto's anti-communism, but throughout the 1970s and 1980s it had little practical significance because international capital was scarce. What little capital Indonesia did attract was from public sector sources, such as aid donors. This changed abruptly in the late 1980s.

The dramatic growth of international investing was matched by a ravenous appetite for capital on the part of Indonesian corporations. Borrowing domestically was expensive: the central bank, or Bank Indonesia

(BI), sought to stem both inflation and speculative lending by keeping rupiah lending rates high. It was far cheaper for Indonesian companies to borrow in dollars offshore, and the free capital regime ensured that there were no restrictions on doing so. It was risky to borrow in foreign currency—if the rupiah dropped in value relative to the dollar, the borrower might be rendered insolvent—but borrowers and lenders alike had strong faith in a crucial policy: the government's implicit exchange rate guarantee.

Indonesia's fixed exchange rate was the foundation on which Soeharto had built his house of cards. But the rate at which BI 'pegged' the rupiah to the US dollar was, in effect, a contrivance. A more fundamentally sound alternative would have been a 'free-floating' system, in which the buying and selling pressure of market players determines the value of a currency. A central bank can influence the currency's value through monetary policy tools, such as changes in interest rates or money supply, but such tools are blunt. The drawback of a floating exchange rate, therefore, is its unpredictability: business planners have little certainty about the currency's future value.

Another alternative to the currency peg would have been a currency board system, in which a government simply does away with its central bank and monetary policy tools, tying its currency to that of a major economy (say, the United States). A key condition is a sufficient level of foreign reserves, so that markets believe that the government possesses sufficient dollars to convert every unit of local currency at the stated exchange rate. Another key condition is that the government surrender its control over monetary policy. Interest rates are dictated by the US Federal Reserve, while money supply is determined by the international flow of capital. The advantage of a currency board is that investors can have a very high degree of confidence that the currency will not devalue—the economy is, in effect, run on dollars. Governments, however, loathe the loss of control required by an orthodox currency board.

Throughout most of Southeast Asia, governments eschewed both of these systems and turned instead to the 'peg'. Governments simply decreed that their exchange rate would remain fully convertible to the US dollar at a certain rate, while continuing to forge their own monetary policy without regard to the direction of US monetary policy. At once they achieved both the certainty of a currency board system and the policy-making flexibility of a floating system—or so they thought.

This 'unorthodox' policy had several drawbacks which were often overlooked at the time. The most obvious was that these pegged currencies were prone to becoming overvalued. Because Southeast Asian economies were experiencing rapid growth and monetary expansion, abundant capital was chasing scarce goods. This fuelled higher inflation than in the United States, to whose dollar these currencies were pegged.

Inevitably, Southeast Asia's economies became overpriced, particularly for non-tradeable goods such as labour and land.[7]

Indonesia, meanwhile, differed somewhat in that BI had long used a variant of the peg system, known as the 'crawling peg'. Rather than letting it remain at a fixed rate in perpetuity, BI wisely allowed the currency to depreciate by 3–5 per cent per year. In 1995, for example, the currency weakened from Rp2200/$ (US dollar) at the start of the year to Rp2308/$ by year-end, a depreciation of 4.9 per cent.

This 'crawl' against the dollar was designed to compensate for the difference between annual inflation of around 10 per cent in Indonesia versus only 5 per cent or so in the United States. Without any movement in the exchange rate between the countries' two currencies, prices for goods and services in Indonesia would quickly outstrip prices in the US. The Indonesian economy would become overpriced, or 'overheated'. A crawling exchange rate was often likened to a tea kettle slowly releasing steam—rather than bottling up pressure and boiling over.

Thus in mid-1997, while other currencies in the region seemed over-valued and were thought to be in danger of mild devaluation, it was frequently argued that Indonesia was a special case. Unlike the Thai baht, Malaysian ringgit or Philippine peso, the Indonesian rupiah had already been depreciating gradually for years. The other currencies, it was argued, now needed a modest devaluation to put them back in line with the rupiah. Indonesia was still recording strong export growth, while most of its neighbours were experiencing a slowdown; this was cited as further evidence that the rupiah was still competitively valued.

Moreover, the rupiah was not simply crawling along a fixed course, but instead was permitted by BI to trade freely within a narrow range of values as it crawled. Thus in 1995, as the currency crawled from Rp2200 to Rp2308, BI might have allowed the rupiah to trade freely in the range Rp2240–2260 during the month of July. This range might have then shifted to Rp2250–2270 during the month of August. As time went on the band was gradually widened, but the currency would almost always bump up against the stronger end of the range (i.e. Rp2250/$ in the example of August 1995). This implied that the market believed that the rupiah, if anything, was undervalued—not overvalued.

Meanwhile, Southeast Asia's pegged currencies had another draw-back: vulnerability to sudden outflows of capital. This proved to be the region's Achilles heel. Much of the capital invested in Southeast Asia had been deliberately placed in easy-to-liquidate instruments, such as heavily traded stocks, precisely in case the investors needed to quickly sell their local holdings and convert their capital back into safe dollar investments. When a sudden political or economic event triggered such a wave of selling, tremendous pressure could be exerted on the exchange rate.

In a free-floating system, in which the local currency's value would be determined by market forces, a stampede by investors could drive the currency down sharply. This would not happen in a currency board system: as long as the board was backed by adequate reserves, there would be no reason to doubt that the government would exchange foreign currency for local currency at the stated rate. Pegged systems, however, offered far fewer assurances.

Because Southeast Asian governments conducted their own monetary policy, rather than adhering to the US Federal Reserve, there was often ambiguity about whether their pegs reflected the 'true' values of their currencies relative to the dollar—and whether they would continue to reflect true values well into the future. Any anticipated downturn in the economy would have implications for monetary stability and thus the accuracy of the peg. Moreover, in countries with low foreign reserve levels, there would be reason to fear that if hit by a crisis the government might lack the resources to support its peg.

Fears about a peg's durability could eventually give rise to a vicious cycle, whereby heavy selling of a local currency would cut deeply into central bank reserves, thereby feeding more fears about the peg's durability, prompting more selling and so on. Exacerbating this vicious cycle would be the role of currency traders and hedge funds, which could speculate on a currency and use 'derivative' instruments to amplify the selling or buying power of their assets. A central bank could soon find itself in a quandary: faced with an avalanche of local currency sales but possessing only a finite sum of reserves with which to buy up the local currency, the central bank might finally decide to abandon the fight. Rather than committing precious reserves in a battle against the combined might of market forces, the central bank might choose to simply float the currency, allowing it to fall in accordance with market pressure—precisely as the original sellers of the currency had feared from the start.

Prior to 1996, Southeast Asia's currency pegs had survived primarily because they had been relatively untested since the advent of volatile, short-term capital flows. Sentiment towards the region's economies had been positive for years, such that more capital consistently flowed in than out. But in 1996 investors in Thailand began to have doubts. Returns on investments were declining, as the country was awash in capital. It became apparent that local banks and, especially, finance companies had been channelling credit into corruption-plagued projects for years, and their portfolios contained far higher bad debt levels than they had been publicly admitting. An overbuilt property sector, surplus industrial capacity and declining export growth prompted a gradual but profound reassessment of Thailand's economic prospects.

As investors began to lose faith in the sustainability of Thailand's breakneck rate of growth, they sought to sell their positions and pull their funds out of Bangkok's capital market. This was particularly true of

portfolio investors: guarding against just such a downturn, they had deliberately invested in easy-to-sell assets, which they now liquidated in herdlike
fashion. As sellers of baht outstripped buyers, the Bank of Thailand (the
central bank) watched its reserves steadily decline. The bank faced a
difficult decision: it could simply give in to the relentless pressure and
allow the exchange rate to slip, or it could continue using foreign reserves
to buy baht from all sellers in a brave attempt to calm fears and prove that
the peg was durable. The gamble, however, was that it would run dry of
reserves before the selling pressure abated.

The Bank of Thailand chose to resist. Rather than accepting the pain
of a modest devaluation, the bank mounted a stubborn defence of the
baht's peg—hoping, meanwhile, that the selling pressure would finally
abate. Instead, it grew worse. International hedge funds exerted massive
pressure, but this was soon surpassed by the pressure from domestic banks
and corporations. Many of these local companies had borrowed offshore
and were 'short dollars'—that is, they owed more dollars than they
possessed. If the baht devalued, they would suffer losses and might even be
rendered technically bankrupt. Scrambling to buy dollars lest the peg gave
way, these companies only exacerbated the Bank of Thailand's plight.
Soon they were joined by vast numbers of baht holders—no one wanted to
hold the currency if it was destined to suddenly plunge in value.

It was not until June 1997 that the Bank of Thailand finally ran out of
resources. It had committed over two-thirds of Thailand's reserves, or
around $23 billion, in forward contracts to buy dollars. It had fought for
over a year to demonstrate to all that it possessed enough resources to
defend its currency, but in so doing it only undermined its own argument
and nearly bankrupted the country in the process. On 2 July the government had no alternative but to finally float the baht. The ensuing outflow
of domestic capital drove the currency to a mere 50 per cent of its pre-
crisis value. Had the devaluation happened earlier, the Bank of Thailand
might have contained the damage to more manageable levels. But
whether that would have prevented Asia's so-called financial market
'contagion' is another question.

It has often been argued that, in the wake of Thailand's devaluation,
neighbouring economies were made victims of an irrational financial
market mania that swept the region like a contagion. Soon after the
collapse of the baht, the Philippine peso and Malaysian ringgit also
devalued. The ensuing Asian crisis was therefore viewed as an unstoppable
malady introduced by external agents, such as hedge funds and panicky
investors. In fact, the crisis was driven by far more than speculation and
panic—there were sound economic reasons for Asia's financial malady.

If a downturn in a financial market could easily 'infect' and destabilise
markets in neighbouring countries, regional or global crises would be far

more frequent than has been the case.[8] Rather than contagion, Southeast Asian markets in 1997 were driven down by a dramatic reassessment of their long-term growth potential, bred by lessons learned in Thailand. In particular, investors increasingly realised that corruption and 'cronyism' had serious economic consequences.

Foreign investors learned some bitter lessons in Thailand. In particular, 'tiger cub' status did not necessarily guarantee uninterrupted growth in perpetuity. Thailand suffered from asset inflation, misallocated capital and inadequate regulation—and all these factors contributed to a devastating loss of investor confidence. Investors quickly applied these lessons to similar economies elsewhere in the region. In reassessing Indonesia, they realised that Soeharto's economic miracle shared many features with Thailand. In fact, it could be argued that Indonesia was even more prone to collapse given the pervasiveness of KKN: *korupsi, kolusi dan nepotisme*— 'corruption, collusion and nepotism'.

Soeharto-era Indonesia professed a strong commitment to capitalism, but it was a false, or 'ersatz', capitalism that conspicuously lacked several critical ingredients, such as fair competition and the rule-of-law.[9] Well aware that wealth could equate to power—which could then be used to challenge his rule—Soeharto was exceedingly careful to ensure that large amounts of wealth accrued only to those whom he trusted. Entire industries were elaborately structured to discourage competition and produce economic rents; that is, payments in excess of what could have been earned in a competitive market. Rent-yielding structures imposed severe costs on economic efficiency, but they enabled Soeharto to reward his loyalists and keep unknown upstarts at bay.

Soeharto used a wide array of the instruments of state to keep a tight rein on who grew rich in Indonesia. State enterprises, state banks and governmental departments were key instruments used for directing the accumulation of wealth. The executive branch formulated rules specifically designed to benefit Soeharto-family cronies; these rules were dutifully rubber-stamped by the legislative branch and zealously defended by a corrupt judiciary. Instances of KKN—or the standard injustices which constantly confronted ordinary Indonesians living under Soeharto's New Order—were merely the outward manifestations of an elaborate system, refined over decades, whose overriding purpose was to reinforce Soeharto's rule. Rather than a market economy state tainted by KKN, Soeharto's Indonesia was, more appropriately, a 'KKN economy' masked by ersatz capitalism.

Indonesia's KKN economy was far less stable than it seemed on the surface, and its sustained growth since the mid-1980s was due in no small part to the ever-larger inflows of foreign capital. In effect, Indonesia was living on borrowed wealth. Some ventures were generating sufficient returns to repay their borrowings with ease—others, however, were not.

Indonesia's economic boom was rife with investment projects undertaken, not for legitimate commercial reasons, but rather for the opportunities they afforded to profit from KKN.

A hypothetical example from the property sector, which was one of the worst affected by malfeasance, can serve to illustrate how the KKN economy worked in practice. To build a new project, property developers must typically invest their own equity to cover at least 20 per cent of the project's estimated total cost, while bank lending covers the rest. But rather than using cash, property developers in Indonesia would often contribute their equity in the form of land—and this land was often acquired through dubious means. For example, government officials could be bribed to sell public land at a fraction of its market value, then military units could be bribed to forcibly evict those living on the land.[10] Appraisers could be bribed to inflate the land's true value, thereby inflating the sum of credit that could be borrowed against it. And when building commenced, developers could siphon off big portions of these loans by hiring workers and purchasing materials from related companies— at inflated prices.

It mattered little if the completed project was marketable: if so, it was added upside; if not, the developer could rest assured that sufficient proceeds had already been extracted just from the project's building phase. In the event that the development failed commercially and the developer defaulted on its loans, the property and building could be surrendered to creditors as collateral. It was more likely, however, that the developer would simply hide behind the judicial system, secure in knowing that the court system's malleable judges would provide ample protection from bankruptcy suits.

This hypothetical example helps explain why Jakarta's skyline continued to sprout new developments even though the property market was already vastly oversupplied. It also helps explain why so many of the projects were poorly designed and poorly constructed. But this model applied to more than just the property sector: it applied to countless capital-intensive projects, including toll roads, power plants, chemical refineries and cement mills. The ulterior purpose of far too many investment projects in Soeharto's Indonesia was to borrow heavily, mark up construction costs and siphon off funds during the development stages.[11] In fact, the Indonesian word for 'project', *proyek*, eventually became a commonly used byword for corruption.

The KKN projects of the 1990s were nothing new: such affairs had been rehearsed for decades, if not for several centuries, of Dutch colonial rule. Soeharto himself pioneered rent-seeking in the military as a divisional commander in Central Java in 1957: two of his unit's 'charitable foundations' assumed the lucrative role of importing and distributing key agricultural commodities, assisted by ethnic-Chinese financiers such as Mohammad 'Bob' Hasan and Sudono Salim.[12] Soeharto was later censored for corruption by the then armed forces chief, A.H. Nasution.[13] Later, in the 1970s, the state oil monopoly Pertamina invested Indonesia's oil windfall in a vast array of projects—most of which were found later to have been marked up by a factor of two.[14] Following Pertamina's collapse in 1976, state banks moved to the fore.

By the 1990s, projects riddled with corruption were being funded by private banks, international banks and equity investors. It was accepted as fact that doing business in Indonesia automatically meant incurring 'hidden costs' in the form of bribes, kickbacks and unofficial levies.[15] One famous example of this practice occurred in 1995, when Deutsche Telkom bought a 25 per cent stake in cellular operator Satelindo. The official acquisition price was $586 million, but Deutsche Telkom's 1996 IPO documents showed that the company had actually paid $676 million. Citing investment bankers familiar with the deal, the *Asian Wall Street Journal* affirmed that the $90 million gap was a 15 per cent 'facilitation fee' paid to Bambang Soeharto, Satelindo's controlling shareholder.[16]

By the mid-1990s bribes alone were sometimes insufficient. To ensure that particularly large-scale projects were allowed to proceed, it was often necessary to give sizeable shareholdings to high-profile figures, free of cost. The recipients were typically members of the Soeharto family—or 'Cendana', as the family was collectively known, after the street on which most of its members lived.[17] Free shareholdings became so commonplace that investment advisors invented a special term for them: 'negative equity', or free equity that co-investors had to fund themselves.[18]

Kickbacks, bribes and gifted shareholdings were prominent features of the KKN economy, but the real cornerstone of the system was easy credit. Once the funds were in hand, the siphoning-off process was a relatively straightforward affair. Those who excelled in the KKN economy were those who excelled at securing capital—and unscrupulous businesspeople therefore invented countless schemes for mobilising funds. The details of these schemes help illustrate how Soeharto's economic miracle was built on exceedingly shaky foundations.

The most straightforward method for raising credit for dubious ends was to simply visit a state-owned bank. According to 1993 BI data, 20 per cent of state banks' loans were non-performing.[19] Although this official figure later declined, it was widely believed that the bad debt levels of state banks were vastly understated.[20] This was largely because of 'ever-greening'—the common practice of adding accrued interest to the outstanding balance of loans, rather than declaring them overdue.[21]

For the state banks, marking up projects and ever-greening bad debt were sustainable practices only so long as new deposits continued to flow in and, more importantly, the government continued to inject fresh equity to sustain further growth. When Indonesia's donors demanded an end to further capital injections in the early 1990s, access to state bank loans was restricted only to a privileged few—primarily consisting of several dozen associates of the Soeharto family. By the mid-1990s the demands made by Cendana and its cronies had so weakened the state banks that most became virtually moribund, even though they should have been thriving amid the economic boom. One of the seven major state banks, Bapindo, was so riddled with fraud by 1994 that it collapsed in spectacular fashion, sending tremors through the financial system.[22]

Besides the state banks, a host of other avenues existed for securing credit. For large business groups, obtaining funds offshore was easy: many commercial lenders and investment banks were eager to forge relationships with Indonesia's burgeoning conglomerates, who were willing to pay premiums for capital. Smaller groups who were less well known often found that they could raise big sums offshore by issuing short-term (270-day tenure) notes known as 'commercial paper' (CP). In the US, the term 'CP' referred to the short-term notes that were issued only by US blue-chip corporations under strict regulations; in Indonesia, CP was issued by companies that were anything but blue-chip—and under no regulations whatsoever.

South Korean banks demonstrated a particularly hearty appetite for CP: they craved the unusually high yields and they interpreted the short maturity as meaning that the paper was relatively low-risk. In fact, Indonesian CP was typically very high-risk, as much of the proceeds were used to fund long-term property developments. The CP market's first major victim was Bank Pacific, a mid-sized bank that collapsed in 1995 after having guaranteed around $1 billion in fraudulent CP.[23] By 1997 the total sum of CP issued in Indonesia was officially estimated at $3.8 billion, but unofficial estimates ranged as high as $15 billion. Even so, issuing CP was only one of the many methods used to mobilise capital in Indonesia's boom years; perhaps the favourite method used by capital-hungry conglomerates was to simply start a bank.

For visitors to Jakarta a stunning feature of the urban landscape is the staggering quantity of signage and billboards erected by banks throughout the city. Faced with the need to diversify the economy away from oil in the late 1980s, Indonesia's economic managers took the highly unusual step of liberalising the financial sector before freeing up the real sector.[24] The deregulation triggered a vigorous financial boom. With the minimum capital required to establish a bank set at a paltry $12 million, nearly every significant business group—regardless of how far removed its core competency might be from finance—jumped at the opportunity to establish its own bank. Within the space of a few years, the total number of banks in Indonesia nearly doubled from 124 in 1988 to 240 in 1994.[25]

The reason for the proliferation of new banks is not difficult to discern: establishing a bank provided conglomerates with an easy and inexpensive way to borrow money. For a conglomerate eager to borrow, a loan from a third party bank was an expensive alternative: assuming that the borrower could find a bank willing to lend, the lending rate would be of the order of 20–25 per cent per annum. It often made more sense for the conglomerate to simply set up its own bank and borrow at 16–18 per cent from public depositors. Regulations prohibited conglomerates from using their banks to channel customer deposits to other companies in their groups—but, in practice, these regulations were rarely enforced and easy to circumvent.[26] Most banks therefore functioned, in effect, as the fundraising arms of their affiliated conglomerates.

While it was very rare for BI regulators to punish banks for imprudence, it was rarer still that auditing firms would express doubts about the veracity of banks' financial statements.[27] With little interference from BI and with cosmetically acceptable audited accounts, few major banks were prevented by the capital markets regulator from listing on the stock market and raising fresh equity from investors. This equity enabled the banks to further expand their balance sheets and borrow yet more funds from the public—to be used, primarily, by the bank's own group.

Few conglomerates cared that raising fresh equity on the stock market required them to dilute their shareholding in their banks. Since most banks were designed to serve their groups rather than to profit in their own right, conglomerates were willing to surrender shares to outside investors. As long as a conglomerate kept its shareholding above a bare minimum of 50.1 per cent, it could retain management control and continue using the banks to fund its own groups. Most conglomerates therefore listed their flagship banks and conducted a quick series of rights offerings to raise yet more capital. When their shareholding was eventually diluted to the bare minimum required to maintain control, they simply 'restructured'—by listing the banks' parent companies.

The Lippo and Sinar Mas groups pioneered the strategy of listing 'financial services holding companies' that, in turn, owned the flagship banks. By diluting their ownership of these holding companies to 50.1 per cent, conglomerates could raise yet more equity without losing management control of their banks—even though their effective shareholding in the banks would have fallen to only 25.1 per cent. A host of other groups soon adopted this strategy. Later it was discovered that most major banks had been lending the bulk of their loans to affiliated companies, more than a few of which were simply conduits for laundering bank loans into cash.

This funding pattern depended, of course, on the faith of both stock market investors and depositors. This faith held up despite ample signs of banks' ill-health, such as the massive oversupply in the property sector (to which banks were heavily exposed) and widespread awareness that prudential regulations were not being adequately enforced. But local affiliates of international auditing firms, such as Arthur Andersen Prasetio Utomo, continued to pass clean bills of health, while the banks themselves continued to expand their earnings.

With no end in sight to Indonesia's prolonged record of rapid economic growth, many investors and depositors simply assumed that the major private banks would continue to benefit from a robust economy. Meanwhile, portfolio funds were flooding into Asia and domestic investors were also becoming increasingly active; this meant that for every investor or depositor who turned sceptical about the banks' prospects, another was ready to step in and invest. Moreover, conglomerates had yet other ways to raise large sums of capital—such as by tapping offshore markets.

Well before the height of the financial boom, in the mid-1980s, clove cigarette maker Bentoel vividly illustrated the pitfalls faced by international banks that lent funds in a KKN state. Along with its blue-chip reputation, Bentoel lost over $350 million in domestic and foreign loans that were embezzled by the majority shareholder.[28] Accounts were fabricated and commercial operations languished for years as the company's owners stashed the company's funds abroad. Because of their strong connections (allegedly to the military), the shareholders were never punished by the ministry of finance, the attorney general or the state banks which lent to them alongside foreign creditors.

The Bentoel imbroglio was viewed as an aberration at the time but, in retrospect, examples of imprudent lending and fraudulent borrowing were common. Many companies borrowed heavily, marked up projects and siphoned off funds; Bentoel only did so more recklessly and was therefore among the first to collapse. One of the next major cases involved Indonesia's leading pharmaceutical manufacturer, Kalbe Farma.

Viewed in the early 1990s as one of Indonesia's premier blue-chips, Kalbe Farma burdened its balance sheet with $240 million in mostly offshore debt.[29] Kalbe's creditors were not concerned that the company had no firm plans for utilising the capital—they trusted the company because it commanded a leading position in a booming sector. The bankers failed to realise that, in fact, Kalbe's marketplace was growing increasingly competitive, and Kalbe's management had been exaggerating earnings by growing its sales to an affiliated distributor.[30] The practice of dumping stock on its distributor finally became unsustainable in 1996; having been one of the market's highest flying stocks, Kalbe's share price suddenly collapsed.[31]

Subsequently, there were strong indications—supported by confidential communications from company insiders—that the company's owners had misused the debt. According to the allegations, Kalbe's controlling shareholders chose not to invest their borrowed funds in secure bank deposits; instead, they purchased CPs issued by other companies that they themselves fully owned.[32] The implication is that the owners used an ailing, partly owned company as a front—to secure relatively inexpensive capital that could be siphoned off for private concerns. Creditors and minority shareholders would shoulder the loss.[33]

As the 1990s wore on, certain market investors increasingly realised that such fraudulence was, in fact, quite widespread among publicly listed companies. Nonetheless, the market continued to boom and Kalbe's collapse hardly dampened the overall sentiment. Then, in 1997, investors witnessed the JSE's most spectacular financial scam: the initial public offering (IPO) of Putra Surya Multidana (PSM), a consumer finance company that leased motorcycles. Essentially a start-up company, PSM pursued a reckless rate of expansion, but investors were mesmerised by the company's persuasive assessment of the pent-up market demand for lucrative motorcycle financing on Java.

Initially valued at $1.4 billion in its May 1997 IPO, within two months PSM's market capitalisation had risen by nearly two-thirds to over $2.2 billion.[34] At that point, however, sizeable amounts of stock began to be dumped on the market. It soon became clear that the owners themselves were selling furiously, and most concluded that the company had been spurious from the start. Within a year from the IPO, PSM was virtually worthless. The shares were eventually delisted.

Kalbe and PSM were hardly isolated cases: the 1990s witnessed hundreds of projects undertaken despite dubious economic feasibility. Capital-intensive projects—such as power plants, petrochemical refineries and pulp mills—were favoured precisely because they offered greater scope for marking up investment costs and misappropriating funds. Sometimes these projects were carried out directly by the government, such as Soeharto's ill-fated rice farm covering one million hectares in the Borneo province of Central Kalimantan. Most, however, were private sector ventures. For instance, Prajogo Pangestu's Chandra Asri Petrochemical Centre—a project which was never viable in its own right but relied on state protection in the form of tariff protection—was built at a cost of $2 billion.[35] According to international consultants who audited the project, the cost should have been only half that.[36]

Some conglomerates justified their headlong expansion by claiming that they were carrying out 'vertical integration' and moving into upstream industries. Sjamsul Nursalim's Gadjah Tunggal Group, for instance, started with rubber plantations and expanded into tyre manufacturing, nylon cord production and, finally, petrochemicals. Other

groups invested in seemingly haphazard fashion: Hashim Djojohadikusumo's Tirtamas Group, for example, simultaneously expanded in
cement, olefins and power generation.

While recklessness and greed coloured much of the lending activity of
international banks in Indonesia, in some instances loans were disbursed
for political considerations as well. A famous example involved the under-
writer of the PSM IPO, Peregrine Securities. The aggressive Hong Kong
investment bank raised eyebrows in mid-1997 by extending a $265 million
short-term loan to a Jakarta taxi operator of questionable repute, Steady
Safe.[37] This unsecured 'bridge' loan—which was more than three times
Steady Safe's total equity—was to be repaid through the proceeds of a
massive rights issue and bond offering later in the year. Steady Safe entertained grandiose plans to diversify from cabs to commuter trams and
high-speed ferries, but the company's earnings prospects interested
Peregrine less than its political connections.

Steady Safe's brash young owner, Yopie Widjaya, was rapidly making
political inroads as a leading crony of Tutut Soeharto, the eldest daughter
of the president.[38] Tutut was Indonesia's leading constructor of toll-roads,
and Peregrine's bridge loan was meant to fund Widjaya's purchase of
infrastructure assets that Tutut wanted to sell. In effect, Peregrine was
trying to curry Tutut's favour by helping her cash out of some hard-to-sell
assets.

By forging ties with Tutut, the Peregrine bankers hoped to win the
lucrative lead-underwriter position for the planned privatisation of Jasa
Marga, the massive state-owned toll-road operator which was, in effect,
Tutut's personal fiefdom. More importantly, it was said that the bankers
believed Soeharto would retire in 1998 and tap Tutut to succeed him.[39]
Peregrine's investment bankers expected that their generosity to Yopie
Widjaya would then be repaid many times over—by a string of coveted
privatisation deals awarded by President Tutut Soeharto.

Peregrine's plan was interrupted. The bridge loan to Steady Safe was
disbursed just weeks before Thailand's devaluation, which threw regional
markets into turmoil and scuttled plans for the rights offering and bond
issue. Steady Safe soon defaulted on Peregrine's bridge loan and, in
January 1998, Asia's largest non-Japanese investment bank finally declared
bankruptcy—because of the sour debt of an obscure Jakarta taxi company.
Ironically, Peregrine's chairman, Philip Tose, ranked alongside Malaysia's
Prime Minister Mahathir Mohamad as one of the most adamant believers
in the superiority of 'Asian values'.

Another episode from 1997 stands out as perhaps the crowning
example of financial excess in Indonesia: the Busang gold scandal. In
late 1996 a start-up Canadian prospecting company, Bre-X, announced a
rich gold find at Busang, deep in the forests of Indonesian Borneo. Duplicitous securities analysts promoted the Bre-X story while the company's

president director—a veteran stock manipulator—ramped the share price. The regulators of Canada's notorious Calgary Stock Exchange were negligent and investors were gullible. Soon the Bre-X find was being touted as the largest gold discovery in world history and the share price reached astronomical valuations. International mining companies began bidding for access to the Busang find, and they did so, typically, by courting access with Soeharto's children.

One of these 'gold majors' made the mistake of seeking the wrong first-family member as its partner: Soeharto's eldest son, Sigit Haryoyu- danto. Since reputedly incurring enormous gambling losses in the late 1980s, Sigit had been virtually ostracised by Soeharto and was rarely seen or heard in public.[40] The Busang bid was his first serious venture in years—but he was quickly upstaged by his sister Tutut, who was backed by a different gold major. Within weeks this sibling rivalry had grown very intense and very public. Soeharto finally decided to put the matter to rest by announcing that the coveted partnership with Bre-X would go to neither Sigit nor Tutut—but rather to himself, through the presidential business foundation run by Bob Hasan, Nusamba Group.

A strange sequence of events followed soon after Soeharto's announcement. First, a mysterious fire at the Busang site destroyed the Bre-X drilling samples. Next, the lead geologist who had made millions on his stock options reportedly jumped from a helicopter in what strongly appeared to be a staged suicide. Finally, an independent assayer deter- mined that the exploration conducted by Bre-X had been a hoax: there was no gold at Busang. The multi-billion dollar fraud was exposed as the greatest mining scam of all time.

B entoel, Kalbe Farma, PSM, Steady Safe and Busang are just a few examples of the financial chicanery that characterised Indonesia's boom-time economy in the 1990s. The boom was sustained by a combi- nation of abundant resources, a long track record of steady economic growth and Indonesia's irresistible allure to foreign financiers who were awash in capital. But the key ingredient that sealed Indonesia's fate was a conspicuous lack of prudential regulation. In fact, Indonesia's regulatory superstructure didn't just turn a blind eye to corruption: it actively took part in propagating the KKN economy—systematically and at virtually all levels of government.

Soeharto himself actually liked to argue, in his private discussions with foreign officials and representatives of donor organisations, that Indonesia's development proved that there was nothing wrong with corruption, as long as the people's basic needs were met and the popu- lation grew gradually better off. Although it took more than 30 years, Soeharto was eventually proven wrong.

3

CRISIS OF CONFIDENCE

Indonesia's boom years brought unprecedented prosperity to large swaths of the economy, but none benefited as much as the financial services sector. In the seven bustling years leading up to 1997, an entire securities industry had sprung up to serve Jakarta's booming capital market. Nearly every major international investment bank established an office in Jakarta to take part in the lucrative business of channelling foreign funds into local shares and, especially, assisting Indonesian firms to raise capital.

For foreign investment bankers, Jakarta represented a frontier of finance. Opaque accounting made financial analysis particularly challenging, while the market's myriad inefficiencies and rapid growth created lucrative opportunities. Investment banks therefore spent lavishly to attract expatriate analysts and salespeople, who were provided with sprawling houses complete with servants, pools and chauffeured sedans. Newly built five-star hotels catered to a constant flow of foreign fund managers and corporate financiers scouring the market for new companies in which to invest.

As the financial bubble created a burgeoning class of Indonesian *nouveau riche*, local stockbrokers and domestic investors joined the fray. Some saw the Jakarta Stock Exchange (JSE) as an irresistible venue for legal gambling—something otherwise discouraged in the world's largest Islamic country. To cater to these investors, local banks launched a bewildering array of mutual funds, high-yield portfolios and margin-trading instruments—thereby inflating the bubble farther still.

The frenzy of demand for Indonesian shares prompted a scramble among companies of all sizes to list their shares on the JSE, conduct rights offerings or launch bond issues. Annually, some 10–12 billion dollars was descending on Jakarta and most of it coursed through the veins of the city's small but giddy capital market. The combination of fast riches, high growth and permissive regulators bred a distinctive culture among

Jakarta's capital-market crowd, characterised by greed, conceit and—most notably—euphoria.

Nowhere was the collective euphoria of the boom years celebrated in more ostentatious fashion than at the annual Capital Markets Conference, a gala event in which analysts, financiers, salespeople and corporate executives all congregated to promote themselves to each other. These convocations grew increasingly grand each year, and the 1997 affair was by far the grandest yet. Indonesian businesspeople and bankers mixed with expatriate stockbrokers and foreign investors. The exhibition hall was rife with free souvenirs, high-tech gadgets and sleek fashion models. Corporate publicity booths ranged from flashy to downright garish: the booth erected by the Soeharto family's preferred investment bank, Makindo, actually flaunted gold gilt.

Overseeing the elaborate preparations for the event was the conference organiser, the Capital Markets Society. As befitted an organisation so closely associated with splendid wealth, the chair was a first-family member, Siti Hediyati (Titiek) Haryadi, the president's second daughter. On the first morning of the conference around 1500 eager attendees packed the main auditorium to hear the keynote speech from an in-law of Titiek: the powerful but well-respected BI governor, Soedradjad Djiwandono.

Djiwandono's soft-spoken oratory style seemed oddly out of place amid the usual bluster and bravado of the Capital Markets Society, but his words stunned the crowd like hammer blows. Unbeknown to all, the central bank chief had decided the previous evening to abandon the peg and float the rupiah. In his keynote morning address he revealed that the momentous policy change had been implemented just moments before the start of his speech.

Some of those in the crowd struggled to grasp the implications of a free-floating currency, while others frantically barked orders into their mobile phones. Still others simply bolted for the door. Throughout the day the mood in the conference hall deteriorated in lock step with the rupiah's relentless dive. By late afternoon the currency had lost 9 per cent of its value. The cornerstone of Jakarta's prolonged financial excess—the rupiah's managed peg to the US dollar—had been plucked out from under the top-heavy house of cards that stood above it.

An era had come to an end, though few realised it at the time. Indonesia's economic crisis had crept up quietly. The Bank of Thailand had floated the baht on 2 July 1997 but that event was accompanied by relatively little concern in Jakarta. Most analysts argued that, compared to Thailand, Indonesia had stronger export growth, a lower current account deficit and a higher ratio of foreign reserves to months of imports.[1] Moreover, unlike the Thai baht, the rupiah had not become markedly overvalued, thanks to Indonesia's peculiar 'crawling peg' system.

Indonesia, therefore, did not appear vulnerable to a standard balance-of-payments crisis, such as the one that had hit Mexico three years earlier. As well, there was strong faith in Soeharto's macroeconomic managers. During various crises that confronted Indonesia in 1966, 1978 and 1986, Soeharto had consistently turned to his respected team of economic ministers—the so-called 'technocrats'—to devise and implement the tough, market-oriented policies required to avert recession. He was expected to do so again.

Furthermore, the traditional maxim regarding Soeharto-era economic doctrine had been 'Bad times make good policy'—that is, crises were opportunities to push through reform. Some therefore believed that the 'scare' of Thailand's devaluation might enable the current crop of technocrats, including Djiwandono and Finance Minister Mar'ie Muhammad, to finally impress Soeharto with the need to fortify the economy by curtailing rent-seeking.[2] Even in the days after Thailand's devaluation, therefore, the JSE index continued to climb, reaching 749 on 8 July. Few at the time realised that this level would not be revisited for years. Within days, the first signs of trouble started to appear.

On 11 July, in a move acclaimed as an appropriate response to the mounting pressure of currency speculators, Djiwandono widened BI's 'intervention band'—or the range of values in which the rupiah was allowed to trade before BI intervened in the currency market.[3] This was designed to deter currency speculators by making the rupiah's movements less predictable and therefore increasing the risk of trading the rupiah.[4] In fact, the move backfired.

At the time, speculators were hungry for risk, having profited handsomely on large bets against currencies around the region. In addition, the 11 July move unfortunately coincided with the flotation of the Philippine peso. Amid sharp drops in the peso and the Malaysian ringgit, BI's move to widen the intervention band inadvertently discouraged investors of all sorts from holding the rupiah—the currency was suddenly seen to have more 'downside' potential than had generally been anticipated.[5] On 21 July the rupiah abruptly plunged to the weak end of its trading band: Rp2600/$. This was a 7 per cent drop—the exchange rate's largest single move since 1986. It was also one of the first signs that Indonesia was facing a 'new' kind of crisis: it was true that Indonesia's balance of public-sector payments were sound, but the balance of private-sector capital flows was another question.

Private capital flows had never been problematic for Indonesia. In the 1970s and 1980s such flows had been negligible and in the 1990s they had been overwhelmingly inward-orientated. Amid the boom in international investing and emerging markets mania, Indonesia received a veritable flood of capital from multinational corporations, international banks and, especially, short-term portfolio investors. Because this investment was fuelling breakneck economic growth, domestic investors generally chose to reinvest their capital in Indonesia. Gradually, however, the same investors who had witnessed the corrosive effects of corruption and reckless lending in Thailand began to reassess Indonesia. As they did so, currency traders identified opportunities—and domestic investors began to stash funds offshore.

There was a momentary calm in the markets as investors waited to see whether the rupiah's 11 July drop was an aberration, but it soon became clear that the currency would not rebound. In fact, over the next three weeks, BI depleted its foreign reserves by around $1.5 billion in its efforts to prevent the currency from sliding farther.[6] And to entice investors to hold rupiah, BI sharply tightened money market liquidity, causing interbank borrowing rates to spike. The high interest rates drove prudent investors out of the stock market, which began to decline in earnest.

As had been the experience of the Bank of Thailand, BI soon found that it was powerless to steer the currency market by dumping dollars and hiking rupiah interest rates. Demand for dollars was far outstripping what BI could afford to sell, and those buying dollars seemed not to care that rupiah interest rates were highly attractive. Had dollar demand been limited to foreign currency traders or short-term portfolio investors, the high interest rate policy should have helped protect the currency. Instead, the dollar demand was being driven by domestic corporations who were desperately short of dollars.

Around 800 Indonesian companies had borrowed offshore and others had borrowed dollar loans from local banks. In most cases the dollar liabilities of these companies exceeded their dollar assets—often by a wide margin. A decline in the rupiah's value caused the companies' liabilities to swell relative to their assets. Ignoring Indonesia's history of periodic devaluation—the most recent of which had been in 1986—remarkably few corporations had insured themselves against currency risk. They might have done so by purchasing special derivative instruments known as swaps, but swaps were expensive and sometimes unavailable.[7] Some managers eschewed hedging simply because they had strong faith that the government would maintain the rupiah's stability, and others may have simply failed to appreciate the risks of being 'unhedged'. But by early August many Indonesian companies were moving to correct their mistakes.

Corporate Indonesia owed offshore creditors an estimated $80 billion —a sum roughly four times greater than BI's gross reserves and many times greater than its liquid reserves. If Indonesian companies bought dollars to cover only a small portion of this sum, it would quickly overwhelm BI's meagre resources. This is precisely what happened on 13 August. After the Philippine peso and Malaysian ringgit floated along with the baht, expectations rose that the rupiah would follow suit. That the crawling peg differentiated the rupiah from other currencies no longer assuaged nervous Indonesian corporations.

Amid the scramble for dollars, the rupiah broke through its new trading band and weakened to Rp2650/$. Recognising that a vigorous defence would only prove futile, BI floated the currency the following morning—the first day of the Capital Markets Conference. The currency fell another 3 per cent the following day. Another interest rate hike helped the rupiah momentarily, but by the end of August it had weakened beyond Rp3000/$. It was now clear that the rupiah's weakness was not a one-off aberration; 53 years of a pegged exchange rate policy had come to an end.

As the implications of a fluctuating rupiah sank in, investor sentiment plummeted. By the end of August the JSE index had lost a staggering 35 per cent from its peak the previous month. In the past, whenever confidence slumped or the economy encountered problems, the technocrats would unveil a list of reforms designed to stimulate investment and productivity. During the 1990s, however, such 'deregulation packages' had become rare. Good times had made bad policy, and the increasingly aggressive cronies surrounding Soeharto successfully fought off threats to their lucrative rent-seeking arrangements. On 3 September, therefore, the market was cheered by a deregulation package introduced by the cabinet's key technocrat, Finance Minister Mar'ie Muhammad.

Muhammad was the virtual antithesis of the stereotypically bland officials who dominated the ranks of Soeharto's government. A career finance ministry official, he was known as a keen reformer, while his unusually modest lifestyle won him the moniker 'Mr Clean'. Alongside these strengths, however, Muhammad had key weaknesses: he was a poor administrator and he lacked media savvy. Poor policy co-ordination and clumsy public relations efforts were hallmarks of his tenure.

The main thrust of the 3 September package was fiscal belt-tightening. Anticipating a budget shortfall, Jakarta's provincial administration had already postponed four large-scale public works projects; now Muhammad's package promised the postponement of many more throughout the country. It also raised import tariffs on luxury goods. And to address concerns about the banking system, Muhammad promised to provide liquidity support to troubled banks.

It was not clear how public spending cuts would stem the outflow of private capital, but nonetheless Muhammad's package was well received. Because all the projects slated for cancellation involved powerful tycoons, Muhammad's package was viewed as a signal that the technocrats would exert their authority over Soeharto's cronies—and this alone was reason for optimism. The JSE rebounded furiously from 479 to 600. But unnoticed by many was an event that actually foreshadowed the duplicitous style of economic policy-making that lay ahead.

At the same time that Muhammad announced government spending cuts, a rival minister disclosed that six companies were being granted generous multi-year tax holidays. Two of these firms belonged to groups that epitomised hubris in the KKN economy: Bob Hasan's Nusamba Group and Marimutu Sinivasan's Texmaco Group.[8] Although the technocrats were promising a return to responsible economic management, other ministers were doing precisely the opposite. Meanwhile, investors were increasingly recognising that, with the rupiah at the level of Rp3000/$, corporate Indonesia faced a plethora of grave problems.

One of Indonesia's currency-related problems pertained to corporate balance sheets. Hundreds of companies with unhedged dollar debts would report large foreign exchange losses on their year-end profit and loss statements. For some companies, these 'forex' losses threatened to wipe out their entire capital base—but this was only part of the problem.

The majority of Indonesian companies earned their revenues in rupiah but had some costs that were linked to the US dollar. For such firms the rupiah's fall relative to the dollar meant that their income fell relative to their costs—in effect, the devaluation squeezed their profit margins. Income was also affected by the general economic slowdown: in a recession, most firms would experience slower unit sales, particularly those in vulnerable sectors like finance, construction, property, building materials and luxury goods. And the companies with unhedged dollar loans suddenly found that their interest payments were one-third more expensive in rupiah terms. This, in turn, had serious implications for the banking system.

Few banks had worried about the creditworthiness of their borrowers when the rupiah was fixed and revenues were perpetually expanding. Now, however, the rupiah was floating freely and revenues were slumping—and widespread defaults were imminent. Meanwhile, those companies that had eschewed offshore debt and borrowed domestically were also threatened with insolvency: BI's policy of hiking interest rates (to encourage investors to hold rupiah) had the regrettable side effect of burying local currency borrowers under ruinously high lending rates.

Securities analysts frantically scrutinised corporate balance sheets to find 'safe plays'—that is, dollar-earning exporters with rupiah costs and low debt. These companies were enjoying unprecedented windfalls but precious few were listed on the JSE. In any event, even these exporters soon encountered difficulties: the degradation of Indonesia's financial system meant that international banks were unwilling to do business with any local banks at all. For exporters this was catastrophic: most relied on trade financing to import raw materials. The devaluation should have made these exporters far more profitable, but lacking credit, many faced severe cashflow constraints. Throughout Indonesia potentially profitable firms that exported garments, shoes or electronic components were forced to stop operations and dismiss workers.

The gravity of the devaluation was causing mounting concern by late September. Moreover, questions were arising about the authority wielded by Djiwandono and Muhammad. Like many Javanese, Soeharto was stubbornly age-conscious—and both Djiwandono and Muhammad were far younger than he.[9] Whereas Soeharto had vested past technocrats with considerable trust, he now tended to overlook his official cabinet and rely on advice from his children and confidants. Few within this inner circle had the expertise to evaluate complex policy options. More importantly, even fewer were ready to sacrifice their personal business interests for the sake of reform. Muhammad encountered trouble, therefore, when he finally unveiled his list of 15 mega-projects that the government would cancel.

Muhammad's list included several of the most ostentatious examples of excess in the KKN economy—but it also included several projects belonging to the first family. These included Tutut Soeharto's improbable plan to erect the 'Malindo' bridge connecting Malaysia and Sumatera, as well as her $2 billion project to burrow a subway line through the swampy soil of Jakarta. Also cancelled were several Cendana-backed power plants that appeared overpriced and rife with rent-seeking arrangements. Muhammad was already unpopular among Soeharto's cronies for having challenged rent-seeking arrangements in the past; now he was raising their ire even further. The finance minister needed to demonstrate that the government was finally intent on smashing the invidious nexus of corruption that weakened the economy—but in doing so he undermined his own authority, by souring his relations with Soeharto.

By early October Indonesia's woes were compounded by nature. The periodic weather phenomenon known as El Nino was creating the worst drought in over 50 years. In addition to causing misery for millions of rural Indonesians, the drought encouraged plantation companies to prepare logged-over land for planting by burning scrub bush. Virgin forests also caught fire. This happened on such a large scale that Singapore and Malaysia were inundated by heavy smoke. That no plantation companies were censored for setting illegal fires only highlighted the extent of corruption in the legal system. The rupiah touched a new low of Rp3800/$.

The combined collapse of the currency and the JSE index meant that foreign equity investors had seen the dollar value of their stocks drop by precisely two-thirds—in just three months. The economy was being devastated by a vicious cycle of pessimism, capital outflow, devaluation and renewed pessimism. Desperate to break this cycle and restore confidence, Soeharto's ministers recommended that Indonesia follow the example of Thailand and the Philippines: both countries had invited assistance from the International Monetary Fund (IMF). On 8 October Soeharto agreed.

Typically, the IMF acts as the world's 'lender of last resort' for governments that have been living beyond their means and have depleted their resources. But in this instance it was unclear what actual support the IMF could provide: Indonesia's foreign reserves were still adequate at $20.5 billion and the government already had a $2 billion World Bank standby facility that it could draw down if needed. This was not a crisis of public resources; rather it was a crisis of private-sector confidence. Soeharto may have hoped to revive confidence by inviting hands-on policy guidance from the world's foremost experts, but the IMF's arrival also drew attention to the severity of Indonesia's predicament. By falling under IMF care, an emerging 'Asian tiger' had joined the ranks of the world's most troubled economies—in the short space of three months.

After a series of delays that dismayed the markets, the IMF's negotiators finally announced the details of the 'rescue package' they had hammered out with the technocrats on 31 October. In the first 'Letter of Intent' between the government and the IMF a deliberate effort was made to awe the market by brandishing a vast sum of resources that would be 'pledged' to help stabilise Indonesia: $43 billion.

In fact, most investors realised that most of the pledged funds were unlikely to ever be disbursed—and, in any event, the government had little immediate need for these funds.[10] More important were specific policy measures to restore investor confidence. Unfortunately, the IMF kept most details of these agreements confidential—undermining the purpose of restoring confidence.

In addition to monetary tightening, the other main thrust of the 31 October package was 'structural' reform. These measures targeted some of the more egregious examples of rent-seeking activity, such as the $5 billion per annum plywood industry. Indonesia's largest export sector was elaborately structured to ensure that a significant chunk of the profits that would have otherwise accrued to wood producers flowed instead to Indonesian Plywood Association (Apkindo), which was run by Indonesia's timber magnate, Bob Hasan. Among Soeharto's oldest financiers, Hasan was Soeharto's golfing partner and was known to be the president's closest confidante.

Although the Plywood Association probably ranked as the country's most ostentatious rent-seeking arrangement, others affected virtually every sector of the economy. For instance, the National Logistics Agency (Bulog) enforced a host of monopolies that favoured well-connected individuals, such as the Bogosari flour-milling monopoly enjoyed by the nation's largest conglomerate, Sudono Salim's Salim Group. Similarly, the world's second largest clove-farming industry was deliberately structured to enrich Soeharto's family.

In 1968 Soeharto's half-brother Probosutedjo joined Salim to enjoy monopoly rights to import cloves and sell them on to Indonesia's massive clove cigarette industry at a mark-up of nearly 100 per cent.[11] Thirty years later the rent-yielding structure had been inherited by Soeharto's youngest son, 36-year-old Hutomo (Tommy) Mandala Putra. All Indonesian clove farmers were forced to sell their crop to Tommy's Clove Marketing and Bufferstock Agency (BPPC) at Rp2500 per kilogram, while clove cigarette-makers were obliged to buy cloves from BPPC at Rp12500 per kilogram.[12]

In 1996 the government granted Tommy another rent-seeking arrangement: Soeharto decreed that Timor Putra Nasional, Tommy's newly formed joint-venture with South Korea's Kia Motors company, had 'pioneer' status to develop a national car. Four state banks and twelve private banks were instructed to disburse a staggering $690 million toward the construction of an assembly plant. And until its completion Timor was permitted to import 45 000 fully built-up Kia sedans—free of the import duties or luxury taxes that formed at least 60 per cent of new car prices in Indonesia at the time.[13] The dispensation for Tommy inflicted a blow to one of the country's most prestigious and promising industries, car assembly.

The Timor program was modelled on the lines of an even larger state-sponsored industry: B.J. Habibie's Nusantara Aircraft Industry (IPTN). With Soeharto's enthusiastic support, the technology minister sought to develop an Indonesian aircraft industry from the ground up. The effort, which had begun in the mid-1970s, was doomed to failure, but Habibie secured massive sums from the state budget to fund IPTN. According to some estimates, this funding surpassed $1 billion a year during the 1990s.[14]

The abundance of protected industries and rent-seeking structures was the main reason why the Indonesian economy was consistently rated as among the world's least competitive.[15] Having long railed in vain against the waste and inefficiency caused by these schemes, the World Bank finally saw the crisis as an opportunity to make progress. At the same time, it was hoped that the implementation of structural reforms would help attract investors again and thereby begin reversing the debilitating crisis of confidence.

Past experience did, indeed, suggest that structural reforms would encourage the market. When there had been downturns in the past, investors had been heartened by deregulation packages that chipped away at market distortions and opened new opportunities. This time investors were eagerly looking for more deregulation, and the stakes were far higher than before. Sentiment was far worse, the distortions were bigger and the scope of reform needed to restore confidence was far broader. The World Bank and IMF soon found that, against this backdrop, restoring confidence through structural reforms was an exceedingly tricky task.

Investors cheered when it was revealed that the 31 October package targeted the Plywood Association, Bulog, Bogosari, BPPC, the Timor and others—but, by demanding so many reforms from Soeharto all at once, IMF officials turned the stubborn president against them. Especially when, in conjunction with the reform package, the IMF initiated a move that backfired badly: the abrupt closure of sixteen troubled banks.

R umours of imminent bank closures had been circulating since September, but it was thought that insolvent banks would be merged into larger banks, rather than resorting to outright closures. It therefore came as a complete surprise when Muhammad and Djiwandono announced on 1 November that sixteen banks would be immediately closed. At first the move was cheered: the closed banks were generally small (their combined assets represented a mere 3 per cent of the total sector, and one of the banks had actually ceased operating seven years before), and most were longstanding and well-known examples of mismanagement.

The largest bank on the November list of closures was Hendra Rahardja's Bank Harapan Sentosa. Rahardja's father had embezzled another family bank in the 1960s—while Rahardja's brother, Eddy Tansil, famously embezzled $600 million from state-owned Bank Bapindo in 1992.[16] Tansil later escaped from prison, and Rahardja himself fled Indonesia rather than stand trial for misappropriating over $1 billion from Bank Harapan Sentosa.[17] As early as 1995, Mar'ie Muhammad reportedly knew that Rahardja was bilking his depositors through fraudulent property projects and affiliated loans, but because the bank's board of commissioners included a brother-in-law of Soeharto, Muhammad was powerless to act.

The second largest bank on the closure list, Bank Pacific, was among the very few banks that went insolvent during the height of the boom—even though BI itself owned 38 per cent of the bank. The balance was owned by Gen. (ret.) Ibnu Sutowo, a favourite peer of Soeharto who became the country's most powerful business figure in the early 1970s as head of the state oil monopoly, Pertamina.[18] During the oil boom Sutowo embroiled Pertamina in a host of uneconomical ventures, burying the company—and thus the government—under contingent liabilities totalling $10.5 billion.[19] After being eased into retirement in 1976, Sutowo entrusted his Bank Pacific to his daughter, Endang Mokodompit, who also proceeded to embezzle funds on a grand scale in the early 1990s. In addition to lending around a third of the bank's assets (some 500 million) to her own companies, Mokodompit raised a further $1 billion by using the bank to guarantee CPs issued by an affiliated finance company.[20] Gullible investors snapped up the CPs simply because the guarantor bank was jointly owned by BI and a close associate of the president. BI was eventually forced to make good on the CPs itself.

Also among the closed banks were three smaller banks whose share-holders included first-family members. Muhammad and Djiwandono were clearly trying to show that economic management took precedence over Cendana's interests—but Soeharto's relatives were not ready to back down yet. The president's second son, Bambang, lashed out at the technocrats upon hearing about the closure of his bank, Bank Andromeda: 'This is an attempt to sully our family name in order to indirectly topple my father, so that he won't be chosen president again.'[21] The president's foster brother, Probosutedjo, also challenged the closure of his own bank. Within a week, Muhammad capitulated and granted Bambang permission to transfer Andromeda's assets and liabilities to a Salim-owned bank.[22] If the tech-nocrats were trying to show that they were in charge, they had achieved the opposite: Soeharto's relatives clearly outranked the minister of finance and the central bank governor.

The bank closures also produced a far more serious misfortune—one that highlights the inherent instability of an economy built on cronyism. Two distinct sets of market expectations were operating at the time: those of professional investors versus those of the local public. Professional investors were initially pleased to see crony banks being liquidated; such investors generally judged bank soundness according to performance ratios, audited accounts, management quality and so on. The closure of bad banks suggested that the government would finally promote pruden-tial regulation.

Many public depositors, however, were dismayed by the closures. Knowing that regulations were rarely enforced and accounts were often falsified, these investors tended to view the safest banks as those most closely affiliated with Cendana. When the technocrats, thinking like professionals, attacked these very banks, local depositors panicked and withdrew their funds from all but the state-owned banks. Exacerbating the panic were poor communications regarding deposit guarantees and the likelihood that other banks might be closed. IMF officials later admitted that the closures, which had been made at their behest, were ill-advised.[23] A move designed to restore faith in the banking system had produced precisely the opposite effect.

S ome argue that the turning point in Indonesia's crisis occurred in November: had the bank liquidations been managed better, or had they not taken place, the technocrats might still have been able to stabilise the economy. Many investors still seemed to believe that Indonesia's problems were only temporary; and precipitously high interest rates finally seemed to be having the desired effect on the exchange rate. Having touched a low of Rp4000/$ in early October, the rupiah strengthened to Rp3200/$ by mid-November. Just then, though, an ominous event occurred.

Mar'ie Muhammad visited parliament on 19 November to fulfil a summons for testimony. Parliament had always been a rubber-stamp body, but occasionally it would exert its constitutional privilege to question policy-makers—particularly when those policy-makers had fallen out of favour with Cendana. On this occasion Muhammad was questioned about rumours that BI had been quietly lending out large sums over the past two months—in contravention of its own tight monetary policy. In particular, parliamentarians questioned whether it was true, as they had 'heard', that BI had disbursed some Rp8 trillion (or around $2.4 billion at prevailing exchange rates) to five large banks. Muhammad refused to answer. And in an indication that rifts were now developing between Indonesia's two main technocrats, he recommended that parliament instead ask BI's governor, Djiwandono.[24]

In fact, BI was well on its way to lending out far more than Rp8 trillion. Before the crisis Indonesia's private banks were already fragile: they were generally undercapitalised, tight on liquidity and overreliant on short-term deposits. In August BI's measures to bolster the exchange rate—draining rupiah liquidity from the banking system and hiking interest rates—placed the weakest banks under severe stress. Amid this monetary tightening, some banks depleted their cash reserves and were unable to borrow from other banks. They then turned to the central bank as the 'lender of last resort'.

In a cabinet meeting on 3 September, Soeharto instructed Muhammad and Djiwandono to lend central bank funds to such cash-strapped banks, lest they default on their depositors.[25] This lending was known as Bank Indonesia Liquidity Support, or BLBI lending. Injecting liquidity into troubled banks contradicted BI's own policy of reining in liquidity, but it was deemed necessary lest panic spread. If a few banks defaulted on a few depositors, other depositors might rush other banks to withdraw their funds all at once—thereby presenting BI with even larger demands for liquidity.

The implicit danger was that an avalanche of demands for liquidity would overwhelm the resources of BI itself—forcing BI to print new rupiah banknotes to fulfil the demands of bank depositors. Printing new currency would only further devalue the rupiah, thereby fuelling a vicious cycle of devaluation, bank rushes, monetary expansion and further devaluation. Muhammad and Djiwandono hoped to avert such a predicament by ensuring that no banks defaulted on their depositors. And as long as BLBI lending was kept to modest levels, BI could (in theory) offset the lending by draining funds from banks with surplus cash, such as state banks. The technocrats therefore hoped to safeguard the bank system while keeping the money supply in balance.

Through September and October, BI's strategy seemed to work. Deposits were withdrawn, but overall liquidity remained tight and the money supply was kept in check. But this all changed with the abrupt closure of the sixteen private banks on 1 November. Depositors, large and small, no longer trusted private banks—particularly the private banks closest to Cendana, which also happened to be the largest private banks. BLBI lending, combined with dollar demand from corporations belatedly trying to hedge their offshore debts, caused the currency to slump to Rp3600/$ by month-end. And amid the atmosphere of mounting crisis the BLBI lending would soon become susceptible to abuse on a large scale.

M eanwhile, depositors were given more reasons to withdraw their savings. While the IMF demanded sweeping structural reforms to restore confidence in economic management, several of the mega-projects that Muhammad had postponed were surreptitiously renewed. Soeharto specifically decreed that construction should resume on the massive Tanjung Jati C power plant, partly owned by Tutut.[26] Similarly, the government commissioned a $3.2 billion petroleum refinery involving Bambang Soeharto.

While some investors and depositors worried that the technocrats lacked the authority they needed to handle the worsening crisis, others soon had reason to worry about the abilities of Soeharto himself: the president suddenly fell ill in early December. Palace officials said that Soeharto was suffering fatigue from an overseas trip in which he logged 62 hours of flying time in a mere twelve days.[27] But when doctors prescribed a ten-day rest, panic spread that the president had been incapacitated by a stroke.

Soeharto-era Indonesia had always been stalked by fears of mayhem in the event of the president's sudden demise. This was a particularly awkward time for such fears to arise again. And only three days later an explosion ripped through the top two floors of BI's newly built office tower, killing fifteen bank employees. Indonesia's increasingly brazen press immediately speculated that the perpetrator was Bambang Soeharto, who was still locked in bitter conflict with BI over the fate of Bank Andromeda.

The mysterious bombing of BI seemed emblematic of the country's plight. Although Soeharto soon re-emerged in public, bank runs continued and private capital fled the country. From net private capital inflows of around $3 billion per quarter prior to the crisis, Indonesia witnessed a staggering reversal in the fourth quarter of 1997: an estimated $8 billion was transferred offshore.[28] The JSE index plummeted to 330 and the rupiah continually sank to new lows, finally reaching Rp5800/$ on 16 December. At this level, the closing of company accounts at year-end would render much of corporate Indonesia technically bankrupt.

There was, however, a far worse tragedy: the rupiah's devaluation caused the price of tradable goods, such as food, to soar in price. While this benefited some farmers, it spelled a sharp drop in purchasing power for rupiah wage-earners and, especially, the poor. Prior to the crisis 11 per cent of the population, or some 22 million people, were living below the poverty line—which was calculated not on income levels but on daily caloric intake.[29] As food prices rose by 3–4 per cent per month during the final months of 1997, decades worth of poverty alleviation—Soeharto's most important achievement—were in danger of being reversed.

Soeharto's efforts to address the crisis did little to restore confidence. Rather than heeding the IMF's advice to reform rent-seeking structures, Soeharto empowered a new 'Business Taskforce' to recommend policy initiatives; heading the taskforce was Anthony Salim, who had taken control of the country's largest conglomerate from his father, Sudono Salim. Again the technocrats were being circumvented in favour of cronies.

Next, Soeharto summarily dismissed four of BI's seven managing directors, without even notifying Djiwandono beforehand. The attorney general began investigating the dismissed directors in connection with a Rp1.5 trillion embezzlement scandal. It strongly appeared, however, that the BI directors were being punished not for corruption but for having attempted to liquidate banks owned by the first family.

As 1997 drew to a close, Indonesians grappled with the notion that the foundations of growth and prosperity had unravelled in less than five months. The country had entered into a recession—a phenomenon that the majority of the population had never experienced. Businesspeople were baffled and consumers were panicky. The devaluation was devastating the banking system, while inflation threatened to impoverish millions. And as many rightly feared, conditions would only grow worse—except, that is, for a privileged few with access to the president.

4

PREDATORY STATE

January 1998 overlapped with the ninth month of the Islamic calendar, Ramadhan, during which all healthy adult Muslims forgo food and water between sunrise and sunset. Jakarta was typically characterised by a distinct feeling of good cheer during Ramadhan; this year, however, the city was overcome by only one emotion: intense anxiety.

As the rupiah plummeted in value, Jakarta's middle class converged on grocery stores to hoard food before prices rose again. The government appealed for calm, but food riots erupted in a host of towns across Java. Perhaps not knowing that food prices inevitably soar following a devaluation, mobs levelled accusations of price-gouging at shopkeepers— particularly those who were of ethnic-Chinese descent. Members of this group accounted for only around 4 per cent of the population, but they dominated trade and attracted widespread prejudice. Anti-Chinese attacks would only grow worse as the rupiah continued its inexorable plunge.

The rupiah had already slid to Rp6350/$ by 6 January, the day that Soeharto addressed parliament to unveil the state budget for 1998. As the markets had feared, the budget rested on hopelessly unrealistic assumptions. Soeharto anticipated 9 per cent inflation, 4 per cent GDP growth and an average exchange rate for the year of Rp4000/$. In fact, the inflation target was likely to be surpassed within a week, and a 4 per cent GDP contraction was far more likely than 4 per cent growth. As for the exchange rate assumption, the rupiah fell to Rp8800/$ the next day.

Meanwhile, an unnamed IMF official planted a statement in the *Washington Post*: the Fund was displeased with the government's performance and it doubted Soeharto's commitment to reform. This further soured the president's relations with the technocrats, and some feared that the president was considering scrapping IMF assistance altogether.[1] Regional stock markets tumbled along with the rupiah's nosedive and the effect was felt as far afield as Wall Street.

Soeharto was suddenly bombarded with telephone calls—US president Bill Clinton, German chancellor Helmut Kohl and Singaporean prime minister Goh Chok Tong all urged Indonesia's president to adhere to IMF advice. But according to some diplomats it was only after a three-hour meeting with the Japanese prime minister, Ryutaro Hashimoto, that Soeharto finally relented.[2] An IMF team arrived days later to negotiate a new 'memorandum'.

By mid-January the IMF team had secured Soeharto's agreement to revise the budget assumptions and, most significantly, institute a breathtaking array of reforms. Major rent-seeking and racketeering operations—the Plywood Association, Bulog, BPPC, the Timor car program and others—would be curtailed or eliminated. BI would be given full autonomy to devise monetary policy and set interest rates, while the finance ministry would implement extensive tax changes. A host of government monopolies and cartels would be ended, costly subsidies for fuel and power would be dramatically reduced and export restrictions on palm oil would be ended. Extensive privatisation would take place and investment restrictions in the banking and retailing sectors would be lifted. Fiscal transparency would be applied to hidden government accounts—such as the reforestation fund, from which B.J. Habibie had famously tapped $600 million for his aircraft plant.

The reform package had been hammered out in a late night session between IMF and World Bank officials and Soeharto himself. Some took this as a sign that the ageing autocrat had finally awoken to the threats he faced. Elsewhere, however, the package was viewed with scepticism. It was vague regarding the central issue of resolving the massive overhang of private sector debt, and investors were growing jaded about the likelihood that Soeharto would implement reforms in good faith.

To make matters worse, the IMF crippled the agreement from the start by committing another public relations blunder, this time at the signing ceremony. As a seated Soeharto bent over the documents and applied his signature, IMF managing director Michel Camdessus stood above him and watched—arms folded and wearing a frown. By the standards of Indonesian etiquette this behaviour was distinctly rude. In footage broadcast throughout the country it appeared that Indonesia was being forced, in its moment of weakness, to bow to Western demands.

Soeharto suffered loss of face in the signing ceremony, and this may have contributed to his unco-operative attitude to the IMF. More likely, the president never intended to co-operate in the first place. In any event, the government was 'backpedalling' on the agreement within days.

The IMF agreement had demanded the dismantling of rent-seeking cartels in major sectors, and it specifically mentioned Bob Hasan's Plywood Association. The cartel channelled enormous rents to the Nusamba Group, which Hasan administered on Soeharto's behalf. But just days after the IMF agreement was signed, the minister of forestry told reporters that it might not be necessary to abolish the Plywood Association after all. He actually admitted that he was awaiting instructions from Hasan before taking any action.[3]

The IMF targeted the Plywood Association in an effort to show the markets that Indonesia was prepared to make its economy more efficient, productive and resilient. But the IMF may have been aiming too high: Bob Hasan was fighting reform with the utmost tenacity.[4] Given his proximity to Soeharto, this indicated that the president himself was at odds with the Fund.

Meanwhile, the government was loath to abandon the mega-projects that the technocrats and donors were trying to halt. The projects invariably involved kickbacks, commissions and bribes that were the lifeblood of Soeharto-era governance. With the economy reeling and a new cabinet scheduled to take office in just four months, some government officials seemed desperate to commission projects while they still had time to do so.

In an angry public letter to the government, the World Bank finally ended Tutut Soeharto's Tanjung Jati C power plant project, but Tutut persisted with other projects—such as a $2.5 billion project to build a triple-decked toll road and commuter train line above Jalan Sudirman, Jakarta's main thoroughfare. On 12 January Tutut told the press that the project's costs could be contained by using domestic suppliers, rather than importing materials at a disadvantageous exchange rate. Citing an example of a good local supplier, Tutut mentioned Citra Lamtoro Gung—her own business group.[5]

Similarly, on 22 January—the day that the rupiah finally sailed through the Rp10 000/$ level—the minister for mines and energy formally commissioned Indonesia's grandest power project to date: the coal-fired Cirenti plant in Sumatera. Designed to supply power to Malaysia, the total construction costs were estimated to reach $6 billion. Cirenti's shareholders included Nusamba, the group controlled by Bob Hasan, and Soeharto himself.[6]

Cendana's mega-projects projects were of limited economic significance in their own right, but the first family's worsening antics cast grave doubts on Soeharto's intentions. Even as international heads of state and Indonesia's principal donors urged him to curtail corruption, the president allowed his children and cronies to perpetuate the very behaviour that had originally helped precipitate the crisis. Soeharto's pragmatism—the hallmark of his 32 years in power—seemed to fail him. And while donors and investors fretted about what they observed on the surface, even more serious acts were being perpetrated behind the scenes, unbeknown to all but a tight circle of Soeharto-family insiders.

The Indonesian term '*katebelece*', derived from Dutch, literally means the tolling of a cat's bell-collar; figuratively, the term is used to refer to the way New Order cronies cadged favours from their patrons in government.[7] *Katebelece* was used to obtain sinecures, largesse or rent-earning structures. And among the most successful users of *katebelece* was Indonesia's polyester king, Texmaco Group owner Marimutu Sinivasan.

In a country consisting of hundreds of ethnic groups the 61-year-old Sinivasan belonged to one of the most unusual: Indonesia's tiny Tamil-Indian community. When Britain's Sir Stamford Raffles ruled Indonesia from 1811 to 1816 (during the Napoleonic wars), he imported a small number of Tamil labourers to work on plantations in Sumatera.[8] Nearly 200 years later their descendants still occupied a distinct neighbourhood in the Sumateran city of Medan. Like many from this community, Sinivasan entered the textile trade at an early age.

The first three decades of Sinivasan's career were lacklustre. Having started in 1963 as a weaver of *batik* cloth, he gradually expanded into polyester and the assembly of weaving looms. Sinivasan's fortunes changed dramatically, however, after meeting Soeharto in 1992. At the time, the president was concerned about maintaining control over those who were accumulating fortunes amid the economic boom.

Soeharto seemed worried that his political enemies might grow powerful through business success. If wealth were allowed to accrue to businesspeople who were *pribumi* (i.e. 'indigenous' Indonesians such as Javanese, Sundanese, Malay and so on), such tycoons might threaten Soeharto politically. The president therefore worked to ensure that the bulk of corporate Indonesia was controlled by a handful of ethnic-Chinese tycoons, whose ethnicity prevented them from pursuing political office. But when Soeharto began courting political Islam in the early 1990s, he was forced to alter course: Indonesia's political Islamists were particularly jealous of the non-Muslim ethnic-Chinese. This may be one reason why Soeharto then promoted a group of *pribumi* whom he could trust absolutely—his own children—but this soon gave rise to complaints of nepotism. In 1992, therefore, Soeharto was looking for a non-threatening and non-controversial front-man. Sinivasan—who was non-Chinese, non-*pribumi*, non-Muslim and non-Christian—fitted the mould.

Soeharto's overt favouritism fuelled breathtaking growth within the Texmaco Group.[9] By 1996 Sinivasan's flagship company, Polysindo, had reputedly become the world's largest producer of polyester. But not content to be known only as a polyester king, Sinivasan emulated other tycoons and branched out. Spearheading an Habibie-esque 'high-technology drive', Sinivasan planned to expand his assembler of weaving looms, Texmaco Perkasa Engineering, into a manufacturer of heavy trucks. Sinivasan mesmerised Soeharto with his grandiose plans and by 1997 the pair were making frequent public appearances together.[10] When the economic crisis struck, however, Texmaco was overextended and unprepared.

Texmaco owed massive sums of unhedged dollar debt, and its largest project—the truck manufacturing plant—was focused towards the domestic market, which was atrophying. There was even serious trouble in Polysindo, an exporter that should have been thriving amid the crisis. The devaluation had shrunk Polysindo's rupiah costs relative to its dollar revenues, but still the company was struggling to service its debt.

In retrospect, it seems likely that the firm's profits were whisked away through common techniques used in the KKN economy: transfer pricing and inflated costs. At the time, however, Sinivasan complained that Polysindo was having trouble obtaining trade finance credits. Indonesia's soaring country risk-ratings meant that international banks were no longer willing to deal with Indonesian counterparts. This rendered many exporters unable to obtain post-shipment facilities and finance their cashflows.

Soeharto made a show of responding to the exporters' predicament by summoning 170 businessmen to the presidential palace in October 1997. Immediately following the closed-door meeting, minister of industry and trade Tunky Ariwibowo announced that a specially designed instrument would be created to assist troubled exporters. He called it a 'pre-shipment' export facility and portrayed it as an improved version of the common 'post-shipment' export facility provided by commercial banks. In fact, there was a world of difference between the two.

A post-shipment facility is a standard trade-financing instrument, whereby a bank pays an exporter for goods that have already been shipped to an overseas purchaser. The purchaser, upon receiving the goods, reimburses the bank, which collects a fee from the original exporter. In effect, the bank is providing a 'bridging' loan for several weeks to help an exporter's cashflow. The bank faces very low risk: it disburses the loan only after the exporter shows proof that the goods, which serve as collateral, have been loaded on board a container ship and insured.

Exporters would have benefited if the government had simply improved the availability of such relatively simple post-shipment facilities. Instead, Ariwibowo introduced an instrument that was far from being a genuine trade-financing facility. The pre-shipment facility enabled exporters to receive payment for their exports before the goods had even been ordered by buyers—much less produced or shipped. By merely forecasting its expected total export revenue for the upcoming twelve-month period, an exporter could tap a state bank for a loan equivalent to 50 per cent of that amount. In effect, the bank would be underwriting the exporter's future revenue—relying on nothing more than the exporter's assurance that it would, in fact, receive orders, produce the goods, earn the revenue and repay the loan.

Ariwibowo's instrument was a classic product of the KKN state. In fact, the facility bore a curious resemblance to a scheme carried out in 1993, when the state-owned bank Bapindo issued 'pre-shipment import facilities' to Eddy Tansil's Golden Key Group—to import $600 million worth of goods that had never even been ordered. This time, however, there was a hitch: Indonesia's state banks were already far too feeble to support Ariwibowo's plan.

Forced to pay out sky-high deposit rates while their loan books soured, the state banks lacked sufficient liquidity to lend heavily to exporters. To circumvent this problem, both Ariwibowo and Djiwandono issued decrees that allowed pre-shipment facilities to be financed with funds from the central bank (BI). State banks would only act as middlemen, identifying 'needy' exporters and channelling funds to them from BI's reserves. Several days after the decrees were issued Sinivasan obtained Texmaco's first pre-shipment facility.

To circumvent the rule that exporters could borrow only up to 50 per cent of their expected annual export revenues, Texmaco simply inflated its revenue forecast.[11] The channelling bank, BNI, disbursed $276 million, or 45 per cent of the forecast. But Sinivasan soon needed more funds. By his own admission, he secured the credit through the personal intervention of Soeharto.[12]

Sinivasan requested $340 million from BNI on 24 December, and he carbon-copied his request to the president on 29 December.[13] Soeharto immediately forwarded the letter to State Secretary Moerdiono, with a note scribbled in the margin: 'State Secretary—I've already authorised this, but it hasn't been acted on yet . . .'[14] Moerdiono relayed the order to Djiwandono, but the central bank governor baulked at issuing such a large sum of foreign currency while the rupiah was in free-fall. He requested that the facility be disbursed in rupiah, but his request was denied.

On 13 January 1998, with the rupiah at Rp8500/$ and with IMF officials hammering out a new reform package with Soeharto, Djiwandono finally authorised the loan. He did not, however, authorise the full amount: Texmaco was lent only $240 million. Sinivasan sought the balance of $100 million from BNI, but the bank's liquidity was too tight. The solution was to turn back to BI, at which point a new mechanism was devised for funnelling funds from BI to BNI: a bilateral SBPU sale.[15] This was a highly unorthodox method.

BI buys SBPUs, or money market papers, from banks to inject liquidity into the banking system. The purchases are typically made through open auctions, but at the time BI had suspended such auctions in order to drain liquidity, support the exchange rate and deter currency speculators. For Texmaco, however, BI conducted a special 'bilateral' auction exclusively for BNI—at below-market interest rates. BNI then re-lent the funds directly to Texmaco. In effect, Sinivasan not only secured coveted pre-shipment export facilities; he also borrowed subsidised funds directly from BI through an unorthodox mechanism contrived especially for him—all amid a catastrophic economic collapse.

Sinivasan soon began asking for more. He invited Soeharto to visit his truck factory in early February, where the president posed for photos in a shiny new vehicle. Later that day Soeharto signed a presidential order dismissing Djiwandono as BI governor, even though his term was due to expire in less than two months.[16] The following day, Sinivasan asked BI for another $200 million. Soeharto, he said, had explicitly instructed him to complete Texmaco Engineering's massive expansion program.

Apparently receiving no response, Sinivasan requested the funds again two weeks later—but this time he asked for an additional Rp450 billion, sending a copy of his request to Soeharto. As before, Soeharto immediately instructed Moerdiono to follow up by scribbling: 'State Secretary—BI agrees. Carry this out.'[17] BI responded, though only in part: the rupiah funds were released, but the dollar loan was short $75 million. As he had done before, Sinivasan immediately demanded the full amount—which was finally disbursed on 12 March. Again a combination of pre-shipment facilities and bilateral auctions were used to direct the funds to Texmaco.[18]

Pre-shipment facilities were finally abolished in mid-1998. Only 20 companies ever received Ariwibowo's coveted pre-shipment facilities. The total funds disbursed through the program reached Rp6.2 trillion—but 75 per cent of this total, or Rp4.6 trillion, went exclusively to Texmaco.[19] Moreover, Texmaco was one of only two borrowers who received these facilities predominantly in dollars. And while it was borrowing pre-shipment facilities, the group was also securing another $300 million through indirect bank loans at below-market interest rates.[20]

In short, during four of the worst months of the crisis—amid a collapsing currency, soaring interest rates, escalating food riots and pro-tracted negotiations over the terms of emergency IMF lending—BI sur-rendered around $900 million of its dwindling foreign reserves to Sinivasan. This sum was equivalent to 7 per cent of Indonesia's net inter-national reserves as of March 1998, or stated differently, equivalent to nearly one-third of the IMF funds disbursed to BI between November 1997 and March 1998. In effect, one out of three IMF dollars had flowed to Sinivasan.

To what end Sinivasan used these funds remains unclear. The poly-ester mogul admits that they were not used for their legally authorised purpose (export financing), but rather for a combination of debt repay-ment and capacity expansion.[21] This seems implausible: the vast majority of Indonesian conglomerates had simply ceased servicing their offshore loans by early 1998; it is difficult to see why Sinivasan would have been an exception. In fact, Polysindo continually defaulted on its creditors throughout 1998. Sinivasan's claims that he was financing the expansion of his truck-assembly facility are also suspect; even during boom times, the feasibility of the project was dubious.

Djiwandono later directed blame to Soeharto. In parliamentary testimony, Djiwandono explained that 'the disbursal of funds to Texmaco took place because BI was not independent. The BI governor's role was as the president's helper. Tycoons had better access to the president than the governor of BI.'[22] Later still, in a foreign press interview, Djiwandono was more frank in explaining why he authorised the lending: 'I was afraid. I have a family.'[23] His replacement, Syahril Sabirin, also said that he was acting on direct orders from Soeharto.[24]

It seems doubtful that Soeharto would have issued his orders merely as a favour for Sinivasan. There is reason to believe that Texmaco's borrowings were used for political purposes: Sinivasan's brother, Manimaren, was an important deputy treasurer of Golkar. Investment bankers familiar with the Texmaco Group claim that its companies acted as a Golkar slush fund, with funds leaked out through practically every post in the profit-and-lost statement.[25] It is also possible that Texmaco's borrowings were simply embezzled, perhaps for the benefit of Soeharto or his family. But regardless of how the funds were used, it is clear that Texmaco was not an isolated case.

In addition to funding Texmaco, BI was accused of disbursing as much as $1 billion in imprudent loans during the crisis through its fully owned commercial bank in the Netherlands, Bank Indover.[26] A former subsidiary of the colonial-era De Javasche Bank, Indover has long been the subject of controversy: Dutch regulators criticised its finances; the IMF demanded that BI divest its shareholding in the bank; and two former BI directors were charged on suspicion of corruption in connection with the bank.[27]

But the Texmaco and Indover episodes stand out only in regard to the amount of detail that later surfaced. The two episodes, in fact, paled in comparison with a far larger use—or depredation—of the state treasury: BLBI lending.

The bank runs that followed the abrupt closure of the sixteen banks in November had still not abated by late December. If anything, they were growing worse. The technocrats vowed not to carry out any more abrupt closures, but depositors seemed to pay no heed. The rupiah's rapid devaluation fed fears that other private banks would be shut down or simply collapse on their own accord. Rumours regarding Soeharto's health only exacerbated the situation. On 27 December, Soeharto reiterated to his economic ministers that BI should provide liquidity to cash-strapped banks to avoid defaults on depositors.[28]

In effect, the government would be bailing out bank depositors, rather than allowing banks to default on their customers. BI Governor Djiwandono agreed with the policy: defaults had to be avoided, lest the banking system collapse under the pressure of worsening bank runs.[29] But ironically, while the provision of liquidity was intended to forestall further bank runs, several private banks continued to report massive withdrawals.

As usual, the instructions that Soeharto issued to BI on 27 December were sent by letter through State Secretary Moerdiono. The letter was marked confidential, but a parliamentary investigation later discovered that copies were leaked to certain bankers.[30] Soon thereafter, demand for BLBI loans skyrocketed. As of mid-November, BI had disbursed around Rp8 trillion in such loans; by the end of January, this had mushroomed to Rp85 trillion, and it would eventually reach Rp145 trillion—or around $14 billion at prevailing exchange rates.[31]

Historically, monetary stability had been a hallmark of the New Order, but suddenly that discipline was lost. BI's lending caused a massive inflation of the money supply. Bank customers throughout Indonesia noticed the circulation of a vast quantity of newly minted banknotes, most of which bore Soeharto's beaming visage. From the end of October to the end of January, cash in circulation increased by a staggering 50 per cent, while the supply of base money (M1, or currency plus demand deposits), rose by 38 per cent.[32] The expansion dismayed the IMF: the government had promised to limit M1 growth to 10 per cent for full-year 1998, but this level had been surpassed before the end of January.[33] For the economy, the consequences were ruinous.

Ironically, BI was implementing two contradictory policies at once. The central bank forced up interest rates (to more than 60 per cent per annum for short-term bank deposits) to tighten the supply of rupiah and thereby boost the currency's value. At the same time, however, the BLBI lending was inflating the supply of rupiah, thereby undermining its value. Far more rupiah were injected into the system than BI could (or did) absorb through 'sterilisation' measures. Punitively high interest rates imposed hardship on banks and borrowers, but the benefits of those high rates were nullified by the BLBI lending.

As the supply of rupiah swelled, the currency's value plummeted. Having lost around half of its value during the second half of 1997, the rupiah halved in value again during the month of January. Following the monetary expansion and the rupiah's sharp devaluation, the near-doubling of consumer prices was unavoidable. This was felt most by wage-earners who were already living under or near the poverty line, and whose real incomes contracted by nearly 40 per cent. In effect, therefore, the cost of protecting a few million bank depositors was born by tens of millions of working Indonesians—most of whom were too poor to even own bank accounts. Moreover, there is ample reason to believe that much of the BLBI lending was driven by malfeasance and was therefore avoidable.

Of the total BLBI lending of Rp145 trillion, Rp116 trillion was disbursed from November 1997 through March 1998—ostensibly to private banks suffering depositor withdrawals. However, BI data show that depositors only withdrew around Rp50 trillion from all private banks during this period.[34] And whereas the bulk of the BLBI lending took place after 31 December, most of these withdrawals took place before that date. The BLBI lending had clearly been subject to egregious abuse. One Indonesian banking expert, David Cole, later concluded that:

> Politically powerful banks seized upon the BLBI facility as a means for obtaining immediate, unrestricted liquidity directly from BI . . . Providing such liquidity without being able to exercise any control over the uses that the banks made of it was an invitation to disaster. Over a period of eight months, a few protected banks borrowed in excess of Rp100 trillion, much of which was used to buy foreign exchange and shift assets abroad.[35]

State auditors later provided documentary evidence of widespread fraud.[36] For instance, some recipient banks used their BLBI funds to repay subordinated loans from their majority shareholders—even though such loans are regarded as equity and should only be repaid after all debts to all other creditors are settled. Other banks used BLBI funds to make new loans, settle derivative contracts, earn returns in the money market or simply fund operational expenses. In some cases, banks borrowed BLBI funds in excess not only of their total third party deposits, but of their total liabilities and equity.[37]

In total, the auditors declared that 96 per cent of BLBI funds, or Rp138 trillion, were subject to some form of abuse. The auditors refrained, however, from differentiating between minor infractions (such as procedural errors in the administration of the funds) and more serious forms of abuse, such as embezzlement. The auditors also refrained from naming which banks were the worst abusers. But among the 48 private banks that received BLBI funds, four stood out: Sudono Salim's BCA, Sjamsul Nursalim's BDNI, Usman Atmadjaya's Bank Danamon and Bob Hasan's Bank Umum Nasional.[38] Of the BLBI funds disbursed for liquidity purposes, these four banks consumed around two-thirds to three-quarters of the total.[39]

Subsequent due diligence on the banks' loan portfolios confirmed that the banks had been channelling credit to their own groups for many years—in contravention of BI regulations and in contradiction to what they declared in their audited accounts. Investigators found that affiliated loans—that is, loans disbursed not to third parties but to sister companies—formed around 60 per cent of total loans in BCA and Bank

Danamon, 78 per cent in Bank Umum and, in BDNI, a staggering 91 per cent.[40] This fraudulent lending suggests that these banks were inclined to misuse their BLBI funds in similar fashion.

In fact, a senior minister later disclosed that BDNI had channelled 90 per cent of its BLBI borrowings to affiliates, rather than to third party depositors.[41] Indeed, BDNI and Bank Danamon borrowed BLBI funds well in excess of the total third party deposits that appeared in their 1997 audited accounts.[42] The Atmadjaya family used the bulk of Bank Danamon's BLBI funds for their own purposes, according to a confidential letter between government officials.[43] In effect, the owners of these four banks enjoyed privileged access to the state treasury, and BI 'blew out' the money supply to fulfil their fraudulent demands for liquidity.

Djiwandono later stated that his belief at the time was that 'speed was of the essence': BI had to react promptly to demands for liquidity lest defaults arise and a catastrophe ensue.[44] But a catastrophe ensued nonetheless—and it was fuelled by BI's baffling inability to distinguish between genuine and fraudulent appeals for liquidity. Some allege that BI officials colluded with bankers but Djiwandono maintains that, amid the panic and frenzy of the crisis, BI personnel were simply overwhelmed.

An alternative theory is that Soeharto specifically ordered the disbursal of BLBI credits, just as he had for Texmaco. This might explain why BI lent more than was necessary to pay out depositors, but it would be inconsistent with Soeharto's track record of pragmatism. The seasoned ruler must have been aware that needlessly inflating the money supply would wreak havoc on the economy—while exacerbating his worst political problem, the relentless decline of the rupiah. Soeharto was less than ten weeks away from being elected to a seventh term in office, but the collapsing rupiah was eroding the cornerstone of his political legitimacy: economic progress. It seems improbable that he would have directed BI's lending when doing so would ultimately imperil his own presidency.

Yet another alternative theory, therefore, is that Djiwandono and Moerdiono were receiving instructions not from Soeharto but from people far less savvy—namely, Soeharto's children. Indeed, BCA, BDNI and Danamon were the main private banks that were most closely associated with the first family. Sigit and Tutut Soeharto actually owned a combined 30 per cent stake in BCA, while Danamon had financed a host of first-family projects. BDNI maintained close ties to the military, and Bank Umum's Bob Hasan was the ultimate Cendana insider.[45]

It therefore remains unclear why the wanton abuse of BLBI lending was to take place, but the fact remains that Indonesia's grandest financial scandal had severe consequences for the economy. The lending inflated the money supply, which drove down the rupiah and triggered rampant inflation. This in turn presented Soeharto with the most serious political predicament of his long presidency.

The question of who might succeed Soeharto as president began looming over Indonesia in the early 1970s. Because Soeharto steadfastly refused to anoint a clear successor—in fact, he refused to even brook public comment on the matter—the 'succession issue' had been the burning, unanswered question of Indonesian politics for more than two decades.

Because Soeharto's position had long been considered unassailable, it was generally assumed that the autocrat would die in office rather than surrendering power or succumbing to opposition. Conjecture about the succession issue, therefore, tended to focus on the office of the vice-presidency. And the more Soeharto aged, the more crucial this office became. After a hard-fought, behind-the-scenes struggle in 1993, the military succeeded in wresting the vice-presidency away from Golkar and filling it with one of its own figures, the charismatic but lightweight Gen. Try Sutrisno. But by the end of 1997 the competition for the office had grown even more intense. At nearly 76 years of age, Soeharto was quite likely to be succeeded by whoever he picked for the vice-presidency this time.

A front-runner for the job was Sutrisno, while another military candidate was the liberal-minded minister of defence, Gen. (ret.) Edi Sudrajat. Other candidates included a pair of Golkar figures: Soeharto's longest serving cabinet minister, the faithful Harmoko, and the powerful head of the national planning agency, Ginandjar Kartasasmita. But in choosing a vice-presidential candidate Soeharto was not seeking a figure who could wield authority in the event of his own demise; instead, even at his advanced age, Soeharto was still intent on prolonging his own political survival—and he settled on a candidate who helped him do just that.

Soeharto had always been able to repudiate his critics by simply pointing to Indonesia's booming macro-economy, but the onset of the crisis turned the tables and the pressure on Soeharto was mounting. This pressure came not from Megawati, who had been sidelined through the PDI Headquarters raid, or Wahid, who had been enticed into supporting Golkar in 1997, but rather from the Islamic fold. Amien Rais had turned overtly critical of the president in early 1997 and was ousted from Icmi in July. Immediately thereafter he audaciously declared his candidacy for the presidency. Another symbolic campaign was launched when Emil Salim nominated himself for the vice-presidency in November. As an esteemed former technocrat, Salim engendered support from secular intellectuals, while as the son of a Muhammadiyah founder (Haji Agus Salim), he drew sympathy from Islamic circles as well.

Rais and Salim were not acting in concert, and Indonesia's Islamic leaders were far from mounting a united front against Soeharto, but the president nonetheless perceived a nascent threat. In a move that stunned the nation on 20 January, Soeharto unveiled his surprise choice for vice-president: the minister for research and technology, B.J. Habibie. Some cited the move as evidence that Soeharto had lost his political acumen; in fact, it was a political masterstroke.

Habibie had been a 'dark horse' candidate, but the other vice-presidential front-runners lacked a crucial quality that he possessed: as chair of Icmi, Habibie garnered considerable support from political Islam. The incipient movement to oppose Soeharto was therefore rent asunder: while some Islamists remained critical of Soeharto, others prepared to ride to power on Habibie's coat-tails.

Three days after Soeharto tapped Habibie for the vice-presidency, the rupiah dived to Rp17 000/$ during inter-day trading. At the time, many assumed that this was a sentimental reaction to Habibie's nomination: investors and donors had long bemoaned the waste and corruption of his fanciful high-tech projects, and they doubted that the quirky engineer would make a capable president. But although sentiment may have played a role, the currency's free-fall was probably due more to the monetary expansion from the BLBI lending. If so, by authorising that lending, Soeharto had unwittingly helped undermine his own political legitimacy, because the rupiah was now his biggest political problem.

For each day that the currency remained at abysmally low levels, more Indonesians concluded that the New Order's vaunted achievements—stability, progress and prosperity—had been little more than illusory dreams or hollow promises. Moreover, the contracting economy threatened to constrict the amount of largesse that Soeharto could distribute through his patronage networks. Having placed himself in a predicament, the president began casting about for solutions. The sweeping structural reforms recommended by the IMF and other donors would have helped restore confidence, but they would unravel those same networks of patronage that Soeharto was relying upon to stay in power. By late January the president was desperately looking for a quick fix—and at just that time he was introduced to an American professor named Stephen Hanke.

Hanke was an ardent 'free-marketeer' who was renowned for extolling the virtues of the currency board system (CBS)—a solution to the problem of volatile exchange rates that, under the right circumstances, could be highly effective. A group of Jakarta finance professionals who were attracted to Hanke's theories had introduced him to one of their finance ministry contacts, the director-general for taxation, Fuad Bawazier.[46] In turn, Bawazier referred the professor to Tutut Soeharto. Within days Hanke was appearing in public alongside a beaming President Soeharto, who told astonished reporters that he was seriously considering the implementation of a CBS.

Soeharto hinted at a CBS exchange rate of Rp5000/$. For a currency board to succeed at this rate, the government would need to convince all rupiah holders that every Rp5000 was backed by one US dollar in the state treasury's foreign reserves. Thus, to cover the broad (M2) money supply, Indonesia would probably need reserves of around $70 billion to make a CBS credible. At the time, however, gross foreign reserves stood at a mere $20 billion.[47]

Moreover, a CBS system would work only if all holders of rupiah were assured that the government would keep the supply of rupiah rigidly fixed to its supply of reserves—otherwise the durability of the CBS would be called into question. If holders of rupiah suspected that the supply of rupiah was increasing without a corresponding increase in reserves, they would doubt the government's ability to exchange one US dollar for every Rp5000. The CBS would then come under pressure: nervous rupiah-holders would begin exchanging their rupiah for dollars. As they did so, the government's foreign reserves would decline, fuelling more doubt and more demand for dollars. This 'negative feedback cycle' could quickly lead to an all-out scramble to abandon the rupiah. Without sufficient reserves to cover the M2 money supply, the treasury could be depleted within days and the CBS would collapse. Thereafter the rupiah would plummet and hyperinflation would ensue.

Given Soeharto's incessant interference with BI's monetary policy over the previous two months, there was ample reason to doubt that the government would rigidly adhere to the strict monetary discipline required by a CBS. But Hanke regarded a CBS as the paragon of free-market virtue, and this zeal seemed to blind him to the practical obstacles posed by Indonesia's circumstances. Hanke blithely dismissed concerns about Indonesia's foreign reserve levels and monetary discipline. Because he was promising a quick and easy fix to the nation's complex crisis, rival economists began labelling him the 'Rupiah Rasputin' and the 'snake-oil salesman of international finance'. But Hanke's promises were precisely what Soeharto wanted to hear; by early February the professor had clearly won the president's favour.

As soon as Soeharto made his stance known, key government officials fell into line. Harmoko, the Speaker of parliament who rarely missed an opportunity to ingratiate himself with the president, declared on 10 February that all 500 parliamentarians favoured a CBS. Other cabinet members voiced their support. Within days, Finance Minister Mar'ie Muhammad asserted that a CBS would be put in place. He clearly had misgivings about the plan, but he was apparently abiding by a decision made by Soeharto in a closed-door meeting of top economic advisors.[48] Meanwhile, the official most staunchly opposed to a CBS, BI governor Djiwandono, was summarily sacked—even though his term was due to expire in a mere six weeks. Soeharto replaced him with Syahril Sabirin, who immediately began drafting plans for a CBS. A currency board was expected to be put in place by the end of February.

Fearing the worst, the international community leapt into action. The IMF threatened to withdraw its support if Indonesia imposed a CBS, while US treasury secretary Robert Rubin urged Indonesia to address other pressing priorities before experimenting with the risky scheme. President Bill Clinton registered his opposition to the move in a telephone call to Soeharto, and the governments of Japan, Australia, Germany and Singapore soon followed suit.

Soeharto was urged not only to abandon the CBS plan but to energetically pursue the structural reforms called for by the IMF. The cabinet had made virtually no headway on such reforms—in fact, it seemed to be doing the opposite. The co-operatives minister had moved to revive Tommy Soeharto's clove monopoly, while Fuad Bawazier had granted tax exemptions on 15 000 of Tommy's Timor sedans.[49] As the end of February approached, Soeharto continued to neglect structural reforms—while continuing to toy with the idea of a currency board.

It was clear that the CBS plan was inextricably tied to the upcoming MPR session, scheduled to convene on 1 March. The MPR was packed with loyalists, but Soeharto was apprehensive about what might take place outside the assembly, on Jakarta's streets. If he could implement a CBS and, in one fell swoop, double the rupiah's value, Soeharto apparently believed that he would thereby neutralise his mounting critics. Foremost among these were Indonesia's boisterous university students.

It was often remarked that the president tended to approach dissent in a 'typical' Javanese fashion—that is, his responses often reflected ideals of kingship and power that could be found in Javanese literature and drama, especially the *wayang kulit* (shadow play) epics that the president loved. In the traditional Javanese worldview, three notions are particularly important: a ruler's power is signified by the tranquillity of his society; there is a finite amount of power to be had in the universe; and the possession of power is self-legitimising.[50]

From the standpoint of idealised Javanese concepts of power, Soeharto had compelling reasons to contain student protesters from the outset. Noisy protests indicate that society is becoming less tranquil and that therefore the ruler is weakening. Mounting protests indicate that the opponents' powers are increasing and that therefore the ruler's power is suffering a corresponding decrease. And as a ruler's power diminishes, so too does his legitimacy.

Soeharto also had concrete historical reasons for being wary of student activists: Indonesia's youth had been instrumental in forcing political change at several critical junctures in the past. Soeharto himself had been among the youths who waged a remarkable guerilla campaign against the Dutch, and his own rise to the presidency had been achieved with the critical support of student groups. As president, therefore,

Soeharto had always taken special precautions to co-opt campus organis-ations or crack down on radical groups. The 1996 crackdown on the youths at PDI Headquarters was one example. Another was the govern-ment's response to the Matraman riot that followed that raid.

Immediately after the riot on 27 July Soeharto's kaster, Lt Gen. Syarwan Hamid, pinned blame for the rioting on a radical student group, the Marxist-inspired Democratic People's Party (PRD). Following trials marked by a host of procedural irregularities, PRD leader Budiman Soed-jatmiko and ten other party members were jailed for sentences ranging from one to thirteen years.[51] In one blow the government had procured scapegoats while dealing a harsh warning to student protesters. However, by turning the PRD figures into martyrs, Hamid inadvertently invited more radical dissent.

Goaded into action by the July 1996 crackdown, a small vanguard of ideological firebrands continued to stage campus demonstrations and to agitate against the government. In mid-1997, Soeharto finally decided to take stern action. He called upon the figure who specialised in regime maintenance tasks: Maj. Gen. Prabowo Subianto, commander of the Special Forces.

P rabowo was still a junior figure in the military leadership in 1997, but he commanded a key unit and his pedigree attracted more attention than his rank. Prabowo belonged to one of Java's most aristocratic families: two of his uncles died fighting the Dutch in 1946 and his father, economist Sumitro Djojohadikusumo, was among the drafters of Indonesia's Con-stitution. In 1958 Sumitro opposed Soekarno's leftist-authoritarianism by joining a rebel government in Sumatera. When Jakarta crushed the rebellion several months later, Sumitro entered self-imposed exile until Soekarno fell.

Prabowo therefore spent much of his youth in foreign boarding schools. His brother, Hashim Djojohadikusumo, pursued a business career by founding the Tirtamas Group, but Prabowo was fascinated by military culture. After graduating from the Indonesian military academy in 1974, he became one of several hundred Indonesian officers who received Pentagon funding to study at US military schools. He completed an advanced course for infantry officers at Fort Benning and a course for Special Forces officers at Fort Bragg. In the latter course Prabowo came first in his class, ahead of US students.[52] Afterwards he trained with an elite anti-terror squad in Germany—an experience that apparently left a deep impression.[53]

Although he seemed destined to reach high command, the over-achieving Prabowo left nothing to chance: in 1983 he married Titiek Soeharto, the president's second daughter. Jakarta's gossip circuit viewed the marriage as having been arranged, and Prabowo soon made rapid headway in his career. Helping matters was the financing he was able to secure from his wife and brother. As Hashim stated to a foreign journalist in 1992: 'Prabowo needs funds. As a loyal and dutiful brother, I'll provide them. He has a lot of soldiers to take care of.'[54]

Despite never having held a territorial command—typically a prerequisite for higher promotion—he assumed command of the Special Forces in 1995. He thereby became the first member of his graduating class to reach the rank of brigadier general, at only 44 years of age. The following year Prabowo almost doubled the size of the Special Forces to nearly 7000 men, and the unit's increased size was used as a pretence for his promotion to two-star general.

At this point the Jakarta cognoscenti began citing Prabowo as a potential successor to Soeharto. He was a Cendana insider and a military man, but as a foreign-educated Indonesian he could also interact with outsiders. His father was a Javanese Muslim while his mother was a Christian from the Outer Islands, such that Prabowo could conceivably appeal to all major cross-sections of Indonesian society: Javanese and non-Javanese; Muslim and non-Muslim. But Prabowo lacked a critical quality: political savvy.

Prabowo's military career was plagued by allegations of human rights abuses, while he marred his public image by currying favour with hardline Islamist groups such as the Indonesian Committee for World Muslim Solidarity (Kisdi).[55] Within the military, Prabowo annoyed older officers by using presidential connections to obtain promotions. And most seriously, Prabowo tried too hard to ingratiate himself with Soeharto—not just by flattering the president but by serving as his chief strongman.

Dating back to the 1950s, the Special Forces was typically the first unit called upon to perform the military's most difficult and distasteful jobs. Soon after Soeharto assumed control of the military in 1965, he used the commando unit to comb the countryside of Java in search of Communist Party members, communist sympathisers and sundry other opponents of the military.[56] Thereafter the unit functioned as Soeharto's principal instrument for gathering intelligence and conducting covert operations against internal security threats, both real and perceived. The threats included armed guerilla movements in East Timor, Aceh and Irian Jaya, but they also took the form of political 'subversives', such as student activists.

Prabowo embraced Soeharto's regime maintenance tasks with zest. His expansion of the Special Forces was carried out with such tasks in mind: to an existing force structure of two regular combat groups and a counter-insurgency group, Prabowo added a covert operations unit ('Group IV') and a secretive anti-terrorist and psychological warfare unit ('Group V').[57] Prabowo modelled Group V on the lines of the US army's top secret Delta Force—a well-trained, well-equipped force that typically operated undercover. Prabowo called upon personnel from this unit when he received orders to 'deal' with student activists in July 1997. Seven captains and three sergeants were placed under the command of Prabowo's personal assistant, Major Bambang Kristiono. Prabowo dubbed the squad 'Rose Team'.[58]

The highly secret Rose Team limited its activities to 'research' and surveillance for about six months. In early 1998, however, Rose Team began conducting its research in underhanded ways. This change in tactics, which coincided with Soeharto's growing anxiety in the approach to the 1 March MPR session, would ultimately cost Prabowo his career.

As he stood on a curb waiting for a taxi on a humid afternoon in early February, Pius Lustrilanang became one of the first individuals to learn of Soeharto's intention to crack down on student protesters. The gaunt, thoughtful 30-year-old was standing on a street, Jalan Diponegoro, that resembled thousands of others in Jakarta—it was crowded, noisy and polluted. But the bland surroundings belied the neighbourhood's status as Jakarta's main hotbed of political activity.

Around the corner from where Lustrilanang stood was the front gate of the Salemba campus of the University of Indonesia, the country's largest school and a centre of student activism. In a ramshackle house across the street was the Legal Aid Foundation, founded in the early 1970s by Adnan Buyung Nasution. The Foundation was still Indonesia's only genuinely independent human rights organisation, and Buyung would crop up repeatedly in the years ahead as one of Indonesia's most active and influential pro-democracy campaigners. Finally, two blocks to the west stood the PDI Headquarters building that had been raided nearly two years before; to the south and east were the lower income *kampung* neighbourhoods that had produced thousands of rioters within hours of that raid.

In fact, it was the raid on PDI Headquarters that had inspired Lustrilanang to found a group called Siaga—a word that means 'readiness' but was also a local acronym for 'Indonesian Solidarity for Amien and Megawati'. Unfortunately for Lustrilanang, Siaga eventually attracted the attention of Bambang Kristiono's Rose Team, which finally went into action on that afternoon in February.

As Lustrilanang patiently waited for one of Jakarta's battered taxis to give him a lift, a sleek grey sedan suddenly rolled to a stop instead. Two large men emerged from the car, pinned his arms behind his back and jabbed his ribs with the muzzles of their military-issue 9mm pistols. Lustrilanang was placed in the backseat and blindfolded. The car travelled through city streets for about twenty minutes before accelerating on a road that, Lustrilanang felt, could only be the Jagowari tollroad, leading towards the town of Bogor on the outskirts of Jakarta. Forty-five minutes later the car arrived at its destination and Lustrilanang was ushered into his new home: a darkened underground cell.

Handcuffs and a blindfold were kept on Lustrilanang at all times, except when he was forced to write statements or identify photographs. When he provided unsatisfactory answers during interrogations, his abductors responded with punches and kicks and electric shocks administered to his arms and legs. At one point he was forced into a water tank; whenever he surfaced to breath he was kicked in the head. 'I thought I was going to die,' he later said.[59] To prevent him from sleeping, rock music was played at high volume around the clock.

Lustrilanang eventually learned that other pro-democracy activists were being brought into neighbouring cells, but the noise hampered communication. Nonetheless, Lustrilanang discovered that one of his neighbours was Haryanto Taslam, a young but influential aide to Megawati who had been pleading with her to embrace the burgeoning student movement. As a vice-secretary-general of PDI before its takeover by Suryadi, Taslam possessed a high public profile. Another relatively well-known figure was Desmond Mahesa, a human rights activist associated with Buyung Nasution's Legal Aid Foundation. A new activist was added to the cellblock every few days, and Lustrilanang gathered that the political temperature in Jakarta was steadily rising.

The abduction of democracy activists was but one of several measures used by Soeharto to respond to the country's mounting political tension. The rapid unravelling of Indonesia's economy emboldened Soeharto's critics, including academics, civic leaders and journalists. More worrisomely for Soeharto, Indonesia's campus protest movement was spreading from a small radical vanguard to the mainstream student population. Following the rupiah's shocking collapse during January, noisy rallies were taking place on a growing number of campuses around the country—and with increasing frequency.

None of the students had known any other president than Soeharto during their lifetime, and none were old enough to recall the Soekarno-era depression that the New Order had rectified. All, however, were suffciently educated to feel that their future was jeopardised by the current crisis. Moreover, the students harboured pent-up frustration at what they saw as systematic larceny on the part of Soeharto's children and cronies.

Soeharto must have recognised that he was facing a formidable threat, and this probably affected his decision to announce a surprising change of military commands in mid-February. The centrepiece of the reshuffle was the promotion of a new armed forces chief to replace Gen. Feisal Tanjung. Soeharto apparently wanted to ensure that his military was in reliable hands, and he therefore called upon a general whom he had been grooming for the past decade: Wiranto.

Unlike many generals, Wiranto was not related to revolutionary heroes or Javanese aristocrats. In fact, he had whiled away the first half of his career in some of the army's most mundane jobs.[60] In 1980, after twelve years in a sleepy outpost in North Sulawesi, Wiranto contemplated early retirement to become a county magistrate (*camat*), but instead he secured a position in the army strategic reserve (Kostrad). There he finally received his break. While conducting a routine field drill Wiranto's unit was chosen for observation by the visiting armed forces chief, Gen. Muhammad Yusuf. Impressed by the tall, well-spoken officer, Yusuf brought him to Jakarta and groomed Wiranto for higher duty. By 1989 he was serving in one of the army's most coveted posts: personal adjutant to President Soeharto.

The president's adjutants and bodyguards inspired jealousy among their peers because they tended to rise quickly through the ranks. Wiranto was no exception. In 1995 he received what was arguably the army's most strategic two-star position: command of the Jakarta Garrison. The following year he received his third star as commander of Kostrad, the army's primary combat force of 40 000 well-equipped, highly mobile troops. Next, in June 1997, he received his fourth star as chief-of-staff of the army.

Whereas most generals wait three or four years for each promotion in rank, Wiranto had been handed three promotions in as many years. Soeharto was rotating Wiranto through each of the military's top commands in quick succession, as if giving the general a chance to sample each post. Suddenly, the Jakarta cognoscenti recognised that, in contrast to the increasingly controversial Prabowo, Wiranto was a far more likely answer to Indonesia's enduring succession issue. It strongly appeared that Soeharto was grooming the young general as his eventual successor.[61]

To be sure, Wiranto possessed many of the qualities that Soeharto sought. The general was not from an aristocratic background: he had been plucked from obscurity; and therefore he owed his rise entirely to Soeharto. Moreover, as a fellow native of Central Java, Wiranto shared many of Soeharto's notions of hierarchy and fealty. While he was in close contact with Soeharto as his personal adjutant, the pair were said to have developed a relationship that resembled that between a father and son.[62] And perhaps more importantly, Wiranto practically became part of the Cendana family. Although Soeharto's children fought viciously among themselves, Wiranto seemed uniquely able to negotiate the poisonous atmosphere and maintain friendly relations with all six at once.

Thus, in February 1998, when Soeharto was growing increasingly concerned about unrest in advance of the March MPR session, he stunned the Jakarta elite by handing Wiranto yet another promotion—his biggest yet. Wiranto replaced Gen. (ret.) Edi Sudradjat as minister of defence, while also replacing Gen. Feisal Tanjung as armed forces chief. Wiranto would hold both jobs at once—something no officer had done since the 1970s. Moreover, Wiranto's age, 50, was well below the average for these jobs. The general was clearly being promoted not for his proven ability but for his (presumed) loyalty.

Similarly, Soeharto promoted several other confidants to key positions: Gen. Subagyo Hadisiswoyo (a former bodyguard) was made army chief-of-staff, while Maj. Gen. Syafrie Syamsoeddin (another former adjutant) was made Jakarta Garrison commander. And soon after, Soeharto promoted his son-in-law, Prabowo, to commander of Kostrad. These changes side-lined a number of more senior and well-qualified officers, but Soeharto's goal was to ensure that the reins of power were held by his own inner circle. The changes served another purpose: denying power to any one clique of officers.

A long army career had taught Soeharto the importance of managing the political forces within the military. He bore first-hand witness to the factional disputes that divided the military after independence, and he later benefited from an internal military *putsch* that cleared his path to the presidency. Thereafter Soeharto managed the military leadership with consummate skill. He kept authority fragmented lest any one general gain sufficient influence to challenge him. He diffused direct control over combat-ready troops among more than a dozen generals—thereby ensuring that, for a *coup d'état* to have any chance of success, at least four key commanders would first need to overcome their own mutual suspicions.[63] And most importantly, Soeharto deliberately fostered such suspicions by balancing commands between arch-rival officers. Thus the 1998 command changes were unusual in that Soeharto consolidated two key posts under Wiranto, but Prabowo's promotion provided balance: the two officers could barely conceal their animosity for each other.

Upon taking command of the armed forces, Wiranto's orders were clear: at a gathering of more than 300 military leaders on 12 February, Soeharto had instructed his officers to 'act firmly—without hesitation—against any violations of the law'.[64] The president was clearly referring to the students. He was keen to prevent campus rallies from spilling out on to the streets lest the activists garner broader support from the general population.

For their part the students were intent on making themselves heard, with the goal of exacting reform measures from the MPR assembly. The students cautiously refrained from denouncing Soeharto directly (a punishable offence), but they adamantly demanded an end to KKN—*kolusi*, *korupsi* and *nepotisme*. This was Soeharto's Achilles heel. The authorities could hardly take issue with demands for clean government: parliament had passed (but rarely enforced) many such laws and Soeharto himself had been brought to power in 1966 on the back of such demands.

In fact, the anti-KKN chorus was joined at one point during February by an unlikely figure: Tutut Soeharto. The president's eldest daughter publicly stated that responsible government could only be achieved by eliminating KKN—a comment that only elicited more anger from students.[65]

Wiranto moved assertively to contain the students lest their protests disrupt the MPR session. A force of 25 000 security personnel was mobilised to safeguard the session—more than twice the number of troops employed at the previous session in 1993. Jakarta's schools were to be closed while the MPR was meeting, street rallies were strictly prohibited and large gatherings of any form were banned from mid-February through to mid-March. Many students challenged these prohibitions, and the security forces arrested over 200 protesters during February. And in brazen defiance of Wiranto's ban, Amien Rais called on Jakartans to flood the streets on 1 March and demand reforms from the MPR. He was briefly detained by police.

By the time the MPR was ready to convene, Wiranto was able to take credit for having prevented any serious demonstrations or disturbances. The rupiah had collapsed and the economy was rapidly contracting, but the security forces had kept anti-government protesters at bay. Defying the mood of the nation, 1000 MPR members prepared to re-elect their 76-year-old president to his seventh five-year term.

5

FORCING REFORM

Indonesia's MPR members had long joked among themselves that their duty was summed up by the Five D's: *datang, duduk, dengar, diam, duit* (arrive, sit, listen, keep quiet, collect pay). Sometimes, however, a few errant members would interject at critical moments to voice their opinions or attempt to waylay the proceedings. In 1993 this tactic was used to great effect by the PDI faction (which was outspoken at the time). The PDI's strength had been neutralised prior to the 1998 session; nevertheless, MPR leaders trusted no one and feared the worst. A terse statement by MPR Chair Harmoko, speaking in his alternative capacity as chair of Golkar, warned party members not to interrupt with needless dissent. The armed forces faction head actually threatened to punish faction members who spoke out of turn—as did the head of the United Development Party (PPP), ostensibly an opposition party.

The threats from the MPR faction leaders were apparently effective: hardly a murmur of dissent was heard in the MPR throughout the 11-day session. As 1000 representatives sat in rapt attention on the first day, Soeharto read his annual address in the familiar tedious monotone that now seemed emblematic of the nation's rigid political structures. Amien Rais' million-person rally never materialised and student demonstrations were minor, but the soporific proceedings in the assembly hall nonetheless stood in stark contrast to the general economic and political upheaval gripping the nation.

Although Soeharto did not neglect the economic crisis in his 1 March address, he took pains to remind listeners of Indonesia's pre-crisis achievements—such as increased per capita income, GDP growth, lower morbidity, etc. He also repeatedly complained that the reforms demanded by the IMF had failed to produce results—omitting, of course, that most structural reforms had yet to be implemented. 'A number of heads of government visited or telephoned me', he explained, 'and they expressed their views on what they consider to be good solutions to resolve our problem.' But Soeharto called for a better alternative: 'I refer to the more appropriate concept as "IMF Plus". I myself am carefully and cautiously contemplating the possible adoption of the currency board system.'

Yet another round of hurried telephone calls ensued as world leaders beseeched Soeharto not to jeopardise his nation's hard-earned foreign reserves by implementing an ill-advised CBS. On 6 March the IMF postponed payment of the second $3 billion tranche of its standby lending facility. Two days later Soeharto struck back by declaring that certain features in the IMF's package contradicted clauses in the 1945 Constitution—specifically the mystifyingly vague Article 33, which states that 'the economy shall be organised as a common endeavour based upon the principle of the family system'. As pundits wondered aloud to which family Soeharto was referring—Indonesia's or his own—Soeharto was preparing a move that would supply them with the answer.

After securing his re-election on a ticket with B.J. Habibie, Soeharto unveiled the membership of his Seventh Development Cabinet on 14 March. Tutut Soeharto played a large role in formulating the cabinet's roster—in fact, in a snub to student demands for an end to nepotism, she herself was included as minister for social services.[1] Never before had a member of the first family served in the cabinet. A general closely associated with Tutut, Hartono, was made minister of home affairs. The new minister of state-owned enterprises was Tanri Abeng, a Bakrie & Brothers executive who was Tutut's partner in the Tanjung Jati C project.

Replacing Mar'ie Muhammad as finance minister was Fuad Bawazier, formerly the director-general for taxation. In addition to granting tax exemptions for Tommy Soeharto's Timor car project, Bawazier had served under Bambang Soeharto as the deputy treasurer of a foundation that culled an extra 2 per cent of taxable income from all Indonesian taxpayers.[2] The foundation collected around $270 million in fiscal year 1996–97, but the use of the funds was never disclosed. Although the tax was ostensibly for poverty alleviation, some alleged that the money had helped finance Golkar's 1997 election campaign.[3]

Meanwhile, there were other signs that the cabinet appointments valued family loyalty over professional ability: Subiakto Tjakrawerdaya was retained as head of the co-operatives ministry, where he continued defending Tommy Soeharto's clove monopoly; Sanyoto Sastrowardoyo stayed on as minister of investment, despite persistent complaints from the business community about the 'hidden costs' of obtaining investment licences; and Abdul Latief, who admitted to having misallocated $3 million from state pension funds, was moved from being minister of labour to minister of tourism.

Yet another example was Haryanto Danutirto, the former transportation minister who had funnelled rents to the first family by restructuring

Indonesia's state-owned airlines.[4] A 1996 investigation headed by Vice President Try Sutrisno had actually found Danutirto guilty of misusing public funds—but, as punishment, Sutrisno merely ordered him to 'undertake introspection'.[5] Danutirto was retained in the 1998 cabinet as minister for food and drugs.

The cabinet's most notable feature, however, was Soeharto's choice for the key economic post of minister of industry and trade: timber baron Bob Hasan. The irony was remarkable: the man who epitomised the cronyism that had largely precipitated the crisis was now charged with engineering a recovery; and the man who was a main target of the IMF's structural reforms would now be a key figure in the government's negotiations with Fund officials.

Meanwhile, the announcement of the cabinet roster coincided with an extraordinary measure taken by the MPR: the assembly conferred upon Soeharto special 'emergency powers'. These would enable the president to disband parliament or outlaw political parties as he deemed necessary. This immediately conjured fears of the dreaded Operational Command for the Restoration of Security and Order (Kopkamtib), the covert agency established by Soeharto in 1965 to fight communism. Kopkamtib had quickly outgrown its original mandate to target a wide array of supposed threats to internal security, using extra-judicial powers of arrest and inter-rogation until the mid-1980s.[6]

The prospect of Kopkamtib's return suddenly lent an air of menace to national politics, especially given that the embattled Soeharto was clearly falling back on his inner circle of loyalists. Key military commands had been filled by former aides and relatives; the new vice-president was a protégé whom Soeharto had patronised for decades; and the cabinet that urgently needed to tackle the debilitating economic crisis was packed with Cendana cronies. With his inner circle empowered to dominate events, Soeharto was circling his wagons in preparation for a showdown.

During the first week of March, revelations that foreign reserves had fallen to a mere $16 billion helped sway opinion against a CBS. On 18 March—one day after a visit to Jakarta by IMF official Hubert Neiss—the powerful Ginandjar finally weighed in on the subject. In his opinion, foreign reserves were insufficient to attempt a CBS 'for the time being'.[7] Although Ginandjar emphasised that he was not articulating official policy, he was now the cabinet's senior economics official and his position effectively put the CBS issue to rest once and for all.

Having surpassed the hurdle of the MPR session, Soeharto was appar-ently willing to compromise. This should have been encouraging, but the markets took little solace. One reason was that other members of the new cabinet were already generating alarm. The minister of co-operatives summarily announced that the government would grant distribution monopolies for soap, toothpaste and similar items to PT Goro—a company owned by Tommy Soeharto.8 Soon after, Finance Minister Fuad Bawazier unveiled a potentially disastrous tax on capital flows. Both measures were overturned, but worse damage was being wrought by Bob Hasan.

On his second day as minister of industry and trade, Hasan rejected IMF demands to disband government-controlled monopolies. 'Which monopolies are we talking about? If they provide for the needs of the people, then there's no problem.'[9] When asked about distribution arrangements for cooking oil, cement and paper, Hasan simply denied these were examples of monopolies. Hasan portrayed structural reform as a concerted effort to weaken Indonesia: 'Foreigners are nice to us only if they want something from Indonesia—but if they can no longer benefit from our commodities, or if they feel threatened by our exports, they start attacking us.'[10]

A central topic of debate was the longstanding ban on exports of raw logs. By depressing domestic log prices, the ban protected inefficient plywood mills and encouraged them to overconsume raw logs. This was the key distortion that had long enabled the Plywood Association to reap extraordinary rents from the plywood sector. In early 1998 the IMF had succeeded in having the ban removed, but Hasan proceeded to reimpose it soon after taking office. He claimed, misleadingly, that banning log exports helped protect Indonesia's forests.

Meanwhile, Hasan's denunciations of the IMF worsened over the following weeks. 'We are not the IMF Republic!' he bellowed at one stage.[11] Ginandjar invariably sought to patch up relations with the Fund in the wake of Hasan's outbursts, but all were aware that Hasan had been the president's closest confidant for over four decades. That he was sounding such strident tones did not bode well for reform. Soon Soeharto himself was voicing such sentiment. In April the president declared that after having achieved political independence from colonial domination, Indonesia's economic independence was being jeopardised by foreigners who were seeking to buy up national assets at distressed prices. This was particularly unfair, he noted, given that the blame for the crisis laid squarely with foreign exchange traders.

Before mid-March many students had still harboured some hope that progress towards reform would be made within the MPR assembly. Those hopes were rudely dashed by the re-election of Soeharto and Habibie, the conferral of emergency powers on Soeharto and, most blatantly, the new cabinet roster. Anger swept through campuses across the country. Even the more conservative or apolitical students were finally turning out for anti-government demonstrations. By the end of March large demonstrations were regularly taking place not only in Yogyakarta and Jakarta but also in provincial towns across the archipelago.

By now it was clear that the students wanted more than an end to corruption—they wanted an end to the New Order. They shouted '*Harga turun!*'—a phrase that literally meant 'lower prices' but was also soon recognised as being a clever play on the words '*Soeharto dan keluarga turun!*', or 'Soeharto and family step down!' The protesters seemed convinced that, because political authority was centralised in the hands of one figure, the removal of that one figure would bring about an end to corruption, abuse and injustice. Antagonism towards Soeharto galvanised students of all religions, races and income levels.

A seemingly typical rally began on the morning of 2 April on the campus of Yogyakarta's Gadjah Mada University (UGM). This was the school with the highest admission standards (save the military academy) and UGM students regarded themselves highly. They felt that their status made them less vulnerable to abuse from the security forces, and they also felt a sense of responsibility: if they did not spearhead and invigorate the nascent student movement, who would?

Students started gathering on the campus lawn around 8 a.m., wearing headgear in preparation for a day in the sun and carrying brightly painted banners and placards. A handful lugged jury-rigged 'personal address systems'. These contraptions, which were slung over the shoulder, consisted of hand-held microphones plugged into battery-powered loud-speakers. They enabled students to hold raucous rallies anywhere, any time. And on this day the UGM students had finally resolved to take their rally out on to the streets, in direct defiance of Gen. Wiranto's orders to remain on campus. Galvanised by their opposition to Soeharto—and intoxicated by the fervour sweeping students across the nation—the students planned to march straight across Yogyakarta to the provincial assembly building, some two kilometres away.

As the throng of several thousand poured through the campus gates and turned to head downtown, a small group of police decided to make an orderly retreat and summon support from the local military garrison. But before the reinforcements arrived the marchers' ranks swelled with several busloads of students from two other campuses in Yogyakarta, plus hundreds of high school pupils and local residents. The resultant strength of numbers was exactly what the military had been trying to avert by restricting students to the campuses.

Since the embarrassment of July 1996—when television cameras recorded police and troops scattering haphazardly before rock-wielding youths—some units had received special crowd-control equipment and training. Nonetheless, most troops remained poorly trained and under-paid, and the incessant abuse and epithets hurled their way were affecting morale. In the heat of midday, a minor scuffle broke out between the UGM students and soldiers. Within minutes it escalated into a melee.

Soldiers fired tear gas canisters and attacked with batons, while students responded with rocks and fists. The fighting was lopsided but raged on throughout the afternoon. At least 88 protesters fell injured. Two days later another battle in Yogyakarta injured twelve.

News of the Yogyakarta clashes triggered similar violence between protesters and troops elsewhere in the country. Soeharto responded by instructing his education minister to ban university students from 'participating in practical politics', but the measure accomplished little. And as the president called for 'clear thinking' and 'togetherness', student groups began to flaunt their ability to organise.[12] On 15 April, 25 campuses across the country staged simultaneous demonstrations—precisely the type of co-ordinated mass action that the New Order regime had always feared.

Still Soeharto showed no signs of bending. In response to the 25-campus rally, the president upbraided his information minister and blamed the press for 'distorting the true situation'.[13] He repeated his call for students to return to their studies.[14] And at an annual celebration honouring the Special Forces—a symbolic occasion—Soeharto issued a veiled threat: 'I expect that the general security situation will be managed by the people themselves, by local governments and by the police. In this way the involvement of the Special Forces will not be necessary.'[15] In fact, an element of Special Forces Group V, Prabowo's Rose Team, had been deeply 'involved' for the previous three months.

P ius Lustrilanang had been detained in the underground cellblock at the Special Forces compound for nearly two months when he was joined by Andi Arief. On 28 March the 27-year-old had been exiting a music studio in Bandar Lampung, a town on the southeastern tip of Sumatera, when he was abducted by three armed men. Arief's captors blindfolded him and drove him straight to Jakarta, an eight-hour journey. A graduate of Yogyakarta's prestigious Gadjah Mada University, Arief chaired the student wing of the PRD, and as such he was the pivotal link between students and the fringe Marxist party that Syarwan Hamid had tried to crush in July 1996.

Detained in a cell similar to Lustrilanang's, Arief was kept blindfolded for three weeks. Although he was not tortured, he was questioned repeatedly about links between PRD and Megawati, Amien Rais and Abdurrahman Wahid. He was also asked about ethnic-Chinese businessman Sofjan Wanandi and former intelligence official and armed forces commander Benny Moerdani (both were despised by Prabowo). When he was instructed to write out his master plan for taking over the Soeharto government, Arief recommended that Soeharto cut off his cronies, hand back his wealth and undertake national reconciliation. 'That plan would be good for you, wouldn't it?' Arief quoted his captors as saying. 'You and all your Communist friends would get off the hook!'[16]

While in captivity, Arief heard the story of Deddy Hamdun, reputedly a *preman* boss who worked for PPP in the May 1997 general election. The burly 44-year-old was abducted along with two associates around that time, and none of the three ever resurfaced. Arief says that a young guard, with whom he became friendly, intimated that Hamdun had been assassinated. And when Arief was being questioned his interrogators issued a stern warning: 'Answer the questions truthfully, or you'll be Deddy Hamdun-ised.'[17]

The Legal Aid Foundation later concluded that at least fourteen activists went missing and never reappeared. Some, such as the poet and labor activist Wiji Thukul, disappeared as early as August 1996. Two Megawati supporters, Yanni Afri and Sonny, were detained in April 1997 and never returned, but both were identified in captivity by Lustrilanang and Desmond Mahesa. Three PRD activists—Suyat, Herman Hendrawan and Bimo Petrus—were kidnapped around the same time as Arief but remained missing. But in addition to the whereabouts of the missing activists, another mystery surrounded Rose Team's abductions: namely, the reasons for releasing the nine activists who survived.

The activist kidnappings might have been forgotten about if they had remained secret: the Legal Aid Foundation and student groups would have called attention to the disappearances, but the military could have simply denied any involvement. It was only when Lustrilanang was released—and his story conveyed to the public—that the kidnappings became problematic for the government and, especially, Soeharto himself.

It remains unclear, therefore, why Rose Team's orders appear to have suddenly changed around mid-April. After 40 days of captivity, Haryanto Taslam was released from custody on 19 April. Lustrilanang, Mahesa, Arief and others followed him over the next few days. Taslam demurred from speaking to the press, fearing that the kidnappers might retaliate by killing activists still in detention. Similarly, Lustrilanang was told that if he spoke about his abduction to anyone, he would be hunted down and killed. 'If we don't find you in a week,' his abductors had warned him, 'we will find you in a month. We are very patient.'[18]

Nonetheless, Rose Team must have realised that releasing the activists would risk exposure, which in turn would damage Soeharto. And this is precisely what finally happened on 28 April, when the Legal Aid Foundation convened a press conference and introduced Pius Lustrilanang. The activist amazed reporters by recounting the details of his abduction and torture; immediately afterwards he boarded a flight to the Netherlands, where he sought refuge in a safe house. Soon after, Arief and Mahesa provided matching testimony. Eventually, Prabowo himself admitted to forming Rose Team and ordering the kidnappings, although he claimed (implausibly) that the team only kidnapped the nine activists who were returned—not those who remained missing.[19]

The revelations injected vigour into the nationwide wave of demonstrations, which was now being referred to as a 'people's power' movement. It was ironic that Rose Team, which had originally set out to defend Soeharto, ultimately damaged his cause. This is particularly ironic given that, at the time, Soeharto clearly wanted his generals to deal sternly with protesters. In fact, the release of the student activists might have been one of the first indications that the military leadership, or at least certain elements of it, were beginning to defy Soeharto's authority.

The president had already punished one official who was deemed too 'soft' on student protesters: Gen. (ret.) Edi Sudradjat. After issuing words of encouragement to student protesters in February, the independent-minded minister of defence was conspicuously excluded from the cabinet formed in March. Nonetheless, by late April, a number of other generals seemed to be cautiously following Sudradjat's lead.

Few generals explicitly endorsed the students' protests, but neither did many issue threats or make uncompromising stands. Syarwan Hamid, the former kaster who was known as a hardliner, adopted a 'middle-of-the-road' stance with students in mid-April: 'Feel free to express yourselves, so long as your actions do not create security problems.'[20] Wiranto himself was soon taking the same stance. 'The military will accept and support reform measures,' he repeatedly told students, 'as long as those measures are required for the progress of the nation.'[21] Across the country, military commanders were stressing the importance of dialogue and acknowledging that it was possible to tolerate 'differences of opinion'.

Wiranto had been groomed for command precisely because of his loyalty to Soeharto, but nonetheless he now seemed reluctant to bully student protesters. A career staff officer who had had only two brief combat tours, Wiranto could be amiable and persuasive when he so chose. Rather than threatening to use force, as Soeharto apparently would have liked, Wiranto staged a series of 'open dialogues' with student activists. The largest of these dialogues took place on 25 April, when several hundred students from regional Muhammadiyah chapters assembled in Jakarta to meet with the newly appointed kaster, Lt Gen. Bambang Yudhoyono.

Yudhoyono had cropped up earlier as one of the officers involved in planning the 1996 PDI Headquarters raid. Following that event the imposing but articulate officer received two quick promotions, such that he now held the military's key 'socio-political' post at the young age of 49. The son-in-law of Special Forces founder Sarwo Edhy, Yudhoyono had excelled in officer training courses in the United States and was renowned for being a quick student. And despite his role in the 1996 crackdown, Yudhoyono had cultivated a reputation for being a reform-minded officer.

This reputation was put to the test on 25 April.

The kaster faced an auditorium filled not only with Muhammadiyah activists but with the press as well. For three hours Yudhoyono manned the podium and fielded questions, occasionally mopping his brow when he broke into sweat. The exchanges grew heated, especially when the general received pointed questions about military backing for illegal businesses such as gambling, prostitution and narcotics rings. 'I'm sure you've all noticed the press reports,' he answered unconvincingly, 'about how the military leadership has punished soldiers involved in "backing" illegal operations . . . The military police are dealing sternly with those involved in manipulation, embezzlement or corruption.'[22]

Yudhoyono was interrupted more than a dozen times by angry students, but he never lost his temper. When asked about nepotism—specifically, the inclusion of Wiranto's spouse and son in the MPR—Yudhoyono's response elicited groans from the audience: both of Wiranto's family members, he claimed, were included in the MPR to reflect their roles as social activists.

But the main focus of the discussion was the military's stance on reform. A student from West Java rose at one point and asked point-blank: 'With whom does the military side—the government or the people?'

'Both,' answered Yudhoyono. 'The military is part of the government, so it is impossible for it to oppose the government. At the same time, the military originates from the people and belongs to the people—so the military cannot possibly betray or oppose the people.'[23] The military's chief policy-maker was not yet abandoning Soeharto—but neither was he denouncing the students' reform movement.

Around the same time, other generals were growing more explicit. Maj. Gen. Agum Gumelar, the Sulawesi Garrison commander who was also a former Special Forces commander, stated on 24 April that the students' demands were 'appropriate, just and representative of aspirations at all levels of society'.[24] This was hardly the same message being sent by the president. While Soeharto acted tough, Wiranto and the bulk of the military leadership were ambivalent or, in some cases, openly tolerant.

The military's forbearance was promptly noticed by the shrewd chair of Muhammadiyah, Amien Rais. Through several meetings with military leaders during March and April, Rais seemed to sense that the military was wavering in its support for Soeharto.[25] Aware that this could mean Soeharto's end, Rais vigorously sought to associate himself with the student movement, while escalating his attacks on Soeharto. And in so doing, he distinguished himself sharply from Indonesia's better known 'reformers': ousted PDI leader Megawati and NU chair Abdurrahman Wahid.

Against all odds, the opposition movement that was dispensing Soeharto's severest drubbing in 32 years was inspired and executed almost entirely by students, with scant support from the nation's political elite. Three decades of repression had cowed the opposition into submission. Potential opponents had been coerced, co-opted or simply jailed. Only a handful of independent politicians commanded sizeable national followings—and the most prominent of these, Megawati, consistently spurned the student movement.

Megawati's stance frustrated her supporters and disappointed the students. Here, presumably, was the opportunity of her career: Soeharto was vulnerable and the students had succeeded, remarkably, in igniting a genuine 'people's power' movement. The only missing element was a popular figure to lead the charge—but Megawati remained inert. Some suspected that she feared reprisals or was misreading the political trends. More likely, Megawati was simply too passive and unprepared. Her political experience consisted mainly of reading prepared speeches at party congresses and parliament assemblies; taking to the streets and leading a people's power movement was an altogether different endeavour.

Wahid, meanwhile, remained just as reticent, but for different reasons. In his days with Forum Democracy in the early 1990s, Wahid had been among the government's most nettlesome critics; by 1998, however, the tables had turned. He conspicuously refrained from either endorsing the student movement or criticising Soeharto. Some suspected that a stroke in January had incapacitated him, but Wahid made his stance clear in a carefully prepared statement that he delivered in April: 'The student movement is more emotional than rational, and signs of destructive anarchy have started to appear.'[26]

Wahid's stance puzzled many—particularly because it was made soon after the revelations of kidnappings and several violent clashes between students and troops. But while Wahid had supported pro-democracy efforts in the past, the driving force in his career had been his adamant opposition to the Islamicisation of politics. As such, his puzzling stance might have been explained by his determination to thwart Amien Rais. Because Rais had been quick to align with the students, Wahid may have felt compelled to reject them—lest he become indirectly allied with the aggressive Muhammadiyah chair. In Wahid's mind, opposing political Islam apparently took precedence over opposing Soeharto.

In addition, Wahid may have been calculating that it was more important at this stage to protect his relations with the establishment. Having already garnered reformist credentials in the early 1990s, Wahid's higher priority may have been to maintain his links to Cendana, which he had cultivated through the military and Tutut Soeharto just one year before. Perhaps Wahid sensed that even if Soeharto suddenly lost power, establishment interests would still retain considerable influence. If this was his reasoning, it was remarkably prescient.

While the reticence of Megawati and Wahid created a void at the pinnacle of the anti-Soeharto movement, Amien Rais made every effort to fill this void himself. He appeared almost daily at student rallies and public demonstrations. And as he issued criticisms of the government and demanded reform, he carefully sought to tailor his message. Rais needed to expand his support base beyond modernist Muslims, and he therefore abandoned the anti-Chinese, anti-Christian and anti-foreign rhetoric that he had been famous for issuing in the past. His new 'inclusivist' message targeted Indonesia's influential non-Muslim and non-*pribumi* minorities. But given that he attracted relatively few of his own supporters to the student rallies, many students wondered whether Rais was helping their movement or feeding off of it. In any event, it was becoming clear that the student movement was gaining ground.

By the third week of April student rallies were being attended by academics, civic groups and professional organisations of all types. Demonstrations occurred in seemingly every corner of the archipelago, from Aceh to Irian Jaya. Violence was not uncommon, especially since many student groups had learned to use Molotov cocktails in combat with security forces, who typically responded with tear gas. The students were difficult enemies for Soeharto to deal with: they were too numerous to crush, too idealistic to be co-opted, and too persistent to be ignored.

Soeharto addressed the worsening problem on 1 May. Summoning more than 30 leaders of the major political parties and parliamentary factions, he emphasised that he was constitutionally obliged to carry the five-year plan that the MPR had produced just seven weeks before. That plan, he said, already included several elements of reform; if these were deemed insufficient, the public would need to wait until broader reforms could be implemented in the next MPR session in 2003. And for the second time in two weeks, Soeharto threatened to 'take action' against parties who were 'forcing reform'.

The public was well aware that Soeharto had stayed in power as long as he had because he delivered economic growth and controlled the military—therefore his sophistry about the MPR's binding mandate carried little weight. Moreover, several constitutional scholars had been telling the public that an emergency MPR session could be convened at any time. Not surprisingly, media reports invariably conveyed Soeharto's message in one way: no reform for five years.

The following day Soeharto dispatched both the former and current information ministers, Hartono and Alwi Dahlan, to clarify his message. They said that there had been a misunderstanding and that the president embraced reform. In fact, they said, he favoured direct elections for all members of parliament in the next parliamentary poll, due to be held in 2002. In effect, Soeharto had brought the start date for reform forward by one year—which fell far short of what the student protesters were demanding. Soeharto's intransigence only seemed to spur more protests.

The first weekend of May witnessed the worst unrest to date. Violence occurred in Jakarta, Yogyakarta and Bogor—but the worst episode by far took place in Medan, the capital of North Sumatera and Indonesia's third largest city. When student protests gave way to widespread rioting, nearly 200 buildings were destroyed in what represented Indonesia's worst episode of mass unrest since the 1970s. Around 30 people were injured by rubber bullets. Reports surfaced that female students had been raped by soldiers. Ethnic-Chinese residents were targeted by mobs, and hundreds of families fled across the Straits of Malacca to Penang, Malaysia.

The nation was shaken by the weekend of unrest. Before the fires in Medan had stopped smouldering, Soeharto took to the airwaves on Sunday evening. The impromptu address to the nation was televised on all channels. In the wake of the activist kidnappings, his rejection of reform, his threats of a crackdown and the gruesome weekend of violence around the country, there was plenty to discuss. Many hoped that Soeharto would propose a resolution to the political turmoil and thereby start remedying the crippling economic crisis—but Soeharto had ideas of his own.

The ageing autocrat baffled his nationwide audience by focusing his comments on a specific structural reform called for by the IMF: the repeal of Tommy Soeharto's clove monopoly. Ignoring recent political and economic events, Soeharto embarked on a rambling discourse on the history of the Indonesian clove industry. As he reclined in an easy chair and spoke pleasantly into a hand-held microphone, he seemed to revel in explaining the arcane points of the government's clove policy. He strove to absolve Tommy from blame, while implying that his decision to relinquish the clove monopoly—something the IMF had been requesting for nearly six months—should be greeted as an act of munificence.

Instead, many wondered whether the president's 'fatigue' in early December had actually been a debilitating stroke. Following more than three decades of impeccably pragmatic rule, Soeharto was misreading the mood of the nation. His preoccupation with defending his son—set in contrast to the economic deprivation and political unrest affecting all Indonesians—was only likely to feed the nation's disillusionment. The time was clearly ripe for a popular figure to unite the nation and make a strong stand, but Indonesia sorely lacked such a figure.

Wahid refrained from speaking out against Soeharto, while Megawati refrained from speaking almost entirely. Within the establishment, the key figures in the parliament and the cabinet lacked not only the initiative to take action but also the power to do so. Soeharto had deftly spread authority among so many state actors—and for such a prolonged period of time—that no one individual could rise to the fore. In fact, no single institution seemed able to take action unilaterally: the MPR commanded supreme constitutional authority but the military monopolised coercive force—and the two exerted a check on each other.

Moreover, the MPR's 1000 members had been carefully screened for their loyalty to Soeharto—and, only eight weeks before, they had unanimously handed Soeharto not only a mandate to govern but sweeping 'emergency powers' as well. It hardly seemed likely that the MPR would move to overthrow Soeharto now. And even if it did, the dearth of national leadership would make it exceedingly difficult for the MPR to reach a decision about who should replace Soeharto as president.

As the second week of May began, therefore, the initiative was still very much with the students. Against all odds, the student movement had pushed Soeharto farther than ever before. They had stood up to their elders, organised with remarkable skill and displayed extraordinary courage for the sake of principle. While 'reformists' in the political elite dithered or fought among themselves, the students broke the impasse. The burning question at the time, therefore, was whether the students would maintain their momentum and overcome Wiranto's military, or falter and be overpowered by it.

In fact, the outcome was more complex. In rapid-fire succession, Indonesia witnessed an extraordinary string of political events. Thirty-two years of stagnant politics suddenly gave way in the space of two weeks.

6

'CLOSER TO GOD'

If Soeharto was worried about domestic stability, it certainly wasn't reflected in his most dramatic economic policy measure during the final month of his rule: a sharp hike in fuel prices implemented on 5 May.

Government subsidies for petrol and diesel fuel were among the foremost peeves of the IMF and World Bank. The subsidies burdened government finances and bred inefficiencies throughout the energy sector. Moreover, they conferred savings on industry and car owners, when the substantial sums involved could have been spent instead on poverty alleviation or growth-promoting projects such as infrastructure. But Soeharto had always been loath to implement price hikes—they not only angered industrialists but had also sparked street riots on several occasions in the past.

Thus when the IMF requested price hikes as part of its April agreement with Soeharto's new cabinet, Fund officials were expecting increases of 5–10 per cent around the end of June. They were taken aback, therefore, when Soeharto told them on 4 May that the price of petrol would be raised by a staggering 71 per cent—to be implemented the next day. Soeharto even decreed a 67 per cent increase in bus fares—and nothing was more prone to sparking riots than this. The policy dealt a grave blow directly to the most restless and combustible element of society, the urban poor. In fact, the government had always been so anxiety-ridden about the issue that bus fares had remained static for years: in early 1998 a ride across Jakarta cost less than five US cents.

Given the unprecedented level of unrest already evident by early May, it seemed risky indeed to increase prices just then. Yet this is precisely what Soeharto chose to do, and he did so in grand style. It almost seemed that Soeharto—or someone within his cabinet who persuaded him to sign off on the policy—was spoiling for a fight.

Predictably, the fuel price increases triggered more rioting in Medan, with mobs burning cars, looting shops and attacking security forces with Molotov cocktails. In over a dozen other cities students staged angry demonstrations, often supported by crowds of urban residents. Protesters now explicitly demanded a change in national leadership, to be effected through an extraordinary session of the MPR.

Crowd control efforts around the country were haphazard affairs. Sometimes security forces would allow students to march unhindered through the streets, and sometimes the students themselves would peacefully retire when confronted by police barricades. It was by no means uncommon, however, for violence to break out. One episode in the Central Java town of Solo reportedly claimed a staggering number of casualties: over 400 students and 31 police were injured in one afternoon clash.[1] Emerging from a private meeting with Soeharto on 5 May, Wiranto demanded that the students end their protests, and threatened to crack down if they continued. Most suspected that Wiranto was merely mouthing Soeharto's words—that he was not serious about a real crack-down, such as the 1989 Tiananmen Square massacre in Beijing.

Indeed, only two days later the general softened his tone. 'We get the message,' he told student protesters. He disclosed that the armed forces would form a team to draft its own proposal for reform measures. This encouraged protesters to clamour louder still, because the military was clearly starting to give way. Moreover, other government institutions were beginning to do likewise.

Indonesia's parliament had been little more than a rubber-stamp institution for over two decades, and under the leadership of Speaker Harmoko few expected anything more of it. The parliament had not initiated its own legislation for years—it only ratified bills introduced by the executive branch, and rarely did it even alter these drafts. The press was accustomed to dismissing parliament's affairs as irrelevant, so few newspapers took notice when Harmoko made an uncharacteristic pronouncement on 5 May: parliament would initiate its own set of political reforms to address the student movement's demands. Supported by the leaders of parliament's four factions, Harmoko vowed to revise the repressive electoral laws and introduce anti-corruption and anti-monopoly laws. He also called on the authorities to 'seriously investigate' the activist kidnappings and he slammed the government's decision to raise fuel prices.

In retrospect, Harmoko's pronouncement marked the beginning of the end of parliament's role as a rubber-stamp institution. This was made clear in a matter of days—by none other than Lt Gen. Syarwan Hamid. The former kaster who had orchestrated the PDI Headquarters raid and jailed the PRD leaders now occupied a crucial position in government: Deputy Speaker of parliament from the armed forces faction. In the New

Order's peculiar version of 'checks-and-balances' the military controlled 75 senior active officers who sat in parliament; this pivotal faction ensured that parliament was hamstrung without the military's backing. As the military's chief figure in parliament, Hamid was positioned at the junction between what were probably the only two institutions capable of challenging Soeharto's authority.

Unlike Harmoko, therefore, Hamid commanded attention when he decided to speak. Not only was he a no-nonsense figure but, as a hardliner, he represented a benchmark for attitudes within the governing elite. On 8 May Hamid appeared on a live television program and issued a startling statement: 'There is now a wide consensus among government, legislators and the public that thorough reform—as demanded by the students through their nationwide protests—is the only thing that would save the nation.'[2]

Hamid added that demands for change were not only acceptable but justified. Because it was clear that the 'thorough reform' being demanded by students was actually Soeharto's resignation, Hamid was implicitly turning against Soeharto. If this was the position of a hardline stalwart, the autocrat was clearly in peril. Nonetheless, Soeharto did well to keep up appearances.

With generals waffling, parliament asserting its authority and devastating riots rocking the country, Soeharto departed the country on a ten-day trip to Egypt, where he was scheduled to chair an assembly of the G-15 (a bloc of major developing countries). Friends and foes alike were stunned that he was willing to leave Indonesia under such conditions. Soeharto may have reasoned that cancelling the trip at a late date would only have made him look weak—but making a show of strength by leaving the country was a heady gamble nonetheless.

Just before leaving Jakarta on 9 May, Soeharto held a press briefing at South Jakarta's Halim Perdanakusuma airport—something he had rarely done in the past. He dwelt on the need for peace and stability and said that he commiserated with the people's suffering, noting that he himself used to be poor. He also used the opportunity to issue yet another warning: 'For those who break the law through the use of force, the armed forces will take action to protect national stability and political stability.'[3] With that parting shot, the president departed. In the airport a doughnut vendor joked with a reporter: 'Will he be allowed to come back?'[4]

As if on cue, mayhem followed hard on the heels of Soeharto's departure. Several hours after his takeoff the clashes between security forces and students claimed their first casualties: a police officer was killed in a student demonstration in Ciawi, West Java, and an innocent bystander was beaten to death by troops during a rally in Yogyakarta.

The next day Amien Rais promised to form a 'People's Mandate

Council', consisting of 55 prominent reformists representing a broad spectrum of society. The coalition included some familiar figures, such as Emil Salim, Sumitro Djojohadikusumo and Buyung Nasution. It also included a highly esteemed Islamic scholar who would play a prominent role in the month of May: Nurcholish Madjid. Rais's Mandate Council promised to pose the most significant challenge to Soeharto's authority in many years—but a mere two days later its declaration was overshadowed by an even more calamitous development on the campus of Jakarta's Trisakti University.

Unlike the top three state schools (UGM, UI and ITB), Trisakti was a private university that catered to the wealthy. Perhaps because of their privileged upbringings, Trisakti students had not been at the forefront of the student movement. Their rallies lacked the hardened edge that could be found in demonstrations at other schools, particularly the less prestigious state schools and teacher-training academies that served lower income youths. Rather than waving banners on the side of the road in the midday sun, Trisakti students liked to joke that they could better induce change by going home and talking to their parents—many of whom were military officers, civil servants or parliamentarians. Nonetheless, by early May the student movement had mushroomed to such an extent that even Trisakti students were holding rowdy protests on a regular basis.

Members of Trisakti's student senate led several hundred demonstrators out of the campus on Friday 8 May. The group stood on Jalan Parman, part of the chaotic 12-lane freeway that rings inner Jakarta, shouting slogans, singing songs and waving as police and marines looked on. Other student groups were amassing across the highway, but while some senators wanted to join them in a march down Jalan Parman, other senators were against it. It was a typical quandary: some wanted to amplify their impact by joining forces, while others feared associating with less disciplined groups.

With their elected leaders arguing among themselves, the rank-and-file students did not know whether to advance or sit still. A late afternoon downpour finally settled the question—everyone went home rather than be soaked. But the rally was deemed a success nonetheless, especially considering that it had taken place spontaneously. It seemed like a good omen for an upcoming event that would be Trisakti's most ambitious undertaking to date: a campus-wide rally followed by a five-kilometre 'long march' to the parliament building.

Some 6000 students gathered for the rally on 12 May.[5] Before he left for Egypt, Soeharto had finally pledged to reform the nation's political laws, but this still fell far short of what the student demonstrators were seeking: his resignation. By noon the students had swarmed out of their campus and were marching swiftly east, towards the parliament. As they made their way down Jalan Parman, traffic was thrown into confusion and eventually brought to a halt. Most of those in the crowd were Trisakti students, dressed in their signature green cotton jackets and red-and-white headbands. Tagging along, however, were pockets of groups from UI, Atma Jaya and Gunadarma—many of whom were dedicated activists who roamed the city each day looking for a rally to join.

The students had only progressed about 500 metres before their path was blocked by a company of riot police. Part of the 'Fast Reaction Unit', these police were equipped with shields, padded vests, shin protectors and visored helmets; the students dubbed them 'Robocops'. The police lacked side-arms, but they carried heavy canes and were supported by units from the Police Mobile Brigade, Brimob. Brimob troops were more heavily armed: they carried teargas guns and rifles loaded with rubber bullets, which were thought to be non-lethal. Joining these forces were four armoured vehicles with water cannons.

When the students were halted, Trisakti's senate leader conferred with the police. He returned to explain to the students that it was impossible to proceed. He suggested that only a small group of student representatives carry on to meet with members of parliament. He cited the reason provided by the police commander: the demonstration was blocking traffic.

Howls of protest rose up from the students. Some in the crowd had been waiting for this rally for weeks. They had watched as fellow students in Yogyakarta waged pitched battles with troops for nearly six weeks, while they themselves had been able to do little more than chant a few slogans at poorly attended rallies. Against all odds, the student movement had injected national politics with a degree of popular furore not witnessed since 1966; this, finally, was their chance to make their mark, and they were determined to continue.

The senate leader tried again to negotiate with the police, but was unsuccessful. Rain started to fall, but unlike the previous Thursday, no one ran for shelter. The students became increasingly impatient for progress. Better to press on, some said, rather than wait for the police to carry out a 'sweeping' action. There was a general belief that at 5 p.m., if the students were still blocking traffic, the police would move in to disperse them by force. It was already 3.45 p.m. The students milled about or sat on the pavement. Some students circulated among the troops pinning flowers to their uniforms.

The police, meanwhile, were growing impatient. Since the senate leader lacked the authority to persuade the demonstrators to leave the street, they summoned the university's president, former Supreme Court justice Adi Andojo Sutjipto. If the students refused to clear the road, said the police, they would crack down with force. Adi Andojo rose to the makeshift podium that the students had erected on the asphalt and urged them to return to campus. The rector was popular among the students— Soeharto had cut short his career in the judiciary because he had been too enthusiastic about attacking corruption—but his appeals to the students failed on this occasion. The students declared that if the police wanted them to move, then let the police commander say so himself.

Finally, around 4.15 p.m., Adi Andojo handed the microphone to Lt Col. Timur Pradopo, commander of the West Jakarta police force. Pradopo told the students he was genuinely concerned about the snarled traffic. Once again the students jeered. Pradopo then offered a compromise: the police would retreat 10 metres for each 10 metres that the students retreated. This way both sides would back down simultaneously and no one would lose face. Out of options and with the afternoon wearing on, the students accepted, although some were unhappy.

With a designated leader shouting the orders, the students slowly and gradually moved back from the police, who did the same. By 5 p.m. the tension between the police and students appeared to have abated. Adi Andojo had already left the site, convinced that everything had been concluded peacefully. Only a small determined band of students were left sitting and standing on the roadside, doggedly chanting their slogans and waving their banners to the traffic which, at last, was able to flow.

Suddenly the lull was broken by a middle-aged man whom the students did not recognise. Claiming to be a Trisakti alumni, he shouted abuse at the students and accused them of being cowards. They in turn immediately accused the lone individual of being a 'provocateur' or an undercover agent deliberately trying to provoke them into violence. Later it was determined that the man's name was Mas'ud. Although police commanders denied that he was acting in their service, witnesses later saw him run for protection in a nearby police office.[6]

The few remaining students traded insults with Mas'ud; the police line began to advance. The police and students were once again face to face and tension was high. Once more the two sides retreated in turn, but around 5.20 p.m., just as the situation seemed to have been defused again, the police sprang into action. Troops suddenly fired rubber bullets, lobbed teargas canisters and charged towards the students.[7] They attacked not only those on the street but those who had already receded to the campus grounds as well. They lashed out with their long batons and kicked at students who had already fallen to the ground. One was dragged and thrown into a grimy canal that ran alongside the highway.[8] Female students—perhaps including some that had been passing out flowers earlier that afternoon—were groped and beaten before being thrown to the ground.[9]

Students on the street ran in all directions to seek cover, while others inside the campus poured back out on to the street to counter-attack the police. Armed with only bricks and bottles, the counter-attacking students were no match for the police. Brimob troops armed with rifles seemed to be firing at will, but the students were convinced that the troops were only firing rubber bullets, which were presumed to be non-lethal unless fired at very close range. The shooting was intense for over half an hour, until 6 p.m., although the last victim did not fall until after 7 p.m. In addition to dozens of students harmed by tear gas, more than twenty were wounded by rubber bullets.[10]

A policewoman who witnessed the scene, Lt Anneke Wacano, later testified that she saw a military-style Land Rover approach the base of a pedestrian overpass near the Trisakti gates. She said that two men wearing black uniforms took up position on the overpass, carrying rifles fitted with telescopic sights. From about 100 metres away, she saw one of them fire in the direction of the crowd and heard a single loud gunshot. The time was about 5.30 p.m., ten minutes or so after the battle between police and students began.[11]

Another participant in the action, police captain Agustri Heryanto, heard several loud gunshots around 5.45 p.m. He recognised the shots as live rounds, which make more noise when fired than rubber-tipped rounds do.[12] Adi Andojo later reported that several students noticed red targeting beams emanating from a building that was under construction on the northeast corner of the plaza—one full block from where the protest had been staged on Jalan Parman.[13] Somewhere in the melee, shooters were firing real bullets.

The first fatalities were Hendriawan Sei, 20, and Elang Mulya, 19. The pair were on the staircase in front of the rector's building on campus when they were shot in the neck and chest. An ambulance tried to approach their position, but the vehicle itself came under fire and the drivers were forced to turn back.[14] Sei and Mulya therefore bled to death. The third and fourth victims were also shot on campus—inside University Plaza, an area enclosed on all sides by tall university buildings. The victims were Hafidin Royan, 21, and Hery Hartanto, 21. Royan was killed by a shot to the head, while Hartanto was hit in the back. Both died where they fell. At least three other students were severely wounded by what appear to have been live rounds.[15]

The shots that killed the four students appeared to have been deliberate and well aimed. Three 5.56mm rounds were recovered, two from victims' corpses and one from a wall on campus (the latter could have first passed through the body of a victim). The bullets were examined in two ballistics labs in Indonesia before being examined by specialists in Montreal, Canada and Belfast, Northern Ireland. The main conclusions were that the bullets designated APB-1 and APB-2 were fired from SS-1 rifles, while APB-3 was from a Steyr rifle.[16]

These findings were insufficient to determine whether the shooters were from the police or the military: the SS-1 is standard issue in both services, while the lightweight, Austrian-made Steyr assault rifle is used by both the Gegana anti-terrorist unit of the police and the army's Special

Forces. The only other conclusion that could be drawn pertained to the distances: APB-1 and APB-2 were fired from distances of between 125 and 200 metres, while APB-3 was fired from less than 100 metres.

One of the most persistent explanatory theories for the shootings is that Special Forces troops might have posed as police officers. The theory rests on a rumour that four Brimob troops mysteriously disappeared several days before the shooting—and their uniforms went missing as well.[17] This raised speculation that rogue military units may have been trying to frame the police while inciting student riots. The proceedings of a subsequent military court lent credence to this view.

The court was convened in June 1998 to try six police lieutenants who were accused of causing the deaths of the four students. The lieutenants were commanding the Brimob squads that fired warning shots. Indonesia's well-known human rights lawyer, Buyung Nasution, suspected that the young police officers were being framed as scapegoats; he therefore volunteered to defend them. He soon proved that there was insufficient evidence to convict them of manslaughter, but the judge summarily changed the charges against the accused. The lieutenants now stood accused of disobedience—that is, giving the order to fire warning shots without having first secured the permission of senior officers. Buyung argued that the court had no right to alter the charges midway through a trial, and he pointed out that disobedience was a matter to be handled internally, by the officers' respective units. The judge not only ignored these arguments but also refused to allow the defence to call Mas'ud as a witness. He then sentenced the lieutenants to prison sentences ranging from two to ten months.

But well before the military court convened, on the day after the Trisakti shootings, funeral ceremonies were held for the four slain students. The date was Wednesday 13 May. Several opposition leaders who were associated with the student movement appeared on campus to deliver orations. These included Amien Rais, Emil Salim, Buyung Nasution and two stridently pro-reform members of Golkar: Sarwono Kusumaatmadja and Siswono Yudohusodo. Significantly, Megawati finally emerged in public to express her condolences. The speakers urged the students to be careful but they also pledged firm support for their cause.

The four slain students were dubbed *Pahlawan Reformasi* (Heroes of Reform), a play on the name for veterans of the revolution against the Dutch. The name stuck. Parallels were also noted with Arif Rachman Hakim, a student shot dead by Soekarno's palace guards in 1966. Hakim's martyrdom had hastened Soekarno's political demise, and now many wondered whether the Trisakti shootings would do the same for Soeharto.

Upon arriving in Cairo on Saturday 9 May, Soeharto and his 64-person entourage were greeted by the last thing that any of them wanted to see: a student protest. The event was staged by Indonesian students studying in Egypt.[18] Soeharto was incensed, but the worst was yet to come. The delegation received word on Tuesday evening about the killings at Trisakti. When international journalists asked Foreign Minister Ali Alatas about the shooting, he explained that the government had warned students not to take their protests to the streets.[19]

The next evening Soeharto gave an informal talk before a group of Indonesian citizens and reporters at the embassy in Cairo. In the same wistful and nonchalant tones used in his clove lecture the previous week, Soeharto hit on all the standard themes: *reformasi* was a nonstop process that had been taking place since before the revolution; the military should be appreciated for its contributions to governance; the Soeharto family had no personal wealth; and so on. Weary from a long day, some of the Indonesian journalists were actually beginning to nod off—but suddenly the president said something that none had heard before:

> Actually, if the Indonesian people no longer have confidence in me, then it's no problem [*tidak apa-apa*]. I myself have already said, 'If I'm no longer trusted, then fine [*ya sudah*]'. I will not stay on through the force of arms. Not like that. I'll become a sage [*pandito*], bringing myself closer to God.[20]

Every reporter in the room was suddenly wide awake.

Even before Soeharto had finished his address, some of the journalists were already scrambling to find phones. Embassy phones, however, could only be used by journalists from Antara, the state-owned news agency. An Antara reporter registered a call to Jakarta, but he chose to relay the wrong bit of information: he reported that Soeharto had publicly denied that his family was the fourth richest in world—hardly an earth-shattering pronouncement.

Meanwhile, a reporter from Indonesia's leading daily, *Kompas*, searched for a telephone outside the building. He found one in the booth that housed the security guards, but a guard explained that it was only for communicating within the embassy compound. The reporter nonetheless tried punching in the numbers for a long-distance call. Within seconds, he was speaking to his editor in Jakarta. 'Is it important?' the editor asked. 'It's already 12.30 a.m. here ...'

'Just take down one sentence,' said the reporter. 'President Soeharto said, "If the people no longer support me, then fine, I'm not going to hold on through the force of arms".'

Following the *Kompas* reporter's example, the same news was reported to Jakarta by journalists from the *Jakarta Post*, *Media Indonesia*, *Republika*, *Bisnis Indonesia* and others—all using the guard booth telephone. Then, after a late dinner, the jubilant reporters retired for the night.

They were awakened at seven the following morning by a reporter from *Suara Pembaruan* who was frantically looking for a cassette recording of Soeharto's talk at the embassy. The reporter explained: 'The president wants to hear exactly what he said last night!'

The banner headline on the Thursday edition of *Kompas*, Indonesia's most widely read paper, declared: 'Soeharto Ready to Resign.' At 9 a.m. in Cairo, reporters were told that the entire entourage would be returning to Jakarta immediately—four days ahead of schedule. A presidential aide found the *Kompas* reporter and told him that there would be no seat on the aircraft for him—he would have to find his own transport home. Ali Alatas met the assembled journalists and told them, angrily, that Soeharto's comments were nothing out of the ordinary. The president, he claimed, had said essentially the same thing on many occasions in the past and it in no way signalled that he was 'ready to resign'.

On the return flight to Jakarta, members of Soeharto's inner circle joked menacingly with journalists in the back of the aircraft. 'We're above the Arabian Sea right now. Which would you prefer: to be pushed out here or to wait until we reach the Bay of Bengal?'[21] Other presidential aides tried to impress the reporters with the crucial difference between 1998 and 1965. When Soekarno fell, it was because the military had backed the demonstrators; now, they said, the military was against the students, and their protests were therefore in vain. 'A great deal of blood,' they said, 'is bound to be shed.'

But while Soeharto's aides were correct about the prospect of bloodshed, their confidence in the military was misplaced.

7

IMPECCABLY AMOK

Indonesians take pride in their rich culture, warm hospitality and refined manners. Their capital might be hectic and disordered, yet it was far safer than many other mega-cities in the world. Despite its problems, Jakarta was generally viewed as a city that was not only improving but gradually developing its own charm and grandeur as well. But the month of May 1998 called all this into question.

The conclusion of the funeral ceremonies at Trisakti University were followed almost immediately by rioting in the surrounding Grogol area. Around 10 a.m. small groups of *preman* began vandalising flower tubs, uprooting trees and knocking down street signs. A truck was set on fire and by 1 p.m. a gas station was burning furiously.[1] Between their acts of vandalism the *preman* exhorted onlookers to take part. Racked by seven months of economic hardship, residents of the densely packed, low-income *kampung* surrounding Trisakti needed little encouragement to take part in venting their frustration; they did, however, require the forbearance of the security forces.

It soon became clear that the police were tolerating the rioting.[2] Riot police under the command of the Jakarta Garrison vigorously defended a nearby mall owned by Ciputra, a property mogul whose business interests overlapped with those of the military; but security forces took little action to stop the rioting elsewhere in the area, particularly along the road leading to Pluit, an ethnic-Chinese neighbourhood.[3] The only forces that seemed intent on defusing the situation were several small units of marines, who tended to act independently from the mainstream police or army.[4] By late afternoon hundreds of people were rampaging through Grogol and Pluit, burning vehicles, vandalising buildings and looting stores.

Traffic resumed through Grogol by early evening, but vandalism continued in several sections of northern Jakarta until morning.[5] Nonetheless, Thursday started off as a typical workday for most Jakartans. Some shopping malls closed for the day, yet many of the city's residents did not fully appreciate the magnitude of the rioting that had occurred the previous evening in Grogol.

Jakartans had already grown somewhat jaded in the face of reports of demonstrations, protests and riots. They might have had warning of what was to come had they paid heed to the events on Tuesday and Wednesday in the cities of Sumatera: Medan had already experienced bad rioting, while Palembang, Pekanbaru and Bandar Lampung had also been affected by unrest. But Jakarta's myopic residents tend to disregard events in the provinces. It was not until mid-morning that most finally realised that this day—Thursday 14 May—was unlike any they had ever experienced. Jakarta's infamous May riots had begun.

Looking west from the top floors of one of Jakarta's highest office towers, the Jakarta Stock Exchange building, office workers saw several plumes of smoke rising from the Grogol area by 9 a.m. on Thursday. Within an hour the plumes were too numerous to count.[6] Fires were also burning in virtually all points of the greater Jakarta area, including twenty kilometres to the west in Karawang and ten kilometres to the south in Depok. Most of the buildings set on fire were shop-houses (tall narrow buildings built in blocks, throughout Jakarta), but all manner of buildings were set ablaze, including banks, homes, markets and shopping malls.

While there were murders and rapes, most of the mayhem that occurred on Thursday was opportunistic looting. There are no shortages of images showing people of all ages taking advantage of an unexpected opportunity to avail themselves of expensive items—such as electronics, appliances, clothing and food—for free. The sheer number of men and women stealing goods seems to have encouraged normally law-abiding citizens to take part also. Along some main streets where looting was taking place, women and children gaily looked on as fires raged and stores were pillaged.

Police made some 2000 arrests on Thursday.[7] Riot police fought pitched battles with mobs on the very doorstep of the Jakarta Police Head-quarters, just south of the Semanggi interchange on Jalan Sudirman, in the heart of the city. After firing dozens of warning shots and dousing the area in tear gas, Jalan Sudirman was secured, but elsewhere the city was a war zone. By mid-afternoon, the city was covered by an even thicker pall of smoke than usual.

Large portions of Kota, the historic ethnic-Chinese district of North Jakarta, were burned out and razed. Mobs invaded more than 1000 homes, most owned by ethnic-Chinese, who saw their possessions stolen, their households burned and, in many instances, their families brutally attacked. The route to the airport—a long, straight toll-road with few exits—was strewn with hazards. When vehicles were stopped at toll booths, the passengers discovered that the booths were manned not by state workers but by *preman* bandits who extorted hefty sums.

Jakarta's police were neither trained nor equipped to respond to such wide-scale rioting—but this was precisely the task for which Syafrie Syamsoeddin's Jakarta Garrison was designed. In fact, as recently as early April, Syamsoeddin's units had rehearsed drills whereby anti-riot troops were inserted by helicopter into Kota, deemed (correctly) to be the district most prone to riots. But as the looting and arson engulfed a metropolitan area of some 15 million residents, many wondered and lamented at the absence of Syamsoeddin's forces.

Finally, in the late afternoon, troops gradually moved in to secure key parts of the city, but elsewhere the rioting carried on into the evening. By this time many people were beyond help: over 130 had already burned to death in East Jakarta when Plaza Central Klender went up in flames. In Ciledug over 50 died in a similar fire; witnesses reported that most of those killed were looters, who continued to re-enter the building despite the flames.

At Harmoni, a key intersection demarcating Kota from the central business district, heavily armed soldiers established a cordon to prevent rioters from moving into the central business district. The soldiers remained impassive, however, as huge mobs attacked storefronts just several hundred metres from their position and in full view. Shop-houses exploded in huge, bright orange bursts—but the soldiers only stirred restlessly and the marauding looters carried on.[8]

The worst rioting generally occurred on main roads that bordered on extensive *kampung* areas. In South Jakarta, Jalan Kapten Tendean and Jalan Warung Buncit were two such thoroughfares. Both were choked with rioters well into Thursday evening. A large department store, Golden Truly, was looted all day long and reduced to an empty shell. A nearby supermarket was destroyed by fire, while around a third of the shop-houses on Jalan Tendean were burned, looted or vandalised. Nearly a dozen cars burned on either side of the road; fuelled by the petrol in their tanks, the cars invariably continued to burn until all that remained were the charred frames.

Throughout the evening, something of a festival atmosphere prevailed along Jalan Kapten Tendean. Although the mobs were mostly men (with many *preman* among them), women, children and the elderly were also evident, and some were revelling in the mayhem. Nearby, in the Widjayakarta housing complex, nervous ethnic-Chinese residents manned the compound's flimsy front gate, wielding golf clubs and softball bats. They prepared for an attack, but the mob remained preoccupied with looting the nearby stores.[9] But while Widjayakarta remained secure, dozens of similar complexes around the city witnessed some of the most terrifying episodes of the May riots. *Preman* bands raided predominantly ethnic-Chinese neighbourhoods throughout the night—looting homes, accosting women and worse.

By Friday morning, troops maintained a heavy presence throughout Jakarta. It seemed as if the army had dredged up every tank in its armoury to occupy key intersections, such as the Hotel Indonesia roundabout and the Tendean–Warung Buncit intersection. Personnel carriers were dispatched to ethnic-Chinese neighbourhoods, such as Pluit, that had been ransacked during the night. An artillery unit stood guard over the Lippo Karawaci Supermall, which was so badly burned-out that deep cracks were visible in the cement of the building's thick outer walls.[10]

By the time the city returned to normal—which was not until the afternoon of Saturday 16 May—over 1217 people had been killed and 31 were missing. Property damage was officially estimated to be around $500 million, but this estimate was probably very conservative because more than 6000 buildings were damaged or destroyed. The official tally was 2547 shop-houses, 1819 stores, 1026 private homes, 535 bank offices, 383 office buildings, 40 shopping malls, 15 markets, 12 hotels, 11 police stations, nine gas stations and two churches.[11] Bank BCA—jointly owned by the Salim Group and the Soeharto family—had 122 of its branches damaged or looted.[12] Vehicles burned included 1100 private cars, over 800 motorcycles and 66 buses.

A number of provincial towns also sustained heavy damage from rioting. On a per capita basis, the destruction in Jakarta was probably exceeded by that in Solo, Central Java, and Palembang, South Sumatera.

In addition to the looting, arson and deaths, the May riots were characterised by brutal episodes of sexual assault, rape and gang rape. In the immediate aftermath of the riots, investigations of rape reports were made by a 'Volunteer Team for Humanity' (Truk) made up mostly of assorted human rights activists. In a 19-page document submitted to the Human Rights Commission in July, Truk provided gruesome details of sixteen rapes, which included assorted methods of physical and psychological torture meted out to the victims and other household members.[13] Most of these cases took place in shop-houses owned by ethnic-Chinese, and in some instances the attacks were carried out by organised gangs transported in vans or heavy trucks. In total, the document cited 168 cases of rape and sexual assault, almost all of which were from Jakarta.[14]

Truk was unable to substantiate its allegations that the rapes were carried out systematically, but it compiled reports of anonymous death threats made to team members, rape victims and counsellors.[15] After four months of such threats, Marthadinata, an 18-year-old team member who some say was also a rape victim, was brutally murdered under mysterious circumstances—just before she was due to depart to the United

States with five others to provide testimony to international human rights organisations. Truk asserted that the girl's death marked the peak of a concerted effort to cover up the rapes and to intimidate witnesses. In contrast, Jakarta police chief Noegroho Djadjoesman proclaimed that Marthadinata's murder was a routine homicide perpetrated by a thief, even though the coroner reported signs of sexual assault on the girl's body.[16]

In the wake of the May riots, the rape reports created an international furore. Because the victims were mostly ethnic-Chinese, the Indonesian authorities came under particularly intense criticism from NGOs and government figures in Taiwan. In a highly unusual display of regional assertiveness, the People's Republic of China issued sharp criticisms of the Indonesian authorities and allowed large anti-Indonesia protests to take place in Beijing. Noisy protests were also held as far away as Boston, in the United States.

Eager to salvage Indonesia's international reputation, the military and certain members of the government strenuously sought to downplay the estimated number of rapes, or even to deny that any had ever occurred. The police claimed to have investigated 103 of Truk's reported rapes without ever finding 'concrete evidence'.[17] Meanwhile, certain activist groups apparently overstated the number of rapes in attempts to attract attention to the issue. Some say that these groups bribed journalists and editors to print stories about the rapes. (The press was riddled with corruption after decades of censorship, and payoffs to cover 'research expenses' were common.) In their efforts to dramatise their stories some journalists apparently doctored photos taken from Internet pornography sites and from reports of human rights abuses elsewhere, such as in East Timor. Several of these photos were debunked as frauds in an *Asian Wall Street Journal* exposé, and this helped the authorities persuade the public that no rapes had taken place at all.[18]

In July the government set up a Joint Fact-finding Team (TGPF), consisting of notable figures with a wide variety of professional backgrounds, to investigate the events of May 1998, including reports of mass rapes submitted by Truk and other groups. In its final report made six months later the TGPF identified 66 rapes (most of which were gang rapes), ten cases of sexual assault and nine cases of molestation. These figures, however, met as much controversy as had Truk's. The main critique was that the TGPF had relied on second-hand reports and had received testimony from only three rape victims.[19] Given that rape victims are wary of reporting to police even in countries with well-functioning legal systems, Indonesian victims had ample reason to remain reticent; nonetheless, the TGPF was criticised for not trying hard enough to gather evidence.

A special United Nations commission finally spoke out on the subject in December 1998, affirming that rapes 'were conducted in a widespread manner, and seemed to be conducted in an organised manner'.[20] But questions still surround the actual number of women assaulted and the identities of their attackers. The TGPF report made little progress in these areas, but it was far more effective in collecting eyewitness reports of the looting and arson. These reports clearly showed that the May riots were not spontaneous.

The May riots not only damaged Indonesia's international repu- tation—they scarred its national psyche. Indonesians were shocked that their own countrymen could behave in such a way. Even before the riots subsided, questions arose that have never been fully answered: were the riots orchestrated, and if so, by whom and for what purpose?

Indonesia in the late 1990s possessed many of the conditions that can produce violent unrest: severe economic collapse; a disorientated security apparatus; and the uncorking of social animosities (which had been glossed over for decades by the Soeharto government). Jakarta was tense even at the best of times, as the newly rich flaunted their wealth while the city's margins were ringed by urban squalor. Jakarta's upper-class homes were invariably surrounded by high walls topped with broken glass and metal spikes—testimony to the occupants' fear of the slum-dwelling masses. The economic collapse only exacerbated these fears and jealousies.

Large numbers were therefore ready to take part in the mayhem once it started—but latent tension in society does not adequately explain why the May riots happened when they did. Two conditions were still required: someone to start the rioting and forbearance on the part of the security forces. It is readily apparent that in May 1998 both of these conditions were deliberately fulfilled. Indeed, even before eyewitness accounts are considered, logic dictates that the May riots did not happen spon- taneously.

First, Jakarta's rioting began early in the morning, with looting starting as early as 8 a.m. and dozens of fires blazing two hours later. Whereas genuine riots would be preceded by a period of mounting tension, those on 14 May broke out with stunning speed.

Second, Jakarta's early-morning rioting was not confined to the Grogol area (where unrest had occurred the previous afternoon): by 10 a.m., looting and arson were under way in locations as far west as Tangerang, as far south as Depok and as far east as Bekasi. In total, at least 47 districts (i.e. distinct sections of the city) were affected by the rioting.[21] Metropolitan Jakarta sprawls across 60 square kilometres, and its poor transport and communications mean that residents can remain unaware of severe rioting that is taking place only a few kilometres away. Whereas a spontaneous riot could well break out in one particular place, the chances are slim that it would spread so quickly, so far and in so many directions at once.

Third, the nature of the arson suggests that some degree of preparation was involved. Scores of large buildings were razed by fire. Bonfires are common in Jakarta but destroying entire shopping malls requires planning, along with resources, such as significant amounts of fuel and combustible materials. Moreover, had the riots been purely spontaneous the mobs would presumably have been preoccupied with looting merchandise rather than destroying entire malls filled with valuable goods.

Fourth, it is odd that so many urban residents were bold enough to riot at that particular time. In Jakarta, unrest was rare because Jakartans knew that the security units were always ready to crack down with force. The Trisakti shootings only reiterated that fact—so much so, in fact, that most student groups confined themselves to their campuses on 13–14 May, rather than risking another deadly clash with troops.[22] Throughout the course of Indonesia's 'people's power' movement, these students had always been more adventurous than urban residents—but suddenly their roles were reversed and residents rioted just when the students hesitated. This supports anecdotal evidence that looters were promised immunity; in effect, it was apparently made clear that the security forces would not intervene.

Finally, similar riots erupted simultaneously in a number of other cities. Medan had been suffering sporadic unrest for nearly two weeks, but Palembang, Padang, Bandar Lampung and Surabaya were all hit by looting and arson on 13–14 May. Rioting also occurred in Bandung, Samarinda (East Kalimantan), Pekanbaru, Makassar and Jayapura. Perhaps the worst violence outside Jakarta was in Solo, where mayhem began just after a city-wide power outage at 8 a.m. on 14 May.

But apart from the circumstantial evidence, eyewitness reports also show that the rioting was not spontaneous. For instance, some of the rioters in West Jakarta on Wednesday night admitted to having travelled to the capital by truck from the West Java town of Tasikmalaya—250 km away.[23] After collecting testimony from riot participants and onlookers from around the Jakarta region, the TGPF asserted in its final report that teams of 'provocateurs' were widely active.

The TGPF report described a four-step procedure that the teams of provocateurs generally followed. First, a team would arrive in a certain place and spread word that riots were about to erupt. Next, team members would attract attention by starting bonfires, yelling inflammatory remarks (such as 'the students are cowards', 'the police are dogs' or 'Chinese are pigs'), and urging onlookers to gather. They would then initiate vandalism by hurling rocks and smashing windows. When they began looting they incited others to follow, but often they urged them to burn or destroy the merchandise rather than making off with the looted goods.[24] Finally, the instigators would set about burning buildings, frequently using tools and materials which they had brought with them, such as crowbars, flammable liquids, torches and Molotov cocktails.[25]

The TGPF report describes some provocateurs as being equipped with walkie-talkies and travelling in trucks, jeeps or motorcycle convoys. Their identities were rarely recognised by local witnesses, although the TGPF reports that it uncovered evidence in Medan that members of Pemuda Pancasila were directly involved in provoking riots.[26]

Similarly, a report made by Truk states that in several locations, including Depok, Tanah Abang and Tangerang, mobs were directed by 'commanders' moving about in vehicles, issuing orders and directions.[27] For example, in a robbery of a Bimantara car showroom in Central Jakarta, witnesses claimed to have recognised intelligence personnel from the local military post. In the attack on a plaza in Tangerang, the men directing the arson looked like military personnel and carried walkie-talkies and handguns. In Cikini, Central Jakarta, the leaders of the rioting were recognised as *preman* who routinely worked for the local branch of Kosgoro, a business association that was a main pillar of Golkar.[28]

The Truk report also described a standard modus operandi for the gangs that perpetrated some of the main acts of arson, such as the attacks on Jatinegara Plaza, Goro and the Lippo Supermall. In some cases, fore-warned crowds had gathered to watch the destruction even before the fires started. The gangs arrived with special equipment and set to work in an organised manner. Once the fire was burning well, they would board their vehicles and leave the scene.[29]

In Jatinegara, East Jakarta, paramedics working for Truk found a badly injured adolescent on 15 May. After being brought to the team's head-quarters the youth told Father Sandyawan, the team's co-ordinator, that he was one of the arsonists responsible for destroying Jatinegara Plaza. He said that he and hundreds of other youths had been housed in a military compound outside Jakarta for two weeks, where they were trained to foment riots and perpetrate arson. He said he was part of a group of eight who were supplied with petrol bombs and transported to Jatinegara; he believed that the other seven had been killed in the fire.[30] Although the boy would not describe those who trained and transported him, there is ample reason to suspect that elements of Indonesia's own security forces were responsible for the wanton destruction of May 1998.

Perhaps the clearest sign implicating the military in the May riots is the simple fact that the riots were allowed to happen. As the destruction raged throughout Jakarta and other cities on 14 May, most security forces stood idly by and took no preventive action.[31] For example, a man named Yanto who was looting shops in North Jakarta's Mangga Dua district was quoted as saying: 'When I came here at eight o'clock, looting had already begun. At first I just watched, but I joined in when I saw that the security forces were doing nothing to stop them.'[32]

Similarly, a looter of the Golden Truly supermarket on Jl Kapten Tendean recalled that he was leaving the building with a bundle of stolen clothing when he was startled to see several armed soldiers standing by the front entrance. One of the soldiers turned toward him and he suddenly feared he would be arrested, beaten or worse. Instead, the soldier just said: 'Walk, please, don't run.'[33]

Riot instigators reportedly told crowds that looting would not be punished, while others spread the same message by cruising through the narrow alleys of *kampung* neighbourhoods on motorbikes. Suddenly presented with the chance to loot valuable goods with no fear of arrest, many of the urban poor simply could not resist the temptation—especially since so many others were already taking part in the crime.

Syafrie Syamsoeddin later claimed that he had too few troops at his disposal to adequately secure Jakarta in the face of such unrest. He said that he had 6000 troops before the start of the riots, some of whom were used to guard vital installations such as the palace, government buildings and the state-owned television station (the men also, however, guarded at least four upmarket shopping malls whose shareholders included generals or military-linked businesses). Although his force levels were brought up to 20 000 by the end of the week, Syamsoeddin claims that logistical constraints prevented him from deploying troops promptly on the morning of 14 May.

The trouble spots were many, but this is hardly a convincing explanation for the garrison troops' remaining out of sight until very late in the day. Police units and even firefighters reportedly received orders to stay put.[34] One of the few units that did take action early in the day was a battalion of marines, who were not under the direct command of Syamsoeddin. This small force of troops was able to easily pacify Jalan Matraman Raya—ordinarily one of the city's most riot-prone areas.

Finally, on Thursday evening, Syamsoeddin's troops moved into the city and the mayhem was quickly brought under control, although sporadic looting continued in northern Jakarta through Friday.

While troops of the Jakarta Garrison remained passive, witnesses claimed to have spotted evidence that military elements were involved in in provoking the riots. There were sightings of gangs driving military vehicles, using military-style equipment or wearing army crewcuts and boots. Pro-Jakarta East Timorese militias, which were trained by the Special Forces, were said to have been transported to Jakarta by military aircraft a week before the rioting. Other Special Forces troops were said to have escorted *preman* gangs into Jakarta from the nearby province of Lampung.[35]

Reports also emerged that military officials, including members of the

Special Forces, had been involved in planning meetings with local *preman* gangs, such as Pemuda Pancasila. One such meeting in Medan was reported to the Legal Aid Foundation by a Pemuda Pancasila 'defector'.[36] A similar meeting in Solo was actually investigated by police before being covered up. Solo police did confirm, however, that the rioting started in a neighbourhood with a strong Pemuda Pancasila presence.[37] In Tangerang, west of Jakarta, a group from a local mosque claims to have captured four thugs who were instigating the rioting. The thugs, who said they were from Surabaya, were turned over to the police, and the police in turn took them to the local military headquarters—from where they disappeared overnight.[38]

There are also indications that the military high command at least had prior warning that rioting would break out. The director of the Legal Aid Foundation, Bambang Widjojanto, says that a non-territorial troop commander (i.e. the commander of a unit not attached to a regional garrison) told him that he received an emergency alert on the morning of 12 May, just before the Trisakti shootings.[39] The message ordered Jakarta's security forces to be on Level One alert—the highest state of readiness.

As for those involved in the violence, *Tajuk* magazine printed the confession of an anonymous Special Forces commando, who asserted that the May riots were perpetrated by select troops from his unit, Kostrad and the Jakarta Garrison—all of which were co-ordinated by Syafrie Syamsoeddin.[40] He claimed that several thousand *preman* were also used, including several hundred shipped in from Eastern Indonesia. Immediately after printing the article, *Tajuk* was sued for slander by the Jakarta Garrison.[41]

In addition to anecdotal evidence linking the military to the May riots, the general way in which the rioting was carried out suggests that it could have been a military operation. The Indonesian military has a long tradition of fostering civilian para-military groups—in fact, irregular youth organisations formed themselves into entire battalions during the struggle for independence. Later, when the military was threatened by the fundamentalist Darul Islam rebellion in West Java in the 1950s, armed forces chief Gen. Abdul Haris Nasution placed high priority on inculcating a thorough understanding of guerilla warfare tactics within the army. The purpose was two-fold: it prepared the under-strength military to mount a guerilla defence against a potential invader, while enabling the army to better understand and cope with domestic guerilla insurrections. A key feature of this strategy was the cultivation of links with civilian militias and para-military groups.

Amid the prolonged corruption of the Soekarno and Soeharto eras, A.H. Nasution's doctrine veered off course. To supplement meagre budgets and to enrich themselves, garrison commanders commercialised their units—that is, troops were hired out to provide protection services for various enterprises ranging from mine sites and factories to discotheques and drug rings. More enterprising commanders escalated their activities from providing security to extorting protection money and racketeering, particularly in remote provinces with heavy concentrations of natural resource industries, such as East Kalimantan, Riau and Irian Jaya. For these and other unsavoury activities, military commanders preferred to work in a symbiotic relationship with mafia groups or *preman* gangs, particularly Pemuda Pancasila.[42] The military would provide 'backing' for illicit businesses, while the gangs supplied *preman* for regime maintenance chores—a well-documented but otherwise typical example of which was the PDI Headquarters raid.

By the 1990s the guerilla warfare doctrine had evolved to such an extent that the military worked with a vast array of quasi-militant organisations. These ranged from military-trained neighbourhood security guards to heavily armed para-militaries such as East Timor's pro-Jakarta militias. In the middle were the *preman* gangs, such as Pemuda Pancasila and its sister organisation, Pemuda Panca Marga. Political roles were sometimes played by the military's own youth groups, such as FKPPI, the youth wing of the military veterans association that was long chaired by Bambang Soeharto. Another such group was IPK, a group for the offspring of military personnel posted to the civilian bureaucracy.[43] The military also supported youth sporting associations—particularly martial arts clubs—which in turn would routinely assist local military units.[44]

The chief agency that fostered and maintained this vast network of gangs and militias was the military's strategic intelligence agency, Bais. For intelligence-gathering and routine operations, Bais would work through regular intelligence officers assigned to all but the lowest levels of the military's vast territorial system. For delicate regime maintenance tasks, Bais would often call upon the Special Forces. In effect, these two units had inherited most of the functions of the disbanded Kopkamtib: Bais inherited intelligence-gathering and planning functions, while the Special Forces took over covert operations. In addition, most senior Bais officials hailed from the ranks of the Special Forces.

Bais therefore sat astride a sophisticated nationwide network of civilian militias, *preman* gangs and covert operatives. It could mobilise these forces through its officers in the territorial system or it could call upon the Special Forces to carry out specific tasks. These powers occasionally caused Bais to be accused of being a 'military within a military'.

Nowhere did Bais better demonstrate its abilities than in East Timor in September 1999. As will be discussed later, the military armed and trained civilian militias in each of East Timor's thirteen districts prior to the ballot on self-determination for the territory. After the ballot, the militias orchestrated a 'scorched-earth' campaign that levelled entire towns and prompted a mass exodus of refugees. Bais and Special Forces troops were heavily involved in forming and directing the militias, and the chief officer orchestrating the militia campaign was Maj. Gen. Zacky Anwar Makarim, a planner of the 1996 PDI raid and reputedly the military's foremost expert on covert operations.

At the time of the May riots, Makarim was serving as the head of Bais. But while Makarim wielded influence from behind the scenes, public scrutiny was deflected towards a general with a far higher public profile: Lt Gen. Prabowo Subianto.

Prabowo admitted to having ordered the kidnapping of student activists, and less than a week after the May riots he was sacked as Kostrad commander and appointed commandant of the armed forces staff college. This move was a humiliation for Prabowo; moreover, it sidelined him from strategic influence. The abrupt sacking fed suspicions that Prabowo was behind the calamities of May: the Trisakti shootings and the riots. Indeed, in November 1998 a government-sponsored fact-finding report pointed to Prabowo as the prime suspect in the riots. The report stated, cryptically, that the riots and Trisakti shootings could not be viewed in isolation from the kidnapping of the students.

In fact, there was a crucial distinction to be made between the three events: while the kidnappings were perpetrated in defence of Soeharto's presidency, the Trisakti shootings and the May riots were clearly designed to destabilise it. All Indonesians are aware of the Javanese maxim that mayhem reflects poorly on the ruler: an orderly kingdom denotes an able and legitimate ruler, while anarchy signals the opposite. Whoever ordered the shootings and fomented the riots was undoubtedly working towards a single purpose: to discredit Soeharto and drive him from power.

While Wiranto fostered the impression that Prabowo alone was to blame for the riots, Prabowo himself maintains his innocence. In fact, the truth may lie somewhere between these two extremes: Prabowo may have had knowledge of the riot plans or he may even have served as an accomplice—willingly or otherwise—in a wider plot. In any event, it is almost certain that Prabowo was not the prime actor, much less the sole mastermind.

One reason to doubt Prabowo's culpability is the lack of a motive. Prabowo had long benefited from Soeharto's patronage, and in early 1998 he needed this patronage more than ever. Prabowo's meteoric rise and his impolitic manner had alienated a clutch of senior generals who outranked him, possessed more experience and commanded greater support among the officer corps. With Soeharto out of power, Prabowo's career progress would be jeopardised by these unsympathetic generals.[45]

In fact, Prabowo apparently continued to defend Soeharto even after the riots took place. When asked on 15 May whether it was true that his father (Sumitro) had joined Amien Rais's People's Mandate Council, Prabowo adamantly denied it. He went on to denounce the council as an 'unconstitutional shadow government'.[46] If Prabowo's motive was to overthrow Soeharto by orchestrating the May riots, his defence of Soeharto at this late date would seem contradictory.

Another explanation put forth is that Prabowo fomented the riots with the idea of helping Habibie attain the presidency, after which he would be appointed armed forces chief. But betting on Habibie would have been a risky proposition: it was by no means certain that, if Soeharto stepped down, Habibie would take over. Most expected the MPR to hold another presidential election; if so, Wiranto or even Harmoko would be stronger candidates than Habibie.

Another reason for doubting that Prabowo was the sole mastermind of the riots pertains to his operational capability. As the newly installed commander of Kostrad, the army's main battle-ready combat force, Prabowo was not well positioned to launch a sophisticated covert operation on his own. Preparations for an operation that size—in which some 47 districts were hit simultaneously—would surely have been noticed by the intelligence chief, Makarim. Moreover, mobilising sufficient manpower was a delicate task to which Kostrad units were unaccustomed; instead, this was the speciality of the Special Forces, which had been placed under the command of Maj. Gen. Muchdi two months prior to the riots. Finally, fomenting riots would have been impossible without the complicity of the Jakarta Garrison commander, Syamsoeddin.

As Kostrad commander, Prabowo outranked Makarim, Muchdi and Syamsoeddin, but he had no authority over them—all reported to Wiranto. Some later assumed that Makarim and Syamsoeddin were personally loyal to Prabowo, because the three had spent several years together in East Timor. But, more recently, Makarim and Syamsoeddin had shared the experience of working in the rarified atmosphere of the presidential palace, as had Wiranto and Subagyo. Syamsoeddin was a former presidential adjutant, while Makarim had been the Bais official responsible for palace security.

It was generally assumed that Soeharto's adjutants and bodyguards were diehard loyalists, but proximity to power may have also fostered an appetite for power—combined with a better understanding of the underhanded means for acquiring it. And whereas Prabowo was far from being subtle or discreet, both Syamsoeddin and Makarim had spent their entire careers in the Special Forces, where they became experts in furtive intrigue—the signature ingredient of the Trisakti shootings and the May riots.

Finally, whereas Prabowo was cashiered in the aftermath of the events in May, both Syamsoeddin and Makarim were spared punishment. Even though both could have been faulted for failing to predict, prevent or even control the riots, Wiranto posted both to coveted jobs. Syamsoeddin's new post had a vague title—'special advisor for political affairs attached to the personal staff of the armed forces commander'—but it actually entailed as much or more responsibility than that of garrison commander. In effect, Syamsoeddin served as Wiranto's de facto envoy to Aceh, arguably the military's highest priority area of operations. He later came close to receiving a promotion to kaster.

Likewise, Brig. Gen. Sudi Silalahi—Syamsoeddin's top aide at the Jakarta Garrison and the officer who would have been responsible for issuing operational commands while the riots were happening—received command of the East Java garrison less than a year later. Another aide to Syamsoeddin, Brig. Gen. Adam Damiri, was promoted to commander of the Udayana Garrison, which encompassed East Timor. Makarim, meanwhile, later obtained a role comparable to that of Syamsoeddin: he became Wiranto's envoy to East Timor. In short, the pattern of promotions suggests that, rather than working for Prabowo, these officers were doing Wiranto's bidding all along.

The same might also have been true for the Special Forces commander, Maj. Gen. Muchdi. Having spent much of his career in the elite anti-terrorist unit, Muchdi had accumulated an extraordinary amount of combat experience in Indonesia's simmering guerilla wars.[47] He was also a deeply devout Muslim. In short, he epitomised the qualities that Prabowo tried to project. The two had served together in East Timor and Irian Jaya, and although Muchdi was three years older than Prabowo his career soared on Prabowo's coat-tails.

The only conceivable way that Prabowo could have masterminded the May riots on his own was by possessing the full co-operation of Muchdi. It was generally intimated that Prabowo relied on his loyalists within the Special Forces to carry out the riots. Soon after Prabowo was sacked as Kostrad commander, Muchdi was sacked as Special Forces commander, and it was believed at the time that he would be discharged from the military along with Prabowo. Instead, Muchdi remained on active duty and continued to be a significant figure in the military high command.[48]

Thus the respective fates of five critical officers—Syamsoeddin, Silalahi, Damiri, Makarim and Muchdi—cast doubt on the theory that Prabowo orchestrated the May riots by using his personal influence with these men. If he had done so, it remains unclear why only Prabowo was punished—while the other five escaped blame or actually benefited.

A main reason for Prabowo's being associated with the May riots was a particular passage in the government-sponsored fact-finding report produced in November 1998. The passage recommended further investigations of a meeting that took place at Kostrad Headquarters on the evening of 14 May. The implication was that the meeting, which was attended by Buyung Nasution and several other pro-democracy activists, involved a cabal of plotters. In fact, the meeting appears to have had little significance. At the time, Buyung and his group were seeking an explanation for the unrest, and Prabowo was the general who was easiest to access.[49] When Prabowo finally arrived at the headquarters where Buyung was waiting, the human rights lawyer launched into a tirade, berating Prabowo for his role in the kidnappings.[50] Buyung demanded to know whether Prabowo had orchestrated the shootings or riots. Prabowo professed his innocence on both charges, noting that he had already sworn on a Qur'an that he had taken no role in the shootings. Had this been a cabal of plotters, the meeting presumably would not have taken place in such an open environment and with such a diverse cast in attendance.

A few members of the team that produced the fact-finding report suggested that the passage highlighting the Kostrad meeting had been included at the behest of Wiranto.[51] They questioned a meeting that took place on 10 October, three weeks before the report's publication, when Subagyo and another Wiranto ally, Maj. Gen. Djamari Chaniago, met in private with several team members. The Officers Honour Council that later discharged Prabowo included Subagyo as its chair and Chaniago as a key member.[52] These officers were clearly interested in steering blame toward Prabowo, and there is ample reason to believe that they pressured the fact-finding team into politicising the final report. Consequently, ten of the eighteen team members refused to endorse the final version of the report—including the team's head, Marzuki Darusman.[53]

While it appears, therefore, that the May riots were organised and did involve military elements, it seems doubtful that Prabowo was the master-mind, as has often been alleged. He may have been aware of the planned riots, and he may even have acted as an accomplice, but he lacked the motive and capabilities to carry out the rioting himself. But because he was ruthless, power-hungry and bigoted—and because he had confessed to kidnapping activists who were tortured—the public was perfectly ready to accept him as the sole scapegoat.

The fact-finding report that shifted blame towards Prabowo made no mention of a far more suspicious event than the Kostrad meeting: Wiranto's insistence that a bevy of senior generals leave Jakarta on the morning of 14 May to attend a ceremony of middling importance in Malang, East Java. The ceremony was to mark the handover of command of a special unit within Kostrad, the Fast Reaction Strike Force. Previously under the command of Kostrad Division I, the strike force was being moved under the command of Kostrad Division II. Ordinarily, such a ceremony would be attended only by the division commanders or, at most, the Kostrad commander.[54] On the evening of 13 May, as rioting was breaking out in Grogol and Senen, Prabowo says that he repeatedly called Wiranto to protest the orders to leave Jakarta—but Wiranto remained inflexible.[55]

Prabowo might have known what was in store. During the Soeharto era it was a common precautionary measure to herd the senior echelon of military commanders together in one place during periods of political tension. For instance, when Soeharto suddenly left the country for emergency medical treatment in Germany in 1996, a large pool of generals were required to huddle together for an entire week at a golf resort in Bogor.[56] By not letting each other out of their sight, the generals could feel secure that no one among them was plotting a coup in the event that Soeharto died. Conversely, if a surprise plot did unfold, each general had a solid alibi with which to prove his innocence.

Wiranto clearly sought to remove all commanders of troops—save Syamsoeddin—from Jakarta during the peak of the rioting on Thursday morning. Therefore, at dawn on 14 May, Wiranto's generals assembled at Halim Airport and boarded a flight to Malang. In addition to the military's two senior figures (Wiranto and Subagyo), this group included all three commanders of battle-ready troops near Jakarta who were not under Syamsoeddin's command: Prabowo, Muchdi and Marine Commandant Maj. Gen. Soeharto (no relation to the president). The only troop commander who remained in Jakarta was Syamsoeddin, an officer with a long background in Special Forces intelligence work.[57]

Given the scale of the rioting that had erupted the night before—and given that Jakarta was already under Level One emergency alert—it is extraordinary that Wiranto ushered so many top commanders to a town 650 kilometres away. If Wiranto was indeed trying to keep tabs on his fellow generals, this would imply two things: that the armed forces commander possessed prior knowledge that the riots would worsen on 14 May, and that he had faith in his fellow former presidential adjutant, Syamsoeddin. Moreover, Wiranto also left his kaster behind in Jakarta. As will be seen, Yudhoyono sat out the rioting in armed forces headquarters—conferring with civic leaders about plans for asking Soeharto to resign.[58]

In the wake of the May riots, few suspected that Gen. Wiranto himself could have been behind the outbreak of unrest. Having catapulted to the military's top ranks from relative obscurity (as Soeharto's adjutant) just three years before, Wiranto was still unfamiliar to the Indonesian public. Neither the international press nor Western defence analysts knew much about him: unlike other officers whom the Pentagon had trained and worked with, Wiranto had not risen up through the Special Forces or the territorial system. He was from a traditional Javanese background and had rarely had occasion to leave Indonesia.

Given this background, few at the time recognised Wiranto's well-honed abilities for manoeuvring in the New Order's Byzantine corridors of power. And because he was charismatic, sociable and, above all, media-savvy, even fewer suspected that he was capable of perpetrating brutality. Weary of cynical leaders, Indonesians and foreigners alike wanted to see Wiranto as a principled, upstanding and dynamic leader. One year later, as will be seen, events in East Timor would finally deconstruct this image.

Had Wiranto's track record been scrutinised, it would have revealed that he had a history of working with civilian para-military forces. As Jakarta Garrison commander in 1995–96, Wiranto oversaw the creation of a 15 000-strong force of youths, dubbed 'Discipline Enforcement Cadres'.[59] This quasi-militant youth regiment was assigned the task of implementing Wiranto's National Discipline Campaign (purportedly concerned with traffic safety, litter and the like), but in fact they were also used to track down certain *preman* groups that were causing trouble for the authorities. In early 1996 large numbers of Jakarta *preman* were arrested, many of whom were believed to have been murdered. Others, such as those that took part in the subsequent PDI Headquarters raid, were encouraged to co-operate with the Jakarta Garrison. Later, as armed forces chief, Wiranto invariably ensured that whenever a vital MPR session occurred civilian 'auxiliaries' took part in its defence.

While Wiranto's past use of para-military units was overlooked in early 1998, there was also a strong belief that Wiranto was unquestioningly loyal to Soeharto. In fact, this might not necessarily have been true. It was generally assumed that because Wiranto and Soeharto shared a traditional Central Javanese upbringing—in which patrimonial fealty is extolled—the general was incapable of betraying his patron. Such notions of loyalty are emphasised, for example, in the ancient Hindu epics depicted in *wayang* shadow plays—which served as fundamental reference points for many traditional Javanese. But the historical chronicles conveyed by the *wayang* also contain countless tales of kings being overthrown by their trusted advisors, lieutenants or even their own brothers. The New Order's obsession with cultivating loyalty by no means precluded betrayal; in fact, it is probably more accurate to regard the obsession with loyalty as a reaction to the constant threat of betrayal.

By late April, Wiranto's military had a number of good reasons to betray Soeharto. They knew as well as anyone that Soeharto was not ruling effectively. The economic crisis was savaging the country, and it had become abundantly clear that only with Soeharto removed would there be an opportunity to restore order and set about repairing the economy. Indonesia's senior generals had extensive business interests at stake and they, like everyone else, were suffering from the collapse.

Another consideration was that some generals chafed under Soeharto's yoke. Soeharto had relegated the military from a proud and professional defence force to a crude implement used for bludgeoning his enemies. Soeharto's overthrow might allow the current generation of military leaders to finally restore the military's long-lost independence.

Finally, the lure of power might have tempted Wiranto and his fellow generals. For the generals who commanded what was arguably Indonesia's most powerful political institution, Soeharto's weakness represented an extraordinary opportunity. These generals could occupy positions of considerable power in a post-Soeharto era—provided they themselves steered the process of change, rather than being buffeted by it.

On the forefront of many minds in late April was Amien Rais's pledge to mobilise 'one million' supporters on 20 May. Rais was urging the public to march on the National Monument, a massive park that abuts the presidential palace. It was a scenario that the military had always feared. The greater Jakarta area contained around 15 million people; even if only 2 per cent of that number heeded Rais's call, the security forces would be overwhelmed. And given that student demonstrations seemed to be attracting growing support from urban residents, it seemed that Indonesia's 'people's power' movement was inexorably headed towards a cataclysmic outcome.

The armed forces chief therefore faced a difficult decision as the month of May began. To remain passive meant yielding the initiative to others, such as the students, Amien Rais or perhaps even the Speaker of parliament and the MPR, Harmoko. And if Soeharto was toppled through a cataclysmic uprising, Wiranto—a figure closely associated with Soeharto and Cendana—might fall with him. However, to continue defending Soeharto was equally undesirable. With the president's position growing increasingly untenable, it was only a matter of time before the president explicitly ordered Wiranto to fire on protesters. If Wiranto obeyed, it might only exacerbate the situation by creating martyrs and provoking yet more unrest; if he disobeyed, Soeharto might sack him in favour of a more subservient general.

An alternative, therefore, was to ease Soeharto out of power. In addition to deflating the student movement, this also afforded promising opportunities for Wiranto. By toppling Soeharto while keeping the New Order apparatus essentially intact, he might at least protect himself and the institutional interests of the military. At best, he might emerge with an opportunity to commandeer Soeharto's elaborate power structure for the express benefit of the military—or even himself. Wiranto's meteoric rise through the ranks had brought him within close reach of the pinnacle of authority. As such, he had both a great deal to lose—and a great deal to gain.

There are plentiful signs that the military had, in fact, tacitly turned against Soeharto by late April. As noted above, one influential hardliner had already, in effect, turned against Soeharto nearly a week before the May riots: Lt Gen. Syarwan Hamid, the key figure in the military's parliamentary faction. Other generals had indicated that they were wavering by conceding that dialogues with students should broach the topic of presidential succession. These included Subagyo and the kaster, Yudhoyono. The latter actually recommended in early May that the government should consider convening an extraordinary MPR session (which would have been empowered to change the president). Never before had an active kaster even allowed the possibility to be entertained.

For their part, Wiranto and Syamsoeddin had also been involved in efforts to engage students in dialogue, and both seemed reluctant to carry out Soeharto's repeated threats of force. A host of officers—including the Bais chief, Makarim—had met on various occasions with Amien Rais; while they warned him against mobilising the masses, they clearly tolerated his incessant verbal attacks on the regime.[60]

Finally, another possible sign of a change of course by the military leadership was the abrupt decision in mid-April to release the nine activists abducted by Rose Team, which was now under a new Special Forces commander, Maj. Gen. Muchdi.

But if the military had, indeed, turned against Soeharto, it possessed relatively limited room in which to manoeuvre. In particular, the generals faced three overriding priorities: end the debilitating unrest; defend the military's extensive institutional interests; and above all else, adhere to the Constitution. Indonesians revered the 1945 Constitution: it was the product of a heroic revolutionary experience, and both Soekarno and Soeharto upheld its exalted status (if for no other reason than because it conferred sweeping powers on the president). Desecrating the Constitution through an outright military coup was undesirable; moreover, it was infeasible, given the proven strength of the student movement. If the military wanted to take Soeharto's place, they would need to find another way.

It is likely that some relatively liberal military figures would have welcomed an extraordinary session of the MPR and a democratic presidential election. This would certainly appease the students and abide by the Constitution, but less reform-minded generals no doubt worried that it would not serve the military's best interests.

An alternative, therefore, was for the military to be handed power by Soeharto—much the way he had been ceded power by Soekarno. The constitutionality of this route was dubious, but it might have been made feasible by the special Emergency Powers that Soeharto had recently obtained from the MPR. The president might simply recede from the scene and allow the military to assume control, perhaps through martial law. This scenario would not permanently allay the student protests, but it might at least buy time. Democratic elections might eventually have to be carried out, but in the meantime the military would at least be in an excellent position to dictate the course of events—while looking after its own interests. And in this scenario Wiranto might have eventually emerged as a leading presidential candidate.

Thus, nudging Soeharto from power made eminent sense for Wiranto and the military leadership. An outright coup d'état was infeasible, but alternative routes to power were potentially available once Soeharto was removed. The keys were to guide events, rather than be guided by them, while forcing Soeharto's hand and compelling him to resign. But confronting Soeharto directly risked angering all of Cendana, and the wealth of Soeharto's family and cronies ensured that they would still possess considerable influence even after Soeharto's political demise. What was required, therefore, was a more circuitous route for deposing the president—a coup *à la* Java.

In Javanese tradition, as noted earlier, harmony and tranquillity served to legitimise an emperor's rule. Pandemonium and chaos would, therefore, do the opposite. It seems clear that the Trisakti shootings were designed to serve as a triggering mechanism, while the deliberately insti-gated riots of 14 May were meant to 'de-legitimise' Soeharto. For several weeks prior to the May riots the broad military leadership appeared distinctly ambivalent about defending the president. As the main pillar of his rule, the military had the most to lose from a tumultuous overthrow of Soeharto—but it had a great deal to gain from controlling the process itself.

Actually perpetrating the May riots could not have been achieved without the complicity of Syafrie Syamsoeddin, the officer with responsi-bility for ensuring security in Jakarta. Similarly, it is extremely unlikely that the preparations for such a large-scale operation could have escaped the attention of the intelligence chief, Zacky Makarim—in fact, it seems likely that his active participation would have been required in such an operation. By 1998 both of these officers had worked with Wiranto in close proximity to Soeharto for over five years. Both would continue to retain Wiranto's trust in the year ahead. Indeed, Makarim would later reappear in East Timor, where he proved adept at organising destructive para-military campaigns similar to the one carried out in Jakarta in May.

An essential ingredient in this plan was a scapegoat. Prabowo Subianto—Wiranto's arch-rival, a confessed kidnapper and an officer who was notorious for his ambition and brutality—fitted the role well. That Prabowo abetted a circuitous plot to oust Soeharto is possible, but remains unclear. What is more clear is that the Kostrad commander almost certainly could not have masterminded the May riots on his own volition. To have any chance of success, he would have had to rely on assistance from his successor as Special Forces commander, Maj. Gen. Muchdi. But whereas Prabowo was later sacked by Wiranto, Muchdi was not. Soeharto's son-in-law kidnapped pro-democracy activists to defend the New Order, but it seems doubtful that he singlehandedly masterminded the subsequent events: the release of the surviving activists, the Trisakti shootings and the instigation of the May riots.

A whirlwind of subterfuge and deception therefore awaited President Soeharto as he flew home from Egypt on 14 May. Several months beforehand he had gone to great lengths to install proven loyalists in the MPR, the military leadership and the cabinet. He would soon discover, however, that these loyalties were not what he had presumed.

8

COUP À LA JAVA

Throughout the hastily arranged flight home from Egypt, Soeharto is said to have complained bitterly about the ingratitude of his people. As Indonesia's president he had succeeded where Soekarno had failed: he had delivered economic growth, raised living standards and achieved rice self-sufficiency. Once the basket case of Asia, Indonesia had become an emerging tiger. There was corruption, yes, but what did it matter if a few officials enriched themselves, as long as the vast majority were steadily growing better off?

The answer might have been readily apparent from the window of his bulletproof Mercedes. A convoy of nearly 100 military vehicles escorted the president from Halim Airport to his residence in Menteng in the small hours of Friday 15 May, 1998. Debris and devastation littered the streets from the previous day's frenzy of violence. Entire buildings were reduced to blackened shells.

Soeharto conferred first with Wiranto and then with his four co-ordinating ministers before retiring in the afternoon to recover from jet-lag. Before going to bed, however, he ordered that fuel prices be slashed. By hiking them so precipitously less than two weeks before, Soeharto had apparently been trying to steer the public's frustrations toward the IMF. If so, that effort had backfired, and now the partial repeal of the price increases was apparently intended to appease the public. It was, however, a laughable concession in light of what had transpired while the president was away.

The weary Soeharto rose early on Saturday. He had a busy day ahead. Never in 32 years had his regime been in such disarray. On top of the convulsions of previous days, calls for his resignation were coming from all directions. The president's political support was beginning to crumble. Just the previous day a host of prominent Nahdlatul Ulama figures— exasperated with Abdurrahman Wahid's intransigence—had taken the initiative themselves and issued a press release. Referring to the newspaper reports of Soeharto's statement in Cairo, the NU leaders 'commended' the president's offer to relinquish the presidency and become a *pandito*, a revered figure who held no formal office. The statement seemed mild-mannered on the surface, but Javanese are renowned for their powers of circumlocution. The subtly worded statement was, in effect, a brazen call for Soeharto to quit.

In addition to the NU statement, Soeharto found that three important Golkar affiliates had formally turned against him on Friday. These were: Kosgoro, a co-operatives association that was one of the main sub-groups within Golkar; the Indonesian National Youth Organisation (KNPI), a key Golkar constituency whose alumni, such as Housing Minister Akbar Tandjung, figured prominently in the party leadership; and a collection of fifteen high-ranking revolutionary war veterans, most of whom had been influential supporters of Soeharto in the past.

The statements from Kosgoro and KNPI showed that defections were now taking place at relatively high levels in the New Order hierarchy. The statement from the veterans was even more worrying: the vast majority of retired officers always hewed closely to the official policies of the military's active leadership, and the statement therefore suggested that Soeharto's support was wavering in military circles. The damage was not yet irreparable, but the president was probably aware that he needed to move swiftly.

S oeharto's first order of business on Saturday was to receive a delegation from the University of Indonesia, led by Rector Asman Boedisantoso. Formally conveying his students 'aspirations', Boedisantoso explained that the president's offer to stand down, as quoted by the reporters in Cairo, was 'well received'.[1] The delegation was unimpressed with the president's response. Soeharto denied having made the offer in Cairo, but in the petulant manner that had become his trademark, he said: 'There's no problem with my resigning. Let's just leave it up to parliament.'[2]

There obviously was a problem with his resigning, and apparently Soeharto felt sure that his obedient servant, Harmoko, would defend his presidency at all costs in his powerful, twin role as Speaker of both parliament and the MPR. By deferring to parliament, Soeharto was falling back on his trusted technique of 'legal formalism'—the tactic of insisting that the game be played according to constitutional rules, even though all but Soeharto's own players were excluded from the pitch. This time the tactic would backfire. Relying on Harmoko was the first of the several miscalculations Soeharto would make during the last days of his rule.

Soeharto had the opportunity to recognise his mistake just minutes after Boedisantoso left the president's office: Harmoko himself was the next visitor, accompanied by the four Deputy Speakers of parliament. Harmoko had spent most of his long political career quashing proposals for reform but suddenly his stance had changed. Perhaps the public pressure exerted upon him had made an impression: for weeks he had been hounded by social organisations, student groups, intellectuals, alumni associations and others who were clamouring for political change. And just two days before, in the Central Java town of Solo, Harmoko's family home had been attacked by rioters and gutted by fire.

But perhaps the most important factor affecting Harmoko was the example set by one of the Deputy Speakers, Syarwan Hamid. The former kaster had become one of Indonesia's most ardent proponents of change—and he still ranked among the most influential generals in the military high command. As he strode into Soeharto's office, Harmoko must have believed that the military was no longer solidly behind Soeharto.

Harmoko began by explaining that parliament had been deluged by citizen groups that were pressing for reform. As the Speaker of parliament, Harmoko wanted to formally convey the three main demands that were being made. These were: the convening of an extraordinary session of the MPR; the reshuffling of the cabinet; and Soeharto's resignation, as had reportedly been offered in Cairo.

Soeharto addressed the last point first. As he had told Boedisantoso, he had never offered to resign in Cairo—he had been misquoted. Nevertheless, Soeharto made a remarkable suggestion: if all factions of parliament could agree that he no longer possessed the full support of the Indonesian people, then he would willingly resign. Perhaps Soeharto did not realise that Harmoko was wavering, or perhaps he felt assured that Hamid and the military's faction would exert a check on Harmoko's parliament. In any event, Soeharto clearly volleyed the ball back to parliament.

Harmoko then put a question regarding procedure: in order to determine whether the people still supported Soeharto, would it be necessary to consult the factions of the larger MPR, or just parliament alone? This may have been a veiled threat, because there was a profound difference between the two choices. The MPR, as Indonesia's highest authority, could summarily replace the president if it so chose. And as the MPR's most powerful figure, Harmoko would then be well positioned to dictate the course of subsequent events. In contrast, parliament lacked the authority to dismiss the president. Not surprisingly, Soeharto told Harmoko that it would not be necessary to convene the MPR.[3]

Before the close of his meeting with the parliamentary leaders, Soeharto briefed them on his three-pronged strategy for battling his way out of his predicament. First, he would restore order and 'safeguard the nation by taking stern measures', including the use of his Emergency Powers. Second, he would continue implementing reforms, and he hoped that parliament would assist him on this front. Third, he would reshuffle the cabinet, including the removal of Tutut Soeharto—even though, as he said, 'she was fully qualified for her job'.[4] If the people still wanted him to resign even after implementing these measures, then he would do so.

Deputy Speaker Ismail Hasan Metareum, an Acehnese from the PPP faction, cautioned that if 'taking stern measures' involved the revival of Kopkamtib, there was likely to be a domestic and international backlash. Soeharto assured him that he need not worry: international opinion was inconsequential, he said, because this was an internal matter. As for domestic opinion, he would avoid parallels to Kopkamtib by reviving the secret police under a new name.

Soeharto concluded the meeting by ordering the parliamentarians to keep most of its proceedings confidential. The only items for public consumption were Soeharto's promise to safeguard the nation and to reshuffle the cabinet.[5]

Harmoko announced the two items to reporters as soon as he emerged from Soeharto's office. The news infused the public and the student movement with a combination of dread and hope: dread because 'safeguarding the nation' meant the revival of Kopkamtib, and Kopkamtib promised grisly consequences; and hope because, by offering to reshuffle the cabinet, Soeharto was starting to bend. Against a ruler who had been uncompromising for decades, the students felt they had finally scored a breakthrough.

Some prominent reformists, such as former environment minister Sarwono Kusumaatmadja, recognised that a turning point had been reached. 'Whenever a dictator starts making compromises,' he later recalled, 'you know it's all over.'[6] Having long stood out as the most outspoken member of the previous cabinet, Kusumaatmadja chose that day to become the first cabinet minister to appeal for Soeharto's resignation.

The events of May so disrupted Indonesia's political order that a mild-mannered Islamic scholar, Nurcholish Madjid, found himself thrust into the thick of the worsening fray. The venerable university rector seemed an unlikely figure amid the coarse world of Jakarta politics, but he possessed a unique set of credentials. Nurcholish's political philosophy had been encapsulated by the famous soundbite: 'Islam, yes! Islamic parties, no!' His eminence as an Islamic scholar won him the trust of modernist Muslims, while his reservations about politicising religion allowed him to maintain constructive relationships with Soeharto and nationalist-minded generals.

Nurcholish could bridge two key groups: the most effective source of organised political opposition was emanating from a loose coalition of Islamic groups, while the arbiter of political change was the military. If these two key institutions—organised Islam and the military—could come to terms on a plan, it would represent a major step forward. Rejecting Wahid as too conservative and Rais as too controversial, the Islamic groups chose Nurcholish to serve as their envoy to the military and Soeharto.

While rioting and mayhem crippled Jakarta on Thursday 14 May, Nurcholish was invited to the armed forces' vast headquarters compound on the outskirts of the city. More than twenty generals, led by the kaster, Yudhoyono, spent much of the day coolly discussing various alternatives for bringing about a political transition. Nurcholish proposed a plan that was hardly radical: he wanted to move the parliamentary elections forward from 2003 to January 2000—which was still a full twenty months away. An extraordinary session of the MPR and a presidential election should take place by April 2000. The proposal also demanded a formal apology from Soeharto and the return of his family's ill-gotten wealth.

Yudhoyono advised against the apology and the return of wealth, but he was receptive to the idea of moving elections forward.[7] In effect, the military's key policy-maker was endorsing a transition plan—while riots were raging just a short distance away. Encouraged by this endorsement, Nurcholish convened a press conference two days later, on Saturday 16 May. Facing a phalanx of television cameras in the lobby of the Hotel Wisata, Nurcholish called on Soeharto to hold new parliamentary elections.

Meanwhile, just two blocks away, another press conference was being convened at the ministry of defence. The military's spokesman, Brig. Gen. Mokodongan, issued a press release that encouraged citizens to augment their neighbourhood security patrols. It was a mundane message, but around the same time reporters were handed another release that proved far more significant. The statement was simple and brief: it explained that the military endorsed the views expressed the previous day by the NU.[8]

The military press release was another example of Javanese circumlocution, referring as it did to the NU statement that had welcomed Soeharto's ('misquoted') offer to resign. Prabowo claims that as soon as he obtained a copy, he reported directly to Soeharto and alerted him to the danger: 'This means the military is asking you to step down!'[9] The implication was that Wiranto had turned against Soeharto.

If it was true the military had withdrawn its support, Soeharto had no hope of surviving. He immediately summoned Subagyo and demanded an explanation, but the army chief-of-staff disavowed any knowledge.[10] Soeharto then explained that he wanted to revive Kopkamtib, with Subagyo as its head. The president had already signed three decrees authorising the revival of the secret police. With intelligence agencies, commando units and conventional forces at his direct disposal, the Kopkamtib commander would have more operational authority—and even less legal scruples—than the armed forces commander. For whatever reasons, Subagyo declined the offer.[11] Again, Soeharto had miscalculated:

his former bodyguard was apparently not as loyal as he had presumed. Soeharto stayed awake all night, chain-smoking cigars.[12]

While Soeharto was meeting with Subagyo, Bambang Soeharto contacted Wiranto to ask him about the press release. Like Subagyo, Wiranto disavowed any knowledge.[13] In fact, Wiranto's aides worked until three that morning, contacting every media publication in Jakarta and warning them not to make any mention of the press release in the morning papers.[14] Wiranto then reported to Soeharto around dawn to plead his innocence in person.[15]

According to Wiranto, Soeharto not only accepted the general's claim of innocence but extended the same offer he had made hours before to Subagyo: command of a revived Kopkamtib. Wiranto says, however, that 'the military, and I myself as the leader of the armed forces, did not pursue [that route] because I realised that if I did so there would be enormous bloodshed'.[16] If Wiranto's story is true, it provides further evidence that the armed forces commander was treading cautiously to protect his own interests. He was not openly antagonistic towards Soeharto, but neither was he eager to fight for the ageing autocrat.

As for the military press release, its origin remains a mystery. Mokodongan, the military's spokesman, later claimed that the release was circulated anonymously without his knowledge, but a reporter present that night recalls him reading the statement out loud.[17] Although a host of explanations are possible, it would seem that the military leadership was divided, indecisive—or both.

O n the morning of Sunday 17 May—around the time that Soeharto and Wiranto were meeting—Nurcholish awoke to a telephone call from State Secretary Saadillah Mursjid. Although he had only recently vaulted on to the national political stage, Saadillah was functioning as Soeharto's right-hand man during these critical days. The morning newspapers reported the demands that Nurcholish had made the previous evening; upon reading the news, Saadillah promptly invited the scholar to the presidential palace. He also invited Fahmi Idris, a businessman and Habibie supporter who had helped Nurcholish formulate the demands. Saadillah was interested in the call for new elections as a potential starting point for arriving at a political compromise, and the three discussed the best method for presenting the idea to Soeharto.[18]

While the three men were conferring, Prabowo arrived unexpectedly.[19] After perusing Nurcholish's proposal, the Kostrad commander called the plan 'crazy'. Soeharto had no 'ill-gotten wealth', he claimed, and he recommended that Nurcholish concentrate on backing Habibie for president instead. Nurcholish argued that Habibie lacked support from the military, but Prabowo told him not to worry: 'I will protect Habibie.'

Before departing, Prabowo asked Nurcholish to recommend to Soeharto that he be made armed forces commander, replacing Wiranto. 'Why not ask Soeharto yourself?' Fahmi Idris asked.

'Because Soeharto doesn't like me,' said Prabowo.

Prabowo had clearly lost Soeharto's favour, presumably because Soeharto knew by now that the Kostrad commander favoured Habibie for president. But whether Prabowo was actively trying to topple Soeharto remains unclear, and, in any event, he was not the only senior general engaged in backroom politicking. While Prabowo was meeting with Nurcholish, Wiranto's kaster, Yudhoyono, was meeting directly with Rais. The two undoubtedly discussed Rais's plan to mobilise Jakarta's masses on 20 May, but alternative succession scenarios were probably touched on as well. And meanwhile, Jakarta Garrison commander Syafrie Syamsoeddin was aiding Soeharto's opponents in a much more tangible way—by extending assistance to the very groups that had been his adversaries for the past four months: student demonstrators.

After Soeharto told the University of Indonesia (UI) delegation on Saturday that the question of his resignation should be left up to parliament, student groups swung into action. According to Prabowo's version of events, UI alumni leader Hariadi Darmawan, who had been instrumental in helping students organise their rallies, approached Wiranto on Sunday evening. Darmawan explained that large numbers of students planned to march on parliament the next morning and he wanted to avoid a clash with security forces. Wiranto agreed. He instructed Syamsoeddin to use garrison vehicles to transport the students at ten on Monday morning.[20]

Students began pouring into the grounds of parliament well before ten. Most used their own transport, rejecting the buses sent to their campuses by Syamsoeddin. But were it not for the acquiescence of the security forces, the students would not have been able to enter the parliamentary compound.[21] A host of garrison units surrounded it and the troops had repelled student demonstrators in the past. On this occasion, however, the students were given free passage: their goals and the military's had finally converged.

Student organisations of all stripes—from modernist Muslim groups to Marxist radicals—were represented in the throng that converged on the 1960s-era parliament building, which also housed MPR assemblies. Scores of students clambered atop the two massive green concrete domes that formed the building's roof and constituted one of Jakarta's most famous landmarks. They draped the building with banners that descried the New Order and called for the overthrow of Soeharto and his cronies. By mid-morning hundreds of students wedged themselves on the broad, tall staircase that formed the front of the parliament building. Thousands more filled the parliament's grounds. It was, by far, the most dramatic student rally to date.

In Harmoko's plush office the Speaker and his four deputies engaged in earnest discussions from 9 a.m. onwards. They gazed through their fourth-floor window at successive waves of students pouring through the compound's gates. Each new busload was greeted with a massive cheer from those already in place. Finally a student delegation presented the parliamentary leaders with a simple demand: call for the president's resignation.

Harmoko and the deputies discussed their alternatives. They had already formally conveyed 'the people's aspirations' to Soeharto on Saturday, and he had specifically indicated that the ball was in their court. At some point they would have to do something—on that much they could agree. It was tempting to sit back, monitor events and determine a course of action once the situation was easier to read, but with thousands of students outside and hundreds more pouring through the gates every hour, this option was simply too risky.

For the moment, the troops outside the front gate were apparently under orders to usher the students into the compound, but Harmoko's group worried that, if the students suddenly turned violent, there was no telling what might happen. If the students lit fires, vandalised buildings or forced their way inside, the troops might intervene. And if the troops intervened, blood would be shed—perhaps including their own. In the end, the parliamentary speakers decided to take action.[22]

One by one, Harmoko summoned each of the four faction chairs. Each agreed in principle to Harmoko's suggested course of action: to formally ask the president to resign.[23] There was, however, a procedural constraint: because parliament was not in session that day, a formal resolution—ratified by the full membership—could not be produced. If Harmoko and the deputies wanted to make a hasty call for Soeharto to resign, it would have to be done merely as an expression of their personal opinions, not as a formal pronouncement of parliament.

Harmoko's deputies had no choice but to accept this compromise. At 3.20 p.m. they entered a press room packed with journalists and camera crews. Harmoko was flanked by Abdul Gafur, Syarwan Hamid, Hasan Ismail Metareum and Fatimah Ahmad. Indonesian television audiences were all too familiar with Harmoko's visage: during his nearly two decades as information minister, Harmoko appeared on state-run television on an almost nightly basis, tediously reading out the text of newly enacted government decrees. This occasion bore the same appearance as countless stale press conferences of the past, but this time Harmoko's audience was riveted. He read from a prepared statement: 'The Speaker and Deputy Speakers, who are concerned with the good of the nation, call on President Soeharto to act with wisdom and erudition and do what is right: resign.'[24]

At this, Hamid punched the air with his fist to silently demonstrate that he, the leading armed forces representative in parliament, concurred. Metareum clapped his hands emphatically. Harmoko closed with an appeal for calm and order to allow the country's leaders to adhere to the Constitution. Television stations interrupted their normal programming to air the conference, and the event was reported on news networks around the world. The ball was now in the military's court.

The nation waited with bated breath for Wiranto's response to Harmoko. It came early on Monday evening, when the armed forces commander appeared on television flanked by his four service chiefs, plus Prabowo, Muchdi and others.[25] Expectations soared—many viewers imagined that Soeharto's regime was about to come to a close, after 32 years.

Instead, the public was fed yet another sour dose of legal formalism. 'Today's statement by parliamentary leaders,' said Wiranto in a bland voice, 'was a statement of individual opinions, even though it was presented by a group.' Wiranto went on to explain that, for Harmoko's statement to have a sound legal basis, all members of parliament would first need to be consulted through a regular session of parliament.[26]

Technically, Wiranto was correct. Harmoko, Gafur and the other deputies had debated for nearly an hour over whether to explicitly state that they were acting in their personal capacities when they called on Soeharto to resign. In the end they chose to make the point implicitly: they mentioned that the factions would formally debate and ratify the matter the following day. Harmoko and his deputies therefore felt justified in delivering the statement without the key words '*secara pribodi-pribadi*' ('in our private capacities').[27]

A possible reason why the deputies had decided to omit these words was that Harmoko had apparently been assured by Hamid that the military would support the call for Soeharto to resign.[28] Harmoko might have been misled by Hamid, Wiranto might have been indecisive, or perhaps the military simply wanted to ensure that parliament's procedure took place with indisputable constitutionality. In any event, it was widely expected that, when the deputies consulted the full parliament the following day, an overwhelming majority would support a formal resolution calling for Soeharto's resignation. In effect, Wiranto had merely bought another 24 hours for Soeharto.

Saadillah summoned Nurcholish to meet Soeharto on Monday evening. The venue would be the president's residence, on the quiet, leafy Jalan Cendana. Since his health began deteriorating in 1996, Soeharto had been conducting the bulk of his presidential affairs from home, rather than from his presidential office complex.

As Nurcholish strode into the president's private study, Soeharto, who was sitting with his half-brother Probosutedjo, immediately told Nurcholish that he agreed in principle to the scholar's proposal, which he had already read. Nurcholish, however, told the president that the events that had transpired that day had already rendered his proposal—which was a mere 48 hours old—obsolete. Not only had the parliamentary speakers called on Soeharto to step down that afternoon, but the influential Islamic organisation, Icmi, had done so as well.

Nurcholish explained that his election timetable, originally set for January 2000, now seemed far too distant. 'The people's understanding of reform,' he delicately told Soeharto, 'is that you step down.'[29] He therefore asked that parliamentary elections be held within six months and that Soeharto not run in the ensuing presidential election.[30] Although this was not what the president had been expecting, Soeharto seemed nonplussed. He even explained—to Nurcholish's amazement—that he had already hinted at resigning while in Cairo. This is precisely what he and his aides had been adamantly denying for nearly a week. He went on to declare that he was 'fed up' (kapok) with serving as president. Nurcholish presumed that he meant fed up with the nation's ingratitude.[31]

But Soeharto still would not commit to a date for new elections, claiming that he first wanted to consult with a delegation of Islamic leaders. He named Nurcholish and Abdurrahman Wahid. Saadillah cited the names of several others who would be suitable for the occasion—most were moderates who had collaborated with Soeharto in the past. But when Saadillah was finished, Nurcholish asked: 'What about my old classmate?'

Soeharto asked whom he meant. 'Amien Rais,' was the reply.

'Well,' said Soeharto, 'let's hold off on that.'[32] The president had no interest in meeting with the ill-mannered Muhammadiyah figure.

In summoning a number of Islamic leaders Soeharto seemed to be making one last attempt to 'divide and conquer'—a tactic that had long been a hallmark of his rule. Soeharto hoped that Wahid, who had refrained from criticising him recently, would use his authority to persuade other Islamic leaders to relent.[33] The Islamic camp had never been unified at the best of times, and if Wahid and his followers could be compelled to make a pact with Soeharto then Rais and the others would be isolated. This was the same divisive strategy that Soeharto had used in the approach to the 1997 parliamentary elections. On that occasion it had worked flawlessly; this time, however, Soeharto would only succeed in isolating himself.

Nine Muslim leaders were invited to Jalan Cendana the next morning.[34] Four were NU leaders and only two were from the Muhammadiyah. Before proceeding to Soeharto's residence most of the group assembled at a nearby house where Rais was staying. Nurcholish briefed them on what to expect: Soeharto wanted to establish a reform committee, or Komite Reformasi, to draft the guidelines for political reforms and to select a new cabinet. Nurcholish suspected that Soeharto would invite some of the nine Muslim leaders to join the committee. Sensing that Soeharto was weak, and fearful of being branded as traitors to reform, the group pledged not to accept any positions offered by the president.

The Muslim leaders arrived at Jalan Cendana at 9 a.m. As expected, Soeharto opened the meeting by outlining his plans for a Komite Reformasi and a new 'Reform Cabinet'. When all nine refused to take part in either, Soeharto was visibly shaken. He had enjoyed close working relationships with some of these figures, such as Ali Yafie, for many years. He had expected them to remain loyal—but he had miscalculated once again.

Nurcholish proceeded to explain that no reform measures would succeed without the president's resignation. 'You must find a way to end your presidency gracefully and honourably. Not in the Latin American way. And not a repeat of our 1965–66 experience.' Nurcholish was referring to the anti-communist pogrom that had claimed a huge death toll. The delegation demanded elections within six months, but Soeharto would only promise to hold them 'as soon as possible'.

The group did not press Soeharto to resign immediately, in part because of the crucial role played by Abdurrahman Wahid. The normally loquacious cleric remained silent throughout most of the meeting. One of his few contributions was to register surprise that Nurcholish was trying 'to hammer' Soeharto—a comment which most of those present took to mean that Wahid opposed Soeharto's immediate resignation. In fact, in a public appearance later that same afternoon, Wahid brusquely demanded that the students quit demonstrating and give Soeharto a chance to work on reforms.

For many, the intransigence of this formerly staunch advocate of democratisation was puzzling. The only explanation for his continued support for Soeharto was that his arch-nemesis, Amien Rais, was leading the anti-Soeharto movement. Even amid this national drama, it appeared to many that Wahid was more concerned with defeating his modernist rivals than with bringing down Soeharto.

Soeharto's meeting with the Islamic leaders was scheduled to last only 30 minutes; instead, it lasted well into mid-morning. At one point the subject of Habibie arose. A member of the delegation proposed that Soeharto simply resign and hand power to the vice-president. Legal experts had generally decided that this was a constitutional alternative, although Indonesia's vague Constitution made the matter somewhat debatable. But Soeharto rejected the idea for a different reason. Referring to the loyal acolyte who had spent more than two decades currying his favour, Soeharto said: 'There is a question of whether the vice-president is capable.'[35]

This dig at Habibie surprised some of those in the room. The two men had been regarded as close friends for years, but now some wondered whether Soeharto had been using Habibie all along. Perhaps Soeharto had installed Habibie as vice-president not because of his merits but precisely because of his deficiencies. Soeharto had apparently felt that, with enemies mustering around him, he was safer with an unpopular replacement waiting in the wings. But another interpretation is also possible: Soeharto might have already sensed that Habibie coveted the top job, and he might have felt betrayed that the vice-president was not signalling his readiness to resign with him, in solidarity.

Whatever Soeharto's reasoning, the president had made yet another miscalculation. The tide of anti-Soeharto momentum was so strong that even Habibie seemed like a palatable alternative to many of those who were demanding change. Habibie's supporters were few, but at this point they outnumbered Soeharto's. And by denigrating Habibie behind his back, Soeharto only made matters worse for himself: the comment quickly found its way back to Habibie.

When one of the nine Islamic leaders recounted Soeharto's comment to him, Habibie expressed outrage and humiliation. He had known Soeharto for 47 years—since the age of thirteen—and he had served in his cabinet for over twenty years. Speaking privately with his friends in his home, Habibie complained that Soeharto's slight was an affront to the institution of the vice-presidency.[36] But at the same time, of course, the slight was convenient: it provided Habibie with the pretext he needed to break ranks with Soeharto and promote his own candidacy. And while he was doing so another key power broker was finally abandoning the president: Ginandjar Kartasasmita.

As one of the four co-ordinating ministers who managed the cabinet, Ginandjar was responsible for fifteen other ministers with economics-related portfolios. Early on Tuesday morning most of these ministers assembled in his office in the headquarters of the National Planning Agency, a colonial-era building that faced a wooded park in Menteng, not far from Jalan Cendana. After several days of intense politicking, Ginandjar and all but two of his fifteen ministers signed a formal memo to the president. Although they refrained from resigning outright, the signatories stated that they were not willing to serve in the next 'reform cabinet'.[37]

In addition to Ginandjar, the memo's signatories included some of the government's most powerful figures, such as Housing Minister Akbar Tandjung, Mines and Energy Minister Kuntoro Mangkusubroto and State Enterprise Minister Tanri Abeng. Surprisingly, the list also included some who were widely viewed as being little more than agents of the first family, such as Haryanto Danutirto and Subiakto Tjakrawerdaya. And perhaps most significantly, the list included an active and influential three-star general, Transmigration Minister Hendropriyono—yet more evidence that Soeharto had lost the support of the armed forces. The only two who declined to sign were Industry and Trade Minister Bob Hasan and Finance Minister Fuad Bawazier, both of whom were particularly close to the first family.

To be sure, the fourteen ministers accounted for less than half of the cabinet, and a host of powerful ministers, such as Defence Minister Wiranto, were not among the signatories. However, many of the fourteen shared an important trait: they had close links to Vice-President Habibie. In effect, Soeharto was facing a mutiny from within and it appeared to be spearheaded by his executive officer.

The events of Tuesday morning revealed that Soeharto had lost the support of his vice-president and nearly half of his cabinet. At the time, however, the president was not yet aware of these facts. He might have suspected that Habibie had turned against him, but he would not meet with the vice-president until later that evening. The ministers' memo, meanwhile, was delivered by courier and remained unopened. Akbar Tandjung—reputedly the prime mover in the effort to enlist the ministers' signatures—showed the letter to Saadillah on Tuesday, but the state secretary neglected to inform Soeharto until the next day.[38] Thus, rather than discovering about the loss of his vice-president and fourteen ministers, Soeharto first heard about a mutiny on a different front: in the halls of parliament.

All four parliamentary factions endorsed Harmoko's resolution calling on the president to resign.[39] The resolution was backed by the entire armed forces faction—consisting of 75 active senior officers from all four branches of the military. Finally, it was confirmed: the military high command wanted rid of Soeharto. With both the parliament and the military turned against him, it was clear that Soeharto was doomed.

Less clear, however, was what might follow in Soeharto's wake. The dictator had been weakened, but popular reform leaders such as Megawati and Wahid remained inert. The students and Amien Rais were exerting relentless pressure for change, but they had little ability to affect the delicate manoeuvring taking place at the highest levels of Soeharto's New Order. The only reformer with influence at this level was Nurcholish Madjid, and even his impact was limited. There was a consensus that Soeharto must go, but the process would be steered by two entities that were hardly reform-minded: parliament and the military. Neither Harmoko nor Wiranto wanted to be outmanoeuvred by the other—and neither wanted to fall victim, along with Soeharto, to a mass uprising in Jakarta. Both were well aware that Amien Rais was still calling for a 'million person' march on the morning of Wednesday 20 May—which was now less than 24 hours away.

Following parliament's announcement, Soeharto received a steady stream of visitors on Tuesday afternoon. Most were active or former members of the New Order's highest ranks, and most apparently urged Soeharto to resign peacefully. A few, however, remained defiant. Home Affairs Minister Hartono, a retired four-star general who was a stalwart member of the first family's inner circle, refused to admit defeat. 'According to my understanding of the Constitution,' he told reporters, 'the president cannot dissolve parliament—nor can parliament topple the president.'[40] It was a last-ditch stab at legal formalism. But Hartono no longer held a military command and his views did not necessarily reflect those of the current military leadership. Wiranto, it was noted, had no comment for reporters.

Before making his own visit to Soeharto, Habibie requested a favour from the three former vice-presidents who were still living: Gen. (ret.) Umar Wirahadikusumah, Sudharmono and Gen. (ret.) Try Sutrisno. Habibie asked them to request Soeharto to resign and the three sent Soeharto a letter to that effect on Tuesday afternoon.[41] Afterwards, Habibie himself met with the president. Presenting a four-page written statement, Habibie advised Soeharto to retire—but to do so on his own terms, rather than being pushed to do so by others. Habibie also emphasised that, in fact, he was perfectly capable of taking on the presidency.

Soeharto seemed fatigued and despondent. He apologised for his earlier comment, and eventually dismissed Habibie with a remark that startled the vice-president: 'Just leave everything to me. I'll finish it off. You just stand by and monitor events.'[42] As Habibie recalled, it seemed that Soeharto was finally ready to capitulate.

The early hours of Wednesday 20 May were among the most nerve-racking in Indonesia's independent history. The capital and a number of other cities around the country were braced for a massive show of force by students, Islamic groups and other pro-reform demonstrators. In Yogyakarta the revered sultan, Hamengkubuwono X, was encouraging Javanese from the countryside to converge on the historic city. Bandung was also expecting massive rallies. But the epicentre, of course, was Jakarta, where Amien Rais had been working assiduously to mobilise a march on the National Monument.

Military commanders had been preparing feverishly. Main arteries began to be sealed off on Tuesday evening, and by five the next morning all roads leading to the National Monument were heavily barricaded with multiple rows of coiled barbed-wire. Thousands of troops guarded this perimeter with assault rifles. Around 160 tanks and armoured vehicles were stationed at major intersections and strategic buildings, while some 40 000 troops were deployed throughout the city.[43] In sharp contrast to just one week earlier, Syamsoeddin now seemed intent on using his forces to maintain order.

For days the military had been urging Rais to call off the rally, but he remained undeterred. The rally was driven by 'mass psychology', he said in a parliamentary hearing on 18 May, and it represented a historic opportunity for the Indonesian people. He added: 'If we miss this chance, we'll suffer regrets until the end of our days.'[44]

But in the early hours of Wednesday morning Rais was finally dissuaded. According to him, one of Prabowo's chief lieutenants, Kostrad chief-of-staff Maj. Gen. Kivlan Zein, contacted him and made it clear that the military was prepared to turn the sprawling grounds of the National Monument into a sea of blood, comparable to Beijing's Tiananmen Square crackdown.[45] Rais relented and took to the airwaves at dawn to call off the rally.

Jakarta residents heeded Rais's call and stayed off the streets, so that the city was like a ghost town. The central bank remained closed, businesses were shut and the normally jammed streets were devoid of traffic. But in other cities throughout Indonesia—from Aceh to Irian Jaya— huge processions filled the streets. Various governors and garrison commanders, such as Sulawesi's Maj. Gen. Agum Gumelar, supported the peaceful rallies, attended by students and local residents alike, in town squares and legislative assembly grounds.

Overall, 20 May was a tribute to Indonesia's civility—in contrast to the intrigues of the elite. Moreover, the contrast between the non-violent gatherings and the previous week's rioting reinforced beliefs that Jakarta's riots were premeditated. The rallies on 20 May demonstrated that when Indonesians assembled of their own accord they tended to do so peacefully.

While an eerie calm prevailed on Jakarta's streets, a frenzied atmosphere filled Saadillah's state secretariat on Wednesday morning. Saadillah and his staff—a key member of which was presidential speechwriter Yusril Ihza Mahendra, who would later emerge as a pivotal figure in post-Soeharto politics—were working frantically to enlist credible figures to join Komite Reformasi. They phoned a huge number of civic leaders, esteemed academics and policy experts, but few expressed any interest.

Across town, students had converged on the parliament compound for the third consecutive day. Some had been camping there since Monday, sustained by meals contributed by activist groups and alumni organisations. By this time Harmoko felt more at ease in his office overlooking the scene below. For the third time in as many days, he issued another challenge to Soeharto: respond to parliament's demands by Friday, he exclaimed, or parliament will call for an extraordinary MPR session. The implicit threat was that the MPR—which had the constitutional authority to revoke the president's mandate—would depose Soeharto.[46]

Harmoko's call lent credibility to the resolution that had been passed the previous day, but it also frightened many in the pro-reform movement: if some sort of resolution to the crisis was not found within a matter of days, Harmoko, as the chief figure in the MPR, might emerge from the political vacuum as the country's foremost power broker. This prospect alarmed reformers, who generally regarded Harmoko as being no better than Soeharto.[47] It also, presumably, alarmed the military.

Wiranto certainly did not want to yield the initiative to Harmoko and the MPR. He therefore spent much of Wednesday shuttling the short distance between Jalan Cendana and the department of defence, giving last-minute consideration to various alternatives for a transition. It is possible that the general and his aides had been hoping for an arrangement that would confer substantial powers on themselves, such as the imposition of martial law or the appointment of Wiranto as a caretaker president. If so, the pressure of the student demonstrations and concerns about constitutionality may have finally dissuaded them from pursuing such arrangements. Wiranto reportedly considered the possibility of shifting power to a triumvirate of ministers, but this was eventually rejected on constitutional grounds.

Finally, Wiranto and his aides resolved on a course of action that was, in effect, a compromise solution: handing power to the vice-president.[48] For Wiranto and the military, this alternative was less than ideal because it did not guarantee that their own interests would be safeguarded. However, it would satisfy public demands for Soeharto's ouster, while preventing Harmoko from seizing the initiative. There were some concerns about the constitutionality of Habibie's assumption of power, but it was a far more constitutional alternative than, for example, a ministerial triumvirate. If the military supported the plan, it would almost certainly be endorsed by the Supreme Court—whose chief justice, Sarwata, was a retired three-star air force marshal.

Meanwhile, at Jalan Cendana, Harmoko's ultimatum on Wednesday afternoon was followed by more bad news for Soeharto: US secretary of state Madeleine Albright had publicly called on Indonesia's president to step down. Next, the memo from the fourteen ministers was shown to Soeharto. Since the signatories included a number of individuals who had profited immensely from their proximity to the first family, Soeharto was taken aback.[49] But for the ageing autocrat the worst was yet to come.

The president surrounded himself with his children and relatives as the steady stream of callers resumed. The three former vice-presidents who had submitted their letter the previous day were among those who visited. Just after 9 p.m. Saadillah and Mahendra arrived to report on their recruitment efforts for Komite Reformasi: of 45 candidates contacted, three were willing to sit on the committee. It was yet another sign that the president's authority was nearly gone. And finally the crowning blow was delivered by Religion Minister Quraish Shihab, who explained that his dogged efforts to enlist Nurcholish Madjid on Komite Reformasi had proved fruitless. Hearing this, Soeharto finally caved in. 'That's it,' he said, 'I'll just resign.'[50]

Around 11 p.m. Soeharto summoned Saadillah, Mahendra and Wiranto. He told the group that he had made up his mind: he would transfer power to Habibie.[51] He then summoned the vice-president and told him that, in a ceremony to take place the next morning, he would hand him the presidency.

On Thursday morning, at 8.30, Soeharto left his residence for the first time in days. Accompanied by Tutut, he arrived at the presidential palace and strode directly into the plush Jepara Room. Waiting in an adjoining stateroom were a host of ministers, generals and parliamentarians. The president was forthright and unemotional: 'Ladies and gentlemen, I will use Paragraph 8 of the 1945 Constitution and declare that I am resigning from my post as the president of Indonesia.'[52] He then moved next door to the Credentials Room, filled with journalists, photographers and camera crews.[53]

Flanked by Habibie, Wiranto, Saadillah, Sarwata and several ministers, Soeharto delivered a short but historic speech to the press. In dispassionate tones he explained that he fully understood the people's aspirations for reform and wanted to ensure that changes took place peacefully and constitutionally. He noted that his efforts to establish a new Reform Cabinet had failed to garner enough support, and that this made it difficult for him to continue carrying out his duties.

> Consequently, having taken into account the input from parliament and its
> constituent factions, I have decided to announce my resignation as the
> president of the Republic of Indonesia effective from the moment I read
> this statement on Thursday 21 May 1998 . . . To the people of Indonesia,
> I express thanks and ask forgiveness for any mistakes or shortcomings that
> may have occurred.[54]

Soeharto explained that Vice-President Habibie would serve out the remainder of his term through 2003 and that a new cabinet would be formed imminently. In front of Chief Justice Sarwata, B.J. Habibie took the oath of office and became Indonesia's third president. Habibie thanked Soeharto for his service to the nation and the two shook hands. Both then departed.

But in the Credentials Room Gen. Wiranto stepped up to the microphone. Speaking on behalf of the armed forces, Wiranto welcomed Soeharto's resignation and expressed support for President Habibie. He urged the Indonesian people to do the same. He also pledged to continue guarding against threats to national unity. And before closing with a call for calm and an end to the violence and unrest, Wiranto made a pledge that would burden Indonesia for years to come: the military, he vowed, would safeguard the security and honour of former presidents—including Soeharto and his family.[55]

Thus did the New Order come to an end, after 32 years. Soeharto had remained in power so long primarily because his regime produced economic growth; but while that growth lasted for more than three decades, it ultimately proved unsustainable. *Korupsi, kolusi dan nepotisme* eventually brought down the economy, which in turn triggered Soeharto's own downfall. The nation was saddled with an additional burden of debt which, in effect, represented decades of New Order excess. Moreover, the dictator bequeathed few government institutions capable of upholding the rule of law. Had he implemented a democratic transition in, say, the early 1990s—before the worst of the excess—Soeharto might have won esteem in the annals of history. Instead, like most dictators, he clung to power for too long.

PART II

TYRANNY OF
THE ELITE

9

ZING-A-BUST

Bacharuddin Jusuf Habibie liked to refer to himself as 'PBA'—or 'president by accident'. Conventional wisdom had maintained that any successor to Soeharto would have to be from Indonesia's political heartland, Java, but Habibie was a native of Sulawesi in eastern Indonesia. Although his mother was Javanese, his father was descended from members of three different ethnic groups on Sulawesi: Bugis, Makassar and Gorontalo. Given its name, the family was also thought to have Arabic ancestors. The elder Habibie had been educated in Dutch, and he was a prominent agricultural official working in South Sulawesi when Bacharuddin was born in 1936.[1]

The fourth of eight children, the young 'Rudy' attracted attention for being extraordinarily clever in school. In 1948 his father obtained a place for him in an elite school in the provincial capital of Makassar, but two years later there was an outbreak of severe unrest. A band of rebels under a Dutch-trained officer, Captain Andi Aziz, sought to break away from the fledgling Republic of Indonesia and establish Sulawesi as an independent state. To quell the revolt, the Indonesian military dispatched the Garuda Mataram Brigade from Central Java. The Habibie family's new neighbour was the brigade's 29-year-old commander, Lt Col. Soeharto.

Perhaps because his own upbringing had been unsettled, Soeharto took to Tuti Marini Puspowardojo, Habibie's mother, as if she were his own mother. Both were from the same region of Central Java and therefore spoke the same dialect. Tuti Marini's husband died of a heart attack in 1950 and the widow fretted over how she would educate her eight children. Impressed by Rudy's talents, Soeharto vowed to help.[2] The young Habibie soon gained entry to Indonesia's best technical college, ITB, in West Java. At that time the Soekarno government, impoverished though it was, gave a priority to higher education and provided generous scholarships for study abroad. In 1955—perhaps aided by the clout of the now Brig. Gen. Soeharto—Habibie gained admittance to the Technische Hochschule in Aachen, Germany.

By all accounts Habibie excelled at Aachen. In 1960 he obtained a bachelor's degree *cum laude* in engineering and in 1965 earned a PhD *summa cum laude* in aeronautical engineering. To support his family he worked in part-time jobs throughout, and soon obtained employment at the German aircraft manufacturer, Messerschmitt. There he pioneered studies of a key problem in aeronautical engineering: the propagation of cracks in aircraft wings. The patented 'Habibie Theorem' described how to calculate the random movement of wing cracks at the atomic level—an area of expertise that earned Habibie the nickname 'Mr Crack'.[3] In the early 1970s he contributed to the development of the Airbus A-300B and in 1974 was promoted to vice-president, then the highest rank ever attained by a foreigner at Messerschmitt.

That same year, however, Habibie decided to return to Indonesia. It was the height of the oil boom, and Habibie's old family friend was now the president of Indonesia. Soeharto offered Habibie an opportunity he could not refuse: he was to become special assistant to the second most powerful man in Indonesia after Soeharto himself: Ibnu Sutowo, head of the state oil monopoly Pertamina.

Working under Ibnu Sutowo was an ideal way for Habibie to learn a lesson that guided his later career: Soeharto adored grandiose projects that brought prestige to his regime. Habibie was just the person to provide him with ideas. The energetic engineer espoused a theory of development that had powerful allure: the use of state resources to build high-tech industries that would allow Indonesia to 'leapfrog' from a less developed country to a modern global economy. The theory defied neo-classical economics—frustrating the economic technocrats who were trying to maintain fiscal discipline but it mesmerised Soeharto.

Given Indonesia's size and geography, Habibie argued, Indonesia should build its own aircraft. The technocrats replied that Indonesia lacked both the technical expertise and the basic manufacturing industries needed to support such a venture—but Habibie argued that the effort would naturally give rise to skills and ancillary industries which, in turn, would raise the economy's total productivity.[4] Habibie founded the Nusantara Aircraft Industry (IPTN) in 1976. Two years later he replaced Sumitro Djojohadikusumo (Prabowo's father) as minister for research and technology—a post he would occupy for twenty years. Habibie soon developed his portfolio into one of the government's most highly funded ministries, with a host of 'strategic' state-owned industries under its purview. In addition to IPTN, these soon included ventures in ship-building, steel, locomotives, communications, munitions and even atomic energy.

By 1991 Habibie's ten strategic industries were estimated to account for over half of the total losses recorded by Indonesia's 164 state enterprises.[5] All of Habibie's firms relied on trade barriers for protection from foreign competition, and most survived on sales to other state entities, which were directed to buy from Habibie's firms. By 1993 economists estimated that the strategic industries were consuming nearly $2 billion a year in state resources.[6] Not all of these funds were from the state budget: when direct allocations to the technology ministry fell short, Habibie would find alternative sources. In 1994, for example, IPTN obtained $190 million from a fund that was ostensibly set aside for the reforestation of clear-felled land.[7]

While the economic technocrats complained that scarce state resources could be used far more efficiently, the military also turned against Habibie, for a different reason. Procuring weapons (at marked-up prices) had long been a lucrative field for Indonesia's generals. When the technology minister began making ambitious forays into defence contracting, they resented the fact that he was both cutting into their margins and burdening them with unwanted gadgetry.

Habibie's most celebrated debacle occurred in 1994, when he procured 39 corvettes, landing ships and minesweepers from the former East German navy—ships that the Indonesian navy had said it didn't need. Habibie tried to parlay the $13 million purchase into a $1.1 billion public works program to build fifteen shipyards and several deepwater ports.[8] Had the program proceeded as planned, it would have transformed Habibie's shipping company into another mini-fiefdom that would have rivalled IPTN in size. In the end the plan was scaled down, but not without controversy. Indonesia's leading news weekly, *Tempo*, pushed the limits of Soeharto-era censorship and ran an in-depth story that criticised Habibie's ship purchases. Within weeks the magazine was shut down by the ministry of information—although at whose behest remained unclear.

Meanwhile, Habibie retained Soeharto's confidence, in part by employing shameless flattery. Habibie took to referring to the president as 'SGS', an acronym that stood for 'Super-Genius Soeharto'. His proximity to the president enabled him to defy opposition from the technocrats and, more significantly, the military mainstream. He eventually cultivated support from certain generals, such as Prabowo, and he frantically tried to build constituencies elsewhere, by chairing a host of organisations, foundations and committees. By 1998 Habibie had no less than 26 official titles to his name. Nonetheless, his main political support base never expanded beyond the ranks of Icmi and political Islam, and even there his support was shallow.

Habibie may have hoped to attain fame through feats of technology, but IPTN failed to live up to his dreams. Despite the resources lavished on IPTN for two decades, the firm never became more than an assembler of Puma helicopters and Cassa turbo-props—built largely by expatriate engineers using imported parts. Its main customer was Merpati, a state-owned airline. In 1995 IPTN succeeded in flying a prototype of its own 70-seat commuter turbo-prop, the N-250 Gatotkaca, but the aircraft found few interested buyers. Habibie therefore unveiled an even grander project: a full-fledged jet airliner, the N-2130.

With Soeharto's energetic backing, in 1996 the technology minister raised $400 million from domestic investors as seed capital for the $2 billion project. At the same time he announced plans for a national car, the Maleo, which would presumably rival Tommy Soeharto's 'national' car imported from South Korea, the Timor. Finally, Habibie continued to pursue long-range plans for building twelve nuclear power stations throughout Indonesia.[9] The economic crisis halted all these projects—but that same crisis also propelled Habibie to the presidency, albeit 'by accident'.

When Habibie assumed the presidency, few had high expectations. Moreover, the nation was in disarray. Jakarta and other cities had been traumatised by the May riots, the economy was in severe crisis and the financial sector was in ruins. Millions of Indonesians had been thrust into poverty. And to make matters worse, Habibie was facing all these challenges from a position of acute political weakness.

Never a popular figure at the best of times, the new president was suddenly deprived of his chief source of political strength: the formidable patronage of Soeharto. Habibie commanded only a small fraction of the authority wielded by his predecessor, and his opponents were many and vociferous. Some, such as sizeable portions of the student movement, denounced his presidency as unconstitutional. Others, such as Amien Rais, demanded prompt elections to install a democratic government. But at the outset of his presidency Habibie overlooked these groups to focus on a more pressing concern: reaching an accommodation with Wiranto's military.

Habibie's first order of business as president was to produce a new cabinet roster—a task which needed to be carried out within less than 24 hours of taking office. His cabinet line-up needed to satisfy the nation's demand for reform, but two other goals took precedence: consolidating his own power and, most importantly, appeasing the military.

Habibie took office on the morning of Thursday 21 May. That afternoon he was visited by Prabowo. The Kostrad commander had been close to Habibie for years, and he had been overtly lobbying on Habibie's behalf for at least the past few days. Prabowo clearly expected to receive a promotion for his services. He asked Habibie to sideline Wiranto and promote Subagyo to armed forces chief, thereby opening the position of army chief-of-staff for himself.[10]

Naturally, Wiranto was adamantly opposed. He met Habibie on Friday morning, just hours before the new president was scheduled to announce his cabinet roster. In a tense encounter the two wrangled over who would head the armed forces in the new administration.[11] Habibie apparently wanted to tap Lt Gen. Hendropriyono, a member of Soeharto's last cabinet, to take over the role of armed forces chief from Wiranto, who would then be left with only the largely ceremonial position of defence minister.[12]

What took place in the meeting remains unclear, but the showdown with Wiranto caused the president to run late. The cabinet announcement was delayed for several hours. When Habibie finally read out his roster, Wiranto was included with both of his titles—defence minister and armed forces chief—still intact. Later that day Prabowo received a telephone call from army headquarters asking for his insignia. He knew immediately that he had been sacked.[13]

Prabowo's response eventually became one of the most talked-about events of 1998: the Kostrad commander's alleged coup d'état attempt. There are at least two markedly different versions of this episode. According to his own version, Prabowo called on Habibie at his home around midday on Friday. He arrived with his staff entourage in three Land Rovers, but finding that Habibie was not at home he proceeded to the presidential office complex.

In the lobby to Habibie's office Prabowo's progress was checked by Habibie's personal assistant, Lt Gen. (ret.) Sintong Panjaitan.[14] Some versions of what ensued claim that Sintong prohibited Prabowo from seeing the new president, while others claim that Sintong forcibly disarmed Prabowo before granting him access.[15] Prabowo himself claims that he removed his holster of his own accord. Prabowo says that he then met with Habibie, who explained that he'd had no choice but to dismiss him.[16] Wiranto insisted that Prabowo surrender Kostrad that day; Soeharto's son-in-law was then moved to a lacklustre position as commandant of the armed forces staff college.[17]

While Prabowo's version is undoubtedly watered down, claims that Prabowo threatened the newly installed president with force likewise appear exaggerated. For example, some allege that Prabowo deployed hostile troops outside the president's home on 22 May. In some renditions of the story these troops were Kostrad personnel, while in other renditions they were Special Forces commandos who were still personally loyal to their former commander, Prabowo.

In fact, Wiranto and the Jakarta Garrison commander had issued instructions for securing key points of the city in the aftermath of the May riots. Kostrad units were ordered to secure commercial centres and strategic buildings, while marines secured foreign embassies and Special Forces troops guarded the homes of the president and vice-president. Therefore, while it is correct that both Kostrad and Special Forces elements were present outside Habibie's home on 22 May, the former could have been part of Prabowo's personal staff entourage, while the latter were probably troops officially assigned by Wiranto to guard the residence.

In short, there is ample reason to believe that Prabowo's famous 'attempted coup d'état' was actually something less sinister. In any event, Wiranto emerged from the presidential succession with his powers intact—and Habibie learned, early on, that Indonesia's generals were an obstreperous lot. And as soon as Habibie resolved his tense standoff with Wiranto, he was forced to turn his attention to another group of rivals for power: pro-democracy advocates who were calling for free and fair elections.

At the start of Habibie's presidency a democratic future for Indonesia was far from a foregone conclusion. The president's cabinet included a dearth of genuine reformers. The large majority of the cabinet's 36 ministers were from Golkar or the military. Twenty had been in Soeharto's last cabinet, including ten who had signed Ginandjar's letter to Soeharto. Habibie retained all four co-ordinating ministers from the previous cabinet, including Feisal Tanjung as co-ordinating minister for politics and security.

Habibie's allies in the cabinet generally came from one of three backgrounds. Some had been his underlings in the technology ministry or in various strategic enterprises, such as Minister for Industry and Trade Rahardi Ramelan. Others were fellow Sulawesi natives who formed a tightknit clique around Habibie; prominent among these was State Enterprises Minister Tanri Abeng. Finally, the cabinet included a number of Islamic politicians from Icmi, notably the new co-operatives minister, Adi Sasono. This cabinet roster did little to encourage those demanding reform, nor did Habibie's inaugural speech touch on the foremost reformist demand: free and fair elections in the near future.

Habibie was not constitutionally obliged to hold elections: Article 8 of the 1945 Constitution stipulated that if the president 'stopped serving', the vice-president would complete the remainder of the president's term.[18] Habibie therefore had a constitutional mandate to carry out Soeharto's term through 2003. The nation's general mood, however, urged otherwise.

Ginandjar Kartasasmita, who still served as co-ordinating minister for the economy, was the first member of the administration to advocate fresh elections to produce 'a new government with a new mandate from the people'. The comment, made on Habibie's second day in office, infuriated the president.[19] Amien Rais grabbed headlines the following day by demanding fresh parliamentary elections within six months, to be followed by a presidential election in the MPR.

To seek input on how to proceed, Habibie summoned six credible reform figures to his home on 23 May. In addition to Rais, Nurcholish, Emil Salim and Buyung Nasution, the group included an independent-minded retired general, Rudini. As home affairs minister in 1988–93, Rudini had tried unsuccessfully to liberalise Indonesia's draconian election laws; he was conspicuously excluded from the next cabinet as a result. Following the discussion with this group, a spokesman announced that the president wished to hold new parliamentary elections as soon as the election laws could be revised. Since this would take time, said the spokesman, the president would study the matter further before announcing a firm timetable.

Habibie had apparently consulted the military beforehand, because within hours of the spokesman's statement, the kaster, Bambang Yudhoyono, held a press conference of his own. A prerequisite for solving the economic crisis, he said, was a government that was genuinely empowered by the people.[20] The military therefore endorsed Habibie's call for parliamentary elections. It was a stunning reversal for the institution that had defended Soeharto for decades, but Yudhoyono's pronouncement was nonetheless met with suspicion.

Perhaps other, more hardline, generals were simply biding their time before intervening. Another suspicion was that the military hoped that the elections would ultimately confer the presidency upon one of their own—namely Wiranto. While the parliamentary elections would be important, the crucial contest would take place in the MPR, where the next president would be chosen. Elected parliamentarians only accounted for less than two-thirds of the MPR's membership—the balance comprised appointed members, including military officers. Thus, even if national elections produced a democratic parliament, the MPR's presidential election might still be subject to manipulation. This point would remain very poorly understood by the Indonesian public.

Meanwhile, Habibie remained evasive about when, exactly, elections would take place. The question arose every time he encountered the media, and even the US State Department publicly urged the president to set a firm date. In inimitable fashion, Habibie groped for excuses to explain the delay: 'I am not a genie who can say "Zing-a-boom!" and everything is there. I have to take care that the election is correct, based on the law, and legal.'[21]

Habibie was equally equivocal about whether he would run for another term himself, or whether he would usher in democracy by serving only as a transitional president. If he wanted to remain in power, it was generally believed that Habibie could do so by manipulating the levers of patronage and coercion that Soeharto had put in place—and which were still in good working order. Conversely, by overseeing a peaceful transition, Habibie could emerge as the father of Indonesian democracy. The public was anxious to see which alternative Habibie would choose.

The Habibie administration's most assertive strides towards democratisation were taken, ironically, by two generals with hardline reputations: Lt Gen. Syarwan Hamid and Lt Gen. Yunus Yosfiah. Both had
previously served as kaster. Hamid surprised the public in early June by
abruptly lifting the ban on political party formation—the key prop behind
Golkar's six consecutive electoral triumphs. Within a matter of weeks the
decades-old political cartel of Golkar, PPP and PDI had given way to a
proliferation of parties of all stripes. Various groups around the country
began announcing the formation of new parties, and although most
lacked established bases of support, these new parties soon numbered well
over 100. Hamid's initiative was soon upstaged, however, by an even more
momentous policy introduced by Yosfiah.

Over the course of a long army career, much of which was served with
the Special Forces in East Timor, Yosfiah had gained a reputation for
toughness. He had also been the subject of international controversy
because of his proximity to the Balibo affair, in which five Western journalists were massacred in East Timor in 1975. The British and Australian
governments upheld Yosfiah's assertion that the reporters were cut down
accidentally in crossfire with East Timorese guerillas, but a 1998 investigation by the International Commission of Jurists found evidence that
the five journalists had been deliberately targeted for assassination.[22]
Moreover, an East Timorese man who claimed to be fighting alongside the
Indonesians at the time said that Yosfiah had given the orders to shoot.

Given his track record, Yosfiah's appointment as minister of information, the post long held by Harmoko, disappointed those who were
seeking keterbukaan—or Indonesia's version of glasnost. But within days of
taking office Yosfiah stunned the nation by opining that the information
ministry—which employed 51 000 civil servants and strictly regulated all
news outlets—should simply be dissolved. 'We're spending all this money
to pay civil servants,' said Yosfiah, 'when all they do is obstruct the free flow
of information to the people.'[23]

It remains unclear whether Habibie had originally intended to
promote keterbukaan when he tapped Yosfiah, a fellow Sulawesi native, as
information minister. In any event, Yosfiah later recalled that, in his first
working meeting with Habibie, he flatly informed the president that he
intended to lift press controls. He remembered Habibie responding with
a simple 'thumbs up' gesture, saying: 'That's right. That's democracy!'[24]

Yosfiah then set about issuing press licences to all who sought them,
while reversing Harmoko's decisions to shut down outspoken publications
such as Tempo. The message was sinking in: the press was finally being
permitted to speak its mind. Throughout his tenure as information
minister, Yosfiah spoke emphatically, and sincerely, about the need for
transparency and truthfulness. The message was soon made explicit when
Feisal Tanjung launched a slander suit against the press.[25] To the surprise

of many, Tanjung lost his suit—and the freedom of the press was firmly established.

Habibie, meanwhile, was embracing democracy less enthusiastically than were ministers such as Hamid and Yosfiah. It was not until the third week of his presidency that the president finally declared, on two separate occasions, that he would not run in the next presidential election.[26] Both declarations, however, were made only after reporters pushed the president to answer—and both were received with considerable scepticism. The doubts were well founded: only three weeks later, on 30 June, Habibie clarified his remarks and stated that he had not yet decided whether to seek election to another term.[27]

Scepticism also surrounded Habibie's timetable for elections, which he finally produced on 22 June. Based on input from Rudini, the schedule seemed unnecessarily protracted. Habibie allowed until December 1998 for the passage of new political laws, accompanied in the same month by an extraordinary MPR session to set a date for parliamentary elections. Habibie proposed to hold those elections in mid-1999, and a new MPR would form some four to six months thereafter. Thus the presidential election would not start until December 1999—a full eighteen months away.

Habibie's election schedule drew staunch criticism from reformers such as Emil Salim, who argued that delaying political reform would only delay an economic recovery. Salim pointed out that Thailand and South Korea had responded to the Asian financial crisis by instituting swift political change, and they were already beginning to recover. Indonesia needed political change even more urgently, because it was readily apparent by June 1998 that its economic crisis was exceedingly severe.

I ndonesia was experiencing the sharpest contraction ever recorded by a major market-oriented economy in the modern era.[28] The protests, rioting and political tumult had taken their toll: in the second quarter of 1998 real GDP was a staggering 16.5 per cent below the same quarter of 1997. By the end of May the exchange rate was languishing at the ruinously low level of Rp11 000/$, compared to Rp2300/$ a year earlier.

One effect of the rupiah's extraordinary plunge was that imported goods became extraordinarily expensive in rupiah terms. By mid-1998, therefore, total imports had fallen by 44 per cent from the pre-crisis level.[29] Foreign products began disappearing from store shelves and, more seriously, bottlenecks arose in certain sectors. For example, the number of public buses plying Jakarta's streets declined by around half due to a lack of imported spare parts,[30] and some areas of the country were reporting shortages of imported medicine. The most serious effect of the devaluation, however, was inflation.

Food prices had risen by 53 per cent since the start of the year and they were still climbing fast. For the lucky few who owned land and farmed exportable cash crops (such as coffee, cocoa or rubber) the devaluation was a windfall: their products still fetched the same prices in dollars as before the crisis, but this now translated into three or four times as much in rupiah. A mini-consumer-boom suddenly hit certain rural regions of the Outer Islands where small farmers grew cash crops. In these areas, sales of motorbikes, cars and appliances soared. These beneficiaries of the crisis, however, were the exception.

The pressure on Indonesia's poor was twofold: while prices rose, job opportunities shrivelled. The United States had endured years of so-called 'stagflation' in the 1970s, as growth stagnated but inflation raged. Indonesia was experiencing the same symptoms—but to a far worse extent. Indonesian wage earners saw their real incomes implode by a staggering 35 per cent.[31] The poverty level was destined to rise to around 27 per cent of the population, or about 54 million people.[32] This percentage was more than double the pre-crisis level, and approximately the same as the level that prevailed in the early 1980s. Intersections in Jakarta and other cities suddenly became filled with beggars and street children—symbols of poverty that had not been seen since the earliest years of the New Order. The incidence of environmentally damaging practices—such as illegal logging, 'rogue' mining and coral bombing—increased amid economic hardship and negligent law enforcement.

Exacerbating the mounting poverty was the unusually severe El Nino weather phenomenon, which created one of the worst droughts of the century and depressed the 1997 rice harvest by a substantial 3 per cent. This contributed to a sharply higher incidence of food riots. The worst-affected region was Java, where the impoverishing effects of the devaluation and economic slowdown were felt most. In scores of incidents during July and August, large groups attacked shops, looted rice mills and pillaged plantations growing cash crops. Food affordability threatened to create a significant humanitarian crisis. President Habibie responded, early in his presidency, by unveiling the 'People's Economy' program.

The Habibie administration's ability to respond to Indonesia's looming humanitarian crisis was curtailed by its drastic shortage of resources. Alongside the financial crisis, political tumult and drought, the government had yet one more problem: the price of oil was mired in the range of $10–12 a barrel—its lowest level in two decades. This worsened government finances at a time when tax receipts were falling and expenditures were rising. Ordinarily, the twin challenges of surmounting a huge budget shortfall and responding to a humanitarian crisis would be sources of great anxiety; but in Indonesia fears of a budget shortfall rarely arose, thanks to support pledged by the World Bank and the Asian Development Bank.

From the initial stages, Indonesia's donors had made it clear that they would provide adequate resources to see the government through the immediate crisis. They also agreed that the government should reschedule its 1998 payments on its foreign debt—the first such rescheduling in decades. These measures significantly alleviated budget pressures; in total, international financing was expected to account for 43 per cent of total government expenditure in fiscal year 1998.[33]

The foreign assistance made possible a program that the World Bank and the Indonesian government had already been formulating and implementing on a small scale for several months: the social safety net. Designed to prevent those most in need from falling into malnutrition, the program provided for the distribution of basic foodstuffs, particularly rice, to around ten million needy families throughout the country.[34] The program also funded make-work programs to provide jobs for the unemployed.[35]

Steered by the new co-operatives minister, Adi Sasono, Habibie capitalised on the social safety net program and parlayed it into a broader package of populist policy initiatives—the People's Economy concept. Drawing on tenets of the economic agenda of political Islam, Habibie and Sasono promised to put the 'little people' first and cease favours for the privileged few. This was an ironic approach for a president who, shortly after taking office, unwittingly admitted that he had never walked through one of Indonesia's ubiquitous wet-markets—the traditional bazaars where most Indonesians buy their daily requirements.[36] The People's Economy idea was also a dramatic departure from the elitist, high-tech approach that had been the hallmark of his career. But after assuming the presidency himself, Habibie no longer needed to indulge Soeharto's vanities, and he no longer needed to found new industries simply to secure new sources of patronage. He deftly converted to the doctrine of what was now his most important constituency, political Islam.

Endorsing the People's Economy concept may have helped Habibie's political popularity at first—after all, few could argue with helping the poor and stopping cronyism—but in practice the program soon generated criticism. Habibie himself helped to undermine his pro-people image when he suggested, in a nationwide radio address during an Islamic holiday in July, that all Muslims join forces to conserve the nation's supply of rice by fasting two days per week.[37] The suggestion was hardly an off-the-cuff remark: Habibie explained that if a person's daily rice consumption averaged Rp220 grams, and if 150 million people fasted twice per week, the country would conserve three million tons of rice per annum, which was equivalent to the amount that Indonesia was then importing to cover the shortfall in domestic production. Ironically, with rice priced at about $300 per tonne, Indonesia's annual rice imports were costing around $1 billion—approximately the same sum that the central bank had disbursed to the Texmaco group earlier in the year. In effect, Habibie was asking the entire country to fast twice a week for a year—just to save the equivalent of what had been squandered through one loan to a Soeharto crony.

Meanwhile, Adi Sasono, who oversaw much of the social safety net spending, was increasingly accused of seeking to attack ethnic-Chinese or non-Muslim businesses in favour of *pribumi*-owned concerns. Sasono also sponsored a program to lend Rp8.3 trillion to state-controlled village co-operatives. Such co-operatives had always functioned as conduits of patronage, rather than genuine economic entities; the heads of most co-operatives typically doubled as local Golkar officials. Only a quarter of Sasono's lending was ever repaid.[38] Later, the head of the state planning agency revealed that a substantial portion of the social safety net funds, which reached around Rp18 trillion for the full year, were misused for political purposes or lost through corruption.[39]

Corruption in the social safety net program was merely one symptom of a broad, fundamental problem that was obstructing economic recovery at every turn: an absence of law enforcement. Indonesia was governed by what legal experts termed 'Ruler's Law', as opposed to rule-*of*-law.[40] Over four decades of authoritarian rule, every component of the legal system had been crafted to defend the supremacy of the ruler, rather than the supremacy of law. Indonesia's legal system was not dysfunctional; in fact, it functioned efficiently and effectively—but towards the wrong ends. The system worked to uphold the interests and authority of the ruler, rather than upholding justice.

By necessity, Indonesia's legal system was rife with corruption. Legal system actors—such as judges, prosecutors, police and lawyers—were not motivated by professionalism, principles or ideals of public service, as the system placed little value on these qualities. Instead, the regime recruited and promoted legal system actors on the basis of their loyalty—loyalty that was induced by financial incentives. Over time, the practice of rewarding loyalty with money conditioned legal system actors, who became highly susceptible to bribery while conducting their routine tasks. Thus, with the exception of decisions that directly affected the regime, legal system actors routinely sold their services to the highest bidders. Eventually, the legal system became a mechanism through which the wealthy and powerful were able to consistently exploit the poor and weak.

The implications of Ruler's Law were profound: the government continued not to be accountable to the people and ordinary Indonesians faced considerable injustice in their daily lives. There were also direct economic consequences: corruption in the legal system obstructed progress on a crucial precursor to economic recovery—asset restructuring.

The Indonesian Bank Restructuring Agency (Ibra) had inherited around Rp530 trillion in assets from collapsed banks, most of which was in the form of non-performing loans. In addition, Indonesian companies owed about $80 billion to offshore creditors, and much of this sum was also non-performing. Without asset restructuring, the government and other creditors would realise a very low recovery rate on their non-performing assets. Moreover, the absence of restructuring would ensure that the bulk of corporate Indonesia remained in the hands of bankrupt, cash-strapped conglomerates, many of which owed their prominence to cronyism rather than business acumen. In effect, the private sector would remain mired in debt and corruption until restructuring took place.

The restructuring process, however, hinged on the legal system. To foreclose on the collateral of insolvent debtors—and to press other recalcitrant debtors into resuming payments on their overdue loans—Ibra and other creditors needed to win bankruptcy suits. But as long as judges remained susceptible to corruption, rulings would continue to favour the debtors and the restructuring process would never commence. Judicial reform therefore ranked among the highest priorities of Indonesia's reformers. In the Habibie administration the official with responsibility for this area was Justice Minister Muladi.

Initially, Muladi's appointment was welcomed by reformers, because the new minister had developed a reputation for being a progressive in his former role as the rector of Central Java's Diponegoro University. Muladi's first act as justice minister was to release hundreds of political prisoners, some of whom had been languishing in New Order jails for over 30 years. Reformers urged Muladi to follow this promising start with a shake-up of the Supreme Court—a key bastion of Soeharto's regime.

Most of the country's various court systems were controlled by the Supreme Court, which in turn was dominated by its chief justice, Sarwata— a retired three-star air force marshal. Sweeping personnel changes were needed in the court before legal system reform could proceed; according to the Supreme Court's most reform-minded member, Paulus Lotulung, only three or four of the court's 51 members supported reform.[41] Other reforms that were urgently needed included a watchdog agency to monitor judicial procedures, to guard against corruption. Even simple reforms would have made an impact: for instance, justices were rarely required to write out their decisions, and judges were forbidden from issuing dissenting opinions.

Muladi, however, made virtually no progress on personnel changes or procedure reforms. Amnesty for political prisoners, one of his first undertakings as minister, marked the high-water point for legal system reform during the Habibie administration. Habibie unshackled the press and lifted the ban on political parties, but Indonesia would continue to be governed by Ruler's Law. In effect, it seemed that Habibie was inclined to govern in largely the same way that Soeharto had done. Meanwhile, his opponents were working assiduously to ensure that he would fall from power—in the same way that Soeharto had done.

10

PHOTOCOPYING SOEHARTO

Less than a month after Soeharto's fall from power the armed forces chief, Wiranto, appeared before parliament and pledged to continue supporting the Constitution, but without favouring any particular political party or politician.[1] This was the crux of the military's 'new paradigm' in the *reformasi* era. But around the same time that Wiranto was pledging his neutrality before parliament, several of his trusted aides were making a visit to East Java. There they met several influential clerics in Abdurrahman Wahid's Nahdlatul Ulama.

Long opposed to Habibie's patronage of modernist Islamists through Icmi, Wahid's NU clerics were among the new president's staunchest opponents. Their hope was that the upcoming MPR session—which Habibie was obliged to convene to endorse new elections—could be used as an opportunity to depose the new president and replace him with a figure less sympathetic to political Islam. The clerics were amazed, but gratified, to hear from Wiranto's aides that the general would also welcome such a change.[2]

Presumably, Wiranto was eyeing the nation's top job for himself. He probably could have seized power from Soeharto in May, but Wiranto was well aware that the presidency was meaningless without constitutional legitimacy. The popular force that deposed Soeharto would only be redirected against a general who seized power illegitimately. If Wiranto wanted the presidency, the best route to take was through the MPR: the assembly's overweening constitutional authority meant that, in effect, it could grant the presidency to whomever it wished.

Not coincidentally, a group of 400 NU clerics gathered a short while later in East Java to formally express their support for the man whom they regarded as 'the most suitable future leader of the country': Wiranto.[3] Suddenly, Habibie's 18-month election timetable seemed like wishful thinking—there was now a strong chance that the new president would be ousted before the year's end. If he wished to remain president, Habibie would clearly have to fight for his survival, and his first bout was for control of Golkar.

Habibie had little time to prepare for his first major political test: Harmoko was finishing his term as Golkar's party chair and a national party congress, held every five years to a elect a new leader to the crucial post, was due to convene in early July. With Soeharto no longer around to carefully orchestrate the proceedings, the contest for control of Golkar would be a free-for-all—and the stakes were high.

To survive beyond the MPR session Habibie needed to retain control of Golkar. True, the party was in disarray and huge swaths of voters had apparently turned against it, but Golkar was still the ruling party. Golkar's infrastructure was massive: an estimated 12 million 'cadres' represented the party in over 70 000 towns and villages.[4] Because Suryadi's PDI had atrophied in size following the illegal Medan congress in 1996, PPP was the only other party with established infrastructure—and it paled in comparison to Golkar's network. And most importantly, Golkar had a formidable ability to raise funds. If resources such as these fell into the hands of Habibie's enemies within Golkar, the president would almost surely be replaced in the upcoming MPR session.

Golkar leadership contests had always been tense affairs. Traditionally, these contests pitched Golkar's civilians against the party's powerful military contingent. In 1988, for instance, the military reportedly invested vast sums in a campaign of 'money politics' to persuade party delegates to elect a retired general, Wahono, rather than the civilians' candidate, Vice-President Sudharmono.[5] In the subsequent 1993 contest, however, this military–civilian rivalry was disrupted by the introduction of a powerful third force: the Habibie clique, which backed Harmoko for party chair.

Habibie's profligacy and proximity to Islamists—combined with Harmoko's corruption and sycophancy—alienated both the military and the party's more progressive-minded civilians in the approach to the 1993 election. Golkar's progressives were led by two former ministers and protégés of Sudharmono who had been student leaders in the 1960s: Sarwono Kusumaatmadja and Siswono Yudohusodo. Popularly called 'Team Sarwono-Siswono', these two forged an awkward 'anti-Habibie alliance' with the generals they had opposed five years earlier—but their efforts were fruitless. Soeharto intervened to ensure that Habibie's faction won. The position of party chair went to Harmoko.[6]

The 1998 leadership contest once again pitted Habibie's faction against an anti-Habibie alliance of progressives and retired generals. Both sides had difficulty selecting suitable candidates. Habibie had a number of loyalists in Golkar but most were either provincial figures from Sulawesi or Icmi members—none had enough nationwide name recognition to succeed as Golkar's party chair. Habibie therefore turned to a figure who was not exclusively associated with any one camp within Golkar but who maintained good relations across the spectrum—through his extra-ordinary talent for political manoeuvring. This figure was Akbar Tandjung.

Unlike most Golkar politicians, Tandjung possessed an uncanny, and invaluable, ability to bridge gaps in Indonesian politics. For instance, while he was a longstanding member of the Soeharto-era establishment, he possessed a modicum of reformist credentials as a former student leader. He was from an elite family, but he managed to portray an affable, down-to-earth manner which played well in public. And while his policy stances were generally aligned with those of secular-nationalists, he maintained important links to modernist Muslims as a former leader of the powerful Islamic Students Alumni Association. Finally, and perhaps most impor-tantly, Tandjung was a Sumateran Batak who identified with outer islanders but who had nonetheless mastered the subtle art of Javanese politics. He rarely raised his voice and he had the knack of asserting his authority with seemingly effortless ease—much, in fact, like Soeharto.

But while these characteristics differentiated Tandjung from other politicians, he had at least one trait that typified Golkar's culture: Tandjung was motivated by no discernible doctrine other than political expediency. He was the type of politician who sought power for the sake of power, and he did so with remarkable success. Within the short space of ten years Tandjung had risen from the cabinet's lowest post, state minister for youth and sports, to one of its most powerful, state secretary—a position which was pivotal in terms of drafting legislation, formulating presidential decrees and administering the presidential palace.

In contrast to the relatively youthful Tandjung, Golkar's anti-Habibie faction turned to Golkar's most senior figures to lead them through the party congress. The highest ranking figures in their camp were former vice-president Gen. (ret.) Try Sutrisno and former defence minister Gen. (ret.) Edi Sudradjat. Both were former armed forces chiefs. After much internal wrangling it was finally decided that Edi Sudradjat would stand for party chair, and in the event of victory the party could then nominate Try Sutrisno—one of the few Indonesian politicians with a household name—for the presidency.[7] Many believed that the move to win the presi-dency would take place at the November 1998 MPR session.

These nominations made sense from the standpoint of seniority and name recognition, but they had their weaknesses. Try Sutrisno had com-manded the Jakarta military district in 1984, when troops fired on Muslim demonstrators in the Tanjung Priok port district, killing 33 and injuring 55.[8] This event won him lasting enmity from a wide spectrum of Islamic organisations. But there was also another problem: Try Sutrisno was a political klutz.

Among the public gaffes that blemished his political career, perhaps the most infamous came in response to the 1991 Santa Cruz massacre in

East Timor: 'It is necessary,' said the armed forces chief of the day, 'to fire upon whoever deviates from the official line. Whoever disturbs stability will be eliminated.'[9] The statement, which was more a product of wit-lessness than ruthlessness, created a minor international uproar. Such blunders repeatedly hindered his career. As a four-star general who had held the vice-presidency as recently as March 1998, Try Sutrisno should have been able to rise to the fore in the post-Soeharto power vacuum. Instead, he proved consistently unable to negotiate the political currents.

Edi Sudradjat, in contrast, was known for his substance as a relatively reform-minded liberal. In a famous speech to army commanders in 1989, Sudradjat warned that the military was in danger of being marginalised for its 'foot-stomping, father-knows-best attitude'.[10] Later, as defence minister, Sudradjat dared to criticise Soeharto in cabinet meetings and he publicly encouraged the nascent student movement in February 1998. But, like Try Sutrisno, he too had deficiencies: he was tainted by business ties to Tommy Winata's Artha Graha Group, he suffered from poor health and, most importantly, he was inept at media relations. Nonetheless, Edi Sudradjat emerged as the best candidate for party chair among a field of relative unknowns.

Edi Sudradjat's backers, at the time, included the influential Sarwono and Siswono—and all were confident of victory. Their faction could claim better reformist credentials than Akbar Tandjung's, and they also believed that Habibie's influence in Golkar was weak. Although the president commanded formidable levers of patronage, he had never been particularly popular within Golkar—his influence had always stemmed from his proximity to Soeharto. Most importantly, Edi Sudradjat's backers counted on the support of Golkar's sizeable military contingent. As the National Party Congress convened, their optimism seemed justified.

In the first significant vote of the congress—the vote to elect a presiding officer to chair the proceedings—the winner was Siswono. Siswono then helped arrange for an election mechanism intended to favour Edi Sudradjat: Golkar's 27 provincial chapter heads would be called on to elect the new party chair. Every chapter head also served as a provincial governor, and 21 of the 27 were members of the Retired Armed Forces Officers Association (Pepabri).[11] Central to Siswono's strategy was the consideration that Pepabri was headed by Try Sutrisno himself. And in the unlikely event that the former vice-president's influence proved insufficient in canvassing votes from the chapter heads, additional support was bound to come from Wiranto. As of mid-June, Wiranto still seemed to be favouring Habibie's ouster, and as the active armed forces chief he commanded considerable sway over the retired officers serving as chapter heads—notwithstanding his oft-repeated pledge to remove the military from practical politics.

Before long, however, events began to go awry for Edi Sudradjat. In particular, a controversy soon arose over who wielded authority in Golkar now that Soeharto was out of power. Traditionally, the Executive Board had been the highest tier of authority within Golkar, but after the 1988 leadership contest the president had added an extra layer to the party superstructure: the Patrons Board. Playing a limited role in routine affairs, the Patrons Board was designed to make a crucial intervention once every five years to ensure that Soeharto's preferred candidate won the party chair election. Now, in 1998, Soeharto's role as chair of the Patrons Board was called into question.

Because Soeharto had resigned as president, did this also mean that he was no longer Golkar's top official? Habibie acted as if this was so, and in his capacity on the Patrons Board as its 'chair for day-to-day affairs' the new president began paving the way for Akbar Tandjung's election. The first step was to hold a closed-door caucus with the 27 chapter heads in late June. Habibie's opponents feared that the president would sew up the election in this meeting—perhaps through the application of what was popularly termed 'brown-bag politics', or bribery.

Edi Sudradjat's faction was alarmed. By pulling the strings that Soeharto had put in place years before, Habibie was threatening to rig the party chair election from above—in the same way in which Soeharto had arranged Harmoko's victory in 1993. To thwart Habibie's caucus, Try Sutrisno intervened. He succeeded in having the meeting cancelled, but in the process the general who was famed for his bungling committed the costliest gaffe of his career. Asked by reporters why he had denounced Habibie's planned caucus as 'improper', Try Sutrisno explained that Habibie had scheduled the event without first obtaining the permission of the Patron Board's chair—Soeharto.[12]

Akbar Tandjung needed no prompting to pounce on the opportunity this afforded. Through a quick succession of press interviews, he successfully fostered the impression that Try Sutrisno was merely a puppet of Soeharto. 'Frankly speaking, Habibie and Soeharto never meet, so the message to cancel the meeting was sent through someone else for whom it was relatively easier to meet with Soeharto,' Tandjung carefully explained. 'In this case, that was Pak Try.'[13]

Over the next several days Try Sutrisno readily repeated his story about conversing with Soeharto—apparently incognisant of the victory that Tandjung was scoring at his expense. As Jakarta's pundits wondered whether Try Sutrisno was deliberately courting defeat, the public soon came to believe that Soeharto was plotting a 'comeback' through his former military chiefs, Try Sutrisno and Edi Sudradjat. That Try Sutrisno was also a former presidential adjutant only reinforced this impression. Soon, false rumours surfaced that Edi Sudradjat's campaign was financed by Bambang and Tutut Soeharto.[14]

Tandjung gleefully intimated that the generals were stooges of the 'status quo'; he and Habibie, of course, were the agents of change. In fact, the opposite was closer to the truth. Try Sutrisno's gaffe was just that: his meeting with Soeharto had little real significance and Try Sutrisno was simply using it, unwittingly, as a pretence for cancelling Habibie's caucus. The irony of the situation was that it was actually Habibie who, in practice, was actively protecting Soeharto at the time. This was apparent from his relations with his attorney general, Soedjono Atmonegoro.

Atmonegoro was a holdover from Soeharto's last cabinet, but immediately after Soeharto's fall the little-known state prosecutor had initiated extensive research on the former president's culpability on corruption charges. According to Atmonegoro, in a matter of days he had gathered enough evidence to imprison Soeharto for years.[15] His research alarmed the Soeharto family, who responded by hiring a legal team (the 'Cendana Consultation Team') to prepare a defence. But only three hours after Atmonegoro presented his research findings to President Habibie on 15 June, he was sacked.[16]

The new attorney general, Andi Ghalib, was an active two-star general —and he would prove far less inclined to challenge Soeharto. Although Atmonegoro's sacking was largely overlooked at the time, the episode provided one of the first clear indications that the Habibie administration was unwilling to prosecute Soeharto, his family or their cronies. This also explained the administration's reluctance to reform the judiciary or the legal system in general—doing so would wear down the defences protecting Soeharto and other New Order power-holders.[17]

Atmonegoro's sacking—and Tandjung's energetic attack on Try Sutrisno—underscored the intensity with which Golkar's leadership contest was being fought. Edi Sudradjat's supporters were in a difficult predicament that was rapidly growing worse. In the final days before the election Wiranto began to waver. Many believed that Habibie was expressly ordering the general to intervene on Tandjung's behalf. Habibie was not in a strong position to dictate terms to Wiranto—the new president needed the military's support to govern—but at the same time he did, on paper, outrank the armed forces chief. Habibie also had three loyal, three-star generals in the cabinet (Hendropriyono, Yunus Yosfiah and Syarwan Hamid) whom he could call upon at any time, if necessary, to replace Wiranto.

With Habibie pressuring him and with Edi Sudradjat's faction being branded as lackeys of Soeharto, Wiranto was left with little choice. Less than two days before the election was due to start, he abandoned Golkar's retired generals and sided with Akbar Tandjung. Publicly, Wiranto hinted at his preference by stating that the military expected Golkar to remain loyal to the nation's constitutional leaders (meaning Habibie).[18] Privately, Wiranto and Home Affairs Minister Syarwan Hamid drafted a message to

be sent down the chain of command. Relayed through an assistant to Kaster
Yudhoyono, Maj. Gen. Mardiyanto, the message instructed all garrison
commanders to contact the Golkar chapter heads (cum governors) in their
territories.[19] Vote for Tandjung, they were instructed to tell the chapter
heads, or face dismissal in Golkar's upcoming provincial congresses.[20]

On the morning of 11 July, the day the vote would take place, Wiranto
met personally with 17 chapter heads at Jakarta's Shangri-La Hotel.[21] The
armed forces chief was finally applying the leverage that accompanied
his office. As the voting commenced that evening, the race was still too
tight to predict. Habibie, according to Tandjung, followed the event
'like a Brazilian watching his team in a World Cup match'.[22] When the
votes of all 27 chapter heads had been tallied, Akbar Tandjung prevailed
with 17 votes, versus 10 for Edi Sudradjat. Wiranto's impact had been just
sufficient to tip the result.[23]

Tandjung's victory in Golkar's leadership contest was, after Habibie's
choice of a cabinet roster, the second major signal that the new president's tenure would not usher in sweeping political reform. Rather,
Habibie seemed inclined to make only small changes to the New Order
system. If there were any doubts about this, Tandjung soon put them to
rest in one of his first actions as Golkar chair: purging the party leadership
of Edi Sudradjat and his allies, including the principled progressives
Sarwono and Siswono. Golkar's top figures in the new, 13-member
executive board included a host of Soeharto-era conservatives, including
Harmoko's deputy Abdul Gafur. Beneath the executive board, Tandjung
filled the key organisational post of secretary-general with a retired two-
star general—despite his promises to end Golkar's links to the military.

Meanwhile, in an embarrassing indictment of Tandjung's leadership,
nearly 10 per cent of the people offered positions on his new 138-member
Leadership Board declined to join. In response, Tandjung made a concession to reform: he lent Golkar a more reformist look by promoting one of
his faction's few progressive figures, the Soeharto critic and human rights
advocate Marzuki Darusman. Tandjung placed Darusman on Golkar's
influential 13-member executive board.

As for Wiranto, the Golkar leadership meeting demonstrated that the
armed forces chief was politicking on behalf of Tandjung, while simultaneously telling the press—with considerable emphasis—that the military
was staying aloof from practical politics and would cease siding with
Golkar.[24] In fact, Wiranto was not only siding with Golkar; he was siding
with one internal Golkar faction against another.[25] The military's involvement was so blatant that Habibie's controversial meeting had actually been
scheduled to take place in Cilangkap, at military headquarters.[26]

Golkar's National Party Congress may have been marked by back-
biting, intrigue and coercion from above, but from Habibie's perspective

the affair was a resounding success. As he embarked on a challenging term as president, the Golkar leadership contest had inadvertently brought the powerful military to Habibie's side. Having begun with the military quietly agitating against him, the president emerged from the contest with Wiranto allied to him—albeit in an alliance of expediency. And in the process Habibie had also secured the explicit backing of the country's most powerful and well-heeled political machine, Golkar. Or at least, so it seemed at the time.

In fact, Habibie would soon discover that the backroom manoeuvring that coloured the leadership election was far from over. Akbar Tandjung had already mutinied against one president, and he would soon show that he was prepared to do so again.

By mid-July Habibie had already turned his attention to his next political hurdle: the extraordinary MPR session, now scheduled for 10–13 November 1998. The MPR was often likened to a 'queen-bee': convening once every five years for a two-week flurry of activity, before returning to hibernation. Having just convened in March 1998, the MPR was not scheduled to meet again until 2003, but its consent was required before new elections could be held. Only the MPR, as the highest law-making authority in the land, could change Indonesia's election schedule. And until the MPR formally repealed the five-year mandate it had issued to Soeharto and Habibie the previous March, Habibie would still be constitutionally obliged to serve out Soeharto's full term through to 2003.

For Habibie, however, there was a catch: the MPR assembly would undoubtedly do more than just rubber-stamp his proposed changes to the election schedule. The assembly's membership was expected to issue a raft of 'MPR resolutions' that would (in theory) bind the president and his administration to certain courses of policy. In addition, the MPR was expected to amend the Constitution to limit presidential terms to two five-year periods. Beyond this, no one could predict what else the MPR might attempt. In particular, it was within the MPR's power to terminate Habibie's presidency and elect a replacement—and this is precisely what the MPR was being pushed to do by a potentially powerful array of interests.

At the forefront of these interests was the National Front, a small band of former Revolutionary war veterans and esteemed former ministers who had served in the early days of Soeharto's New Order. Many of the National Front's fifteen or so members were household names in Indonesia, and since most were over 70 years old they wielded formidable powers of suasion in Indonesia's age-conscious society. This group also included some figures who were fearless when it came to challenging established power structures, such as Maj. Gen. (ret.) Ali Sadikin.

A popular governor of Jakarta during the first few years of Soeharto's rule,[27] Sadikin grew increasingly disenchanted with Soeharto's corruption and manipulation. When the president overtly coerced the military leadership into supporting him politically in 1980, Sadikin and a host of other senior retired officers formed the 'Petition of 50'.[28] The group's actions were tightly restricted by security forces (to the extent that Sadikin's ally H.R. Dharsono was jailed from 1984 to 1990), but the Petition of 50 had formidable symbolic significance as Indonesia's most prominent group of political dissidents.

Another independence-era veteran in both the Petition of 50 and the National Front was Lt Gen. (ret.) Kemal Idris, a garrulous Sumateran still prone, at age 73, to pounding his fists and roaring out loud. Idris had proven his mettle in the past: as Soeharto's Kostrad commander in March 1966, Idris trained the barrels of his tanks on the presidential palace while the cabinet was meeting inside. He maintains that he was only trying to arrest an alleged communist minister (Subandrio) who was inside the building at the time; nonetheless, his actions inadvertently helped persuade Soekarno to sign the 11 March Letter, or Supersemar, that ceded executive authority to Soeharto.[29] Having helped install Soeharto in office, Idris (like Sadikin and others) soon grew disillusioned with what he saw as the president's betrayal of independence-era ideals.[30]

Under Sadikin and Idris the National Front was a vehement force—and it adamantly demanded Habibie's dismissal from the presidency. The president was only willing, they argued, to make minor changes to the New Order system, when what was needed was a thorough overhaul of the most corrupt government in Asia. They called for an impartial 'presidium'—comprising credible and venerable figures—to replace Habibie, oversee national elections and usher in democracy.

These battle-hardened dissidents were not the least deterred by qualms about the MPR's constitutional rights to change the president in mid-term—they were determined to finish the job that had only just begun with the overthrow of Soeharto in May. Coming from some of the very individuals who played significant roles in the actual formation of the Indonesian Republic and the 1945 Constitution, their appeal attracted considerable attention and carried considerable moral force. If some of those who risked their lives to found the republic were themselves advocating the overthrow of a president, surely the younger generation should be even less squeamish about pushing the bounds of constitutionality.

While the National Front was delivering its hardline message to the nation, it sought to protect its flanks by claiming that it was only acting as a 'moral movement'. 'We are nothing but toothless old grandfathers', claimed the former chair of Opec, Subroto.[31] In fact, behind the grandfatherly guise, the National Front was busily mobilising tangible power—by turning to the student movement.

The alliance was a potent combination. The National Front provided guidance and press attention—as well as access to financing for food, transport, banner production and all the accoutrements needed by a large-scale protest movement. The student movement, meanwhile, provided numbers, determination and courage. This was a marriage of brains and brawn, and it caused serious consternation in Habibie's camp. It was also a vexing problem for Wiranto.

In the event that Habibie was ousted, Wiranto could not feel secure about his own political future. He had backed Akbar Tandjung in the Golkar congress—and now many of Edi Sudradjat's backers, such as Siswono and Sarwono, were allied with the National Front. If the National Front succeeded in toppling Habibie, they were likely to go one step farther and replace Wiranto as well. At that point Wiranto would have to choose between relinquishing power and mounting an extra-constitutional challenge to the MPR.

There was no precedent in Indonesia for an outright military coup. Although the military had pressured presidents in the past (such as Idris's own confrontation with Soekarno), it had never directly repudiated the MPR. And even if Wiranto did choose that route, he could not be certain that his officer corps would be willing to follow. After all, as of August 1998 Wiranto had been in the military's top job for a mere six months—a small fraction of the time needed to win the personal loyalties of the subordinates he had inherited. If Habibie was vulnerable in the months preceding the November MPR session, so too was Wiranto.

It must have been cold comfort for Habibie and Wiranto to think that all that stood between themselves and the virulent students and the National Front were the 1000 members of the MPR. Habibie sought to cleanse the MPR's ranks by appointing around 65 of his own supporters to fill vacated seats (most of which were opened when spouses and offspring of Soeharto-era officials chose to resign).[32] But the real authority in the MPR was held not by the membership but by the Speaker, Harmoko, and his clutch of deputies. Habibie enjoyed a friendship and alliance with Harmoko that dated back to the 1970s—but then so too had Soeharto. Harmoko certainly had his reasons to resist reform, but if his own political survival depended on sacrificing Habibie, there could be little doubt about which choice he would make.

The 10–13 November MPR session was therefore shaping up to be a test of strength. Habibie and Wiranto needed to exert more pressure on Harmoko, his deputies and the assembly's members than that exerted by the National Front and the student movement. This equation would be affected by three crucial variables: Megawati, Abdurrahman Wahid and Amien Rais. As the only politicians with proven mass support, these three could potentially sway the outcome. If the National Front and the student movement joined forces with one or all of these popular leaders, events on the streets of Jakarta might just prove capable of swaying the course of action within the MPR assembly. Aware of the impending danger, Habibie began mending fences and building bridges in earnest.

One of the first objects of Habibie's attention was the student movement. The president conducted a well-publicised visit with the families of the Trisakti victims in late June, vowing to achieve 'full justice' for those who had been slain, whom he acknowledged as 'heroes of reform'.[33] Although no action was ever taken to find the true perpetrators, Habibie's promise persuaded some at the time. Combined with his initiatives to free political prisoners, liberalise the press and repeal the political party ban, Habibie's popularity was growing.

But then came the Independence Day debacle. The annual ceremony on 17 August was the country's grandest national holiday. Before a massive television audience, Habibie delivered a speech that was roundly criticised for lacking 'urgency' amid the crisis. He then proceeded to bestow the nation's highest medal of honour, the *Anugerah Bintang* (the Blessed Star), on his wife, brother and a number of others who were distinguished only by their proximity to him.[34] The press—newly freed and eager to vent decades of pent-up frustrations—seized on the symbolism and drew parallels to the nepotism of Soeharto. This elicited a celebrated response from the president: 'I am not,' he fumed, 'a photocopy of Soeharto.'[35]

Meanwhile, Wiranto's preparations for the upcoming MPR session were equally artless. The military chief's prime concern was security: he wanted to avoid the embarrassing clashes with students that had taken place earlier in the year. To curb street protests, therefore, Wiranto's staff drafted the euphemistically titled 'Freedom of Expression' bill. The legislation required permits for gatherings, defined the locations at which they could take place and limited the number of attendees to 50.

Marzuki Darusman and other human rights proponents accused Wiranto of abrogating his promises to restore democracy.[36] At first Habibie demurred from sending the draft bill to parliament, hoping instead to pass the unpopular measure as a less conspicuous government regulation. By October, however, the military prevailed and parliament obediently passed the bill into law. Nonetheless, Wiranto knew that a law alone would not deter the students.

Soon after the Golkar congress the general installed one of his protégés, Maj. Gen. Djaja Suparman, as Jakarta Garrison commander. Wiranto apparently wanted a trustworthy hardliner to handle security in the capital. The move also meant that the city's two critical security posts— the governorship (held by Lt Gen. Sutiyoso) and the garrison command —were now in the hands of Wiranto's former aides when he himself commanded the Jakarta Garrison in 1994–95.[37] Wiranto, Suparman and Sutiyoso had worked together in 1994 to form 'volunteer security forces', or civilian para-military units, and now they replicated those efforts on a larger scale. Rather than using troops to confront boisterous students head on, Wiranto wanted to use hastily assembled para-militaries instead.

While preparing for a battle on the streets, Wiranto also paid careful heed to his image in the media. The public wanted explanations for the recent trauma: the kidnapping of 23 dissidents, the Trisakti shootings and, most importantly, the May riots. Wiranto needed to designate a guilty party and put the events behind him. The perfect candidate was Prabowo. The former Kostrad commander had already confessed to kidnapping the nine dissidents who had been released; his abrupt sacking from Kostrad on 22 May only fed the impression that he was also at fault for the Trisakti shootings and the May riots.

In August, Wiranto convened a military tribunal chaired by Subagyo. After a 15-day inquiry conducted behind closed doors, the tribunal discharged Prabowo without honour.[38] In the only explanation provided to the public, Subagyo claimed that Prabowo had admitted to misinterpreting orders.[39] The public was left to draw its own conclusion.

In general, the conclusion was that Prabowo had been the culprit behind all the mayhem. This impression was reinforced by the subsequent issuance of the official fact-finding report, which deliberately sought to steer suspicion in Prabowo's direction. Question marks remained and doubts about Prabowo's culpability persisted, but Wiranto had largely succeeded in deflecting blame for the events of May. His only critics were those who complained that Prabowo had been dealt with too leniently.

At the same time, Wiranto dealt differently with an officer whose culpability was far more compelling than Prabowo's: Maj. Gen. Syafrie Syamsoeddin, the Jakarta Garrison commander in May 1998. Rather than following Prabowo into retirement, Syamsoeddin obtained a post with considerable strategic significance: advisor on territorial affairs, attached to the general staff. Wiranto was clearly refraining from punishing the officer who had been responsible for Jakarta's security while rioters rampaged through its streets on 13–15 May.

No sooner had Wiranto cashiered his rival, Prabowo, than new sources of controversy emerged. In early September a team from the Human Rights Commission conducted a brief tour of Aceh, the strife-torn province on Sumatera's northern tip which had long been home to a determined, Islamic-inspired guerilla movement seeking secession from Jakarta. The team's brief tour was sufficient to conclude, unsurprisingly, that widespread abuses had taken place over the preceding ten years, during which time the province was designated an 'area of military operations'. The team asserted that at least 780 civilians had been killed and hundreds more were missing.[40] Other teams from various legal aid foundations uncovered more than a dozen mass graves in northern Aceh.[41]

The findings helped undo whatever goodwill Wiranto had generated for the military since the downfall of Soeharto—and they would be only the first of many revelations concerning the military's past activities in Aceh and other provinces. As more skeletons tumbled from the military's overstuffed closets, it would become increasingly difficult for Wiranto to cultivate the positive image for which he was striving. And in the meantime the armed forces chief faced increasingly strident protests from Indonesia's irrepressible students.

Early September coincided with the time when most university students in Jakarta returned to campus. Many wasted no time in mounting street protests reminiscent of those which triggered Soeharto's downfall. On 8 September 300 students from the radical group Forum Kota (Forkot) forced their way on to the grounds of parliament, demanding the dismissal of President Habibie. But unlike May, when troops actually facilitated the students' invasion of the parliamentary grounds, this time the band of Forkot demonstrators were swiftly dispersed by marines and riot police.

A worse confrontation followed the next day. As President Habibie arrived for an official visit in Surabaya, Indonesia's second largest city, a force of 2000 student protesters blocked his path. Youths flaunting pro-Megawati placards began attacking the motorcade, pelting it with rocks and chunks of asphalt. The presidential entourage eventually manoeuvred to safety and police moved in, scattering the crowd with warning shots.[42]

The Surabaya attack showed that tension was rising throughout the country. Indonesians had already endured more political tumult in the previous twelve months than most had witnessed in a lifetime, and still no one knew for sure what the next few weeks held in store. The politicians jockeyed for position, the students agitated on the streets and the generals prepared for a showdown. Yet less than three weeks before the MPR session was due to convene, the nation's scrutiny was torn away from events in Jakarta and, incredibly, diverted to one of the most overlooked corners of the archipelago: Banyuwangi, East Java.

11

'CRUELISM VERSUS CRUELISM'

Throughout the rural, impoverished and densely populated province of East Java, religious traditions figure prominently in everyday life. This is especially true in Banyuwangi: among East Java's 37 *kabupaten*, or administrative districts, Banyuwangi arguably stands out as the most distinctive—both religiously and culturally. Because of these distinctions, the remote district of Banyuwangi became the unlikely focus of the nation's attention during a few critical months in late 1998.

Situated 830 kilometres from Jakarta, Banyuwangi occupies Java's far eastern tip, separated from Bali by a strait that is only a few kilometres wide. As the historical crossroads between the two islands, Banyuwangi possesses a blend of the distinctive cultures of Muslim Java and Hindu Bali. This created a hybrid culture, language and, most notably, religion.[1] Islam throughout East Java is heavily flavoured by mysticism, while the Hinduism of Bali places emphasis on the role of spirits; combining elements of both traditions, the million and a half people of Banyuwangi harbour strong beliefs about the supernatural world.

Banyuwangi's residents believe in assorted types of occult arts, including enchantment (*santet*), sorcery (*sirih*) and black magic (*tenung*). The practitioners (*dukun*) of these arts often occupy prominent positions in village society, whether as respected leaders or feared evil-doers. And sometimes the levels of fear reach the point of hysteria: on over a dozen occasions during the 1990s, frenzied mobs murdered *dukun santet* who were believed to have cast spells on their neighbours.[2] Few took notice, therefore, when five alleged *dukun tenung* were mysteriously murdered in July 1998.

But when a string of unexplained killings were reported the following month, it became clear that this was no ordinary crime wave. By the end of August over 50 murders had taken place. The killings garnered no press attention in Jakarta, isolated as they were in Java's most far-flung corner; in Banyuwangi, however, the local population was gripped by fear. The district's residents were alarmed not only by the frequency of the killings but also by the bizarre and menacing way in which *dukun tenung* were being murdered.

In numerous instances, witnesses or survivors claimed that attacks were perpetrated in the dead of night by men who wielded knives, swords or scythes. Rather than quickly despatching their victims and fleeing, the killers often mutilated the victims' bodies, dismembering the corpses and severing their heads. Sometimes the mutilated corpses were strung from trees, while at other times body parts were flung into mosques.[3] These were not the typical ways in which frenzied mobs killed suspected *dukun tenung*—these killings bore the characteristics of an intimidation campaign.

In at least a third of the cases the perpetrators reportedly wore black outfits and masks that covered all but their eyes. In local parlance, attackers who used this guise were termed 'ninjas'—and their repute bred terror in Banyuwangi and other neighbouring districts. Villagers organised night patrols to guard against intrusions from outsiders whom they could not recognise. But to circumvent these patrols the killings began to take place around twilight and dawn, and sometimes victims were pulled out of their paddy fields in broad daylight.[4]

During September the frequency of killings increased to nearly three per day. Murders were being reported not only in Banyuwangi but throughout the southeastern peninsula of East Java and the large island of Madura to the north. By month-end the death toll had surpassed 100; with much of East Java in a fervour, the national press finally began running short articles about the strange 'ninja killings' of Banyuwangi.[5]

As the killings continued into October, the violence and terror escalated. Nervous villagers conducted night patrols, which often transformed into angry and dangerous vigilante mobs. Soon vigilante groups were manning roadblocks and imposing curfews throughout much of East Java. Rumours spread that the mysterious ninjas possessed the power to fly or make themselves invisible; in response, villagers formed 'anti-ninja' squads and rehearsed magical counter-spells.[6] The level of fear was so high that three men who received death threats chose to commit suicide rather than be hunted down by the terrifying ninjas.[7]

Amid the delirium, any outsider entering a village in certain parts of East Java was in danger of being mistaken for a ninja. In the town of Pasaruan a man who faced the wrong direction while praying in a mosque was presumed to be a ninja; a mob therefore hacked him to death.[8] Others were murdered simply for trying to drive through roadblocks. By the end of October vigilante mobs in East Java had lynched at least 35 suspected ninjas.[9]

By this time the paranoia in the countryside had spread to the heart of East Java's second largest city, Malang. On 18 October an excited mob seized two people suspected of being ninjas, beating one to death. The second suspect was taken into policy custody and whisked away, but before reaching the station the police were intercepted by the mob. The suspect was seized and killed on the spot. His body was mutilated and decapitated. Mounting motorbikes, the mob paraded through Malang's normally placid streets carrying the severed head mounted on a spike. Only days later, a virtually identical episode took place in the nearby town of Batur, as a mob decapitated a suspected ninja and towed his corpse behind a motorbike.[10] Finally, East Java had captured the national media's strict attention.

In late October and early November every major news weekly ran cover stories on ninja stalkers, slain sorcerers and tales of blood and gore. The flurry of investigations by the print media soon revealed that *dukun tenung* were not the only victims of the murder spree. Although the killings had initially been concentrated in the three sub-districts of Banyuwangi in which *tenung* is widespread, cases later occurred in nearly all of Banyuwangi's 21 sub-districts, as well as a number of kabupaten that neighboured Banyuwangi. And while the victims in the early stages had mostly been alleged *dukun tenung*, large numbers of those killed in September and October were mainstream Muslim clerics (*kiai*), Islamic boarding-school teachers and ordinary citizens who happened to be devout Muslims.

In total, over two-thirds of the murder victims were traditionalist Muslims who belonged to NU. That fraction does not differ substantially from the percentage of all adult males in rural East Java who are NU members, but nonetheless a perception grew that the 'NU fold' was coming under deliberate attack.[11] By the end of November, official figures put the death toll from the Banyuwangi killings at 140, while local sources claimed that at least 180 had died.[12] By this time a host of different explanations had emerged to account for the killing spree.

Some theories cited mass hysteria and this was certainly an important element in the murders. Several groups of villagers openly admitted to having despatched certain neighbours whom they suspected of having practised black magic. Because they heard that a wave of *dukun* killings were taking place elsewhere, they felt justified in forming a vigilante mob to rid their own community of suspicious *dukun*. These cases, however, seemed to be reactions to a broader trend.[13] Something more than local vendettas was at play.

Witnesses and survivors of attacks often asserted that the attackers were not local residents. Sometimes the attackers used their own vehicles, and the same vehicles were seen by witnesses at different murder scenes. A large number of episodes shared characteristics that seemed designed to instil terror.

Banyuwangi's police officials and district administrators asserted that the killings were organised, and Maj. Gen. Djoko Subroto—East Java's garrison commander and the province's senior security official—

acknowledged that 'most of the killings shared the same *modus operandi*'.[14] The provincial police chief declared that the killers were hired assassins who had been paid up to Rp1 million per 'hit'; a fact-finding team from the National Commission for Human Rights corroborated this claim.[15] What remained to be explained was who was organising the killings and what purpose they were hoping to achieve.

One explanation put forth was that the killings were related to the anti-communist pogrom of 1965–66. Banyuwangi was a communist stronghold at that time and the NU's quasi-militant youth group, Ansor, had played a leading role in massacring confirmed or suspected Communists.[16] Some therefore suspected that the murdered *dukun* had been former Ansor members—and that the friends and relatives of those murdered over 30 years ago were finally taking revenge.

It seems doubtful, however, that the victims' relatives could have perpetrated the murder spree with such speed, efficiency and brutality. It is also unclear why vengeance murders would have occurred just then, in October 1998, and not before or after. Moreover, the way that the bodies were mutilated bore the hallmarks of a campaign designed to sow terror, rather than eliminate specific targets. For similar reasons, explanations blaming Christians, ethnic-Chinese, Muhammadiyah or Icmi were even less convincing. Suspicions therefore began to focus on the military.

NU sent a credible and independent fact-finding team to Banyuwangi in the wake of the killings. Headed by the organisation's senior *ulama* in Banyuwangi, the team asserted that military elements were involved in the killings.[17] At a special assembly convened on 14 October in Tuban, East Java, over 2000 NU *ulama* met with the province's security officials and accused them, point-blank, of having backed the murder spree. NU's top *ulama* in the southeastern region of Java, Yusuf Muhammad, declared that 'the tragedy affecting these humble people is a direct result of disputes between opposing elements of the political elite. We call on the political elite to cease these disputes'.[18]

The NU *ulama* in East Java cited the security forces' slow response to the killings, the actions of the Banyuwangi district chief (a retired colonel who later resigned in disgrace) and instances in which police prematurely released or otherwise protected suspects.[19] The NU *ulama* were particularly perturbed by what they claimed were deliberate efforts by police to conceal the identities of suspected killers. In several cases police allegedly orchestrated the escapes of suspected killers who had been turned in by vigilantes. But in what may have been the most bizarre aspect of the ninja killings, police were repeatedly accused of filling the escaped suspects' places in prison with mentally handicapped people.[20]

In fact, a large number of mentally disabled people were reportedly found wandering around parts of East Java during September and October often, it seemed, dropped into the vicinity of a recent murder.

By the end of October, around 30 mentally ill people were either found by local residents or produced as suspects by police in the areas of Banyuwangi, Jember and Probolinggo.[21] Most of these people were strangers to local residents. In the vicinity of Malang, police took custody of 40 mentally ill people, some of whom were from the Outer Islands. More than a dozen mentally disturbed people who were found wandering alone were mistaken for ninjas and killed by mobs.[22]

The frequency with which mentally ill people were cropping up around East Java at the time reinforced suspicions that the killing spree was backed by elements of the armed forces. One explanation was that the real perpetrators were deliberately inserting mental patients, who were apparently taken from asylums, into the vicinity of a murder to provide scapegoats and deflect suspicion from themselves.

In late October several retired officers with a military intelligence background publicly aired suspicions that their former agency, Bais, was behind the Banyuwangi killings. Lt Col. (ret.) Rudolf Baringbing, a retired Bais officer and former instructor in the agency's school for intelligence techniques, claimed that 'only fools would believe that these killings were purely criminal acts'.[23] Baringbing noted several hallmarks of military intelligence work: the killings were well organised, methodical and apparently designed to inflame communal tensions. He also questioned why the authorities had produced no explanation for the killings, despite having detained 157 suspects. 'In the intelligence profession,' he said, 'if more than three conspirators are captured, even the tidiest of scenarios will be untangled.'[24]

Two other retired colonels, both of whom possessed intelligence experience, concurred with Baringbing. They affirmed that the Banyuwangi killings bore striking resemblance to past Bais operations.[25] They also noted that criminal acts or vengeance killings would have been less consistent, less widespread and less professional—especially considering that the killers seemed undaunted by the local security patrols organised by villagers.

Several months after the killing wave subsided, a team of investigative journalists cited off-the-record military sources from the East Java Garrison as saying that the military's intelligence agency, Bais, was behind the killings.[26] The journalists found evidence that a team of intelligence officials headed by a lieutenant colonel resided in Situbondo, a district neighbouring Banyuwangi, from early August through to mid-September (the period during which the killings of *dukun tenung* began in earnest). The intelligence team claimed to be gathering evidence on organised gambling, even though gambling was virtually unknown in rural Banyuwangi.

Few at the time believed that the Banyuwangi killings were a covert intelligence operation. A parliamentary probe confirmed that the murder spree had claimed 182 lives—and its chief investigators said they were 'fairly certain' that the killings had been organised—but like the Semanggi shootings, May riots and Trisakti murders, no conclusions were drawn about who was responsible.[27] The bizarre killings simply went unexplained.

In retrospect, it seems that the most convincing explanation is that the Banyuwangi killings were among the first instances in which political interests in Jakarta deliberately provoked communal tensions for political ends. It seems that at least some military elements were involved, with the goal of influencing the outcome of the November MPR session.

Around the time that the killings began, the military was vulnerable. Pressure was mounting to try Soeharto, curtail the military's role in politics and push Habibie out of power. Student protests had been virtually uncontrollable in May 1998, and in mid-1998 all indications suggested that Habibie would face as much or even greater pressure from demonstrators. And if they were joined by a popular opposition figure, such as Megawati, the resultant united front could imperil the MPR session, the Habibie administration and, quite possibly, Wiranto's own career.

The military's overriding mission at the time, therefore, was to safeguard the MPR session from outside pressure. The most straightforward way to prevent the MPR from working against the military's interests was to simply prevent it from convening in the first place. A possible explanation for the Banyuwangi killings, therefore, is that they may have been an attempt to ignite a conflagration which would, in turn, justify the postponement or even the cancellation of the MPR session.

To pursue this line of reasoning further, the perpetrators of the killings might have been trying to revive Indonesia's last great social upheaval: the Muslim–PKI strife of 1965–66. That military-backed anticommunist pogrom did more than just neuter Soeharto's chief political enemy, the PKI—it also plunged Indonesia's political heartland, Java, into several months of severe turmoil. Thus, by targeting local mystics and NU *ulama*, the perpetrators of the Banyuwangi killings may have been trying to reignite grassroots Muslim–Communist strife in Java.

Military and administration officials undertook a concerted campaign at the time to pin the blame for the Banyuwangi killings on latent Communists. For instance, in a high-profile media interview published in early November, on the eve of the MPR session, Wiranto declared that 'the armed forces want to remind the nation that the latent threat of communism still exists and must be countered'.[28] Referring explicitly to the Banyuwangi killings, Wiranto asserted that 'those who reject, *a priori*, the possibility that Communists are involved in these acts of brutality are, in effect, defending or at least sympathising with Communists'.[29] Wiranto dwelt on the need to stop this 'radical group' in order to resolve the nation's crisis, and emphasised that the military intended to support the nation's constitutional government—meaning the Habibie administration.

Wiranto's generals followed suit. Lt Gen. Agum Gumelar, head of the National Resilience Institute at the time, told reporters that he believed the Banyuwangi killings were perpetrated by Communists.[30] The national police chief, Lt Gen. Roesmanhadi, concurred.[31] Claims of communist involvement were also being made by Habibie's allies, such as Lt Gen. (ret.) Zen Maulani, who headed the intelligence agency Bakin, which reports directly to the president.[32] Habibie himself grabbed headlines in early October by announcing that 'radical revolutionaries' were attempting to breed instability and defeat the MPR session.[33]

But if the Banyuwangi killings were intended to revive widespread Muslim–PKI strife, the campaign failed. Those who were blaming Communists had apparently fallen prey to their own propaganda: they failed to realise that, unlike in 1965–66, grassroots Java no longer harboured a latent PKI force. NU members were provoked and whipped into frenzies, but they refrained from lashing out at latent Communists in their community, simply because no more latent Communists existed. The killings produced considerable mayhem, but if they were designed to ignite a conflagration they must have been a 'botched job'.

This leads to an alternative explanation. Rather than an attempt to ignite a conflagration, the killings may have had a more limited aim: namely, to split the political opposition. At the time, there was a common belief that if any one of the country's three main opposition leaders threw their support behind the radical students demanding Habibie's dismissal, the MPR would have no choice but to depose the president. The student movement had already demonstrated its potency against Soeharto; backed by Megawati, Wahid or even Amien Rais, it would be unstoppable. A gradual political transition would give way to an abrupt overthrow of old regime elements. The influence of the military—and Wiranto himself—might be severely curtailed.

It therefore seems that by creating instability in East Java the perpetrators of the Banyuwangi killings hoped to drive a wedge between Wahid's NU and Megawati's new mass-based party, PDI Perjuangan. Megawati launched her new party in Bali on 8 October in a rally which attracted massive support and fanfare. The campaign in nearby Banyuwangi—the departure point for PDI Perjuangan supporters travelling by ferry to Bali—may have been intended to disrupt the congress. This explanation was put forth by an unnamed military source quoted in the international press.[34] Another unnamed military source reportedly claimed that his outfit, the Special Forces, was involved in perpetrating the killings. The original plan, he said, had been to instigate trouble in Bali prior to the congress; but because the Balinese were too vigilant, the operation was moved to nearby Banyuwangi, where it was easier to operate.[35]

Again, the planners might have fallen victim to their own propaganda: it was assumed that PDI Perjuangan was supported by significant numbers of PKI sympathisers, but in fact this was not so. No antipathy emerged between Wahid and Megawati, nor between NU supporters and those of PDI Perjuangan. But while the campaign may have failed from this standpoint, it succeeded in another way.

The mysterious victimisation of NU members created extreme apprehension among the NU leadership during September and October. In an interview on 13 October, Wahid expressed fears that if the Banyuwangi killings were not quickly put to a stop they could spiral out of control.[36] 'People will take things into their own hands—burning, looting, violating women.' He seemed unclear about who was responsible for the killings but he warned that, if the mysterious perpetrators were allowed to have their way, Indonesia could join the ranks of countries such as Myanmar, Iran or Iraq. Indonesia would witness, as he put it, 'cruelism [sic] versus cruelism'.

Ironically, while NU officials in East Java blamed the military for condoning the killings or perhaps even actively abetting them, Wahid took a different approach: he purposely curried favour with Wiranto in order to obtain security assistance in East Java. As the NU chair explained: 'I said to General Wiranto, "Please, do something. Please take control so that I can control the *ulama* in East Java." I urged him to send more troops, including troops from those units defending Jakarta—not just those defending East Java.'

When asked about his views of the military chief, Wahid added: 'Wiranto's a democrat. He believes in people power. This I'm sure of.' Wahid's views on Wiranto would later undergo a dramatic change, but at the time he was clearly siding with the general. 'Unlike in the past,' he said, 'we are now working with the authorities—and it feels strange!' On 18 October, when Wahid staged a massive rally to launch NU's new political party, he ensured that Wiranto and a host of other military leaders attended. Military leaders rarely attended such rallies, but Wahid pointedly chose to sit squarely between the military's two highest ranking generals: Wiranto and Subagyo.

In effect, the Banyuwangi killings had pushed the icon of NU, Indonesia's largest mass-based organisation, firmly into the arms of Wiranto's military. Wahid had secured military protection for his followers—but this left him indebted to Wiranto. When the MPR session convened in November, the military chief would expect NU to defend the military's interests. Wiranto would not be disappointed.

12

'STAY INDOORS'

F or an avowedly Islamic party, PPP had a distinctly non-Islamic name: the 'United Development Party'. This was deliberate. PPP was founded in 1973 when Ali Murtopo, Soeharto's chief political advisor at the time, forced the merger of the country's main Islamic parties into one entity.[1] Along with PDI, PPP became one of only two 'opposition' parties that were allowed to exist. Its main function was to help make Golkar's uninterrupted string of landslide victories seem like real contests. By foisting a bland name and nondescript symbol on the party, Murtopo helped ensure that these contests never proved too real.

Government pressure and interference gradually took its toll on PPP: by the mid-1990s the party had lost a quality which Indonesian politicians refer to as 'dynamism'. Leadership posts were filled with malleable figures and the party rarely strayed from the doctrine of Soeharto, Golkar and the military.[2] This alienated PPP's constituents: the party's official share of the national vote fell to a mere 16 per cent in 1987, from nearly a third in the preceding three elections.[3] When PDI staged an aggressively pro-reform campaign in 1992, PPP slipped even farther. By 1996 it seemed that the next year's election would relegate PPP to an even more distant third—until the authorities raided Megawati's PDI Headquarters.

With PDI usurped by Suryadi, PPP suddenly became, by default, the only remotely 'reformist' alternative for anti-Golkar voters in the 1997 election. Events had conspired to thrust this moribund, faux-opposition party into the national spotlight. Even those who cared little for PPP's Islamic agenda flocked to the party, which won its highest ever vote tally in the 1997 election. PPP's chiefs were suddenly looked upon as Indonesia's foremost 'opposition leaders'—a role in which some of them were far from comfortable.

None of this, of course, stopped PPP from endorsing the Soeharto–Habibie ticket in the March 1998 MPR session. Only a few courageous delegates voiced reservations about the re-election of Soeharto. With only

14 per cent of the assembly's seats, PPP was powerless to achieve anything even if it had had a mind to do so. But when Soeharto fell from power only two months later, PPP's delegates suddenly lost their inhibitions. In the approach to the special MPR session in November 1998, PPP's delegates began to portray themselves as Indonesia's champions of reform—the roles their constituents wanted them to play. They still only commanded the same 14 per cent bloc, but this time they were determined to make their presence felt. For the first time in decades, an MPR session would be coloured by meaningful differences of opinion.

Three factions controlled over 80 per cent of the MPR's seats in 1998: Golkar, the military and the appointed regional representatives.[4] All three wanted the November session to proceed as smoothly as possible, hoping only to endorse the Habibie administration's timetable for elections and perhaps perform a few other uncontroversial tasks. PPP, in contrast, was determined to produce 'MPR resolutions' which would guide government policy. PPP did not want to go so far as to oust Habibie—he was, after all, a powerful patron for Islamic interests—but the party did push for two key points of reform: curtailing the military's political role and investigating those suspected of corruption, specifically Soeharto and his family.

To stave off these and other pro-reform resolutions, Golkar, the military and the regional representatives resorted to a time-tested technique. Throughout the Soeharto era potentially embarrassing controversies were typically resolved within special 'working committees' comprising of around 90 MPR members. Meeting behind closed doors several weeks before an MPR session, the working committee would prepare the session's agenda and compose draft resolutions—which would then be rubber-stamped by the full MPR. Adhering to New Order precedents, MPR Speaker Harmoko convened just such a committee in September 1998.

PPP delegates comprised less than one-fifth of the working committee's membership, but this small delegation proposed over half of the 23 draft resolutions put before the committee.[5] None of PPP's resolutions were passed, however, because all were considered too controversial by the Golkar-dominated committee. PPP's leaders were incensed. They vowed that when the full MPR met in November they would take the virtually unprecedented step of resubmitting their proposals on the assembly floor—particularly those regarding the military's political role and the investigation of Soeharto.

As the month of October progressed, radical students continued to demonstrate, sometimes clashing violently with para-military units. Other student groups, however, demurred from attacking Habibie. Some did so because they were Islamic organisations which tacitly supported Habibie for his proximity to political Islam. Although Habibie was a part of the old regime, he was from the part that had helped advance modernist Islam; that fact alone enticed powerful student groups such as Kammi to call for a peaceful MPR session and democratic elections in 1999.

Other student groups that refrained from denouncing Habibie were simply being fastidious about constitutionality. This category included the bulk of students from the University of Indonesia. 'Although I realise the MPR is dominated by elements of the old regime,' said UI senate leader Rama Pratama, 'we can't toss them out of power just like that. A democracy can't be formed overnight.'[6] Earlier in the year, Indonesia's students had been galvanised by their common antipathy toward the Soeharto family. Toward Habibie, however, the students' attitudes were more ambivalent. Lacking unity, the students were a far less effective political force.

Qualms about deposing Habibie were evident not only among students but, more critically, among Indonesia's big three opposition leaders. All three—Wahid, Megawati and Amien Rais—had their own reasons for refraining from challenging Habibie's legitimacy through the MPR. All three could see that Wiranto backed Habibie and that therefore a confrontation could prove bloody. Given that Habibie had promised to hold open elections by mid-1999—and given that all three leaders were confident about winning legitimate electoral support—none felt it worthwhile to confront Habibie and Wiranto just for the sake of accelerating elections.

In fact, all three opposition leaders felt that they needed time to build up new political parties and carry out campaigns across the vast archipelago. Megawati and Wahid had been particularly slow to start: both waited until October to finally launch their new parties. Wahid dubbed his the National Awakening Party (PKB); in effect, it was the political vehicle of NU. Megawati, meanwhile, had wanted to regain control of her former party, PDI. The Habibie administration, however, upheld the illegal Medan congress of 1996, thereby depriving her of PDI's well-known symbol and party infrastructure. Megawati was forced to found a new party from scratch: the Indonesian Democratic Party of Struggle, or PDI Perjuangan. Public confusion over the two parties' similar names and symbols would linger for months.

Lacking both infrastructure and experienced cadres, Megawati and Wahid estimated that they would need at least six months to recruit party officials and advertise their new political vehicles to an electorate of more than 100 million people. And for Megawati there was another reason for not confronting Habibie: the PDI Perjuangan chair was held back by a curious trait for an opposition politician—passivity. Steeped in Javanese culture, Megawati wanted to avoid the appearance of being power-hungry, which traditional Javanese regard as unseemly. For years Megawati had been expressing the firm belief that one day she would become president.[7] A corollary of this determinism seemed to be that power would, and should, simply accrue to her without undue exertion on her part. It was a belief that she would exhibit, usually to her own detriment, on repeated occasions in the years ahead.

Amien Rais, meanwhile, embarked on a challenging experiment. As Indonesia's most notable Islamic politician, he received offers to join either PPP or a new party that united a host of strident Islamists, the Crescent and Star Party (PBB). Instead, Rais founded his own party, the National Mandate Party (Pan). Rais attempted to cast the party as an 'inclusivist' reform party that was open to all segments of society: Muslims and non-Muslims, *pribumi* and non-*pribumi*. It was a risky strategy: Rais faced stiff competition for the Islamist vote from more avowedly Islamic parties, while many secular-nationalist voters mistrusted him.

From the outset, therefore, Pan was divided into two wings. One comprised secular reformists who saw Rais as a pro-democracy campaigner. Sympathising with the students and concerned that the government would not conduct fair elections, members of this wing generally wanted to replace Habibie with a neutral caretaker government in the upcoming MPR session. Rais, however, chose to follow the lead of a more powerful faction within Pan: the 'Muhammadiyah wing', whose members emanated from Rais's traditional constituency. Many within this group sympathised with Habibie, whom they saw as a reasonably effective patron of political Islam. Some within the group even harboured ambitions to forge an alliance between Pan and Habibie's Golkar.[8] Thus, despite having been stridently opposed to Soeharto's New Order several months before, Rais conspicuously refrained from calling for Habibie's ouster in the November MPR session.

Thus Indonesia's opposition leaders demurred from challenging Habibie so that they could pursue their own political interests. But there was another reason for their hesitancy: they viewed each other with too much mistrust. Publicly, Megawati could barely conceal her disdain for Rais; privately, among her advisors, she would emphatically declare that she 'hated' the former Muhammadiyah chair.[9] Wahid, meanwhile, had been publicly bad-mouthing Rais, his longstanding rival, for years. November 1998 would not be the first occasion in which personal differences would prevent Indonesia's vaunted opposition leaders from taking concerted action.

The inaction of the opposition leaders frustrated anti-Habibie student groups. On 9 November—one day before the MPR was due to convene—a group of students finally succeeded in meeting separately with all three opposition leaders.[10] Due in part to this student lobbying, the opposition leaders decided, at last, to hold a joint summit the following day. The venue would be the home of Abdurrahman Wahid, in the semi-rural

Jakarta suburb of Ciganjur. The three figures expanded their ranks by inviting another popular civic leader, Yogyakarta's Sultan Hamengku-buwono X.[11]

After a one-hour meeting the 'Ciganjur Four' produced an eight-point communiqué. Apart from a perfunctory refrain about upholding national unity, the 'Ciganjur Declaration' demanded that a new government should take office no later than three months after elections in May 1999. Other demands were that Wiranto disband the para-military units that had been clashing with students, and efforts to investigate and punish KKN should begin with Soeharto. Finally, the Ciganjur Four declared that the military should withdraw from politics—but only over an exceptionally long period of time, six years. The communiqué made no mention of a caretaker government.

In effect, the Ciganjur Declaration implicitly endorsed both Habibie's presidency and the military's political role. Only Soeharto had been singled out for attack. In effect, the Ciganjur Declaration was a victory for Wiranto—a victory that had been made possible by the declaration's main driver, Wahid.

Anti-Habibie student groups and the National Front claimed that the Ciganjur Four had betrayed the ideals of reform, but when the MPR session finally commenced, the declaration did have some impact. Apparently influenced by the Ciganjur Declaration, several influential Golkar politicians suddenly endorsed PPP's demand for a resolution on investigating Soeharto. Attached to a measure on 'clean governance', the demand read:

> Measures to eradicate corruption and nepotism must be carried out swiftly against anyone, be they state officials, former state officials, their families and cronies, as well as private entities/conglomerates, and including former President Soeharto, with attention paid to human rights and the principle that a suspect is innocent until proven guilty.[12]

The MPR was explicitly ordering the Habibie administration to investigate Soeharto. Few had expected the Golkar-dominated body to act so assertively. Some attributed the assertiveness to the executive board's most notable newcomer: Marzuki Darusman.[13]

Another controversial resolution pertained to 'economic democracy'. The crux of the measure was a passage that read:

> The control over the nation's land should be handled fairly by eliminating all forms of centralised control and concentrated ownership, through a framework of capacity-building for the economically weak, small-to-medium enterprises and co-operatives—as well as for the broader public at large.[14]

At the end of the final sentence, the PPP faction wanted to add an additional phrase: 'especially for *pribumi*'. Parliament's other four factions killed the proposal, but the incident suggested that Indonesia's Islamists harboured some crude concepts about economic management. PPP's proposal seemed to hint that if an Islamic government took power, the state might embark on a program to redistribute assets along ethnic or religious lines.

As the MPR session wound down to its final hours, the assembly finally considered the most hotly debated resolution: namely, PPP's proposal to exclude the military from parliament.[15] Having been rejected once in the working committee in September, PPP's proposal was refused again when it was resubmitted to a subcommittee of the MPR. Indignant PPP members had staged a walkout from the subcommittee, thereby forcing the matter to an open vote on the floor of the entire 1000-member assembly.[16]

A genuinely open vote in the MPR was virtually unheard of in the lifetime of most Indonesians. Javanese political culture has high regard for the concept of consensus, and both Soekarno and Soeharto encouraged this mindset to quell dissent. But when the members of this MPR addressed the role of the military in parliament, consensus eluded them.

Most of the Golkar faction wanted to preserve its longstanding, symbiotic relationship with the military; the party's leaders therefore ensured that when PPP's resolution reached the floor, it was so watered down that it bore scant resemblance to its original draft. Rather than ousting the military from parliament, the measure finally put before the MPR merely reduced the military's seat total. And the sticky question of how many seats the military would relinquish, and by when, was delegated to parliament to decide. In effect, the MPR was dodging the tough decisions.

The watered-down measure passed with ease. The vote took place near the end of the session's final day, 13 November, and it was broadcast live on nationwide television. When MPR Speaker Harmoko asked all those in favour to stand, the 136-member PPP delegation resolutely stayed seated. Nearly everyone else in the assembly stood, including all but one of the 585-strong Golkar delegation.[17] Harmoko, pleased with the outcome, declared: 'There! That's how democracy is carried out in the *reformasi* era: transparent for all to see!' Wiranto, also beaming, milled around the assembly floor accepting congratulations. But interspersed with these pictures, the television broadcasts cut away to scenes taking place on streets not far from where the MPR was meeting—but where the prevailing mood was far less jovial.

By mid-November anti-Habibie student groups had been demonstrating on an almost daily basis for six weeks. The most determined activist groups, such as Forkot and Famred, had tried on several occasions to occupy the MPR complex, but to no avail. Other groups staged raucous rallies on campuses, particularly at UI's Salemba campus and at Atmadjaya University on Jalan Sudirman. The latter was a particularly popular venue for staging rallies because it was in a visible place in the heart of the business district. It was also ideal for launching marches on parliament: immediately adjacent to the Semanggi interchange, the campus was just over one kilometre from parliament.

In the weeks prior to the MPR session the incessant demonstrations elicited a concerted response from the military. To provide security in the capital Wiranto and his Jakarta Garrison commander, Djaja Suparman, authorised the formation of civilian militias.[18] These militias, or 'para-militaries', included veteran Golkar-affiliated gangs such as Pemuda Pancasila and Pemuda Panca Marga. Others were formed from the ranks of Jakarta's unemployed. The bulk of the manpower, however, was mobilised by the Front for a United Islamic Ulama (FUIB), an alliance of some twenty Islamist groups that explicitly backed Habibie.[19]

Few of these Islamist groups, however, were genuine, mass-based organisations. Most were creations of Icmi, PPP, Golkar or, especially, the military. The leaders of at least three Islamic militia groups acknowledged that their members received training from military personnel before the start of the MPR session.[20] Another group, the Indonesian Committee for World Muslim Solidarity (Kisdi), had long maintained close links to Prabowo and other generals.[21] Leaders of another group, the Islamic Defence Front (FPI), admitted that their ranks included Jakarta *preman*.[22] FPI would later become one of Jakarta's most notorious gangs, along with another group that took part in defending the MPR, Laskar Jihad.

In total, an estimated 30 000 para-militaries were deployed in Jakarta several days prior to the start of the MPR session.[23] At night they camped in large mosques, on the grounds of the Forestry Ministry (adjacent to the parliament building) or inside the Senayan sports complex. During the day they patrolled the city wielding heavy bamboo spears—long poles with the ends sliced off to form razor-sharp points. Several gangs rode in a convoy of about ten trucks, plying Jalan Sudirman, the capital's main thoroughfare.[24] Chanting oaths and brandishing their spears as they passed beneath the office windows of Jakarta's main banks and brokerage houses, the militias inflicted far more damage on the stock and currency markets than on enemies of Habibie.

The security forces gave the para-militaries free rein to stone the Atmadjaya campus and vandalise its buildings—which represented a double standard on the part of Wiranto, who had been complaining at length that student protests disrupted public order. Other militias joined police vehicles in patrolling the city, while still others stationed themselves at spots where student groups were expected to convene rallies.[25] In instances where student demonstrators confronted security forces, militias were deployed in the front line, acting as buffers between the students and the troops.

In one such location in Menteng, on 10 November, a large force of para-militaries prepared to attack a massive procession of students approaching from UI's Salemba campus.[26] A violent clash was narrowly avoided, but the next day violence finally broke out in the same place. When students were prevented from marching downtown by a barricade on Jalan Imam Bonjol, several activists in a Volkswagen van deliberately hurtled through the barricade, injuring nine soldiers. In the ensuing melee, security forces meted out severe beatings to several students and three journalists.[27]

The next day, Thursday 12 November, Jakarta witnessed its worst bout of violence since May. At one point during the day, MPR members were led to believe that protesters were on the verge of descending on the MPR complex—news that prompted the entire Golkar faction to prepare for evacuation by helicopter.[28] In a clash in Slipi, West Jakarta, a teenager named Lukman Firdaus was severely beaten by security forces. Before dying from his wounds in a hospital the next day, Lukman, according to his father, asked for permission to watch the live television broadcast of the MPR's final day-long session.[29] In total, Thursday's clashes killed one police officer and caused over 100 students to be hospitalised.[30] But the worst was still to come.

Friday 13 November started off with a special message to the residents of Jakarta from Gen. Wiranto: 'Stay indoors.'[31] From the short shrift given to PPP's proposed resolutions, students had concluded that the MPR was ignoring their demands, and their protests therefore grew more intense. Another trend was that ordinary residents were joining forces with the students. In Cawang, East Jakarta, a mob of local residents brutally attacked a small militia unit deployed in front of a company of troops. The mob beat three of the para-militaries to death.[32]

Meanwhile, student groups were congregating at various campuses around the city. The military's primary concern was to prevent these groups from coalescing. A key crossroads was the centrally located Semanggi interchange, a four-way cloverleaf connecting Jalan Sudirman with the equally congested Jalan Gatot Subroto. One group of students was assembling just to the northeast of the Semanggi interchange at Atmadjaya University, while another was forming about five kilometres to the southeast on Jalan Gatot Subroto. If the two groups merged at the Semanggi interchange, they would then be able to make the short northwesterly march to the grounds of parliament, where the MPR session was taking place.

The large number of students at the Atmadjaya rally was augmented by residents from surrounding neighbourhoods. Journalists reported that the crowd numbered in the tens of thousands by midday.[33] Although some were there strictly as onlookers, many of the local residents, particularly youths, began taking part in the noisy protests being staged by students. Security forces were stationed on the clover leaf just a few hundred metres to the southwest of the students. Around midday, militias arrived from the north and the day's first altercation broke out.

The para-militaries began scuffling with a mixed group of students and local residents. When the local crowd swelled into an angry mob, the fighting escalated and the militia units began to yield ground. Soon they were retreating, pell-mell, to the north. The chasing mob overcame two para-militaries and began beating them. Before long the two men had been stabbed to death, their bodies mutilated.[34]

Soon after that, about 3 p.m., the students on and near the Atmadjaya campus were hurling bottles, rocks and chunks of asphalt towards the security forces assembled on Jalan Sudirman. At least one witness spotted a flaming object, thought to be a petrol bomb (or Molotov cocktail), thrown toward troops.[35] Around 4 p.m. warning shots were fired in the air and teargas canisters were launched. Armoured personnel carriers fitted with water cannons were also used, firing jets of high-pressure water to push the students away from the interchange.

Not all of the warning shots, however, were fired into the air. By 4.30 p.m. several dozen protesters had suffered wounds from rubber-coated bullets, and a private hospital confirmed that one student protester had been killed.[36] A BBC report one hour later cited three deaths. Soldiers were seen firing rubber bullets at students from close range, at which the supposedly non-lethal ammunition can kill. Students responded by uprooting street signs and hurling them at soldiers.[37]

There was a lull in the fighting after 5 p.m., but the violence was far from over. Because a number of local residents had been among those injured in the afternoon clash, even larger groups from nearby neigh- · bourhoods crept forth to join the students. Around 6.30 p.m., just after dark, a small group attempted to break through a police barricade. Shots rang out again.[38]

Troops continually fired rubber bullets into the crowd, sometimes crouching and carefully taking aim. When they temporarily forced the students to retreat, some soldiers were seen dancing a jig in the street. Others picked up rocks that had been thrown at them and hurled them back towards the students. The students, for their part, lobbed dozens of flaming Molotov cocktails towards the troops.[39] Some students showed their bravado by standing directly in front of the troops, taunting the soldiers as they fired.[40] Other students crouched behind makeshift wooden shields. Some observers, including a radio reporter providing live coverage of events, reported seeing helicopters delivering armed men to roofs of the GKBI and BRI office towers, both of which overlook the Semanggi area.[41] Some reported seeing red targeting beams, such as those used by snipers, emanating from these roofs.

Television cameras were recording the scene at Semanggi and airing it live for domestic and international audiences. As an armoured personnel carrier advanced toward the line of students, viewers watched an army officer, mounted atop the vehicle, empty his handgun into the crowd. He then reloaded and fired again. The handgun was later determined to be a non-lethal gas-powered gun, but few viewers knew that at the time.[42] Somewhere, however, shots were being fired with live ammunition. By 8 p.m. five protesters were dead and over 50 injured.[43] 'Jakarta,' said foreign correspondents covering the scene, 'is a battle zone.'[44]

Domestic broadcasts interspersed scenes from Semanggi with views inside the MPR assembly. Cameras zoomed in on MPR members who were slouched down in their chairs, sleeping soundly as the proceedings wore on—and as the street combat raged only a short distance away. Around 9.30 p.m. President Habibie delivered the closing speech of the session, in which he expressed regret that 'two students and one civilian volunteer' had been killed in street protests.[45] Apparently he had not been informed of the latest situation at Semanggi.

As the session came to a close, Sarwono Kusumaatmadja—whom Golkar had recalled from the MPR the previous month—repeatedly tried to contact Marzuki Darusman and other MPR leaders to urge them to postpone the session's close, so that the MPR could address the demands of demonstrators who had lost their lives that day. 'Since gaining independence, never has Indonesia held an MPR session as bloody as this,' Sarwono told reporters that night.[46] A different reaction came from Feisal Tanjung, speaking in his capacity as Indonesia's co-ordinating minister for politics and security: 'In a democracy,' said Tanjung, 'this is what happens. We'll investigate later.'[47]

After Harmoko's gavel marked the official close of the MPR session at 10 p.m., the tempo of the street combat increased again. The fighting carried on intermittently until the early hours of Saturday morning. Soldiers chased students into surrounding buildings and, in several instances, inflicted serious injuries by hurling them down stairwells.[48] After a pre-dawn lull, more shots were fired after daybreak. Around 8 a.m., police firing from the flyover wounded a sergeant of the marines in the leg.[49] Whether the shot was an accident, and whether live ammunition was used, remained unclear; soon after, however, police units made a hasty withdrawal. Suspicion arose that separate elements of the security forces were at odds with each other.

By mid-morning on Saturday some 1500 demonstrators remained at Semanggi. The only security forces left in the area were marines, who enjoyed a better rapport with protesters than the police or Jakarta Garrison troops did. Escorted by about 60 armed marines, the student protesters finally made their way to the parliament building—but by this time, of course, the building was empty.[50] The final casualty toll from the Semanggi shootings was 16 dead and around 200 injured.[51] Before the incident had even finished, Jakarta's rumour mill was rife with speculation about who ordered the shootings—and why.

One explanation for the 'Tragedy at Semanggi' held that poorly disciplined troops and incompetent commanders were responsible for the mayhem. 'Certain radical elements' among the protesters had started the violence, according to Wiranto, and the troops at Semanggi had been 'overdefensive and tended to deviate from established procedures'.[52] Wiranto vowed to punish those responsible and eventually 163 soldiers, including twelve officers, served detention periods of 14–21 days for indisciplinary conduct.[53]

Wiranto's explanation, however, is not convincing. Indiscipline and incompetence may explain why troops flagrantly violated procedures— such as by firing rubber bullets from close range, beating students and hurling rocks. They may also explain why the violence was allowed to carry on for more than twelve hours. The use of live ammunition, however, was attributable to more than indiscipline and incompetence.

According to military spokesman Maj. Gen. Syamsul Ma'arif, the troops deployed that day were authorised only to use blanks and rubber bullets, and no 'shoot on sight' orders were in effect.[54] Yet forensic experts found metal bullet fragments in most of the nine victims who died from bullet wounds. The experts said that bullets were 5–6mm in diameter and were shot at high velocity. Significantly, the experts said they found no evidence of close-range shooting—which suggested that the fire could have come from snipers.[55]

More clues emerged a week after the shootings. On 22 November newspapers ran front-page stories on the emotional testimony provided to the Human Rights Commission by a 21-year-old former Trisakti student named Wiwid Pratiwo.[56] Pratiwo related a detailed story about how he had been befriended by Private Budi Leksono of the presidential security guards (Paspampres), whose colleagues eventually coerced Pratiwo into spying on student activists. Pratiwo said that his first job was to help collect militia personnel from points in rural Java and transport them to Jakarta. His second duty, he said, was to attend student rallies at Atmadjaya University and relay information to Leksono.

Around noon on 13 November, Pratiwo says, he received a message from 'headquarters' on his pager: 'All those at Atmadjaya should withdraw because between 1 p.m. and 4 p.m. there will be a shooting spree.'[57] Pratiwo ignored the warning lest his absence arouse suspicion among his fellow activists; in any event, the shooting at around 4 p.m. was relatively light. But Pratiwo received another warning at about 7.30 p.m.—by which time heavy shooting had already begun.[58]

At the Trisakti campus the following day, several student activists confronted Pratiwo and accused him of acting as an informant. Pratiwo confessed and, several days later, sought protection from the Human Rights Commission. More than a week after Pratiwo's story became public, it finally elicited a response from the commander of the military police, Maj. Gen. Djasri Marin. Marin acknowledged that Leksono was a member of the Paspampres security group that had previously served President Soeharto and his family.[59] Marin said that he had deserted on four occasions, including a period surrounding the November MPR session.

When Marin summoned Leksono for questioning, the latter acknowledged that he knew Pratiwo well and that he had lived for several months as a lodger with Pratiwo's parents.[60] Leksono denied, however, that he had used Pratiwo as an informant, and in early December he therefore lodged a slander suit against the former Trisakti student.[61] Marin, meanwhile, told the press that he doubted Pratiwo's story for lack of corroborating evidence—but Pratiwo's lawyers from the Legal Aid Foundation asserted that Marin had deliberately ignored the evidence they put forth.[62]

The possibility that Paspampres was involved raised several avenues of conjecture. Paspampres is an elite army unit with a high degree of operational autonomy—and its members typically possessed strong personal loyalties to the Soeharto family. Interestingly, it was clear at the time that Cendana was angry at Habibie. One day after the shootings, Soeharto's half-brother Probosutedjo relayed a quote from the former president to reporters:

> [The Semanggi shootings] happened because the students' aspirations
> were not heard and appreciated. If the government had respected them,
> the problem could have been overcome. I stepped down in May to avoid
> bloodshed—but unfortunately, it happens now.[63]

In effect, Soeharto was heaping scorn on his former protégé, Habibie. Few believed that the criticism was motivated by genuine grief for the slain students; instead, it seemed likely that Cendana was reacting to the previous day's decision by the MPR to explicitly name 'Soeharto and his family' in the resolution on investigating KKN. One possible explanation for the Semanggi shootings, therefore, is that Cendana perpetrated the Semanggi violence to discredit Habibie's government, or perhaps simply to sow disorder.

Alternatively, the shootings may have been part of an internal military power struggle. At the time, some members of the Habibie administration were reportedly seeking to sack Wiranto as armed forces chief and replace him with someone more loyal to Habibie, such as Lt Gen. Hendropriyono.[64] Indeed, when a raft of weekly magazines hit news stands two days after the shooting, only two had front covers that vehemently demanded

Wiranto's ouster: *Ummat* and *Adil.* Because these were the two magazines most closely associated with Icmi, this fuelled speculation that the shootings had been perpetrated by an anti-Wiranto/pro-Habibie clique within the army.

In any event, the reason behind the use of live ammunition in the Semanggi shootings remained a mystery. The possibility that Wiranto's rivals sought to discredit him cannot be discounted. On the other hand, Pratiwo's story—although it was soon forgotten by the press and the public—would not be the last time that Paspampres personnel (or other elements tied to Cendana) would surface in connection with an unexplained episode of violence in Indonesia. In fact, the next such episode occurred less than two weeks after the shootings, and only a few kilometres from the Semanggi interchange—in the notorious district of Kota.

The Kota area of North Jakarta is a notorious hotbed of narcotics, prostitution, gambling and crime. Among its many crowded, polluted and run-down neighbourhoods, one, Ketapang, stood out in late 1998 because it laid claim to being the home of the Paradiso, said to be Southeast Asia's largest gambling den.

Although most Ketapang residents were *pribumi* Muslims, the Paradiso's clientele was mostly ethnic-Chinese and its formidable security force was staffed by Christian Ambonese. Natives of the Maluku archipelago in eastern Indonesia, the distinctive-looking Ambonese are famed for their martial qualities—a stereotype deriving, perhaps, from their prominent role in the Dutch colonial army. In the early morning hours of 22 November a dispute took place in front of the Paradiso between two Ketapang residents and the Ambonese security guards.[65] Witnesses characterised the dispute as a minor affair that appeared to be quickly resolved, but nonetheless a massive escalation took place. By 6.30 a.m. well over 100 Ambonese *preman* had assembled in the area, ready to wreak violence on the residents of Ketapang—supposedly in revenge for the scuffle with security guards several hours before.[66]

As dawn broke, the *preman* combed Ketapang's narrow streets, smashing flowerpots, destroying motorbikes and vandalising buildings. In the mayhem a window was broken in the local mosque; this in turn triggered reports that the Christian Ambonese were on an anti-Islamic rampage.[67] Within hours, trucks arrived carrying crudely armed men from mosques as far away as Tangerang, twenty kilometres to the west. Mobs set fire to the gambling den as well as a church in which the Ambonese were hiding. From then on the rioting spread out of control. Mobs attacked churches and Christian schools throughout North Jakarta, including several located more than ten kilometres from Ketapang.

In addition to the damaged mosque, four churches were burned down and twelve others damaged. Over 30 other buildings were vandalised. Six people, most of them Ambonese, were hacked to death by mobs, and ten others burnt to death in fires.[68] Another 81 were injured.[69] As the rioting peaked, the security forces sent in a convoy of trucks—specially equipped with cages to protect the passengers—to extricate 159 Ambonese who were under attack from angry mobs.

T he Ketapang riot marked the second public appearance of the Islamic Defence Front (FPI), one of the militia groups that had defended the MPR session just two weeks before. Founded in mid-1998, FPI's leaders instructed their followers not only in their own peculiar version of Islamic doctrine but also in martial arts and physical training. Structured like a military outfit, FPI members were accorded ranks and given command responsibility for specific neighbourhoods, especially in North Jakarta. The FPI maintained close relations with key security officials in Jakarta, such as the garrison commander, Djaja Suparman, and the police chief, Maj. Gen. Noegroho Djadjoesman.[70]

Rather than protesting issues that offended much of the Muslim community, such as abuses of Acehnese women or the religion ministry's extortion of *haj* pilgrims, the FPI's activities typically seemed designed to support the military and police.[71] FPI members took part, for instance, in defending the MPR session as militia personnel. Upon hearing news that Ambonese Christians had attacked a mosque in Ketapang, they sprung into action again: several truckloads of FPI men rushed to the scene, wielding hand-held weapons and clashing with the Ambonese.[72] The FPI would reappear again on a host of occasions in Jakarta and elsewhere over the course of the next two years.

As in previous episodes of violence, there were indications that the Ketapang riot was not spontaneous. There appears to be scant reason why an ordinary scuffle would have prompted such massive retaliation— and at such an odd hour. How the Ambonese *preman* were assembled is also unexplained: identification cards from those killed indicated that they were not from Ketapang; rather, they resided in disparate locations throughout Jakarta.[73] Finally, the speed and efficiency with which the *preman* were extracted suggested that the security forces were not making arrests but, rather, were carrying out a pre-planned rescue operation. Police detained 187 people, most of whom were Ambonese. Three of those detained were former Special Forces soldiers. All but thirteen of the detainees were released.[74]

Furthermore, there is an important link between those who instigated the Ketapang riots and the former first family: the security guards at the Paradiso worked under an Ambonese man named Sadrakh Mastamu, a *preman* gang leader who was also the right-hand man for Yorrys Raweyai, the operational head of Pemuda Pancasila.[75] Raweyai was known to be close to Bob Hasan and members of the Soeharto family, and he made at least two startling public appearances at Soeharto's side in late 1998.[76]

Given that one side of the Ketapang conflict consisted of thugs employed by Cendana's chief henchman, while the other side was supported by military-backed 'Islamic militants', it strongly appears that the Ketapang affair was contrived. Security forces were somehow able to rescue more than 150 men in specially equipped trucks, yet were unable to prevent sixteen churches and over 30 other buildings from being damaged around North Jakarta. No one was held accountable for the arson and deaths; on the contrary, the FPI continued to cause targeted disruptions in Jakarta with seemingly no censure from police.

As for the Ambonese, some 300 Pemuda Pancasila *preman*—including Sadrakh Mastamu's thugs—cropped up a few weeks later in their native Maluku, where similar communal strife soon commenced.[77] The bureau chief for the *Far Eastern Economic Review*, John McBeth, ascertained that the *preman* had been sent via naval landing craft—on the orders of the governor of Jakarta, Lt Gen. Sutiyoso.[78] As mentioned, Sutiyoso had worked with Suparman under Wiranto in 1994, when the Jakarta Garrison officers organised civilian militias. It is likely that, when he shipped the Pemuda Pancasila *preman* to Maluku, Sutiyoso was doing so at Wiranto's behest.

Together, the Semanggi shootings and Ketapang riots demonstrated that Indonesia's violence had not ended with the riots of the previous May. For Indonesians familiar with Javanese legends this came as no surprise: when a paramount ruler cedes power, his realm is expected to unravel and fall into disarray. Modern Indonesia seemed to be no different—except that in this case Indonesia was not unravelling of its own accord.

13

NAIL OF THE UNIVERSE

By the end of 1998 Habibie's position as president was far more secure. Having surpassed the hurdle of the MPR session, he no longer needed to be as wary of the military and other potential opponents. Moreover, he now had a large incentive to seek Soeharto's prosecution: if he disobeyed the MPR's explicit orders to investigate the former autocrat, he would have little chance of winning another term from the following year's MPR—which was likely to be far more reform-minded than the present one.

Habibie therefore took a tentative step in late November. His cabinet unveiled an official inventory of the Soeharto family's landholdings nationwide. Officials in the forestry ministry, the national land agency and the attorney general's office had contributed to the report, which revealed that Cendana-related companies owned land in 26 of Indonesia's 27 provinces. The aggregate holdings totalled more than nine million hectares, an area equivalent to the island of Java, or around 10 per cent of Indonesia's total land area (excluding territorial waters).[1] Forestry concessions represented the largest category of the Soeharto-related land-holdings, followed by plantations, industrial estates and tourist resorts.

The land inventory startled the nation, but not all of Habibie's lieu-tenants were acting in unison. While some officials were publicising Cendana's property assets, others were scrambling to downplay estimates of the family's wealth. Akbar Tandjung, speaking in his ministerial role as state secretary, told the nation that an investigation of domestic bank accounts in Soeharto's name found that the former president possessed $2.6 million, which Soeharto claimed were his life savings from a career as a public servant.[2] Tandjung brushed aside the possibility that Soeharto had stashed wealth abroad, in clandestine accounts or under the names of others (such as his offspring).

Meanwhile, Attorney General Andi Ghalib was investigating the management of seven charitable foundations that were headed by

Soeharto and had assets of around $530 million. Ghalib acknowledged that there was evidence of wrongdoing—such as the transfer of vast sums to private companies—but he claimed that the former president could not be held accountable because the foundations were not legally considered to be his personal property.[3]

The claims of Tandjung and Ghalib sparked outrage from the press and the students. Many Indonesians knew full well that estimates of Cendana's total wealth started at $4 billion and ran as high as $40 billion.[4] The US business magazine *Forbes* had recently stated that the family owned stakes in around 3000 Indonesian companies.[5] Yet the Soeharto family, comfortably shielded by the state's top government officials, obstinately denied the reports of its wealth.

In late November Tommy Soeharto lashed out at students who were accusing his father of corruption. 'Don't just talk!' the fiery Tommy barked at students, addressing them through a specially convened press conference. 'Don't just stage demonstrations or voice demands—prove [your allegations]!'[6] Tommy was echoing the sentiments of his older brother, who had earlier denounced those who were 'condemning and humiliating' his father. 'If people talk about the corrupt, collusive and nepotistic practices of my father's administration,' said Bambang, 'why don't they also attack similar practices found in the ruling administration of today?'[7] Soeharto himself had taken to the airwaves in September to deny that he had amassed wealth, and he had challenged his detractors to find any foreign bank accounts held in his name.[8] For their part, student protesters told the press that their resolve was only hardened by what they saw as Cendana's insolence.

Faced with public pressure and needing to build his popular support ahead of the parliamentary elections, Habibie made an attempt to break the deadlock on the Soeharto issue in late November. He contacted Buyung Nasution and asked for help.[9] Although he and the human rights lawyer had been longstanding political opponents, the two men actually had much in common: they were of similar age, they were both non-Javanese and they had both earned PhDs in continental Europe. Both had eccentric personalities and, perhaps most importantly, each tolerated the other's viewpoint—an uncommon trait in Indonesian politics.

At a Sunday brunch meeting on 29 November Habibie explained to Buyung that he wanted to establish an independent commission to investigate Soeharto and that he needed a credible and capable figure to head it. Buyung immediately declined the offer, but he agreed to advise Habibie on how to go about the chore properly. Undeterred, Habibie pressured Buyung to accept the post, vowing to meet whatever demands Buyung made.

Sensing that Habibie might finally be sincere about pursuing

Soeharto, Buyung became intrigued. The lawyer responded with an inventory of conditions: the commission must be small, it must be manned only by Buyung's handpicked people, and it must have real power. For instance, the commission needed to be able to issue subpoenas, seize evidence and punish perjury. In effect, it needed to be empowered to work above the attorney general's office—not as a mere advisor to it. Buyung Nasution was also well aware that the Swiss government had offered to assist in a search for any Soeharto-family wealth held in Swiss-domiciled banks, but only on the condition that the Indonesian government take the initiative by establishing the legal necessity for doing so.[10]

Habibie understood Buyung's demands and, much to the latter's surprise, agreed to them. Objections were raised by Habibie's aides, particularly Akbar Tandjung and Justice Minister Muladi, but after seeing that the president was serious, they too relented. A final point of concern was that the commission would make the administration look bad; Buyung therefore agreed that, while he would work independently, he would announce his final findings with Ghalib and Muladi at his side. But there were also objections from other quarters—such as Cendana.

Within hours of Habibie's first, private meeting with Buyung, members of Soeharto's family were aware of the plan to erect an independent commission. There was obviously a leak close to Habibie. The next day Soeharto's legal advisor, a little known attorney named Yohanes Yacob, publicly issued a brash threat. 'If Soeharto is tried, it's going to embroil the government, senior officials, former ministers and cronies— all of whom are suspected of accruing ill-gotten wealth—in messy litigation.'[11] If Soeharto were faulted for enacting presidential decrees which fostered corruption, Yacob vowed to implicate the ministers who drafted and helped implement the decrees. 'We have our trump cards ready,' warned Yacob.[12] Press reports claimed that Yacob had spent months compiling data on the personal wealth of active government officials, as well as stories of extra-marital affairs.[13]

Shortly after Yacob's threat, Habibie called Buyung and told him that the plan was off. In its place Habibie issued a presidential order to Ghalib to move forward with the investigation; this, in effect, sent the signal that nothing would be done. Despite the heavy public pressure on Habibie to prosecute Soeharto, the New Order system of Ruler's Law continued to function—in fact, it seemed to be working harder then ever to shield government officials from accountability and protect vested interests. But given President Habibie's apparent initial enthusiasm for the independent commission, the strange sequence of events left many wondering what had transpired behind closed doors.

More than two years later Ghalib stated in his autobiography that Wiranto intervened, blocking Habibie's plan to name Soeharto as a suspect.[14] Other reports supported Ghalib's assertion.[15] But if so, it remains unclear how Wiranto did this—whether it was simply by stating his objection, cajoling, or through more underhanded means. Although few drew the connection at the time, clues to the answer might have been apparent in events that were taking place in another far-flung corner of the archipelago: Kupang, the capital of East Nusatenggara.

Situated on the western half of the island of Timor, some 1900 kilometres southeast of Jakarta, Kupang is a provincial backwater that is home to around 300 000 residents, around 90 per cent of whom are Christian.[16] Beginning on 29 November—the day that Habibie decided to establish an independent commission, and one day before Yacob threatened blackmail—a mob tore through Kupang attacking mosques. The attacks were supposedly in retaliation for the targeting of churches in Jakarta's Ketapang riot the previous week.[17]

According to priests and government officials who witnessed the attacks, the mob consisted not of local Kupang residents but, rather, uniformed youths trucked in from outlying towns and points as far away as Dili, East Timor.[18] Although Kupang possessed a large contingent of security forces (the town was a base for military operations in East Timor), the anti-Muslim mob was able to rampage through town for two full days. Not only did security forces allow the mob free rein, but in some instances they reportedly protected it from local residents who tried to counterattack.[19] In total, the mob killed three, injured 27 and damaged over 100 buildings, including nine mosques.[20] The streets were finally brought under control on 2 December—after Habibie had scrapped the independent commission.

Even more so than other unexplained outbreaks of violence in November, the Kupang episode appeared to have been staged. Its pretence seemed hardly plausible: that remote Timorese would care so much about Jakarta's Ketapang riot stretched credulity—particularly since the news of the Ketapang riot was already a week old by the time the Kupang episode happened. Moreover, religious tensions in the West Timorese town were not considered particularly strained. As Nurcholish Madjid noted, when religious tensions erupt in Kupang they are typically between Catholics and Protestants—not Christians and the tiny Muslim minority.[21] In fact, Muslim leaders in Kupang later asserted that, when Muslims were attacked, many local Christians helped defend them against the unknown marauders.[22]

In a report made in December the Human Rights Commission cited indications that the Kupang riot was 'plotted by a third party so that it looked like an inter-religion conflict'.[23] Like the appearances of Paspampres, FPI and Ambonese *preman*, this would not be the last time that violent bands of rural West Timorese youths would be involved in an unexplained act of violence in Indonesia.

The Kupang riot was followed by yet more protests against Cendana and by more riots around the country, such as in Ujungpandang, South Sulawesi and Ciamis, West Java.[24] Then, at 5 a.m. on 1 January—only five hours into the new year—a medium-size explosion rocked Jalan Sabang in Central Jakarta. The blast occurred just outside a vacated department store that belonged to a major retail chain, Ramayana.[25]

Police investigators quickly produced a detailed explanation: the bombing arose from a land dispute in which one party wanted to acquire the land on which the Ramayana store stood; when they failed to do so, they sought revenge by bombing the location. The police also insinuated that two members of the marines were accomplices in the bombing.[26] In light of the incident in which a marine had been shot by police officers at Semanggi six weeks before, this allegation heightened the speculation that there was a rift between the police and the marines.

The police never found the guilty party, but there was ample reason to believe that the event did not, in fact, arise from a land dispute. Farther down the street from the Ramayana store, a bomb squad found two other explosive devices that had failed to detonate. Had all three bombs gone off at once, the damage would have affected far more than just the Ramayana store. Most of Jalan Sabang—a well-known commercial street in downtown Jakarta—would have been destroyed.[27]

Contrary to the prompt explanation put forth by police, the Jalan Sabang bombing seemed designed to sow terror. Over the course of the next month a host of downtown office buildings, malls and hotels received bomb threats. And on 8 January a riot in Karawang, 60 kilometres east of Jakarta, claimed 26 casualties, including two dead. The attention of Karawang police had been mysteriously diverted by a false report of a disturbance elsewhere, and local police officials asserted that military personnel had been involved in fomenting the riot.[28]

Strife was also erupting in a place far removed from Jakarta: on 19 January a severe riot between Christians and Muslims broke out in Maluku's capital of Ambon. Local police acknowledged that the violence had been started by the Pemuda Pancasila *preman* who had recently been shipped there from Jakarta, following the Ketapang riot.[29] Elsewhere, riots erupted simultaneously in Sumatera, Kalimantan, Sulawesi and Central Java.[30]

Meanwhile, the mounting regional violence coincided with increasing pressure in Jakarta for Soeharto's trial. Students waged incessant protests throughout December and January—and their foremost demand was the prosecution of the former president. Troops maintained a heavy defensive cordon in a 100 metre radius around the Soeharto-family compound on Jalan Cendana, but students launched repeated attacks on the position.[31] A clash on 9 January claimed 160 casualties.[32]

Some accepted the increased incidence of violence and the attacks on

Soeharto as being coincidental; others, however, believed otherwise. One was Abdurrahman Wahid.

Amid a worsening atmosphere in Jakarta in December 1998, Wahid determined that he would attempt to diffuse the tension. Having just recovered from a minor stroke in late October—his second in eighteen months—Wahid repeatedly admonished student protesters to cease their demonstrations and return to their books. Meanwhile, he commenced a series of controversial visits.

First, Wahid met Wiranto on 9 December, in part to discuss the general's plan to recruit, train and equip another 70 000 para-militaries to provide security for the election.[33] Following the debacle of using Islamic militias to defend the November MPR session, Wiranto's plan was roundly criticised. Wahid, however, said that 'after being assured that Wiranto would lead these units personally, I was able to rest easier'. He then urged NU youth to volunteer for Wiranto's units.[34] Next, on 12 December, Wahid met with Habibie at the president's residence. The following day, he made the first in a series of visits with Soeharto.

Among the nation's major popular leaders, Wahid was in the best position to approach Soeharto: he had lent his support to Golkar in the 1997 election and, more importantly, he had refrained from calling for Soeharto's resignation in May 1998. Wahid therefore received a cordial greeting from the former president when he arrived at the agreed-upon meeting place: the home of Bambang Soeharto. But Soeharto's grin did not tell the complete story—the former president used the occasion to send an ominous signal to Jakarta's political elite. Greeting the press at Soeharto's side was none other than Yorrys Raweyai, Pemuda Pancasila's *preman* boss.[35] By appearing with Raweyai, Soeharto was sending an explicit message: he was no longer president, but he still commanded formidable powers of coercion.

Wahid renewed his 'shuttle diplomacy' on 19 December. His first stop that day was at the Centre for Strategic and International Studies (CSIS), where he met former armed forces commander Benny Moerdani. As Soeharto's most trusted lieutenant throughout the late 1970s and 1980s, the Catholic general won political Islam's lasting enmity for brutally repressing Muslim leaders. He then fell out with Soeharto after criticising the president's penchant for indulging his children, but since Soeharto's resignation the two men had apparently reconciled their differences: Moerdani was known to have frequently visited Soeharto in late 1998. Now he was apparently offering Wahid advice on how to handle the former president, whom Moerdani understood as well as anyone. Immediately following his one and a half hour meeting with Moerdani, Wahid proceeded to Soeharto's residence on Jalan Cendana. Again he was greeted by Yorrys Raweyai.

Although he refused to repeat what he discussed with Soeharto, Wahid's comments to the press following the visit left little to the imagination: 'Soeharto still has many loyal supporters—even among those in power.'[36] Given Raweyai's presence, there could be little doubt that this included elements of the military, which was close to Raweyai and Pemuda Pancasila. Whether Wiranto was counted among them was less clear. Wahid did, however, claim that 'angry supporters of Soeharto' were responsible for the violence of the preceding weeks.[37] He said: 'Soeharto did not order them, but they took their own initiative. If their idol, Soeharto, tells them to desist, they'll stop. That's why we must engage Soeharto.'[38] Later Wahid implicitly accused Raweyai of provoking the severe Christian–Muslim violence in Ambon.[39]

Wahid's seemingly cordial meetings with Soeharto—combined with his newfound friendliness toward Wiranto and Habibie—earned the NU leader sharp rebukes. Some called him 'pro-status quo', while others criticised him for abandoning his principles and excessively pursuing romantic Javanese ideals of social harmony.[40] Others alleged that Wahid was, in effect, running for president; however, given the NU leader's eyesight, which by this time was nearly gone, few believed that Wahid could be a serious contender for high political office. Instead, he was expected to use his influence to act as a 'king-maker'.

The next round of shuttle diplomacy began on 24 January, when Wahid persuaded four other popular opposition leaders to meet with Wiranto and Yudhoyono at army headquarters. Present at the opening of the meeting were Megawati, Sultan Hamengkubuwono X and Nurcholish Madjid. Amien Rais arrived late, but abruptly confronted Wiranto upon entering the room. Referring to the recent spate of violence that the military had failed to stop or even explain, Rais called on Wiranto 'to instruct the military to apprehend all those whose hands have been bloodied, so that the public's faith in the security forces can be restored'.[41] Rais was insinuating that the military had been condoning the violence, but Wiranto pleaded innocence: 'Who doesn't want to bring the perpetrators to justice?'[42]

Three days later Wahid shuttled back to Jalan Cendana to meet Soeharto for the third time. The NU cleric beseeched the former president to tell his loyalists to cease fomenting violence. Wahid specifically referred to the particularly bloody strife taking place in Ambon.[43] Just 30 minutes after the end of the closed-door meeting, Wahid delivered a forceful message to a host of politicians and Islamic figures who had assembled at the home of a well-connected businessman.[44] The gathering included Nurcholish, Buyung Nasution, Pan officials and leaders from several new Islamic parties. Wahid told the assembled crowd to cease pressuring Cendana and cease trying to remove the military from politics. 'We have to be realistic,' Wahid stressed. 'Soeharto still commands the loyalty of many people in high places.'[45]

Wahid's message received relatively little attention because the public was beginning to grow weary of his enigmatic behaviour. The NU leader continued to equivocate about whom his new party, PKB, would support for the presidency, and he had hurt his credibility when he wrongly accused Adi Sasono of helping to perpetrate the Banyuwangi killings. But with regard to Soeharto, Wahid was not indulging in mere speculation. The long series of closed-door meetings with Wiranto, Moerdani and Soeharto himself had led Wahid to a conclusion from which he would never depart: efforts to challenge Soeharto would only elicit violent reprisals.

Privately, a high-level official in the Habibie administration asserted that the increase in violence around the country was no coincidence— instead, Soeharto loyalists were deliberately fomenting the strife.[46] Several press reports also cited anonymous government sources who made the same claim.[47] The perpetrators of the violence, said these sources, were deliberately targeting communities with deep ethnic or religious rifts that could be exploited and inflamed. In some places, such as in Maluku and Poso, Central Sulawesi, conditions were fertile for prolonged strife. Elsewhere, such as North Sumatera, provocation failed to take root and small-scale riots remained isolated events.

Mob violence is an unwieldy instrument to use for political ends, but it nonetheless could have served several aims. For instance, outbreaks of unrest served to distract public attention from demands for Soeharto's trial. Riots could also be used to intimidate or coerce government officials. More generally, widespread unrest could discredit or possibly even de- stabilise Habibie's government. Entrenched interests had a huge incentive to cling to power—and an even greater incentive to avoid defeat.

Some suggested an analogy to the legends in *wayang* operas, whereby deposed kings would sow destruction to ensure that their own downfall was accompanied by that of the entire kingdom. The royal sultans of Solo were named 'Pakubuwono', or 'nail of the universe'. Figuratively, the name implied that if the nail came loose the universe would unravel.

Wahid concluded that 'to further the cause of reform, we must focus on carrying out free and fair elections'. It was becoming increasingly clear that, to confront entrenched Soeharto-era interests, Indonesia's reform leaders would first need to secure an irrefutable popular mandate. This, in turn, meant that Indonesia's future hinged on the 7 June parliamentary polls. It was clear to all that, in Indonesia's first free election in over four decades, the stakes would be exceedingly high.

14

OLIGARCHY OF THE PARTY BOSSES

fter nearly five months of work, a blueprint for Indonesia's new democracy was finally unveiled in November 1998. A team of seven esteemed political scientists had produced three draft laws that promised to fundamentally reconfigure Indonesia's electoral system. This 'Team Seven', under the leadership of Ryaas Rasyid, was working under the auspices of Syarwan Hamid's ministry of home affairs. Ironically, this was the same ministry that had been responsible for engineering the long succession of lopsided elections in the past—but under Hamid the Byzantine ministry was rapidly changing.

Hamid had little chance of reaching any higher office, and people close to him claimed that he was genuinely concerned about atoning for his past actions as Soeharto's kaster in 1996. Ushering in a healthy democratic system was one way in which Hamid could alter the historical record on his career in public office. Consequently, Rasyid and his six handpicked academics—who included the astute 'young Turk' of Indonesian political science, Andi Mallarangeng—enjoyed free rein to draft the best electoral laws they could.

When Team Seven presented the results of its work to President Habibie in a cabinet meeting, State Secretary Akbar Tandjung voiced ardent objections. The proposed system departed too radically from past precedent. Although he need not have said as much out loud, the state secretary objected because a host of features in the drafts would create difficulties for him in his other job: chair of Golkar. Habibie was therefore required to decide between the drafts recommended by his home affairs minister, Hamid, and the objections raised by his state secretary (and chair of his own political party), Tandjung.

For a president seeking re-election in less than a year, it might have made sense for Habibie to defer to his party chair and order Hamid to make changes to the draft bills. But this was the *reformasi* era, and it would not do for Habibie to win another term through an electoral system which was seen to have been rigged in his favour. In any event, Habibie knew that after his executive branch passed the draft bills on to parliament, the bills might be amended and rewritten until they were virtually unrecognisable. Tandjung himself, as chair of the largest party in parliament, would have a central role to play in that process.

Finally, Habibie had yet another consideration: to win another term he would probably need support from other parties in addition to Golkar. The party that seemed to be most solidly behind him—even more solidly, in fact, than Golkar itself—was PPP, the 'United Development Party'. Because PPP was striving to project a reformist image, it was likely to fight Tandjung and Golkar on a number of controversial issues in the political laws. It was better for Habibie to take a 'pro-reform' stance that would please PPP and others, rather than an 'anti-reform' stance that would satisfy only Golkar. In the end, Habibie overruled Tandjung and endorsed Hamid's drafts. Soon after, parliament's working committees began picking the draft bills apart, piece by piece.

When parliament received Hamid's proposed political laws a number of parliamentarians recognised the apparent contradiction in their position: a parliament handpicked by Soeharto—and dominated by Golkar—was preparing to write political laws that would determine the framework for democracy in Indonesia. To deflect accusations that they were preparing to rig the system in favour of the 'status quo', parliamentarians invited comments from academics, civic leaders and, most significantly, the newly formed, mass-based opposition parties that were not represented in parliament.

For years Megawati had been strenuously advocating the direct election of Indonesia's president, rather than his or her election through the elitist MPR. Only by winning a majority of the votes of Indonesia's 100 million or more voters could a president claim to have a popular mandate and, therefore, unequivocal political legitimacy. Megawati professed a strong belief in this principle—except when it came to deciding on an election system for Indonesia's parliamentary representatives. Rather than supporting the direct election of parliamentarians—which would have been consistent with her support for the direct election of the president—Megawati opted for a much less democratic system.

By far the most fundamental issue at stake in the political laws was the mechanism for electing parliamentarians. In a direct system, voters vote for an individual candidate to represent their district.[1] In a proportional system, however, they merely vote for a party. A party's seat total in a given district is proportional to its share of the total vote tally: for example, if a party wins 20 per cent of the vote in a district with ten seats, it wins two seats. The party leadership then determines which individuals will fill the seats won. The difference between these two systems, therefore, is profound: in a direct system representatives are directly accountable to their constituents, whereas in a proportional system they are accountable almost exclusively to their party leaders.

Because she was not a member of parliament, Megawati had no formal influence over the choice of an electoral system; nonetheless, she could have used her popularity to highlight the issue, mobilise public pressure and influence parliament from outside. Promoting a direct electoral system was of paramount importance as it would have furthered democratisation and the spirit of *reformasi*; however, Megawati was content to go along with a proportional system.

Megawati justified her preference by claiming that Golkar would enjoy certain advantages in a direct system. During the New Order, only Golkar had been permitted to establish offices below the district level, and it was believed that the preponderance of village heads—who played pivotal roles in local politics—were Golkar sympathisers. It was feared that, on election day, these village heads would use their overweening authority to ensure that their entire villages voted for the ruling party. Megawati ostensibly wanted to avoid clashing with Golkar at this grassroots level; in a proportional system, voters would only choose between party symbols and therefore the campaigning would primarily take place at the national level.

Ironically, Megawati's fears about Golkar's grassroots strength were unfounded. Golkar itself was not confident about campaigning at the local level and therefore it, too, opted for a proportional system. In fact, most major party leaders, including Wahid and Rais, quietly expressed their preference for a proportional system—even though, all the while, they vowed to channel Indonesians' 'aspirations' for reform through democratic elections, public accountability, people's sovereignty and so on.[2] But behind the rhetoric, Megawati, Wahid and Rais preferred an electoral system that aggrandised the power of the party boss. A proportional system vested them with far more leverage over their party followers and parliamentary delegations.

When Ryaas Rasyid's Team Seven, working within the home affairs ministry, submitted its proposed Election Law to parliament, the draft provided for a mixed system. Around 84 per cent of parliament's seats would be elected through direct voting, while the remaining 16 per cent would be determined through the proportional distribution of 'lost votes'.[3] This was similar to the system used in Germany, Japan, Taiwan, Thailand and the Philippines. Parliament scrapped this proposal in favour of a proportional system, but at Team Seven's insistence one modest element of a direct system was retained: parties were required, before election day, to assign candidates to specific districts and to post rosters of these assignments at polling booths.

In theory, these candidate rosters would allow voters to know who would be representing them if a given party won their district's seat. In practice, parties blithely ignored the law. Rather than adhering to their candidate rosters in the post-election period, party leaders inserted individuals in whichever seats they saw fit.

More than any other decision made in the drafting of Indonesia's new political laws, the choice of a proportional system, rather than a direct system, helped determine the outcome of the election before the voting ever took place. Whatever vote breakdown was produced on election day, the choice of electoral systems ensured that political power would remain firmly in the hands of the Jakarta elite rather than directly elected representatives accountable to their voters. Parliament would be filled by political hacks serving their party bosses—not representatives serving the long-disenfranchised mass of ordinary Indonesians.

While the choice of a proportional system was the most portentous part of the political laws debate, it was also one of the easiest decisions for the Soeharto-era parliament to agree upon. A far more contentious issue was whether civil servants should be allowed to join political parties. Golkar had won past elections by relying on what Jakarta's politicos aptly dubbed 'Tim Buldoser': the team consisting of the party, the military and, perhaps most crucially, the bureaucracy. There were about 5.1 million civil servants in Indonesia (4.1 million in government departments and around one million in state-owned enterprises).[4] In accordance with the New Order's so-called 'mono-loyalty' policy, all civil servants were members of Golkar.

Team Seven's draft Political Party Law required that all civil servants remain politically neutral. Those who wanted to become members or leaders of a political party would have to first retire or at least take leave of absence. Of course, given the state of Indonesia's court system, it would be difficult to enforce a ban on political activity by civil servants in the lower echelons of the bureaucracy. But at the higher ranks the proposed ban would devastate Golkar. Some 10 000 of Golkar's senior officials, or 'functionaries', also served as high-level bureaucrats. Some of the party's most influential figures derived their influence from their positions in the cabinet. Most notable among these was Akbar Tandjung himself—the state secretary who simultaneously served as Golkar chair.

In the debates within parliament on the crucial civil servants question, Golkar was alone. PPP and the tiny PDI faction opposed the measure—as did the military, to the surprise of many. This was one instance in which Wiranto stayed faithful to his pledge to keep the military equidistant from all political parties in the *reformasi* era. The military doubted Golkar's vote-winning potential in the upcoming parliamentary elections. At this point it was in Wiranto's interest to remain neutral—or at least appear to remain neutral—until the results of elections shed more light on the political landscape. Thus, with even its erstwhile ally, the military, calling for civil servants' neutrality, Golkar was cornered.

Naturally, Tandjung was panicking. 'Forbidding civil servants from expressing their political aspirations through a specific political party,' the Golkar chair pontificated, 'is an egregious violation of their human rights.' The issue was of such importance that even the normally reasonable-sounding Marzuki Darusman was forced to echo Tandjung's awkward argument: Indonesia had signed the workers' rights conventions of the International Labour Organization (ILO) which, he said, prohibited Indonesia from enforcing civil servants' neutrality.[5] 'Imagine that that could come out of Golkar!' fumed Mallarangeng. 'After 32 years of raping the human rights of civil servants of Indonesia by the mono-loyalty policy, now they are using the ILO's human rights convention to argue their case! It's B.S.!'[6]

Golkar's overwhelming majority in parliament could allow it, in theory, to ride roughshod over its opponents. But not only would that contravene Javanese norms of consensus, it would also create a public relations fiasco—Golkar desperately needed to begin projecting a reformist image to keep pace with the mood of the nation. And if it pushed the civil servants issue through and then performed well in the elections, the party's detractors would undoubtedly cry foul.

Tandjung was desperate to find a solution. He could not tolerate losing the civil servants, yet neither could he override his opposition. He therefore devised a tactic: lest the deadlock drag on, he proposed that the nettlesome issue be dealt with in a separate piece of legislation, a Civil Servants Law, to be considered at a later date.[7] But Tandjung's opponents were not so easily misled: there was no guarantee that such a law would be submitted to parliament and passed before the June elections. They rejected his offer and the debate remained deadlocked.

Indonesia's election schedule had initially assumed that the pivotal political laws would be passed during December, but the MPR had moved the date back to 28 January. This allowed a scant four months in which to plan one of the largest democratic transitions in world history. Thus with only two weeks remaining before the end-January deadline—and with parliament set to recess for a full week to celebrate the Muslim holiday of Lebaran—Mallarangeng warned that the civil servants deadlock might delay, and even derail, the entire election process.[8] This triggered alarms in Jakarta. And in parliament, Golkar finally gained the upper hand.

PPP's leaders agreed to a regulation that made it seem as if they had won the debate: civil servants were required to take a temporary leave of absence in order to be active in a political party. The regulation's fine print, however, stipulated that the civil servants need not report their political activities until three months after the regulation took effect. With elections just over four months away, civil servants still had ample time to help Golkar. And if there were any delays in issuing the regulation (which was put not in the political laws but in a presidential decree), the civil servants might stay active through early June. Golkar had prevailed.

Meanwhile, another issue was proving almost as troublesome to resolve as the civil servants issue. This was the number of parliamentary seats to be reserved for the military. The MPR had already determined that the military would retain seats in parliament—contrary to the insistent demands of student protesters and pro-reform activists—but how many was to be determined by parliament. The military had held a 15 per cent share of the previous parliament, but Wiranto recognised that he needed to make a concession. As a gesture towards *reformasi* he indicated a willingness to see the military's quota reduced to 10 per cent. PPP, however, was adamant that in the post-Soeharto era the military should be afforded no more than two per cent of parliament's seats. Golkar recommended 5 per cent.

After prolonged wrangling over the tortuous logic used to justify various percentages, parliament finally agreed to 7.5 per cent, or 38 seats in a 500-member chamber.[9] The agreement attracted considerable fanfare —so much, in fact, that the military's parliamentary faction generally came to be seen as its primary source of political influence. Wiranto and his staff were happy to foster this impression. They trumpeted the fact that they had allowed their parliamentary allocation to be halved—the implication being that the military now possessed only half as much political influence. The truth, however, was different.

Compared to its parliamentary role, the military wielded far more political influence through *kekaryaanisasi*, the system whereby officers are seconded to civil service posts. These include cabinet positions, Supreme Court seats, provincial gubernatorial posts, district *bupati* posts and executive positions in state-owned enterprises. In 1995 there had been around 6000 active personnel serving in such posts, plus an even greater number of pensioned officers who, though retired, typically remained subservient to military headquarters.[10] But even the influence wielded through *kekaryaanisasi* was eclipsed by the territorial system.

The army's territory-based organisational system made it resemble a force that was occupying its own country. From the two-star generals commanding regional garrisons to the sergeants assigned to individual villages, the army maintained an influential physical presence at virtually every administrative level of the state.[11] Territorial commands were the most coveted positions for young officers, and territorial commanders were often more powerful, in practice, than their civilian counterparts.[12] But in public discussions about the military's controversial socio-political role, the fanfare about parliamentary seats typically distracted attention from *kekaryaanisasi* and the territorial system. The controversy over the military's seats also deflected attention from a larger issue: the number of appointed seats in the MPR.

Soeharto had controlled previous MPR votes by reserving more than half the seats for appointees from the military, regional representatives and 'functional groups'.[13] Team Seven had proposed limiting the latter two categories of non-elected members to 21 per cent of the full MPR, but parliament expanded this to 29 per cent. Taken together with the appointed military seats, this meant that a full third of the MPR would be non-elected.[14] Moreover, parliament failed to clarify the process for selecting the non-elected regional and functional group representatives—which created ample reason to fear trickery and money politics. If Golkar and the military used their combined might to secure control of these 238 non-elected seats in the 700-member MPR, they could then secure a clear majority in the presidential election with the addition of only 113 of the elected seats—or about 25 per cent of the seats at stake in the 7 June elections.

The election laws therefore made Indonesia's political outlook highly unpredictable. There would be a large number of parties taking part in parliamentary elections, there were no reliable polls to gauge voter predilections and, in any event, the outcome of the subsequent presidential election hinged on the process used for selecting 200 non-elected MPR members. And complicating the picture was the fact that, once the full MPR was formed, there would be nothing stopping individual MPR members from breaking ranks with their parties and forming ad hoc alliances with other factions for the purpose of the one presidential vote. But despite these complexities Megawati remained supremely confident that she would emerge as Indonesia's next president.

In fact, the only true winners of Indonesia's electoral contest would be the party bosses. The election laws passed by parliament represented an improvement over their New Order precedents, but they nonetheless stopped far short of vesting the political system with true democratic accountability. A third of the MPR would be non-elected, while the proportional system rendered the remaining two-thirds loyal only to their party bosses, rather than to voters. In effect, the autocracy of Soeharto would be replaced by an oligarchy of the party bosses.

In early 1999 Indonesia's most popular party leader was clearly Megawati. 'Mega mania' swept the country as the daughter of Soekarno campaigned for PDI Perjuangan. Over half of Indonesia's population were too young to have experienced her father's rule: these young people knew that Soekarno had been brilliant and inspirational, but they forgot that he had also been reckless and ruthless. They knew that he had won independence and had united a disparate archipelago, but they forgot that he had fostered despotism, deprivation and communist hysteria. For young Indonesians weary of Soeharto's cynical pragmatism, Soekarno symbolised an Indonesian golden age which, they believed, his eldest daughter would restore. Megawati lacked the oratorical flair of her father, yet her beneficent image, magical pedigree and ten-year track record of stoic opposition to Soeharto were more than enough to captivate supporters.

Abdurrahman Wahid was the only other Indonesian who could even approach Megawati's popularity—but his appeal was tightly confined to Java, particularly the NU stronghold of East Java. Like Megawati, Wahid also had an exalted lineage, as the grandson of NU founder Hasyim Ashari. And the two leaders had much else in common: antipathy toward political Islam; dissident status (notwithstanding Wahid's capitulation to Golkar in 1997); and, perhaps most importantly, a common Javanese outlook. Wahid had spent some years studying in the Middle East, but otherwise neither he nor Megawati were particularly cosmopolitan. Like Soeharto, both were heavily imbued with Javanese concepts of hierarchy and both believed strongly in mysticism. With these traits in common, Megawati and Wahid were a comfortable pair: their joint public appearances were typically marked by private jests and hearty laughter. Their friendship, however, was also grounded on serious considerations of practical politics.

Java had long been characterised as being divided into two main 'cultural streams': orthodox (or *santri*) Muslims and nominal (or *abangan*) Muslims. In addition to their different attitudes toward Islam, the two broad groups possessed deeper cultural differences that had, at times, given rise to violence. As a 20-year-old, Wahid had been traumatised by the involvement of NU groups in the anti-communist pogrom of 1965–66— a pogrom that largely took place along the lines of the *santri-abangan* divide. NU and other Islamic organisations generally drew their followers from the ranks of *santri*, while Communist Party members were more likely to come from the *abangan* fold.

Plagued by guilt for NU's actions, Wahid seemed determined to make amends—or at least prevent a repeat of the catastrophic cleavage between NU Muslims and secular parties. In 1999 the largest secular party by far was PDI Perjuangan, which seemed to be drawing the bulk of its support from *abangan*. Wahid was determined to build bridges between Java's two cultural streams and thereby create an indomitable political following. There was plenty to unite the two streams. *Santri* and *abangan* alike were eager for change, and Wahid and Megawati were the most widely known figures opposing the ruling party, Golkar.

At the same time, both Wahid and Megawati wanted to stem the influence of political Islam, as represented by modernist parties such as PPP, PBB and a host of others. Thus Indonesia's political map could not be aligned on a linear spectrum. Rather than a binary affair between the 'status quo' and 'reform', the election would be a tripartite contest between the secular-nationalists, political Islam, and the incumbents.

In the early stages Wahid was confident that the vast bulk of the Indonesian electorate would reject not only Golkar but political Islam as well. He expected a landslide victory for PDI Perjuangan and his own party, PKB. 'These two parties,' he predicted in an October 1998 interview, 'will, together, take around 70 per cent of the votes in the parliamentary elections.' His calculations were simple. Citing Indonesians' hatred of Golkar, he predicted that the ruling party would win no more than 5 per cent of the vote.[15] He then presumed that Islamic-oriented parties such as PPP, Pan and PBB would combine to win no more than a quarter of the electorate. That left 70 per cent for PDI Perjuangan and PKB to share between them.

'Such a wide margin of victory,' Wahid joked, 'actually isn't healthy.'[16] Wahid believed that he and Megawati had the presidency locked up— barring fraud or money politics. He vowed to back Megawati for president, though he claimed that, in the event that something prevented her from serving, Megawati would instruct her party to put him in the presidency instead, regardless of his physical disabilities.[17] Even though he had ex-perienced two strokes, suffered diabetes and lost his eyesight, Wahid declared his readiness to serve as president if he was 'called upon to do so'. Few took him seriously at the time, especially as it became increasingly clear that his electoral calculations were far too simplistic—and overly optimistic.

Before Wahid had even proposed his vaunted alliance with Megawati, complications were already arising. The first sign of trouble came in early October, just after Megawati's massive rally in Bali to mark the official launch of PDI Perjuangan. Megawati was one-quarter Balinese and the densely populated island of three million Hindus was her foremost strong-hold. Nearly every village was plastered with banners and placards in red, the colour symbolising secular-nationalism and the official hue of PDI Perjuangan. The party congress was therefore a resounding success—until Megawati attended prayers in a Hindu temple.

Balinese ceremonies are open to people of any faith, and Megawati— herself a Muslim—approached the ceremony as a typical campaign event. But after newspapers ran photos of her wearing a Balinese dress and kneeling in front of Hindu idols, Megawati's opponents leapt into action. First off the mark was the caustic and combative A.M. Saefuddin, PPP's most vocal Islamist.

Years of loyalty to Habibie within Icmi had won the German-trained agronomist a seat in the cabinet as food minister. After only a few weeks in the new job, Saefuddin sparked controversy by suggesting that looters of rice mills should not be faulted so long as they took 'less than 5 per cent' of inventories.[18] But the comment that won him even more opprobrium was delivered in mid-October. 'A Hindu,' said Saefuddin, pointing to a photo of Megawati's visit to the Balinese temple, 'is not fit to serve as president of the world's largest Muslim country.'[19]

Saefuddin was being snide—and Megawati ignored him—but similar attacks soon followed. The food minister had kicked off an Islamist campaign to portray Megawati as 'religiously incorrect'. The PDI Perjuangan candidate should have recognised the serious threat that this posed. Islamists feared that if Megawati gained power she would systematically disenfranchise Islamic leaders while promoting non-Muslims. This is precisely what her father had done as president, and modern-day Islamic leaders noted with alarm that Megawati was following Soekarno's example.

The PDI Perjuangan leader insisted on allying closely with religious minorities—be they Protestant, Catholic, Hindu or Buddhist. She engendered near-fanatic support in non-Muslim regions such as Bali, North Sulawesi and Flores. She specifically appointed a Christian Ambonese, Alex Litaay, as PDI Perjuangan's secretary-general, a crucial organisational post. The party's more seasoned politicians objected to Litaay's inexperience, but Megawati wanted to demonstrate her solidarity with marginalised religious and ethnic groups. From the viewpoint of Indonesia's Islamists, there seemed to be little point in supporting Megawati's quest for the presidency: she seemed unlikely to grant them any more access to power than had Soeharto—and even less than that promised by Habibie.

From the standpoint of electoral politics, Megawati's strategy made little sense. Megawati was courting religious minorities who accounted for a mere 14 per cent of Indonesia's population. Of the Muslims who accounted for the remaining 86 per cent, a substantial portion was disturbed by Megawati's proximity to non-Muslims. Although she was Muslim, she did little to publicly demonstrate her faith. By simply appearing in mosques, visiting key Islamic groups or performing the *haj* to Mecca, Megawati might have assuaged many sceptical Muslim voters.

Moreover, a strategy of portraying Islamic piety was essentially 'risk-free': non-Muslims would support Megawati regardless of her outward image, simply because they had no other reformist, secular alternatives from which to choose. Megawati could easily afford to court Islamic groups without losing non-Muslim votes—but she refused to adjust her approach. It was unclear whether she was adhering to principle or simply bumbling. Either way, a sizeable portion of the electorate was being rubbed the wrong way.

One of the first signs of Muslim aversion to Megawati emerged when 2000 leaders from every significant Islamic organisation in Indonesia gathered in Jakarta in November. The Islamic Clerics Conference marked the first time in Indonesia's history that such a wide array of Muslim interests were able to unite in one spot—infighting or Soeharto's meddling had repeatedly frustrated past attempts. The clerics sought to express their unity as a step towards reversing decades of perceived discrimination against political Islam. But some of those in attendance also wanted to deliver a calculated blow to Megawati: they proposed that the conference definitively state that Islam forbids a woman from serving as head of state.

A few of the clerics who backed the anti-Megawati ruling genuinely believed that certain traditions of the Prophet Muhammad forbid females from ruling over Muslim communities. Others simply didn't trust or didn't like Megawati and were willing to use the decree as a way to lash out at their political rival. In effect, the clerics in the latter category were demonstrating their willingness to manipulate religious authority for tactical political ends. By the end of the conference the proposed rule was voted down—but only by a slim margin.

Less than a month after the conference Megawati's Islamist rivals tried another stratagem. Rather than targeting Megawati directly, they focused instead on one of her closest advisors, Maj. Gen. (ret.) Theo Syafie. Syafie had already engendered considerable controversy when ardent pro-democracy activists decried Megawati's willingness to accept one of Soeharto's former generals into the pro-reform party.[20] Now Syafie was attracting criticism from Islamists as well. A fervent Protestant, Syafie was accused of spreading anti-Muslim hatred in speeches he delivered to church audiences. An alleged recording of Syafie's speeches circulated Jakarta, and when the venerable Islamic scholar Nurcholish Madjid heard it he declared the evidence irrefutable.

But Syafie's opponents went one step further: they claimed that Syafie's anti-Muslim diatribes were responsible for inciting the Christian mob in Kupang to attack mosques and other Muslim buildings on 30 November. The claim was obviously contrived. As mentioned earlier, there was strong evidence that Soeharto loyalists fomented the Kupang violence—not Syafie.

In fact, there was ample reason to believe that the true perpetrators of the Kupang violence were also responsible for blaming Syafie. In so doing they deflected suspicion away from themselves while casting aspersions on their chief enemy: Megawati. This type of tactic, according to one seasoned Indonesian politician, was the hallmark of Feisal Tanjung—the Soeharto loyalist who was a former military chief, a self-professed Islamist and a schemer with a penchant for furtive tactics.[21] However, no direct evidence of Tanjung's involvement ever emerged.

B y the start of 1999 the criticism of Megawati and PDI Perjuangan was taking a toll. With Islamists harping on the importance of Islamic credentials on one hand, and with Megawati continuing to consort with non-Muslim interests on the other, two parties were stuck in the middle: Amien Rais's Pan and Wahid's PKB. Rais was attempting to bridge his natural Muhammadiyah base of support with a more broad-based, liberal constituency—but the increasingly acerbic tone of the religious debate was polarising the two sides of his party. Wahid, meanwhile, was experiencing even greater difficulties.

PKB was the party officially endorsed by the NU leadership, but this by no means meant that NU's leadership was uniform in its political outlook. Several NU leaders openly rebelled against Wahid and established their own parties.[22] The most significant of these parties, PKU, was lead by Yusuf Hasyim. Although he was Wahid's paternal uncle, Hasyim had long been Wahid's bitter rival for control over NU, and he had allied closely with Habibie through Icmi in the early 1990s. There was little doubt that Hasyim would throw his new party's support behind the incumbent president; whether he would be followed by large numbers of NU voters was more difficult to predict.

But even more serious than these defections were the deep splits emerging within PKB itself. The divisive issue was Megawati. On the surface, the debate was about gender; underneath, the tensions arose from memories of Soekarno and worries about Megawati's proximity to Christians. NU clerics from Central Java tended to be more moderate in their outlook than those from the extreme eastern portion of East Java. Thus, while the former held a series of seminars and congresses that implicitly supported Megawati, the latter did the opposite, vehemently maintaining that Indonesia's next president must be a male.

Facing a large-scale rebellion within his own flock, Wahid began waffling about his party's alliance with Megawati. His support for her presidential campaign seemingly varied with his mood at the moment: one day he would reaffirm it, the next day deny it. On various occasions he also mentioned alternative candidates as compromise figures; chief among these was Yogyakarta's sultan, Hamengkubuwono X. His father, Hamengkubuwono IX, had served as vice-president under Soeharto. The sultan was revered by millions on Java, and he had kept a relatively low profile throughout the New Order. He did, however, serve as the honorary president-commissioner of Syamsul Nursalim's BDNI, the second largest consumer of Bank Indonesia liquidity credits.

That Wahid was seriously contemplating the candidacy of the sultan was a sign of how desperate Megawati's plight had already become. Megawati had always had her share of political enemies, but she enjoyed such a massive advantage over other politicians in the post-Soeharto era that there was really no reason for her to lose a democratic presidential election. Yet even her closest ally, Abdurrahman Wahid, was already equivocating at an early stage of the campaign.

Several efforts were made by lower level party officials from PDI Perjuangan, PKB and Pan to join Indonesia's three main opposition figures in a united front against Golkar, but the efforts consistently failed.

Rivalries between the party leaders—combined with Islamic-secular rifts within both Pan and PKB—rendered unity impossible. Indonesia's political landscape was a fragmented mess in which anything might transpire. To make matters worse for Megawati, the electoral system produced by parliament featured a built-in regional imbalance—which favoured Golkar at her expense.

G olkar expected to fare poorly in Java. The party's own leaders freely admitted as much. Compared to the Outer Islands, voters were more sophisticated and better informed in Java, and therefore anti-Golkar sentiment ran deeper on this island of 115 million inhabitants. Moreover, Golkar's competitors were strong in Java: whereas new parties could canvass the densely populated island with relative ease, reaching the scattered inhabitants of the remote Outer Islands was a different matter altogether. Only Golkar (and, to a far lesser extent, PPP) had organis-ational structures that extended to the distant nooks and crannies of the vast archipelago.

Another consideration pertained to fraud. While new opposition parties had difficulty reaching remote Outer Island locations, so too did election monitors. In Java, Golkar officials would be hardpressed to use the dirty tactics employed by Tim Buldoser in past elections, as the electorate would be vigilant, the polling stations would be crowded and university-based monitors would be in close proximity. In the Outer Islands, however, none of these conditions would prevail. Polling stations would be smaller, more widely dispersed and therefore more difficult to monitor.

Poverty was also a factor, especially in the eastern provinces. More than a few voters who were trapped in grinding poverty would be willing to sell their votes. Where bribery failed, coercion could sometimes be used: many impoverished villagers were at the mercy of the local civil service—usually dominated by Golkar. Various government agents might be responsible for furnishing agricultural inputs, extending subsidised credit, buying farm produce or maintaining basic infrastructure. All these functions could be used for political ends. A remote village that failed to deliver its votes to Golkar might, for example, see the one vital road linking it to the outside world fall into disrepair and become impassable.

The Golkar-led parliament had produced a political system that favoured their own party's strengths: votes in the Outer Islands, where Golkar was strongest, mattered more than votes in Java, where Megawati and Wahid were strongest. The newly made political laws provided for parliament's 462 elected seats to be broken down equally between Java and the Outer Islands—even though the country's population breakdown between the two regions was 59 per cent to 41 per cent, respectively.

This 'regional imbalance' was even more skewed for the MPR, where the members of parliament were augmented by regional representatives.

Each province would send five regional representatives to the MPR, and the Outer Islands possessed 22 of Indonesia's 27 provinces. In total, therefore, seats from the Outer Islands would constitute 49 per cent of the new MPR's 700 seats, whereas seats from Java would form only 36 per cent (with the balance held by 'regionally neutral' representatives such as the military and functional groups).[23]

It was not necessarily 'wrong' that the electoral system should be skewed in favour of the Outer Islands—in fact, Java's historic dominance over the Outer Island regions could be cited as a good reason for giving those regions more say in government. But parliament almost certainly produced the '50/50' electoral system with practical political consider-ations in mind. The decision was also kept out of the limelight, such that there was little public discussion of an issue that would significantly affect the election's outcome. PDI Perjuangan officials grumbled about the structure, but did little to attract public scrutiny.[24]

Thus Golkar enjoyed a built-in electoral advantage, but the ruling party also had its share of challenges. One was the need to recast itself in a more reformist image. Another was to find a viable presidential candidate.

B y early January Habibie had made it clear that he was intent on run-ning for another term in office. But at the same time Akbar Tandjung was beginning to equivocate about whom Golkar would nominate as its presidential candidate. This was becoming increasingly embarrassing for Habibie. After having gone to such great lengths to ensure that the pivotal post of Golkar chair went to a trusted ally, Tandjung was now wavering.

The crafty party chair had ample reason for betraying Habibie: Golkar faced an uphill battle in the elections, and Habibie's past—combined with his inability to prosecute Soeharto or account for recent atrocities—was too heavy a burden for Golkar to carry. The party's best hope was to find a more inspiring candidate—although who that might be still remained unclear. But Tandjung undoubtedly had more than just his party's interests at stake; if Habibie was indeed destined for defeat, Tandjung's best chance for surviving into the post-Habibie era was to help defeat Habibie.

Faced with Tandjung's possible defection, Habibie did not remain passive. He knew that many of the Golkar veterans surrounding Tandjung resented the sudden ascendancy of Adi Sasono. A newcomer to party politics, Sasono had been catapulted into Golkar's highest tier, the executive board, and was trying to steer the party in a more populist, Islamist direction.

More than ideology, however, the issue that seemed to rankle the Golkar mainstream was Sasono's incursions into their traditional pat-ronage domains. As minister of co-operatives, Sasono was bending one of

Golkar's most formidable patronage networks toward an altogether different set of beneficiaries—Islamic boarding schools and NGOs. Moreover, Sasono was skilfully using the media to advertise himself and was clearly pursuing higher political ambitions.[25] Habibie therefore began distancing himself from his erstwhile ally—a move designed to appease Tandjung and the Golkar mainstream. From having been the most influential cabinet member only months before, by the start of the new year Sasono was already a 'has-been'.

Meanwhile, Habibie's decision to sack his speechwriter Yusril Ihza Mahendra, the chair of the stridently Islamist PBB, provided further evidence that the president was deliberately distancing himself from political Islam. When someone praised him for this 'move to the centre', Habibie famously feigned surprise: 'I haven't moved anywhere! I'm always in the centre—it's other people who keep moving about.'[26] But before Habibie could gauge the success of his manoeuvre away from political Islam, he took a bold step that put him in deeper trouble than ever before.

East Timor had long been the foremost thorn in Indonesia's diplomatic side. Indonesia forcibly annexed the tiny territory when Portugal suddenly granted independence to its centuries-old colony in 1975. The United Nations' refusal to acknowledge Indonesia's claim over East Timor—combined with the military's longstanding record of human rights abuses there—helped ensure that East Timor consistently attracted far more international attention than, for example, Irian Jaya or Aceh.

Soeharto had warded off repeated attempts by the international community to equitably resolve the plight of East Timor. In 1991, for instance, an international uproar followed a massacre at East Timor's Santa Cruz Cemetery, prompting two donors to suspend aid.[27] But while Soeharto's power at home allowed him to treat the international community in highhanded fashion, Habibie was in no such position. He needed to cultivate support wherever it could be found, and in the throes of an economic crisis, the international community was an even more valuable ally than before. Goodwill from diplomatic circles could help him stay in power, and there was no better way to obtain it than by thawing Indonesia's long-frozen position on East Timor.

After only one month in office, Habibie showed more flexibility on East Timor than Soeharto ever had: he promised to grant 'special autonomy' for East Timor and to reduce troop levels in the territory.[28] Few expected much concrete action, but after more than two decades of an uncompromising stance, the gesture represented a breakthrough.

Habibie's overture elicited objections from conservative politicians; in particular, they feared that concessions to East Timor would only bolster secessionist movements in places such as Aceh and Irian Jaya. In a diverse, archipelagic nation which had suffered its share of secession movements in the past, the theme of national unity—at all costs—enjoyed strong currency. Soeharto had ardently propounded this hardline nationalism, implying that his stern rule was required to keep the nation intact. But there were some who harboured radically different views. One of them was a woman who, like Habibie, was an accomplished intellectual and pious Muslim from the Outer Islands: Dewi Fortuna Anwar.

In her official role as Habibie's assistant state secretary for foreign affairs, Fortuna Anwar had witnessed first-hand just how harmful the East Timor imbroglio had become for Indonesia's relations with foreign donors, OECD states and the UN. On the basis of her input, the president was finally convinced that Indonesia could generate considerable goodwill from the international community—while laying to rest a constant source of controversy—by finally taking bold action. In a routine press conference on 27 January 1999 President Habibie held forth, for the first time, the possibility that Jakarta would entertain a 'ballot' (he studiously avoided the odious term 'referendum') on independence for the East Timorese.[29]

Habibie genuinely believed he was doing the right thing. He felt that his policy was in Indonesia's interests and was mandated by the political realities of the post-Soeharto era. He would remove, once and for all, the foremost stumbling block in Indonesia's foreign relations. Events began to move rapidly. Within two weeks Habibie disclosed that he personally favoured independence for East Timor.

Given East Timor's tiny size—it represented less than 1 per cent of Indonesia's population and land area—Habibie apparently felt that Indonesia had little to lose in real terms. He even used this argument to persuade sceptics that East Timor was not worth keeping. 'What have the East Timorese given us?' he asked an audience in February. 'Natural resources? No. Human resources? No. Technology? No. Abundant gold? No. Rocks? Yes!'[30]

Habibie's ground-breaking initiative won applause from the international community and made most East Timorese ecstatic, but the Indonesian public felt differently. Few recognised the circumstances by which East Timor had been annexed—the New Order had suppressed the facts of its forcible invasion in 1975. Many Indonesians viewed East Timorese independence as a repudiation of national integrity. It was on this basis that Megawati, the purveyor of her father's patriotic rhetoric, opposed Habibie's initiative. Wahid joined suit.[31] More critically, opposition also came from Habibie's own party chair, Akbar Tandjung. Just as Habibie was trying to appease Tandjung and win Golkar's unequivocal nomination, his sudden East Timor initiative stood in the way.

What few realised at the time, however, was that by far the most dangerous opponent to East Timorese independence was Wiranto's military. If the East Timorese voted to remain part of Indonesia, all might be forgiven; if not, Habibie's political future would be in grave jeopardy.

15

UNDER-DEMOCRACY

As soon as Indonesia's new political laws were passed at the end of January 1999, the minister of home affairs Syarwan Hamid faced a conundrum. His first essential task in preparing for parliamentary elections—Indonesia's first competitive contest since 1955—was to determine which of Indonesia's 130 or so new political parties would be eligible to take part. The political laws specifically delegated the screening of new parties to the General Election Commission (KPU), but Hamid's problem was that the KPU itself was to consist of one representative from each eligible political party (plus five government representatives). It was a 'Catch-22': party eligibility could not be established until the KPU was formed, but the KPU could not be formed until party eligibility was established.

Hamid did not hesitate. He unilaterally decided to appoint an independent team to screen parties, even though the KPU was the only body legally empowered to perform that task. As so many Indonesian officials were accustomed to doing, Hamid was in effect turning a blind eye to the letter of the law. But to demonstrate that he was in fact acting in good faith, Hamid went to great lengths to ensure that the newly created team consisted only of individuals whose reputations for integrity were strong. 'Team Eleven', as it was known for its number of members, was headed by Nurcholish Madjid and included Buyung Nasution, Adi Andojo Sutjipto and Andi Mallarengeng, in addition to a complement of noted academics, legal reform advocates and a student leader.[1]

Team Eleven followed the eligibility guidelines set out in the new Political Party Law. The law's initial drafts required parties to have branches in all 27 provinces and signatures from one million supporters, but the law's final version was far more lenient. To help upstart parties (and perhaps to fragment Golkar's opposition), the Golkar-led parliament lowered the requirement for provincial branches from 27 to nine, while scrapping the signature requirement altogether.

But despite the more lenient rules Team Eleven still faced a daunting task. The team was charged with verifying whether prospective parties actually maintained representative offices in at least half of the districts in at least nine provinces. Some provinces, such as Yogyakarta, had as few as three districts, but others had dozens. Most of the 137 parties claimed to have representative offices in at least 40 districts. Thus there were several thousand physical locations throughout the archipelago that the eleven team members would, at least in theory, need to inspect. And they had two weeks within which to work. The deadline was urgent: the longer they tarried, the less time the KPU would have to implement its long list of administrative chores to ensure that the election took place on time.

Nurcholish's team split up and began travelling intensively. The job was simplified by the fact that some parties had no branches at the provincial level, much less the district level. Team Eleven also received assistance from civic groups such as religious organisations and university networks. Nonetheless, the task was too big and Team Eleven risked sparking messy disputes over the accuracy of its rulings.

Nurcholish's team therefore opted for the least controversial alternative: allowing a larger than expected number of parties to pass. Just before its deadline expired, the team recommended eligibility for no less than 48 parties. Even arriving at this number had not been easy. As the deadline neared, Team Eleven was criticised for resorting to questionable and non-transparent means to winnow down the number of parties.[2] Nonetheless, the government endorsed the team's recommendation. Hamid had been suspected of wanting to manipulate the process to disenfranchise his enemies, but instead he and Team Eleven went to great lengths to ensure that the process was fair; the result was a bewildering array of parties contesting the election.

Team Eleven was so fastidious about demonstrating its impartiality that it even granted eligibility to the Marxist-inspired PRD. This was the same party whose leader, Boediman Soedjatmiko, was still in jail—having been blamed by then-Kaster Syarwan Hamid for masterminding the July 1996 Matraman riots. Now, as home affairs minister, Hamid was granting Soedjatmiko's party a chance to compete in elections. Team Eleven was less openminded, however, with regard to parties that had obviously been erected by Soeharto family surrogates. Eligibility was granted to the overtly pro-Soeharto Republican Party, but six other parties allied to it were rejected.[3]

Completion of the party screening process marked the crossing of a difficult hurdle—but in producing a large number of parties it also created new problems. When 28 parties existed in 1957, Soekarno complained that Indonesia suffered from 'over-democracy'—and he used that fact to help justify the imposition of authoritarian rule, or 'Guided

Democracy'. By Soekarno's standards Indonesia now had an even greater dose of over-democracy. With 48 parties competing, campaigning would be boisterous, ballots would be confusing and the KPU itself would be unwieldy. Forty-eight parties meant that the KPU would have a total of 53 members (one from each party plus five from the government), and many doubted whether a commission that large could prove effective.

Another problem was more mundane, but no less serious: the sheer logistical challenge of printing ballots with such a vast array of party symbols. Because Indonesia was using a proportional electoral system, only party symbols would appear on the ballot (whereas in a direct system, candidate names would appear). The act of voting only required voters to pierce the party symbol of their choice on the ballot. Thus the ballot would simply be a large sheet of paper bearing 48 party symbols, with party names beneath each symbol. The size of a small poster, Indonesia's first democratic ballot since 1955 was a bewildering sight to behold.

Megawati faced a special problem. Many voters still associated her with the long-established PDI, not the new PDI Perjuangan. Megawati there-fore had to run a massive educational campaign: 115 million voters needed to be informed that her party symbol was no longer the familiar white bull in a triangle, but a new one: a rather sinister-looking black bull set against a red circle. Compounding matters was the fact that five other symbols on the ballot also portrayed bulls. In practically every campaign speech she delivered, therefore, Megawati carefully told voters that, of all the bulls on the ballot, only hers had a white nose.

Wahid's PKB, meanwhile, used a symbol that was pirated and altered only slightly by PKU, the rival NU splinter party headed by Wahid's uncle. PKB voters might also be confused if they relied on the party's initials to find the symbol on the ballot: in addition to the PKU, at least four other parties had similar acronyms.

Pan's symbol, meanwhile, was a white starburst on a blue background. It was emblematic of Rais's campaign: it eschewed both the green associ-ated with Islam and the red associated with nationalism. Rais was studiously avoiding taking sides in the debates over religion that were cleaving the anti-Golkar opposition. His refusal to align with either Megawati or political Islam meant that his vote-getting potential was the foremost question mark of the election campaign.

B y February Megawati was campaigning in earnest. On one typical day during the month, she and her entourage flew from Jakarta to the Central Java capital of Semarang. Although it was only shortly after dawn, the small airport was mobbed with tens of thousands of supporters uniformly dressed in red. After visiting with several local dignitaries, Megawati boarded a campaign bus and proceeded to the town of Magelang, home to the armed forces academy.[4]

Passengers on the bus later claimed that, throughout the 75-kilometre journey, hardly a kilometre passed when the roadsides were not filled with jubilant, red-clad PDI Perjuangan supporters. When the bus reduced speed, throngs would run after it in the road, attempting to touch its sides or even, if it stopped for a moment, kiss the glass behind which Megawati sat, smiling and waving. By the time Megawati reached Magelang she had been seen by an estimated half a million supporters. In Magelang itself another 200 000 stood waiting for the candidate to arrive and deliver her speech. And the Magelang visit was not unique: huge gatherings met Megawati wherever she went.

Some criticised Megawati for delivering campaign speeches that were too simplified or lacklustre, but others praised her as a speaker. She generally dwelt on themes of national pride, unity in the face of adversity, and respect for pluralism. She would typically note that she herself was not purely Javanese but rather of mixed ethnic heritage (her mother, Fatmawati, was from Bengkulu, Sumatera, while her paternal grand-mother was from Bali). All Indonesians, she said, should think of themselves as Indonesian first, and Javanese or Sumateran second. Megawati also maintained that women needed to turn out to vote and should take a greater role in politics: as evidence of this she would typically point out that most of those attending her rallies were teenage boys or young men.

Another theme that Megawati emphasised in many of her speeches and press interviews was the need for the rule-of-law. She seemed to understand the difference between the supremacy of law and what had prevailed during the Soeharto era, and pressed the point more consistently than the other presidential contenders did. But while she would freely denounce Soeharto and the excesses of his rule, she refrained from calling for his punishment and she strenuously avoided criticising the military.

In fact, in most of her speeches Megawati took pains to praise Wiranto's military for implementing internal reforms. She declared that the military was changing from a tool of Soeharto to a professional defence force. Megawati shared the secular-nationalist ideology which prevailed among generals; more importantly, however, she expected that she would need the potentially pivotal support of their 38-member faction when the new MPR convened to elect a president. And she knew that in practice the military's backing would make it far easier to rule—although whether it would make it easier to implement change remained to be seen.

The messages Megawati delivered seemed to resonate with supporters, but it was still her aura that attracted the masses. Understandably, Indo-nesians craved a respectable leader. Amid a dearth of noteworthy national figures, Megawati filled the void and her persona took on legendary proportions. People would travel vast distances and camp outdoors for days to hear her speak. Some of her rallies in Java attracted over 800 000 supporters. Her appearance in some locations incited such euphoric frenzy that injuries were common and the candidate herself had to be whisked out of harm's way on more than one occasion. The magnitude of the rallies turning out for Megawati was sufficient to convince many that PDI Perjuangan would win the upcoming parliamentary elections in a landslide. It seemed that Megawati was a shoo-in for the presidency. In fact, the reality was different.

Megawati garnered the support of many millions on Java, but on an island of 115 million inhabitants—and some 68 million voters—the massive crowds that Megawati was attracting did not necessarily point to a clear majority of Java's electorate. In any event, as mentioned, votes on Java counted for less than in the Outer Islands, where Megawati's support was sometimes much less strong. The heavily populated province of South Sulawesi, for instance, was staunchly pro-Golkar: B.J. Habibie was the province's native son. And regardless of voters' preferences, Megawati would surely lose if the elections were rigged against her. The work of Team Eleven set an encouraging precedent in this regard, but it was immediately followed by an event which raised more suspicions about the Habibie administration's intentions: the appointment of government representatives to the KPU, the General Election Commission.

In early February the home affairs ministry was due to announce the five individuals who would represent the government on the KPU. According to the new election laws, these five would collectively possess a 50 per cent share of the voting rights within the KPU—with the other 50 per cent collectively held by the 48 party representatives. Given the overweening authority the KPU would possess in implementing the often vaguely worded election laws, the choice of these five government representatives was crucial. The government was urged to select impartial figures with integrity, rather than surrogates for those who were in power, such as Golkar, the bureaucracy and the military.

Several days before the announcement was due to be made, the names of the five leading candidates were leaked to the press. All were Soeharto-era officials who were closely aligned to various conservative interests in the government. Feisal Tamin, for instance, was the unpopular head of Korpri—the civil servants association that had long campaigned alongside Golkar and the military as part of Tim Buldoser. Another candidate was a retired two-star general, Dunija, who headed the key 'socio-political affairs' unit within the ministry of home affairs.[5] The most controversial member, however, was an active two-star general, Sudi Silalahi.

Were Silalahi included on the KPU, he would clearly be serving as the surrogate of the military in general and of Kaster Bambang Yudhoyono in particular. But Silalahi had only recently been installed as Yudhoyono's chief assistant; until mid-1998 he had been chief-of-staff of the Jakarta

Garrison under Syafrie Syamsoeddin, his chief patron in the military. As
the garrison's operations officer, Silalahi had been Syamsoeddin's 'right-
hand man'—and if Syamsoeddin was implicated in the 1998 May riots, so
too was Silalahi.

Wiranto was ardently pledging to remove the military from practical
politics and to allow the parliamentary elections to take place unhindered—but the move to place Silalahi on the KPU provided reason to
doubt Wiranto's sincerity. It remains unclear who proposed the slate and
who leaked it to the public, but the episode suggested that there were
those within the Habibie administration who were intent on using
whatever means they could to ensure a favourable election outcome.

Criticism of the leaked slate delayed the final announcement of the
government's five representatives to the KPU, but after several days of
intense, backroom haggling the decision was finally made. The five individuals were of high standing. Rather than Tamin, Dunija and Silalahi, the
final slate included Buyung Nasution, Andi Mallarangeng and Adi Andojo
Sutjipto.[6]

The delay over the announcement had been rumoured to be the
result of the military's qualms about not having a seat on the commission.
In the end, it appears that a compromise may have been reached: when
the full KPU elected Buyung Nasution to serve as the commission's chair,
the lawyer declined and ceded the top position to the runner-up in the
vote—Rudini, a retired four-star general who had helped Habibie devise
the election schedule. Rudini sat on the commission as a representative of
a small Golkar splinter party.[7] Thus the military obtained no seats among
the five government representatives, but the KPU's most important post
ended up in the hands of a former army chief-of-staff.

Rudini's election did not, however, signal an outright victory for the
military: he was more liberal than the mainstream military. Rudini had
administered the 1992 elections as minister of home affairs from 1988 to
1993, but he had done so in a way that was considerably more impartial
than the actions of past officials in that position. In response, Soeharto
had ended his ministerial career after only one term.

In effect, Rudini's background made him an ideal compromise
candidate. He was generally trusted by the military and Golkar, yet he
was palatable to opposition groups. And as a former head of the election
bureaucracy that produced the lopsided results of 1992, he knew just
what types of unfair practices needed to be outlawed. This was an
important quality for the KPU chair to possess: by the end of February,
it was clear to all that foul play might jeopardise Indonesia's first attempt
at free elections in more than 40 years. President Habibie and Attorney
General Andi Ghalib had become embroiled in the administration's most
embarrassing scandal to date—the scandal of the so-called 'Ghalibie
tape'.

Although he had been in office for only six months, Ghalib was already highly unpopular for his foot-dragging on the Soeharto case. In addition, he had been ridiculed for providing seven of his assistants with extravagant vehicles: BMW sedans. 'Hopefully,' said Ghalib at the time, 'these will help my staff perform better under difficult conditions.'[8] But these controversies paled in comparison with the scandal exposed by the 24 February issue of *Panji* magazine. The magazine's cover depicted a caricature of the president whispering into the ear of Andi Ghalib, above a caption that read 'The Circulation of the Ghalib–Habibie Tape'.

The magazine, which sold out in hours, contained a transcript of a four-minute telephone conversation that had taken place between the president and his attorney general on 10 December 1998. The conversation started with Habibie asking Ghalib, in an urgent tone of voice, about the status of corruption investigations of three businessmen.[9] Habibie mentioned two by name: Arifin Panigoro, a *pribumi* oil baron allied with Megawati; and Sofyan Wanandi, an outspoken ethnic-Chinese businessman supporting Abdurrahman Wahid.[10] The third figure being investigated (although he was not mentioned by name) was Tommy Winata, a controversial property developer who had long been associated with military-run businesses. Winata was allegedly backing Edi Sudradjat and Try Sutrisno, who had left Golkar to found their own party, the 'Justice and Unity Party' (PKP).

In response to Habibie's inquiry, Ghalib said that the investigations of the three tycoons were under way. 'Well, that's good,' said Habibie, 'because people are asking me about this.'

'They're under way,' said Ghalib, 'but we have to keep looking [for evidence], because we're worried that these measures could be counter-productive . . .'

Habibie interrupted him. 'But they're already manoeuvring!' he exclaimed. 'These people are starting to make moves!'

'Yes, we've got them under investigation, but we want to move towards some sort of . . .'

Again Habibie interrupted him. 'Look, why don't you just write me a brief report, okay? Explain what's going on and how much progress has been made.'

'Right. This is actually connected to the case of Pak Soeharto.' The day before, on 9 December, Ghalib had summoned Soeharto to the attorney general's office for a much-publicised interrogation. Reminded of this useful service, Habibie softened his tone.

'Yes, I understand—you can't move too fast because you've got the Soeharto case to handle. How did that go, anyway? Did it turn out all right?'

'It went very well. He [Soeharto] seemed to realise that this was a measure that had to be taken—otherwise he might have had to face justice in the streets.'

'So he was ready.'

'Yes, because the public is so impatient now. But as soon as we summoned him, the tension seemed to abate. People are starting to feel more sympathetic toward him. So things are improving.'

Habibie then asked what the next phase of the Soeharto investigation would be. 'We don't know yet,' answered Ghalib. 'We haven't made an announcement.'

'Well then, why don't you fill the time with those three?' asked Habibie, returning to the original purpose of his call.

'God willing [*Insya Allah*]', said Ghalib.

Habibie then explained the reason for his concern: he had just received 'feedback' from Achmad Tirtosudiro, the septuagenarian retired general who had succeeded Habibie as chair of Icmi. 'Pak Tirto asked me why Panigoro and the others were not included [on the list of suspects under investigation]. Because they're the ones who are financing these other [parties].'

'Ya, *Insya Allah*.'

'Okay, then. Everything else is okay, right?'

'*Alhamdulillah*.'

Habibie was ready to conclude the conversation. In closing, he cracked a joke to Ghalib, an active two-star general: 'You've already had a five-star take the stand over there!' Along with generals Sudirman and A.H. Nasution, Soeharto was the only other five-star in Indonesian history. This prompted a hearty laugh from Ghalib, but before the conversation ended the attorney general wanted to explain the circumstances behind an embarrassing incident that had occurred when Soeharto was questioned. The attorney general had inappropriately borrowed a helicopter from another agency to provide standby transport, and a television news station had run a critical story about it.

Habibie was not interested in Ghalib's excuses, but the story reminded him of something else: 'You didn't forget to tell the Pangab [Wiranto] about what you were doing, did you?'

Apparently, Habibie was suddenly fearful that the interrogation of Soeharto might have irked his military commander. 'Not until after Pak Soeharto was already under way,' said Ghalib. 'Only then did we let Wiranto know.'

'And did you explain everything to him?' demanded an agitated Habibie.

'Well, it was like this. He [Wiranto] was terribly worried. I said to him, "Leave it to me. Trust me." It seems that he did trust me. After all, I was given this task from you. I knew what my duty was. I told him that there was no need to worry. Finally, he understood. And in the end, we were able to speed up the investigation. It didn't last all afternoon. The others, for instance, were seven or eight hour interrogations. Bob Hasan's interrogation lasted for eight hours.'

'How many hours in the case of Bapak [Soeharto]?'

'Just over three hours.'

'Yes, that's enough.'

'That's right,' Ghalib answered. 'However,' he added with a laugh, 'if it had been only two hours, people would have said, "What kind of comedy routine is this, anyway?"'

Habibie shared the laugh, albeit halfheartedly, and thanked the attorney general for his efforts.

Some of the president's advisors claimed the tape was a fake, but forensic experts confirmed its authenticity and Ghalib himself eventually admitted to having held the conversation.[11] Habibie himself implicitly acknowledged that the tape was genuine: he said that he was the victim of an 'intellectual criminal act' that violated his human rights, and he ordered Wiranto to find the perpetrators—thereby admitting, unwittingly, that the eavesdropping had taken place.[12]

The leaked tape confirmed several things about high-level Indonesian politics at this time. First, Habibie was misusing the attorney general's office for political ends—just as Soeharto had always done. Second, neither Habibie nor Ghalib was serious about prosecuting Soeharto. Third, it seemed that Wiranto was even more determined to protect Soeharto than they were, and that the level of co-ordination and trust between Habibie and Wiranto was low. None of these conclusions, however, came as a great surprise to the Indonesian public.

Opposition leaders denounced Habibie, and some PPP parliamentarians threatened to initiate impeachment proceedings, but the affair soon blew over. The main effect of the tape was simply to remind the public that the Machiavellian nature of Indonesian politics had changed little since Soeharto's downfall. Ruler's Law was still in force. More interesting than the substance of the tape, therefore, was the question of how it had surfaced in the first place.

Copies of the Ghalibie tape had begun circulating as early as mid-December 1998—only days after the conversation took place. Several 'mass-based organisations' (presumably including the Muhammadiyah and/or the NU) claimed to have received copies of the recording in early January, and a little-known tabloid, *Berita Keadilan*, ran a feature story on the tape soon afterwards.[13] But because the tabloid circulated only outside Jakarta the story went unnoticed until the *Panji* report appeared.

Meanwhile, rumours abounded that tapes of two other conversations were circulating: one between Habibie and Feisal Tanjung, and another between Habibie and Akbar Tandjung. Who was blackmailing the president? Although most of the president's advisors were cautious and circumspect in their public comments about the Ghalibie tape, the man who had by now come to be Habibie's most influential advisor was quite forthright in voicing his suspicions.

Arnold Baramuli was a man who was grossly at odds with the *reformasi* era. Having served as governor of South Sulawesi during the Soekarno era, Baramuli's political and business career spanned nearly 40 years. In 1998 he finally reached the zenith of his power: Habibie had tapped him to head the president's supreme advisory council (DPA). The council had little tangible power but it possessed an exalted status. And because he enjoyed longstanding ties to Habibie—and because he was a master of backroom deal-making—Baramuli used the position to become Habibie's de facto chief-of-staff. As elections approached, the DPA chair was becoming increasingly influential, as evinced by a particularly odd event that took place in mid-February.

Just one week before the *Panji* transcript appeared on news stands Baramuli persuaded the president to summarily sack one of Ghalib's assistants: Maj. Gen. Syamsu Djaluluddin, the assistant attorney general for intelligence.[14] Although he had been appointed to the position only a few months before, Djaluluddin occupied a post that had been a linchpin of Ruler's Law throughout the New Order. Within an attorney general's office that had long been geared towards punishing enemies of Soeharto, the assistant attorney for intelligence kept tabs on opponents of the regime and helped steer the course of investigations. As such, the post was arguably the country's third most powerful intelligence-gatherer, after Bais and the civilian-controlled agency, Bakin.

The administration provided no official explanation for Djaluluddin's dismissal, nor why Baramuli appeared at Djalaluddin's resignation ceremony—even though there was no official reason for him to attend as chair of the DPA. Some newspapers speculated that Djalaluddin, like the former attorney general Soedjono Atmonegoro, had been too aggressive in investigating Soeharto—but this speculation was off the mark.[15] A far more likely reason for Djalaluddin's dismissal became apparent several days later, when the transcript of the Ghalibie tape appeared in public.

In response to the public furore generated by the transcript, Baramuli lashed out at the military: 'It's obvious that this is an intelligence game.'[16] This was the first instance in which a high-level administration official had levelled a public allegation against Wiranto's military. Baramuli seemed to be implying that Djalaluddin was responsible for the leak, and that the active two-star general had been working on behalf of the military intelligence agency, Bais.

To be sure, Djalaluddin's track record seemed to indicate that he was a New Order stalwart and Wiranto loyalist. Until September 1998 he had served as head of the military police, the investigative unit that had found no guilty parties in a string of military abuses, including the July 1996 PDI Headquarters raid, the March 1998 kidnapping of political activists, the Trisakti shootings and the May 1998 riots and rapes. Moreover, Djalaluddin was alleged to have received kickbacks in exchange for using the military police to 'back' (or provide security for) gambling dens and other types of vice in North Jakarta.[17] However, the fluid politics of *reformasi* often meant that loyalties were blurred. After being transferred to the attorney general's office, it is not inconceivable that Djalaluddin was actually working against Wiranto, on behalf of others.

It remains unclear, therefore, whether Baramuli was correct in assuming that Djalaluddin had been working for Bais. Officials from the intelligence agency examined the recording and maintained that it had not been made by wire-tapping, but rather was produced by a cassette recorder installed on the telephone of either the president or the attorney general. The implication was that the tape was made by insiders, not by spies. An independent forensic expert, Roy Suryo of Gadjah Mada University, later concurred with the Bais officials.[18]

In any event, it made little sense that Wiranto and his allies would want to circulate a tape that made the military chief look nearly as bad as Habibie and Ghalib. Nor would Wiranto want it known that the interrogation of Soeharto was contrived. A more likely explanation, therefore, is that Djalaluddin was working on behalf of one or more of the three tycoons being targeted by the attorney general's office.

Suspicions focused on Tommy Winata, the owner of the Artha Graha Group who was closely tied to two former armed forces commanders, Edi Sudradjat and Try Sutrisno. The retired four-star generals shared a plausible political motive: they had grand ambitions for their new party, PKP, and they were staunch opponents of the president and Wiranto. Moreover, they were rivals of the two other figures whose voices had purportedly been captured on embarrassing tape recordings: Feisal Tanjung and Akbar Tandjung. (Feisal had long been their enemy within the armed forces, while Akbar had only recently expelled them from Golkar.) But while Winata and the two retired generals may have had a plausible motive for committing political blackmail, no proof of their complicity ever emerged.

The origins of the Ghalibie tape therefore remain unclear, but the choice of a new intelligence assistant attorney was revealing. Djalaluddin was replaced by Lt Gen. (ret.) Yusuf Kertanegara, a member of the military honour council that had cashiered Prabowo six months earlier. Kertanegara was known as a close ally of Wiranto and the current military leadership.[19] For instance, both Kertanegara and the new intelligence chief, Tyasno Sudarto, were former commanders of the Central Java Garrison—a position reserved for stout Cendana loyalists.

Thus, while Djalaluddin had been insufficiently loyal, Kertanegara was apparently inserted to ensure that the attorney general's office would protect, rather than attack, Soeharto and other Cendana-related interests. This change caused a minor stir at the time—and the Ghalibie tape had inflicted serious damage on the president's credibility—but the controversy soon subsided nonetheless. Elections were approaching and public excitement was mounting. So too was election-related violence.

A series of events in late March spawned fears that Indonesia's first democratic election in over 40 years would be a brutal and chaotic affair. In Yogyakarta, in the heart of Java, youths supporting PDI Perjuangan clashed with a rival group supporting PPP; one died and fifteen were injured.[20] A week later, in nearby Purbalingga, more PDI Perjuangan supporters wreaked havoc on a Golkar rally attended by Akbar Tandjung. The mob destroyed Golkar's tents, podiums and banners, while setting fire to a Golkar vehicle. Tandjung's Land Cruiser was pelted with rocks while he was inside. Most disturbing, however, was the violence perpetrated on women attending the rally: at least fifteen female Golkar supporters were forced by the mob to shed their yellow (i.e. Golkar-coloured) garments.[21]

Megawati refused to apologise for the Purbalingga attack, asserting that the attackers were not formal party members and that, in any case, their anger was simply an expression of public antipathy towards the ruling party. In a competition with 48 parties—most of which were mobilising support by manipulating emotive symbols, including religious symbols—the prospects for a peaceful election campaign seemed dim. Wealthy residents of Jakarta began making plans to stay abroad during May, when campaigning was expected to peak. But campaign-related violence was not the only concern for Indonesians in early 1999: an even more troublesome development was the increasing incidence of communal strife.

By the end of March several hundred had been killed in the religious infighting in the Maluku archipelago. Wiranto openly admitted that some of the soldiers that had been sent to the provincial capital of Ambon to quell the strife had themselves taken sides and contributed to the bloodshed.[22] At first the public generally believed Wiranto's explanation that the soldiers were taking sides because they had familial ties to local victims of the conflict and therefore felt compelled to seek vengeance rather than keep the peace. But as the conflict wore on, doubts grew about the actions of Wiranto's units.

Meanwhile, communal clashes were beginning to occur outside Maluku. Sambas, a district in West Kalimantan on the island of Borneo, suddenly became the scene of grisly bloodshed in March. The frontier region had long suffered social tensions between indigenous Dayak and more recently arrived settlers from the island of Madura, near the coast of East Java. A third group consisted of ethnic Malays. What triggered the fighting between the groups remains unclear, but around 300 people died in a bloodthirsty rampage which garnered worldwide media attention.[23] International television crews arrived in Sambas to capture footage of roads lined with decapitated heads. Evidence emerged that the warring sides would sometimes devour the flesh of those they killed.

In light of the conflicts and disasters afflicting Indonesia—from the disclosure of the Ghalibie tape to the violence in Maluku and Sambas—many were amazed that the campaign's leading candidate, Megawati, steadfastly shunned attention. Megawati claimed that she was listening and contemplating, rather than speaking out in a way that might only lead to more problems.[24] Although she diligently toured the country to hold campaign rallies, she refused to take part in public debates with other party leaders, asserting that debates were 'not in accordance with Eastern culture'.[25] She also shied away from press interviews.

Megawati seemed to presume, like many Indonesians, that her election to the presidency was a foregone conclusion, given the huge crowds attending her rallies. However, Indonesia lacked accurate opinion polls, so that it was difficult to be certain of what the electorate really thought. Voter surveys never existed during the New Order, and the low prevalence of telephones required pollsters to interview voters in person. Thus it was not until late March—less than ten weeks from the election—that results emerged from Indonesia's first statistically significant survey of nationwide voter opinion. The poll, conducted by the International Foundation for Election Systems (Ifes), surveyed more than 1500 eligible voters in 22 provinces. Its findings surprised more than a few: Megawati's lead was not nearly as strong as many believed.

The good news for Megawati was that the Ifes poll showed her with a high favourability rating: 49 per cent of respondents declared that they had a 'favourable' impression of her. This, however, only put her in second place—to Habibie. The president had a favourable rating of 56 per cent, while his unfavourable rating was the same as Megawati's, at 11 per cent.

Habibie's high score may have reflected Indonesians' lingering reluctance to speak their minds freely. Only a year earlier, few would have dared criticise the president to a pollster. Moreover, the survey work had actually taken place in January and February, before the Ghalibie tape had embarrassed the president. Nonetheless, it was clear that Megawati was not without challengers for the presidency. Three other candidates enjoyed generally favourable ratings (albeit with lesser name recognition): Abdurrahman Wahid, Sultan Hamengkubuwono X and General Wiranto. Only two contenders could be ruled out of the running for president because of high unfavourable ratings: Akbar Tandjung and Amien Rais. The latter, it seemed, lacked popularity because he was seen as being too unabashedly power-hungry.

But the most important feature of the poll was not the favourability ratings but the party affinity scores. Voters had favourable impressions of Megawati—but this did not ensure that they would vote for her party. PDI Perjuangan was supported by a mere 20 per cent of a highly fragmented electorate. Golkar, PKB and PPP followed, with shares of 17 per cent, 12 per cent and 9 per cent respectively. Amien Rais's Pan was supported by a mere 7 per cent of respondents, and a large 27 per cent were either undecided or too wary to disclose their preference.

The figures on party affinity showed that Megawati would need to invite partners into an alliance if she was to win a clear majority in the MPR's presidential election. The poll results suggested that even with the full support of Wahid's PKB—which at this stage was beginning to look questionable—Megawati would still command only 32 per cent of the electorate. Assuming this alliance garnered around one-third of the undecided votes, the total would still be short of a majority, at around 41 per cent. Moreover, when the total vote share was translated into actual seats in parliament and, especially, the MPR, the percentage controlled by Megawati and Wahid would be even smaller, due to the regional imbalance in the electoral system. This was because Megawati and Wahid derived the bulk of their support from Java, where votes counted for less than in the Outer Islands. Thus, even if Megawati received support from the military, which held a 5 per cent share of the MPR's seats, she would still fall short of a clear majority in the MPR.

The clear message from the Ifes poll was that the PDI Perjuangan leader not only needed to campaign aggressively; she also desperately needed to reach out to potential alliance partners. Many pro-reform Indonesians ardently hoped for a united anti-Golkar front—comprising Megawati, Wahid and Rais—but these hopes were fading. The election was about more than reform: it was also about religion. Despite the clear message sent by the Ifes poll, Megawati stubbornly refused to reach out to Amien Rais or anyone associated with the Islamic camp. For their part, many in the Islamic camp were more willing to support Habibie's Golkar than they were Megawati's PDI Perjuangan.

Thus, for those who assessed the electoral system and scrutinised the results of the only reliable poll yet conducted, it was already clear by late March that Megawati's presidential prospects were slim. Nonetheless, Megawati continued to act as if she was destined to win the presidency. Inexplicably, the Jakarta elite and the Indonesian public seemed to believe likewise. There was, however, one politician who saw things differently: Abdurrahman Wahid.

A central question of the election campaign was the potential for an alliance between Megawati and Wahid. If Megawati could not gain Wahid's support, there was little likelihood that any other component of the political spectrum would back the PDI Perjuangan leader. Worrisomely for

Megawati, Wahid statements during March showed that his support was wavering. His stance seemed to change on a daily basis. 'I will support the party led by Mega,' he declared in a press interview during the third week of March.[26] But in a speech delivered in Singapore on 24 March, Wahid seemed to take the opposite stance:

> I am close to Megawati—she is like a sister to me—but the most important thing is that we abide by democracy, by the rule of the majority, and I don't think the majority will elect Megawati . . . In a Moslem country, it is difficult to realise. Why? Because we are tied to Islamic law. Many members of PKB are still clinging to the idea of Islamic law [barring a woman from becoming president].[27]

This comment seemed to rule out PKB support for Megawati, but Wahid soon changed his stance yet again.

In early April he declared that the PKB would not officially decide on a presidential nominee until after the 7 June elections. Moreover, he asserted that either Megawati or Sultan Hamengkubuwono X would be fit to serve as president. He ruled himself out of the running unless he experienced an unexpected improvement in his eyesight, which was so bad that he could distinguish vague shapes only a few inches from his face. Wahid also vowed not to co-operate with Amien Rais, whom he suspected of harbouring ambitions for transforming Indonesia into an 'Islamic state'.[28] In short, Wahid's only predictable quality was unpredictability.

But while it was unclear whom Wahid might support for the presidency, it was readily apparent that the NU leader occupied a central position on Indonesia's fragmented political map. In a tri-polar contest, Wahid's PKB appeared capable of moving in almost any direction. Wahid himself seemed inclined to back Megawati, but much of his party leaned toward Wahid's old rivals in the Islamic camp. Wahid's waffling was one of the strongest indicators that Indonesia's election campaign was barrelling towards an indecisive outcome—precisely the result that would most favour Golkar.

Many presumed that Golkar was widely reviled and would be trounced in the upcoming elections, but the incumbent party had some crucial advantages, such as experience and financial resources. Golkar also expected to benefit from the regional imbalance in the electoral system, as well as the addition of appointed members in the MPR. Golkar leaders admitted that they would only win around 10 per cent of the votes on Java, but they hoped to garner over 30 per cent throughout the Outer Islands, thereby producing a nationwide total of 20–25 per cent. Such a result would make the ruling party well positioned to forge an alliance with other components of a fragmented 'opposition'. Golkar's key problem, though, was its crippling internal divisions.

Less than six weeks away from the parliamentary elections, these divisions had prevented the party from being able to decide on a single candidate to nominate for president. For months Habibie had been expecting his erstwhile ally, Akbar Tandjung, to hand him the nomination—but Tandjung had deep reservations. Habibie's candidacy was hurt by the Semanggi shootings, the East Timor referendum and, perhaps most importantly, the Ghalibie tape, which proved that Habibie was side-stepping a central issue: trying Soeharto. But Tandjung was also concerned about his own political future.

In practice, Habibie was delegating power only to a tightknit circle of loyalists and aides, many of whom were Sulawesi natives or associates from Icmi. Despite holding two key offices—state secretary and Golkar chair—Tandjung consistently found himself cut out of the loop. If Habibie won re-election to the presidency, Tandjung calculated that his own political career would suffer. Tandjung's quandary, however, was that Golkar was bereft of other visible figures to carry the party's mantle. He therefore stalled for time.

In March, rather than nominating a single presidential candidate as most other parties had done, Golkar merely put forth a slate of five potential nominees. In addition to Habibie, these included Wiranto, Ginandjar, Sultan Hamengkubuwono X and Tandjung himself. Out of the rival factions formed around each of these potential nominees, two main factions gradually emerged: one which advocated the immediate nomination of Habibie, and another, led by Tandjung, that wanted to postpone nominating anyone until after 7 June.

The central issue was that, if Golkar won a better-than-expected election result, Tandjung might win the party's nomination for himself. To prevent this, Habibie's allies tried three times to persuade Golkar's 106-member leadership board to convene a national leadership meeting (known as a 'Rapim') prior to the elections. The Rapim would be empowered to nominate Golkar's sole candidate. On all three occasions they failed: around two-thirds of the leadership board remained loyal to Tandjung. Habibie's allies would still have one more chance to push the issue to a vote. First, however, the administration would try to make progress on the matter that most affected Habibie's public image: prosecuting Soeharto.

The Soeharto question was the hottest topic of the election campaign. Wahid, the only significant politician to be openly meeting with Soeharto, was advocating leniency towards the former president. Megawati seemed similarly inclined: she reportedly wanted to treat Soeharto better than he had treated her father.[29] But a further consideration for both Wahid and Megawati was that Wiranto's military was determined to protect

Soeharto and his family, and whoever won the presidency needed to accommodate the military. Both 'reform' leaders trod carefully to avoid antagonising Wiranto, and this included taking a soft stance with regard to trying Soeharto.

President Habibie, meanwhile, was in a different situation. Unlike Wahid, Megawati and Rais, Habibie desperately needed to earn reformist credentials if he hoped to win another term. He too needed to court the powerful military, but distancing himself from his Soeharto-era past was an even higher priority. Making this all the more urgent was the pressure from Tandjung and Darusman to undermine Habibie's candidacy. If Habibie wanted the presidency, he needed to sacrifice his former mentor, 'Super-Genius Soeharto'. Ironically, Soeharto's former flatterer was now, in effect, Soeharto's most dangerous political adversary.

In December Habibie had explicitly ordered Attorney General Ghalib to investigate the former president, but by March virtually nothing had been achieved. Meanwhile, incessant student demonstrations were exacerbating the embarrassment. In one of the most creative and successful protests, students demonstrating in front of the attorney general's office donned paper masks of Soeharto's face. The striking scene—which seemed to depict Ghalib's staff as being 'mini-Soehartos'—captured widespread press coverage. And in another famous incident students presented Ghalib with a live chicken—a gift meant to symbolise his lack of courage in pursuing Cendana.[30] Soon afterwards, in mid-March, Ghalib endured a more serious embarrassment: journalists in the United Kingdom stumbled upon some intriguing indicators of the scale of the Soeharto family's wealth.

London had long been one of the favourite retreats for the Cendana clan. Sigit, Tutut, Titiek, Tommy and Probosutedjo all owned high-end properties in Britain which they used for frequent vacations and shopping trips and as homes for their children who studied in British schools. As long as Soeharto was in power the family was welcome, but soon after his downfall the British government instituted an abrupt policy change: visas were denied to a host of Soeharto relatives. Family properties began appearing on London's property market soon after that.

According to a report by the *Independent*, Soeharto relatives were disposing of three properties worth an estimated £11 million, the most valuable of which was an eight-bedroom home in Hampstead, London.[31] A grandchild of Soeharto, Eno Sigit, had used the home while she attended fashion school—to which she was chauffeured in a Rolls Royce. Another house for sale had been used primarily for storage: most of its rooms were filled with packages, from places such as Selfridges and Harrods, that had never been opened. In addition to the three houses for sale, family members were believed to own at least four other upmarket properties in London and Brighton.[32]

The report of family properties in Britain brought widespread publicity in Indonesia, where the public was starved for details of Cendana's legendary but mysterious wealth. *Tempo* magazine catalogued a short list of Cendana assets which showed that the London properties were not unique: properties of similar worth were owned in Beverly Hills and Boston. Other homes were owned in Singapore, Geneva, the Cayman Islands and Hawaii. Tommy Soeharto was seeking to sell Lilybank Lodge, his secluded hunting retreat at the head of a glacier in the New Zealand Alps, for NZ$10 million.[33] Other relatives and friends owned high-end property on New Zealand's South Island: Titiek, former finance minister Radius Prawiro and former Bulog director Bustanil Arifin all owned lakeside chalets near Queenstown.[34]

Reports of Cendana's luxuries were not limited to property. The family owned a number of aircraft, and Tutut's children, who were studying in Boston, reportedly owned a small fleet of Ferraris, Porsches and Rolls Royces. Tommy Soeharto, whose Humpuss Group had bought Italian sports car manufacturer Lamborghini, was an ardent enthusiast of off-road rallies. Tommy raced Mitsubishis for Goro Rally, a team he sponsored himself. He sometimes competed against his nephew, Ari Sigit, who drove Audis for a team of his own: Sexy Motor Sport.[35] In addition to hunting and motor sport, Tommy also liked sailing: he owned a half share of a A$16 million yacht berthed in Darwin, Australia.[36] The yacht was named *Obsession*.

The initial *Independent* report immediately brought Ghalib and Justice Minister Muladi under fire from the press. Why, reporters asked, had the administration's three-month long investigation of Soeharto not turned up evidence of these assets? Ghalib's forthright but unsatisfying answer was that his office had been looking for properties that were explicitly listed under Soeharto's own name—not those of his relatives. Muladi kept reiterating that the administration needed to move cautiously: 'If we are not careful with regard to the juridical aspects of the case, the political ramifications could be serious.'[37] Presumably Muladi was alluding, like Wahid, to the threat of a backlash from Cendana, the military—or both.

But President Habibie was in no position to be cautious. By March his presidential campaign was in full swing. Having been ordered by the MPR to investigate Soeharto and his family, Habibie needed to show results. Perhaps this explains why, in late March, Ghalib finally made a move: the attorney general initiated the trial of the 'Goro-Bulog' scandal.[38]

R icardo Gelael was a *pribumi* entrepreneur who owned a small chain of supermarkets. He was also a car-racing companion of Tommy Soeharto. In 1994 he founded Goro, a warehouse-style supermarket chain modelled on the lines of European hypermarkets such as Makro and

Carrefour. Gelael was president-director and Tommy was president-commissioner.

The key to the venture was location. Gelael wanted to build the first Goro store in Kelapa Gading, a vast residential suburb in East Jakarta that was rapidly becoming more affluent. The Kelapa Gading Mall, built in the early 1990s, had been a superb success primarily because East Jakarta had virtually no other modern shopping outlets. A Goro store in Kelapa Gading was bound to be profitable. The main challenge was to find a plot of real estate in the densely packed suburb—and this is where Tommy helped.

Gelael and Tommy noticed that right in the middle of Kelapa Gading was a sprawling, 50-hectare warehouse complex belonging to the National Logistics Agency, Bulog. Ostensibly designed to stabilise food prices by dominating the distribution of key commodities such as rice, flour, sugar and cooking oil, Bulog had long been a lucrative domain for Soeharto-family cronies. The agency's wrongful losses for the years 1996–97 alone totalled some Rp3 trillion, according to an IMF-mandated audit conducted in 1999.[39] Tommy's presence in Goro ensured that Gelael's venture would have little difficulty in securing the valuable Kelapa Gading real estate from Bulog.

A close associate of Cendana, Beddu Amang, was made head of Bulog in February 1995. On his first day in the job he authorised a land swap—known in Indonesia by the Dutch term *ruilslag*—with Goro. The *ruilslag* provided that Bulog would exchange its warehouse complex in Kelapa Gading for a plot of land owned by Goro in North Jakarta. The two plots were of similar size, but the similarities ended there. Bulog's plot was prime real estate, while Goro's was marshland—in a remote location, surrounded by slums, and polluted with industrial waste. Goro was therefore required to clear and improve its land before giving it to Bulog. But Gelael and Tommy demurred from spending their own funds on the land clearance; instead they chose to borrow.

In July 1996 Goro obtained a loan worth Rp20 billion, or around $8 million at the time. Officially, the lender was Bank Bukopin, but Bukopin was controlled by Bulog and the loan to Goro was backed by a Rp23 billion deposit from the logistics agency. If Goro defaulted, Bukopin would be entitled to Bulog's deposit. In effect, the Goro deal was a prime example of how Soeharto's children enriched themselves at the state's expense: they not only bilked a state-owned agency but also forced the agency to finance their bilking of it.

By late 1996 Soeharto himself had commemorated the opening of Goro's Kelapa Gading store, but meanwhile Goro had defaulted on its loan from Bukopin and the polluted marsh in North Jakarta remained unimproved. Gelael claimed that more funds were required to complete the land clearance, and Beddu Amang therefore lent an additional

Rp33 billion to the supervisor of the clearance work, Hokiarto, a banker who also happened to be a longstanding business partner of Amang's. But still the land remained unimproved. And while waiting for the North Jakarta land to be cleared, Bulog continued to use two warehouses on the Kelapa Gading site—for which it was forced to pay rent to Goro.

In the grand scheme of Soeharto-era corruption the Goro scandal was a trifling affair: state prosecutors estimated that the Goro *ruilslag* caused losses to the state of Rp94 billion—a pittance compared, for instance, to Tommy Soeharto's deals with Pertamina. Yet the Goro scandal was ideal for prosecutors in that it was straightforward and clear-cut. The key to winning conviction in a corruption case was to prove that the accused had caused losses to the state. The evidence that Tommy, as president commissioner of Goro, had caused such losses was quite clear. State prosecutors had listed Tommy as a suspect on 10 December, but it was not until 12 April that they finally summoned him to court to stand trial.

Tommy's appearance in court marked the first time that an offspring of Soeharto had stood trial on formal charges. But despite facing a maximum penalty of twenty years imprisonment, Tommy's mood was distinctly buoyant. When he arrived at the courtroom the gallery was packed with cheering young women, one of whom broke through his cordon of bodyguards to hand him a bouquet of flowers. Tommy's defence team had arranged the supporters beforehand—as they had done when other Soeharto family members had been made to appear at the attorney general's office. And in photos that became some of the most famous images of Indonesia's post-Soeharto era, Tommy was pictured wearing a wide, cocky grin as he sat in the centre of the courtroom, seemingly mocking the gravity of the situation.

Apparently Tommy was already confident of victory. His defence team included two former senior members of the attorney general's office (one of whom was yet another race-car enthusiast). As the trial progressed, it became clear that the prosecutors' case might not be so clear-cut after all. Three key witnesses—officials from Bulog who included the agency's new director, Minister for Industry and Trade Rahardi Ramelan—changed their testimony during the course of the trial.

Ramelan claimed, vaguely, that he had found new information that was different from that which he had used in his earlier testimony. Bulog's *ruilslag* transaction with Goro, he said in early May, had not caused any material losses for the logistics agency. Prosecutors threatened to try Ramelan for providing false testimony, but he had nonetheless provided the judges with a basis for dismissing the case. Tommy walked away unscathed.

The outcome of the case was puzzling. To boost his political prospects, Habibie needed to convict Soeharto or, failing that, one his children. This was presumably why Ghalib initiated the Goro case in the first place. Yet, by early May, Habibie's loyal aide Rahardi Ramelan had reversed his testimony in Tommy's favour. What was Ramelan's motive? One possible explanation might be discerned from a sequence of events that attracted relatively little attention at the time, and that few observers connected to the trial of Tommy Soeharto.

Ghalib first levelled formal charges against Tommy as a suspect in the Goro–Bulog case on 10 December 1998. One day later a small shopping centre in Central Jakarta, Plaza Atrium, was rocked by an explosion. Later that month Tommy's older brother Bambang was forced to appear at the attorney general's office. He was questioned for three hours regarding his role as the treasurer of a charitable foundation, run by Soeharto, that was being investigated for 'signs of abuse'.[40] Bambang's interrogation was followed less than 72 hours later by the 1 January explosion, mentioned above, that damaged the Ramayana department store and nearly wrecked the length of Jalan Sabang, a bustling commercial street.

Later, on 27 January 1999, Ghalib summoned Tommy to his office and formally charged him with corruption in the Goro–Bulog case. Less than two weeks later, on 9 February, an explosion took place in the Kelapa Gading Mall—the same mall whose popularity had encouraged Ricardo Gelael to undertake the Goro project in the first place. And on 15 April, three days after Tommy was forced to appear in court, a third explosion occurred in front of Plaza Hayam Wuruk in North Jakarta.

Finally, on 19 April, Tommy made his second appearance in court. His lawyers requested an 'exception' to halt the proceedings against their client, but the judge denied their request. Later that afternoon, at 3.20 p.m., Jakarta witnessed its fifth bomb blast in as many months: an explosion destroyed several rooms in the basement of the administrative building on the grounds of Central Jakarta's Istiqlal Mosque, the largest mosque in Southeast Asia. The blast injured four.[41]

Thus five attempts to punish Tommy or Bambang for corruption were followed soon after by bomb blasts; in four of the cases the intervals were three days or less. But the day after the Istiqlal blast—just as suspicions were finally beginning to focus on Cendana—police officials announced that the perpetrators belonged to the Indonesian Mujahidin (Amin), a hitherto-unknown band of Islamic terrorists who were supposedly based at a 'training camp' near Bogor.

The investigators' prompt indictment of Amin immediately generated scepticism. The police had failed to produce any explanation for the half dozen episodes of violence and terrorism that had afflicted Indonesia over the past year, yet in this instance they found the culprits within hours. The Legal Aid Foundation and a host of NGOs accused the police of fabricating the allegations. Several Islamic leaders decried the use of underhanded tactics 'à la Benny Moerdani'.[42] Indeed, Amin's very existence was dubious: journalists who investigated the area that the police claimed was Amin's training camp found nothing of the sort.[43] There was also the problem of explaining why Islamic terrorists would target the nation's largest mosque.

Police detained twelve suspected members of Amin, most of whom were living in dire poverty as rickshaw drivers, cassava vendors and the like. Six months later, all were released for lack of evidence.[44] Like the explanation for the Ramayana department store bombing, Amin appeared to be a crude fabrication created to distract attention from the true culprits.

In fact, police sources later told John McBeth, the bureau chief of the *Far Eastern Economic Review*, that they had been told by their superiors to 'switch off' their investigation into the Istiqlal bombing.[45] Their investigation had homed in on former and serving members of the Special Forces' covert operations unit, Group IV.

Meanwhile, Jakarta's rumour-mill claimed that Cendana had commissioned the bombing through a Rp200 million payment, with the involvement of a former minister and an obscure Islamic proselytiser employed by Tommy Soeharto's Humpuss Group.[46] The minister was presumed to be Bob Hasan, while the proselytiser was presumed to be Toto Tasmara, an Islamic activist with an unusual background. Having been imprisoned in the 1980s as an Islamic militant, Tasmara was not only later released but employed as a vice-president of Bank Duta, a bank controlled by Bob Hasan and Soeharto. He later became a corporate secretary of the Humpuss Group, owned by Tommy Soeharto.[47] The complicity of Hasan and Tasmara was never proved, but it would not be the last time that Cendana-linked Islamists were alleged to be involved in episodes of unexplained violence.

Thus the explosions that took place during the first few months of 1999 shared a host of similar characteristics. They corresponded to dates on which Tommy or Bambang appeared in court or at the attorney general's office. The bombs were of similar magnitude, no one claimed responsibility and the authorities failed to provide plausible explanations. If it was true that the Special Forces had been involved, this would suggest that the military's most notorious unit was perpetrating a terror campaign on behalf of Cendana. More indications to this effect would emerge later. Meanwhile, mysterious violence was also raging elsewhere: the Istiqlal explosion was overshadowed at the time by bloodshed in the distant Maluku archipelago.

Since the initial outbreak of Christian–Muslim strife in January, the death toll in Maluku's communal killings was growing steadily higher. Having begun in the capital of Ambon, the violence had spread to distant reaches of the Maluku archipelago. In the Kei Islands—sandy atolls renowned for their natural beauty—the small number of local residents began slaughtering each other with reckless abandon.

In early March a two-star general and native Maluccan, Suaidi Marasabessy, took charge of a special military taskforce assigned to investigate and resolve the worsening violence in Maluku. Wiranto, however, gave the taskforce only one month in which to work. At the end of that time Marasabessy concluded that the violence was being fomented by 'provocateurs at both the local and national levels', but he was unable to identify those involved.[48] And despite having failed to impose peace in Maluku, Marasabessy soon received rapid promotion through military ranks.

Meanwhile, on 15 April, former president Soeharto granted a brief interview with a Japanese newspaper.[49] His primary message: the 7 June election should be postponed. Soeharto claimed that the Indonesian people were not ready to vote because the IMF's demands had burdened them with undue hardship. He also doubted whether the election could be free and fair, with 48 parties competing. Finally, he warned that unscrupulous politicians would exploit divisive issues simply to further their own interests—thereby worsening the potential for local conflicts.

Soeharto's ominous warning strengthened the impression that a clandestine intimidation campaign was being carried out, the object of which was to coerce the Habibie administration and possibly thwart the 7 June elections. There was ample reason to believe that the incessant violence in Maluku was part of this campaign. Not only was the military incapable of stopping the strife, but reports were surfacing that individual units of the security forces were taking sides in the conflict. Apparently, the aim was to incite inter-religious conflict in Maluku that would raise tension nation-wide—thereby interfering with plans for the election. This would benefit Soeharto and his allied interests who were threatened by reform.

Although some still doubted that a campaign of political sabotage was under way, episodes of violence were occurring with increasing frequency. In addition to the Maluku violence, a mysterious killing spree which resembled the Banyuwangi killings was taking place in the West Java district of Ciamis. Unrest simmered, as usual, in Aceh and Irian Jaya, while persistent reports emerged from East Timor that the military was arming pro-Indonesia militias in advance of the referendum on independence.[50]

With such episodes of violence taking place around the country, it was remarkable—and encouraging—that Habibie's administration remained committed to carrying out the election on schedule. In part, this was attributable to the fact that postponing elections would trigger the same street rallies that had toppled Soeharto. But there was also another reason for Habibie's determination to carry out elections: he was determined to win the presidency for himself.

Given Habibie's need to make progress on trying Soeharto or his children, it initially seemed that Ghalib's failure to convict Tommy in the Goro–Bulog case was a serious blow to the president's campaign. Habibie had repeatedly failed to carry out the MPR's explicit instructions to investigate Soeharto, and his chances of winning Golkar's nomination therefore appeared even more remote than before. Nonetheless, the president doggedly pressed ahead.

Habibie's allies on Golkar's leadership board had been defeated three times in votes over whether to convene a Rapim (the leadership meeting empowered to nominate Golkar's presidential candidate). They nonetheless tried for a fourth time on 7 May. In a strikingly different result, more than two dozen votes on the 106-member board switched sides. A Rapim was scheduled for 10 May. Habibie's faction had finally prevailed.

The surprising result immediately triggered allegations of money politics. Board members that switched sides were said to have been paid sums ranging from one to three billion rupiah each.[51] Marzuki Darusman was particularly bitter: votes had been bought, he said, and the same would take place on a grander scale within the Rapim itself.[52]

Darusman's prediction proved accurate. Golkar's candidate would be nominated through a vote of Golkar's provincial chapter heads, and Habibie's allies began lobbying these 27 figures vigorously. Leading the effort was Arnold Baramuli, the DPA chair who, earlier in the year, had already been implicated in a highly publicised money politics scandal in his native Sulawesi.

Baramuli recognised that Golkar had deep regional divisions and he deliberately played upon anti-Java sentiment among the chapter heads from Outer Island provinces. Habibie's strongest support was from his native region of Eastern Indonesia, and Baramuli formed these ten chapters into a distinct caucus within Golkar—the 'Iramasuka' caucus. The name was taken from an acronym for the eastern provinces: Irian Jaya, Maluku, Sulawesi, Kalimantan and Nusa Tenggara.[53] Iramasuka was the bedrock of Habibie's support, but with only 24 hours remaining until the Rapim commenced the president still had only these ten chapters in his camp. Twelve chapters supported Tandjung and five remained undecided.

In a last-ditch effort to avert defeat, Habibie called on six high-level administration officials to assist Baramuli's lobbying effort. These included Minister of Justice Muladi, Youth Minister Agung Laksono, Labour Minister Fahmi Idris, Deputy Speaker of Parliament Abdul Gafur and National Co-operatives Board Chairman Nurdin Halid. All were veterans of Soeharto-era lobbying campaigns. Working alongside them was Marimuta Manimaren, the Golkar treasurer whose elder brother, Marimutu Sinivasan, owned Texmaco—the textile group which had long served as a slush fund for Golkar.[54] Together, this group became known as 'Tim Sukses Habibie'—or the 'Habibie Success Team'.[55]

Since a large Texmaco textile plant was located in Central Java, Manimaren was specifically assigned to lobby the chapter head from Central Java, Mohammed Hasbi. Muladi, a former rector of the leading university in the province, assisted. Although Hasbi's chapter had explicitly instructed him to support Tandjung, Hasbi succumbed to the lobbying pressure and switched sides the day before the vote.

Rumours abounded that Tim Sukses was carrying out its lobbying efforts through purely financial means. The chapter heads were staying in Hotel Indonesia, and Habibie's lobbyists made visits to their rooms to undertake private negotiations in the hours before the vote was due to take place.[56] By the end of the day Tim Sukses had confirmed support from twenty chapter heads. When the Rapim delegates convened that evening in the hotel's conference hall, members of the Iramasuka caucus were in high spirits—slapping one another on the back and leading cheers. Some of Tandjung's supporters, meanwhile, sulked in the lobby chain-smoking cigarettes.[57]

As the final vote was about to start, a Tandjung supporter interjected and proposed a change to the rules of order. Rather than restricting the vote only to provincial chapter heads, the delegate from Yogyakarta proposed that the far more numerous district heads also be allowed to vote. When the Habibie faction opposed this manoeuvre, another was put forth from Tandjung's camp: rather than allocating one vote to each province, votes should be allocated in proportion to provincial populations. The intent was clear: Habibie was supported by many small provinces, while Tandjung was supported by a few densely populated ones. Again the proposal was shot down.[58]

The voting commenced and, when the ballots were tallied, Golkar confirmed Habibie as its sole presidential candidate. Less than a month from the crucial parliamentary elections the ruling party had finally thrown its support behind Indonesia's 'President-by-Accident'. Despite the debacles of the East Timor policy, the Ghalibie tape and the lack of progress on trying Soeharto, Habibie was nonetheless one major step closer to winning a full five-year term in office.

16

'SLANDER IS WORSE THAN MURDER'

P arty rallies had been taking place for months, but May marked the start of the official period for *kampanye*, or campaigning. In Indonesia, party supporters campaign by parading through the streets in huge, noisy convoys. Vehicles of all sorts are used, from rickety three-wheeled taxis to flat-bed trucks and buses. People stand on the roofs of cars, cling to the sides of buses or even perch on the front bumpers of trucks as they barrel through the streets. In the 1997 election this campaigning had been marked by anger and the constant threat of violence; in 1999 many assumed that the dire economy made violence even more likely.

Exacerbating fears of violence was the fact that most major parties were mobilising bands of quasi-militant youth brigades to provide 'security' during the campaigning. It was expected that such brigades, which were modelled after Golkar's Pemuda Pancasila, would clash with rival party supporters in the streets—and in late April at least five bloody clashes occurred in rapid succession in Central Java, involving supporters of PKB, PPP and PDI Perjuangan.[1] Upper-class residents of Jakarta—particularly wealthy ethnic-Chinese and expatriates—took the news of these clashes as their cue to leave. As the capital braced for another onslaught of mayhem, many who could afford it sought temporary refuge in Bali, Singapore or Australia.

In fact, the fear was misplaced. The violence in Central Java was not repeated elsewhere. The rancour and frustration that had marred the 1997 campaign were virtually gone in 1999: although the economy had collapsed, the political system had been opened and Indonesians were genuinely optimistic about the future. Far from being a calamity, the campaigning period in Jakarta and elsewhere actually resembled a prolonged festival.

With 48 parties competing, only certain parties were permitted to campaign on any given day. The thoroughfares of central Jakarta remained quiet on Golkar's campaign days, but they were filled with green-clad supporters on the days reserved for PPP. And on the PDI Perjuangan days, traffic was brought to a halt by throngs of Megawati supporters.

The final PDI Perjuangan campaign day was 3 June and it was by far the largest mass rally in years, if not in Jakarta's entire history. The city was awash in a sea of red. It was estimated that well over a million people took to the streets, which were so choked that the only way to move about was to walk. But despite the heat, smog and crowds, Jakarta was a seamless mass of smiles and laughter. Campaigners sang, waved banners and pounded on drums well into the night. Supporters of other anti-Golkar parties joined in the revelry—which was, in essence, a mass celebration of political freedom. Indonesians clearly cared about the fate of their nation, and they clearly yearned for change—or *reformasi.*

The pro-Megawati euphoria must have been disheartening for Golkar and Habibie. To make matters worse for the president, demands for Soeharto's prosecution dogged him throughout May. And near the end of the month yet more revelations emerged about Cendana's wealth, when *Time* magazine published an eye-opening cover-story on the Soeharto family's rent-seeking, infighting and freewheeling spending.[2] Photocopies of the article sold briskly at footpath vending stands, and the local press gleefully reproduced the details reported by *Time.*

The report estimated that Bambang and Tommy each earned over $100 million a year from nearly 200 rent-seeking contracts with Pertamina, the state oil monopoly that, according to a Cendana associate, 'they milked like a cow'. An unnamed government source estimated that Bulog contracts provided the family with $3–5 billion over an 18-year period, while Bambang's free acquisition of telecommunications licences inflated the value of his telecom firm, Satelindo, to $2.3 billion. *Time* also described the heavyhanded techniques used by family businesses to seize land from farmers for property developments. And it mentioned that, when the crisis struck, Soeharto's grandson Ari Sigit was planning a 'national shoe project'—whereby all elementary-school children would be required to buy shoes for their school uniform from his company.

Soeharto responded to the report by making his first public appearance in months. 'Slander is worse than murder,' he declared in an unscheduled address on five television stations. 'It's a crime and I have the right to take legal action.'[3] The former president initiated a defamation suit against the New York–based magazine.[4] Unwittingly, this only raised further publicity for the story.

Meanwhile, Attorney General Andi Ghalib initially responded by defending Soeharto: he summoned *Time*'s reporters and commanded them to reveal their sources.[5] Soon, however, public pressure forced him to change direction. His staff summoned Soeharto's children one by one and queried them about *Time*'s assertions.

The interrogations were widely viewed as being cosmetic, but one comment provided another hint of the extent of the Soeharto family's assets: in talking with reporters one of Ghalib's investigators read a list of places in which Titiek was alleged to have holdings. They included: Moscow, Uzbekistan, Canada, Jordan, India, Yemen, Cambodia, Spain, Sudan, South Africa, Madagascar, Singapore, the Netherlands, Vietnam, Hong Kong, Myanmar, the Virgin Islands and Florida.[6] Presumably the holdings were related to her international barter-trade concession, which she owned in partnership with her brother-in-law, Hashim Djojo-hadikusumo.

The most highlighted aspect of the *Time* article was its mention of reports that had emerged the previous year regarding a massive transfer of funds from Switzerland to Austria.[7] The transfer, which totalled $9 billion and reportedly caught the attention of the US Treasury, was attributed to the Soeharto family. Soeharto and his children had reportedly visited Switzerland on at least three occasions between 1996 and 1998.

Habibie reacted to the *Time* report by stating that he was sure Soeharto was telling the truth about not owning assets abroad: 'He never lies—if he doesn't want to tell you something, he'll just smile.'[8] Although Habibie despatched Ghalib and Muladi to Switzerland and Austria to investigate reports of the massive transfer, it was clear from the outset that their journey would accomplish little. According to the Swiss ambassador, his government was ready to order Swiss banks to reveal any accounts owned by Soeharto or his family, but the Indonesian government first had to submit an official application for international judicial assistance. Habibie's government never produced the request—without which the much-publicised trip by Ghalib and Muladi was pointless.[9]

The renewed attention on Cendana's wealth was a public relations setback for Habibie—and it was only made worse by Akbar Tandjung. The Golkar chair acknowledged that if Habibie did not make progress in trying Soeharto before the October MPR session the president's campaign could encounter 'difficulties'. This was yet another sign of the ruling party's discord: the Golkar chair was snapping at the Achilles heel of the Golkar candidate. But Habibie was not the only presidential candidate to suffer an embarrassment on the eve of elections: Megawati had problems of her own.

In late May PDI Perjuangan finally submitted its final list of legislative candidates. Compiled by the party's central leadership, the list assigned individual candidates to each electoral district. This was the crux of the proportional system: people voted for party symbols, not individuals. Voters had only one way to find out who would represent them if a certain party won their district's seat: they had to consult a list—which was to be posted at each polling booth on election day—detailing the names of the candidates assigned to that district by each of the 48 parties. But even if this list was available, the voters were unlikely to recognise most of the names of the candidates, because a large portion were Jakarta residents rather than locals.

On 25 May PPP chair Hamzah Haz ignited a controversy by declaring that PDI Perjuangan's candidate lists included disproportionate numbers of non-Muslims. Neither Megawati nor her aides provided an adequate response to the allegation, which therefore snowballed. Several days before the election the powerful Indonesian Council of Ulama (MUI), headed by Habibie's ally Ali Yafie, denounced Megawati in harsh terms.

In a formal edict disseminated through mosques throughout the country just before election day, the MUI declared that Muslim voters were religiously obligated to vote for a Muslim party.[10] The target was obviously PDI Perjuangan. Similar digs at Megawati's party also came from Muhammadiyah and even the NU—although the NU statement lacked the endorsement of Abdurrahman Wahid.

Megawati's supporters claimed that the Islamic camp was perpetuating the divisive, spiteful tactics begun eight months earlier by Food Minister A.M. Saefuddin—but in fact Megawati herself was to blame for exercising exceedingly poor judgment. Non-Muslims barely comprised 14 per cent of the nation's population, yet more than half of PDI Perjuangan's candidate list was non-Muslim. The list had been drafted with considerable input from three PDI Perjuangan figures who were politically conservative and ardently Protestant. Apart from being insensitive to Muslim interests, Megawati had blundered by further distancing herself from the Islamic camp—precisely when she needed to be reaching out to potential alliance partners.

The nasty debate over Megawati's candidate list threatened to inflame religious tensions on voting day, but all remained peaceful. On the morning of Monday 7 June some 103 million Indonesians flocked to over 298 000 polling stations in 66 000 villages and neighbourhoods throughout the country. They did so in such an orderly and peaceful fashion that observers were astonished. Far from being marred by violence, 7 June was a proud day for Indonesia. Whether Jakarta's political elite was ready for democracy remained highly questionable, but if anyone doubted whether the Indonesian people themselves were capable of participating in democracy, this day laid that doubt to rest.

In the absence of accurate polls no one knew what to expect when the first results began filtering in from polling booths. The reporting of the results was exceedingly slow: ballots were counted first at the polling booth and then at the village levels before being counted for a third time at the sub-district level. From there some results were reported directly to

Jakarta, while others were re-counted again at the district and provincial levels before reaching the capital.

The system provided ample opportunities for the cross-verification of vote-counts, but the counting took place by hand at each level and therefore consumed weeks. But in the first days after the vote it was already clear that Megawati had failed to win an outright majority of the votes cast. Indonesia's first experiment with democracy in over 40 years was providing no single candidate with an irrefutable popular mandate to lead.

Before reliable election results were available the question already being asked was whether the voting had been fair. The balloting had been monitored by around 350 foreign organisations and, more importantly, tens of thousands of student volunteers. In addition, a small group of Indonesian statisticians, called the 'Rector's Forum', sampled results at the polling booth level around the nation, forming a statistically signifi-cant prediction of the outcome of the vote. The findings of the Rector's Forum largely converged with the official vote-count, suggesting that the vote-counting process had been fair overall.[11] But there were, of course, exceptions.

The worse instances of fraud appeared to have occurred in North Sulawesi. To investigate a horde of complaints, the KPU dispatched a respected lawyer from the Legal Aid Foundation, Todung Mulya Lubis. Although there were ample signs of wrongdoing, the agency responsible for adjudicating the complaints was the Panwaslak, or Election Oversight Committee. Because the Panwaslak consisted largely of judges from the notoriously corrupt court system, it took no action in North Sulawesi—and the KPU was powerless to do anything about it. The same scenario was played out all around the country: election complaints elicited little or no response from the Panwaslak.

As more election results were reported, tougher questions were asked about the integrity of the vote. This was because of the reported results for Golkar: the ruling party's vote totals seemed to rise in direct proportion to a district's distance from Jakarta. As some in Golkar had admitted prior to the poll, the party's popularity in the politically savvy heartland of Java was poor. In total, less than 10 per cent of Java's voters chose Golkar—a thun-dering rejection of the status quo. But in the distant reaches of Eastern Indonesia, Golkar generally placed first or second with shares that ranged from 40 to 65 per cent. The ruling party's second strongest performance was recorded in the backwater of Southeast Sulawesi, where Golkar claimed 63 per cent of the vote. Due to indications of fraud and voter coercion, only five of the 48 party representatives on Southeast Sulawesi's provincial election committee agreed to endorse the result.[12]

In effect, Golkar scored its best returns in the districts that were most remote, underdeveloped and impoverished. Sceptics charged that Golkar had bought votes, coerced voters or manipulated the vote-count. It was also possible, however, that voters in remote locations were simply ignorant of their choices. Others may have genuinely supported the ruling party—particularly in Outer Island areas where the devaluation was a boon to freeholders growing cash crops. But because Panwaslak was unable to adjudicate disputes—and because there was a broad array of interests that simply wanted to finalise the results and move swiftly on to the presidential election—the true reasons for Golkar's mystifyingly strong performances in remote provinces were never officially determined. Questionable results simply went unquestioned.[13]

The nationwide vote tally, which was finally confirmed on 17 July, showed that PDI Perjuangan had won a 34 per cent plurality of the votes cast, followed by Golkar with 22 per cent. Wahid's PKB and Hamzah Haz's PPP received 12 per cent and 11 per cent respectively. The main surprise was Rais's Pan, which won a mere 7 per cent of votes cast. The results mirrored the Ifes poll that had been conducted four months before the election.

The nationwide vote-count therefore showed that nearly 80 per cent of Indonesian voters had, in effect, voted against Golkar by choosing parties opposed to the ruling party. But this opposition was highly frag-mented between Megawati's PDI Perjuangan, Wahid's PKB and a host of Islamic-leaning parties. Furthermore, Megawati's slim lead over Golkar was narrowed farther by the regional imbalance in the electoral system.

Because PDI Perjuangan and PKB won most of their votes on Java, their shares of parliament were smaller than their shares of the national vote, at 31 per cent and 10 per cent respectively. In contrast, Golkar benefited from its strong performance in the Outer Islands, receiving 24 per cent of parliament's seats. The shares of PPP and Pan remained the same. Another 9 per cent of parliament's seats were shared by sixteen small parties, most of which were Islamic-orientated, plus 8 per cent allocated to the military.

The breakdown of the new parliament was therefore known by July, but its 500 members were not due to convene until 1 October. And before the presidential election could begin, it was still necessary to determine the complement of 135 regional representatives and 65 functional group representatives who would sit alongside the parliamentarians in the 700-member MPR.

The process of appointing functional group representatives required the KPU to choose which groups should be entitled to representatives; then those groups—mostly religious organisations, professional guilds, minority associations and the like—selected the individuals they wanted to represent them. The KPU attempted to perform a screening function to reject individuals who were clearly partisan, but in practice this proved impossible. In this way Abdurrahman Wahid gained entry to the MPR as the representative of the NU functional group. More significantly, a bevy of pro-Habibie politicos obtained functional group seats. Mahadi Sinambela—Golkar's representative on the KPU and a staunch ally of Akbar Tandjung—lamented in late August that around half of the 65 functional group representatives were inclined to support Habibie.

As for the regional representatives, each of Indonesia's 27 new provincial assemblies was assigned with electing five representatives to the MPR. This is where Golkar enjoyed a distinct advantage: the ruling party was pre-eminent in many small provinces—each of which was entitled to five representatives—whereas PDI Perjuangan and PKB were strong in a few very large provinces. Although many regional representatives did not disclose their party preference, it was generally assumed that over half of the 135 appointees favoured Habibie.

As was the case with the functional group representatives, many Jakarta politicians from the Soeharto era resurfaced as regional representatives in the MPR. This produced allegations that the election results from the 27 provincial assemblies had been produced by money politics. And as if these dubious results alone were not proof enough that money politics were skewing Indonesia's democratic transition, evidence began emerging that Tim Sukses had long been using graft and extortion to mobilise funds for Habibie's campaign.

The first money politics scandal to affect the Habibie administration had surfaced in May, when the World Bank postponed funds for the government's social safety net because of worries that the funds would be misused. In June US customs officials apprehended a woman who was attempting to enter Hawaii without declaring that she was carrying $600 000 in US currency; Minister of Industry and Trade Rahardi Ramelan angrily denied allegations that the woman was his wife, but suspicions lingered nonetheless.[14] Later, state auditors disclosed that in his capacity as head of Bulog the minister had authorised Rp88 billion in spending on 'state needs'. Subsequent ministers later asserted that the funds were allocated to Golkar.[15]

Another serious scandal was revealed in July by a new offshoot of the Legal Aid Foundation: Indonesia Corruption Watch. The group publicised bank documents that showed that Attorney General Andi Ghalib had received over Rp50 billion paid directly to his personal bank accounts. The payments were made by tycoons who were under investigation by Ghalib's office. The implication was that Ghalib had been using his office's powers to extort bribes from wealthy individuals. Indonesia Corruption Watch produced receipts showing that Ghalib's wife had used Rp500 million from one such account to purchase jewellery.[16]

Rumours that Ghalib had been raising bribe money had already been circulating for several months. For instance, indebted bankers who had been blocked from travelling abroad were said to have been able to remove themselves from the embargo list by simply paying off Ghalib's office. Now, however, there was strong evidence of wrongdoing, and Habibie was forced to sack his loyal ally and fellow Sulawesi native.

As a replacement for Ghalib, Habibie initially chose Feisal Tanjung. When this created a public furore, the president relented and temporarily filled the position with one of Ghalib's deputies, Ismudjoko. A meek career bureaucrat, Ismudjoko was clearly out of his league in the politically pivotal position of attorney general. Soon after his promotion, he reminisced to an interviewer about the happiest period of his career: the seven years he had spent in the sleepy town of Wates, a tiny, peaceful outpost in Central Java. It was clear from the outset, therefore, that Habibie's promises to implement rule-of-law were not likely to be fulfilled by the humble Ismudjoko.

As for Andi Ghalib, the evidence against him was never taken to court. One of Ghalib's aides later asserted: 'If the case had been thoroughly investigated, it would have produced connections to bank accounts controlled by other ministers, such as Feisal Tanjung and Rahardi Ramelan.'[17] In any event, attention was diverted from the Ghalib scandal in late July. A heretofore little-known banking analyst, Pradjoto, suddenly occupied centre stage.

After more than three decades of tightly controlled public discourse, the advent of *reformasi* gave rise to countless seminars, forums and conferences in which political and economic issues were debated with unprecedented fervour. It was at one of these seminars that Pradjoto fielded a question regarding the status of Bank Bali, a medium-sized private bank that had consistently won management quality awards before the crisis. The finance ministry planned to recapitalise the bank and hoped to invite foreign participation. Standard Chartered was scrutinising Bank Bali's accounts; it was hoped that the British bank would help fund the recapitalisation costs in exchange for taking over Bank Bali's management from its Indonesian owners, the Ramli family.

The business community was anxiously waiting for the outcome: the crisis was already two years old and the Bank Bali sale would finally mark the first instance in which the state sought to defray its financial burdens by selling a significant asset to foreign investors. If all went well, the Bank Bali transaction would provide a model for subsequent deals. Australia's ANZ Bank, for instance, was watching the Bank Bali deal closely before deciding whether to bid for Bank Panin. To kick-start an economic recovery Indonesia needed to encourage foreign investors to take over moribund assets, such as banks, that were under state control. The government needed to recapitalise the banking sector swiftly and with foreign participation, and on both counts Bank Bali was a crucial test case.

At the seminar on 30 July, therefore, Pradjoto was asked why Standard Chartered had still not decided whether to invest in Bank Bali. The foreign bank had been conducting 'due diligence' since April and its three-month deadline had already passed in mid-July, with no decision made.[18] Pradjoto responded by dropping what proved to be a political bombshell: the transaction was derailed, he declared, because Bank Bali was 'a victim of money politics'.[19]

Pradjoto claimed that a gaping hole had been discovered in Bank Bali's balance sheet. During the crisis the bank had extended a number of large 'inter-bank' loans to banks that were later shut down by the government. These loans were of various types, but in total they amounted to a staggering Rp3 trillion—or nearly a third of the bank's total assets. Of this amount, Rp904 billion was a claim on Syamsul Nursalim's BDNI. Bank Bali's owner, Rudy Ramli, believed that the government's deposit guarantee scheme, which was introduced by Soeharto in January 1998, covered the claim. He therefore felt that the government, through Ibra, owed him the Rp904 billion.

According to Pradjoto, Ramli tried for more than a year to secure his claim from Ibra and BI officials. Finally, in early 1999, he was forced to use the 'facilitation' services of a private company, whose owner acted as a middleman between the bank and the government. This middleman's fee, or 'kickback', was a staggering 60 per cent of the claim.[20] In effect, Ramli had been the victim of extortion: to avoid a Rp904 billion loss, he was forced to pay a Rp546 billion bribe. But the most alarming feature of Pradjoto's story was the identity of the middleman: he was a member of a major political party, and his kickback was being used in a campaign of 'money politics'.

While the public gradually digested Pradjoto's story a startling comment came from the president's chief advisor, Arnold Baramuli. Even though Pradjoto had not mentioned Golkar by name, Baramuli nonetheless branded Pradjoto's claims as slander against the ruling party. He hotly denied that Golkar had been involved in money politics. 'If I were the chair of Golkar,' said Baramuli, chiding Akbar Tandjung, 'I would sue Pradjoto for slander in accordance with the law.'[21]

Meanwhile, Ibra Director Glenn Yusuf contributed another piece of information: on 1 June, Ibra had indeed instructed BI to pay Bank Bali the Rp904 billion it was owed by BDNI.[22] Pradjoto's story, therefore, was partly verified. Moreover, BI made the payment immediately upon receiving Ibra's instruction, even though it was outside normal banking hours—at 7.30 on a Sunday evening.[23] The press began to take more interest.

Some enterprising reporters had somehow surmised that the middleman in question was Setya Novanto, one of several deputy treasurers involved in fundraising for Golkar. In addition to being a member of Tim Sukses, the young *pribumi* businessman had been given a parliamentary seat from East Timor, even though he was a West Java native. Novanto also had business links to Baramuli and the minister for state enterprises,

Tanri Abeng. One day after Yusuf's comment, Novanto acknowledged that he was the president director of EGP, an 'investment services' company owned by the ethnic-Chinese property magnate Djoko Tjandra. In January, said Novanto, EGP had forged an 'asset swap' with Bank Bali.

Under the terms of the swap, or *cessie*, as it was referred to in Indonesian business parlance, EGP was entitled to collect Bank Bali's claim on Ibra, in exchange for a payment made to Bank Bali. As Novanto explained: 'The use of an investment company, like EGP, to make Bank Bali's claim on Ibra is standard practice in banking.'[24] In fact, the public was not so gullible. It was clear that EGP should have had no role to play: either Bank Bali was entitled to the full claim or not, but the bank certainly should not have had to split the claim with an intermediary. Meanwhile, the public was also aware that the acronym 'EGP' had a dual meaning: in Jakarta slang, it was also a commonly used epithet meaning 'I don't give a damn' (*emang gue pikirin*). The homonym was obviously deliberate.

EGP's kickback was a minor affair set against the context of Indonesian corruption: at the prevailing exchange rate, Novanto's fee amounted to around $70 million, or less than a tenth what Marimutu Sinivasan had borrowed a year earlier from the central bank, and less than 1 per cent of the widely misused BLBI liquidity credits. But the scandal was significant for other reasons. First, it undermined the credibility of the institution that was the most crucial for an economic recovery: Ibra. More importantly, it strongly appeared that one of the people responsible for extorting funds from the bank recapitalisation process (Novanto) was a fundraiser for the president.

Naturally, Habibie's loyalists in Tim Sukses desperately wanted the affair to be quickly forgotten, just like the Andi Ghalib scandal and several others before that. The attorney general's office claimed that the newly passed Central Bank Law, which provided for BI's independence, rendered the government powerless to investigate the case. In fact, the opposite was true: it was precisely this law that empowered the authorities to open bank accounts and uncover the perpetrators. Yet again the Indonesian public was being fed Soeharto-era 'legal formalism'. Meanwhile, the police conducted perfunctory interrogations of officials within Ibra and the ministry of finance, but little progress was expected. But just as it was beginning to seem as if the scandal might fade away, new momentum was injected from a seemingly unlikely source: a vice-chair of Golkar.

Convening a press conference on 12 August, Marzuki Darusman stunned the Jakarta press by exhorting investigators to find the true perpetrators of the Bank Bali scandal—even though the weight of evidence to date suggested that those perpetrators were fellow members of Golkar. Furthermore, Darusman told reporters that the police investigations were headed in the wrong direction: the officials at Ibra and the finance ministry were merely lesser actors and should not be allowed to be used as scapegoats for the true masterminds.[25] Darusman sounded as if he possessed a wealth of information on what had actually transpired—in effect, he was acting like a traffic cop, directing the flow of the investigation away from dead ends.

Darusman's press conference provided the Bank Bali scandal with an entirely new dimension. The scandal started as a serious financial crime and quickly became political when it embroiled presidential aides. Now it was larger still: Golkar politicians were apparently using the scandal to derail the presidential campaign of their own party's candidate, Habibie. In fact, it soon became clear that Tandjung and Darusman had been responsible for leaking the original information to Pradjoto.[26]

The problems of Tim Sukses grew worse in the next few days. On 13 August the IMF issued a stern warning.[27] Because the scandal pertained to the crucial process of bank recapitalisation and, therefore, investor confidence, the fund demanded a thorough investigation before it would disburse the next instalment of its liquidity support to the central bank.[28] And the following day more details emerged about the involvement of Habibie's highest advisor, Arnold Baramuli.

The 15 August edition of *Gamma*, a new investigative news weekly, printed the transcript of a recorded conversation, similar to the Ghalibie tape exposed five months earlier by *Panji*. This conversation was between Baramuli and Setya Novanto, with several other unidentified voices in the background. The recording, which experts later certified as authentic, had been made on a Saturday afternoon during the first week of August. It captured Baramuli coaching Novanto on how to justify EGP's receipt of the kickback. The chair of the supreme advisory council told Novanto that he need not worry: 'I'll do all your thinking for you.'[29]

Baramuli's first point was to emphasise that EGP's kickback did not, in fact, derive from the bank recapitalisation program, as some media reports had construed. 'Those funds belonged to Bank Bali,' he said, 'and they were paid according to a contract. There's nothing wrong with making a contract, is there? Why all the fuss?'

Next, Baramuli likened the transaction to a distressed debt sale.[30] At the time, most debts from private Indonesian companies were trading at steep discounts in secondary markets, reflecting the low likelihood that the debts would ever be repaid in full. Baramuli emphasised this point: 'People are attacking you for taking too much. [But] it was not much, only 60 per cent—er, 40 per cent—from the [face value] of your *cessie*. Other people take 80 per cent! [You can say:] In my case, I didn't take much—only a 40 per cent discount from the claim.'

Baramuli and Novanto were apparently confused about whether EGP's kickback was equivalent to 40 per cent or 60 per cent of Bank Bali's claim on Ibra. In fact, the kickback was roughly equivalent to 40 per cent of the principal plus interest, but around 60 per cent of the principal alone, which is all that Bank Bali ultimately collected. Baramuli went on: 'If you want to sell the debt of Bakrie [Bakrie & Brothers, a heavily indebted conglomerate], you would have to give the Americans 80 per cent! It's a discount, not a fee. Why do [creditors who sell their claims] want to give discounts of 40, 50 or 60 per cent? Because they profit, don't they? If he collects cash today, he profits. So if you collect on a claim, you only take 40 per cent.'

'So, the payment is only 60 per cent of the total,' said Novanto.

'Sixty per cent discount,' answered Baramuli.

'From the claim?' asked Novanto.

'From . . . ya . . . the claim. You collect, you only get 60 per cent. You only pay 60 per cent.' By repeatedly contradicting himself, Baramuli was only confusing Novanto. Nonetheless, the chair of the supreme advisory council carried on: 'So, the discount is 40 per cent from the claim. If other people take over claims, they take up to 80 per cent. That's over twice as much—that's not healthy! You have to make this clear . . . 40 per cent is normal.'

The difference, of course, was that Bank Bali's claim was not on a commercial entity but on the government. It should have been for the courts to decide whether Bank Bali was eligible to be paid or was not. Before concluding the meeting Baramuli admonished Novanto to keep his identity secret: 'Eh, don't use our name—use Djoko's name, ya?'

Revelations of the Bank Bali scandal threatened to finally sink Habibie's dogged bid for the presidency. And at the same time—and perhaps most worrisomely for Tim Sukses—the deadlocked process of political alliance-forming finally witnessed a breakthrough.

Apparently finally aware of her political predicament—and perhaps eager to mend the damage wrought by her fiery speech in July—Megawati made an effort to reach out to a potential alliance partner. On 13 August two nationwide alumni organisations co-hosted a banquet at Jakarta's historic Hotel Indonesia. Both organisations were politically influential: Kahmi embodied alumni from the Islamic Students Association, while GMNI comprised alumni from the Indonesian National Students Movement, a secular-nationalist organisation.

Just as the two giant student groups vied with each other on campuses around the country, the two alumni associations were longstanding rivals in national politics. The banquet was meant to portray a rapprochement between the two groups in the interest of *reformasi*. It also, therefore, symbolised a truce between the two groups' chief luminaries: Megawati from GMNI and, from Kahmi, Akbar Tandjung.

There was no mistaking the meeting's intent. In effect, it was a political summit between two arch-rivals. Aides to the two politicians had spent over a week preparing the groundwork for the event.[31] Seated at the same table, the pair engaged in polite conversation while successive speakers harped on the merits of a Megawati–Tandjung alliance, implying that the pair would make an ideal presidential ticket. In comments to the press at the end of the evening, the two politicians reminisced about their middle school days—at the ages of thirteen, Tandjung and the daughter of then-president Soekarno had been classmates.

After months of being aloof, Megawati was finally reaching out to build an alliance with a common enemy of Habibie: Tandjung's faction in Golkar. Ardent reformists within Megawati's party were dismayed by her willingness to embrace figures from the 'status quo', but the results of the 7 June elections—and the vehement antagonism of the Islamic camp—had left Megawati with no alternatives. The question, therefore, was simply how many votes Tandjung could command in the MPR session. Not only were the divisions within Golkar unclear, but the MPR's functional group and regional representatives had not yet been appointed. There were, however, some indications of where sentiment within the party was heading.

Several days after Megawati's summit with Tandjung there occurred a seemingly obscure event: Ginandjar Kartasasmita engaged legal assistance from Muchyar Yara, an attorney who was also a mid-level Golkar official.[32] Beneath the surface the news carried more significance than most realised—in fact, it marked a turning point in the presidential election. Ginandjar was defending himself from allegations, levelled by Mulia Group owner Djoko Tjandra, that he was implicated in the Bank Bali scandal. This alone suggested that Tim Sukses had turned against the powerful economics official. Moreover, Ginandjar's decision to retain Yara was significant: the lawyer was a staunch supporter of Akbar Tandjung. A native of Sumatera's remote Bengkulu province (the home of Megawati's mother, Fatmawati), Yara had helped orchestrate the Tandjung–Megawati summit.[33]

That Ginandjar was turning to Yara strongly suggested that Habibie's senior economics minister had defected to Tandjung's camp. As confirmation of this fact, Tim Sukses member Muladi decried Ginandjar's choice of Yara, claiming that Yara was not 'objective'. Ginandjar was Golkar's senior politician from West Java, the province with the party's largest delegation in the new parliament. If he supported an alliance between Tandjung and Megawati, all 23 members of his province's delegation were likely to do so as well.

Thus, if Megawati were backed by Tandjung, and if Tandjung were backed by Ginandjar, the PDI Perjuangan candidate would be practically certain of sufficient votes to win the presidency—if, that is, she secured the support of the military and Abdurrahman Wahid's PKB. The military was expected to back whomever was poised to win: Wiranto understood that amid the uncertainty his best interest was to remain neutral for as long as possible. Rumours that Megawati had offered him the vice-presidency had been circulating for months. It only remained to be seen whether, and to what extent, the support of his MPR seats was needed to ensure victory.³⁴ And as for Wahid, Megawati seemed confident that the support of his PKB would ultimately revert to her.

Meanwhile, Megawati's apparent alliance-building with Akbar Tand-jung was accompanied by worsening disarray within the third major element of the presidential contest: the Islamic camp. Rife with cleavages and jealousies, the Islamic parties were unable to find a single viable pres-idential candidate to unite them. Rais, having failed to win broad-based support in the election, seemed to be reverting to his traditional role as an Islamist, but he was simply too unpopular (especially with the military) to win the presidency. Other Islamic party leaders, such as Yusril Ihza Mahendra and Hamzah Haz, had even narrower bases of support.

Faced with a dearth of candidates, Rais surprised many in mid-July by blurting out the possibility of supporting a candidacy by, of all people, his arch-rival: Abdurrahman Wahid. But few took Rais seriously. Wahid was still presumed to be tacitly supporting Megawati, and his disdain for Rais and the political Islamists was famed. In any event, Wahid appeared too frail to run. Leaders of Islamic parties immediately dismissed Rais's suggestion as a 'personal opinion' which they did not—and would not—support.³⁵

After more than a year of uncertainty Indonesia's political transition finally seemed to be nearing a conclusion. The Bank Bali scandal had delivered a crippling blow to Habibie, while the Islamic camp was in disarray. Tandjung and now Ginandjar were leaning toward Megawati. It appeared that the presidency was all but assured of going to Megawati. But, not for the first time in Indonesian politics, appearances would prove deceiving. Habibie's Tim Sukses was not yet ready to concede.

T im Sukses scrambled to contain the damage sustained by the Bank Bali transaction. Events moved rapidly. First, Setya Novanto resigned as a deputy treasurer of Golkar.³⁶ Next, Baramuli made a pronounce-ment: on 14 August he told reporters that the Rp546 billion payment to EGP would be returned to Bank Bali. This was a stunning promise from one who disavowed any connection to the transaction.³⁷ Ironically, Baramuli issued the statement immediately after a ceremony in which the president awarded him with the nation's highest honour, the *Anugerah Bintang*.³⁸

Just as Baramuli predicted, EGP transferred the funds to Bank Bali several days later.³⁹ Apparently, the perpetrators hoped that by simply putting the funds back where they belonged the scandal could be laid to rest. In fact, it only raised further suspicion: the prompt mobilisation of

$70 million demonstrated that whoever perpetrated the deal commanded access to vast sums of money; this, in turn, suggested that the Bank Bali deal was but one of many such transactions.

Having tried to placate the public by returning the funds, Baramuli next sought to intimidate his opponents. A petition began circulating among the executive boards of provincial Golkar chapters; it demanded the removal of Marzuki Darusman from the party leadership. Twelve chapters endorsed the letter, which Tandjung branded as 'a terrorist act by political guerillas'.[40] Darusman was sure that the initiative for the petition came from 'amateurs who feel jealous, angry, threatened and insecure'.[41] Tempers within Golkar were clearly running high. Baramuli openly admitted that he had signed the letter, and many suspected that he was actually its chief sponsor.[42]

It seemed odd to some that Baramuli was going to such great lengths—but the reason soon became clear. On 22 August Indonesian Corruption Watch provided reporters with a document called the 'Chronicle of Rudy Ramli'. Baramuli had obviously been anticipating this event. The corruption watchdog group maintained that Ramli, as Bank Bali's owner and key manager, was the key to unlocking the case. The 'chronicle' was his recollection of how the scandal unfolded, and it pointed to the involvement of a host of cabinet members, administration officials and senior politicians.

In the chronicle, Ramli asserted that those pressuring him to engage EGP were Baramuli, Abeng, Tjandra and Novanto.[43] He said that in a meeting on 11 February this group secured the support of BI Governor Syahril Sabirin, who Baramuli ordered to facilitate Bank Bali's Rp904 billion claim. Thereafter, says Ramli, BI officials were much more co-operative with Bank Bali.

Because, he says, he felt coerced, Ramli informed a World Bank official of his predicament in March, before finally seeking help from Finance Minister Bambang Subianto in mid-May. According to Ramli, 'Bambang promised that he would find a way out. He promised to make sure that those involved in the transaction would start fighting among themselves.' Subianto then arranged for Ramli to meet Marimutu Manimaren, the younger brother of Texmaco owner Sinivasan. Like Novanto, Manimaren was a deputy treasurer of Golkar and a member of Tim Sukses—according to some, he ranked second only to Baramuli in terms of his influence with the president.[44]

Manimaren provided little solace to Ramli: he offered to help retrieve Bank Bali's inter-bank loan from Ibra, but he too demanded a facilitation fee that was only slightly smaller than EGP's. Manimaren and Hariman Siregar, a longstanding friend of Habibie who was also prominent on Tim Sukses, advised Ramli to take their offer and simply cancel the transaction with Tjandra. According to Ramli:

They said that it would be better if the transaction did not go through Djoko [Tjandra]. Manimaren informed me that 'RI 1' [the president] only needed Rp300 billion. It was feared that Djoko would ask for more than that. They also said that they themselves were not asking for anything . . . I felt pessimistic that Tjandra would agree to cancel the deal . . . but they told me not to worry. They knew who was behind Djoko—namely Tanri Abeng and Baramuli.

Manimaren and Siregar were apparently trying to take the deal for themselves. But in his subsequent meeting with Tjandra, Ramli not only failed to cancel his deal with EGP but also let slip that it was Manimaren who had asked him to try.

A short while later Ramli was summoned to yet another meeting—this time with both teams, Manimaren's and Baramuli's, in attendance. 'The meat of the discussion,' said Ramli, 'was that they had already talked and had come to the conclusion that the one who was making things difficult was Bambang Subianto.' Without delay, Manimaren and Tjandra brought Ramli to Subianto's home to straighten out the entire affair. Afterwards they planned to visit Habibie. Ramli recalled:

At 9 p.m. we reached Bambang's home, and Manimaren first entered alone. Ten minutes later Djoko and I were asked to come in. Inside, Bambang said, 'So, everything's settled then, right? There's no problem.' After that the conversation revolved around Djoko's debts to Ibra. I didn't understand what they were on about. When the meeting finished, Manimaren again spoke privately with Bambang for several minutes. After that Manimaren said that we need not meet with the head of the government, and Bambang said that he would straighten everything out the next day. Around 10 p.m. we returned to Hotel Mulia to report to Tanri Abeng. After reporting, I went straight home.

If Subianto had had any qualms about Bank Bali's transaction with EGP, they were apparently put to rest, somehow, in the course of his brief discussion with Manimaren. In effect, Manimaren had joined forces with Baramuli and Tjandra—much to Ramli's chagrin.

Djoko Tjandra repeatedly implored Glenn Yusuf to authorise the Rp904 billion payment to Bank Bali, but Yusuf refused.[45] Finally, while the Ibra director was in New York on 1 June, his two deputies (Pande Lubis and Farid Harijanto) authorised the payment in his absence.[46] Despite its being a Sunday evening, Bank Indonesia made the Rp904 billion payment.

Meanwhile, Ramli had already fled to Singapore and checked into the penthouse suite of an inconspicuous hotel—using a false name. He claimed, in his chronicle, that he was suffering from severe stress and wanted to be able to ponder his predicament without being disturbed. On 3 June he finally decided to contact Manimaren and ask whether it was still necessary to transfer the Rp546 billion to EGP. Manimaren said that it was, and so Ramli made the transfer. But in so doing, his saga did not end—in fact, it was only just beginning.

Less than three weeks after the transfer, Ramli claimed, he was contacted by Anthony Salim, the son of Sudono and heir to the Salim Group. Anthony warned Ramli that his transaction with EGP was bound to create problems, and he invited Ramli to his office to meet the president's brother and close aide, Timmy Habibie. According to Ramli:

> In the meeting Anthony said that I must be careful because Djoko had already been boasting—even in Singapore—that he had 'bought off Kuningan [the president]' with Rp300 billion. However, Timmy Habibie said that the actual sum was less: he said that they had only received Rp200 billion.

Anthony contacted Ramli in early July and reassured him that the affair had been 'cleared up', but Ramli says he was still concerned. And as he feared, the transaction was leaked to the public, through Pradjoto, before the end of the month.

The circulation of Ramli's chronicle represented a public relations disaster for the administration, Tim Sukses and Habibie himself. Some of the president's closest associates—such as his brother Timmy, Baramuli, and Hariman Siregar—were implicated in wrongdoing. So were at least three cabinet ministers: Sabirin, Subianto and Abeng. But just as it seemed that Habibie's presidential aspirations might be sunk, the scandal took yet another strange twist.

Following a cabinet meeting on 26 August, Muladi (now serving as state secretary as well as justice minister) appeared before reporters to read out a startling letter. He attributed the letter to Rudy Ramli and claimed that he had acquired it from a trustworthy source. The letter disavowed the contents of the chronicle, claiming that the document was a fake. 'I have never produced a chronology of the Bank Bali case, either in typeset or oral form,' the letter read. 'The chronology did not come from me and I therefore bear no responsibility for its contents.'[47]

Muladi was clearly elated: the letter destroyed the most damaging testimony against Tim Sukses, which could now distance itself from the transaction between EGP and Bank Bali. But the press soon began to have doubts. Reporters noted that, at the bottom of the letter they had been handed, the signature was written as 'Rudi Ramli'. Until now the banker's first name had always been spelt with a 'y'. A controversy immediately arose: which testimony was authentic, and which was fake? But before anyone could find out, the focus of the press in Jakarta—and throughout much of the world—shifted to a tiny territory over 2000 kilometres from Jakarta: East Timor.

17

HEROES OF INTEGRATION

In East Timor the normally staid and bureaucratic United Nations was taking a daring gamble. President Habibie, as mentioned before, startled the UN in December 1999 by offering the East Timorese a referendum on self-determination—or, as he preferred to put it, a 'popular consultation'. This had long been the dream of Alexandre 'Xanana' Gusmao, East Timor's hugely popular independence leader, but both Xanana and the UN had hoped that demilitarisation would take place first. They anticipated a process of several years in which to prepare East Timor for a fair and peaceful vote—instead, in January 2000, Habibie insisted that the vote take place before the next MPR session. This was less than nine months away.

Habibie may have believed, like a great many in the Indonesian elite, that a fair ballot in East Timor would produce a pro-integration result—thereby 'confirming' the territory's status as Indonesia's 27th province and boosting Habibie's prestige just prior to the MPR's presidential election. Conversely, if the ballot produced a pro-independence result, Habibie may have believed that this would earn him valuable international kudos. Some say he even expected to win the Nobel Peace Prize. But if that was the case, the president was sorely underestimating the depth of domestic opposition to East Timorese independence. Like the UN, he was committing himself to a very high-stakes wager.

The UN had two paramount concerns in the hastily arranged ballot: fairness and security. From the outset there were serious doubts on the latter score—but because Habibie's offer might never be granted again, the UN accepted the risks and forged ahead. Preparations were made to establish a United Nations Assistance Mission in East Timor (Unamet), manned by about 1000 foreign and 4000 East Timorese staff. Meanwhile, the Indonesian military proceeded with a program of its own.

Gen. Wiranto adamantly opposed Habibie's ballot offer. So too did almost every army officer. The army had been fighting East Timor's guerilla force, Falintil, for 25 years. Though the army had whittled Falintil down to a tiny force camped high in East Timor's towering mountain range, the army lost thousands of its own troops in the process. This bred a deep emotional resistance to East Timorese independence, but military leaders also voiced fears of a 'domino theory', whereby concessions to East Timor would encourage secession movements in Aceh and Irian Jaya.[1] And finally, the military had its own institutional interests at stake.

Indonesia's military is largely self-funded. Government defence spending is estimated to cover only around a quarter of the military's operational needs. Unlike military leaders elsewhere in the world, Indonesia's generals rarely push for increases in defence spending—the modest state support provides them with a rationale to justify their business interests. But rather than being legitimate ventures many of these business interests are, in fact, rent-seeking structures and protection rackets. The military maintained business activities in Jakarta and at all levels of the nationwide territorial system, but perhaps the most obvious venue was East Timor.

Although East Timor's population was a mere 880 000 people— and although it was consistently rated as Indonesia's most impoverished province—its gross domestic product was not inconsiderable at $400 million a year.[2] The military played a central role in this economy. In partnership with Tutut Soeharto, the local military command controlled East Timor's top export crop, coffee. Military commanders were also well positioned to benefit from central government spending in East Timor, which reached $33 million in fiscal year 1997.[3] Others possessed interests in property, infrastructure and sandalwood.[4] East Timor was not the world's richest occupied territory, but neither was it without spoils.

Thus, several weeks before Habibie announced his idea for a 'popular consultation', military commanders were already alarmed to discover that the president was even contemplating such a plan. Habibie saw the ballot as a way for Indonesia to shed a diplomatic burden and perhaps gain international fame for himself; the military, in contrast, regarded East Timor as a proving ground, a strategic battlefield and a cash cow. Wiranto therefore issued a swift response.

In a command reshuffle on 4 January 1999 Wiranto surprised military analysts by removing Maj. Gen. Zacky Anwar Makarim from command of the military intelligence agency, Bais. Only later would the reasoning behind the surprise move become clear: Wiranto had an even more important task for his trusted lieutenant. Within days of the reshuffle, Wiranto quietly formed a new command that would eventually come to be known as the Taskforce on the East Timor Consultation (P3TT). The command was based in East Timor's capital, Dili. Although its name sounded innocuous, the taskforce would actually have paramount control

over all military operations in the troubled territory.[5] To head P3TT,
Wiranto discreetly selected Makarim.[6]

A career Special Forces intelligence officer, Makarim had served in
East Timor from 1983 to 1989. Later, as a lieutenant colonel, he ran
counter-insurgency campaigns against the Free Aceh Movement in the
northern tip of Sumatera, eventually earning repute as the military's
foremost expert on covert operations.[7] As mentioned before, a key feature
of covert operations since the 1970s had been the use of *preman* gangs
and other para-militants. This strategy made imminent sense for Bais and
the Special Forces. With unskilled manpower readily available throughout
Indonesia, the military could amplify its existing troop strength quickly
and inexpensively by raising such civilian militias. Militias also shielded
more highly trained military personnel from combat risks and, perhaps
most importantly, they provided the military with 'plausible deniability' of
its own involvement.

Makarim's command of Bais coincided with a period in which para-
militants were particularly active. The military organised Islamic militias to
defend the November 1998 MPR session, and *preman* gangs had been put
to use—apparently by Makarim and Syafrie Syamsoeddin—to perpetrate
the May riots. As soon as Makarim took command of the P3TT taskforce
in Dili, such para-militant groups were put to use again. Makarim
launched a crash program to raise, train and arm pro-integration militias
in East Timor.[8]

In its earliest days the militia-raising program was not a secret. Col.
Tono Suratman, commander of East Timor military district, actually told
reporters in early December 1998 that his troops would train five to ten
volunteers in each village to serve as a civilian militia and to fight against
the pro-independence guerillas—the Falintil (*Forcas Armadas in Timor
Leste*, or East Timor Armed Forces). 'This is what the people want,' said
Suratman, a career Special Forces officer. 'Through their local representatives they have asked the military to come and train them to defend their
villages.'[9] Suratman denied that the military would arm the militias, but he
said that 'if they use other weapons [such as knives and guns], then that is
their own initiative'.

Wiranto later denied any military involvement with the militias whatsoever, describing the armed gangs as having developed spontaneously.
But in fact a number of militia members and pro-integration leaders
readily admitted to having received arms and funding from the military.[10]
By February 1999 the military's militia-forming program was already
receiving criticism from the Human Rights Commission, East Timorese
activists and various church organisations.[11] Around the same time, militia
activity caught the attention of several international journalists. Most
notably, Dan Murphy noted in the *Far Eastern Economic Review* that 'the
military has a record of using civilians to sow fear . . . Given that track

record, many East Timorese fear the military will play on existing divisions to undermine the independence process'.[12] Murphy also quoted a local officer who admitted to distributing rifles to newly recruited militia members.

Wiranto's denials that the military was backing the militias were hurting the general's credibility. In fact, the military had been using para-militaries in East Timor for at least a decade, but in 1999 the crash program dramatically boosted their size, number and strength. Their ranks were supposedly filled with East Timorese civilians who ardently supported integration with Jakarta, but in fact they included ample numbers of military troops in civilian garb, as well as some West Timorese *preman*. A total of some 6000 men were recruited or gang-pressed into militias, often with the involvement of organisers from the Special Forces. At least 1500 militia members were said to have received training from Special Forces troops in West Timor or Jakarta.[13]

Organisationally, the militias mirrored the military. In East Timor, as elsewhere throughout Indonesia, the military maintained a permanent presence in districts, sub-districts and (most) villages. Militia 'battalions' were therefore formed in each of East Timor's thirteen districts. 'Companies' and 'platoons' were formed at the sub-district and village levels. At each level, militia members co-operated with—and sometimes doubled as—resident military personnel.[14]

The militias adopted fiery names such as Blood of Integration, Thorn, Red Dragon and Thunderbolt.[15] One, Mahidi, was ostensibly an Indonesian acronym for 'Live or Die for Integration', but many believed that the name was also a tribute to the chief-of-staff of the Udayana Garrison, Brig. Gen. Mahidin Simbolon. A former Special Forces intelligence chief who took credit for capturing Xanana Gusmao in 1992, Simbolon was a protégé of Zacky Makarim and he was presumed to have played a prominent role in forming militias.[16] His nickname was Mahidi.

It was not long before the militias were put to use. Only days after 27 January, when Habibie made his formal offer of a ballot, militia violence erupted in several western districts of East Timor. Next, in mid-February, a Special Forces intelligence officer addressed militia leaders from twelve districts. According to one of those present, the officer told them to prepare for a full-scale assault on suspected sympathisers of the CNRT (*Concelho Nacional da Resistencia Timor*, or National Council of Timorese Resistance)—the umbrella organisation for pro-independence groups, including Xanana's Falintil.[17] Since Soeharto's fall, many CNRT leaders had grown more daring and were no longer in hiding. The assault began the next day.

The precise goals of the military's crackdown remain unclear. Militias were reportedly ordered to kill CNRT's leaders and sympathisers, but the military could not have been hoping to simply eradicate the East Timorese resistance movement, as some have speculated. Nor does it seem that military officials genuinely hoped to coerce voters into backing integration. For example, militias were directed to enforce a policy whereby all adult males were required to support integration.[18] Sometimes this meant that men were gang-pressed into serving in militias, while at other times they were simply forced to man barricades and carry out other menial duties. On at least one occasion reported by witnesses, a militia leader flatly declared that all males over fifteen years of age in a certain village were to be killed outright. Perhaps more than any other policy, this targeting of adult males cemented anti-Jakarta attitudes among the bulk of the population—and military commanders must surely have known this when the policy was created.

Thus, rather than being agents of intimidation, it appears that the militias were used, knowingly or otherwise, as bait designed to lure guerillas out of their mountaintop cantonments and into pitched battles with regular army and Special Forces troops. Xanana Gusmao's Falintil guerillas were estimated to number no more than 3000—versus some 6000 police and 14000 soldiers stationed in East Timor—but they were well equipped and determined. A Falintil offensive would provide more than enough of a conflagration to suit the military's purposes.

In Aceh and Irian Jaya, generals such as Makarim had long since learned how to publicise guerilla atrocities—real and contrived—and use them to their advantage in larger campaigns. This was precisely why, in 1983, Xanana resolved to transform his independence drive from a hopeless and ugly armed insurrection into a broad-based civil resistance movement. Doing so hoisted his stature among East Timorese, while generating the moral authority needed to mobilise support from the UN and governments throughout the world.

After being captured by the Special Forces in 1992, Xanana used his moral authority to wage East Timor's struggle from his jail cell in Jakarta, by writing letters and, when permitted, meeting diplomats and journalists. By 1999, therefore, the 53-year-old Xanana knew better than anyone that Falintil attacks would be self-defeating. They would undermine international support while handing the military a convenient pretext for cancelling the ballot. East Timor's chances for self-determination hinged on the ability of his guerillas to exercise restraint. In essence, the contest for East Timor was a contest of wills—guerilla wills.

Throughout his years in prison Xanana remained unrivalled as Falintil's supreme commander. By early 1999 he had been moved to house arrest in Jakarta. When the militia crackdown commenced, he issued strict orders to his followers in Falintil: resist provocation and remain inside the cantonments. Even though the guerillas were dispersed across East Timor's mountain peaks—and even though their home villages were being pillaged—Xanana's orders were obeyed. As he remarked at the time: 'One of the principles of the guerilla movement is to have the moral strength to be patient. When we want to come out to fight, we'll fight. If we don't want to fight, we won't. When we want to provoke, we'll provoke. But we can ignore their provocation.'[19]

Makarim's militias soon put Xanana's bold assertion to the test—at a historic seaside town called Liquica.

L iquica's quaint Portuguese architecture stood amid abject poverty and a grim social atmosphere—produced by years of bitter civic resistance to the town's army and police garrisons. On 4 April the town was electrified by news that pro-integration militias had killed five people not far from town. The reports prompted some 2000 unarmed civilians to seek refuge in a compound that contained a church and a priest's house. Soon they were confronted by a militia known as Besa Merah Putih (Red-and-White Steel). The militia's ranks were augmented by East Timorese men serving in the local garrisons. First, the attackers fired tear gas into the compound. When this flushed out the civilians, they opened fire with automatic weapons, cutting down those trying to flee.[20]

Jakarta military officials denied that security forces were involved. An Australian journalist followed up these claims by interviewing witnesses and survivors, and she provided this account of the event:

> The priest's house was encircled by the militia, and then behind that were rows of mobile police and troops from the local military command, who were out of uniform. But the people inside the house knew these people personally. They recognised them. They even named some of the sergeants who were involved in the attack, and they said these soldiers carried semi-automatic weapons and that they were involved in the shooting. The original attack began when the mobile police fired teargas canisters into the house. So the military certainly can't say that there is no blood on their hands.[21]

The military also claimed that there were only five deaths in Liquica. Although this matched the number of bodies buried in the immediate vicinity, locals witnessed army troops removing several truckloads of bodies, which were later found dumped in a nearby lake.[22] The death toll was estimated at 45.[23]

Col. Suratman promised an investigation, but meanwhile local soldiers renovated the Liquica church and priest's house to remove all traces of the shooting. According to a journalist who visited the scene before and after the renovation: 'Where on Thursday I saw walls full of bullet holes and floors caked with blood, only freshly applied paint and shiny tiles are now visible.'[24]

The Liquica massacre elicited a stunning response from Xanana Gusmao. 'I am compelled to authorise all necessary action in defence of the population,' he declared in an angrily worded press release, rifled off only minutes after the first reports of the massacre. 'I authorise the East Timorese population to undertake a general popular insurrection.'[25] The statement was titled 'East Timor on the Brink of War'. Given its contents, the title was apt.

Diplomats puzzled over Xanana's action. He was well aware that armed conflict would be self-defeating. The military would cancel the ballot and the East Timorese, having compromised their 'moral high ground', might never gain another chance for self-determination. But Xanana's stern words were not without reason: he may have been trying to placate Falintil lieutenants who were yearning to strike back—and, more importantly, he was almost certainly trying to goad the torpid UN into action.[26] In effect, he was playing a heady game of brinkmanship.

Xanana promised to retract his call to arms if the UN pledged a peace-keeping force for East Timor. This triggered a whirlwind of diplomatic activity, as UN member states contemplated the possibility of sending blue-helmeted troops to remote East Timor. It was soon apparent that Jakarta stridently opposed this option, but the UN did elicit a pledge from Wiranto to begin disarming the militias. Xanana had at least succeeded in alerting the UN to the gravity of East Timor's situation; within a few days, he retracted his call-to-arms and reaffirmed Falintil's ceasefire orders.

The next test of Falintil's discipline came just a few weeks later. Xanana faced a new nemesis: a 26-year-old thug who would soon earn international notoriety, Eurico Guterres. As a teenager, Guterres had landed in a military prison in Dili. Although he was not detained long, he never left the military's employ.[27] He distinguished himself as a para-military throughout the 1990s, and when the dramatic militia expansion took place in 1999 Guterres obtained command of the key militia in the Dili area: Aitarak. In Indonesian, the name meant 'Thorn'.

Guterres won fame for a fiery speech he delivered in Dili on 17 April. His audience included several thousand integration supporters, as well as a clutch of provincial-level officials from the government and military. 'From this day forward,' said Guterres, 'I order all pro-integration militia to conduct a thorough cleansing of the traitors of integration! Capture them and kill them!'[28]

Within hours of Guterres's speech Aitarak attacked the Dili home of a prominent pro-independence figure, Manuel Carrascalao, whose brother had been a popular governor in the 1980s. Around 150 refugees were taking shelter in the house. Guterres's men killed between 14 and 25 people, including Carrascalao's teenage son.[29] Some bodies were dismembered and thrown down a well. Irish Foreign Minister David Andrews, head of the European Union observer team, then watched the mob ransack the nearby office of East Timor's main newspaper—in full view of idle security personnel.

Several days later Wiranto responded by arriving in East Timor to preside over a well-publicised disarmament ceremony with a small militia group. Afterwards, journalists recounted how the weapons were returned to the same militia members.[30] In turn, these and other press reports prompted Guterres to threaten the safety of foreign journalists in East Timor. 'Better to sacrifice one journalist,' he declared, 'than 800 000 East Timorese.'[31] Meanwhile, more killings took place in at least three other districts during April—but still the Falintil guerillas remained in their camps.[32]

In retrospect, April marked the turning point in East Timor's quest for self-determination. Falintil's restraint in the face of relentless provocation ensured that the military remained the sole aggressor. Meanwhile, Wiranto's disarmament charade illustrated a central flaw in the military's campaign: it lacked 'plausible deniability', a cornerstone of successful covert operations.[33] The military was trying to provoke Falintil under the watchful eyes of diplomats, UN workers, election observers and a horde of skilled journalists. In addition, Australian defence officials possessed clear evidence of the militias' subordination to the military. According to one intelligence expert at Australia National University:

> Detailed intelligence came in through the course of April and May from both our [Australia's] external intelligence service, ASIS, and the Defence Signals Directorate responsible for monitoring communications. This provided very detailed evidence of particular working relationships between units of the Indonesian army and particular militia elements and militia leaders. It also provided even more direct and explicit evidence of Wiranto's direct involvement in the arming and supporting of the militia.[34]

After the Liquica massacre, Wiranto and his subordinates could no longer deny their true role. Set against Falintil's forbearance, this convinced the international community—including the UN, the Pentagon and the US Congress—that the chief threat to a peaceful ballot was none other than Wiranto's military.

When UN officials met their Indonesian counterparts in early May to set the rules for the upcoming ballot, security issues were the UN's chief concerns. Key stipulations of the '5 May Accord' were that the Indonesian police would be assigned to ensure security in the territory, and that the military would cease supporting the militias. To oversee security measures, the accord also provided for a 'Peace and Stability Commission', composed of both pro-integration and pro-independence officials.

The New York agreement made little impact on the situation in East Timor. Police and military personnel blithely ignored the rules of the 5 May Accord. In fact, militia threats drove all but one of the Peace

Commission's pro-independence officials into hiding. By the end of May UN Secretary-General Koffi Annan was exasperated. 'Truckloads of pro-integration militia,' he complained, 'are able to roam about freely and set up checkpoints along the roads—without any intervention from the army or the police.'[35] For their part, army officers in East Timor liked to claim that they were powerless to stop the militias—because the 5 May Accord explicitly vested that authority with the police.

UN pleas for security continued to go unheeded through May and June. The 1000-strong foreign Unamet contingent included 270 unarmed police officers (most of whom were from Australia or New Zealand), but these UN police were only permitted to 'advise' the Indonesian police. It soon became clear that the latter were taking their orders directly from the military.

Following a restructuring in early 1999, the national police chief no longer reported to the armed forces commander but rather to the minister of defence. This seemed significant on paper, but in practice it meant little: Wiranto held both posts. Moreover, the police were generally believed to be dependent on the military for operational funding. Little, therefore, had changed since the fall of Soeharto: the chief mission of the police was simply to follow military orders, in keeping with the Soeharto-era system of Ruler's Law. In East Timor, this meant giving militias free rein. In fact, police personnel sometimes seemed subordinate not only to their local military counterparts but to local militia leaders as well.[36] For the police to stay neutral was difficult enough; for them to actually confront the militias was expecting far too much.

As UN officials and diplomats gradually realised that the police would not stop the military's militia campaign, support grew for a UN-sponsored peace-keeping force. This, however, presented an entirely new realm of problems—on the diplomatic front.

Although a few Indonesian voices expressed concern about the atrocities perpetrated by the militias, there was generally little sympathy for pro-independence East Timorese. A generation of Indonesians had been taught that the military had been invited into East Timor in 1975 and that the territory's annexation was just. In Jakarta, news of East Timor was drowned out by election excitement, and when reports did surface in the local press they were sometimes incongruous with what foreign journalists had witnessed. For these reasons the Indonesian public showed no support for an armed UN presence—in fact, many regarded the mere suggestion as belligerence on the part of the international community, and particularly Australia. For Habibie, the introduction of foreign soldiers would be politically ruinous.

In any event, Habibie himself was powerless to authorise peace-keepers: there were ample signs that, in the post-Soeharto power vacuum,

Indonesia's East Timor policy was being formed by a large number of actors. Among others, these included Wiranto, East Timor governor Abilio Soares, parliament and opposition leaders, among others. To force the issue of peacekeepers with Habibie would only jeopardise his fragile relations with Wiranto—thereby jeopardising Indonesia's commitment to carrying out the ballot. But at the same time, as militia killings continued throughout June and July, it was clear that a large segment of the East Timorese population was living in fear and danger.

Finally, an event which helped break the impasse occurred on 20 July, when foreign journalists obtained an internal document from the co-ordinating ministry for politics and security—Feisal Tanjung's department. The document, which was labelled 'secret' and dated 3 July, discussed the military's options for the post-ballot period. The document was addressed to Tanjung and was signed by Tanjung's chief aide, Maj. Gen. Garnadi—who was also serving at the time as the vice-chair of Makarim's P3TT taskforce.[37]

The 'Garnadi document', as the memo came to be called, described the East Timorese as a 'floating mass who would vote for whoever provided them with food and medicine'.[38] And because of the prominent humanitarian role played by UN-backed NGOs, the rambling document predicted that the upcoming vote would favour independence. 'Indonesia,' it read, 'has been left behind in the effort to win the hearts of the East Timorese people.'

Ironically, the Garnadi document voiced the opposite of the UN's fears: it worried that Falintil would launch post-ballot attacks on all those aligned with Jakarta. 'After the ballot, horrifying things will happen to civil servants and the militia members, who are the real heroes of integration.' The document therefore called for the post-ballot evacuation of all integration supporters to West Timor.

Finally, in a cryptically worded conclusion, the Garnadi document recommended that the military 'secure withdrawal routes, if possible destroying facilities and other vital installations'. The meaning of this concluding recommendation was unclear at the time, but the leaked document nonetheless demonstrated that high-level Indonesian officials expected—and indeed were perhaps planning—an apocalyptic aftermath to the referendum.

According to the anonymous source who made it public, the Garnadi document had been widely circulated among civil servants in Dili following a visit by officials from Jakarta. The government denounced the document as a '100 per cent fake', but it looked and sounded authentic—and Garnadi himself admitted that the document's signature was his own.[39]

Soon after the Garnadi document surfaced, Australian defence officials acknowledged that the UN might assemble a 'transition assistance force', with Australian and New Zealand troops forming the 'core of

expertise'.[40] This marked a significant departure from previous UN assertions that no peacekeepers would be used, but still the transition force was
only envisioned for use in the post-ballot period. The UN still lacked ideas
on how to protect the East Timorese until then. Meanwhile, the crucial
process of voter registration had already begun.

Militia attacks impeded the voter registration process, but an even
greater obstacle was East Timor's growing refugee problem. By the
end of July the UN High Commissioner for Refugees estimated that
the militias had driven 35 000 people from their homes, while church
groups put the figure at 60 000.[41] Most of these 'internally displaced
persons' had seen their houses burned down and were seeking refuge in
Falintil cantonments. They wanted protection to visit registration centres,
but Unamet was unable to help.

Still, the East Timorese found ways to cope. For example, a Unamet
political affairs officer in Ermera described how one contingent of Falintil
guerillas descended from a mountain and braved detection to visit a registration centre:

> Falintil members wanted protection to register, but . . . Unamet told them
> they had to take risks like the rest of the population. On a pre-arranged day,
> the registration centre at Fatubolo, in Falintil territory, opened early. Over
> 150 active Falintil members crowded into the building, their weapons stored
> in a nearby house. They were very nervous, afraid of a possible military
> attack . . . By 9.00 a.m. most of the guerillas had melted away into the forest.
> The police who always guarded the centre had kept their distance. It felt like
> a small victory that at least these Falintil members had been able to
> register.[42]

Despite the obstacles, the number of registrations mounted toward
the end of the period, ultimately reaching 446 000—a staggering 98 per
cent of the territory's estimated number of eligible voters.[43] Clearly, the
East Timorese were more than an apathetic 'floating mass': they cared
deeply about their political future.

The high registration totals alarmed the military. In a cabinet meeting
on 28 July Wiranto strenuously argued that the ballot should be
cancelled.[44] Civilian ministers countered that the international backlash
would be too costly. The meeting lasted all day, but finally the civilians
prevailed. Indonesia would abide by the ballot process.

Meanwhile, in New York, Koffi Annan and his aides were also wrestling
with the question of whether to proceed with the next phase of the ballot
process: a ten-day campaigning period. Twice the UN had pushed back the
ballot schedule because of militia violence, but still the attacks continued.
Militias erected roadblocks, discharged weapons, attacked local Unamet

staff and flagrantly defied election rules in all parts of the territory. The military's role was obvious to all who visited East Timor, including Unamet officials, visiting diplomats and scores of foreign journalists. Militias were seen using military weapons, riding in military vehicles, frequenting military installations and perpetrating killings in full view of passive soldiers.

Annan insisted that, for the ballot to proceed, the security situation must improve. But to bring about that improvement the UN was still relying on a force that was grossly inadequate: the Indonesian police. Either UN officials were misinformed about the nature of the police or, more likely, they were willing to indulge in wishful thinking. To some extent, the voter registration period may have instilled the UN with a false confidence: having surpassed that hurdle amid considerable violence, the UN apparently felt that a fair ballot result was also within reach. The campaign period was set for 20–28 August, and the ballot itself for 30 August.[45]

By mid-August, tension was rising within diplomatic circles. The World Bank warned that its aid could be disrupted if the ballot failed. Sharp criticism also emanated from the Carter Center, an election-monitoring organisation that was headed by former US president Jimmy Carter, and which had ten monitors in East Timor. The organisation denounced the military for backing militias and later accused 'top representatives of the Indonesian government' of trying to undermine the ballot.[46] A host of US officials, including Secretary of State Madeleine Albright, voiced serious concerns about Indonesia's security efforts. The British government did likewise, and even the normally reticent Japanese held high-level talks with Jakarta. But Indonesia's staunchest critic, by far, was Australia.

For many Australians East Timor commanded special importance. In World War II thousands of East Timorese volunteers had fought heroically with several hundred Australian commandos, pinning down a large Japanese force in a strategically critical campaign.[47] In 1975, when Indonesian troops killed five journalists working for Australian television stations, renewed attention was focused on the tiny territory located just 600 kilometres from Darwin. Many Australians were angered, therefore, when in 1985 Canberra granted de facto recognition of Indonesia's annexation of East Timor, even though the UN itself had not yet done so.

Canberra's decision was particularly unseemly because it appeared to be motivated by crass commercialism: recognition paved the way for the 1989 Timor Gap Treaty, whereby Indonesia and Australia shared rights to a deep-sea gas field off Timor's southern coast.[48] By 1999 there was overwhelming public pressure for the Australian government to make amends for its prior cynicism, and support for East Timor's independence therefore became a political imperative.

Added to Australia's historic links to East Timor was the general excitement surrounding a rare Australian foray into international politics. Unlike, for example, the apathy sometimes shown by Americans towards US involvement in Central America, Australians were riveted by East Timor. An international drama was unfolding on their doorstep, and key actors included their own journalists, diplomats and UN representatives.

Australia's concerns about the fate of the East Timorese were certainly justified, but the Howard administration was often clumsy in handling its relations with Jakarta, which quickly soured as a result. In early August presidential spokeswoman Dewi Fortuna Anwar—the aide who, ironically, was a prime mover behind Habibie's original overture on East Timor— lashed out at Australia:

> Sometimes we wonder whether Australians really value Indonesia as Indonesia—you know, the fourth largest country in the world with 211 million people—or whether they think that Indonesia is worth knowing only because of East Timor . . . Australia cannot act as East Timor's godfather. We reject intervention.[49]

This was only the first of many barbs that Indonesian officials would aim at Australia. The war of words grew worse as the ballot date approached: it became increasingly clear that the East Timorese would vote overwhelmingly for independence, which frustrated the militias and prompted them to intensify their attacks.[50] The attacks, in turn, elicited more calls from the international community for a peace-keeping force—which only hardened attitudes in Jakarta. Increasing numbers of moderates, like Dewi Fortuna Anwar, seemed to side with the military in protesting against Australia. Tiny East Timor's campaign for self-determination was spiralling into an international imbroglio and it was all happening just as Indonesia itself was preparing for a tense presidential transition.

B owing to the torrent of international criticism, Wiranto finally made a gesture on 13 August: he removed Col. Suratman from command of the East Timor military district. Few, however, viewed the change as anything more than cosmetic. The key officer in East Timor was not Suratman but Makarim. Moreover, Suratman was hardly being punished: he soon received both a promotion in rank and a choice assignment as deputy defence spokesman. Meanwhile, his replacement was a fellow Special Forces officer, Col. Mohammed Noer Muis, who continued to give the militias free rein. And four days after the changeover, Eurico Guterres's Aitarak militia killed five people in a day-long rampage in Dili.[51] Immediately after Guterres's attack, Habibie and Wiranto were contacted by Japanese Prime Minister Keizo Obuchi; Madeleine Albright;

US Defence Secretary William Cohen; the vice-chair of the US Joint Chiefs of Staff, Gen. Joseph Ralston; and Australia's foreign minister, Alexander Downer. Koffi Annan 'demanded' that the Indonesian security forces restore law and order. Finally, several days before the ballot, Wiranto recalled Makarim to Jakarta, temporarily replacing him with Maj. Gen. Tyasno Sudarto. And in compliance with personal entreaties from US senators, Wiranto also removed the commander of the Maliana district, Lt Col. Burhanudin Siagian, whom observers accused of carrying out executions.[52]

Still, Wiranto's measures were viewed as window-dressing. Tyasno was Makarim's successor as chief of Bais and the pair had worked closely together for years. Wiranto was therefore replacing like with like, and it was probable that Makarim would continue overseeing operations from afar. As for Siagian, he reappeared in Maliana only days later.[53]

There was therefore little reason to expect security conditions to improve—as the military itself warned in a remarkable press release issued on the eve of the ballot. 'The security forces in East Timor,' said the military's official spokesman in Jakarta, 'cannot guarantee against the outbreak of chaos.'[54] This was a statement of the obvious for UN observers in East Timor, but it was a startling admission for the military to make after having claimed the opposite for months—while steadfastly rejecting UN peacekeepers.

The security concerns presented the UN with an agonising decision over whether to proceed with the risk-fraught ballot. For some UN officials, securing an accurate self-determination vote would rank among the most significant achievements of their careers. Now they felt tantalisingly close to a historic ballot. Moreover, CNRT leaders insisted that the ballot go ahead, even though they expected reprisal attacks.[55] Taking an audacious gamble, UN officials decided to proceed.

On the day of the ballot most observers expected direct militia attacks on voters and polling stations. A few did occur: most notably, militias in Ermera district opened fire on a polling station just as it was being visited by the US ambassador to Indonesia, Stapleton Roy.[56] But apart from these few incidents the balloting was a remarkably peaceful affair.

The militias were not an unruly rabble: they were well disciplined in that they followed military orders, and they had apparently been ordered not to interfere with the actual ballot itself. This lends credence to the view that the military's aim was not to disrupt the balloting or to coerce voters into choosing integration, but rather to lure Falintil into combat. If so, the campaign failed: with a few exceptions—and despite myriad acts of provocation—the guerillas maintained their discipline and confined themselves to their camps.

The absence of violence on 30 August allowed for a remarkable level of voter turnout. Throughout the territory, large groups had camped overnight near voting stations in order to queue when the polls opened at 6.30 a.m. In the end, an extraordinary 98 per cent of those who had registered—virtually the whole of East Timor's adult population—succeeded in casting ballots. But almost as soon as the polls closed in the afternoon, the militias swung into action.

The militias resumed their rampage in typical fashion: targeting pro-independence leaders and Unamet local staff, at least three of whom were killed by soldiers in Ermera district.[57] The next day militias and security forces in the same district held a 150-member Unamet convoy hostage for hours. Throughout East Timor, militia violence forced Unamet workers and journalists to retreat to Dili.[58]

Before the balloting on 30 August had even finished, pro-integration leaders were already denouncing the poll as unfair. There could be few complaints about the mechanics of vote-taking and vote-counting—Unamet had gone to great lengths to ensure that impartial procedures were used—but integration supporters complained bitterly that Unamet workers were biased.[59] East Timor's notoriously pro-Jakarta governor, Abilio Soares, even denounced Unamet for having incited hatred and violence.[60]

Unamet workers were largely sympathetic to the pro-independence side—and, given the one-sided nature of the aggression in the territory, it would have been difficult for outsiders to have been otherwise. Unamet was criticised for employing a large number of East Timorese who harboured pro-independence views, but Unamet's complexion reflected the population at large: most East Timorese had strong views one way or another, and the vast majority were pro-independence.

In any event, the biases of Unamet staff were only material if they swayed East Timorese voters and substantially affected the outcome of the ballot—which they almost certainly did not. Militia harassment turned voters against Jakarta far more than Unamet 'preaching', as Soares put it. And even if Unamet workers did commit infractions of the election rules, the militias obviously did far worse.

As the votes were being counted a new phase of violence commenced. As Unamet workers streamed back into Dili they reported attacks such as the one in the border town of Maliana, where twenty people were gunned down in a schoolyard and scores of houses set on fire.[61] Dili itself became chaotic, with militias roaming the streets, manning roadblocks, burning homes and discharging military-issue assault rifles. Militia men used machetes to hack a man to death in full view of BBC correspondent Jonathan Head; they then seized Head and beat him severely. Thousands of Dili residents fled their homes and sought refuge in the densely wooded mountains to the west. Others converged on the

UN compound, which itself was the target of intermittent gunfire.

Meanwhile, the vote-count proceeded quickly. On the morning of 4 September Unamet chief Ian Martin convened a press conference at Dili's main hotel, the dilapidated Mahkota. In remarks broadcast live on East Timor radio, Martin read the ballot's final results: 78.5 per cent of the votes had been cast for independence. Despite rampant intimidation, coercion and the dislocation of tens of thousands, nearly four out of five East Timorese adults had braved considerable risks to repudiate Indonesian rule.

Most people familiar with East Timor—including many integration supporters—had expected that a fair ballot would favour independence, but few had expected such a lopsided result. In a society where the voices of the 'little people' were rarely heard, East Timor's vote for self-determination struck like a clap of thunder.[62] The tragic irony was there for all to see: in 25 years of trying to subjugate the East Timorese, the military had only succeeded in stiffening their will to resist.

For Habibie the ballot result was a political catastrophe. For decades Indonesia's first two presidents had stressed the paramount importance of national integrity; within only fifteen months the third president had already 'lost' a province. Among Indonesia's political elite a few acknowledged East Timor's unique history and appreciated the territory's triumph of democracy; most, however, viewed Habibie as a bungler. True to his word, the president promptly addressed the press and stated that he accepted the results of East Timor's ballot.

Habibie also expressly ordered all Indonesian security personnel in East Timor to halt the territory's worsening violence, but the order went unheeded. By now it was clear that Wiranto's military was openly defying the president. Habibie desperately wanted to put the East Timor debacle behind him and concentrate on salvaging his presidential campaign, which was already imperilled by the Bank Bali scandal. But for Habibie the East Timor debacle would only grow worse—as it would for the East Timorese themselves.

The announcement of the ballot results should have been a joyous moment for many East Timorese, but an atmosphere of fear prevailed instead. Even the scene of the announcement—the lobby of the Mahkota—was itself struck by violence a mere two hours after Martin's announcement, when a militia gang fired salvos of pistol rounds through the front window, sending journalists and cameramen scurrying for cover.[63] In Liquica an American policeman working with Unamet was shot in the abdomen—by Indonesian police.[64] The relentless attacks prompted Unamet to begin airlifting personnel to Darwin, while in New York the UN Security Council convened an emergency session. Australia hastened to prepare some 3000 troops for possible deployment as 'peace-enforcers'.

The next day, 5 September, a special military unit slipped quietly into East Timor: Detachment 81 of the Special Forces, the elite anti-terror squad.[65] Later that night attackers razed the home of Bishop Carlos Belo— East Timor's senior church official, a co-winner of the 1996 Nobel Peace Prize and East Timor's most popular figure after Xanana. Hundreds of refugees in Belo's home were forced into trucks and taken away.

Elsewhere, reports from Dili's notoriously violent Becora neighbour- hood said that uniformed soldiers were speeding up and down the main street, raking houses with machine-gun fire and hurling grenades.[66] Militia men fired on a convoy of Australian consulate vehicles, and one bullet nearly struck the ambassador to Indonesia, John McCarthy.[67] Amid heavy gunfire refugees continued to pour into the Unamet compound, which was rocked by an explosion when a rocket-propelled grenade struck an adjacent building.[68] Not far away the Aitarak militia attacked the Dili Diocese, burning the building and killing 25 refugees.[69]

Meanwhile, a few kilometres away, a delegation of cabinet ministers arrived at the Dili airport. These included Ali Alatas, the veteran foreign minister who had spent much of his career defending the annexation of East Timor. According to Alatas, the UN was to blame for the violence, because the ballot was fraudulent and it was only natural that the public should vent its anger.[70] Wiranto, who was also present, declared martial law in East Timor. Anyone on the streets after midnight would be shot on sight.[71] Ironically, several perpetrators of atrocities were in Wiranto's presence: the airport meeting was attended by prominent militia leaders from throughout East Timor.[72] No one in the cabinet delegation ventured outside the airport lounge before boarding their return flight to Jakarta.

The next day, 6 September, militias ransacked the headquarters of the International Committee of the Red Cross (ICRC). Swiss doctors were forced to flee, while several hundred refugees were taken from the compound and loaded into trucks, probably headed for West Timor.[73] Meanwhile, the Hotel Mahkota became just one of many Dili buildings that were consumed by flames. Wiranto's promise to restore order had had no effect.

As the scorched-earth campaign forced all UN staff and foreign journalists to seek refuge in Dili, reliable reports from the countryside dwindled. Militia checkpoints and barricades on all roads leading out of Dili contributed to the isolation. And as all 600-odd journalists in the territory departed at once, the world's view of East Timor narrowed to just a handful of locations: the Unamet compound, the Australian consulate and a few churches with foreign missionaries.

Many suspected that conditions in East Timor's interior were as bad or worse than the turmoil in Dili. This was certainly so in Suai, a small town in the southwestern district of Covalima. According to stories corrobor- ated by several survivors, around 100 women and children were seeking

refuge inside Suai's main church on 6 September. Gunmen from the
Mahidi militia entered the church and sprayed the interior with automatic
weapons fire. On their way out, they lobbed three grenades inside. Twenty-
six bodies were later found buried across the border in West Timor, but
the total death toll was estimated to be between 50 and 200, including
three priests and two nuns.[74] Two days later, in Maliana, 33 were reportedly
killed by a combined force of militia and soldiers.[75]

In Jakarta the onset of the scorched-earth campaign triggered a terse
confrontation between the president and his armed forces commander.
Habibie had originally embarked on his East Timor policy to improve
Indonesia's international image; now Wiranto's military had, in effect,
sabotaged that policy, such that Indonesia was being pilloried by the UN,
its donors and its most important allies. Wiranto was implacable—the
barrage of diplomatic pressure exerted upon him appeared to have no
effect—but Habibie nonetheless tried to repair the situation.

The president was particularly concerned about his reformist credentials—he needed the support of some reform-minded Islamic parties to
win the presidency. His cabinet therefore rejected Wiranto's pronouncement of martial law, made the previous day. This infuriated Wiranto.
Several hours after the cabinet decision he visited the president with a
group of generals in tow.[76]

Whatever Wiranto said in his meeting with Habibie proved effective:
early the following day Habibie reversed the cabinet decision and decreed
martial law in East Timor. In a striking display of the military's political
clout, Wiranto had prevailed over both the president and the cabinet.
When asked point-blank by reporters if he had perpetrated a 'silent' coup
d'état, Wiranto said: 'Habibie is my president.'[77] The comment only
created more speculation: to some, Wiranto's use of the possessive, in
Indonesian, sounded overly possessive.

But Habibie did not give in. The president summoned a host of
Sulawesi natives to the home of Arnold Baramuli; those attending
included Tanri Abeng, Yunus Yosfiah, Andi Ghalib and Ulama Council
chair Ali Yafie.[78] Habibie wondered aloud whether he should surrender his
presidency or at least withdraw from the presidential race, but his
supporters urged him to carry on and assert his authority.

Three days later, on 10 September, the president appeared ready to
issue the long-awaited invitation to peacekeepers—without Wiranto's
consent. But according to his aides, just before he made the announcement he was presented with a written ultimatum from Wiranto: if Habibie
admitted foreign troops into East Timor, the military would hand power to
a ministerial triumvirate consisting of Wiranto, Feisal Tanjung and
Syarwan Hamid.[79] All were active or retired generals.[80]

Habibie desisted from summoning peacekeepers, but meanwhile his aides spread word that a coup d'état had been attempted. This in turn triggered a counter-move from Tyasno Sudarto's Bais: intelligence officers spread word that the president was on the verge of resigning. Late that night Habibie's residence suffered a rare power outage, which some of his aides thought was designed to intimidate the president.[81]

To signal its severe displeasure at the turn of events in East Timor, the UN Security Council dispatched a special delegation of five envoys to Jakarta. They arrived to meet with Wiranto on the same day that the general delivered his ultimatum to Habibie. The contents of the meeting were recorded by a clandestine British journalist, David Usborne, who sat in on the meeting at military headquarters by posing as a UN aide.[82] According to Usborne, some twenty senior officers flanked Wiranto as he recited his familiar refrain: the military had good intentions and the unrest was being subdued. He opposed peacekeepers because an armed UN presence was 'relevant to the dignity of the Indonesian military'. He also argued that UN troops would imperil supporters of integration, such as militias, because Falintil would feel emboldened to attack.

Martin Andjaba, the leader of the Security Council team and a former Namibian freedom fighter, rejected Wiranto's reasoning outright. He added: 'You are failing the international community, you are failing the people of East Timor and you are failing Indonesia.' Then, as if to underscore the chasm between the two sides, one of the Security Council envoys received a call on his mobile phone from the Unamet chief in Dili, Ian Martin. Militia gunmen were attacking the compound with rifle fire, said Martin, while grenade blasts could be heard nearby. The attack was preventing the air evacuation of some 1400 refugees sheltering in the compound.

The UN envoy relayed the news across the table to Wiranto, who promptly telephoned his commander in Dili. Wiranto soon informed the UN envoys: 'There is no trouble in Dili. The situation is peaceful.' But minutes later Martin rang back to report that the compound was still under fire. This time, after speaking again to his commander in Dili, Wiranto admitted that there may have been some trouble—but nothing serious, only some 'veterans' protesting because the evacuees included local Unamet staff.

Before the meeting ended, Wiranto invited the UN delegation to join his staff for a round of golf at the military's own course. The Indonesian general, who had rarely travelled abroad during his career, seemed at a loss as to how to behave in the presence of the high-level UN delegation. Rather than playing golf, the Security Council envoys insisted that Wiranto accompany them to Dili.

Following the meeting Wiranto received a telephone call from the Pentagon. It was the chairman of the joint chiefs of staff, Gen. Hugh

Shelton. Only moments before, Koffi Annan had declared that the perpetrators of atrocities in East Timor could face international war-crimes charges.[83] Now the American general reportedly 'laid into his counterpart', bluntly warning that Wiranto was on the verge of ruining his country.[84] Wiranto replied by saying that he planned to inspect the damage in East Timor himself. The next day he visited Dili with the Security Council envoys, and he registered surprise at the devastation.[85] By this time most of Dili had been reduced to ruins.

The envoys reported—as journalists had been doing for seven months—that the military was able to 'switch the violence on and off' at will.[86] In fact, barely half an hour after the delegation's departure, shooting started up again on Dili's streets.[87] In the countryside, meanwhile, the military carried on with its premeditated scorched-earth campaign—the completion of which may have been Wiranto's overriding goal all along. Wiranto's behaviour on his visit to Dili fostered the impression that he had simply been oblivious to events in East Timor; more plausibly, the typically inscrutable Wiranto may have been feigning surprise—using the Dili tour just to stall for time.

Col. Muis had told reporters on 2 September that the military would implement a program to evacuate up to 250 000 people to West Timor if the ballot result favoured independence.[88] Muis estimated that the plan—which echoed the Garnadi document—would require ten to twelve days to implement. The plan was initiated on 5 September and would therefore not be completed until 15 September at the earliest. Wiranto knew that the Australians would need at least 48 hours to land troops after getting the go-ahead for a peace-keeping mission. Perhaps it was no coincidence, therefore, that after months of pressure Wiranto finally gave his consent to a peace-keeping force on the evening of 12 September.

'I have made the decision to give our approval to a peace-keeping force together with the Indonesian military to maintain the security of East Timor,' said President Habibie, in a televised speech. 'Too many people have lost their lives. We cannot wait any longer.'[89] Wiranto, standing at his side, supported the decision. It was the signal that the UN and the international community had been seeking for months. Three thousand Australian troops, augmented by a contingent from New Zealand and a small force of British Gurkhas, prepared to deploy within a few days.

But still Jakarta's intentions were unclear. While the Security Council prepared formal authorisation for the peacekeepers, Habibie stalled on fixing a firm date for deployment. Moreover, Indonesian soldiers and police looted the Unamet compound on 14 September, only minutes after its skeleton staff had retreated to a more secure location.[90] More ominous still was a declaration from the military's spokesman in Jakarta: Indonesia

opposed the inclusion of 'biased' troops in the peace-keeping force, and
he specifically ruled out Australians and New Zealanders.

The announcement threatened to delay the peace-keeping mission
yet again. Australia was the only nation willing and able to mount a meaningful operation within a few days' time. But with an estimated 20 000
Indonesian security personnel in the territory—plus thousands of armed
militiamen—Canberra was naturally unwilling to land troops without first
securing Jakarta's explicit consent.[91] The unspoken fear was that, when the
peacekeepers arrived in East Timor, rash militias or renegade Indonesian
troops might open fire on them, thereby embroiling the two neighbours
in a shooting war.

Within hours US President Clinton weighed in: the peace-keeping
force must include Australian and New Zealand troops, and Indonesia was
in no position to dictate terms.[92] Clinton had already explicitly blamed the
Indonesian military for 'aiding and abetting the militia violence'; now
he cut military ties with Indonesia and warned of dire economic consequences for Indonesia if the violence did not end.

Finally, the military began an organised withdrawal from East Timor
on 15 September—precisely ten days from the start of their scorched-earth
campaign, as per the original plan of Col. Muis. It remains unclear whether
the combined might of the international community prised the military
from East Timor—or whether Wiranto's forces were simply following their
own predetermined schedule, impervious to outside demands.

From the time that the UN Security Council finally authorised an International Force on East Timor (Interfet) on 15 September, five days
elapsed before the first troops arrived. A possible factor for the delay
was an act of diplomatic spite on 16 September by Feisal Tanjung: as the
co-ordinating minister for politics and security, Tanjung unilaterally
revoked Indonesia's military co-operation pact with Australia, forged in
1995. Many wondered what this augured for Interfet's landing, but when
the first Australian, New Zealand and British Gurkha troops arrived on
20 September they met no opposition from the few thousand members
of the security forces still in East Timor. But neither did the atrocities end.

British journalist Jon Swain was among a handful of reporters who
accompanied Interfet into East Timor. The day after the landing he set out
to tour Dili's ravaged Becora district, but his way was soon blocked by
Indonesian army regulars. The soldiers were members of Battalion 745,
under the command of Maj. Yakob Sarosa. The battalion had been
stationed on the eastern tip of the territory and was gradually withdrawing
through Dili toward West Timor. When they encountered Swain's vehicle
the soldiers beat Swain's driver and abducted his interpreter.[93] They
allowed Swain and his cameraman to flee—but the same area was visited
an hour later by a 30-year-old Dutchman named Sander Thoenes.

A reporter for the UK's *Financial Times*, Thoenes stood out among Jakarta's proud community of resident foreign journalists. On arriving in Dili the enthusiastic Thoenes wanted to inspect conditions in Becora, the staunchly pro-independence neighbourhood that was routinely targeted by militias. Thoenes wanted to see what damage had been wrought during the ten days in which the territory had been devoid of journalists. He set out on the back of an *ojek*, or motorcycle taxi, but like Swain he was soon impeded.

The *ojek* driver recalls encountering three motorbikes carrying six gunmen who wore military uniforms. The driver spun the bike around and fled, but the gunmen followed. After a short chase, shots rang out and Thoenes fell from the bike. The driver crashed but escaped on foot. Thoenes' body was recovered the next day by Australian soldiers; he had been killed by one rifle shot through the chest. Battalion 745 soldiers, under the command of Maj. Yakob Sarosa, were nearby. Because their own officers later admitted that troops from that battalion had been involved in the earlier attack on Swain, it is believed that Thoenes had been killed by the same troops.[94]

As Interfet gradually fanned out through the territory, the world witnessed stunning pictures of devastation and deprivation. In footage filmed from helicopters, entire towns were seen to be burned out and virtually devoid of residents. Much of the territory's population had been uprooted, and Interfet forces found tens of thousands living, and starving, in the wooded hills outside Dili. Some 280 000 people—nearly a third of the population—had been removed to West Timor.[95] In one district alone, the tiny enclave of Oecussi, 8000 residents remained when Interfet troops finally reached the secluded area in late October; the enclave's pre-ballot population had been 58 000.[96]

Throughout East Timor the forced removals were implemented with the utmost brutality. East Timorese knew that to refuse evacuation would brand them as independence supporters—and all independence supporters were potential targets for theft, arson, rape and murder. Many naturally agreed to be removed, even though they might have preferred to stay. The evacuations split apart countless families, and militias forced many of those in the West Timor camps to remain there for months against their will.[97]

Dili itself was in ruins: the majority of its buildings were destroyed or vandalised and the city was without power, water or sewerage. The official death toll was estimated at around 1000, but UN officials later conceded that a more realistic figure would be at least twice that. However, the perpetrators of the scorched-earth campaign took pains to conceal dead bodies, and many dead were presumed to have been recovered and buried quietly by family members, lest the bodies be disturbed further. Suspicions also linger that bodies were dumped at sea. According to some aid agencies, the death toll could have been as high as 7000.[98]

The military's motives for the scorched-earth campaign are puzzling. It is possible that the military was making a last-ditch attempt to precipitate a battle with Falintil, which might then be used as an excuse to remain in East Timor. But if so, it remains unclear why military units were clearly undertaking a pre-arranged withdrawal, as per the Garnadi document.[99] In addition to public buildings and infrastructure, military units destroyed their own barracks and bases—which they would not have done had they been hoping to stay and fight.

It is possible that the pillaging had no larger aim and was simply attributable to sheer spite. According to Wiranto, 'mental blocks', as he put it, were the sole reason for the destruction. Individual soldiers and militia members were so emotionally attached to integration, he said, that they simply couldn't stop themselves from wreaking vengeance.[100]

To be sure, an impulse to punish 'disobedient' East Timorese was clearly at play—as was resolute intolerance and anger at having 'lost face'. But if the destruction was purely a psychological phenomenon among rank-and-file soldiers, as Wiranto and his generals contended, this would not explain why the destruction was carried out in such an organised manner. If spite was the only reason for the scorched-earth campaign, it was not merely at the individual level—it was the deliberate policy of military commanders at the intermediate level, if not higher. This, then, raises what was perhaps the most often-asked question associated with the scorched-earth campaign: was it conceived by Wiranto?

Most agreed that the armed forces chief bore full responsibility for the conduct of his troops, but many people—both at home and abroad—still wanted to give Wiranto the 'benefit of the doubt'. It was therefore often argued that Wiranto was merely guilty of ignorance and negligence, and that the mayhem in East Timor was the result of insubordination, lack of discipline or the like. In fact, this argument seems implausible.

Given the input he was receiving from diplomats alone, Wiranto could not have been misled about the situation on the ground. And as for negligence, Wiranto was actually following events in East Timor very closely. He went there three times in five months and he dispatched some of his most trustworthy aides to Dili. When he argued over East Timor with cabinet ministers and the president, he typically did so with great emotion. In fact, Wiranto even took to the stage at a retired officers' party on 12 September—the day that he and Habibie finally relented on UN peacekeepers—to sing the 1970s love song 'Feelings'; Wiranto's hobby was karaoke singing, and he claimed that the song summed up his 'feelings' about losing the province of East Timor.[101] The territory may have been small and remote but it was very much at the forefront of

Wiranto's attention before—and after—the fateful ballot.

Another rationale for absolving Wiranto was the suggestion that he lacked control over his subordinates. But again this seems far-fetched. As mentioned above, Wiranto picked his commanders in East Timor by hand, and the choice of Zacky Makarim to head the P3TT taskforce seemed deliberately designed to keep the general in touch with events on the ground. By all accounts Makarim exerted firm control over the military as well as the militias and police. Moreover, Makarim's successor as head of military intelligence, Maj. Gen. Tyasno Sudarto, was also in Dili just before the ballot, as was another trusted Wiranto aide, Maj. Gen. Kiki Syahnakri.[102]

Rather than having lost control, therefore, it strongly appears that Wiranto invested some of his best resources to ensure control. In fact, rather than random violence, the events in East Timor bear closer resemblance to two notorious operations from the previous year: the May riots and the defence of the November MPR session. The most obvious similarity between these events was the use of para-militaries to perpetrate targeted violence. In the May riots, *preman* gangs attacked over 47 districts in Jakarta simultaneously. In November, military-backed Islamic militias were armed with bamboo spears and used in clashes with students. In East Timor, the same pattern of using civilian militias was repeated again.

Another striking feature of the May riots and the scorched-earth campaign is that a core group of officers played prominent roles in both episodes. Along with the Special Forces, Bais is the agency most adept at training and employing civilian militias; during the May riots the head of Bais was Zacky Makarim. Meanwhile, the commander of the Jakarta Garrison during the May riots was Maj. Gen. Syafrie Syamsoeddin, and according to at least two veteran foreign journalists who recognised him, Syamsoeddin was active in Dili during the post-ballot period.[103] Moreover, one of Syamsoeddin's chief aides at the time of the May riots was the then brigadier general Adam Damiri; during the scorched-earth campaign, Maj. Gen. Damiri commanded the Udayana Garrison which encompassed East Timor. Most of the funds and equipment supplied to the militias was channelled through Damiri's territorial command structure (while Makarim's P3TT taskforce issued the combat directives).[104]

It therefore appears that the scorched-earth campaign was another product of generals in close proximity to Wiranto. The precise roles played by certain figures, such as Feisal Tanjung, remain obscure, but there can be little doubt that Wiranto was in charge of a deliberate campaign, and that his key subordinates were some of the same commanders associated with the May riots. But assuming that the primary aim of the pre-ballot violence was to lure Falintil into combat, the necessity of the post-ballot scorched-earth campaign is not obvious. The question that remains, therefore, is: what were the military's motives in the post-ballot period?

One of the most perplexing aspects of the scorched-earth campaign was that it seemed, at least to outsiders, that the military was losing far more than it was gaining. It appeared that Wiranto and his generals were willing to endure scathing condemnation just for the sake of wreaking vengeance on the East Timorese people. There is, however, one possible explanation for the military's behaviour: Wiranto and his generals may have been trying to send a message to secessionist movements elsewhere in the archipelago.

By exacting a ruinously high price for East Timorese independence, perhaps Wiranto and his advisors sought to intimidate would-be separatists in Aceh and Irian Jaya. Moreover, the message might have also been targeting foreign audiences, warning the UN, Australia and others to think twice before 'interfering' again with Indonesia's national integrity. But if the military was consciously seeking to intimidate domestic separatists and to send a warning to the international community, the cruel irony is that the message was unnecessary—and probably counter-productive.

In effect, the military was repeating the same miscalculation it had been making for decades: in cracking down on regional dissent Jakarta's generals thought they would discourage secession movements—when in fact the action was probably only encouraging secessionists by providing them with yet more examples of injustice. As for the international community, the military need not have bothered to warn anyone against meddling in Irian Jaya or Aceh. In Irian Jaya the UN recognised the province's integration with Indonesia, while in Aceh the Islamic fundamentalism of the Free Aceh Movement ensured that Western powers—particularly the United States—wanted Aceh to remain a part of Indonesia.

Remarkably, none of the military's senior officers ever publicly expressed reservations about the military's actions in East Timor—not even Bambang Susilo Yudhoyono, the kaster who was celebrated as an intellectual reformer. Rather than voicing dissent, other prominent members of the military high command remained conspicuously silent.[105] Privately, however, there must have been more than a few officers who deeply regretted the unsavoury image that the scorched-earth campaign lent to the military.

The Indonesian military possessed a proud past: it had won the struggle for independence from the Dutch, and in so doing it won the pride of the nation. Some 50 years later the military's conduct in East Timor won only lasting ignominy—especially from the international community. Domestically, the Indonesian public took relatively little notice of events in East Timor. The Bank Bali scandal and the approaching presidential election were dominating headlines, and Indonesia's city-dwellers seemed to deem East Timor irrelevant. In fact, nothing could have been further from the truth; the military's campaign in East Timor was, in effect, a prototype for what lay ahead.

PART III

MELEE OF
THE ELITE

18

ACRIMONY AND LARCENY

Millions of Indonesians stopped what they were doing on the afternoon of 9 September 1999 and tuned their radios and television sets to a live broadcast from parliament. The nation had become transfixed by the high-stakes drama of the Bank Bali scandal, and this day promised to yield yet more drama: a parliamentary commission of inquiry had summoned Rudy Ramli to testify in public.

Ichsanuddin Noorsy was the prime mover behind the parliamentary effort to expose the Bank Bali scandal. Although he was a member of Golkar, Noorsy had won renown for being an outspoken, independent thinker. Having failed to win a seat in the next parliament—which was due to convene in less than a month—Noorsy was a 'lame duck' legislator with little to lose. He was therefore following his conscience in his role as a member of parliament's Commission VIII, which had authority over legal matters. Noorsy sat on the special subcommission assembled to investigate the Bank Bali scandal and he immediately emerged as its most prominent member. And because his actions conformed to Akbar Tandjung's goal of stopping Habibie's candidacy, the Golkar chair gave Noorsy free rein.

In late August, at the urging of the IMF, the special subcommission had ordered a thorough financial investigation, or 'forensic audit', of the Bank Bali scandal. An independent accounting firm, Pricewaterhouse-Coopers (PwC), was hired for the task. While the auditors were working, Noorsy's subcommission subpoenaed Rudy Ramli to testify.

When Ramli finally appeared in parliament on 9 September, Noorsy immediately demanded an explanation for the banker's contradictory statements. Which, Noorsy asked, was true: the chronology outlining protracted negotiations with high-level officials, or the blanket retraction read out by Muladi and signed 'Rudi Ramli'? A nationwide television audience waited with bated breath for Ramli's response. The retraction, the banker replied, had been coerced. To signal his unwillingness to sign the document, he deliberately misspelled his signature.[1]

The testimony marked a breakthrough in the case. Muladi was irate. 'Rudy Ramli,' he declared to reporters, 'must be subjected to a lie detector test. I don't have any faith in someone who continually changes his story.'[2] Baramuli reacted even more harshly: 'You should know,' he told reporters, 'that Rudy Ramli is a heavy user of narcotics.'[3] The Tim Sukses members were trying to undermine the banker's credibility, but their efforts proved fruitless: the next day, Ramli's story was lent credence by a startling revelation from Indonesia's esteemed human rights lawyer, Buyung Nasution.

Buyung had served as Ramli's lawyer for a brief period in late August. As such, he was being accused of having drafted the retraction that was read out by Muladi. Buyung admitted that his team had helped Ramli draft four different versions of a retraction, but Ramli had been unable to choose between them because he could not decide on what information to retract. Buyung explained that the famous letter read out by Muladi was, in fact, one of the four drafts that never should have been allowed to leave his office.[4] Buyung then severed his contact with Ramli, but after the banker's parliamentary testimony he felt that he needed to clear his name. He therefore proceeded to the presidential palace on 10 September to meet directly with Habibie.

Addressing reporters after emerging from his meeting with the president, Buyung paraphrased what Habibie had told him: the controversial letter containing Ramli's retraction had been brought forth by Baramuli. Buyung asked Habibie why he had accepted Baramuli's letter, when neither Ramli nor he, as Ramli's lawyer, publicly vouched for its authenticity. 'But Baramuli is the chair of the Supreme Advisory Council!' Habibie replied. 'How could I not trust him?'[5] Soon thereafter, Muladi also confirmed that Baramuli had procured the retraction.[6]

Additional details quickly surfaced. Ramli described a meeting that took place on 25 August, just two days after Indonesian Corruption Watch publicised his chronicle. He had met with a 'go-between': Kim Yohannes, an ethnic-Chinese businessman who knew Ramli and had been a past business partner of Baramuli.[7] According to Ramli, Kim Yohannes said that the attorney general would prosecute Ramli for corruption unless he retracted his chronicle. Ramli believed the threat because Kim Yohannes, at the time, was talking on the telephone to Baramuli. In effect, Ramli felt that the threat was coming directly from the president's chief advisor. The banker therefore produced the draft retraction taken from Buyung's office, and Kim Yohannes sent it to Baramuli.[8] The next day Muladi read it to reporters after a cabinet meeting.

Thus, within several days of Ramli's testimony, the retraction was no longer believed. Muladi and Tim Sukses had lost credibility. But as for the chronology, Ramli remained reticent: he refused to discuss its details before the subcommission. This prompted Noorsy and other commission members to threaten him with 'contempt of parliament'. Ramli countered that he and his family had been receiving death threats.[9] He did, however, admit that he had originally submitted the chronology on 13 August to a lawyer in PDI Perjuangan.[10] The lawyer later forwarded it to Indonesian Corruption Watch.

Ramli's reasons for turning to PDI Perjuangan are not hard to discern: he was seeking protection from the party that he believed would win the presidency. And by supplying Megawati's aides with ammunition to use in their campaign against Habibie, Ramli may also have been trying to ingratiate himself with the would-be ruling party. This detail confirmed that the scandal was being used as a political commodity not only by Akbar Tandjung's Golkar faction but by Megawati's party as well. The two groups were clearly in league in trying to end Habibie's presidency.

Parliament and the public lamented Ramli's unwillingness to discuss the contents of the chronology, but the task of finding the perpetrators behind the scandal did not hinge on Ramli's testimony alone. Tim Sukses was hoping that everyone with knowledge of the affair would keep silent, but the imminent presidential election complicated the situation. During the Soeharto era, high-level scandals were rarely uncovered because witnesses knew better than to cross anyone close to the president. Now, however, the political tides seemed to be shifting in favour of Megawati, and a number of actors were eager to distance themselves from the faltering Habibie. The investigative reporting being carried out by a boisterous free press exacerbated Habibie's predicament. The first to break ranks with the president was one of the administration's least 'political' figures: Ibra's youthful director, Glenn Yusuf.

Appearing before Noorsy's commission on 13 September, Yusuf declared that Baramuli had masterminded the scandal, repeatedly asking him to disburse the claims of Bank Bali and two other banks.[11] Yusuf had refused but, while he was travelling abroad, Pande Lubis authorised the Bank Bali transaction in his absence. The Ibra director also stated that Baramuli had tried to have him fired, so that Lubis could take over and similar transactions could be carried out. Yusuf also indicated that Tanri Abeng and Syahril Sabirin were among Baramuli's accomplices. Moreover, Baramuli's intention was clear: he wanted to raise funds to buy votes in the MPR, and he even discussed his calculations of the MPR seat breakdown— and his estimate of how much a victory would cost.

The following day Yusuf's testimony was supported by Bambang Subianto. The finance minister sought to deflect blame from himself by casting aspersion on Baramuli and, especially, Tanri Abeng. But at around the same time, revelations about Subianto's background appeared in the press. His association with Pande Lubis—the official whose wrongdoing was the most obvious—dated back 36 years. Both worked together at Bapindo, the state bank that collapsed in 1994 under the weight of its own mismanagement and collusion. Upon reaching the cabinet, Subianto drafted Lubis to work in Ibra under Yusuf. He even endorsed Lubis's request to bring more than 40 former Bapindo bankers on board at Ibra. Yusuf had adamantly opposed the idea, which elicited yet more threats from Baramuli, who also had ties to Bapindo.

After Bambang Subianto, Tanri Abeng was summoned to testify before parliament. The state enterprise minister disappointed his audience by simply refusing to answer any questions whatsoever, claiming that the matter had no connection to his official duties. Similarly, Baramuli flatly denied any involvement when he appeared before the subcommission. 'This is a conspiracy!' he exclaimed. 'These people are amoral—they only want to topple me, because it was I who made Golkar win [in the 7 June election]. I always adhere to the teachings of the Prophet Muhammad, and I beseech Allah to forgive them for what they do.'

Following Abeng, the next figure to testify was Setya Novanto, the director of Era Giat Prima (EGP, the company that received Rudy Ramli's kickback). Novanto acknowledged that he had close ties to both Baramuli and Abeng, but he stated that the bulk of the funds received from Bank Bali, Rp426 billion, was transferred to an account belonging to EGP owner Djoko Tjandra. Most of the balance, Rp112 billion, was transferred to Manimaren's textile concern, Ungaran Sari Garment. In effect, the Golkar deputy treasurer was trying to save himself by steering blame elsewhere. But whereas Novanto denied having taken the money, he tried to claim credit for returning it: he claimed that it was he who initiated the repayment of the Rp546 billion to Bank Bali in July. He and Baramuli had hoped that the repayment would put the affair to rest.

Following Novanto's testimony, members of the special subcommission summarised their findings. The subcommission was sharply divided by political loyalties: Noorsy's small 'anti-Habibie faction' was opposed by a larger 'pro-Habibie faction' led by Eky Syachrudin. Also siding with the president were commission members from Hamzah Haz's PPP as well as House Speaker Harmoko and Deputy Speaker Abdul Gafur.

Finally, in a statement issued on 24 September, the subcommission concluded that seven government officials were involved in the scandal: Baramuli, Subianto, Abeng, Sabirin, Yusuf, Lubis and Ibra deputy director Farid Harijanto. The statement also named six non-government officials: Tjandra, Novanto, Kim Yohannes, Ramli and two other Bank Bali executives.[12] Originally, the subcommission wanted to name a total of sixteen figures, but Harmoko and Gafur succeeded in clearing three names from the list: Manimaren, Timmy Habibie and Hariman Siregar. They also tried to clear Baramuli, but failed.

President Habibie received the subcommission's findings with a grand promise: 'If investigations prove that government officials were indeed involved, then I will call on the appropriate authorities to prosecute the case until justice is served, in full accordance with the laws of the state.'[13]

A key to this process was the forensic audit demanded by the IMF—but by this time the controversy surrounding whether and how the audit should be published had mushroomed into another scandal.

With the IMF's backing, parliament had called on PwC in mid-August to investigate Bank Bali's claim on the government, as well as Bank Indonesia's transfer to Bank Bali and the subsequent flow of those funds. The obstacles strewn in PwC's path were almost as incriminating as the contents of the forensic audit itself.

The first indication that the audit would have limited impact was that PwC's work was placed under the supervision of the Financial Inspection Board (BPK), rather than under the police as would have been proper for a criminal investigation. Throughout the Soeharto era, the BPK had never been much more than a showpiece agency. After Soeharto's fall, proponents of reform wanted the respected former finance minister, Mar'ie Muhammad, to be appointed chair of BPK. Instead, Habibie filled the post by rehabilitating a former protégé from the technology ministry: Satrio Budihardjo 'Billy' Joedono.[14]

PwC commenced its investigation by requesting information regarding certain bank accounts from BI. But central bank officials refused to comply: they first needed explicit instructions, they said, from Joedono. With only about six weeks remaining before the presidential election took place, Joedono stalled for time. After the elapse of several valuable days, he finally instructed BI to comply. PwC, however, later complained that BI impeded their investigation in a host of other ways. In particular, BI refused to provide PwC with access to two critical bank accounts, citing supposed restrictions in the Bank Secrecy Law. One of the accounts belonged to Manimaren, the main money-handler for Tim Sukses. Meanwhile, several dozen people with whom PwC auditors requested interviews refused to comply; these included Baramuli and Abeng.[15]

Finally, the IMF had insisted that the audit results be provided to the police, parliament and the newly formed Independent Review Committee (or IRC, an Ibra watchdog agency created at the IMF's behest and chaired by Mar'ie Muhammad). Instead, Joedono ensured that only the police received the full 400-page audit, which detailed the numbers and owners of bank accounts through which funds from EGP flowed. Joedono demanded that PwC produce a 36-page summary that omitted all names and bank account numbers, and even this watered-down summary was circulated on a tightly restricted basis.[16] And in a tortuous twist of logic the BPK chair claimed that the recipients of funds who were named in the PwC audit had not yet been proven guilty; publicising their names, therefore, might sully their reputations. Joedono told PwC auditors that if their 'long-form' audit reached parliament or the press they would face multi-million dollar fines and prison sentences of up to four years.[17]

In a host of press interviews during September, it was clear that the chain-smoking Joedono was determined to 'localise' the Bank Bali affair and prevent Habibie's allies from being damaged—particularly with the all-important presidential election just weeks away. The IMF, presumably, had wanted the findings submitted to parliament precisely in order to circumvent the unreliable police, yet Joedono was claiming that only the police were entitled to BPK audits. Just as Wiranto had used Soeharto-era legal formalism to fend off pressure from the UN in East Timor, Joedono used the same methods to ward off the IMF.

In response to Joedono's intransigence the IMF and World Bank— which had already halted new lending pending a thorough investigation— urged Co-ordinating Economics Minister Ginandjar Kartasasmita to send PwC's 'long-form' to parliament. Two high-level officials, Stanley Fischer from the IMF and Sven Sandstrom from the World Bank, criticised Joedono's BPK for failing to allow PwC to carry out its audit in accordance with its original scope of work.[18] The police, however, were making little progress in their investigation.

In addition to the PwC audit, a cursory audit was performed by BPK itself. A police spokesman stated that, because there were a great many differences between the two audits, police investigators doubted the veracity of the PwC report.[19] They therefore based their investigation on the findings of the BPK audit, which steered blame for the affair almost entirely toward Ibra, omitting any mention of cabinet members or figures closely connected to Habibie. Meanwhile, Joedono's obstructionist efforts had provided time for Habibie's allies to strike back.

During the first week of September a little-known tabloid called *Siaga* revealed what it deemed to be another major political scandal. The paper, which was run by Golkar parliamentarian Eky Syachrudin, published a list of individuals who had allegedly donated around Rp1 trillion to PDI Perjuangan. Although he was formerly a staunch ally of Akbar Tandjung, Syachrudin had abruptly changed sides and was now working on behalf of Tim Sukses.

Pointing to evidence that he himself admitted was 'only about half accurate', Syachrudin repeatedly accused Megawati of having received Rp650 billion from the Lippo Group, owned by James Riady (who had previously been implicated in a campaign finance scandal involving US President Bill Clinton).[20] *Siaga*'s list of campaign donors, however, was hardly credible: besides Riady, it included four Soeharto relatives, several convicted criminals, an active lieutenant general and other improbable figures. But regardless of their accuracy, Syachrudin's claims largely succeeded in creating the impression that Habibie's 'Baligate' was offset by Megawati's 'Lippogate'.

Syachrudin's counter-attack helped stifle the criticism of Habibie coming from PDI Perjuangan officials, but Golkar's Ichsanuddin Noorsy carried on his campaign nonetheless. By 17 September details of PwC's 'short-form' audit had been obtained by the press. The foreign accounting firm had determined that a web of more than 150 sizeable transfers took place within days of EGP's receipt of funds from Bank Bali. Recipients included a host of politicians, parliamentarians and public officials.[21]

In addition, Djoko Tjandra confessed to PwC that he had transferred funds from the Bank Bali *cessie* to government officials and politicians. The audit also tracked the sources of the Rp546 billion that Tjandra returned to Bank Bali after the scandal was exposed. The short-form named nine major sources, including a close business associate of Tanri Abeng and at least one company belonging to Texmaco owner Marimutu Sinivasan. In general, the short-form found no contradictions with the chronicle of Rudy Ramli.[22]

As for PwC's long-form, President Habibie pledged to the IMF that the audit would be made public by 10 October. But citing objections from BPK, BI and Ginandjar, Habibie deferred the decision to the Supreme Court. Several weeks passed. By the time the court finished its deliberations the presidential election was already over. Against pressure from the IMF, the World Bank, parliament, the press and the public, Habibie's Tim Sukses had succeeded in shrouding the scandal in secrecy. Those implicated in the scandal apparently resorted to violence to protect themselves: in late October PwC accountants came under fire, literally, when two bullets were fired through the firm's third-floor windows.

Finally, after exerting relentless pressure, the IMF prevailed and the results were made public in early November. It soon became clear that PwC had uncovered a remarkable amount of information. The firm had had only three weeks in which to work, and a formidable array of barriers had been erected to slow it down. Some 35 people refused to comply with PwC's requests for interviews, including Baramuli and Novanto. Nonetheless, PwC's auditors succeeded in tracking around 70 per cent of the kickback funds to the ultimate recipients. Fittingly, PwC's team of twenty auditors was headed by an accountant named John Wayne.[23]

What was concealed in the secret audit? One conclusion drawn by the report was that Ibra officials either knew, or should have known, about the existence of Bank Bali's *cessie* with EGP. Consequently, Ibra should never have authorised the payment to Rudy Ramli's bank. Moreover, it was unclear whether the government's deposit insurance actually covered the specific type of claim that Bank Bali was making—and this cast more doubt on the propriety of Ibra's actions. But more consequential than the roles of Ibra and BI were the details regarding the flow of funds.

From the Rp546 billion that Bank Bali transferred to EGP on 1 June, the funds went in three general directions: Rp351 billion went to accounts controlled by Djoko Tjandra, Rp120 billion to accounts controlled by Marimutu Manimaren and Rp76 billion to Arung Gauk Jarre, a longstanding business partner of Tanri Abeng.[24] With the exception of Jarre's involvement, this conformed to what Setya Novanto had admitted in mid-September. From these three channels, however, the funds fanned out to scores of destinations.

PwC mapped out a complex web of more than 150 transfers, most of which took place during the first half of June.[25] Ultimately, around 10 per cent of EGP's kickback reached 'dead-ends'—that is, numbered accounts or cash withdrawals by unknown individuals. Other destinations (or conduits) were companies belonging to Tjandra's Mulia Group and the Texmaco Group of Manimaren's brother, Sinivasan. The latter was renowned as a funding vehicle for Golkar.

Among the most commented-upon findings was a relatively paltry Rp15 billion which was paid, prior to the Bank Bali transaction, to Golkar's official campaign fund (Bappilu Golkar). These funds originated from James Riady's Bank Lippo: on 26 May Lippo paid Rp30 billion to Golkar deputy treasurer Marimutu Manimaren, who then transferred half of that sum to the Golkar account. A short while later funds from EGP's kickback were used to repay Lippo for the Rp30 billion loan, which apparently bore no interest.

As chair of Golkar, Akbar Tandjung endured considerable public criticism for the Rp15 billion contribution. This was somewhat ironic, given that he was a prime mover behind the exposure of the scandal. Tandjung dodged the criticism by claiming that the funds were merely a personal loan from Manimaren and that the sum was fully repaid by October. The Rp15 billion sum exceeded the maximum legal contribution to a political party by a factor of 100, but little attention was ever paid to Indonesia's outdated campaign finance rules.

As for the notable figures who received funds from Tjandra, Manimaren or Jarre, those topping the list included the first lady, Hasrie Ainun Habibie, whose charitable foundation received Rp2 billion. Setya Novanto received at least Rp1.5 billion, while another Golkar vice-treasurer, Enggartiasto Lukita, received Rp10 billion. Freddy Latumahina, a Golkar vice-chair from Maluku who was an ardent Habibie supporter, received nearly Rp1 billion which he withdrew in cash. The head of the state family planning agency, Dr A. Mongid, received at least Rp1 billion. Although Arnold Baramuli was not proven to have received any funds, his chief ally on the supreme advisory council, Agus Sudono, received Rp1.5 billion. Likewise, Tanri Abeng did not appear to receive funds directly, but a company he owned received Rp1.2 billion.[26] The PwC audit therefore failed to trace the EGP kickback to a single politically significant recipient, but it actually accomplished something more important: it provided a rare glimpse into the inner workings of the money machine that drove Indonesian politics.

EGP's Rp546 billion kickback was hardly a significant source of campaign funds in its own right—but as suggested by the speed with which Novanto mustered sufficient funds to repay Bank Bali in August, the kickback appeared to be but a small piece of the larger whole. Within days the funds disappeared in a whirlwind of account transfers, cashed checks and currency withdrawals. By mid-1999 the motor that drove Indonesia's political patronage machine was running in overdrive. The administration's success in concealing PwC's findings until after October ensured that the public could only guess at what was taking place behind the scenes as the election approached. Few, however, would have been surprised to know that the engine was only accelerating.

As the controversy over the Bank Bali scandal mounted during September, expectations grew that Megawati would defeat Habibie in the presidential election. Several other events and trends supported these expectations. First, the PDI Perjuangan candidate attended a wedding in Akbar Tandjung's company on 3 September—their second joint public appearance in as many weeks. By Megawati's standards this was a veritable flurry of political diplomacy. It was precisely the sort of politicking she needed to perform if she was to muster a majority alliance in the MPR.

Next, Indonesia's 27 newly elected provincial assemblies began forming. The first to convene was arguably the most important assembly: that of the province of Jakarta. PDI Perjuangan commanded the largest faction, with 30 of the assembly's 84 seats.[27] Amid the turmoil in East Timor and the furore over the Bank Bali scandal, few noticed when the Jakarta assembly conducted an election to produce a Speaker. But the election produced a strange result: the winner was a retired general from the military's faction, which commanded only eight appointed seats.

The odd result came about because most of the PDI Perjuangan delegation rejected their own candidate and crossed factional lines to vote for the military's candidate, in alliance with eleven representatives from Golkar and several from smaller parties. The result outraged PDI Perjuangan youth supporters, who had gathered in front of the assembly building while the vote took place. Said one youth activist: 'It seems that all this time we've been struggling not for reformers but for traitors.' Inside the assembly, reform-minded legislators greeted the result with catcalls of 'Long live the New Order! Long live the status quo!'

Nonetheless, the event signalled something important: PDI Perjuangan was finally building alliances. If it wanted to defeat Habibie and elect Megawati, this was precisely what the party needed to do. The vote therefore suggested that the military, Golkar and the bulk of PDI Perjuangan would work together in the upcoming MPR session. The order to hand the position of assembly Speaker to the military was presumably a small part of a larger political bargain. But while this was encouraging for

Megawati, her designs on the presidency were being put at risk by her erstwhile ally, Abdurrahman Wahid.

To elect Megawati, PDI Perjuangan needed support from Wahid's PKB, but by late August the NU chair was steadily distancing himself from his lifelong friend. On 24 August he captured headlines nationwide by declaring: 'I don't support Mega. Who says I support her? That's only a mistake made by the press.'[28] Wahid's statements had been erratic in the past, but by the end of August his anti-Megawati stance had been reiterated several times, such that it was gaining credibility.

Not all of Wahid's supporters, however, agreed with his change of course. Although some NU clerics opposed Megawati, others adamantly supported her as a way of opposing their traditional enemies, the Islamic modernists in the Central Axis, a new loose alliance of Islamic parties that was being promoted by Amien Rais. Wahid therefore hastily convened a central NU leadership meeting on 28 August. He expressly forbade NU officials voicing preferences for any particular candidate. The move was clearly aimed at silencing Megawati supporters such as Matori Abdul Djalil and Wahid's own nephew, Muhaiman Iskandar.

With Amien Rais having informally nominated Wahid as the presidential candidate of the Central Axis, it seemed that Wahid was now actively seeking the presidency for himself, despite his lack of eyesight. But Wahid adamantly denied this. As he put it, he was simply standing by, ready to accept the job if it was thrust upon him—just as any upstanding NU member would respond to a call to duty on behalf of the community. But the charming analogy was somewhat misleading. In fact, Wahid's public appearances showed that he was earnestly trying to curry favour with Rais's Central Axis colleagues—the same figures he had denounced in scathing terms in years past.

On 30 August Wahid publicly met with leaders of the major Islamic parties: Rais, Yusril Ihza Mahendra, Nur Mahmudi Ismail (chair of Partai Keadilan) and two vice-chairs of PPP. One of the driving forces behind the summit was Fuad Bawazier, a crafty power broker who was determined to find his way back into the cabinet.[29] The finance minister in Soeharto's short-lived sixth cabinet, Bawazier had served for years as director-general of taxation—a role that provided him with close links to the first family. But in addition to Cendana, Bawazier also maintained ties to Icmi-linked modernists such as Rais. As such, he reputedly helped Wiranto recruit and finance several of the Islamic militias that defended the 1998 MPR session, such as Laskar Jihad.[30] Upon leaving the closed-door meeting, Wahid praised the Central Axis and claimed that it possessed the potential to resolve the nation's political crisis.

In response to Wahid's manoeuvring, Megawati's lobbyists attempted to circumvent the NU cleric. Unlike most other major politicians, Wahid did not act as the chair of his own political party: instead, he had entrusted the position to a seasoned PPP politico from the NU fold, Matori Abdul Djalil. By late August Wahid and Matori were clearly at odds, as Matori continued to exude enthusiastic support for Megawati.

The most plausible explanation for Matori's break with Wahid was the rumour that had long been circulating in Jakarta: Megawati's husband, Taufik Kiemas, had promised to make Matori vice-president.[31] Three cabinet posts and several gubernatorial slots were also said to have been included in the political bargain. However, the strength of Matori's support among the PKB's rank-and-file remained unclear—especially since he was openly opposing his party's founder, Wahid. Another problem was that Megawati could offer the vice-presidency to only one person, yet there were already three potential candidates: Wiranto, Tandjung and Matori.

Thus, as preparations were made for the start of the MPR session on 1 October, Indonesia's electoral arithmetic was extraordinarily complex. Habibie's public image had been damaged during August by the Bank Bali scandal and the East Timor referendum; during September, however, Tim Sukses revived Habibie's chances by placing his allies in a large share of the MPR's appointed seats. Megawati attracted support from Golkar's anti-Habibie faction, but lost support from PKB's Wahid supporters. The Central Axis was supporting Wahid, though some within it preferred Habibie. And to further exacerbate the confusion and tension, Wiranto's military began to make some ominous moves.

Wiranto and his aides had been trying intermittently for months to pass a State of Emergency bill through parliament. Ironically, the draft law was known as the KKN bill because of its Indonesian initials, but in fact it had no relation to anti-corruption measures. Instead, the bill would enable the military to legally conduct search-and-seizure, perform summary arrests, impose curfews and order media blackouts. The military would be justified in imposing such measures on any district or province with an outbreak of civil unrest, ethnic clashes or religious strife.

September 1999 was an awkward time for the military to be seeking expanded powers, as its public image had deteriorated drastically in preceding weeks. In July, while abuses were taking place regularly in East Timor, military personnel in Aceh massacred 51 unarmed civilians in the village of Bantiqiyah. In Maluku, meanwhile, Kostrad and Brimob units opened fire on each other on 26 August, killing one soldier. In the internecine religious strife which, at that point, had claimed over 1300 lives, Kostrad units had been siding with Muslims while Brimob sided with Christians.[32]

At the same time, the military was also affected by drug scandals. In early August a second lieutenant in Special Forces Group IV had been apprehended in a hotel room with four kilograms of methamphetamine hydrochloride ('ice', or *shabu-shabu*), plus more than 6000 ecstasy pills and 27 grams of heroin. The 24-year-old officer, Agus Isrok, was the son of Army Chief-of-Staff Gen. Subagyo.[33] Similarly, five active soldiers were apprehended by police while transporting 60 kilograms of dried marijuana from Aceh to Medan.[34] The incident supported longstanding suspicions that military units were intricately involved in Aceh's notorious drug trade.

Despite the military's worsening image—and despite the fact that previous attempts to pass the KKN bill had engendered vehement public protest—Wiranto continued to push the measure through the committees of the old Soeharto-era parliament, which was still in session through to 24 September. Because the next parliament was expected to be more 'reformist', Wiranto's staff apparently viewed September as their last chance to push their bill through.

The military's kaster, Bambang Yudhoyono, promoted the bill by claiming that it was actually less draconian than the existing statute governing the military's emergency powers, which dated from 1957. In fact, legal experts pointed out that the law would continue to allow the military to run roughshod over civil rights.[35] The law's principal innovation was that it curbed the president's powers over the military. Apparently, Wiranto and Yudhoyono wanted to protect the military from the meddling of a newly elected civilian president. But by pushing the bill aggressively without admitting their true motivation, the generals aroused deep suspicion and vehement protests. At the forefront of these protests were Indonesia's university students, most of whom had just recently returned to their campuses.

For more than a year students had been demanding justice for the perpetrators of the killings at Trisakti and Semanggi—but instead of answering those demands Wiranto and Yudhoyono responded by pushing a bill that might legitimise similar acts in the future. The KKN bill therefore became a symbol that galvanised students like no other issue since the presidency of Soeharto. Massive protests in front of parliament paralysed Jakarta on 9 September, followed by an even larger protest the next day.

As a concession to the demonstrators, Wiranto changed the name of the law to a less odious-sounding acronym, but its contents remained the same. And despite the adamant student protests, neither Megawati nor Wahid voiced serious objections to the bill—both were too keen to enlist the military's potentially pivotal support in the presidential election. Finally, on 23 September—the day on which the outgoing parliament finally adjourned—the bill was passed by unanimous acclamation. It was a stunning demonstration of the military's clout within parliament.

Within hours of the bill's passage the students took to the streets in large numbers. Military leaders chastised student demonstrators for failing to register their complaints through 'proper' channels, but the students maintained that it was precisely the lack of proper channels that forced them to protest. The will of the Indonesian people, they said, had been ignored by Soeharto-era parliamentarians—who passed the unpopular measure moments before leaving office. Some students simply sought to vent their anger, while others demanded that Harmoko reconvene parliament and repeal the measure.

After more than two years of protesting, the students were hardened veterans. Many had always been fearless to the point of being reckless; they now augmented their courage with clever tactics and skilful co-ordination. Various groups of students converged on the parliament building from different directions at once, fragmenting the security forces. The students also succeeded in attracting support from youths in local neighbourhoods.

Finally, their protest against military brutality was met with more brutality. In an episode remarkably similar to that of November 1998, troops opened fire with live ammunition and killed four protesters, three of whom were teenagers. Scores were injured.[36] The shootings took place in the same location as the previous year's killings: the Semanggi interchange. The next day, as protests continued, Habibie finally intervened and announced that he would postpone signing the bill into law. After 36 hours of nonstop protest, the students finally dispersed. But from then onwards, whenever they demanded accountability for the military's use of lethal force, their list of episodes included 'Semanggi II'.

The student unrest exacerbated fears of violence surrounding the presidential election. Having won a plurality of the 7 June election, PDI Perjuangan supporters expected Megawati to win the presidency. Although a victory by Habibie was being discounted, it was still viewed as a real possibility—and this raised widespread consternation about Megawati supporters taking to the streets.

Having won 1.9 million votes in Jakarta alone, plus millions more from the suburbs in West Java, there was no doubt that PDI Perjuangan could mobilise large numbers if it chose to do so. In fact, implicit threats of mass action had been issued on several occasions by PDI Perjuangan figures such as Dimyati Hartono and Aberson Marle Sihaloho.[37] If Megawati were denied the presidency, they had warned, a mass of party supporters would descend on Jakarta. These subtle attempts at intimidation helped alienate Megawati from potential political allies, and they elicited elaborate security preparations from the authorities.

In the approach to the presidential election Jakarta governor Sutiyoso summoned the five other governors from Java and Bali; he urged them to prevent large convoys of political party supporters from departing to Jakarta. Meanwhile, the Jakarta Garrison commander, Maj. Gen. Djaja Suparman, mobilised a staggering 70 000 security personnel to guard the city during the MPR session. Amid this mounting tension—and only three days after the Semanggi II killings—Wahid issued a startling statement. If any group interfered with the MPR through force, he vowed, he would surround the parliament building with 100 000 members of Banser, the quasi-militant wing of NU's massive youth group, Ansor. Banser youth are unarmed, but they study martial arts and provide bodyguard and security services for NU officials.

In an attempt to clarify his comment the following day, Wahid claimed that he had not been referring to interference from students. Apparently he meant PDI Perjuangan supporters, and his flippant remark set Jakarta on edge. The threat of mass violence between supporters of Indonesia's two leading reformists was hardly an auspicious start to Indonesia's first 'democratic' election in more than 40 years.

19

GUERILLA POLITICS

When the new MPR convened on 2 October, no one was sure how the forces within the assembly would array themselves in the presidential vote.[1] It was clear that there were three broad groupings: PDI Perjuangan, Golkar and the Islamic parties of the Central Axis. But their relative strengths—and how they might ally with each other in the presidential vote—were obscured by a host of variables.

Most important was the impact of the MPR's appointed members, who formed 200 of the assembly's 700 members. It was still not clear how these regional and functional group representatives would ally themselves with various parties. Meanwhile, most major parties had deep internal cleavages: while Golkar was divided over whether to support Habibie, most Islamic parties were being pulled in multiple directions as well. And because individual members would be able to cross party lines and vote for opposing candidates, the pledges of party leaderships were not always meaningful—a party's rank-and-file members might ignore the pledge and vote differently. But amid these uncertainties one thing was clear: the proceedings would be heavily influenced by money politics.

One strong indication that 'brown-bag' politics would colour the MPR session occurred in September, when most of the new provincial assemblies elected 'regional representatives' to the MPR. Each of Indonesia's 27 assemblies determined its own rules for selecting five representatives. Impartial observers hoped that the party breakdown of the 135 representatives would mirror the breakdown of votes from 7 June; instead, Golkar eventually secured 47 per cent of these seats—even though the ruling party had won a mere 23 per cent of the national vote on 7 June.[2] PDI Perjuangan obtained less than a third of the regional representative seats.

Golkar's strong performance in the provincial assemblies immediately prompted allegations that brown-bag lobbying had been applied. For example, after having secured 49 per cent of the votes in North Sulawesi (amid vehement allegations of fraud), Golkar proceeded to win all five of the province's regional representative slots.[3] Meanwhile, a Tim Sukses member who formerly headed Tommy Soeharto's clove monopoly, Nurdin Halid, openly admitted that Habibie's lobbyists were campaigning in the 27 provinces to secure regional representative seats for themselves.[4] Arnold Baramuli and Abdul Gafur won such seats, as did five cabinet members linked to Tim Sukses.[5] Many other regional representatives had dubious backgrounds: Indonesia Corruption Watch estimated that at least 100 of the regional representatives had links to past corruption scandals.[6]

The next indicators of money politics were the MPR's decisions on procedural issues. The session would not meet continuously until a president was elected; rather, a ten-day break would precede the vote. This was ostensibly to allow a smaller 'MPR working committee' to form state guidelines and conduct routine business. Officials from PDI Perjuangan, however, alleged that the break was intended to provide ample time for brown-bag lobbying away from the MPR session.[7]

The MPR also resolved that it would elect a president using a secret ballot. In a system already lacking in accountability and transparency, this was hardly a democratic way to choose Indonesia's first 'democratically' elected president. MPR members would not even agree to use the assembly's newly installed, state-of-the-art electronic voting devices. Representatives maintained that the devices might be 'engineered' and were therefore untrustworthy. In fact, they were apparently worried that the devices would not be entirely confidential. The reason was clear: a secret ballot would greatly facilitate money politics, by allowing representatives to accept bribes and cross party lines without being noticed. In an open vote they would stand out and look suspicious.[8]

It was unclear to most whether Megawati or Wahid would stoop to the use of vote-buying. But even if they did, it was generally assumed that in an MPR session affected by brown-bag politics the main beneficiary would be B.J. Habibie. Golkar's success in garnering regional representative seats promised to significantly boost Habibie's support within the MPR. Despite the twin blows of the East Timor debacle and the Bank Bali scandal, Habibie's candidacy was regaining strength. But perhaps the biggest boost to his presidential hopes came from an unlikely source: the minutiae of Indonesia's new election laws.

To embark on its first experiment with democracy in over 40 years, Indonesia used a unique and ungainly vehicle: a hybrid electoral system. The original drafters of Indonesia's new electoral laws opted for the more democratic of the two standard models of electoral systems: the 'direct' system. Voters voted for individual candidates at the local level, thereby holding their representatives accountable at the grassroots level. But when the draft laws were submitted to the Golkar-dominated parliament in early 1999, they were changed to a far less democratic alternative: a 'proportional' system.

In a pure proportional system, voters only voted for party symbols, not individual candidates. A party would win seats in proportion to its share of the total vote, after which the party's leadership would have full discretion over assigning individuals to fill its seats in parliament. In practice, this system would concentrate political power in the hands of a few party bosses, as parliamentarians would be accountable primarily to their party leaders—not their constituents.

To avoid the pitfalls of a purely proportional system and to make representatives at least somewhat accountable to the electorate, Indonesia's new laws incorporated a crucial feature of a district system. Prior to elections, all parties were required to assign legislative candidates to specific electoral districts, or *kabupaten*, of which there were more than 400 in Indonesia. These 'candidate lists' were posted at polling stations so that voters could, at least in theory, consult the lists and determine what individual would be representing them if a given party won their district's seat.

The problem, however, was that Indonesia's leaders—from Golkar as well as PDI Perjuangan and other parties—wanted the proportional allocation of seats to take place at the provincial level, not the lower *kabupaten* level. Therefore a compromise was reached: parties would win seats proportionally at the provincial level, but would fill those seats based on their performances at the *kabupaten*. Thus, if a party won three seats in a province, those seats were to be filled by the pre-assigned candidates in the three *kabupaten* in which the party performed best.

Unfortunately, the new laws failed to define 'best'. Did it mean the district in which a party won its largest number of votes, or the district in which a party won its highest percentage of votes? Because the sizes of Indonesia's *kabupaten* varied widely, the difference was consequential. In a large *kabupaten*, a modest share of the total vote might nonetheless equate to the largest aggregate number of votes in the province; in a small *kabupaten*, the opposite might be true—a small number of votes might represent a large share of the total vote.

For months, independent election observers had urged the General Election Commission (KPU) to clarify the rule and enforce a consistent standard nationwide. But the political parties, meanwhile, sought to manipulate the issue for their own ends. Almost all parties asked the KPU to allow the parties themselves to decide which standard to apply. Most parties were struggling with internal cleavages, and the discretion to manipulate the system was valuable. To fill seats with the most desirable candidates, party leaderships could use one definition of 'best' in one province, but the other definition in the next province. This would help them shape the complexion of their parliamentary delegations by screening for loyalists of a particular faction—precisely the type of behaviour that the designers of the hybrid electoral system had intended to prevent.

The KPU should have upheld the original intent of the laws by choosing one standard or the other, but under the malleable Rudini the commission was dominated by party interests. The KPU therefore acquiesced and gave party leaderships the authority to determine which standard they would use. Predictably, this created massive infighting within parties, as rival claimants vied for seats.

Within PDI Perjuangan the infighting developed along religious lines. Because the party's original list of candidates included far too many non-Muslims, the party's secretary general, Alex Litaay, manipulated the 'largest votes' versus 'largest percentage' distinction on a selective basis, from one province to the next, to boost the number of Muslims in PDI Perjuangan's parliamentary delegation. The process gave rise to local disputes that often turned violent, with loyalists of losing candidates attacking the loyalists of winning candidates from the same party.

Similarly, Habibie's allies on Golkar's executive board used their influence to promote their own loyalists—at the expense of Akbar Tandjung's.[9] And in some cases the original list—which had been displayed at polling stations on 7 June and was supposedly unalterable—was simply ignored. The KPU consistently failed to react, to the chagrin of the commission's more responsible members.[10] The issue was critical to the outcome of Indonesia's political transition, but it seemed arcane to the press and public and therefore went largely unnoticed.

Thus, by the time the MPR convened on 1 October, Habibie was in a far better political position than had been expected. Despite East Timor and the Bank Bali scandal, Habibie's Tim Sukses had garnered a large number of regional representative seats, while manipulating Golkar's candidate lists to produce an overwhelmingly pro-Habibie delegation. Against all odds, Habibie was back in contention.

During its first days in session the MPR put various procedural and structural matters to a vote on three occasions. Although none of the issues were particularly consequential, the votes provided crucial measures of Megawati's support within the assembly. It should have surprised none that Megawati's support was low: signs to that effect had been evident for months. Nonetheless, the results of the first three procedural votes shocked the nation: on all three issues PDI Perjuangan lost by a wide margin. Megawati's support never exceeded 250 votes—a level well short of the 351 that would be required to win the presidency.

From rough estimates of how the regional and functional-group representatives would ally themselves with various parties, it now seemed that the MPR's three main groupings were of approximately equal size: the

Central Axis, PDI Perjuangan and Golkar each seemed to control around 25–30 per cent of the assembly's 700 seats. The balance was held by the military (5 per cent), the PKB (6 per cent) and smaller parties. But a host of variables obscured the balance of power.

For Megawati the situation was grim. Her only steadfast allies were two tiny secular nationalist factions, with a combined 4 per cent share of the MPR. Even if she won the full backing of both the military and the PKB— an outcome that was far from certain—she would still fall several percentage points short of a 51 per cent majority. Because the Central Axis was resolutely opposed to her candidacy, she could only turn to support from Golkar's anti-Habibie faction, led by Akbar Tandjung.

The first few days of the MPR session made Megawati's hopes for a winning alliance seem like a forlorn dream. The military faction abstained from the three procedural votes: despite Megawati's unwavering support for the armed forces over the preceding months, Wiranto and his aides were choosing to remain neutral until it was absolutely necessary to take sides. Similarly, Tandjung was also keeping his options open. Despite Megawati's gestures to his potentially pivotal faction within Golkar, it soon became clear that Tandjung had been busy brokering behind-the-scenes deals with the Central Axis and his own party's pro-Habibie faction. Finally, Abdurrahman Wahid continued to promote himself as an alternative candidate, but at the time this seemed to be the least of Megawati's worries—it was generally assumed that at the last minute the blind cleric would recognise the hopelessness of his candidacy and cast his support back to Megawati.

As her critics and some of her aides had been telling Megawati for months, she had done far too little to build alliances with other elements of the MPR. As one of her aides put it: 'We've been fighting a long guerilla war. We've only recently emerged out of the jungle, and suddenly we're expected to be diplomatic. Of course we'll have weaknesses.'[11] But the party's problems ran deeper than this. Megawati failed to act in a 'presidential' way in the MPR assembly: she stayed mute and seemed unable to read the constantly shifting political currents. This stood in sharp contrast to other figures, particularly Rais and Tandjung. Not only did these two posture incessantly to assert their presence within the assembly, they also lobbied tirelessly outside the assembly. Unlike Megawati, therefore, Rais and Tandjung were well prepared for the session's first major contests: the votes for the Speakers of the MPR and parliament.

The votes for the two Speaker positions had considerable political significance in their own right, but they also promised to reveal the hidden balance of power within the MPR assembly. In the days prior to the vote, Golkar leaders met repeatedly with leaders of the Central Axis; their goal was to forge a pact to win the two powerful positions for themselves.

In the early hours of 3 October—only hours before the MPR Speaker vote would take place—the two sides finally reached an agreement.

Initially, Wahid had wanted to run for MPR Speaker himself, but he failed to obtain sufficient votes for a nomination from within his faction (the functional group faction). A different plan was forged: for MPR Speaker, Golkar would back the chair of the largest party in the Central Axis, Hamzah Haz of PPP. In return, the Central Axis would back Tandjung in the subsequent vote for Speaker of parliament. Rais would become Deputy Speaker of parliament, with the understanding that if Tandjung obtained the vice-presidency, Rais would then take over his position as Speaker of parliament.[12] But just prior to the vote, the plan changed again.

Rais was apparently concerned about being left out. His chance for high office was contingent on Tandjung reaching the vice-presidency—an outcome that was far from certain amid the confusion. Rather than being appointed by the president, Indonesia's new electoral rules stipulated that the MPR would elect the vice-president in a separate vote to be held one day after the election of the president. Like the presidency itself, therefore, the outcome of the vice-presidential vote was nearly impossible to predict.

Rais therefore preferred a more secure position, but his problem was that Haz, in effect, outranked him. The PPP chair controlled the third largest MPR faction, whereas Rais controlled the fifth largest. Rais therefore enlisted help from the figure whom he had nominated for president: Wahid. At Wahid's insistence a new 'scenario' was produced in which Haz and Rais swapped positions.[13] Thus the Golkar–Central Axis alliance would back Rais for MPR Speaker, while Haz would wait in the wings of parliament. Meanwhile, PDI Perjuangan backed PKB chair Matori Abdul Djalil, and several other candidates were nominated by small factions.[14]

A huge television audience watched as the vote commenced. The actual vote-taking process was exceedingly slow. Eschewing the electronic voting system, MPR members scribbled their preferences on slips of paper and deposited them in boxes. The secret ballots were then read out one by one and the votes tallied on a whiteboard, in full view of the MPR assembly and television cameras. As the black ticks gradually accumulated over more than an hour, the tension grew.

The race between Rais and Matori was too close to call until the very end. Finally Rais won—but only with a 305-vote plurality of the 650 votes cast. Matori received 279 votes. A portion of Matori's own party had apparently rebelled and voted for Rais, on Wahid's instructions. This was a crucial swing vote. Also crucial was the abstention, in effect, of the military: fond of neither Matori nor Rais, the military pledged its 41 votes to its own candidate.

As soon as the vote was finished the various parties scrambled to prepare for the next contest two days hence: the vote for Speaker of parliament. It seemed that PDI Perjuangan and PKB might nominate Matori again. He had come very close in the race against Rais, and if the military's backing could be secured a winning alliance might be cobbled together. But the position of parliament Speaker was no party's paramount goal; all contestants were jockeying for the presidential vote. That vote, in turn, seemed to hinge on the figure who was emerging as Indonesia's most cunning political operator: Akbar Tandjung.

When Indonesia's presidential transition began in 1998, Tandjung was merely a junior member of Soeharto's ill-fated Seventh Development cabinet. Lacking both mass support and a clear ideology, the soft-spoken housing minister relied solely on his wits to advance his career. Amid the turbulence of Indonesia's post-Soeharto power vacuum, Tandjung navigated with consummate skill. He could ally with anyone—and betray anyone—so long as it served to promote his own advance. By early October 1999 he had successfully taken possession of the ideal position amid the political impasse: all major political factions needed his support for their respective presidential bids. At the time, it was believed that Tandjung commanded the loyalty of only 40–60 members of Golkar's MPR faction, but this bloc represented the assembly's crucial swing vote.

Hours before the vote on 5 October Megawati met with Tandjung and Ginandjar at Hotel Borobudur.[15] Golkar sources said that Tandjung would not discuss the presidential vote—he first demanded that Megawati support him in the vote for Speaker of parliament, and only after that would he broach the topic of an alliance in the presidential vote.[16] Such was the strength of Tandjung's bargaining position at this point.

Most other parties also fell into line behind Tandjung. Golkar's pro-Habibie faction was furious with Tandjung for having hindered Habibie's campaign, yet the faction was still hopeful of finally gaining his support—so even they backed him for Speaker of parliament. And because Tandjung's support had been critical in electing Rais as MPR chair, the Central Axis backed him as well. Soon after the voting commenced on the evening of 5 October, it was clear that Tandjung would win in a landslide. When the ballots were tallied, he had received a staggering 84 per cent of votes cast.[17]

Tandjung's election caused a stir because it was so sharply at odds with the principles of *reformasi*: nearly four out of five voters had voted against Golkar on 7 June, yet more than four out of five parliamentarians picked Golkar's chair to be their Speaker. In a result that highlighted the power still possessed by the 'status quo', the first parliament to be elected democratically in over 40 years would be headed by a paragon of New Order rule. Many began to wonder whether an even more potent display of that power would be demonstrated in the next major decision of the MPR: the vote on the accountability speech of President Habibie.

Because the MPR had given the president his mandate and policy guidelines at the start of his term, the president was required to deliver a speech of accountability to the MPR at the end of that term. If the MPR agreed that the president had complied with its guidelines, it would 'accept' the accountability speech and the president would be eligible to run for another term. These speeches had been perfunctory affairs under Soeharto, but the advent of *reformasi* opened a new realm of possibilities. For Habibie, the accountability speech promised to make or break his campaign. Meanwhile, during the nine days between Tandjung's Speaker election and Habibie's speech, the various party leaders and their lobbying teams started to jockey for position.

On 6 October B.J. Habibie's brother Timmy occupied a rented suite in the Hotel Crowne Plaza, situated not far from the parliament building. He had scheduled a meeting to which he had invited four guests: high-ranking NU clerics who were serving as Abdurrahman Wahid's 'political envoys'. According to the clerics' version of events, Timmy Habibie began the meeting by belittling Wahid for being blind. Faced with their candidate's obvious physical constraints, he said, why did the PKB not simply back B.J. Habibie instead?

Timmy then offered an inducement: a huge duffle bag stuffed with cash. If the clerics pledged PKB's 50 or so votes to his brother's campaign, he would pay Rp250 billion, on which the money in the bag was a down payment. Less than fifteen minutes after the meeting began, the clerics turned down the offer and walked out. They recounted the event to the press and Wahid himself vouched for their story.[18] But in addition to providing anecdotal evidence of the backroom money politics that was presumably taking place on a regular basis, the episode also demonstrated another trend: Wahid's candidacy was eliciting growing consternation.

Even after the MPR session had begun, many still doubted that Wahid's candidacy was serious. Earlier in the year the NU chair had repeatedly said that he was not physically fit for the presidency.[19] Combined with his longstanding alliance with Megawati, these protestations convinced many—both in PDI Perjuangan as well as the Central Axis—that Wahid was carrying out an elaborate ruse. By accepting Rais's nomination, it was believed, Wahid was simply acting to prevent the Central Axis from organising behind another candidate. At the last minute the NU cleric was expected to withdraw from the race and hand the presidency to Megawati.

By the second week of the MPR session, however, Megawati was clearly regarding Wahid's candidacy with alarm. On 6 October an influential PKB official, Alwi Shihab, grabbed headlines: like Matori, Shihab had been a staunch supporter of Megawati, but now he was vowing to back Wahid.

Wahid's dogged campaign was finally galvanising the PKB, and this threat-ened to doom Megawati's presidential bid.

On 8 October, therefore, Megawati embarked with Wahid on a one-day excursion to East Java. The trip's itinerary included visits to the graves of her father, Soekarno, and Wahid's father, Wahid Hasyim. Among other topics, Megawati dissuaded Wahid from punishing Matori for opposing Rais in the MPR Speaker vote. Wahid had publicly alleged that Matori had received a Rp11 billion bribe from PDI Perjuangan.[20]

Upon returning from East Java, Wahid maintained that he was staying in the race and was doing so purely in the interest of democracy. As he put it, if the race contained only two candidates and Habibie's accountability speech was rejected, Megawati would win the presidency unopposed—and that would be an unfortunate lesson in democracy for Indonesia. He was staying in the race, he claimed, to provide some healthy competition. But while Wahid's candidacy was creating problems for Megawati and Habibie, he also faced obstacles of his own—particularly within the Central Axis.

The Central Axis had always been an awkward marriage of rivals. Besides their Islamic identity, the various parties in the alliance were unified only by their common lack of viable presidential candidates. Therefore, as Habibie's prospects improved during the course of the MPR session, the Central Axis was pulled in opposite directions. Pan and the smaller parties that portrayed reformist images remained resolutely opposed to the former technology minister of Soeharto; in contrast, PPP and PBB contained large numbers of delegates who had longstanding ties to Habibie's Icmi and the establishment as a whole. When Habibie's candidacy suffered setbacks in July and August, these conservative elements leaned toward Wahid—but then events during the first few days of the MPR session made them reconsider.

Golkar had demonstrated surprising solidarity in the first five votes of the session, and the PwC long-form audit seemed destined to remain a secret. If anything, the Bank Bali scandal simply demonstrated that Tim Sukses had enormous financial resources at its disposal—thereby making many in the MPR think twice about the wisdom of opposing such a well-heeled candidate. To many within the Central Axis it began to seem that Habibie might have a chance of winning after all. They therefore tempered their support for Wahid, which had never been enthusiastic, and began leaning toward the Golkar candidate. Habibie's biggest problem, however, was that so far he had not completely quelled the rebellion within Golkar's own ranks.

Akbar Tandjung was still mounting stiff resistance to Habibie's candidacy. In a pre-MPR strategy meeting attended by Golkar leaders and Wiranto, the president was said to have exploded at his insubordinate Golkar chair. 'If I lose this race,' he screamed at Tandjung, 'you're finished!'[21] Habibie even demanded that Tandjung recall some 40 Golkar parliamentarians who were opposed to his candidacy—even though the new election laws clearly outlawed the Soeharto-era practice of recalling. Finally, Habibie resorted to outlandish threats: if his presidential bid failed, he said, Eastern Indonesia would secede from the republic.[22]

Immediately after the meeting Tandjung met with reporters and explicitly endorsed Habibie's candidacy. This helped him retain the support of both Golkar factions in the vote for parliamentary Speaker. But as soon as he obtained that post Tandjung promptly switched back to his former tactics: he made sure that Golkar would convene another Rapim, on 11 October, to 'evaluate' Habibie's candidacy. Many believed that Tandjung would stage a last-ditch effort to sabotage Habibie and pledge Golkar's support to an alternative candidate, such as himself, Ginandjar, Wiranto or Sultan Hamengkubuwono X.

The president therefore needed to pass three tests in quick succession: the Golkar Rapim to retain Golkar's nomination; the accountability speech to stay in the presidential race; and finally the presidential vote itself. But just before the first of these tests the political spotlight was stolen by the attorney general *ad interim*, Ismudjoko.

Indonesia's meek public prosecutor faced reporters on 10 October to abruptly announce that his office was issuing an 'SP3', or 'order to halt proceedings', in its investigation of corruption in the charitable foundations headed by the former president, Soeharto.[23] The case had been initiated nearly a year earlier, but it had never been handled seriously. In late September, on the eve of the MPR session, Ismudjoko had upgraded the case from an 'inquiry' to an 'investigation', but he did so without naming Soeharto, or anyone else, as a suspect.

Never before had an attorney general launched an investigation without a suspect.[24] And less than three weeks later, the case was dropped on specious grounds. Ismudjoko explained that Soeharto's management of the foundations had not broken any laws, but the SP3's extraordinary timing—hours before the start of the Rapim—suggested that something far more significant was afoot.

On the surface, the SP3 hardly seemed to serve Habibie's interests: Soeharto's legal status was arguably the most closely watched issue of Habibie's presidency, and another failure to punish Soeharto only further damaged the president's pubic image. Moreover, Jakarta was already braced for violence surrounding the presidential election, and the SP3 only provoked more demonstrations. Most importantly, the previous MPR had explicitly instructed Habibie to thoroughly investigate Soeharto; it seemed to make little sense that Habibie would flout those instructions just days before being held accountable to them.

Habibie, however, was paying little heed at this point to public sentiment or the old MPR's edicts. The presidential election would not be decided by national opinion, but by a select group of 700 political elite. The SP3 was clearly intended to win support from conservative elements of this group. In effect, Habibie was taking a high-stakes political gamble. The identity of the counterpart in this wager became apparent two days later.

As in May, Habibie's prospects of surviving the Rapim hinged on Golkar's 27 provincial chapter heads. And as in May, Habibie enlisted Wiranto's aid. Just before the vote, five chapter heads who were retired military officers—and who possessed critical swing votes—obtained retroactive promotions in rank. The promotions were authorised by the president, at the request of Wiranto.[25] Yet again the military chief was breaking his vow to remain aloof from practical politics.

When the Rapim convened at Hotel Santika on 11 October, the gathering included Marimutu Manimaren, the financier behind the Bank Bali scandal. This reinforced suspicions that Tim Sukses was applying money politics yet again. 'Why would Manimaren show up,' asked an anti-Habibie member of Golkar, 'if not for vote-buying?'[26] The Rapim finally voted the following day and the provincial chapter heads upheld Habibie's candidacy. The president had passed his first hurdle. However, the Rapim stopped short of endorsing Habibie's choice for vice-president.

Golkar's designation of a specific vice-presidential candidate had been the subject of speculation for weeks. If the MPR rejected Habibie's accountability speech, Golkar was expected to throw its support behind its vice-presidential candidate. Tandjung and Ginandjar had therefore been jockeying for the position, while Sultan Hamengkubuwono X was also mentioned as a possible candidate. Because the Rapim was too deeply divided to arrive at a decision, Habibie was allowed to express his own preference, albeit without the official backing of his party. Immediately after the Rapim, therefore, the president made a rare visit to Golkar's national headquarters in Slipi, West Jakarta. He announced that his top choice for a running mate was Gen. Wiranto.[27]

Habibie's announcement highlighted, yet again, the disjunction between public opinion and elite politics in Indonesia's electoral system. The president was offering the vice-presidency to the general who, by most accounts, had threatened a coup d'état the previous month and whose military, in preceding weeks, had perpetrated the Semanggi II killings, the East Timor scorched-earth campaign, the Bantiqiyah massacre and the shootout with police in Maluku. But Habibie was concerned less with public opinion than with his careful calculations of the MPR's delicate balance of power.

Habibie calculated that, even if he won the maximum possible support from Golkar and pro-Habibie elements of the Central Axis, he would still be just shy of the majority needed in a vote on his accountability speech. PDI Perjuangan, PKB and pro-reform elements of the Central Axis were resolutely opposed to his candidacy; this meant that the success or failure of his accountability speech seemed to hinge on the pivotal 5 per cent bloc controlled by the military. It could hardly have been a coincidence that Ismudjoko's SP3 accomplished something that Wiranto had vowed to do the moment Habibie assumed the presidency: protect Soeharto. By halting the investigation and nominating Wiranto for vice-president, Habibie was clearly trying to gain the military's favour.[28]

Wiranto, however, responded in cryptic fashion. He called Habibie's offer 'an honour', but he refrained from explicitly accepting it. Privately, the armed forces chief was said to have been disappointed that Megawati had not nominated him first.[29] Wiranto had reportedly been lobbying Megawati through his Bais chief, Tyasno Sudarto.[30] Moreover, Wiranto's advisors, like everyone else, were unsure whether Habibie would win. Wiranto naturally wanted to avoid aligning with a failure; he therefore waited before making his position known.

O n the day of the accountability speech, 14 October, the presidential motorcade took a circuitous route to the parliament building. The president's handlers were avoiding a heavy concentration of demonstrators in the area. Habibie reached his destination without incident, but the situation on Jalan Gatot Subroto soon deteriorated.

Live television broadcasts cut away from the packed assembly hall to depict thousands of troops and protesters squared off against each other on the highway. Flares, teargas canisters and Molotov cocktails occasionally illuminated the night sky. Lest a full-scale battle erupt, three MPR leaders —Rais, Matori and Kwik Kian Gie—ventured outside and addressed the crowd from the roof of a vehicle. They invited a delegation of protesters inside the assembly, but only four accepted the offer. Finally, around 10 p.m., President Habibie began his long-awaited speech.[31]

The president dwelt on his administration's accomplishments: the return of economic stability, the liberalisation of the press, the carrying out of elections and the passage of regional autonomy laws. But Habibie also addressed his shortcomings at length. With regard to the secession of East Timor, he maintained that international politics necessitated the self-determination ballot. He also acknowledged that, as president, he bore ultimate responsibility for the human rights abuses that had occurred in East Timor and elsewhere during his administration, and he begged forgiveness from the victims' relatives. From this point onward, however, Habibie's speech steadily deteriorated in quality.

As television broadcasts periodically switched to scenes outside the MPR, where troops were using tear gas and water cannon against the protesters, Habibie discussed KKN. He reiterated Ismudjoko's claim that

Soeharto's investigation was halted due to insufficient evidence. He noted that the ministers dispatched to Europe had detected no evidence of bank transfers by the Soeharto family—while neglecting to mention that the Indonesian government had never formally requested assistance from the Swiss government. As for the Bank Bali case, Habibie claimed that an impartial and transparent investigation was being carried out. And as for the larger issue behind rights abuses and corruption—namely, a legal system designed to serve the ruler, rather than serve justice—Habibie simply made no comment.[32]

Scores were injured in the fighting outside the assembly, but none killed. Following Habibie's speech most of the MPR's various party factions convened late-night meetings to prepare their responses, which they delivered the following day. Most factions, including a rancorously divided Golkar, chose to accept the speech with reservations. Only PDI Perjuangan, PKB and two small factions rejected the speech outright. Because it was not clear whether the full MPR would conduct a formal vote on whether to accept or reject the speech, it seemed that Habibie was on the verge of successfully passing his second hurdle.[33]

The protests from the previous night carried on the next day, lasting well into the night. Troops and police used brutality in scores of incidents, not just near the parliament building but also as far as seven kilometres away. For their part, protesters hurled countless Molotov cocktails and destroyed several police vehicles. The security forces refrained from using live ammunition, such that none were killed but some 160 sustained injuries.[34] Meanwhile, amid the incessant street clashes, Indonesia's party bosses resumed their lobbying and politicking with vigour.

O n the day of Habibie's accountability speech Wahid had met privately with Tutut Soeharto. According to rumours that surfaced soon after, Tutut was urging Wahid to draft Wiranto as his vice-presidential running mate.[35] Two days later Wahid visited Habibie's home for a closed-door meeting with the president and the armed forces chief. The NU cleric was presumably trying to muster support for his candidacy in the event that Habibie was eliminated from the race.

Wahid was also shoring up support within his core constituency: on 17 October NU's executive board finally endorsed his candidacy. Wahid's repeated visits to NU *pesantren* in East Java had apparently helped elicit the statement. NU leaders had been reluctant to back Wahid's campaign because they feared he would suffer an embarrassing defeat. Perhaps more importantly, they were also apprehensive about his alliance with their arch-rivals in the Central Axis. Now that NU officially backed Wahid, it was even less likely that PKB—NU's official political party—would continue supporting Megawati, regardless of Matori's wishes. But while Wahid's candidacy was gaining momentum on these fronts, it was suffering setbacks elsewhere: some of his supporters within the Central Axis appeared to be wavering.

A sizeable portion of the Central Axis comprised politicians who were too reform-minded to ally with Habibie, yet too modernist to back Wahid or Megawati. Some favoured supporting Akbar Tandjung. Others, however, proposed a new name as a 'compromise candidate': the esteemed Islamic scholar Nurcholish Madjid.[36] Led by two PPP politicians, this group circulated a nomination petition that quickly acquired 89 signatures.[37]

Support for Nurcholish grew further when, on 15 October, Amien Rais touted his candidacy as a way to break a possible deadlock. The next day, Nurcholish was seen meeting with the US ambassador who, several months before, had publicly mentioned Nurcholish as a possible compromise candidate for the presidency. For what it was worth, Nurcholish presumably had the tacit support of the US government.[38] More significantly, he seemed to be attracting support within Golkar: Marzuki Darusman stated on 17 October that 'in many respects, Nurcholish is a figure who can be accepted by all sides'.[39] He acknowledged that Golkar was considering Nurcholish's candidacy. Nurcholish himself was indicating his willingness to serve as president if needed, but he stated that his term should only last one or two years—just long enough to arrange for a direct election of a new president.

For sincere reformists who were growing disillusioned with both Megawati and Wahid, Nurcholish's candidacy was greeted as the most positive news in weeks. But because his strongest support came from the Central Axis, his candidacy hinged on Wahid withdrawing. This, in turn, depended on Habibie's candidacy: on 18 October the MPR announced that it would conduct a full vote on whether to accept the president's accountability speech. The vote was scheduled for the evening of 19 October—just eleven hours before the presidential election was due to commence. In effect, the vote on the accountability speech would mark the first phase of the long-awaited presidential election. If Habibie obtained a majority in favour of the speech, he would almost certainly have enough support to also win the presidency. If not, a last-minute scramble would ensue.

The day before the vote on the accountability speech, Wiranto convened a press conference aired live on state-run television. He was flanked by the military's entire top echelon: four service chiefs, the kaster, and the commanders of four main combat units (Kostrad, the Special Forces, the Jakarta Garrison and the Marines). But, for all the fanfare, Wiranto's message was deeply ambiguous. In addition to the usual denunciations of mass protests, he also responded—after an interval of six days—to Habibie's offer to become his running mate. Wiranto declined, claiming that the country's security situation required him to devote his full attention to his military duties. But later in his speech

Wiranto also said that, if the people truly wanted him to serve in public office, he would be willing to do so.[40]

Wiranto's statement seemed oddly contradictory on the surface—if he was declining Habibie's nomination to preserve the military's neutrality and to focus on security concerns, why was he keeping open the option of accepting a nomination from elsewhere? Some suspected that Wiranto was deliberately trying to defeat Habibie's candidacy. Others pointed to reports that US Ambassador Robert Gelbard strenuously opposed Wiranto's candidacy in closed-door meetings with political leaders.[41] In fact, it seems likely that Wiranto was merely making a carefully calculated manoeuvre to protect his own interests.

Wiranto and his military wanted to avoid an unseemly situation in which they sided with the losing party. According to an anonymous military source quoted in the press, Wiranto's aides anticipated that Akbar Tandjung's faction would vote against Habibie, and Wiranto was therefore unwilling to gamble on the president's prospects. This explains why Wiranto waited until the last minute before rejecting the nomination. It also explains why Wiranto remained willing to accept other nominations while rejecting Habibie's. In any event, Wiranto's rejection dealt a tough blow to Habibie's hopes—at the same time that Wahid's prospects were gaining strength.

W hile the public was puzzling over Wiranto's odd press conference Wahid was meeting with Nurcholish at the Regent Hotel. The meeting clearly discussed the recent moves to support Nurcholish's candidacy. Afterwards, Wahid told reporters that if he was forced to withdraw from the race he would back Nurcholish; until then, however, he claimed that Nurcholish regarded him as his *Imam* (the temporal and spiritual leader of an Islamic community).[42] Nurcholish stressed that his own candidacy was strictly passive, in that he would play a role only if Wahid was forced out. In effect, Wahid had quelled the incipient movement that had been gathering momentum behind Nurcholish.

Having shored up his support from NU, PKB and now the Central Axis, Wahid was ready to compete. On the morning of 19 October he paid a visit to Megawati at her home, presumably to reiterate his intention to stay in the race.[43] Later that evening he gathered with several NU clerics at the Mulia Hotel; also in attendance was Akbar Tandjung. Wahid's meetings with Megawati and Tandjung probably addressed strategy ahead of the vote on the accountability speech.[44] Around the same time, supporters of Habibie were arriving at the parliament building—and they were wearing grim expressions.

Habibie's candidacy had achieved a remarkable recovery from the blows of just two months before, but many within the president's camp sensed that their luck was running out. Wiranto's rejection of the vice-presidential nomination was inauspicious—it suggested that the military might turn against Habibie. And several Habibie loyalists divulged another problem: all their efforts to enlist the support of Tandjung's faction had failed.[45]

None of Tandjung's two dozen or so followers originated from Icmi, the technology ministry or Sulawesi. They knew that if Habibie won another term as president they would be marginal players in an administration dominated by Habibie's close-knit inner circle. But while they did not want Habibie to win, neither did they want to vote against him: ideally, they could side with Habibie in a losing effort, thereby avoiding being branded as traitors. But as the hour for the vote approached, Tandjung finally decided that this course was too risky. There were too many unknown variables; according to some calculations, Habibie might even emerge with 400 votes. Tandjung decided that he could not afford to cast his group's votes in Habibie's favour. Instead, he ordered his followers to vote against their own party's candidate.[46]

MPR Speaker Amien Rais commenced the voting on Habibie's accountability speech at 9 p.m. The votes were finally ready to be counted around two hours later—just eleven hours before the presidential election itself was due to take place. For the third time in just over two weeks the nation anxiously watched the television broadcast of the MPR's laborious vote-count. As the ballots were read out one by one, and as the votes to accept or reject were marked as ticks on a whiteboard, the tension rose. During the first hour of the vote-count the 'lead' changed hands three times. None could predict the outcome with confidence, and the atmosphere inside the assembly grew heated. Shouts and whistles came not only from observers in the gallery but from MPR members themselves. The total votes cast numbered 690; finally, with only about 20 votes still to be counted, the votes to reject the speech surpassed the halfway mark of 346. In effect, Habibie's presidency had ended.

The final vote-count was 355 against and 322 in favour, with nine votes abstaining and four invalid. Habibie was a mere 17 votes short of victory. Members of Tim Sukses were certain that 24 votes from Tandjung's faction had voted against Habibie.[47] The position of the military was less clear. Wiranto's faction had apparently not voted as a bloc: some military votes accepted the speech, some rejected it and others abstained. Rais finally adjourned the evening's session at 12.30 a.m. It seemed as if a climax had been reached, but in fact the real drama was only just beginning: the presidential election was due to commence only nine hours later.

F ollowing the rejection of Habibie's speech, Megawati reportedly went home to sleep. Virtually all other MPR leaders commenced a frantic, marathon session of lobbying and politicking. One hub of activity was Habibie's residence in the Kuningan neighbourhood, where members of

Tim Sukses and a clutch of other politicians gathered after the vote. Among others, these included Wiranto, Haz, Ginandjar, and Yusril Mahendra.[48] Several of those present urged Habibie not to concede defeat; the margin had been so close, they argued, that there was still the possibility of a reversal in the next day's event. But Habibie refused to continue. He wasted no time in making his decision: around 1.30 a.m. he decided that he was withdrawing. Habibie's erstwhile supporters now needed to find another candidate to back.

Habibie recommended nominating PBB chair Mahendra, but the former Soeharto speechwriter declined, saying that his party was too small. Next, the president asked Haz to stand for election, but the PPP chair demurred.[49] Wiranto was also reportedly offered the nomination, but he too declined. The general may have calculated that pro-reform elements of the Central Axis would never support him. He also might have recognised that his election would spark a domestic and international furore.

Habibie then suggested another former member of Icmi: Amien Rais. The strident Pan leader had been a staunch critic of the New Order regime, but as a former Muhammadiyah chair he was more palatable to Habibie's backers than Wahid or Megawati were. Through a Pan official present at the meeting, Habibie's aides contacted Rais and pledged their support.

W hen he was contacted by the president's aides at Kuningan, Rais was in a suite at the Mulia Hotel with PKB official Alwi Shihab and Muhammadiyah chair Syafii Ma'arif. Also present were two Pan officials who were influential as financiers and strategists, Al-Hilal Hamdi and Hatta Radjasa.[50] The group recognised that Rais had little chance of winning the presidential election, even with the support of Habibie's followers. The military, for one, was loath to back him due to his long-standing criticism of the army's political role and rights abuses. More importantly, his entry in the race would infuriate Wahid, and the NU cleric would undoubtedly pledge PKB's votes back to Megawati. And it was precisely this PKB bloc, Rais realised, that held the key to the election.

The group in Rais's suite had analysed the vote that had taken place that evening. They agreed that all 322 votes that had accepted Habibie's speech would remain firmly opposed to Megawati in the presidential run-off. Added to this total, however, would be a swing faction: Wahid's PKB. According to Alwi Shihab, all 57 PKB votes had rejected Habibie's accountability speech.[51] But with Wahid running in the presidential election, the vast majority of PKB votes were certain to switch sides and join the 322 that would oppose Megawati. This would give Wahid around 370 votes—well above the 351 majority he needed to win. Moreover, Rais also knew that a portion of his own small faction had voted against Habibie but would likewise swing behind Wahid.

In short, there was a broad swath of anti-Megawati sentiment in the MPR, consisting of Habibie's Golkar faction, the Central Axis and most of the PKB. None of Habibie's recommended candidates—Mahendra, Haz, Wiranto or Rais—could unite these disparate elements. Only Wahid could achieve this feat.

Rais realised that he had no choice but to continue backing Wahid, but he nonetheless fulfilled the invitation to join the gathering in Kuningan. He also wanted to make certain that Habibie would withdraw from the race—if not, there was a chance that Wahid would be eliminated in the first round of voting, allowing Megawati to defeat Habibie in the final run-off. Thus, if Habibie ran, Rais's plan would be thrown into disarray.

The group in Rais's suite, with the exception of Shihab, relocated to Kuningan around 2 a.m. Immediately upon entering Habibie's home, Rais was greeted with pleas that he stand for election as the nominee of Golkar and the conservative elements of the Central Axis. He firmly declined. He had forged a pact with Wahid, he explained, and he was indebted to the NU chair for having backed him for MPR Speaker. Ma'arif, the current Muhammadiyah chair, was on hand to help Rais. He argued that if Rais stood for the presidency the manoeuvre would sour the grassroots relations between his organisation and its arch-rival, NU.[52] These relations had improved since Rais backed Wahid for the presidency, but to withdraw that support might trigger unrest.

In response, Habibie's advisors argued that Wahid was not serious about his candidacy. They expected the blind cleric to bow out at the last minute, thereby handing the presidency to Megawati—which, they alleged, had been his ulterior motive all along. Rais therefore telephoned Wahid, who emphatically promised to '*maju terus*'—to keep pressing forward.[53]

In the middle of this discussion Akbar Tandjung suddenly appeared. Considered a traitor by Habibie's supporters, the Golkar chair had already suffered insults and scathing abuse on his way out of the parliament building. Two fanatically pro-Habibie party colleagues had struck him with their fists, and there were reports that another had accosted him at gunpoint.[54] Now Tandjung faced an enraged Habibie. The president grabbed the burly politician by his shirt collar and yelled into his face: 'Why did you let this happen!?'[55] Rais and Mahendra jumped to their feet and separated the two men.[56]

Finally, the Kuningan group accepted Rais's refusal. For his part, Rais was satisfied that Habibie had, indeed, withdrawn from the race.[57] The gathering adjourned around 4 a.m. Rais returned to his hotel to sleep, while the bulk of Habibie's coterie, including Tandjung, departed to Istiqlal Mosque to pray. By this time word had spread that Habibie's eighteen-month presidential campaign was finally at an end.

By the time they returned to Kuningan, Habibie's group had only 90 minutes before the 7 a.m. deadline for registering a candidate with the MPR secretariat. Megawati had been registered several hours before, and several Central Axis parties were registering Wahid. The group at Kuningan was determined to thwart Megawati and they were only slightly less opposed to Wahid. But no one from Golkar, the military or the Central Axis possessed the stature and breadth of support to pose a challenge— with the possible exception of Akbar Tandjung. As the minutes ticked by, the Kuningan assembly degenerated into bitter disputes.[58]

For Habibie's loyal supporters it was galling that Tandjung—the figure deemed responsible for Habibie's political demise—should now be considered for Golkar's nomination. But those who advocated the move argued that it was Golkar's only hope for retaining the presidency. To win a majority of the MPR's 690 votes, the 322 that had accepted Habibie's accountability speech needed to be augmented by at least 24 more—and this was precisely the number that Tandjung controlled.

Habibie agreed to back Tandjung. 'Whatever it takes,' he said, 'to thwart Megawati.'[59] But with three candidates in the race—Megawati, Wahid and Tandjung—the question was whether Tandjung would survive the first round of voting. Much of the Central Axis preferred Wahid. For Tandjung the key was his level of support among the constituency that he had so callously betrayed just hours before: Golkar's pro-Habibie faction. Tandjung had succeeded in his carefully orchestrated scheme to undermine Habibie's candidacy—but the irony was that in so doing, he jeopardised his own chance to ascend to the presidency.

Around 6 a.m. Tandjung arrived at the parliament building and entered a conference room to meet with Golkar's rank-and-file. He knew that it would be no easy task to convince the crestfallen Habibie supporters that he should now become their candidate. As expected, the haggard and cantankerous crowd showered Tandjung with abuse. Many were adamantly opposed to his nomination and some were hysterical. Minutes before the deadline for registering Tandjung's candidacy—amid a cacophony of shouts and curses—a senior official who was loyal to Tandjung stood on a table. Reaching toward a concealed ankle holster, he whipped out a handgun and brandished it over his head. 'Don't bully Akbar!' he shouted. 'Bully him and it means you bully me!'[60]

Marzuki Darusman registered Tandjung's candidacy with the secretariat several minutes before the deadline, but Tandjung immediately began having second thoughts. With several of his allies in his office, he reportedly voiced concern about an outbreak of unrest if a Golkar figure won the presidency.[61] After meeting with Ginandjar he finally decided, around 8 a.m., that he lacked the support to survive a first round of voting. To avoid a humiliating defeat he withdrew his name from the race.

After forcing Tandjung out, Golkar's pro-Habibie faction faced a relatively simple decision: Megawati or Wahid. The group uniformly opted for Wahid, whom they deemed more conservative. Forty members of Golkar's pro-Habibie faction boarded a convoy of vehicles and proceeded to the Mulia Hotel, where Wahid was staying. The NU cleric, accompanied by Alwi Shihab, finally met them in a conference room around 10 a.m.—just half an hour before the election was due to begin. Wahid explained that he had just finished a telephone conversation with US Secretary of State Madeleine Albright.[62] He had slept little, but he was in a jovial mood.

The spokesperson for the Golkar contingent was Arnold Baramuli.[63] He explained that his group had considered abstaining from the election, but if their support was rewarded they would back Wahid. Baramuli reportedly sought the vice-presidency for either Muladi or another influential Tim Sukses member, Fahmi Idris. Wahid agreed. They also demanded ten seats in a 35-seat cabinet. Again Wahid agreed. 'I only want three or four for myself,' he chuckled. 'You can have the rest.'[64] The Golkar politicians wanted a more resolute commitment, but after fifteen minutes their time had already expired. The attendees rushed back to the parliament building to prepare for the vote.

The start of the presidential election was delayed by an hour. At 11.30 a.m., therefore, MPR Speaker Amien Rais announced the names of candidates nominated for the presidency. His name and Akbar Tandjung's were not on the list. Instead, appearing alongside Megawati and Wahid was the name of Yusril Mahendra. As the chair of a party with a mere 13 MPR seats, Mahendra knew that he had no hope of winning. But with three candidates in the race, the voting would take place in two stages: the first would eliminate the weakest candidate, while the second would be a runoff. Mahendra's entry in the race was therefore a tactic.

Even at this late stage some of Wahid's age-old enemies within the Central Axis—such as Mahendra's vice-chair in PBB, Hartono Mardjono—still suspected that the NU leader's candidacy had been an elaborate ruse. Lest he abruptly withdraw and hand the presidency to Megawati, Mardjono had nominated Mahendra. If Wahid stepped out now, Mahendra would still be running—and he might even garner enough anti-Megawati votes to win.

Moments before the first phase of voting was due to commence, Mardjono moved through a crowd surrounding Wahid and posed a stern question: 'Are you serious about your candidacy? Are you planning to back out?'

Wahid's reply was emphatic. '*Bismillah* [in the name of God]—no!'[65] The PBB Islamists were satisfied. Mahendra's candidacy was withdrawn at 11.40 a.m.

Eleven hours of politicking and manoeuvring had whittled the contenders down to two: Wahid and Megawati—two old friends who, until a mere six months before, had been steadfast political allies. Yet again, the vote-count was neck-and-neck for an interminably long period of time. At one point Megawati commanded a lead of 40 votes over Wahid. With each vote that was read, the candidate's name was announced on the loud-speaker and the candidate's supporters in the assembly let out a hearty roar. Indonesia's first 'democratic' presidential election in over 40 years was a thoroughly raucous affair.

Outside the MPR assembly, thousands of pro-Megawati demonstrators had converged on the city's main roundabout in front of Hotel Indonesia. Soon after the voting commenced, an explosion tore through the crowd, injuring several PDI Perjuangan supporters.

As the tally neared the end, Wahid pulled into the lead and widened the gap. As the last few votes were read, Wahid's supporters from the Central Axis switched on their microphones and began chanting prayers in Arabic, which resonated throughout the assembly hall. Indonesia's prolonged political transition was finally at an end. Against all odds, the blind NU cleric had won the presidency, by a vote of 373–313. Megawati looked shellshocked and dumbfounded. Despite being Indonesia's single most popular leader by far, she had managed to lose the presidency that should have been hers for the taking.

The news of Megawati's stunning defeat was greeted with more bomb explosions in downtown Jakarta. Riots also erupted in Solo and, most notably, Bali—an island heretofore renowned as a haven of tranquillity. The Balinese were fanatical supporters of Megawati and within hours of the presidential vote tall spires of black smoke billowed up from the capital of Denpasar. Throughout the heavily touristed island, angry protesters attacked government offices, tore down street lamps and lit bonfires. Hundreds of trees were felled and laid across roads to block traffic. The alarming level of unrest did not go unnoticed—it had a significant impact on events in Jakarta, where the MPR still had one crucial task to perform: the selection of a vice-president.

As predicted by Amien Rais, Wahid appeared to have won the presidency with the 322 votes that had favoured Habibie's accountability speech, plus around 45 votes from the 57-strong PKB faction. Akbar Tandjung's faction remained allied to Megawati, but Wiranto's entire military faction apparently backed Wahid.[66] This suggested that if the military had backed Megawati she would have won the presidency instead. The leaders of these three pivotal factions—Wahid, Tandjung and Wiranto—would again prove pivotal in electing a vice-president.

Wahid had reputedly offered to back Wiranto for the vice-presidency on Monday; he then reportedly made the same offer to Tandjung early on Tuesday morning.[67] Finally, on Wednesday—the day of the presidential vote—he made the offer yet again, to a representative (such as Muladi or Fahmi Idris) of Golkar's pro-Habibie faction. Consequently, as Wahid prepared for his swearing-in ceremony to be held Wednesday evening, he was already facing a plethora of debt collectors. But the violence raging in several spots around the country strongly suggested only one course of action: supporting Megawati for the vice-presidency.

On Wednesday afternoon, immediately after losing the presidential vote, Megawati had expressly ruled out serving as vice-president. But around six that evening—an hour before taking the oath of office—Wahid called on Megawati at her home. 'Don't hold a grudge,' he reportedly said. 'Accept my offer of the vice-presidency.'[68] With Wahid's backing, Megawati would have a strong chance of winning the vote—but nothing was certain.

For her part, Megawati was bitter. In private she deplored the betrayal of someone she had considered to be a close friend.[69] Some of her advisors consoled her by pointing out that, politically, she was probably better off waiting for the next election in 2004. Until then she could lead the opposition—a role in which she was experienced and relatively effective. Megawati therefore declined the offer from Wahid, who departed for the MPR assembly. His aides, however, did not give up: to coax Megawati into running, they would contact her several more times during the night.

Immediately after the swearing-in ceremony, Tandjung concentrated on winning the vice-presidency for himself. He sought to forge the same majority alliance that had elected Wahid earlier in the day. To enter the vice-presidential race a candidate needed the signatures of at least 70 MPR members—plus the official nomination of at least one of the MPR's eleven party factions. Tandjung's first challenge, therefore, was to win the nomination of Golkar. This in turn entailed jostling past another strong candidate who was earnestly seeking Golkar's nomination, Wiranto.

In a nation long traumatised by decades of military-backed dictatorship, Wiranto's candidacy for the nation's second highest political post was a sensitive matter. Never before had an active officer run for vice-president. The military faction therefore refrained from nominating Wiranto or any other candidate. 'This is to safeguard the neutrality of the military and police,' said a faction spokesperson. 'If we nominated a candidate, we would not be neutral.'[70]

In fact, the day before, activists organised by Bais Chief Tyasno Sudarto had strung up banners outside the parliament building. As MPR members arrived for the presidential vote they noticed that some banners called for a Wahid–Wiranto ticket, while others called for a Mega–Wiranto ticket.[71] The point was clear: regardless of who won the presidency, Wiranto was angling for the number-two job. Later that day, after the presidential vote had been concluded, Wiranto's supporters promoted his cause further by circulating a book extolling his military career and service to the nation. They placed a copy on every desk in the assembly. These and other lobbying efforts won over a substantial number of Golkar delegates. Therefore when Tandjung convened a closed-door meeting of the delegation on Wednesday evening, he endeavoured to persuade the party not to back Wiranto. The party chair emphasised that the election of a military figure would invite a public backlash, while further damaging Golkar's public image. Tandjung noted that, although Wiranto had been explicitly tapped by Habibie for the vice-presidency, the Golkar party leadership had made no formal commitment to Wiranto. Before long the assembled party members agreed to consider other candidates instead.

Meanwhile, Megawati was beginning to soften her stance. Earlier she had been determined to spend the night in her own home. Around midnight, however, she and her entourage moved into the Hilton Hotel to be closer to the whirlwind of politicking that would be taking place that night. Megawati was now listening to advice from a different quarter: aides such as Kwik Kian Gie urged her to run for the vice-presidency. To refuse to negotiate, Kwik argued, would only repeat the obstinate behaviour that had already cost her the presidency. Additional persuasion came in the form of news reports filtering in from several cities: Megawati's supporters continued to wreak havoc in response to the MPR's vote that afternoon. Finally, around 10 p.m., Megawati sent a message to Wahid.

The newly inducted president was conferring with a handful of NU and PKB officials—his first meeting in the presidential palace—when he received word that Megawati had agreed to serve as vice-president. She refused, however, to endure another vote, lest it end in yet another defeat. She would only accept the post if the MPR presented it to her through acclamation.

As Wahid and his advisors mulled over Megawati's difficult demand, Golkar's MPR delegation was trying to decide on a candidate of its own. As usual, the bitterly divided party could reach no conclusion. The party's pro-Habibie faction wanted to back Muladi or Fahmi Idris, while Tandjung's faction proposed the party chair himself. Finally, around midnight, a contingent of Golkar negotiators contacted Wahid. Which candidate, they asked, would Wahid prefer: Muladi, Idris or Tandjung?

By this time Wahid was once again growing doubtful that Megawati would enter the race. She adamantly refused to put the matter to a vote, and it was clearly impossible to muster unanimous support for her candidacy. Wahid therefore told the Golkar negotiators that he would back Tandjung, citing his greater experience. This settled the question for Golkar: Tandjung had the full backing of his party and the PKB. But to replicate that afternoon's vote, Tandjung still needed to enlist support from a figure whom he had snubbed just hours before: Wiranto.

Around 2 a.m. Tandjung heard from his party colleagues that Wiranto was still insisting on obtaining the vice-presidency for himself. The Golkar chair therefore departed for Wiranto's home around 4 a.m. The four-star general was livid. His support had been the decisive factor in electing Wahid and he expected the vice-presidency in return. Wahid had even promised as much, in front of Habibie and Rais, just after taking the oath of office.[72] Now, however, the general discovered that he had been out-manoeuvred by Tandjung. Rather than supporting Tandjung, therefore, Wiranto vowed to proceed with his own candidacy.

Tandjung left Wiranto's home around dawn and proceeded to the nearby residence of Habibie. There he was contacted by Wahid. The president's lobbyists, led by Alwi Shihab, had finally persuaded Megawati to run for the vice-presidency through an open vote in the MPR. Wahid therefore told a disappointed Tandjung that he was compelled to back Megawati, lest her party supporters provoke more unrest around the country.

Tandjung realised that without Wahid's PKB his candidacy could not succeed. He promised to bow out of the race later that day and support Megawati—but not before bargaining for several cabinet seats for his supporters. Wiranto, meanwhile, doggedly pressed ahead.

Wiranto would have no trouble collecting 70 signatures to back his candidacy, but securing the formal nomination of an MPR faction posed a greater problem. Unwilling to use the military faction and unable to win Golkar's nomination, Wiranto finally sought out a seemingly odd ally: the 'Sovereignty of the Islamic Community' faction (FPDU).

Although it was the MPR's second smallest faction with a mere ten seats, FPDU gathered attention for being staunchly committed to the promotion of Islamic law. But far from being revolutionaries the five tiny parties within FPDU maintained longstanding ties to Soeharto's regime. All had also been strong supporters of Habibie. Much as Wiranto's military had mobilised Islamic para-militaries to defend the November 1998 MPR session, now Wiranto was turning to these supposedly hardline Islamists for the formal nomination that his vice-presidential campaign required. In a petition drive led by the former home affairs minister and military par-liamentarian, Syarwan Hamid, Wiranto's nomination was seconded by 74 MPR members.

The vice-presidential vote was scheduled for 10.30 a.m. Thursday morning. In addition to Tandjung (who was expected to withdraw his candidacy later that morning) and Wiranto, Megawati faced one other challenger: PPP chair Hamzah Haz. Wahid had had no success in heading off Haz's candidacy: the parties nominating him, PPP and PBB, were resolutely opposed to Megawati. Wahid had better luck, however, in nego-tiating with Wiranto.

Around 8.30 a.m. the new president dispatched Rais, Matori and Shihab to visit the military chief.[73] Wahid's envoys finally persuaded

Wiranto to withdraw his candidacy, but only in exchange for certain concessions: the post of co-ordinating minister of politics and security for himself, and his choice for a new military commander.[74] Wiranto may have also demanded two cabinet seats. With intense politicking taking place, Rais (as MPR Speaker) delayed the vice-presidential vote until 2 p.m. Ultimately, Wiranto's demands were accepted. The military would back Megawati.

As soon as the session commenced, Tandjung promptly announced his withdrawal from the race. 'Political office is not everything to me,' said the Golkar chair. 'I also withdrew my candidacy from the presidential race.'[75] A few moments later the military faction notified the Speaker that Wiranto had withdrawn as well. Only Haz remained in the race. Megawati expected an easy win—but as the vote-count began, Haz quickly took the lead by a commanding margin of 40 votes.

Panic coursed through the PDI Perjuangan faction. If Megawati lost again, it would be her most humiliating defeat yet. Her husband, Taufik Kiemas, kept asking those seated around him whether they were sure of their calculations. Eventually the ticks on the whiteboard evened out and Megawati regained the lead. Much of Golkar's pro-Habibie faction had apparently joined the bulk of the Central Axis in voting for Haz, but Megawati retained the support of PKB, Akbar Tandjung's Golkar faction and the military. Megawati prevailed by a wide margin, 396 to 284. According to Kiemas, who met reporters after the vote: 'It was all due to Gus Dur [Wahid] and the PKB Faction!'[76]

Megawati's election to the vice-presidency immediately quelled the rioting and unrest in Bali and elsewhere. And to many outside observers it appeared as if the historic MPR session had produced an ideal outcome. A few days earlier it appeared that Habibie had a strong chance to win the presidency, while it seemed almost certain that the vice-presidency would go to a Golkar or military figure. Instead, Indonesia's three best known reform figures—Wahid, Megawati and Rais—obtained the country's top three political posts. The likes of Wiranto and Haz had been denied office, and it seemed a small price to pay that Golkar chair Akbar Tandjung obtained the top position in parliament. On the surface, it had been a landslide victory for the 'reformists'; but in fact this superficial appearance was deceiving.

Beneath the surface, the MPR session had been a stunning display of the New Order's tenacity. Despite a popular election in which nearly 80 per cent of the electorate voiced a desire for change—and despite a raft of rights abuses and graft scandals that cast shame on the incumbent administration—the political establishment came exceedingly close to securing another term for Habibie. Although three leaders who professed a commitment to reform obtained high offices, the MPR that elected them displayed a very deep ambivalence about ushering in change.

Most fundamentally, the MPR session demonstrated that political power radiated from the party bosses, not from the people. The press was liberalised and elections had taken place, but the electoral system was flawed and Indonesia's leaders still lacked accountability to the people. The dictatorship of Soeharto had been replaced by the dictatorship of around half a dozen party bosses—of which the military chief was one. Although now touted as a democracy, Indonesia was still run by the elite, for the elite. Ruler's Law still prevailed. Wahid seemed almost to be emphasising these points in his first major action as president: the formation of the cabinet.

20

SHOCK THERAPY

By the end of 1999 Indonesia faced daunting economic problems. Stability had been restored—per capita GDP was just below the level of 1995—but the economy was not yet growing.[1] Bank lending was moribund and foreign investment was negligible. In fact, Indonesia's net private capital flows were still negative, in sharp contrast to the massive inflows before the crisis. President Habibie had taken credit for stabilising the money supply, the exchange rate and inflation, but conditions were still not ripe for doing business.

Some investors were deterred by incessant demonstrations in Jakarta or intermittent violence in several regions of the archipelago. Others had simply been waiting for the election outcome before assessing the country's prospects. But more fundamentally, the main impediment to investment and a resumption of economic growth was the glacial pace of asset restructuring. Indonesia's economy was rife with valuable assets—such as factories, property or brand names—that still belonged to conglomerates that were either unwilling or unable to service their debts. If these assets were restructured—that is, if the conglomerates that owned them were forced to surrender control to new investors—the process would bring a host of benefits.

Most fundamentally, asset restructuring promised to invigorate the economy. As long as potentially productive assets—such as factories, plantations or mines—remained under the control of insolvent or corrupt conglomerates, they would continue to languish for lack of capital or professional management. New investors would be likely to infuse the businesses with fresh cash, better managerial expertise or strategic linkages. On a sufficiently broad scale, such restructuring could provide powerful momentum for renewed economic growth.

In fact, the dire insolvency of Indonesia's private sector could actually be viewed as a rare opportunity: through a sequence of auctions the state could sell assets obtained by cronyism to the highest bidders; if conducted impartially and according to strict rules, such auctions might produce a private sector that was substantially cleaner and more professionally run than during Soeharto's time. Economic growth could resume and it could do so in a healthier manner than before.

Meanwhile, asset restructuring would also help address a daunting economic problem: the sharply higher level of government debt. Indonesia's ratio of total debt to GDP was 102 per cent—a fourfold increase from before the crisis.[2] This was partly due to the decline in GDP and an increase in foreign debt, especially IMF loans. But the most important factor, by far, was the increase in domestic debt. The government had responded to the collapse of the banking system by issuing BLBI liquidity credits, closing certain banks and taking over others. To pay for these actions, and to recapitalise the banks it had taken over, the government issued a staggering amount of domestic debt: Rp657 trillion (or around $88 billion at the December 1999 exchange rate). Stability had been restored, but only at a crippling cost to the state.

Even with strong economic growth, at least a decade would be required before Indonesia's total debt returned to its pre-crisis level. But while the state had become an enormous debtor, it had also emerged from the bank recapitalisation process as the economy's largest creditor by far. Through the state banks and Ibra, the government controlled almost the entire banking sector. The vast majority of pre-crisis loans outstanding—most of which went sour—were now owed to the state.

Ibra was assigned with restructuring the sector's non-performing loans to salvage whatever value could be recovered. The agency had made a promising start in late 1998 and early 1999 by erecting sound internal systems, hiring credible directors and moving decisively to close, take over or recapitalise banks. But when it came to the more difficult step of actually restructuring the non-performing assets in its portfolio, Ibra's progress ground to a halt. Two years after its founding, Ibra had made virtually no progress on debt restructuring. The Bank Bali scandal compounded Ibra's problems, but the agency had already been stymied before that. Private sector creditors had also been trying to restructure non-performing debts owed by Indonesian companies, but they too had made little progress. The main problem was Indonesia's dysfunctional legal system.

In theory, Ibra, as a creditor, should have been able to seize assets that borrowers had pledged as collateral for their loans. By selling these assets to new investors Ibra would recover part of the loan's original value. Meanwhile, the example set by a few high-profile asset seizures should have spurred other recalcitrant debtors to resume payments on rescheduled plans. Either way, Ibra's massive portfolio of non-performing loans would be generating some income—which could then be used to defray the government's debt. The book value of Ibra's assets as of early 2000 was around Rp470 trillion; even though the realisable market value of these assets was probably well below a third of book value, Ibra's asset recovery program could still generate significant funds for the government. The privatisation of state-owned enterprises and property could yield more funds. These efforts would be crucial with regard to a chief problem facing the new administration: balancing the state budget.

The legacy of the crisis would burden Indonesia for years to come. Debt service, or interest payments plus debt repayment, was projected to consume around one quarter of the government's revenues in fiscal year 2000.[3] This ratio would rise in subsequent years unless economic growth resumed. But Indonesia's conundrum was that the budgetary burden threatened to retard economic growth: the high level of debt service would divert spending from development programs or investment in primary infrastructure, while the government's heavy domestic borrowing threatened to 'crowd out' private investment. This conundrum—whereby the debt burden of an impoverished country kept the country mired in poverty—is known as 'crisis equilibrium' or a 'debt trap'. Lest Indonesia enter such a trap, aggressive restructuring was crucial.

In addition to its practical consequences for Indonesia's private and public sectors, asset restructuring also had an ethical dimension. The government's official policy was to bail out the banking system's depositors—but not the borrowers. More than 70 per cent of loans in the banking system had soured during the crisis. Although some of these loans had turned bad purely because of 'exogenous' economic factors that were beyond the control of the borrower, most were affected to some extent by malfeasance. And in many cases, malfeasance, fraud and corruption were the main factors that rendered loans non-performing.

Malfeasance in the banking sector had remained hidden while the macro-economy was growing: new borrowing kept the economy liquid, enabling banks to 'evergreen' bad loans and conceal their financial chicanery. The example of Thailand, which eventually collapsed under the weight of its own corruption, suggests that Indonesia would have done the same in the end. In any event, Thailand's downturn caused investors to reassess Indonesia's prospects; this in turn fed a panic and brought Soeharto's 'house of cards' tumbling to the ground.

By revealing the true state of Indonesia's banking system, the crisis triggered, in effect, a one-off reckoning for decades worth of wrongdoing. Only through a vigorous process of asset restructuring would Indonesia ensure that the cost of this reckoning would be born, as much as possible, by the blameworthy—the handful of relatives, cronies and supporters of Soeharto who had abused the system for 30 years. Otherwise, their excesses would be shifted to the shoulders of the blameless—the hardworking population of Indonesia. The experience of the Habibie administration, however, had demonstrated that asset restructuring would remain moribund without initial progress in a related area: legal system reform.

More precisely, Indonesia first needed to make more progress on a systemic transition from Ruler's Law to rule-of-law. Through the elections of 1999, parliament and the presidency had made substantial progress on this transition. But other institutions had yet to follow; these included the civil service, the security forces and the court system. Consequently, corruption was still rife within the attorney general's office, the police force and the judiciary. Corrupt judges had thwarted virtually every bankruptcy suit put before them—including all but a trivial few of some 50 cases put forth by Ibra.[4]

Without the ability to sue for bankruptcy, creditors such as Ibra lacked legal recourse with which to seize collateral from recalcitrant borrowers. Even compelling such borrowers to negotiate was difficult. Potentially productive assets still belonged to insolvent and unprofessional owners. The government debt issued to bail out the creditors of these owners (i.e. bank depositors) threatened to mire Indonesia in a debt trap. By guaranteeing all bank deposits in 1998 and taking control of the bank system, the government had maximised its potential liabilities from the crisis; by neglecting legal reform, it was now minimising the potential assets with which it might repay those liabilities. For the Indonesian people at large, the cost of the crisis was, in effect, being made as expensive as it could possibly be. Lest the country be forced to work for a generation to pay for Soeharto's wrongdoing, quick strides were needed on legal system reform. This, in turn, required political will. The stakes were high, therefore, when President Abdurrahman Wahid took office.

Relief, jubilation and renewed optimism accompanied Wahid's election to the presidency. For years Indonesians had been clamouring for reform, and now nothing seemed to stand in its way. Cronies notwithstanding, businesspeople generally regarded the Wahid–Megawati ticket as the ideal outcome to the prolonged transition. The executive branch included the immensely popular Megawati, but the presidency itself went to a figure regarded as more intelligent and savvy—Wahid. And despite the financial havoc wreaked by the crisis, there was a sense that Indonesia would now make slow but inexorable progress on the daunting problems that remained. The future looked more promising than the present, and therefore investors once again began seeking out money-making opportunities.

The same basic factors that had underpinned investment rationales during the boom still prevailed: Indonesia was a huge potential market with abundant natural resources, poised in a region with long-term growth potential. The devaluation had been a massive setback to the real incomes of wage-earners, but at the same time it provided a major economic boost to regions, such as Sulawesi or southern Sumatera, where large numbers of smallholders were exporting cash crops. And perhaps most importantly, the reform era promised to uncork entire sectors that had been bottled up for years by the rent-seeking structures of cronies.

In the past an independent entrepreneur with a lucrative business venture was vulnerable, quite literally, to a 'hostile' takeover by a better connected group, such as Salim or a first-family conglomerate. Now there was a belief that entirely new vistas of opportunity would be opened for grassroots entrepreneurs. Indonesia had been able to record consistently high growth rates in the past despite the heavy burden of corruption and cronyism. This implied that, on a more level playing field and amid a thriving global economy, the country should at least be able to achieve moderate rates of growth. It also seemed possible to put this growth on a more stable footing and ensure that its benefits were spread more widely. All this, however, was predicated on political reforms—to enforce the rule-of-law, allow assets to change hands and reduce the state's involvement in the economy.

Few expected Wahid, a Muslim cleric steeped in Javanese traditions and racked by physical disabilities, to understand and champion an aggressive program of political and economic reforms. There was a hope, however, that he would fill strategic cabinet posts with those who did.

W ahid consulted a team of savvy NU officials for advice on how to structure his cabinet. In contrast to the unwieldy 35-member cabinets long favoured by Soeharto, they recommended a compact version with only nineteen full ministers and six junior (or 'state') ministers. But as soon as Wahid began the process of drafting the cabinet roster, its size swelled to accommodate the interests seeking representation.

The new cabinet was officially titled the 'National Unity Cabinet'. Having long espoused pluralism, Wahid included representatives from each official religion and most major regional and ethnic groups. For the first time, the cabinet included a Papuan from Irian Jaya.[5] The main group represented, however, was a small clique of Indonesia's main party bosses.

Wahid readily admitted that, because he had forged pacts during the MPR session, he was obliged to apportion cabinet positions to the parties that had backed him. These included the Central Axis, Golkar and the military. However, PDI Perjuangan also obtained three influential seats, perhaps in exchange for Megawati's agreeing to run for vice-president. As Wahid put it: 'I use the guarantee system, so the cabinet includes those who are guaranteed by Amien, Megawati, Wiranto and Akbar.'[6] In sum, PKB obtained five seats, Golkar and Pan four each, PDI Perjuangan and the military three each, PPP two, and PBB and the Justice Party one each.

Wahid had some success in preventing certain tainted figures from obtaining posts in his cabinet. Muladi and Fuad Bawazier were two such examples. Another was Marwah Daud Ibrahim: a prominent member of Habibie's Tim Sukses, she was promised the ministry of information. Just before the cabinet was announced, however, Wahid heard that Marwah Daud had been involved in fomenting demonstrations in Sulawesi that called for the secession of Eastern Indonesia from the republic. To prevent her from becoming a minister, Wahid took the dramatic but long-overdue step of disbanding the information ministry.

Meanwhile, Wahid was generally praised for including some reputable figures such as Sarwono Kusumaatmadja as minister for maritime affairs, Ryaas Rasyid in the newly created post of state minister for regional autonomy, Erna Witoelar as minister for regional settlement, and Hasballah Saad in a new post, state minister for human rights. Otherwise, though, the cabinet was a disappointment.

As co-ordinating minister of the economy—the cabinet's senior finance post—Wahid tapped Kwik Kian Gie at Megawati's behest. A veteran newspaper columnist who had long been critical of Soeharto with regard to economic topics, Kwik possessed integrity and good political sense. His understanding of financial markets, however, was weak and his administrative abilities were even worse. And working alongside him, as finance minister, was a little-known business professor from Gadjah Mada University: Bambang Sudibyo. 'Guaranteed' by Amien Rais, Sudibyo was widely viewed as a surrogate of Fuad Bawazier.

Several other Central Axis politicians with longstanding ties to the New Order also appeared in key positions, such as Hamzah Haz as co-ordinating minister for social welfare, Zarkasih Noer as co-operatives minister and, most significantly, Yusril Mahendra as minister of law (the new name for the justice minister). This latter appointment elicited bitter disappointment from all those who sought rapid progress in reforming the cornerstone of the Soeharto system: the legal system and particularly the judiciary. But Wahid's toughest adversary in forming the cabinet was Wiranto.

As promised on the day of the vice-presidential election, Wiranto was permitted to remain in the cabinet as co-ordinating minister for politics and security. Under Soeharto and Habibie this post had been influential but its occupant had never been able to exert full authority over the military itself—the armed forces chief had always retained this authority. Wiranto, however, implemented a number of elaborate measures to preserve his influence over the military.

On the day before he surrendered his post as armed forces chief, 4 November, Wiranto carried out a dramatic reshuffling of top military commands. The new armed forces chief was a naval officer, Admiral Widodo. On the surface, this appeared healthy: it fostered the appearance that the long-dominant army was relinquishing its power in favour of the less political services—the navy and the air force. Beneath the surface, however, was the fact that Widodo had little chance of actually exerting much authority over the army. He had been handpicked as Wiranto's successor precisely because of his weakness.[7]

Beneath this figurehead armed forces chief, Wiranto had revived a long-defunct position, vice-chief of the armed forces, which he filled with a hardline loyalist, Fachrul Razi. Razi had spent the previous year serving as secretary-general in the ministry of defence—the key post through which the military controlled the police force. Now Razi, as a four-star general, was positioned to be the military's key power broker—and Wiranto's surrogate.

Meanwhile, Wiranto himself retained his status as an active four-star general—even though his post, co-ordinating minister for politics and security, had only ever been held by retired officers in the past. Wiranto, Razi and Army Chief-of-Staff Subagyo were the military's only four-star army generals, and this helped Wiranto to continue exercising influence over the military command. At the time, it was uncertain whether Wiranto would be required to retire.

Wiranto had promoted a host of other loyalists through the 4 November reshuffle. Coveted garrison commands were typically allocated to officers who had worked their way up through the territorial system; Wiranto, though, filled most of the eleven commands with aides from his own staff. He also promoted his protégé, Maj. Gen. Djaja Suparman, to Kostrad commander.[8]

Wiranto ensured that a civilian was made defence minister and he heralded this move as a symbol of the military's gradual withdrawal from politics. However, the civilian he chose, Juwono Sudarsono, was overtly pro-military. Moreover, when Sudarsono arrived for his first day of work he immediately realised that his staff had been handpicked by Wiranto. Razi's former position as secretary-general in the defence ministry had been handed to Lt Gen. Sugiono, a former adjutant and bodyguard of Soeharto. It was expected that the ministry would be run, in practice, by Sugiono.

Perhaps most importantly, Wiranto sidelined two of his potential rivals: Lt Gen. Bambang Yudhoyono and Lt Gen. Agum Gumelar. Both generals had a high public profile and were relatively independent-minded. Yudhoyono had been hoping to become army chief-of-staff, while Megawati had backed Gumelar to become minister of defence. Instead, Wiranto insisted that both be 'kicked upstairs' to the cabinet.[9] They received portfolios that were important but bore no relation to their experience—Yudhoyono as minister for mines and energy and Gumelar as minister for transportation and communications. Both generals publicly acknowledged their disappointment at having their military careers cut short—especially Yudhoyono, whose meteoric rise meant that he was still five years from retirement age.

Thus Wahid's new cabinet roster failed to assert civilian supremacy over the military. The changes, seemingly, were encouraging: Wiranto was moved to a civilian cabinet post, while a navy officer became armed forces chief and a civilian became minister of defence. However, the reality was different: Wiranto had carefully preserved his influence. No one was in a position to challenge his authority.

The roster of the National Unity Cabinet, therefore, demonstrated the concessions that Wahid had made during the course of the MPR session. Despite being the era of *reformasi*, around a third of the cabinet comprised Soeharto-era figures whose commitment to reform was highly dubious. Another third were of questionable quality. But if there was room for optimism it was provided by two of the cabinet's bright spots: Attorney General Marzuki Darusman and State Enterprise Minister Laksamana Sukardi. After only two weeks in office, the pair worked together to shake up Indonesian politics by launching a corruption investigation of Indonesia's foremost political financier: Texmaco Group owner Marimutu Sinivasan.

L aksamana Sukardi stood out among Wahid's lacklustre cabinet roster in several ways. His portfolio, state enterprises, was among the most important in efforts to stem corruption. Meanwhile, his political clout was among the most powerful of any minister: Laksamana was arguably Megawati's most influential aide, having backed her since before PDI's memorable 1992 parliamentary campaign. Laksamana was also highly popular with international donors and investors: a former executive of a foreign bank in Jakarta, he was highly competent on financial and economic matters. But above all, Laksamana stood out for his passionate drive to rectify Soeharto-era injustice.

After only a month in office, therefore, Laksamana appeared before parliament to present documentary evidence of corruption in Bank Negara Indonesia (BNI), one of the state enterprises under his purview. He regaled the parliamentary commission with details of the Texmaco scandal: how Sinivasan borrowed voraciously from the central bank, through BNI, during the height of the crisis. Laksamana showed how Texmaco's 'pre-shipment export facilities' had been used for other purposes, and how BNI had clearly violated rules on the amount of loans that a bank can lend to one customer. Texmaco was also in default on its Rp10 trillion in debts to BNI.

'If you want to change a corrupt culture,' Laksamana declared in an interview at the time, 'you need shock therapy. We're dealing with the source of the problems, not the symptoms.'[10] Some parliamentarians, alluding to Texmaco's role as a financier of first Soeharto and then Habibie, accused Laksamana of attacking Texmaco for purely political reasons. Others, however, argued that Texmaco's political role only provided all the more reason to prosecute the case. This is precisely what Laksamana—and his ally Attorney General Darusman—proceeded to do.

Only one day after Laksamana submitted his documentary evidence to the attorney general's office, Darusman formally charged Sinivasan as a suspect. This stunningly swift action sent shock waves through the Jakarta establishment: Laksamana and Darusman seemed determined to finally punish those who had looted grand sums from state coffers. Moreover, they were starting from the top—by targeting one of Jakarta's most powerful influence-peddlers. When four out of five Indonesians voted for Golkar's opponents in the parliamentary elections five months before, this was presumably just the sort of vigorous law-enforcement effort they were calling for.

Laksamana and Darusman must have expected that their case against Sinivasan would encounter stiff resistance. Within days of Laksamana's revelations, Sinivasan mobilised a stunning array of lawyers, parliamentarians and economists to spring to his defence.[11] These naturally included a host of officials tied to the Habibie administration, but the most valuable allies enlisted by Sinivasan were figures who possessed credible reputations.

To serve as his attorney, Sinivasan hired the human rights advocate Buyung Nasution. Having briefly defended the owner of Bank Bali, this was the second occasion in recent months in which Buyung lent his reformist image to a dubious cause. He claimed that in the interest of upholding the rule-of-law, it was important to defend controversial figures lest 'witch-hunts' arise. Others, however, accused Buyung of betraying the principles he had followed for decades.

Alongside Buyung, another figure at Sinivasan's side was a well-known economics commentator, Rizal Ramli—a figure whose prominence would rise even further in the months ahead. Although his only credentials as a reformist were his occasional past criticisms of government policy, this was sufficient to lend Ramli a distinctly positive public image. Sinivasan shrewdly capitalised on this image, using the well-polished consultant as his chief spokesperson and media relations manager.[12]

Together Sinivasan, Buyung and Ramli organised an unprecedented media blitz. Sinivasan's visage appeared on countless magazine covers and television talk shows. He and his managers achieved remarkable success in defending themselves in the press. By conveying their message through a wide variety of media outlets, they succeeded in obfuscating Laksamana's case.

The Sinivasan camp generally argued that Texmaco employed many workers and exported to foreign markets—and therefore the group should not be bothered about its mountain of overdue debt to the state. Furthermore, Ramli insisted that other tycoons were more corrupt than

Sinivasan. 'If you want to punish the real KKN,' said Ramli (long a harsh critic of the ethnic-Chinese community), in parliamentary testimony, 'go after Prajogo Pangestu, Sudono Salim and Bob Hasan.'[13] In fact, Sinivasan had borrowed more from the state than any other tycoon: Texmaco was Ibra's largest debtor, with Rp17 trillion in overdue loans.[14]

Sinivasan was being defended with shaky arguments, but few challenged him—such was his clout. Despite Laksamana's protests, Sinivasan's camp won the media relations war within a matter of weeks. But Laksamana might have still had a chance of prevailing in his suit against Sinivasan, had he been able to rely on support from President Wahid.

Having won the presidency through a complex web of political compromises—rather than through a direct vote by Indonesian voters—Wahid lacked a clear popular mandate to govern. Nonetheless, he embarked on his presidency with far more political capital than most new presidents of more established democracies had. The entirety of the Jakarta elite—the 'status quo', Islamists and reformers alike—waited with bated breath to see how he would apply his powers.

Although his cabinet roster received mixed reviews, Wahid made several important gestures during his first days as president, such as emptying Indonesia's jails of all political prisoners.[15] He also formed a special economic advisory team composed of some accomplished technocratic figures, notably Sri Mulyani Indrawati.[16] Wahid also made grand promises to decentralise governmental authority, a long-overdue measure designed to promote efficiency by bringing government decision-making closer to the people it affected. The provinces had long been clamouring for such decentralisation and Wahid's promises raised expectations—especially in Aceh.

Aceh suffered from a long history of injustice. The Dutch first tried to subjugate the powerful sultanate in the 1870s; they never fully succeeded. The fierce resistance of the Acehnese lent force to Indonesia's war of independence in the late 1940s but, under Soekarno, Acehnese leaders began to complain that the central government was intrusive and exploitative. Wanton neglect of local interests continued under Soeharto, eventually giving rise to armed secessionist movements in the 1970s. The military's heavyhanded attempts to suppress these Islamic-inspired separatists entailed widespread human rights abuses among the Acehnese population.

Complicating matters was Aceh's thriving drug trade—the separatists and the military seemed to be vying for control over the province's vast marijuana plantations. Yet another complaint pertained to the wealth generated by the province's natural resources: the Arun natural gas field made the province Indonesia's fourth largest contributor of export earnings from natural resources. The central government netted around

$1 billion per year from Arun, and the Acehnese complained that only a tiny fraction of that sum benefited Aceh itself.

Finally, by the late 1990s, decades of injustice, abuse and upheaval had turned the bulk of the Acehnese population against Jakarta. Demands for independence had originally been voiced by only a small number of Islamic fundamentalists, but now the broad population seemed to view independence as the only readily apparent means to end the central government's dominance and the military's heavyhandedness. These demands—and similar ones from another resource-rich province, Irian Jaya—had driven the Habibie administration to pass the Regional Autonomy Law and the Law on Sharing Natural Resource Revenues. Indonesia needed decentralisation, and these laws were important gestures towards that end, but the bills were poorly conceived and difficult to implement. As a means of ameliorating the discontent in Aceh and Irian Jaya, they failed.

The violence in Aceh only escalated during the latter half of 1999 and assorted episodes of unrest claimed at least 300 lives.[17] Achieving peace would clearly require far more fundamental measures than hastily drafted legislation. The Acehnese placed particular emphasis on the complete withdrawal of military troops from the province, but Wiranto repeatedly refused. As more revelations emerged of human rights abuses by the military, demands grew louder for a referendum on Acehnese independence.

In mid-1999, during the presidential campaigning, reporters had asked Wahid about his stance on a referendum for Aceh—and the NU leader said he supported the demands. At the time, the comment attracted little attention in Jakarta, but it resonated widely in Aceh. Following Wahid's election to the presidency, the Acehnese began staging massive demonstrations to appeal for a referendum. After one such rally President Wahid was again asked for his opinion of the situation. 'I don't know when, but I support a referendum [for the Acehnese], of course,' he said. 'That's their right. If we can do that in East Timor, why can't we do that in Aceh?'[18]

This time the comment caused a moderate stir in Jakarta and Southeast Asian capitals. Unlike that for East Timor, there was virtually no international support for an independent Aceh. The province harboured a large-scale drug trade and its separatist movement was being spear-headed by radical Islamic fundamentalists of the Free Aceh Movement (Gam). More importantly, international and domestic observers alike were alarmed that Aceh's independence would trigger Indonesia's dissolution. Aceh was a far more integral part of the Indonesian state than illegally annexed East Timor had ever been.

Moreover, Aceh's leading role during the revolution made it an emotive symbol of Indonesian nationalism—granting it independence threatened to jeopardise the underlying rationale for Indonesian unity. In contrast to East Timor, the secession of Aceh might very well produce a 'falling domino' effect, whereby other far-flung, distinctive or resource-rich provinces would also agitate for independence.

Wahid soon found that he was bombarded from all sides with these and other arguments against a referendum. Nonetheless, he made a comment in mid-November, while in Tokyo, that only heightened public apprehension. 'The plan,' Wahid told reporters, 'is to hold a referendum in Aceh around seven months from now.'[19] Because this was the third time that Wahid aired this view, the comment now sparked a frenzy of public debate and financial market worries.

The comment also elicited a stern reaction from the military's new spokesperson, a fierce Wiranto loyalist who would play a prominent role over the next few weeks: Maj. Gen. Sudrajat.[20] The two-star general took it upon himself to clarify the president's comment in Tokyo. Wahid, he said, had been expressing a personal opinion—he was not speaking in his capacity as president.[21] In the opaque semantics of Javanese politics this represented a blatant affront to Wahid, and it was one of the first signs that the military was not prepared to follow its civilian leader.

Meanwhile, in Aceh, Wahid's promise of a referendum elicited a combination of joy and dread. Some Acehnese looked forward to independence and, hopefully, an end to injustice. Others began to flee to neighbouring provinces lest the violence witnessed in East Timor be repeated in Aceh. Suddenly, the attention of the nation was focused on the Aceh question. Wahid was digging himself into a hole. But in a hint of what would lay ahead in his presidency, he abruptly changed his mind.

In Jordan, on 24 November, Wahid suddenly told reporters that independence for Aceh was 'out of the question'.[22] He tried to claim that US President Bill Clinton had intervened to rule out a referendum; in fact, the tide of opinion in Jakarta made Wahid's stunning about-face inevitable.

For the Acehnese, meanwhile, Wahid's reversal naturally produced bitter disappointment. They could only hope that the president would find other avenues toward peace, justice and prosperity for the sorely troubled province. But their foremost demand—the complete withdrawal of all central government troops from the province—seemed no more attainable than a referendum, as long as Wiranto's conservatives continued to dominate the armed forces. The Acehnese would have to wait for Wahid to exert his authority and establish civilian supremacy over the recalcitrant military. First, though, the president had to engage another thorny front: legal system reform. Specifically, he was forced to make a decision with regard to the Texmaco case.

A fter only five weeks in office, fissures were already showing between State Enterprise Minister Laksmana Sukardi and Finance Minister

Bambang Sudibyo. A hallmark of Soeharto's rule had been to grant ministers overlapping jurisdictions, and the lines separating Laksamana and Sudibyo were particularly fuzzy. This soon gave rise to a jealous rivalry between the two ministers from rival political parties. Sudibyo publicly admitted that, although Wahid was his boss within the structure of government, Amien Rais was his boss in another 'framework'.[23] In fact, as mentioned, many believed that Sudibyo was also working on behalf of Fuad Bawazier. Consequently, when Laksamana introduced the Texmaco case, Sudibyo did not endorse his rival's 'shock therapy'. Instead, he visited the president on 9 December—with Texmaco-owner Sinivasan in tow.

Immediately after the meeting with Sudibyo and Sinivasan, Wahid issued a cryptic statement: the high-profile Texmaco case would be settled through a 'win-win' solution.[24] The president was not supporting Laksamana's energetic prosecution of Texmaco—a fact that was even more devastating than the formidable media campaign waged by Sinivasan's camp. Soon Wahid himself was spouting Ramli's weak refrain: Texmaco's size should exempt it from having to repay the state.

The real reason for Wahid's lenient treatment of Sinivasan remains unclear. He may have been unwilling to risk alienating Golkar by attacking one of the party's foremost financiers. Alternatively, Sinivasan may have financed not only Golkar but other parties as well—such as elements of the Central Axis or even Wahid's own PKB. In any event, the administration's first high-profile initiative on legal system reform—Laksamana's 'shock therapy'—had fallen flat. But while Wahid faltered on this front, he started to make gradual progress on another front: military reform.

Wiranto's 4 November command changes had left two critical posts unchanged: chief-of-staff of the army and the chief of Bais. This was despite the fact that the former post had been filled since 1998 by Subagyo, who was constantly rumoured to be slated for retirement. The lack of a change in this position was a signal of the rocky relations that would mark civil–military relations in the Wahid era: the president and Wiranto were in a tense standoff over who should replace Subagyo. Wiranto proposed one of his protégés, Lt Gen. Djamari Chaniago. Wahid, on the other hand, reputedly wanted Lt Gen. Luhut Panjaitan, then serving as ambassador to Singapore. Finally, a compromise was reached: Lt Gen. Tyasno Sudarto.

Tyasno's career was skyrocketing. He had obtained his third star only eleven months before, when he replaced Zacky Makarim as Bais chief, and now he ranked as the military's third most senior officer after Widodo and Razi. But the Bais chief was hardly a reformer. Like Wiranto, he too had previously served as an adjutant to Soeharto, and he was reputed to have worked closely in the past with Tutut Soeharto. He had also served as commander of the Central Java Garrison, a position typically reserved for members of the first family's inner circle. And most importantly, Tyasno's tenure at Bais overlapped with the scorched-earth campaign in East Timor, in which the intelligence service played a prominent role.

Nonetheless, the president was familiar with Tyasno from the general's lobbying efforts during the MPR session, and Wahid therefore preferred him to Chaniago. The new president was at least exerting some influence over the appointment of key military commands. This was particularly consequential for a prominent two-star officer who was about to cause an unprecedented stir—Agus Wirahadikusumah.

Like many generals, the 49-year-old Wirahadikusumah had a distinguished pedigree: his uncle, Gen. (ret.) Umar Wirahadikusumah, was vice-president from 1978–1983. But Wirahadikusumah was also noted for his academic credentials: he completed three officer training courses in the US, as well as a master's degree in public policy from Harvard University. Although he was arguably the military's foremost intellectual, Wirahadikusumah had long been forced to cede the pro-reform limelight to his academy classmate, Bambang Yudhoyono. Yudhoyono's cautious pace of reform frustrated Wirahadikusumah, but with the advent of the Wahid era—and with Yudhoyono sidelined in a ministerial role—there was an opportunity to be seized.

Anticipating a push for reform from Wirahadikusumah, Wiranto deliberately sought to place the two-star general out of harm's way. In the 4 November command changes, Wiranto posted Wirahadikusumah to a politically insignificant garrison command in Sulawesi. The move sent a clear anti-reform signal—otherwise Wirahadikusumah would have been kept in Jakarta, where his reformist ideas could have been put to use in a policy-making post. The obscure posting, however, failed to muzzle Wirahadikusumah.

Like all other high-ranking officers, Wirahadikusumah had stayed mute throughout the military's debacle in East Timor, but privately he was sorely disgruntled. In early December Wirahadikusumah watched with interest as the Human Rights Commission announced that it would investigate Wiranto's role in human rights abuses in East Timor. Soon after, President Wahid stunned the nation by declaring that if Wiranto were proven guilty, he would actually be prosecuted. With Wiranto under fire, Wirahadikusumah seized the opportunity to speak out.

In a public appearance on 13 December, Wirahadikusumah issued a sharp criticism of the military's involvement in politics. Days later he publicly sparred with the former Jakarta Garrison commander who had been promoted to the command of Kostrad: Lt Gen. Djaja Suparman. Not only was Suparman a superior officer, but he was also a loyal ally of Wiranto. The two generals traded barbed comments about Wiranto's culpability for the scorched-earth campaign. Suparman claimed that indictments of military leaders made ordinary soldiers 'sick at heart';

Wirahadikusumah countered that ordinary soldiers were loyal to the institution, not to individual personalities. Corruption and abuse of power, he said, were what made ordinary soldiers truly sick at heart.

It had been decades since the public had witnessed such an open confrontation between active generals—but Wirahadikusumah was only getting started. Aware of Wahid's fixation with religious pluralism, Wirahadikusumah announced plans for a multi-denominational religious conference in Sulawesi. Using this as a pretext, he obtained an audience with the president on 16 December. It was rare for a president to meet privately with a two-star general—and given Wirahadikusumah's reputation, there could be no mistaking the political undercurrents of the meeting.

The day after his presidential audience, Wirahadikusumah appeared before a parliamentary commission to discuss military reform. This elicited a sharp rebuke from Maj. Gen. Sudrajat, the military spokesperson who had suddenly taken on a prominent role as a surrogate of Wiranto. Sudrajat declared that, by appearing in parliament, Wirahadikusumah had 'violated the military's ethical code'.[25] But the reprimand failed to deter the Sulawesi Garrison commander.[26] The lowly general from a remote outpost apparently possessed high-level political backing—which he immediately put to use.

Within days of his parliamentary appearance, Wirahadikusumah conducted a media blitz that rivalled Sinivasan's in intensity. Most generals loathed speaking to the press—and on the rare occasions when they did speak they would invariably use the military's peculiar brand of euphemistic 'doublespeak'. A quintessential example of this was the military's title for its reform program: 'Redefining, Repositioning and Reactualising the Military in the Life of the Nation'. But rather than using the standard rhetoric, Wirahadikusumah spoke with stunning candour, conducting more than a dozen press interviews within a week. His square-jawed visage appeared on the cover of almost every major news weekly, plus a host of tabloids and newspapers.[27]

Wirahadikusumah accused the officer corps of corruption, abuse of power, incompetence and feudal thinking. He denounced human rights abuses as shameful, inexcusable and destabilising. He agreed that Wiranto should be punished if found guilty of abuse of power in East Timor. He even issued a formal apology to the Indonesian people for the behaviour of the military. But perhaps most radical of all were his views on the territorial system.

This system, the chief means through which the military exercised its political role on a daily basis, mimicked the Dutch colonial force structure. Military posts or personnel were stationed at every level of the civilian bureaucracy, from provincial capitals down to the village level. Officers regarded territorial commands as the most attractive jobs in the army, largely because they afforded ample opportunities to generate personal wealth. But according to Wirahadikusumah:

> The territorial system is precisely what is obstructing democratisation . . . It
> has been an instrument of domination and political manipulation, and it
> must be curtailed. It must be! How can it not be? Don't we want to promote
> a new Indonesia that is more democratic?

Wirahadikusumah urged that the territorial system's two lowest tiers, at the village and sub-district levels, be eliminated first. In effect, he was proposing surgery on the military's political backbone. But he did not stop there: he also castigated its financing practices—that is, the myriad businesses run by the military's various 'charitable foundations' or by individual units and officers. Said Wirahadikusumah:

> The military's businesses interfere with the economy, because they receive
> so many different types of facilities. And there are all sorts of weaknesses in
> military businesses: their management style is erratic and they continually
> make losses . . . Let's not use excuses about limited budgetary resources!
> What actual benefits have there been for the military as an institution? In
> the end, it's all for the individuals running the businesses.

Wirahadikusumah even denounced the notorious practice of '*beking*', or racketeering. Although Indonesians knew that illicit businesses received protection from military personnel, it was rare for the subject to be discussed in public—especially by an active general. Wirahadikusumah, however, compared the military to 'a parasite':

> Who backs and supports the discotheques, brothels and narcotics if not
> the military or police? . . . No matter how many times citizens report the
> locations of illegal brothels or gambling dens, nothing is done—in fact,
> the crime rings continue to receive backing . . . Anyone can see how
> military officials abuse their authority for personal gain—even becoming
> backers of narcotics rings! This is precisely what turns the public against
> the military.

And this message was precisely what turned the public in favour of Wirahadikusumah himself. Never had such 'heresy' been heard from an active general. Initially, some suspected he was guilty of opportunism, but the zeal with which he delivered his critiques showed that he was sincere. His popularity—outside military circles—soared. The press immediately began speculating that Wahid would soon promote him to army chief-of-staff. But the general also knew that he was pursuing a high-risk strategy: 'My ideas have been well received by President Wahid, but my ideas are dangerous, and you have to realise that the old establishment is still large, wary and clever.'

The warning proved prophetic. The patience of the 'old establishment' was already being tested by investigations into the Bank Bali and Texmaco scandals, in which a total of nine suspects had been named.[28] And in mid-December the old establishment was vexed by two more initiatives. On 6 December Attorney General Darusman reopened the corruption investigation of former President Soeharto—in effect, overturning the controversial SP3 letter that his predecessor, Ismudjoko, had issued two months before on the eve of the MPR session. But this move was overshadowed by a concurrent drama: the start of an official inquiry into human rights abuses in East Timor.

21

EAST TIMOR WRIT LARGE

The Human Rights Commission occupied one of the oldest government buildings in Jakarta: a picturesque four-storey structure built during the colonial era. Unlike most state offices, this one was impeccably neat and well ordered—testimony, perhaps, to the management style of the commission's chair, Marzuki Darusman. Since its founding in 1992 until the end of the New Order, the office had been a sleepy place. In Soeharto's wake, however, it had become a bustling locus of activity. The quiet residential street that it faced was often the scene of noisy demonstrations. Some were authentic, while others were staged by hired protesters (or, in the parlance of the reform era, 'rent-a-mobs'). And since the departure of Habibie the National Human Rights Commission had taken on even more importance—and an even more frenzied pace.

Before leaving office President Habibie had authorised the Human Rights Commission to investigate reports of abuses in East Timor. A special subcommission was formed for this purpose: KPP Ham. Initially, few credible figures were willing to serve on the subcommission—it was expected to only carry out mock investigations, to be used as a counter to a parallel UN investigation that was expected to take place. But when Abdurrahman Wahid was elected to the presidency the tiny subcommission was suddenly infused with vigour and purpose.

KPP Ham was mandated to investigate reports of mass killings, extrajudicial executions and arbitrary shootings in East Timor during 1999. Its jurisdiction was limited to closed-door fact-finding, meaning that if it found evidence of wrongdoing it would have to persuade the attorney general to prosecute. But at the time, this legal distinction was blurred: Marzuki Darusman was serving simultaneously as both the head of the Human Rights Commission (KPP Ham's parent) and attorney general. For those identified by KPP Ham as suspects, Darusman's dual role made the threat of punishment seem very real.

The subcommission therefore became the focus of attention in

Jakarta when, in early December, it subpoenaed testimony from more than 30 prominent government officials, militia leaders and armed forces personnel. The list included Syafrie Syamsoeddin, Zacky Makarim and Wiranto. This marked the second time that these three officers visited the historic headquarters of Darusman's commission: all had been questioned by an official fact-finding team following Jakarta's May 1998 riots.

Since the May riots Syamsoeddin and Makarim had retained Wiranto's trust: by late 1999 they were both serving as expert advisors to the co-ordinating minister for politics and security. In effect, the two figures most likely to have been involved in perpetrating the May riots were clearly part of Wiranto's inner circle. Meanwhile, others involved in East Timor had since received promotions or choice assignments. East Timor's former police commander, Col. Timbul Silaen, was now a brigadier general heading the national police unit responsible for investigating corruption. East Timor's former military commander, Col. Tono Suratman, now served as the military's deputy spokesperson. And Maj. Gen. Adam Damiri, the former commander of the Udayana Garrison which encompassed East Timor, now held a choice assignment as operations assistant to the chief-of-staff for general affairs—a post that was instrumental in co-ordinating military operations throughout the country.

Given the influence wielded by those implicated in the East Timor campaign, the military naturally registered alarm when it became clear that KPP Ham was conducting the most thorough human rights investigation yet witnessed in Indonesia. Barely two months after taking office the new administration was attacking, among others, an active four-star general who was the foremost figure of the powerful military. For members of Indonesia's political establishment, this was precisely the sort of attack they had been dreading since the fall of Soeharto. If Wiranto could be punished, so too could anyone with any connection to Soeharto-era corruption or abuse.

Furthermore, the East Timor investigation represented a clash of institutions: the newly reformed presidency was seeking to assert its supremacy over the politically entrenched military. With Wiranto removed from power, a path might be cleared for ardent reformers to rise to the fore. Wirahadikusumah and other likeminded officers might start rebuilding the military into a professional force—focused on defence rather than corruption, repression and political control. At stake, therefore, was far more than Wiranto's job—an entire system of governance was implicitly under attack.

Wiranto and his allies had a great deal to lose, and even more to fear. If they lost their rank and status, they might be prosecuted and even jailed. And even if KPP Ham faltered, Wiranto had ample reason to worry that the UN would convene a war crimes tribunal in Den Haag, the Netherlands. The trials of Serbian leaders caused consternation for Wiranto, who feared being charged with crimes against humanity in East Timor. Naturally, he and his allies were desperate to cling to power. As the former Golkar reformer Siswono Yudohusodo liked to say, 'a corrupt government has only one alternative: to stay in power'.[1] This is precisely what Wiranto strove to do. His first step was an ironic one: he sought legal assistance from his erstwhile opponent, human rights lawyer Buyung Nasution.

Having just recently worked for Sinivasan, Buyung's decision to join Wiranto's defence team raised jeers from pro-democracy activists. More than twenty years before, Buyung had pioneered human rights advocacy work by founding the Legal Aid Foundation, the predecessor to the National Human Rights Commission. In fact, some of the foundation's current directors now sat on KPP Ham—directly across the table from where Buyung would be sitting with Wiranto. Moreover, the lawyer appointed by Wiranto to accompany Buyung was none other than Ruhut Sitompul—the chief legal counsel for Pemuda Pancasila. Sitompul's presence on the defence team highlighted the close ties between Wiranto's military and Yorrys Raweyai's *preman* syndicate.

Despite their high-powered legal counsel, the officers summoned in KPP Ham's initial rounds of questioning often provided strange and conflicting testimony. One example was Maj. Gen. (ret.) Garnadi, the aide to Feisal Tanjung who signed the secret document calling for a post-ballot campaign of destruction. Garnadi acknowledged the document's signature, stamp-mark and letterhead as authentic—but he claimed that the document's contents had been doctored. He could not, however, recall what the original document supposedly contained.

Meanwhile, Maj. Gen. Adam Damiri, the Udayana Garrison commander, claimed that he had issued shoot-on-sight orders both before and after the balloting. However, his direct subordinate at the time, Brig. Gen. Tono Suratman, denied ever receiving such orders. And as for responsibility for training and funding militias, some of the suspects issued blanket denials, while others shifted blame elsewhere. For instance, Suratman denied any military involvement, arguing that the police had trained the militias. He also said that the provincial government funded the militias— an assertion supported by most of the thirteen district chiefs who were questioned.[2]

Several militia leaders appeared before KPP Ham, but most chose to remain silent. Nonetheless, their mere appearance served as a spectacle: the most notorious and brutal militia leader, Eurico Guterres, arrived in an expensive off-road vehicle, dressed in guerilla fatigues and accompanied by ten bodyguards. He said that his Aitarak militiamen had surrendered some weapons in Gen. Wiranto's much-publicised 'peace agreement' in June, but he admitted that they returned soon after to retrieve the weapons, which included military-issue M-16s.[3]

Zacky Makarim, the former intelligence chief and head of the military's special operations in East Timor, adopted a particularly super-cilious attitude. When asked how militiamen acquired M-16s, he provided a terse explanation: the militias had captured them from Falintil guerillas who, in turn, had captured them from military personnel. 'There is therefore no more reason,' Makarim proclaimed, 'to make an issue of where the weapons came from.'[4]

Makarim admitted that military headquarters had drafted a 'contin-gency plan' for the post-ballot period, but he declined to describe its contents. He asserted that soldiers were prevented from stopping militia activities because of 'their long history and the proximity between the military and militia groups'.[5] Nonetheless, he claimed that foreign-supported forces committed worse atrocities than the militias. He went on to denounce KPP Ham as a tool for those seeking revenge on the military: 'Domestic forces are working together with foreign forces to systematically destroy the military. Their purpose is to ensure that domestic politics can be easily manipulated from abroad.'[6]

Wiranto, meanwhile, stalled for time. In late December and early January, while KPP Ham waited for Wiranto to fulfil his summons, the general's allies in the military leadership mounted sharp public criticisms of President Wahid. Leading this effort was the garrulous spokesperson, Maj. Gen. Sudrajat. Since disputing with Wahid over the Aceh issue, Sudrajat had since been a vocal critic of US and UN efforts to help some 150 000 East Timorese being held in militia-run camps in West Timor. Now, hearing rumours that Wahid wanted to reshuffle certain military commands, Sudrajat disputed the president's authority over the armed forces. 'According to the Constitution,' he declared, 'the president holds supreme authority over the army, navy and air force. This does not mean that he is the commander-in-chief—that term is used only in the US.'[7]

Wahid wanted to sack Sudrajat for insubordination, but the military leadership resisted. Meanwhile, Sudrajat hinted that if Wahid denied the military a free hand in cracking down on Acehnese separatists, the military might try to manoeuvre him out of power. 'If there is no other way to preserve the Constitution,' Sudrajat explained to the *Washington Post*, 'our modality would not be by coup, in taking over the government; our modality would be to go to the parliament and talk to the people.' He added: 'There won't be a formal coup.'[8] Sudrajat's statement was astonishing—especially considering his capacity as the military's official spokesperson. Suddenly, international attention was riveted by the possi-bility of a clandestine coup d'état.

In fact, the military was in no position to grab power—Wahid's constitutional legitimacy was far too strong, and the public uproar in the wake of a military coup would be devastating. Moreover, the military leadership was deeply divided. None of the hardline generals aligned with Wiranto contradicted Sudrajat, but reformers such as Wirahadikusumah denounced the spokesperson's comments. The chief-of-staff of the air force made clear that the military spokesperson was by no means speaking for his branch of the military. These comments were a sign of the times: not even during the worst of the East Timor debacle had senior military leaders broken ranks with their official spokesperson. Nonetheless, Wiranto's allies still possessed considerable influence: they resisted Wahid's order to sack Sudrajat, such that a month passed before the spokesperson was changed.

Meanwhile, Wiranto and his allies prepared for the worse. They were determined to resist summary command changes, human rights inquiries and other painful reform measures imposed by civilians. As his conflict with Wahid escalated, Wiranto defended himself and his institution by resorting to extreme measures. In alliance with Wahid's political enemies, Wiranto's conservative generals employed their crude but time-tested technique of manipulation: *preman* politics.

In the 'inclusivist' fashion that characterised Javanese politics, NU traditions and Wahid's own career, the president had offered governmental posts to all elements of the political spectrum. Logically, his main enemy should have been PDI Perjuangan, given that Megawati felt that Wahid's manoeuvring had deprived her of the presidency. By helping her obtain the vice-presidency, however, Wahid garnered her party's grudging support. It was ironic, therefore, that Wahid's staunchest critics were from the same group that had been his most ardent supporters: the Central Axis.

Hamzah Haz's PPP quickly emerged as Wahid's toughest political opponent, despite having provided a large share of the votes that elected him to the presidency. That election, however, was essentially a vote of expediency; the animosity between PPP and Wahid was more than fifteen years old. The flipside of Wahid's tolerance had always been a rigid intolerance to political Islam—which he identified, rightly or wrongly, with PPP. Thus, while he accommodated a wide range of interests in his new administration, he gave short shrift to PPP and especially PPP's formidable ally: Golkar's Habibie faction.

Although Haz was included in the cabinet as coordinating minister for poverty alleviation, and another PPP official, Zarkasih Noer, was made co-operatives minister, neither post was particularly influential. And while four Golkar officials received cabinet posts, only one of these was from the party's pro-Habibie faction: Minister of Industry and Trade Jusuf Kalla. After having combined to provide Wahid with the bulk of his votes in the presidential election, PPP and Golkar's pro-Habibie faction seemed bitter about their role in the new government. Their power—and, perhaps, their access to the spoils of office—were not commensurate with the votes they had pledged to Wahid.

For his part, Wahid seemed intent on sidelining Haz and his allies. By the end of December Wahid had already shamed Haz into resigning. Speculation was rife that he would soon sack Kalla as well. Wahid apparently felt that he could govern without the support of PPP and Golkar. He may have presumed that, like Soeharto, his position was secure for the duration of his five-year term and he could wield authority without having to defer to parliament. On both counts he was sorely mistaken. Elements of the Central Axis demonstrated just how much influence they could exert when, in January 2000, they openly aligned with Wiranto.

Wiranto's alliance with political Islam had deep roots: as mentioned, the general had used Islamic para-militaries in November 1998, and he had turned to the MPR's most overtly Islamic faction, the tiny FPDU, when he needed a formal nomination to run for vice-president. Now Wiranto's chief source of support was from the Crescent and Star Party (PBB) of Soeharto's former speechwriter, Yusril Mahendra. Although PBB possessed only thirteen seats in parliament, its leaders were skilled politicians who made the most of their foothold in government.

PBB's deputy chair, Hartono Mardjono, contributed his experience as a lawyer by joining the military defence team headed by Buyung Nasution. Mahendra, as minister of law, decried Marzuki Darusman's dual role as attorney general and Human Rights Commission chair—a criticism that was echoed by the head of PBB's parliamentary faction, Achmad Sumargono.[9] Together they exerted sufficient pressure to force Darusman to resign from the commission. Meanwhile, PBB, PPP, Golkar and the military quietly joined forces to obstruct a new human rights law, without which Darusman would have difficulty trying anybody for human rights abuses.

The tactics of this military–Islamic alliance were not limited to political manoeuvres and public posturing—it appears that a more assertive approach was also used. The start of KPP Ham's investigation corresponded with a sudden increase in religious violence around the country. Some of the episodes may have been 'organic'—that is, it is possible that they arose of their own accord in a society racked by a prolonged economic recession and an emotionally fought political struggle. There was, however, ample reason to believe that the sudden wave of violence was being deliberately fomented—to distract attention from KPP Ham or to compel Wahid to halt the investigation.

The first unexplained episode of religious violence occurred just days after KPP Ham began its work in earnest. The scene was Wisma Doulos, a charity and Christian proselytising organisation in East Jakarta. The Doulos compound, which housed around 400 residents, consisted of an orphanage, mental institution and drug rehabilitation centre. The organisation supposedly stood accused of persuading those under its care to abandon Islam and convert to Christianity. Late on the evening of 16 December, Wisma Doulos was targeted for attack.

Several hundred men in traditional Muslim garb surrounded the compound. They wielded machetes, hatchets and scythes. Without warning they doused the buildings in the compound with gasoline and lobbed Molotov cocktails through the windows. As men, women and children tried to flee, the mob hacked at them—killing one boy, maiming seventeen and inflicting cuts and bruises on others.[10] Military personnel were on station at a nearby territorial post, but they failed to respond.

President Wahid, who housed some of the displaced Doulos orphans in his home, ordered the police to carry out a thorough investigation. The Doulos attack was the worst case of religious violence in Jakarta since the Ketapang riot the previous year—and there was reason to believe that the attack had been perpetrated by the same group that was involved in the Ketapang violence: the Islamic Defence Front (FPI). Ostensibly a volunteer band that was determined to combat the 'enemies of Islam', the FPI functioned in practice like a military-backed *preman* gang.

It was generally believed that FPI's military patron was Wiranto's protégé, Djaja Suparman.[11] FPI arose just after Suparman took command of the Jakarta Garrison in mid-1998, and it was among the para-military groups that Suparman recruited to defend the subsequent MPR session. Following its suspicious role in the Ketapang riot—an episode of violence that strongly appeared to have been staged—convoys of FPI trucks carrying hundreds of white-clad youths became a common sight in Jakarta throughout 1999. The group's constant harassment of unsympathetic journalists helped keep FPI out of the mainstream press, but the group attacked liquor distributors, nightclubs and discotheques on a regular basis—and with impunity. But in its choice of targets to attack and issues to protest, FPI belied its roots.

FPI invariably targeted obscure nightspots rather than confronting the huge brothels, gambling dens and narcotic rings in North Jakarta— places that were widely believed to be backed, or owned outright, by the military. In effect, FPI seemed to function as the army's racketeering arm, pressuring businesses that competed with the army in the entertainment sector.[12] FPI's own leaders admitted that they recruited their followers from *preman* gangs, but the organisation served more than a purely criminal function.[13] Like Pemuda Pancasila in the past, the group was also put to use for political ends.

FPI rarely protested the issues that seemed to concern the bulk of Muslim activists, such as usury, violence in Aceh, or corruption on state-run pilgrimages to Mecca. Instead, FPI's interests closely overlapped with those of the army. Besides defending MPR sessions, FPI also protested against the General Elections Commission on behalf of the Islamic parties in the FPDU—the MPR faction that nominated Wiranto for vice-president. And most tellingly, FPI's leaders chose to speak out in December 1999 on an issue that seemed to bear little direct relevance to them: KPP Ham's handling of the investigation on East Timor.[14] FPI later staged a series of raucous demonstrations on the street in front of the Human Rights Commission's office.[15] In effect, FPI was defending Wiranto.

Whether FPI perpetrated the Doulos attack remains unclear: the police never questioned FPI, even though the group had carried out a violent protest against Wisma Doulos only a month before the attack.[16] There was also reason to believe that the Doulos attack was connected to the Abu Sayyaf rebels in Mindanao, in the southern Philippines. In the early 1990s the Abu Sayyaf had bombed the International Floating Library M/V *Doulos*, a missionary ship run by the same UK-based proselytising group that sponsored the Doulos complex in East Jakarta.[17] This may have been a coincidence but, as will be seen, other factors linked Islamic rebels in the Philippines to Islamic militias in Indonesia. Some of these links converged in Maluku, the strife-torn province just to the south of the Philippines. Within days of the *Doulos* attack, Maluku's violence grew markedly worse—and it would be exacerbated further by FPI and its sister organisation, Laskar Jihad.

Upon taking office Wahid explicitly charged Megawati with addressing Maluku's simmering Christian–Muslim strife, which was over ten months old and had spread to remote reaches of the province. Since the start of the fighting, the death toll had already surpassed 1000. The assignment seemed appropriate for Megawati, given her grassroots appeal, but the vice-president was apparently chagrined at being charged with solving a seemingly intractable problem. By the time Wahid finally returned from another overseas tour in early December, Megawati had still not visited the distant archipelagic province. 'If Megawati doesn't want to go to Ambon,' Wahid finally told reporters, 'then I'll go myself.'[18]

In the end, the vice-president accompanied Wahid on a visit to Maluku on 12 December. Their message: only Maluccans can solve Maluku's problems. In fact, there was reason to doubt whether this was true. The day after Wahid and Megawati returned to Jakarta, Maluku's violence entered a new phase of intensity. During the next three weeks fighting claimed over 500 lives.[19] It would soon become clear that the escalating violence was not due to rising passions alone. Maluku's strife was being stoked from outside.

Unlike other regions, such as Banyuwangi, where outsiders had apparently attempted to provoke strife, Maluku was ripe for conflict. The province's population was divided almost equally between Christians and Muslims. There were also ethnic and cultural differences between native Ambonese and Malays who were originally from Sulawesi, Java or Sumatera. Christians had historically dominated provincial politics, but when Muslims gained control of the governor's office and other posts in the mid-1990s bitter jealousies arose. As mentioned earlier, Jakarta's governor shipped some 300 Ambonese *preman* from Jakarta to Maluku just after the Ketapang riot of November 1998. Similar religious rioting broke out in Ambon weeks later. Also present in Maluku at the time was Yakmi, a youth group that had supplied para-militaries for the November 1998 MPR session, and which was believed to be sponsored by Tutut Soeharto.[20]

By mid-1999 reports were emerging that certain elements of the security forces were siding with the combatants and exacerbating the fighting. At first these reports were attributed to biases arising from the heated conflict, but an increasing number of observers began asserting that the security forces were deliberately aiding and abetting rival religious factions—just as in East Timor. In fact, a number of similarities stand out between the military's role in East Timor and its operations in Maluku.

Around the time that Wiranto dispatched Zacky Makarim to head the Taskforce on East Timorese Consultation, he also assigned Maj. Gen. Saudi Marasabessy to a similarly innocuous-sounding position: head of the Taskforce on Restoration of Peace in Maluku. At the same time, the commander of Maluku's Pattimura Garrison, Max Tamaela, wore only one star; every other garrison commander was a two-star general. Therefore, just as Makarim had outranked East Timor's territorial commander (Col. Suratman), Marasabessy outranked Maluku's commander (Brig. Gen. Tamaela). Just as Makarim was ostensibly preparing for a smooth ballot in East Timor, Marasabessy was ostensibly trying to restore peace in Maluku. In fact, both appeared to wield paramount authority over military operations in their regions, and both appeared to work at cross-purposes to their job titles. As in East Timor, Wiranto insisted that the security forces were doing their utmost to restore peace in Maluku—even though the violence escalated all the while.

Marasabessy was a native Maluccan, but he was nonetheless an odd choice for the peace-keeping role: he was known as a staunchly Islamist general and, prior to his posting in Maluku, militant Islamic leaders had cited him as their favourite figure in the military leadership.[21] Although his ten-month effort to restore peace in Maluku was an abject failure, Marasabessy endeared himself to Wiranto. In the 4 November command reshuffle in which Wiranto promoted his loyalists, Marasabessy catapulted over a host of more senior generals to obtain a coveted three-star post: chief-of-staff for general affairs (kasum). This post was on a par with kaster as the most senior three-star position, and it entailed strategic authority over troop deployments and military operations throughout country. And soon after Marasabessy was promoted to kasum, military activities in Maluku expanded significantly.

Some 22 militant Islamic organisations assembled at Jakarta's National Monument on 7 January 2000. They hurled scathing abuse at the Human Rights Commission for being preoccupied with East Timor while

Indonesian Muslims were suffering in Maluku. Some speakers also called for a *jihad*, or righteous struggle, against Christian belligerents in Maluku. The crowd of more than 100 000 passionate activists was whipped into a frenzy. This marked the first time that Maluku's religious tensions had ignited passions in Jakarta. But it remained unclear whether this was a spontaneous and genuine outpouring of emotion—or a carefully orchestrated political manoeuvre.

The event attracted press attention at the time because Amien Rais stood on the podium and called for a *jihad* to Maluku—a blunder that helped undo his painstaking efforts to portray himself as an 'inclusivist' politician. A more striking feature of the event, however, was the number of speakers and organisations that had track records of co-operating with the military. In 1994, Indonesia's first high-profile militant organisation was established: the Indonesian Committee for World Muslim Solidarity (Kisdi). Its founders included two relatives of Soeharto: his foster brother, Probosutedjo, and his son-in-law, Prabowo Subianto, who was then a one-star general. Kisdi had declined since Prabowo's ouster from the military but its chief figures had erected new political parties and militant groups—often in alliance with military figures. Achmad Sumargono, for instance, was the former Kisdi chair who was now supporting Wiranto in parliament. He was among the speakers calling for a *jihad* to Maluku on 7 January.

The following day a concerned President Wahid disclosed that several hundred armed youths had been sent to Maluku as *jihad* fighters.[22] He publicly ordered Armed Forces Chief Widodo to ensure that all travellers entering Maluku be screened, lest troublemakers further enflame the situation. In fact, the security forces failed to carry out this order. One of the groups that had supplied para-militaries in November 1998—a shadowy militant group called Laskar Jihad (Holy War Forces)—was recruiting, training and equipping Javanese youths to fight Christians in Maluku.

Within weeks Laskar Jihad had sent several thousand of these fighters to the troubled province.[23] Their arrival on the scene marked a turning point in the conflict—the scale of the violence was significantly more severe than before.[24] Many wondered why the security forces failed to prevent the staging and shipment of the Laskar Jihad forces. Such large shipments of personnel could not have left Java, nor entered Maluku, unnoticed. And despite having 11 000 personnel stationed throughout Maluku, the military consistently failed to quell the strife.[25] Meanwhile, other episodes of unrest and violence were erupting around the country during January.

In Aceh, at least 30 people were killed in one week alone in mid-January—an abnormally high toll.[26] In West Timor, pro-Indonesia militias made a series of incursions across the border into East Timor, having been explicitly encouraged to do so by Maj. Gen. Adam Damiri.²⁷ In East Java and Central Java, killings of alleged *dukun santet* suddenly resumed for the first time since the 1998 Banyuwangi killings, which claimed 150 lives.²⁸ This time only around eighteen victims were reported, but the modus operandi was the same and East Java's police chief declared that Jakarta *preman* had commissioned the hits.²⁹

Meanwhile, in the remote province of Irian Jaya, the longstanding struggle for an independent West Papua had turned more heated and violent than usual. Certain episodes of violence were backed by an unlikely figure: Yorrys Raweyai, the Pemuda Pancasila leader who was with Soeharto during Wahid's visit to Cendana the year before. Although a native Papuan, Raweyai was not considered a credible independence campaigner—his interests clearly lay in Jakarta. He had a track record of loyal service to Soeharto and the military, and his rabble-rousing in Irian Jaya involved Pemuda Pancasila members—at the same time that Pemuda Pancasila's chief legal counsel, Ruhut Sitompul, was working as Wiranto's personal lawyer in the KPP Ham inquiry.³⁰ In effect, Raweyai seemed to be stoking secessionist and ethnic unrest to exacerbate the sense of crisis in Jakarta.³¹ There was, however, another location where an episode of violence was even more transparently orchestrated: Lombok.

Eggi Sudjana was ostensibly the head of an Islamic labour union, but in fact he was one of the more prominent militant Islamists who often worked on the army's behalf. He had supplied para-militaries to Djaja Suparman, he boasted of close ties to Wiranto and he had long worked closely with the PBB parliamentarians who were now allying openly with the co-ordinating minister.³² On 17 January Sudjana helped stage a rally in Mataram, Lombok's capital, ostensibly to express solidarity for Muslims in Maluku. The event attracted a crowd of around 5000. After the event about half of these people rampaged around the small island, killing five and destroying dozens of churches and public buildings.³³

The attack was obviously pre-arranged. A large number of Christian businesses and homes were destroyed in a short space of time, and the perpetrators were not unruly mobs but local para-military racketeers—similar to those in East Timor.³⁴ Carrying target lists and using walkie-talkies, the rioting gangs split up and hit widely dispersed districts simultaneously.³⁵ While vandalising cars and shops, they deliberately destroyed valuable merchandise such as stereo equipment—rather than looting like a disorganised mob.³⁶ Two senior Special Forces offices were in the vicinity as the riots took place, and a host of military personnel from East Timor had recently been relocated to Lombok.³⁷ Some units of marines and police moved to contain the riots, but their field-radio communications were electronically jammed.³⁸ Soon after, another odd riot took place on another holiday resort island, Bintan, near Singapore.

Indonesia had witnessed considerable turmoil since the end of

Soeharto's rule, but never had so many conflicts suddenly erupted at one time—just at the point, in fact, when the country's political and economic outlook seemed to be improving. Within the space of a month, at least half a dozen separate episodes occurred: the Doulos attack, the escalation of Maluku strife, the killing of *dukun santet* in Central Java, ethnically targeted secessionist riots in Irian Jaya and the religious riots on Lombok and Bintan.

The violence came just three months after a deliberate scorched-earth campaign had been waged in East Timor. President Wahid was convinced that elements of the military were perpetrating a similar campaign—but on a nationwide scale. 'There is a kind of frustration,' he said, 'because we are chipping away at their power. We are trying to make the rule-of-law supreme—and they don't like it.'[39]

Some wondered why the military would want to behave in such a seemingly self-defeating way, but others concluded that the military was trying to deflect attention from KPP Ham. The subcommission's hearings took place from mid-December through late January—the same period in which the worst spate of violence occurred. Others speculated that the military had larger goals, such as sending emphatic warnings that reform measures should proceed no further. Some even suspected that the military sought to precipitate a nationwide conflict, perhaps along religious lines, to justify a military takeover. This would have resembled the military's apparent efforts to provoke Falintil guerillas in East Timor. Finally, there was the possibility that the military was not acting entirely on its own accord but rather at the whims of its financiers, who may have included Cendana cronies and the Soeharto family itself.

While Wahid insisted that establishment interests were waging an organised campaign of intimidation, he carefully refrained from issuing controversial allegations against specific figures. Instead, he seemed determined to complete a thorough investigation on the one specific set of alleged human rights abuses for which detailed data was available: East Timor. Undaunted by the havoc being wreaked around the country, KPP Ham kept chipping away.

On 17 January the latest edition of *Tempo* magazine became available from news stands and sidewalk vendors. Although it was not the cover story, an excerpt from Wiranto's testimony before KPP Ham—which had been carried out behind closed doors three weeks before—was reproduced in the magazine. The transcript had been leaked. Although it was overlooked at the time, Wiranto's own words seemed to provide incriminating evidence. Rather than 'stonewall' KPP Ham as Feisal Tanjung had done—or rather than concocting far-fetched counter-arguments as Zacky Makarim had done—Wiranto grudgingly confessed certain key points. In particular, the general finally admitted that the military had armed militias—something that officers had been strenuously denying for a year:

> Sometimes weapons were provided, but this does not mean that [militias] carried weapons wherever they went—the weapons were stored at sub-district military headquarters. This is because armed gangs were being confronted . . . So there was a force of people's militias that were nurtured since integration.[40]

Next, Wiranto unwittingly destroyed a possible basis for his defence: he might have tried to claim that he was misled by his subordinates, such that he was never properly informed about the situation on the ground in East Timor. KPP Ham investigators therefore asked whether, in addition to what he witnessed himself in East Timor, he received official reports on the security situation. 'Of course', Wiranto replied. 'I received reports regularly and I studied those reports, and at critical junctures those reports were forwarded to the president.' Clearly, the former armed forces chief was not pleading ignorance.

A subsequent question then delved into the crux of the matter—why soldiers allowed the mayhem to transpire. Wiranto did not admit the existence of a concerted operation but he did confess that the military never had any intention to discipline the militias:

> When I inspected the field, and when I received reports from field commanders, it seemed that there was a certain mental block. For twenty-three years they [the soldiers] worked together with the integrationists, and suddenly they have to shoot them—and they were sure that the integrationists were not criminals, but just people who were trying to find justice or uncover fraudulent practices in the balloting process. I'm sure that that is what led to the massive outpouring of emotion. All of a sudden we were required to shoot people who were merely seeking justice . . . We could have used that approach—shooting [militias]—but instead we pursued a humane approach, whereby we contacted militia leaders individually and urged them to reduce the tension.

'But the question,' said investigators, 'was not about shooting them, but simply stopping them. Moreover, how can we explain the arson to government buildings?'

'That was due,' Wiranto insisted, 'to a mental block. And that mental block derived from our policy, which tried for years to resolve the problem of East Timor.' Wiranto was not confessing, but at least he was acknowledging more than other officers had done before KPP Ham.

Immediately after this testimony, Wiranto's lawyers implemented damage control measures. The Pemuda Pancasila lawyer, Ruhut Sitompul,

took a curious tack: rather than trying to deny that Wiranto had implicated himself, Sitompul resorted to the intimidation tactics for which his
organisation was so well known. 'KPP Ham can go right ahead and charge
Wiranto as a suspect. Do they have the guts? We're waiting . . .'[41]

KPP Ham, for its part, was undaunted. Having collected testimony
from scores of witnesses and more than 30 suspects, the subcommission
prepared to announce its findings on 31 January. But before issuing the
final report, subcommission members sought to clear a path forward by
urging that Wiranto be rendered non-active as minister. They launched a
well-coordinated lobbying effort toward this end. On 14 January the US
ambassador to the UN, Richard Holbrooke, announced explicit support
for KPP Ham's investigations. 'What we are witnessing,' said Holbrooke, 'is
a great drama—a struggle between the forces of democracy and reform
and the forces of backward-looking corruption and militarism.'[42]
Holbrooke later revealed that he had obtained Wahid's approval before
issuing the statement.[43]

In parliament Holbrooke's statement drew sharp criticism from PPP
faction chair Achmad Sumargono. This provided yet another sign of the
alliance being forged between Wiranto and the Islamists—and this was
precisely the sort of development that most alarmed Wahid, who had
campaigned for years against political Islam. Finally, Wahid resolved on a
course of action.

Speaking to a visiting delegation of Japanese business leaders, the
president disclosed that he intended to sack Wiranto in the near future.
The comment found its way into a Japanese newspaper on 15 January and
was picked up by international wire services the next day. By 18 January it
was plastered across headlines throughout Indonesia.[44]

Suddenly, frenzied rumours swept through Jakarta and Singapore: the
military was on the verge of launching a coup d'état. In fact, a coup was
simply not a feasible alternative for Wiranto. There was no precedent for
an outright power grab in Indonesia, and the present circumstances were
not favourable: Wahid was still too popular and student protesters
throughout the nation were too formidable a force. Internationally,
Indonesia's creditors and allies would exact heavy punishment if the
country's long-awaited democratic leader were ousted after only three
months in office. But the financial markets and the cocktail circuit
generally ignored these considerations; the frenzied rumours persisted.

In response to the mounting speculation of a coup, Wiranto met with
friendly reporters to emphasise that he had no interest in taking power.
The reasoning he employed, however, was hardly reassuring. 'If you look
back to when I was leading the armed forces,' Wiranto explained, 'there
were several times when it would have been easy for me to seize power.'[45]
He cited the November 1998 MPR session, when student protesters filled
the streets of Jakarta:

From Semanggi to parliament was how far? If I or the military had unwhole-some intentions, we could have easily given the students the opportunity. 'Please, go ahead, take over the parliament building!' After the coup d'état by the mob, all I would have had to do was launch a counter-coup. That would have been possible.

Instead, sixteen protesters were shot dead at Semanggi. Wiranto men-tioned another opportunity: Soeharto's handover to Habibie. 'At that time,' said Wiranto, 'I had in my pocket an order that empowered me to take emergency measures.'

Wiranto's reasoning did nothing to ease tensions in Jakarta. Fears of a coup persisted. And although an outright power grab was not a real possibility, the escalating conflict between Wahid and Wiranto was none-theless a desperate and momentous affair.

The events of January 2000 illustrated that Indonesia's newly elected civilian leaders possessed strictly limited powers. A new figure, Wahid, had won the presidency—but the presidency was but one of several important governing institutions. In the past the presidency had been powerful not because of the institution itself but rather because of the personal authority accumulated by Soeharto over several decades. Wahid was discovering that the title of president, on its own, counted for little. He still faced myriad rivals for authority, including the party bosses running parliament and an elaborately corrupt civil service. But even if Wahid consolidated control over the presidency, the parliament and the civil service, he would still face Indonesia's single most powerful political institution, the recalcitrant and deeply entrenched military.

As KPP Ham prepared to present its conclusions at the end of January, President Wahid escalated the tension in his tacit war with Wiranto. On 27 January he endorsed a measure forbidding active military officers from serving as ministers. This meant that the cabinet's four generals—including Wiranto and Yudhoyono—would be forced to retire from the military. The measure was clearly aimed at undermining the political authority of Wiranto in particular and the military in general.[46] As one of only three active four-star army generals, Wiranto's active status was a critical means through which he continued to exert influence over the officer corps.

Despite the worsening regional violence and mounting tension with his military leaders, Wahid departed on 28 January for a 17-day tour of the Middle East, Europe and Asia. Jakarta was gripped with fears that the military would launch a coup d'état in his absence. But before leaving, Wahid told reporters that he was 'not worried about a very small number of military leaders who actually do not have followers. I can leave the country peacefully because this small number of military leaders are not

obeyed by the personnel under them'.[47] He labelled his opponents within the military as 'cowards'.[48]

Finally, on 31 January, the National Human Rights Commission presented the conclusions of its KPP Ham subcommission. The material was presented by Djoko Soegianto, who had replaced Marzuki Darusman as chair of the commission. After a study of eleven specific episodes of violence—including the fatal shooting of *Financial Times* correspondent Sander Thoenes—Soegianto declared that elements of the military, police and civil government funded, trained and abetted militias both directly and indirectly. Soegianto cited evidence that 'provides a strong indication' that serious human rights abuses took place in East Timor in a co-ordinated, systematic, and large-scale manner.[49] These took the form of massacres, searches and seizures, theft, brutality towards women and children (including rape and sexual molestation), forced evacuations, arson, looting and vandalism. Soegianto said that all these acts represented crimes against humanity.

The subcommission recommended that the attorney general pursue investigations of 31 people, comprising six provincial government officials, ten militia leaders and fifteen officers from the military and police. This list included the entire top echelon of military and government figures associated with East Timor in the post-ballot period. Soegianto emphasised, however, that paramount responsibility rested with Wiranto:

> All crimes against humanity in East Timor, both direct and indirect, occurred due to failure by the armed forces chief to guarantee public security surrounding the balloting process. The structure of the police force, which at that time was under the command of the minister of defence, consistently interfered with efforts to provide public security in accordance with the New York Agreement. For these reasons, General Wiranto, as armed forces chief and minister of defence at that time, is the party that must be held responsible.[50]

At last the principle of accountability was being applied. But the process was only just beginning. The Human Rights Commission had submitted its findings to Attorney General Darusman, but it remained unclear when, or whether, the state prosecutor would file charges. Although he had appeared to be an enthusiastic backer of KPP Ham when the subcommission began its work in November, Darusman had since lost steam.

During his first three months in office Darusman had recorded no progress whatsoever on three high-profile cases: the Bank Bali scandal, Texmaco and Soeharto. In some instances the Golkar politician who had doggedly undermined Habibie's campaign now seemed distinctly hesitant about pursuing convictions in corruption cases. At other times Darusman's prosecutors were thwarted by corrupt judges. The authority to change judicial personnel rested with Yusril Mahendra, the new minister of law, but he consistently refused to take any action.

Thus, even if Darusman wanted to press charges against Wiranto, he might be easily defeated in the courts. This was especially so given that Darusman would have shaky legal grounds on which to punish human rights abuses—Indonesia still lacked an explicit law on human rights. The newly elected parliament had been expected to quickly pass such a law but—in one of the first clear indications of the depth of establishment influence in the new parliament—it had failed to do so. Lacking a human rights law, Darusman's only option might be to prosecute Wiranto for violating military procedures. But such a case would be tried in a joint civil–military court—where the likelihood of a conviction would be even more remote than in the corrupt civil courts. Recognising the obstacles that lay ahead, President Wahid suddenly intervened.

Only moments after the Human Rights Commission concluded its press conference in Jakarta, Wahid met reporters in Switzerland, where he was attending the Davos economic summit. The president was asked whether his co-ordinating minister for politics and security would be sacked as a result of KPP Ham's findings. Wahid replied in the nonchalant fashion that was fast becoming his trademark: 'Oh ya, of course. I'm going to ask him, politely, to resign.'[51] Jakarta's hottest topic of speculation for more than a month—that Wahid wanted Wiranto out of the cabinet—was now fact.

The next day, in London, Wahid reiterated his appeal for the general to resign. Noting that the activities of the attorney general were among those 'co-ordinated' by Wiranto's office, the president recommended that Wiranto resign to avoid a conflict of interest in the East Timor investigation.[52] Wahid disclosed that he had already instructed his defence minister to urge Wiranto to step down. Wiranto refused. He was apparently angry that the president should try to shunt him aside in such a public and unceremonious fashion. He denounced the recommendations of the Human Rights Commission as 'vulgar', while deriding the commission itself as being an unofficial body.[53] He would wait, he said, for the attorney general to take action. Meanwhile, Wiranto's allies leapt to his defence.

The situation elicited a sharply worded response from the deputy armed forces chief—and the most senior army officer in the military command—Gen. Fachrul Razi. The hardline Acehnese general warned against a 'trial by the press'.[54] The military, he said, did not want the East Timor investigation to become a political commodity used to sully the reputations of high-ranking officers. Clearly, Wahid's efforts to impose his authority over the military were meeting stiff resistance. But the president also had supporters within the officer corps—particularly Agus Wirahadikusumah. 'The abuses being investigated now,' said the popular two-star general, 'are just part of a larger culture of brutality within the Indonesian military.'[55] Wahid's frontal attack was cleaving the military's ranks.

Next, Wahid appeared with the Netherlands' Queen Beatrix in Den Haag on 3 February. He told reporters that he had received information about a clandestine meeting held by generals at an office of the modernist Islamic organisation, Icmi. 'I also heard,' said Wahid, 'that there will be a demonstration by Muslim militants on 5 February. I suspect there may be evil hands at work. I don't know if those hands belong to the generals . . .'[56] In fact, the meeting place was frequented by Eggi Sudjana, the militant Muslim labour leader accused of fomenting the rioting in Lombok. Both Sudjana and Wiranto denied that any plots were afoot. In the end, no demonstrations took place on 5 February. That day, however, Wahid appeared in Rome with the Italian prime minister, who publicly implored the Indonesian military to refrain from launching a coup.[57]

Five days later, in Seoul, Wahid claimed that his aides had received expressions of support from a number of pro-reform generals. The claim was disputed by Wiranto's allies, but these allies were beginning to dwindle in number. A key general had broken ranks and publicly endorsed Wahid's call for Wiranto to resign: the new army chief-of-staff, Gen. Tyasno—the former Bais chief who had helped guide Wiranto through the MPR session.[58] Tyasno was nimbly shifting to what he presumed would be the winning side.

Finally, on the eve of his return to Jakarta, Wahid raised the stakes. 'It's up to Wiranto whether he wants to resign. But if he doesn't resign, then I'll change the cabinet's structure to exclude him.'[59] Finally, on the morning of Sunday 14 February—several hours after having returned to Jakarta—Wahid met with Wiranto, Megawati and Darusman. Emerging from a lift on his way out of the meeting, Wahid was confronted by reporters. 'What transpired inside?' he was asked.

'I asked Wiranto to resign,' Wahid answered, 'but he asked that we first wait for the outcome of the legal process. Ya, for me, it's no problem. That's the kind of person I am.'[60]

The reporters were astonished. After vowing for weeks to sack Wiranto, Wahid was apparently backing down. 'Does this mean,' they asked, 'that you've made a compromise with Wiranto?'

'There's no compromise. This has been my stance from the beginning. It's the reporters who made the mistake.' The reporters surrounding Wahid were floored. The president went on. 'I asked Wiranto to resign, and Wiranto asked to follow procedures. There's no problem. In fact, Wiranto and I are close friends. Only reporters portray us as enemies.' Wahid explained what he had decided with Wiranto, Megawati and Darusman: 'We're all close friends, and our decision was to adhere to the law. The attorney general will adhere to the law, Wiranto will adhere to the law, the vice-president will adhere to the law, and I will adhere to the law.'

Wahid's remarks were not impromptu. Soon after the Sunday morning meeting the president's spokesperson convened a formal press conference. His message: the attorney general would form a team to study whether Wiranto should be tried in court. Until then the general would continue serving in the cabinet. After two weeks of tough talk, Wahid had backed down.

The event was more than a tussle between a president and an unruly minister—this was a critical juncture on Indonesia's systemic transition from authoritarianism to democracy, from Ruler's Law to rule-of-law, and from the New Order to *reformasi*. Wahid symbolised the fruit of a costly, tumultuous and heroic campaign for reform that had consumed the nation's attention for a full two years—and that had been kept alive by reformers since Soekarno's original imposition of martial law in 1957. After more than four decades of military-backed authoritarian rule, Indonesia's newly elected civilian president had tried, and failed, to rein in the country's most powerful general. Or at least this was the impression created momentarily.

Late Sunday evening, just prior to midnight, President Wahid summoned reporters again. 'While waiting for a decision from the attorney general's team,' he said, referring to Darusman's imminent investigation of Wiranto, 'and to ensure that its investigation remains neutral, General Wiranto has been made non-active in his cabinet position.'[61] Wahid went on to explain that Home Affairs Minister Surjadi Soedirdja would become the *ad interim* co-ordinating minister for politics and security. Wahid's dizzying policy changes only cast more doubt on his constancy and steadiness as president; nonetheless, his decision to finally oust Wiranto was his biggest achievement to date.

It remained unclear what prompted Wahid to change his mind twice in 24 hours. The president's cabinet secretary said, ominously, that Sunday's late-night announcement had been made 'for the sake of the government's stability'.[62] Wahid was said to have telephoned US Ambassador Robert Gelbard during the day.[63] And on Monday afternoon, hours after Wiranto's ouster, UN Secretary General Koffi Annan declared that the UN would not try the general in Den Haag—something that had clearly worried Wiranto. This created a distinct impression that Wiranto had bargained for his freedom.

22

'RAID CENDANA'

resident Wahid's first four months in office had generally disappointed Indonesia's reformers, but Wiranto's dismissal suddenly
revived their hopes. It seemed that the path stood clear towards
sweeping reform of the military's role in politics—thereby allowing
concomitant progress towards legal system reform and the rule-of-law. In
many ways, the optimism resembled that which followed Soeharto's ouster
nearly two years before. But if anything had been learned since then it was
that toppling a strongman was only a first step towards change. Just as
Soehartoism had outlived Soeharto, so too would military recalcitrance
survive Wiranto—unless Wahid moved assertively to promote reform-
minded officers. High anxiety therefore marked the approach to the next
reshuffle of military commands, due to be announced on 1 March 2000.

By this time Indonesia's generals were no longer hiding their
contempt for one another. During Wahid's tense standoff with Wiranto,
Agus Wirahadikusumah had cheekily—and publicly—advised the four-star
general to abandon the military and pursue a career in Golkar. The
reformer was chiding his senior officer for harbouring political ambitions
and Wiranto was quick to lash back. Moments after the ceremony in which
he surrendered his cabinet post, Wiranto complained bitterly to reporters
about 'a certain two-star general who has been making public comments
about a four-star. Such behaviour violates the ethical code of the officer
corps. But it is my own fault—I have apparently failed to provide adequate
guidance for officers that behave that way'.[1]

It was widely expected that Wahid would promote Wirahadikusumah,
and reformers hoped that he would obtain either one of two key policy-
making posts: kaster or deputy army chief-of-staff. When finally
announced on 1 March the reshuffle did indeed promote Wirahadikusumah, while sidelining two Wiranto loyalists: Djaja Suparman and
Saudi Marasabessy. But the list of command changes included few other
concessions to military reform. Rather than obtaining a policy-making

post, Wirahadikusumah became Kostrad commander—a pure combat role in which he would have no meaningful influence over matters of military policy.

Meanwhile, two powerful conservative generals survived the reshuffle: Gen. Fachrul Razi, the deputy armed forces chief, and Lt Gen. Agus Wijoyo, the kaster. All but one of the regional garrison commanders were also retained; most of these officers were former staff officers in Wiranto's headquarters. But the most significant feature of the reshuffle was the sudden appearance of a little-known officer who was shooting up through the ranks: Lt Gen. Endriartono Sutarto, the new deputy army chief-of-staff.

Sutarto had been promoted to three-star general a mere four months before, along with Marasabessy and Suparman. Prior to that his main distinction had been his service to the Soeharto family: until September 1998, amid the tumult surrounding the student movement and the fall of Soeharto, Sutarto had commanded the elite presidential security unit, Paspampres. A mere twenty months later he was in a choice three-star post—and he was poised to rise farther still.

Sutarto's career trajectory—distinguished by proximity to Cendana and characterised by fast-track promotions—bore striking similarity to that of Wiranto. And like Soeharto and Wiranto, the 52-year-old general was from Central Java.[2] Thus, while certain Wiranto allies were eased out of power, others were ushered in, such that the overall complexion of the military leadership changed little. As would soon become clear, Indonesia's new civilian president still lacked control over a recalcitrant military.

While Wahid was confronting the military during the early months of 2000, the fragile political alliance that had backed him in the presidential election began to crumble. First, Golkar's pro Habibie faction felt betrayed when only one of their number obtained a cabinet post. Second, Wahid compelled Hamzah Haz to resign from the cabinet after only one month in office—a move that drove the party Haz chaired, PPP, into tacit opposition. By the start of 2000, therefore, Wahid had already alienated the two largest groups that had elected him to the presidency. This hardly bothered anti-establishment reformers, but it did have practical political consequences.

Wahid seemed to regard his presidency as being unquestionably secure. He made few efforts to cultivate and maintain political support in parliament; in fact, he actually told a parliamentary commission, which had summoned him to explain why he had dissolved the information ministry, that the parliament resembled a kindergarten. The joke would haunt him later: Wahid's position would prove far less secure than Soeharto's had been.

The new electoral laws provided for an MPR session to be held annually, rather than every five years. Although the rules were somewhat ambiguous, the essential fact was that the MPR was the country's highest constitutional authority, and therefore Wahid could conceivably be removed from office whenever the MPR convened. And in between the annual sessions, which took place in August, the parliament could censor the president through a series of memorandums; the process would consume some four to six months and would culminate in an MPR vote on an accountability speech by the president. If the MPR rejected the speech, the president's mandate would be revoked.

In short, Indonesia's fuzzy new electoral laws had produced what generally resembled a parliamentary system. The president could be frequently subjected to the political equivalent of a no-confidence vote. Antagonising Golkar and PPP was therefore foolhardy, but Wahid seemed not to realise this. In fact, he continued to make new enemies.

E arly in the Wahid administration, a bitter conflict arose over something that had been engendering political controversies for decades: control over the country's state-owned enterprises. The government ran nearly 200 state firms, some of which dominated huge swaths of the economy, such as transportation, telecommunications and energy. Soeharto had deliberately created overlapping lines of authority over these powerful institutions. Consequently, while Laksamana Sukardi held the post of state minister for empowering state-owned enterprises, it remained unclear whether he or Finance Minister Bambang Sudibyo should wield paramount authority over the most notoriously corrupt state-owned enterprises: the state banks.

Control over the state banks entailed control over vast largesse. In the past this had been channelled to crony conglomerates, such that control over the state banks now also entailed the power to crack down on these heavily indebted cronies—or let them off the hook. Sudibyo, who was backed by Amien Rais's Central Axis, and Laksamana, who belonged to Megawati's PDI Perjuangan, had already clashed over how to handle the state's largest debtor: Texmaco's Marimutu Sinivasan, who owed Rp17 trillion to state banks. Sudibyo's intervention to protect Texmaco—combined with his alleged proximity to former finance minister Fuad Bawazier—suggested that Sudibyo's allies sought to commandeer the state banks for their own benefit. In contrast, Laksamana vowed to purge Soeharto-era bank directors and install professional management teams.

To carry through on his promise, Laksamana secured full control over the state banks through a governmental decree signed by Wahid in late December 1999. But Sudibyo and his allies immediately objected. A mere five days later a second decree handed control back to the finance minister—but the matter was still not resolved. Days later a third decree arrived at a compromise that resembled the original overlap of jurisdictions: the minister of finance possessed authority over state-owned financial institutions, but the minister of state enterprises could change their directors unilaterally. Laksamana promptly embarked on a thorough shake-up of state bank directors—and he quickly made a host of enemies.

Laksamana's deputy at the ministry for state enterprises was Rozy Munir, a Wahid appointee. Munir apparently worked with Megawati's husband, Taufik Kiemas, to undermine Laksamana's influence and perpetuate the Soeharto-era style of political patronage. 'Munir and Kiemas,' according to a palace source, 'had already reached agreement on dividing the spoils—but Laksamana refused to go along.'[3] In effect, Laksamana faced opposition from a rival faction within his own party, headed by Kiemas. An unnamed party source commented: 'It's a kind of conspiracy: Taufik's faction asked Wahid to get rid of Laksamana—and it suited Wahid's general goals to do so.'[4] In late April Wahid shocked the country by accusing Laksamana of corruption and sacking him from the cabinet.

It was the president's worst blunder to date. Regardless of whether Laksamana was corrupt, the public viewed him as the cabinet's cleanest minister—and Wahid offered no evidence to prove otherwise. By impugning Laksamana's reputation, Wahid damaged his own credibility—while signalling that his administration was not, in fact, serious about reforming corrupt institutions. But in addition to discrediting himself and setting back reform, Wahid also squandered his political capital. By sacking Laksamana, Wahid alienated the more reformist faction of parliament's largest party, PDI Perjuangan. And before long he would lose the party's support altogether.

Along with Laksamana, Wahid also sacked Minister of Industry and Trade Jusuf Kalla.[5] Corruption allegations against Kalla, a close associate of Arnold Baramuli, were far more plausible than in the case of Laksamana; however, Kalla was the sole cabinet representative of Golkar's pro-Habibie faction, and his disgrace and dismissal therefore cemented Golkar's opposition to Wahid. Thus, by the end of his first six months as president, Wahid had won the enmity of Golkar, PPP, Pan and PDI Perjuangan. Still, he dug himself even deeper.

In April the president decided to push for the repeal of a 34-year-old MPR resolution that outlawed communism. It was a noble gesture that sought to redress the bloody anti-communist pogrom of 1965–66, but it was politically self-defeating. Islamists such as Yusril Mahendra pounced on the opportunity afforded to warn of a communist–atheist resurgence and to heap scorn on the president. Wahid eventually backed down, but his political honeymoon with Indonesia's party bosses had come to an end—and his standing with the Indonesian public was sinking as well.

Indonesians clearly craved action to combat corruption, yet when Wahid fired Laksamana he sent precisely the wrong message. By mid-2000 the public was giving up hope that the Wahid administration would make progress on anti-corruption efforts. The president established various anti-corruption commissions, sacked the Wiranto-era police chief and appointed credible figures to head the state oil and power monopolies, but these were only piecemeal steps. Wahid never presented a coherent strategy for comprehensive legal system reform—a prerequisite for a sustainable economic recovery.

The president's inaction puzzled many. He was obviously not a timid person: with regard to ideological gestures such as reopening Israeli relations or legalising communism, Wahid demonstrated remarkable courage in the face of scathing criticism. Ironically, he displayed far less courage with regard to more popular and tangible goals, such as cracking down on corruption. The paradox was difficult to explain.

Wahid did not appear to be avoiding legal system reform for his own personal interests. Although a few disreputable figures appeared in his inner circle, the president himself was not an avaricious man. He lived humbly and had always displayed a cavalier attitude towards wealth and material possessions. His inaction on legal system reform therefore seemed attributable to a mere lack of understanding: Wahid seemed confused about why or how the goal should be pursued.

A simple starting point for legal system reform would have been judicial screening, whereby judges deemed guilty of bribe-taking would be dealt stiff disciplinary action. The authority for this task, however, rested with the chief justice of the Supreme Court, Sarwata. A retired three-star air force marshal who had served as the cornerstone of Soeharto's judiciary for many years, Sarwata was hardly inclined to make significant changes. Moreover, a newly passed law providing for the independence of the judiciary made it difficult to dislodge him prior to his scheduled retirement in August 2000.

In the jockeying to find a successor for Sarwata, Wahid expressed his support for Benjamin Mangkoedilaga. An ardent reformist, Mangkoedilaga was the lower court judge who had famously ruled against the government in the slander suit against *Tempo* magazine in 1995. Wahid, however, lacked the power (and perhaps the determination) to hasten Sarwata's retirement. Meanwhile, the Golkar faction in parliament adamantly opposed Mangkoedilaga's candidacy—in favour of Habibie's justice minister, Muladi, or another Soeharto-era official, Bagir Manan.

While Indonesia waited for a new figure to fill the pivotal chief justice post, Yusril Mahendra could have been making considerable progress towards judicial reform in his role as minister of law. Mahendra, however, steadfastly defended the judicial establishment. The court system possessed several features that facilitated the buying and selling of verdicts: the legal code was rife with contradictions, judges were rarely required to defend their decisions in written statements, and (in cases involving multiple judges) dissenting opinions were forbidden. In alliance with Sarwata, Mahendra consistently upheld these practices, and the sale of verdicts became increasingly blatant.[6]

In the absence of a functional court system, Attorney General Marzuki Darusman made very little headway in the high-profile corruption cases that his office tried to prosecute. Upon taking office Darusman identified five priority cases: the Texmaco scandal, the Bank Bali affair, the misuse of BLBI liquidity credits, human rights abuses in East Timor and corruption on the part of Soeharto. Despite having failed to make headway in the case against Texmaco, Darusman made a promising start on the Bank Bali investigation by convicting and jailing Pande Lubis, the former deputy director of Ibra whose guilt was clear-cut. But when Darusman's prosecutors attempted to try other suspects in the scandal, proceedings were foiled by political resistance, judicial corruption and questionable acts within Darusman's own office.

Indonesia's corruption law stipulates that, in trying a suspect for corruption, the prosecution must prove that the suspect has inflicted losses on the state. Therefore when Darusman's prosecutors sought to try Djoko Tjandra, the main recipient of the kickback from Bank Bali, a South Jakarta judge dismissed the case on the grounds that Tjandra had returned the kickback and so no losses to the state had been incurred.[7] The ruling was issued by Judge Soenarto, the same judge who had absolved Tommy Soeharto of guilt in the Goro scandal the year before.[8] Meanwhile, another court ruled that the kickback was a valid financial transaction; and therefore Bank Bali owner Rudy Ramli escaped prosecution even though the PricewaterhouseCoopers report had cited a host of disclosure rules that he had violated. Those with strong connections to Golkar, such as Arnold Baramuli, Setya Novanto and Tanri Abeng, never faced charges from Darusman's office.

Ramli even succeeded in retaining control of his bank, by conducting a veritable war of attrition against Standard Chartered, the foreign investor that was seeking to purchase the bank from Ibra. Ramli's directors orchestrated anti–Standard Chartered strikes among the bank's staff and reputedly sabotaged the computer system. In a sustained 'media blitz', Ramli launched angry attacks against Standard Chartered and its directors. The foreign bank finally capitulated and withdrew its bid for the bank—thereby delivering a devastating blow to Ibra's asset restructuring program. When the agency finally sought to sell its controlling stake in BCA through a public offering, foreign demand was extremely weak. The failed Bank Bali divestiture and its knock-on effects on the BCA sale highlighted the importance of bringing unscrupulous businessmen to heel. Nonetheless, the Wahid administration did not even attempt to confront far larger targets, such as the three banking tycoons who had consumed the bulk of the central bank's BLBI liquidity credits in 1998.

Sudono Salim, Syamsul Nursalim and Usman Atmadjaya had together borrowed around two-thirds to three-quarters of the Rp144 trillion in BLBI loans disbursed by the central bank from late 1997 through the first half of 1998. The uncontrolled lending had caused an explosion in the money supply, which in turn closely tracked the decline of the rupiah. In effect, BLBI lending was the most important factor contributing to Indonesia's crippling devaluation—more important, even, than sentiment or panic.[9] Under the circumstances, Salim, Nursalim and Atmadjaya stood out as logical objects of a campaign to impose accountability. Instead, under the Habibie administration, the bank owners had been let off lightly.

In lieu of cash payments, the three tycoons had been allowed to repay their BLBI loans with corporate assets—and the values attributed to these assets were highly questionable. Perhaps the most egregious example involved Nursalim's Dipasena; ostensibly intended to become the world's largest integrated shrimp farm, Dipasena was in fact among the most grandiose KKN projects of the late Soeharto era. Ibra's advisor, Lehman Brothers, valued the asset at $1.8 billion; less than two years later Ibra officials assessed the scandal-plagued shrimp farm at barely $100 million.[10]

Similarly, the companies surrendered to Ibra by the Salim group were valued in September 1998 at Rp53 trillion; two years later different auditors appraised them at a mere Rp30 trillion. The decline in value was partly due to the economy's poor overall performance, but it was nonetheless evident that Salim, like Nursalim and Atmadjaya, had obtained a favourable deal from the government. Moreover, many of the Salim assets were highly illiquid and therefore difficult for Ibra to convert into cash.

Thus, given the ease with which high-profile BLBI borrowers escaped justice, there was ample reason to doubt that Darusman would make meaningful progress on trying either Wiranto or Soeharto. Just as it had done throughout the Habibie administration, Soeharto's legal status was still generating intense public interest. And just as it had done for Habibie, inaction on the case made Wahid look weak. At the end of January 2000 a *Kompas* poll of residents in thirteen cities estimated Wahid's favourability rating at 52 per cent; four months later the same poll revealed a drop to 42 per cent. By July Wahid's favourability rating was at a mere 27 per cent.[11] The president's erratic public statements and incessant foreign travels contributed to his unpopularity, but the core problem was the absence of the rule-of-law. And in addition to injustice and a lack of accountability, this was having devastating consequences for the prospects of an economic recovery.

The judicial corruption under Sarwata and Mahendra effectively blocked the restructuring of the economy's distressed assets and non-performing loans. Creditors were unable to threaten debtors with bankruptcy proceedings, because the bankruptcy courts routinely sold verdicts to indebted conglomerates.[12] It would not have been so surprising if judicial corruption only victimised foreign creditors—but it also inflicted massive losses on the government itself, through Ibra. In the absence of asset restructuring, investment was moribund and Indonesia continued to record net outflows of private capital. From Rp7000/$ at the outset of Wahid's presidency, the exchange rate fell to Rp9000/$ by mid-year.

Ibra's string of failed bankruptcy suits alarmed the World Bank and the IMF. The donors responded by demanding that bankruptcy cases be heard by 'ad hoc' judges (i.e. outside legal experts who would not succumb to bribery). Darusman enthusiastically endorsed the idea, but Mahendra vehemently opposed it—and thereby prevented it from being used. In any event, Darusman complained that he could find few qualified legal experts to serve in ad hoc roles: 'It turns out that some of [the candidates] are hesitant to have themselves appointed because of . . . the risk that they will have to face possible bribes. If they try to reject the bribes then they feel there are further risks . . . which could even include personal consequences.'[13] In fact, there was ample reason for Indonesian reformers to fear for their personal safety. Once again, Indonesia's political arena was turning markedly violent.

At 7.30 a.m. on a Sunday in early March, Matori Abdul Djalil was working in his flower garden when he was approached by a visitor. As a deputy MPR Speaker and the chair of Abdurrahman Wahid's PKB, Matori was easy to recognise, and he was therefore accustomed to being approached by strangers. But when this man in his mid-30s drew near to Matori, he reached behind his back and drew out a machete. His first blow was blocked by Matori's arm, but the second hit home. As Matori screamed, the machete chopped into the back of his head and he crumpled to the ground. Perhaps leaving Matori for dead (in fact, he survived), the attacker and an accomplice turned and fled. But several witnesses chased after them and, as often happens in Indonesia, the excitement soon produced an angry vigilante mob—which eventually caught the attacker and beat him to death. The accomplice was later caught by police.

The attack might have been dismissed as a random act of violence, except for the explanation put forth by police: the attackers belonged to the Indonesian Mujahidin (Amin), the shadowy fundamentalist organisation which police had claimed, unconvincingly, were behind the Istiqlal mosque bombing a year before. As it had done then, this explanation rang hollow. Few believed that Amin actually existed. In the 1980s it had been a common tactic of Soeharto's security officials to fabricate militant Islamist organisations that could then be blamed for mysterious killings.

Moreover, the attacker's identity was established as a *preman* from a distant market in East Jakarta—not a religious fanatic.

Assuming that the attack was an assassination attempt or an intimidation tactic, it was difficult to establish a likely motive. However, one explanation that attracted little attention at the time was that Matori had been the target of a hit backed by elements of the military. The attack occurred only four days after the announcement of the military reshuffle that sidelined several allies of Wiranto. Matori had been advising Wahid on whom to promote, and he had ardently proposed a clean sweep of the military leadership to promote bona fide reformers.[14]

No proof emerged of military involvement, but neither was a more plausible explanation put forth. The press soon forgot about the attack on Matori and, when the accomplice was quietly sentenced to prison some six months later, prosecutors had established no motive.[15] But if elements of the military were connected to the attack, it would only be the first of several such episodes during the course of 2000. The next episode of political violence occurred in April.

When President Soeharto relaxed with old friends in the mid-1990s, it was said that he enjoyed nothing more than regaling his visitors with stories about his children—the favourite of whom was his youngest son, Hutomo Mandala Putra, or Tommy Soeharto. In a family renowned for its eccentricities Tommy stood out. In contrast to his two introverted older brothers Tommy was tough, cocky and enthusiastic. President Soeharto would beam with pride as he talked about Tommy's skill as a rally car driver, success as a big-game hunter and, especially, prowess as a 'lady-killer'.[16] The tabloids kept careful tabs on the steady stream of singers, actresses and fashion models seen dating Indonesia's most eligible bachelor.

Rather than obtaining a college degree, Tommy had attended a flight school in the United States in 1983. A year later he established his own business group, Humpuss. The group's first ventures were in aviation (leasing and maintaining jets for state-owned carriers), but Humpuss soon evolved into an elaborate rent-seeking organisation. It established its own airline, Sempati, which amassed vast debts and unpaid fuel bills from Pertamina. Its shipping arm secured contracts worth hundreds of millions of dollars to transport Pertamina's LNG. And because of his fascination for race cars, Tommy purchased the Italian carmaker, Lamborghini SpA, in 1993. By the late 1990s Humpuss possessed 43 subsidiaries, including Timor Putra Nasional—the national car project that was tapping state and private banks for $690 million when the crisis struck.[17]

Tommy's attitude seemed to be that his father had built Indonesia and that therefore the Soeharto family could do with it as they wished. This was the distinct impression he made through one of his first public ventures, his disastrous foray into clove-trading in 1990. Tommy wanted to become the nation's sole buyer of cloves, which he would then sell at a steep markup to Indonesia's multi-billion dollar clove cigarette industry. But while he wasted several months securing a $350 million startup loan from the central bank, cigarette makers were hoarding cloves, establishing alternative suppliers in Africa and reformulating their cigarettes to reduce their clove content. Consequently, Tommy's monopoly was soon saddled with massive clove inventories that could not be unloaded. Meanwhile, the price of the spice plummeted, inflicting hardship on tens of thousands of clove farmers in Eastern Indonesia.[18]

The solution, Tommy informed parliament in early 1992, was for the nation's clove farmers to burn half of their stocks. This would inflict severe hardship on farmers, but apart from possibly raising the value of Tommy's inventories, it was unclear what else this policy might achieve. While parliament was ordinarily a rubber-stamp body, several Golkar legislators finally grew exasperated with Tommy's callousness: they denounced his plan as 'inhumane' and foolhardy.

Tommy immediately lashed back. He upbraided the parliamentarians for criticising him in public, reminding them that his father had built Golkar—not vice versa. In the end, the parliamentarians apologised and the national co-operatives board baled out Tommy, but not before the 30-year-old tycoon had established a reputation for ruthlessness and greed.

Eight years later, Tommy again faced criticism from parliament concerning the clove monopoly. This time, however, parliament was far more outspoken—and Tommy's apparent reaction was even more emphatic. In March 2000 parliament's Commission V summoned him to explain why his monopoly had not returned Rp1.9 trillion in 'forced savings' that had been collected from clove farmers. Five minutes after Tommy left the building with four bodyguards, a shot rang out.

Forensic investigators later concluded that an armour-piercing bullet had been fired from an SS-1 rifle from the parking lot outside the parliament building.[19] The bullet pierced a first-floor window directly across from the Commission V office. The gunshot incident might have been forgotten, were it not for another mysterious episode that occurred three months later. First, however, Indonesia's minister of defence issued a startlingly candid assessment of what was taking place behind the scenes.

Juwono Sudarsono had been tapped for the defence portfolio by Wiranto, who appreciated the academic's deep, longstanding conservatism. Having served in three successive cabinets, Juwono was renowned for never having voiced serious criticisms of the military. By June 2000, however, his patience had finally run out. Sickened by the incessant violence affecting Indonesia, particularly in Aceh and Maluku, Juwono joined the likes of Wirahadikusumah in breaking ranks. He noted:

Every time there is a court case involving Soeharto or a high official from the past, a riot always ensues. It's very clear that this is the result of conflict between the ruling elite . . . Those who are behind the riots are people defending Soeharto. I strongly suspect that these are former officials from Soeharto's last cabinet who were used again in Habibie's cabinet—i.e. my former cabinet colleagues . . . By defending Soeharto, these people are really trying to defend themselves.[20]

As a former Soeharto supporter, a prominent member of the ruling elite and a conservative-minded defence minister, Juwono's assessment was eminently credible. Of the handful of figures who had served in the cabinets of both Soeharto and Habibie, the press identified the two most likely culprits as Feisal Tanjung and Wiranto. As for whether the military itself was perpetrating the violence, Juwono asserted that 'the military and the intelligence agencies are still evenly split between old forces and new forces . . . The problem is that those financing the unrest have more money than the security forces themselves'.

Although he claimed to know who was funding the operations, Juwono refrained from mentioning names. He insisted, however, that they included 'former high officials, both military and civilian':

These people are aware of the government's difficulty in overcoming the four or five cases of ongoing violence in areas such as Aceh and Maluku— not to mention the tensions surrounding the upcoming annual MPR session. Therefore, I can confirm that there is a deliberate and systematic effort to overburden the security forces, in order to create the impression that the government is ineffective and unable to control the situation.[21]

Because he was normally so cautious and circumspect, Juwono's comments carried considerable weight. Moreover, as minister of defence, Juwono was privy to the information needed to reach these conclusions. And just days after his comments were published by *Tempo*, at 6.05 p.m., an explosion shook the first floor of the attorney general's office. Tommy Soeharto—accompanied by no less than nine bodyguards—had left the building just one hour before.

The exploded bomb was only a small device but it was apparently intended to clear the building of its occupants—ten minutes later a far larger bomb was set to detonate on the third floor. This bomb would have destroyed at least half of the building, including the records library and its files on current corruption investigations. However, the shock from the first-floor bomb damaged a clock needle on the timing device of the larger bomb, thereby disabling it. Thus, rather than a scare tactic, the explosion appeared to be a botched attempt to level the entire building.

Investigators initially made rapid progress on the case. First, they identified the unexploded device as military materiel issued to an arsenal in East Java some four years earlier. Second, they interrogated around 35 witnesses, including the bodyguards accompanying Tommy (who had been queried that day about yet another corruption case, in which his aircraft chartering company stood accused of misappropriating eight helicopters that belonged to the ministry of forestry).[22] All nine of Tommy's bodyguards were former military or police personnel and six of them had arrived at the building together, driving a white Toyota Land Cruiser.[23]

At least four witnesses saw several of the bodyguards carrying a duffle bag from the building to the jeep. A janitor said that he saw the person who planted the bomb on the third floor; his description was translated into a police sketch. Meanwhile, investigators found multiple sets of fingerprints on the unexploded bomb. They also found the Land Cruiser parked along a road in West Java, and determined that it belonged to a man whose initials were BD.

Reporters speculated that 'BD' stood for Boli Diaz, the younger brother of Agus Diaz, the head of Tommy's bodyguard detail. BD was revealed as a former sergeant-major in Paspampres, the military's elite presidential security unit. It came as a surprise, therefore, when police suddenly detained BD and four other passengers who had been in his vehicle on the day of the bombing. After questioning the five as witnesses on 14 July, South Jakarta police chief Edward Aritonang stated that BD had repeatedly delivered conflicting testimony and it was therefore possible that he would be named as the prime suspect in the case. At the same time it was reported that the sketch made from the janitor's description matched the appearance of BD.[24]

It seemed that the police were finally on the brink of solving a high-profile case of political violence—for the first time in years. They possessed suspects who were under custody, positive identification from an eyewitness, and fingerprints from the bomb itself. On 18 July police officials stated that they were merely waiting for the results of the fingerprint tests from the forensics laboratory.[25] But the results were never announced. The case suddenly died.

The police made no more comments on the case and the East Java Garrison commander, Maj. Gen. Sudi Silalahi, never fulfilled his promise to investigate how the bomb went missing from the arsenal in his province. BD and Tommy's other bodyguards were released from custody. The local police official who had been handling the case, Edward Aritonang, was replaced weeks later.[26] Marzuki Darusman dropped his investigation of Tommy's helicopter scandal, and the press eventually lost interest. Yet again an act of violence went unexplained.

The abrupt halt to the police investigation was reminiscent of April 1999, when police sources claimed that they had been told to 'switch off' their investigation into the Istiqlal bombing, perpetrated hours after

Tommy Soeharto's appearance in court in the Goro case.[27] President Wahid later affirmed that the case had ground to a halt because 'certain army members opposed the investigation'.[28]

Juwono, the minister of defence, said that he was convinced that Tommy's bodyguards had perpetrated both the shooting at parliament and the bombing of the attorney general's office. If Juwono's supposition was correct, this would be the second time that Paspampres personnel were implicated in a mysterious crime—the first being the alleged role of Private Budi Leksono in the Semanggi shootings of November 1998. Meanwhile, by mid-July, a much higher level former Paspampres officer was diverting press attention—on the political front.

Endriartono Sutarto, the former Paspampres commander who was now serving as deputy army chief-of-staff, was involved in a concerted lobbying effort to oust the ardent reformer, Agus Wirahadikusumah, from the military leadership. Soon after being installed as Kostrad commander, Wirahadikusumah had incensed Indonesia's conservative generals by hiring an accounting firm to perform the first professional audit of Kostrad businesses since 1964. The auditors determined that Djaja Suparman, Wirahadikusumah's rival and predecessor as Kostrad commander, had illegally withdrawn a total of Rp160 billion from Mandala Airlines, a business owned by Kostrad's pension fund.[29] Another Rp29 billion simply went missing from the airline's accounts. Furthermore, the funds were apparently laundered through a series of fictitious or heavily marked-up purchases of land, equipment and Kia sedans. After Wirahadikusumah disclosed the scandal, Suparman returned Rp41 billion to Mandala.[30]

Wirahadikusumah only pointed out that funds had gone missing, but there was a much deeper implication. The funds disappeared between December 1999 and March 2000—around the same time that several thousand youths were being enrolled in Laskar Jihad militias. These militias were armed, trained and transported to Maluku where they attacked Christian targets with impunity, despite the presence of some 11 000 security personnel in the province. Suparman was widely presumed to have helped create Islamic militias such as Laskar Jihad, and Western diplomats in Jakarta asserted that the missing Kostrad funds had financed the militia operations in Maluku.[31] By disclosing the finances of Kostrad, Wirahadikusumah was obliquely accusing Suparman—and, by extension, his patron Wiranto—for fomenting the bloodbath in Maluku.

Wirahadikusumah's audit prompted an official investigation by the inspector general of the army. This post was held by Maj. Gen. Djoko Subroto, the same officer who had commanded the East Java Garrison at the time of the unexplained Banyuwangi killings in late 1998. When he announced his findings to the press Subroto flatly stated that no funds had been misused, without addressing the evidence of wrongdoing cited by the independent accounting firm, which was not represented at the press conference. Subroto studiously avoided making any mention of Suparman's name. He conceded only that Kostrad's chief financial officer may have been guilty of poor book-keeping.

Meanwhile, the military's conservative generals were desperate to remove the 49-year-old Wirahadikusumah from the military leadership. Despite having been boxed into a combat role at Kostrad, Wirahadikusumah had demonstrated that he could still prove damaging to the military's entrenched interests. A host of senior conservative generals therefore gathered together on 26 July. The venue for the meeting was the private residence of Gen. (ret.) Wiranto.[32]

Among those in attendance were Lt Gen. Sutarto and Lt Gen. Suparman, along with a host of other Wiranto allies. The group resolved that Wirahadikusumah must be removed from his command. To accomplish this, Wiranto approached Megawati several days later. He reportedly urged the vice-president to prevail upon Wahid to sack Wirahadikusumah; for reasons that remain unclear, Megawati agreed to help. All that remained was to convince Wahid.

It was no coincidence that the initiative to sideline Wirahadikusumah coincided with a period of extreme political vulnerability for President Wahid. The president had few allies left and his public popularity had sunk to an alarmingly low level. His travel, erratic comments and tolerance for high-profile corrupters such as Sinivasan had inflicted severe damage on his reputation. Nonetheless, his predicament was attributable as much to his successes as to his mistakes: he had repeatedly thwarted efforts by Indonesia's party bosses to exploit a corrupt state apparatus. For instance, Akbar Tandjung's Golkar had wanted to appoint their own candidate—the discredited former justice minister, Muladi—to the crucial post of Supreme Court chief justice. Wahid refused. Amien Rais's Central Axis, meanwhile, wanted to consolidate control over state enterprises through Finance Minister Bambang Sudibyo. Again Wahid refused. And perhaps most significantly, Wahid had infuriated the military by sacking Wiranto and promoting Wirahadikusumah. But in addition to being spiteful, Wahid's enemies were also power-hungry.

Wahid's two staunchest critics, Tandjung and Rais, emphasised that their only motivation was to rescue the country from Wahid's ineffectual leadership—but this was rhetoric. Had they been purely pursuing the national interest, they could have taken many more proactive measures to correct or assist Wahid. The IMF had requested bills on energy and tax reform, the Human Rights Commission was pleading for a law on human rights courts, and bills on special autonomy were urgently needed to address secessionism in Aceh and Irian Jaya. Tandjung's parliament delivered none of these.

In fact, parliament produced no significant acts of legislation whatsoever during its first ten months in session—the legislature would not even
permit Wahid to change the name of Irian Jaya to Papua, as requested by
the residents of the province. Instead, parliamentarians focused on
combating the president. Rais and Tandjung had already climbed to
power by bringing down two presidents, and they were now keen to climb
farther by toppling a third.

For his part, Wahid afforded plenty of opportunities to his critics. In
May 2000 evidence emerged that a total of around $6 million had been
misappropriated by the president's handlers, in what became known as the
'Buloggate' and 'Bruneigate' scandals. This seemed to provide the party
bosses with the ammunition they needed to oust Wahid before the end
of his first year in office. The opportunity would arise in the annual MPR
session to be held in August 2000. Although there was no historical
precedent for doing so, it seemed quite possible that the MPR would issue
the equivalent of a no-confidence vote, thereby terminating Wahid's
presidency.

Desperately in need of allies, Wahid turned in late July to the military.
When Megawati delivered Wiranto's demand that Wirahadikusumah be
sacked, Wahid agreed—apparently on the condition that the military back
him in the MPR. The deal was struck. The MPR prevailed upon Wahid to
reshuffle the cabinet and delegate more power to the vice-president, but
it refrained from terminating Wahid's presidency.[33] In the process, the
military exacted a host of concessions.

In the new cabinet the number of co-ordinating ministers was reduced
to two (one each for the economy and for politics) and their powers
were enhanced to provide for clear control over the rest of the cabinet.
Wahid dismayed reformers by giving the economics post to Rizal Ramli,
the consultant who had been working for Texmaco the year before. And
as co-ordinating minister for politics and security, Wahid tapped Lt Gen.
(ret.) Susilo Bambang Yudhoyono, previously the mines and energy
minister. Although known as a progressive in the past, Yudhoyono's
reformist credentials had since weakened.

Meanwhile, Wirahadikusumah was stripped of his Kostrad command
and 'parked' at military headquarters. His two loyal allies, Maj. Gen.
Suarip Kadi and Maj. Gen. Romulo Simbolon, were also sidelined—and all
three were later brought before a 'military honour council' to answer
charges of 'indiscipline'. Wirahadikusumah was clearly being punished for
his exposure of the Kostrad scandal, but the charges used against him
pertained to a different case, whereby he was faulted for having deployed
around 100 Kostrad soldiers to help with an earthquake relief effort,
without first obtaining permission from the armed forces commander.
Wirahadikusumah's replacement as Kostrad commander was Maj. Gen.
Ryamizard Ryacudu, the son-in-law of the former vice-president and

retired four-star general, Try Sutrisno. A former Wiranto associate, Ryacudu promptly buried the pension fund scandal.[34]

The military had therefore exacted valuable concessions from Wahid: Yudhoyono obtained the cabinet's most senior political post and Wirahadikusumah was ousted. But the military also exacted concessions from the MPR. Ignoring appeals to curb the military's political role, the MPR affirmed that the military would be allowed to keep its own appointed faction in parliament through 2004 (and in the MPR itself through 2009). The assembly also passed a regulation forbidding 'retroactivity' in human rights courts—in effect, protecting the military from punishment for human rights violations that occurred before 1999.

Thus, within ten months of being elected, Wahid had squandered his political capital and surrendered hard-won territory to military conservatives. But while he struck a deal to remain in office, he nonetheless persisted in trying to assert his authority over the military. At the same time, episodes of violence increased in both frequency and magnitude.

Late in the afternoon on 1 August the Philippine ambassador was climbing into his car in the driveway of his residence on Jalan Imam Bonjol, just several hundred metres from the US ambassador's residence in the neighbourhood of Menteng. Seconds later a massive explosion destroyed the car, emitting shock waves that broke window panes for hundreds of metres in all directions. A piece of shrapnel shattered one such pane on the tenth floor of a bank building one kilometre away. The ambassador survived the blast but suffered very heavy injuries. Three others died and around twenty people nearby were injured.

At first it seemed possible that the blast was unrelated to Indonesia's political power struggle. But when police failed yet again to make any serious investigation, it strongly appeared that another cover-up was taking place—which in turn suggested that senior military figures were at least condoning the terrorism. The best explanation put forth, therefore, was that the car bomb was related to the religious strife in Maluku.

At the time, clear evidence was emerging of the military's prominent role in fomenting Maluku's Christian–Muslim fighting, which by now had claimed nearly 5000 lives. In early July a BBC cameraman filmed a raging gun battle in the rubble-strewn streets of Ambon. The footage clearly depicted Christian fighters trading fire with Muslim militia members— who were fighting alongside regular army troops. Maluku's police chief acknowledged that certain units were taking sides.[35] While army units from outside Maluku tended to side with Muslims (including Laskar Jihad personnel sent, apparently, with army backing), local police units tended to side with Christians.[36]

According to the Maluku Garrison commander, Brig. Gen. Max Tamaela, soldiers in Maluku were behaving according to 'emotional attachments' to one side or the other.[37] At the time, at least five of the 19 assorted military battalions in Maluku were from the East Java Garrison, commanded by the protégé of Syafrie Syamsoeddin, Maj. Gen. Sudi Silalahi. After a promise by Armed Forces Chief Widodo to withdraw partisan troops, one of Silalahi's battalions was abruptly pulled back to Java.[38]

Later the Human Rights Commission concluded an eleven-month study of the Maluku conflict by concluding that human rights abuses were perpetrated by 'both individuals and the state apparatus, both the police and military'.[39] Furthermore, the reasons for the conflict included 'social jealousy, provocation by outside agents, the non-neutral attitude displayed by the security apparatus and local government, religious sentiment, vendetta, and elite political rifts'. The November 1998 Ketapang riot was also cited as a factor in triggering the conflict.

Evidence of the military's involvement in Maluku, combined with the apparent cover-up of the police investigation, suggested that the attempted assassination of the Philippine ambassador may have been a favour for Islamic militants in the southern Philippines. Alternatively (or additionally) the bombing may have been in retaliation for clandestine support that the Philippine military was allegedly providing to Christians in Maluku. In any event, there was ample reason to believe that the car bomb was not an isolated act by fanatics but an escalation of Indonesia's ruthless and desperate political power struggle. What had begun as a campaign of intimidation and provocateurism had now escalated into carefully targeted terrorist attacks. The next such attack, although far removed from downtown Jakarta, occurred after an interval of just five weeks.

Following East Timor's ballot on independence, the UN High Commission for Refugees (UNHCR) had been delivering humanitarian assistance to more than 100 000 East Timorese refugees occupying squalid camps in neighbouring West Timor. Many of the refugees wanted to return to East Timor but were prevented from doing so by the remnants of pro-integration militias that were wielding influence over the camps. As during the approach to the ballot, the international community had repeatedly pressured Jakarta to rein in the militias, but the military refused and the Wahid administration appeared powerless to act.

On 1 September Attorney General Darusman finally initiated legal proceedings for human rights abuses in East Timor. Exactly six months had passed since the National Human Rights Commission had recommended trials for more than 30 military, militia and civilian figures. Darusman's list of 22 'possible suspects' excluded Wiranto and Zacky Makarim, but it did include Maj. Gen. Adam Damiri, four colonels and six lieutenant colonels.

Within days of Darusman's announcement a group of armed East Timorese men from a pro-integration militia stormed the UNHCR compound in Atambua, West Timor. They murdered three foreign relief workers: an American, a Croatian and an Ethiopian. They dragged the corpses behind vehicles before burning them in the street.[40]

There was no mistaking the Atambua attack for a random act of violence: the killings took place precisely at the time President Wahid was seated in an auditorium at UN headquarters in New York.[41] No less than 154 other world leaders had assembled for the United Nations Millennium Summit. Kofi Annan asked for a minute's silence in memory of the three UN workers killed in Atambua; it was a grave humiliation for Wahid.

Still, the attack did not deter Darusman. On 12 September the attorney general issued formal charges against the first of the nineteen suspects, Col. Herman Sediono. In addition to being an active officer in 1999, Sediono also held the top civil service post (*bupati*) in one of East Timor's thirteen districts, Cova Lima. Sediono was charged for his complicity in the Suai church massacre of September 1999. He told reporters that he had attempted to calm the situation by ordering Brimob police to secure the area; in fact, a combination of army troops, Brimob personnel and militia gangs had attacked the church with automatic weapons and grenades, and witnesses saw Sediono directing the operation. The church was filled with refugees, most of whom were women and children. Estimates of the death toll range from 50 to 200. Afterwards, several female survivors were reportedly taken to the local military headquarters and sexually assaulted.[42]

Meanwhile, as Darusman's staff interrogated Sediono and several other suspects during the second week of September, Darusman was preparing to commence the trial of Soeharto on 14 September. Two days before the trial six dilapidated buses delivered a contingent of pro-Soeharto demonstrators to the street in front of Darusman's office. Carrying placards that read 'Hang Darusman!', the scruffy crowd looked very much like a 'rent-a-mob', or hired protesters.[43] The protest was almost comical, but what followed the next day was anything but that. On 13 September—one day before Soeharto's scheduled court appearance and two days after the start of Darusman's interrogations in the East Timor case—Indonesia witnessed its worst episode of terrorist violence to date.

The Jakarta Stock Exchange Building stands out as Indonesia's most prestigious business address. The stately twin towers contain the heart of the financial market, as well as the highest-priced office space in the city. With tenants such as international investment banks, oil companies and the World Bank, the 34-storey building is the workplace for some of the country's most influential businesspeople. It was therefore a symbolic target to attack. Also symbolic, however, was the fact that the attack inflicted the most harm on some of the poorest-paid people in the building.

Many of the executives and office workers in the JSE Building hired drivers to chauffeur them to and from work; during the day, many of these drivers remained 'on stand-by' deep in the underground carpark. Few took notice when, on the morning of 13 September, an old Japanese sedan parked in a space on level P2.

Unbeknown to anyone in the building, the trunk of the sedan contained a large amount of C-4 plastic explosive. Around 11 a.m. the explosion ripped through the carpark, incinerating those in the immediate vicinity, choking others and knocking some unconscious. In the building's cavernous lobby, shards of tile and cement crashed from the ceiling onto the marble floor. Office workers throughout the building heard the blast and felt the floor buckle. Outside, passing motorists saw thick black smoke billowing from ventilation ducts.

In total, the blast killed fifteen and injured at least 46.[44] But in addition to killing and maiming, the bomb also struck fear into the heart of the business community. Most importantly, the JSE bombing made a mockery of President Wahid's attempts to portray Indonesia as being stable and secure.

Suspicions immediately focused on supporters of Soeharto, who was due to appear in court the next day. The newly appointed, pro-military defence minister, Mohammad Mahfud, recommended that the government simply drop the case against the former president—otherwise 'we will continue to be harassed . . . more terror will keep coming'.[45] Concurring with Mahfud, Marzuki Darusman told reporters that the bombing bore the hallmarks of rogue military elements and Soeharto supporters.[46] President Wahid agreed.

Following prayers on Friday afternoon, two days after the JSE bombing, Wahid addressed reporters. In the previous day's cabinet meeting, he explained, he had ordered the arrest of Tommy Soeharto and a member of the Islamic Defence Front (FPI), Habib Alwi al Baaqil. The purpose, he said, was to prevent another act of terror: 'We don't want another explosion like the one in the JSE Building, because the victims were ordinary citizens.'[47] The same day a police spokesman stated that Tommy would be arrested 'today or tomorrow'.[48]

Tommy did, in fact, appear at police headquarters the next day—but not because of any action taken by the police. 'I have come here on my own initiative,' he declared while smiling in front of television cameras, 'rather than being chased here by the police.'[49] He was accompanied by a bodyguard, but no lawyer. After a brief interview he was allowed to return home. Two days later, Wahid sacked the national chief of police, Rusdihardjo, for his failure to detain Tommy. Wahid promoted Gen. Suroyo Bimantoro to the post—but it was a move that the president would later regret.

Bimantoro marked his first full day as police chief with the announcement that the police had suddenly caught 25 suspects in the JSE bombing. According to a deputy police spokesperson, all were 'armed civilians from Aceh'.⁵⁰ Many immediately suspected yet another whitewash. Various police officials produced contradictory explanations of the arrests, and it was later revealed that two of the suspects were not Acehnese civilians but active military personnel (from Kostrad and the Special Forces).

Lawyers from the Legal Aid Foundation represented some of the Acehnese suspects, and they claimed that their clients had been forced to sign confessions under severe duress.⁵¹ In any event, even if some of the Acehnese suspects were accomplices in the bombing, police officials admitted that these were merely the 'perpetrators' and that the mastermind remained at large. Nonetheless, the case against the Acehnese suspects seemed to deflect attention away from Tommy Soeharto; Wahid therefore pursued another approach.

The Goro land scandal—the case that Tommy had won twice in lower courts—was suddenly revived. Marzuki Darusman appealed the lower court rulings to the Supreme Court. Within days the justices handed down a shocking verdict: Tommy was guilty. On 27 September Soeharto's youngest son was sentenced to eighteen months in prison. Wahid clearly wanted to jail Tommy as a result of the JSE and other bombings, and he was using the relatively petty Goro case as a means to an end. It may have been a somewhat unseemly way to proceed, but few objected. The public eagerly waited for Tommy's arrest.

At Jakarta's Cipinang Prison, a special cell had been made ready for Soeharto's son. The prison warden promised to protect Tommy from the other prisoners and ensure that his basic needs were met. 'But alas,' he joked, alluding to Tommy's fame as a rally driver, 'we can't provide him a race track to practise on.'⁵² But while the courts had sentenced Tommy and the prison was prepared to receive him, Gen. Bimantoro refrained from taking him into custody. For each day they delayed, police officials cited a growing litany of technical and procedural constraints that prevented them from seizing Tommy. Meanwhile, Soeharto himself appeared in a South Jakarta court; the former president was formally acquitted of corruption charges, on the grounds of his poor health.

The miscarriage of justice in the two Soeharto cases became an international embarrassment. Moreover, no one was being held accountable for the grisly attack on the UN compound in West Timor. Richard Holbrooke, the US ambassador to the UN, cut to the point: 'We must face facts: elements within the Indonesian military are directly or indirectly responsible for these outrages.'⁵³

Meanwhile, Tommy's lawyers stalled the police by requesting a pardon from the president. Tommy should have been taken into custody while waiting for the pardon, but he wasn't. By the end of September Wahid, who was travelling in South America, was clearly agitated. He declared that every judge involved in the ruling on Soeharto should be replaced by 'clean and honest judges who cannot be bought'.[54]

Next Wahid issued a message to the boisterous students who had been staging daily demonstrations near Soeharto's residence, which was heavily defended by troops and police. The students, he said, should take out their anger by marching directly on Soeharto's home on Jalan Cendana.[55] The advice only highlighted the president's impotence. In Jakarta, however, the comment encouraged the student protesters. In a clash with troops near Jalan Cendana on 28 September, one student died and more than a dozen others were wounded. Unmoved, Wahid repeated his comment the next day while in Buenos Aires. He also called on the security forces to cease defending Soeharto, but the plea was ignored.

Upon returning to Indonesia Wahid made a puzzling move. On the evening of 5 October he visited the Borobudur Hotel and met personally with Tommy.[56] A presidential spokesman later confirmed that Tommy had offered a cash payment in exchange for a pardon but that the offer was rejected. But the mere fact that the president had deigned to meet Tommy caused a grave embarrassment for Wahid. Nonetheless, he agreed to another such meeting on 31 October, at the Regent Hotel.[57] Apparently, no agreement was reached.

Three days later police finally arrived at Tommy's Menteng residence, but they found him not at home. He had apparently been tipped off; reporters who were camped outside his front gate had seen his entourage drive off several hours before the police arrived. Soeharto's youngest son had become a fugitive.

Tommy's whereabouts became Jakarta's hottest topic of gossip. Bimantoro claimed that the police were conducting a nationwide manhunt, combing Tommy's favourite racetracks and luxury resorts. Some said he was hiding in Bali, while others maintained that he was in Hong Kong or China. Wahid himself suggested that Tommy was being sheltered in Jakarta by two retired generals who had been close to the Soeharto family: Hartono and Prabowo Subianto.

Some of Wahid's advisors urged him to sack Bimantoro and appoint yet another police chief, but a majority in parliament seemed to be defending Bimantoro's actions. When the MPR had convened the previous August, it had resolved that the president should seek parliament's approval before appointing new chiefs for the police or military. Parliament had not passed the resolution into law, but if Wahid sacked Bimantoro he would clearly anger his rival party bosses. At the time, the president was already under pressure to testify before a special parliamentary commission (Pansus) regarding the Bulog scandal. Tommy Soeharto therefore remained free.

The escape of Tommy Soeharto demonstrated that Wahid's authority as president was severely limited. He had no control over the police force, and in late October he lost control over the military. Gen. Endriartono Sutarto, Soeharto's former Paspampres commander, became army chief-of-staff—against Wahid's wishes. With a weak navy admiral serving as armed forces chief, and with Wahid having dissolved the post of deputy armed forces chief, Sutarto effectively emerged as the military's single most powerful commander. The move ensured that military reformers would make no further headway.

By late 2000, therefore, Indonesia had entered a period of 'non-governance': the president lacked influence with the corrupt judiciary, he received incessant attacks from the party bosses in parliament and he no longer wielded authority over the police. On the occasions when the president and attorney general did try to prosecute corruption or human rights abuses, their efforts were met with terrorism—which the military never prevented or punished. In effect, the military was carefully cir-cumscribing the authority of the civilian politicians, who were already hampered by their own ineptitude and bickering. Meanwhile, the muddled policies of Jakarta were increasingly ignored by provincial and *kabupaten*-level governments. Indonesia's three-year-old power struggle had produced a devastating free-for-all.

The mood in Jakarta was distinctly downbeat. Most agreed that political and economic conditions would continue to deteriorate. Just as pre-crisis Indonesia had been marked by a collective sense of euphoria, post-crisis Indonesia was consumed by pervasive gloom. In fact, the political turmoil would only intensify in the months ahead.

23

STATE OF EMERGENCY

hile the political elite fought among themselves, the lack of
effective governance exacted a high toll on the economy. Earlier
in the year, Wahid's election and the imposition of monetary
stability had boosted confidence and allowed interest rates to drop. This
sparked a rally in consumer spending—but by year-end the confidence
had evaporated. Following the bombings and the farcical situation with
Tommy Soeharto, investments were shelved and asset restructuring
ground to a halt.

Most investors had long been aware that they lacked legal recourse in
Indonesia; in the latter half of 2000, however, it had become patently clear
that the country was a truly risky place to do business. Throughout the
country, a host of foreign and joint-venture investors found themselves
coming under deliberate attack. In some cases, such as Standard
Chartered's attempted acquisition of Bank Bali, foreigners who tried to
purchase assets from Ibra came under ruthless attack from the management of the target company. In cases where foreign investors had forged
agreements with state-owned enterprises—such as Mexico's Cemex and
Semen Gresik, or Ariawest and Telkom—parochial interests scuttled the
deals. And throughout the archipelago, a host of foreign companies that
mined gold or coal were specifically targeted for attack.

It was widely believed that military elements hoped to commandeer
the lucrative but relatively 'low-tech' mining operations; they therefore
harassed the mining companies by fomenting strikes, imposing new taxes
and sponsoring illegal mining on private concession areas.[1] In the past,
foreign CEOs might have taken their complaints to officials in Jakarta (or
perhaps to Soeharto himself), who would then instruct the security forces
to impose order. But in the era of non-governance that alternative no
longer existed. These concerns had been plaguing mining concerns in the
Outer Islands for over a year, but in late 2000 an extraordinary and high-
profile case occurred in the heart of Indonesia's financial sector.

Jiwa Asuransi Manulife Indonesia (MI) ranks among Indonesia's leading providers of life insurance. The firm was founded in 1985 as a joint-venture between Canada's Manulife Financial and the Dharmala Group. Manulife Financial was the majority owner, while Dharmala Sakti Sejahtera (DSS), a financial services holding company, owned 40 per cent. The remaining 9 per cent was held by the IFC, the private investment arm of the World Bank.

In addition to being the joint-venture partner of DSS, Manulife Financial was also one of its creditors. DSS had already defaulted on a derivatives contract with Bankers Trust in 1995, and in 1998 the crisis rendered DSS insolvent. In fact, the Gondokusumo family, which owned both the Dharmala and Putra Surya Perkasa groups, was mired in debt. Together the two groups constituted Ibra's third largest debtor—and, in terms of reaching restructuring agreements, its most unco-operative.[2]

By 1999 MI was receiving substantial negative publicity as a result of Dharmala's insolvency. For these and other reasons Manulife Financial wanted to increase its shareholding in MI. Manulife therefore joined other creditors, including Ibra, in suing DSS for bankruptcy. After a prolonged case they finally won in the Supreme Court in June 2000—this was the first instance in which any foreign creditors had won a significant bankruptcy suit in Indonesia.

Following the bankruptcy, the court appointed curators to control the assets of DSS, including the company's share certificates for its 40 per cent stake in MI. In October the State Auction House held an open auction for the shares, which Manulife purchased for Rp170bn. The auction proceeds were to be distributed to 23 foreign and domestic creditors, of which Ibra was by far the largest.

For a moment, the Manulife case sent an important signal to all creditors, both foreign and domestic: in a multi million dollar legal battle, it was indeed possible to obtain legal recourse in Indonesia's notorious court system. But just when it seemed that the spirit of *reformasi* was finally affecting the judiciary, the tables turned. Within days the Manulife case changed from a success story to a harrowing example of what could go wrong for investors in Indonesia.

Two days prior to the auction, Manulife had received a protest from Roman Gold Assets International, a company registered in the British Virgin Islands. During one of the court proceedings, Roman Gold's lawyers suddenly appeared waving a share certificate. Manulife had no right to purchase the 40 per cent stake in MI, they told the judge, because Roman Gold had purchased the same shares from a Samoa-based concern just one week before the auction.

Initially, Manulife executives were amused. Their case was ironclad: no such share transaction had been registered, as required by law, with MI. And even if such a transaction had occurred it would have been illegal on

several counts: no shares could change hands during bankruptcy proceedings, nor could a transaction take place without notifying the insurance
regulators, the capital markets supervisory agency and the tax department.
None of these notifications had been made. Moreover, DSS had been
collecting dividend payments throughout the entire time in which others,
it claimed, controlled the shares.

The first court that heard Roman Gold's claim rejected it immediately.
But a few days later, on the same day as the state-supervised auction, the
police launched a criminal investigation—not against Roman Gold, but
against Manulife. In effect, the police were vigorously following up an
obviously spurious complaint made by a previously unknown foreign
entity, Roman Gold. Manulife complained that the Gondokusumo family
was using Roman Gold—and now, apparently, the national police—to
block the sale of the 40 per cent stake in MI.

The Canadian embassy wrote to the national police chief, Gen. Bimantoro, stating that Manulife was being subjected to harassment. The letter
was ignored, because the following day police detained Manulife's senior
vice-president, Adi Purnomo Wijaya. Because Purnomo's signature was on
the auctioned share certificate (which Roman Gold was denouncing as
fake), the police accused Purnomo of forgery. Around the same time, the
wife of MI's president director was mugged by a machete-wielding thief.
The arrest and attack sent a chilling message to prospective investors:
purchase the assets of a legally liquidated company in a state-supervised
auction, and face incarceration by the police, or worse.

Only after Canada's prime minister, Jean Chretien, wrote to President
Wahid was Purnomo finally released from custody—after having spent
three weeks in jail. However, police had also detained the court-appointed
curator, Ari Effendi, who had simply been following standard procedures
in the transaction. Police repeatedly pressured him to sign over control of
the account that held Manulife's Rp170 billion payment to the state
auction house, but he refused. At one point he was held for four days in
solitary confinement, without adequate food, water or sanitation.

Meanwhile, Dharmala succeeded in replacing Effendi with their own
curator, even though the Bankruptcy Law clearly states that curators must
be approved by creditors, not by debtors. Dharmala used the stratagem
to prevent further asset disposals. Creditors protested, but both the
bankruptcy court and the Supreme Court upheld the appointment. These
judgments prompted Rizal Ramli, the co-ordinating minister of the
economy, to publicly call on judges to be 'more responsible' in their
decision-making. As for Effendi, his family lobbied police officials and,
after 35 days, finally obtained his release. Manulife, however, remained
under investigation.

An investigative report from the police headquarters' own legal team
concluded that the guilty party was clearly Dharmala, not Manulife—but

still Bimantoro refused to halt the investigation. The police chief remained impervious to pleas from Chretien and high-level officials from the IFC, the World Bank and the IMF. The capital markets supervisory agency sided with Manulife, while the minister of finance declared that the Gondokusumos should be charged as criminals. Ibra described the Dharmala owners, who were hiding in Singapore, as 'fugitives'.

Meanwhile, in December 2000 the IFC and several other creditors were pursuing a bankruptcy suit against an insolvent finance company, Panin Overseas Finance. Just when it appeared that Panin was destined to lose the case, a consortium of fourteen lenders—domiciled in places such as the Bahamas and Western Samoa—suddenly cropped up. They claimed to have lent Panin $170 million, even though Panin had already defaulted on other creditors before receiving the purported loan. The IFC protested that the consortium was fictitious and was working on behalf of Panin, but the bankruptcy court recognised the consortium nonetheless.

Because the consortium (supposedly) represented the majority of Panin's total debt, it assumed control of the creditors' meetings. It also promptly accepted Panin's proposal to pay creditors a mere ten cents in the dollar. The IFC protested again, but both the bankruptcy court and the Supreme Court upheld Panin's settlement.

The IFC and the foreign press took note that several of Panin's fourteen mysterious creditors were the same companies that claimed to have traded Dharmala's 40 per cent stake in MI. In fact, Panin had used the same lawyer, Lucas, that had worked for Dharmala. Lucas simply used the same offshore shell companies in his legal subterfuge. In both cases the investment arm of the World Bank—Indonesia's largest multi-lateral donor—was among the creditors that were defrauded.

In the meantime, by December the MI case had reached an impasse. The police refused to drop the case against Manulife, but Dharmala and Lucas proved unable to recover the auctioned MI shares. Lucas therefore tried to apply pressure on MI by suing it for bankruptcy.

Indonesia's bankruptcy law states that a company with unpaid debts to two or more creditors is liable for bankruptcy. Lucas based his suit on a disputed rent payment to a Dharmala affiliate (MI's landlord), but for the second creditor he tried to use one of MI's life insurance policy-holders. He argued that an unpaid insurance claim constituted an overdue debt to a creditor. This was a specious argument—and in any case the claim was unpaid because the policy-holder had been proven guilty of insurance fraud (he had concealed a life-threatening illness prior to buying insurance). Nonetheless, the bankruptcy court appeared ready to rule in Lucas's favour.

Rather than risk being declared bankrupt, MI thwarted the suit by paying out the disputed insurance policy, which was worth $680 000. Before doing so, however, MI arranged for forensic auditors to trace the funds; the audit revealed that the money flowed not to the policy-holder's family but to Roman Gold. When this was reported by a Jakarta-based political journal, Lucas threatened a defamation suit.

The Manulife episode demonstrated what could potentially happen to investors operating in an environment of non-governance. The company was an unlikely victim: unlike less scrupulous foreign investors who had exploited New Order corruption to obtain lucrative concessions or large government contracts, Manulife had been a responsible corporate citizen. Having spent fifteen years in Indonesia, Manulife employed 3000 Indonesians and served 400 000 customers. Its only 'transgression' was to pursue its legal rights as a creditor by participating in a bankruptcy suit. Nonetheless, the company fell prey to some of the very agencies charged with upholding the law and facilitating investment. In effect, legal-system actors were now functioning as renegades.[3] Freed from working for Soeharto, they could now work exclusively for the country's richest individuals—such as its largest recalcitrant debtors.

Before mid-2000, legal-system renegades were cast by the government as 'rogue elements' in what were otherwise sound and responsible institutions, such as the judiciary, the police or the military. By year-end, however, such claims were no longer credible. The authorities had made no progress on prosecuting, or even explaining, the three terrorist bomb attacks or the raid on the UN compound in West Timor. Islamic militias from Java continued to wreak havoc in Maluku, despite the heavy presence of government troops. Tommy Soeharto remained at large and no East Timor trials had begun. Bimantoro continued to pressure Manulife. These cases all strongly suggested that Indonesia's legal-system renegades were not rogue elements—the rule-of-law was being subverted, explicitly and implicitly, by the mainstream leadership of the security forces. And, as demonstrated by a shocking occurrence on Christmas Eve, the tactics were growing increasingly savage.

In mid-December Marzuki Darusman finally set a trial date for Aitarak militia leader Eurico Guterres: 2 January 2001. Guterres was easily the most recognised militia leader in East Timor: having served as a military accomplice since the early 1990s, he was among the military's most valuable allies in 1999.[4] But a week before Guterres's trial, on Christmas Eve, bombs exploded at Christian targets in ten cities throughout the country.[5]

A total of 62 bombs were planted in 38 locations, including churches, priests' homes, cemeteries and one private residence. This was Indonesia's largest and most sophisticated terrorist bombing to date. Some bombs were duds and others were diffused, but 24 exploded. In total, the Christmas Eve explosions killed 19 people and seriously injured 120. The nation was in shock, and the East Timor trials were indefinitely postponed.

The perpetrators of the Christmas Eve bombings were never prosecuted, although several suspects were apprehended and a host of clues were available. In Medan, local police detected a bomb several hours before it was set to explode; they warned other churches in the area and nine bombs were defused. In Ciamis, West Java, a bomb exploded while two perpetrators were carrying it towards their destination; one was killed and the other escaped. But the best lead was in Bandung, where a bomb exploded while it was being assembled in a workshop, killing three and injuring two. One of the dead men was carrying an address book—in which he had written the phone number of the Jakarta residence of an active two-star general.[6]

As usual, there were signs of a cover-up. Military police on the island of Batam, where three bombs injured 29 people, apprehended two perpetrators: a member of the Special Forces and a soldier from southern Sumatera's Sriwijaya Garrison.[7] In Jakarta, Franciscan monks identified a mysterious boarder as an intelligence agent; he was implicated in the bombing of the Jakarta Cathedral and arrested by police, but was promptly released.[8]

Meanwhile, journalists from Indonesia's leading news magazine, *Tempo*, conducted their own investigation in Medan. Perhaps because the city's police seemed to be sharply at odds with the military, a number of leads were uncovered, including telephone records. Working from police data, *Tempo* mapped the frequency of telephone calls among a small group.[9] These included three men caught red-handed with bomb-making equipment; two double-agents suspected of working for both the Free Aceh Movement (Gam) and Bais; an ethnic-Chinese financier whom military officials in Medan acknowledged as one of their business partners; and a Special Forces lieutenant colonel who was the intelligence chief for northern Sumatera's Bukit Barisan Garrison. The map strongly suggested that intelligence officials were connected, through their financiers and Gam double-agents, with the suspected bombers. Moreover, the suspected bombers themselves had longstanding ties to the Special Forces.

The minister of defence, Mohammad Mahfud, expressed his certainty that 'the bombing episode . . . had strongmen from the inner circle of the previous New Order regime that were backing it'.[10] He explained:

> We can easily perceive their motive: they don't want to be prosecuted along with former President Soeharto, therefore they use their money to mobilise followers. They divert the attention of the public and the government away from the legal charges levelled against them.[11]

Similarly, the Forum for a Peaceful Indonesia—a group recently formed by respected civic leaders such as Nurcholish Madjid, Emil Salim and Mar'ie Muhammad—carried out an independent investigation. The group concluded that the church bombings were not religiously motivated but rather were political acts designed to destabilise the government and the country.[12] The group said that the involvement of active or retired military personnel could not be ruled out, but the informal investigation produced no hard evidence.

Military conservatives responded; but as they had done in the past, they responded through their Islamist allies in parliament. Abdul Qaedir Djaelani, a member of Yusril Ihza Mahendra's PBB faction, publicly alleged that the masterminds of the bombing were Lt Gen. Agus Wira-hadikusumah and Maj. Gen. Suarip Kadi—the military's two leading reformers.[13] Kadi had actually been sidelined precisely because he had published an insightful and courageous book that inventoried the acts of provocation that had taken place in Indonesia since 1996.[14] Djaelani's allegation suggested that military conservatives were attempting to steer blame towards their enemies—but the tactic failed because Djaelani was not believed.

Finally, Marzuki Darusman aired his frustrations: the main obstacle to investigating human rights abuses and bombings, he declared on 7 January, was the military. Army Chief-of-Staff Sutarto, the military's most influential figure, lambasted Darusman for saying so. 'How could the military be declared an obstacle?' asked Sutarto. 'If I am an obstacle, just report it to the president!'[15] Apparently, Darusman did so.

The day after the bombing, the president had declared that the perpetrators were political actors who were trying to destabilise his administration and oust him from power. By late January Wahid had lost patience. He tried to fire Sutarto, but failed.[16] Apparently the army chief-of-staff refused to step down, and Wahid received no support for the measure from the military leadership or other party bosses. The Christmas Eve bombings simply went unexplained and unpunished, as the president's opponents—including the military—closed ranks against him. Wahid's presidency was imperilled and the hot topic of political debate was when, not whether, he would be ousted from power.

By early 2001 President Wahid faced a diverse array of opponents. The military was annoyed by his attempted command reshuffles, his support for human rights investigations and his refusal to back a hardline military approach in Aceh and Irian Jaya. The Central Axis was apparently annoyed that Wahid had not promoted Islam more forcefully in return for having been elected by Islamic parties. Golkar lamented its small allocation of cabinet posts, and was yearning to regain power. Finally, many PDI Perjuangan legislators wanted Megawati in the presidency, at almost any cost. Even Indonesia's donors and foreign allies were turning against Wahid, exasperated by economic mismanagement, judicial dysfunction and the awarding of 'sweetheart' debt rescheduling deals to tycoons such as Sinivasan. Meanwhile, Wahid's own performance as president did little to help his cause.

Wahid was not guilty of multi-billion corruption as in the Soeharto era, nor even of scandals such as the Bank Bali affair during the Habibie administration. Wahid was, however, implicated in the Bruneigate and Buloggate scandals—and this was sufficient to make him politically vulnerable. The Bulog affair was particularly unseemly: Sapuan, the deputy director of the corruption-riddled logistics agency, had agreed in January 2000 to disburse Rp35 billion from Bulog's pension fund to Soewondo, the president's personal masseur. Sapuan apparently believed that Soewondo had sufficient influence to secure his appointment as head of Bulog.

Within days, however, a little-known group named Government Watch produced evidence that cheques had been cashed against an account belonging to the Bulog pension fund. A Rp5 billion cheque was traced to an official of a startup airline based in Surabaya: AW International. Although the airline's initials officially stood for 'Air Wagon', they were also widely recognised as meaning 'Abdurrahman Wahid', as the NU leader had been made a part-owner in the firm in 1999. Another Rp10 billion cheque from the pension fund was cashed by Soewondo's wife. Yet another Rp5 billion was cashed by a woman named Siti Farika.[17]

Police arrested Sapuan in May 2000, and the deputy Bulog chair claimed that Soewondo had asked for the funds in order to make informal contributions to humanitarian relief in the troubled province of Aceh. Unwittingly, President Wahid declared five days later that the money spent in Aceh had not originated from Bulog but from a $2 million donation made by the Sultan of Brunei. Thus started Bruneigate. Wahid's opponents denounced the president's decision to accept an undeclared cash gift from a foreign head of state. Wahid clarified his remarks and claimed that he was merely facilitating a contribution made by the Sultan to relief agents that Wahid was able to recommend.

Meanwhile, Soewondo's wife and Siti Farika returned the cash they had received.[18] By this time the annual August MPR session was approaching, and speculation mounted that Wahid might be subjected to a no-confidence vote. Instead, the party bosses apparently determined that such a course of action would have been of dubious constitutionality. It also seems that the party bosses were stymied by an inability to agree among themselves on a post-Wahid power-sharing accord. But immediately after the MPR session, parliament resolved to form a special investigative subcommittee, or 'Pansus', to formally investigate Buloggate and Bruneigate.

Initially, Wahid admitted to knowing Soewondo, who had previously worked for President Soeharto. 'I know he's one of Soeharto's people,' said Wahid. 'He provides quite a lot of information about that world over there [at Jalan Cendana].'[19] Wahid denied, however, that he had received a bribe from Sapuan (who never obtained the Bulog post). Wahid was summoned to testify before the Pansus in November, but he declined to attend because he was travelling. The Pansus then summoned Gen. Rusdihardjo.

The former police chief testified that Wahid had personally handed the Rp5 billion cheque to Siti Farika.[20] The press had already aired accusations that the president had been involved in at least one extra-marital affair, and now questions were raised regarding his relationship with Siti Farika.[21]

The following month the president denounced the Pansus as illegal. Nonetheless, in late January 2001 he agreed to meet commission members at a neutral site: the Jakarta Convention Centre. But after only a few minutes of receiving barbed questions from the chair of the Pansus, PPP legislator Bachtiar Chamsyah, Wahid simply stormed out of the meeting. Indonesia was clearly entering into yet another political crisis.

A series of tense meetings between Wahid and the rival party bosses ensued. The public soon gleaned that Wahid was proposing an accelerated election schedule: rather than waiting until 2004, he suggested that elections for parliament and the presidency be held right away, using direct voting.

Depending on the rules used, this might have produced a parliament with greater accountability and integrity. Indonesian Corruption Watch estimated that over half of Akbar Tandjung's parliament comprised Soeharto-era officials; if these parliamentarians were elected directly by their constituents, such entrenched, tainted Jakarta officials would have difficulty competing for seats on the local level. And whoever was elected would be required to work in the interest of local constituents rather than for the party bosses—otherwise they would be voted out of office in subsequent elections. Direct elections could therefore weaken the party bosses while imposing a check on abuses of power.

Wahid, however, articulated his election proposal poorly and the idea garnered scant attention. In any event, the acceleration of elections would have required the approval of the MPR, but the party bosses vehemently opposed any electoral measure that would undercut their own influence. This included Megawati: in a decision that dealt a heavy blow to the prospects for democratic accountability, the PDI Perjuangan leader insisted that Indonesia must continue using a proportional voting system. Political parties were not 'ready', she said, for direct elections, and she claimed that a change in the electoral system would lead to national disintegration.[22]

In any case, electoral reform would not have been a panacea for Indonesia's crisis at this late stage. Direct elections might have remedied certain problems—such as an ineffective president, a weak presidency and an unaccountable parliament—but the problem of the military would still have loomed large. Regardless of whether or how the civilians resolved their infighting, governmental authority would have remained carefully circumscribed by the military. Wahid therefore faced a threefold predicament: his own administration was ineffective; the other party bosses had turned vehemently against him, for various reasons of their own; and as the civilians continued to bicker, the military's influence mounted. Gen. Sutarto was emulating the conservatism and political activism of Wiranto—and this did not bode well for Wahid.

While the party bosses conducted successive rounds of backroom deal-making, Sutarto moved to consolidate his control over the military. The previous August, the military had already benefited from a change in defence ministers, from the outspoken Juwono Sudarsono to the relatively unknown Mohammad Mahfud. Although sometimes outspoken, Mahfud was generally sympathetic to the military leadership. Next, in a small-scale command reshuffle in January 2001, Sutarto promoted a number of Wiranto-era conservatives.

Maj. Gen. Sudrajat, the former spokesman whom Wahid had sacked only a year before, was rehabilitated and given an influential intelligence post in the ministry of defence (director-general for strategic defence).[23] Maj. Gen. Bibit Waluyo, the Central Java Garrison commander who possessed strong ties to Cendana, obtained command of the Jakarta Garrison, replacing a sidelined Wahid loyalist.[24] And Brig. Gen. Mahidin Simbolon, the chief-of-staff of the Udayana Garrison during the East Timor crisis and a protégé of Zacky Makarim, obtained promotion to the coveted two-star command of Irian Jaya's Trikora Garrison. The appointments clearly signalled that Sutarto was moving the military in a conservative direction. Next, he demonstrated that he had no intention of abstaining from political affairs.

The military faction in parliament faced a historic decision on 1 February. The Pansus that investigated Wahid had finally concluded that the president had 'played a role' in the illegal disbursement and use of funds from Bulog.[25] The committee had also faulted him for inconsistency in explaining the Brunei donation. Parliament therefore convened to vote on whether to send the president a 'memorandum'—that is, to formally censure him for the two scandals. The Constitution stipulated that parliament must issue two such censures before convening a special MPR session and holding a no-confidence vote. The entire process would require at least six months, such that the president might be voted out of office on 1 August. While pro-Wahid demonstrators clashed with troops outside, parliament voted overwhelmingly to issue the first memorandum. Eschewing its pledge of political neutrality, the military voted in favour of the motion.

The parliament was adamantly anti-Wahid but the public seemed considerably more ambivalent. The newspaper *Kompas* polled urban residents at the end of January, and only 41 per cent of respondents believed that Wahid was guilty of wrongdoing in the two scandals.[26] At this stage Wahid still might have thwarted the party bosses by appealing directly to the people. In particular, Wahid could have branded his enemies as Soeharto-era remnants—a charge that would not have strayed far from the truth. Akbar Tandjung was a New Order minister, while the heads of most party factions had strong political or business links to Soeharto's regime. Arifin Panigoro, for example, was accused of bene-fiting from crony contracts as the owner of Medco, Indonesia's largest private oil concern; he now headed the parliamentary faction of PDI Perjuangan.

Wahid could have argued that the party bosses simply wanted to topple him in order to acquire more power for themselves. After all, parliament had implemented few constructive measures to improve the government's performance—instead, it had been focused primarily on combating the president. By assuming the moral high ground and turning public opinion in his favour, Wahid might have protected himself. On an issue of such importance the party bosses would have had to pay heed to public sentiment. But instead of generating popular support Wahid continued to grapple with the elite—a contest in which he was sorely outmatched.

Wahid pursued a haphazard approach to salvaging his presidency: in the escalating battle with the party bosses he alternated offers of power-sharing with threats of punishment. One of his first assertive actions in response to the memorandum was to deal with his minister of law, Yusril Ihza Mahendra. Having irked the president by backing Golkar's two candi-dates for chief justice of the Supreme Court, Mahendra finally over-stepped the bounds during the first week of February. On two separate occasions Mahendra publicly advised Wahid to resign from office. He was sacked days later. Wahid then proceeded to launch an array of high-level corruption investigations—targeting, of course, his politial enemies.

Anti-corruption efforts had sunk to a low by this time. For example, a court had recently reversed the verdict on Pande Lubis, the former deputy Ibra director who had colluded with Arnold Baramuli in the Bank Bali scandal. Lubis, the only perpetrator sentenced to jail, suddenly walked out of prison—well before his four-year sentence expired. Meanwhile, parlia-ment had finally passed a long-awaited law on human rights courts—but the legislation was too weak to enable prosecutors to try past abuses, such as those in East Timor.[27] And in February the Supreme Court not only freed Soeharto from house arrest (citing his ill health) but also ordered the attorney general's office to pay for the former president's team of 40 doctors.[28] But perhaps the most egregious miscarriage of justice concerned the trial of Soeharto's premier crony and the country's foremost timber baron, Bob Hasan.

On 2 February the Jakarta District Court finally tried Bob Hasan on two charges of fraud. He was found guilty on only one charge and received a sentence of a mere two years—which could be served in house arrest. Because he had already been detained for nine months, this meant that Hasan would only be required to spend another fifteen months in comfortable lodgings. But just when the press was beginning to lament the ruling, an unexpected reversal occurred.

Hasan's sentencing took place in the same week that Wahid finally sacked Yusril Mahendra from the influential ministry of law. In place of the former Soeharto speechwriter, Wahid appointed the highly respected Baharuddin Lopa. A member of PPP, Lopa represented the best of Indonesia's Islamic political tradition: like Nurcholish Madjid, he viewed Islam not as end to be pursued through politics but as a source of inspiration for ideals of justice and decency.

On his first day in office Lopa required all members of his ministry to solemnly forswear bribe-taking. Next he sacked the head of the Jakarta High Court and reshuffled about a dozen other judges, as a first step towards shaking up the judiciary. Then Lopa turned his attention to Bob Hasan—something that the tycoon's high-paid lawyers had not anticipated. Thanks to Lopa, Hasan was moved from house arrest to the 'Alcatraz' of Indonesia: Pulau Nusakambangan.[29]

Originally built by the Dutch, Nusakambangan was a maximum-security island penitentiary off the south coast of Central Java. Thousands had died there after Soeharto's takeover in the 1960s.[30] When Hasan arrived at Nusakambangan, he saw a sign hanging above the front entrance. A relic of the New Order, it carried a ditty that all inmates were required to memorise and repeat:

Yesterday I broke the law,
Today I'm learning so that
Tomorrow I can join in with development.[31]

Ironically, one of Nusakambangan's spartan cells now held Soeharto's premier crony. Meanwhile, another court verdict extended Hasan's sentence to six years. The 70-year-old timber baron accepted the verdict with equanimity: he apparently expected to be released once Wahid and Lopa were removed from office. For the public, however, Hasan's treatment suddenly raised expectations that more Soeharto-era corrupters would finally be held accountable.

In late February Wahid issued an ultimatum to Attorney General Marzuki Darusman: prosecute ten high-level corrupters within one month or be dismissed. In the meantime, parliamentarians from the president's party, PKB, prepared a class-action suit against Akbar Tandjung and the chair of the Pansus, Bachtiar Chamsyah.[32] Darusman was expected to target several Soeharto relatives, as well as first-family cronies such as timber baron Prajogo Pangestu and BDNI owner Syamsul Nursalim. Iron- ically, the president had intervened in past cabinet meetings to protect Pangestu and Nursalim, citing their importance to the national economy.[33] Darusman's first target, though, was his own Golkar colleague, deputy MPR Speaker Ginandjar Kartasasmita—a longstanding adversary of Abdurrahman Wahid.

Prosecutors charged the former co-ordinating minister with corrup- tion in a relatively trivial case dating from the early 1990s, when a small oil concession had been awarded to PT Ustraindo Petro Gas. The contract allegedly caused $25 million in losses to the state, through the state-owned oil monopoly Pertamina. As minister of mines and energy at the time, Ginandjar sat on Pertamina's board of commissioners. In late March, while waiting to be interrogated in the attorney general's office, Ginandjar suddenly discovered that the authorities were planning his arrest. He hastily left the attorney general's compound—despite efforts by the security guards to prevent him from leaving—and sought refuge in the Pertamina Hospital. He was too ill, he claimed, to fulfil the summons issued by state prosecutors. Darusman's staff finally secured Ginandjar's arrest two weeks later, but the Golkar official would not remain in custody for long.

Ginandjar's lawyer pointed out that at the time the alleged scandal took place his client was an active two-star air force marshal; he therefore argued that this was a matter not for the state court system but rather for the military courts. Prosecutors countered that the case was not related to military issues and that at the time Ginandjar had been serving in a civilian ministerial post. Moreover, Ginandjar was no longer active and therefore could now be tried as a civilian. Nonetheless, the judge referred the matter to Armed Forces Chief Widodo, who promptly ordered Ginandjar's release.

Darusman was immediately questioned for his decision to pursue the obscure Ustraindo case. Ginandjar was allegedly involved in a host of other scandals after his air force retirement, including the construction markup of the Balongan refinery project—a $2.5 billion project that should have cost around $1 billion.[34] Suspicions therefore arose that Darusman chose to prosecute the Ustraindo case precisely because he knew it would fail.

President Wahid, frustrated by the lack of convictions for corrupters and human rights abusers, unveiled a novel proposal in March: in order to speed up corruption cases and circumvent the irresponsible judiciary, he recommended that the burden of proof be reversed. Those charged with corruption, he said, should be presumed guilty until they proved them- selves innocent. For a president who was himself facing allegations of corruption, this was an odd measure to promote. It would have required fundamental changes to the legal code (and perhaps the Constitution) and therefore was never implemented. Nonetheless, Wahid's gesture indicated that he was growing increasingly desperate as Jakarta's political tension escalated.

The Ginandjar case showed that President Wahid lacked the clout to confront his political opponents by trying them for corruption. In fact, Wahid's belligerence only seemed to galvanise the party bosses against him: on 2 March the Islamic parties of the Central Axis hosted a political rally attended by Megawati and her husband, Taufik Kiemas. The venue was the Al-Azhar mosque in South Jakarta, a headquarters for many of the political Islamists who, in 1999, had adamantly rejected Megawati's presidential bid on gender grounds. Now these same figures declared that it was, in fact, acceptable for a woman to rule over a predominantly Muslim country.[35]

Similarly, all the party bosses now agreed that Megawati should become president (although there was intense competition for the post of vice-president). This was a dramatic reversal from eighteen months earlier, when the same party bosses had elected Wahid precisely because they were so stridently opposed to Megawati. Since then, however, Wahid had proven less malleable than anticipated, while Megawati had demonstrated a surprisingly conservative disposition. This served to assuage a political elite that had deepseated reasons to fear change. But perhaps the most important reason for the dramatic change in attitudes toward Megawati pertained to straightforward calculations of power politics: many suspected that the party bosses supported Megawati simply to bring themselves one step closer to the presidency.

If Wahid was replaced by Megawati, the new vice-president would be next in line to succeed her if she, too, were ousted from the presidency. Tandjung, Rais and Haz all seemed to be vying for the vice-presidency. Megawati's advisors feared that these figures might not be trustworthy partners: they had already toppled Soeharto and Habibie and they were now on the verge of toppling a third president within a span of four years. Megawati therefore stated that she would only accept the presidency if her right to serve through 2004 was assured. Ironically, such an assurance could only really be provided by the direct popular election of the president—a measure that Megawati inexplicably opposed.

Meanwhile, as the party bosses focused on their own power struggle, ordinary Indonesians suffered from the deleterious effects of prolonged non-governance. The central bank had once again lost control of money supply growth, such that the rupiah steadily declined to Rp12000/$—compared to Rp8000/$ when Wahid took office. Asset restructuring, impeded by the dysfunctional legal system and the overall uncertainty, remained moribund. The government budget was deeply in deficit, while the decentralisation program and promises of regional autonomy produced bureaucratic confusion at all levels of government. In Aceh the death toll mounted by around 50–100 people per month. Conflicts simmered in Irian Jaya and Maluku.

Virtually all of Indonesia's various crises were attributable, in some form, to the leadership vacuum in Jakarta. By early March the struggle for power among the party bosses was crippling the state. But nowhere were the symptoms more acute than in the hitherto peaceful province in the middle of Borneo: Central Kalimantan.

In 1997 and 1999 West Kalimantan had witnessed deadly ethnic clashes between indigenous Dayak and settlers, or descendants of settlers, from the East Java island of Madura. In early 2001 such clashes suddenly erupted in the neighbouring province of Central Kalimantan. As had been the case in the past, the fighting was ferocious. By late February the confirmed death toll had soared above 300.

President Wahid, travelling in Nigeria and the Sudan, continually insisted that reporters were exaggerating the level of violence in Central Kalimantan.[36] Nonetheless, the strife attracted worldwide attention as the international press captured gruesome images of mutilated corpses and decapitated bodies. The cover of *Time* showed nude, headless bodies in pools of blood; the caption read 'Bloody Borneo: a massacre and cannibalism strike at the heart of Indonesia'.[37]

Dayak bands quickly gained the upper hand in attacks on Madurese settlements, and the port towns of Kalimantan became choked with refugee families seeking safe passage to Java. Tens of thousands were trying to flee. The situation was particularly tense in the town of Sampit: according to a number of witnesses, including a senior member of the Sampit district assembly, Madurese refugees who wanted to board evacuation ships were forced to pay bribes to the security forces.[38] Moreover, the rival branches of the security forces—the military and the police—began competing with each other for control over the lucrative sale of berths.

Finally, on the afternoon of 27 February a scuffle escalated into a deadly clash: on a street next to the port, army soldiers shot and wounded two middle-ranking police officers. Heavily armed Brimob police soon fired back. By nightfall a fierce gun battle raged through the streets of Sampit—involving more than 80 soldiers and police, fighting each other.[39]

The firing killed a bystander and a soldier, while injuring three more soldiers, three police personnel and at least two others.[40] The skirmish damaged dozens of buildings and vehicles in the area, including the evacuation ship itself. The military spokesman confirmed the injuries and attributed them to 'an emotional misunderstanding . . . that led to measures that were not in accordance with standard procedures'.[41] Several days later Vice-President Megawati finally visited Sampit in Wahid's absence.

Shedding tears before reporters, Megawati proclaimed that Indonesia had reached the lowest point in its 56-year history. Her display did little to restore confidence or inspire hope. Central Kalimantan's ethnic strife officially claimed 469 lives, but aid workers in the remote reaches of Borneo estimated that at least 2000 victims had been killed, since many bodies had been dumped in rivers.[42] The strife produced around 50 000 refugees.[43]

The security forces endured harsh criticism for their apparent passivity. Although the riots were not deliberately provoked by outsiders, little was done to quell the fighting. As had happened in East Timor and Maluku, murderous mobs rampaged in full view of Brimob troops.[44] In one episode police fled from a Dayak attack, thereby allowing the mob to massacre 118 Madurese.[45] And throughout the conflict, which lasted for about three weeks, the military proved reluctant to assist. In fact, military leaders seemed to be exploiting the strife to pursue their own ends— namely the acquisition of political power.

The deployment of troops to Central Kalimantan might have deterred the marauding Dayak, who were armed only with knives and sickles. Gen. Sutarto was urged to reinforce the local garrisons, maintain an army presence and secure key towns to protect Madurese refugees. Sutarto, however, implied that if the army took action its only available course of action would be to shoot on sight. But this, he said, was impossible because the military lacked sufficient legal authority. He therefore used the strife as a reason to demand 'a legal umbrella [i.e. expanded military powers] so that our soldiers in the field can be proactive in maintaining security'.[46]

Similarly, the pro-military defence minister, Mohammad Mahfud, argued that the military should reassume control over the police. He cited the Central Kalimantan strife as evidence that the organisational separation of the two branches, as mandated by the MPR the year before, was likely to 'cause a lot of problems'.[47] Sutarto himself complained about the separation of the police from the military following a long, secretive and unusual meeting with all 55 active army generals on 1 March.[48] But perhaps the concern stemmed not from the security needs of the people but rather from the institutional interests of the military.

As active generals had admitted in the past, the military derived its income from business interests that included protection services and racketeering operations. Following its divorce from the police, the military no longer possessed a clear monopoly on coercive force—the police force, although weaker, was beginning to act as a rival. Thus, while the Central Kalimantan strife was reflecting poorly on both the president and the police, the military used the situation to its own political advantage. Amid the debilitating political impasse in Jakarta, the military was answerable only to itself—and its leaders therefore focused their energies on augmenting their own political power.

After returning from his trip through Africa in mid-March, Wahid seemed to make a few gestures toward reconciliation. He had only six weeks before parliament would issue a second memorandum. In a move that may have been designed to win support from one faction of Golkar (the formerly 'pro-Habibie' faction), Wahid changed his minister of forestry. Nur Mahmudi Ismail, the leader of a small Islamic party, was replaced by Marzuki Usman, a veteran Golkar official. Because it controlled a lucrative sector, the forestry portfolio was a coveted post, but Wahid needed to do much more to salvage his presidency.

At the end of March, with a host of parliamentarians pledging to issue a second memorandum just one month hence, Wahid grudgingly apologised for his recent 'unpraiseworthy attitudes'.[49] In the same speech, however, he again denounced the Pansus investigation as unconstitutional and illegal. And in mid-April he signed a presidential decree that established the legal basis for ad hoc human rights tribunals; however, with regard to East Timor, the decree restricted tribunals to trying only those abuses that took place after the ballot of 30 August 1999.[50]

In effect, the decree on tribunals handed a crucial concession to the military. The bulk of cases investigated by the Human Rights Commission and the attorney general's office pertained to pre-ballot abuses—and thus the president had, in effect, awarded immunity to those responsible. These included Aitarak militia leader Eurico Guterres, who still had not been brought to trial. But while Wahid was making hamfisted attempts to appease his opponents, he continued to undermine his position with off-the-cuff, impolitic remarks.

In mid-April Akbar Tandjung and other politicians proposed a power-sharing accord whereby Wahid would become a ceremonial 'head of state', while Megawati assumed all presidential authority. In response, Wahid stated publicly that he doubted Megawati's abilities to serve as president. The remark reflected poorly on Wahid and antagonised PDI Perjuangan. Moreover, it conjured memories of Soeharto's last days in office, when he expressed doubts about Vice-President Habibie's ability to take the helm. By the final week of April it was clear that Wahid's haphazard political strategy was doomed to fail: parliament clearly intended to issue the second memorandum on 1 May. Wahid therefore resorted to the tactics of his enemies.

The NU's para-military youth wing, Ansor, had been threatening for weeks to descend on Jakarta and wreak untold violence. Wahid tacitly endorsed such threats by scheduling a massive NU prayer rally at Jakarta's Senayan Stadium on 29 April—one day before parliament would vote on the memorandum. As thousands of NU supporters arrived in the capital, Jakarta residents feared violent confrontations in the streets. Traffic was sparce and commerce ground to a halt as stores throughout the city remained closed for three days.

In the end, Wahid's supporters perpetrated no serious violence and parliament issued the second memorandum, as expected. The vote was 363 in favour of censuring the president versus 52 opposed. The military faction abstained—but it did so only for appearances. Because it was clear beforehand that the vote would be lopsided, the military was able to feign neutrality without influencing the outcome. In fact, the military leadership reshuffled the membership of its 38-member faction just days before the vote; officers who had expressed reservations about ousting Wahid were replaced by conservatives, such as the former commander of Maluku's Pattimura Garrison, Maj. Gen. Max Tamaela. And in its official comment on the vote, the military faction made clear that it would accept the convening of a special MPR session.

Following the second memorandum, the president had only one month in which to respond. Thereafter, if parliament again deemed the response inadequate, it would have grounds for convening the MPR. Wahid would be required to deliver an accountability speech, the rejection of which would constitute a vote of no confidence, as had been the case for President Habibie. But whereas Habibie withdrew from the presidential race within hours of the vote on his speech, Wahid was vowing to stay in the presidential palace even if it were surrounded by tanks.

Wahid was clearly beginning to panic. Several days after parliament's second memorandum he extended a major concession to Golkar. For nine months the president had resolutely opposed parliament's two nominees for chief justice of the Supreme Court—the position that would be pivotal in any initiatives toward legal system reform. Both candidates were Golkar figures with poor New Order track records. Finally, on the eve of parliament's vote for a second memorandum, Wahid capitulated and accepted Bagir Manan. With a Golkar figure planted atop the judiciary, progress toward the rule-of-law would be that much more difficult.

The concession, however, did little to help Wahid's predicament. The chief justice post was a valuable 'bargaining chip', but Golkar already seemed to be beyond the point of wanting to bargain. And at the same time that he seemed to be offering desperate concessions, Wahid was also issuing even more desperate threats: just five days after the second memorandum, he threatened to decree a state of emergency and dissolve parliament.[51]

There had been second-hand reports that Wahid had attempted to disband parliament several months before, in January, but many had dismissed the story as untrue or just another case of Wahid's whimsy. Now, however, the president readily admitted that he had called on the military leadership to support his 'decree' of a state of emergency. Wahid claimed that such a decree would give him the power to dissolve parliament, although most constitutional experts disputed this fact.[52] In any event, Wahid admitted that the military had refused to comply with his request.

For Wahid the event was politically devastating. He seemed not to realise, or care, that a state of emergency would sharply contradict the spirit and purpose of *reformasi*—and would therefore have no chance of gaining public support. Regardless of parliament's performance, a decree would be blatantly anti-democratic. It would also be certain to elicit a snap MPR session that would revoke Wahid's mandate, within days. Even worse, a decree provided the military with a valuable opportunity to portray itself as the defender of Indonesia's budding democracy—a role that Sutarto played with relish. In short, Wahid's suggestion of a decree was illegal, unpopular, infeasible and counter-productive. Nonetheless, he continued to repeat his desire to implement it.

A vicious cycle ensued: each time Wahid threatened to issue a decree, his political standing fell; and each time his standing fell, he grew more strident about issuing a decree. Ironically, had Wahid couched his demands differently, he might have resuscitated his presidency. Conceivably, the president could have exposed some of the highhanded behaviour of parliamentarians, thereby generating popular support for an accelerated election schedule—using an electoral system that imposes accountability. This might have achieved a major step towards the rule-of-law and responsible government (although the problem of the military's political role might have still loomed large). But Wahid eschewed this route. He seemed not to appreciate the principles of democracy, nor the means for promoting them. Bewildered by the political maelstrom, he resorted to acts of desperation to preserve his presidency.

The threats of a decree were coupled with rumours that Wahid wanted to sack Sutarto, Widodo or both. In response, all eleven garrison commanders issued a joint statement: the military would not obey 'political generals'. The statement was read by the commander of the Udayana Garrison, Maj. Gen. Willem da Costa—a former Wiranto partisan. In effect, the statement meant that if Wahid appointed reformers such as Agus Wirahadikusumah or Suarip Kadi to key posts, the entire military command would openly rebel.

In effect, Wahid's ill-advised attempts to issue a decree had inadvertently relegitimised the military's involvement in politics. Having won nothing but opprobrium since Soeharto's fall, the military suddenly saw its fortunes rise. It had been thrust into the centre of the political fracas and therefore enjoyed more manoeuvring room than it had possessed in years. At the same time, several court decisions went in the military's favour.

For months the UN and foreign governments had been pressuring Indonesia to punish the militia men who had killed three relief workers in Atambua, West Timor. A court finally reached a verdict in early May—but rather than manslaughter, the six perpetrators were charged with a far lighter crime: inciting unrest. And because of 'good behaviour', they were handed the lightest possible sentences: 16–20 months in prison. The UNHCR declared that 'the sentences make a mockery of the international community's insistence that justice be done in this horrific case'.[53]

Around the same time, a sociologist at the University of Indonesia, Thamrin Amal Tomagola, faced a libel suit filed by Gen. (ret.) Wiranto and three other generals. In a speech nearly a year before, Tomagola had named Wiranto and three active generals (Djaja Suparman, Suaidi Marasabessy and Sudi Silalahi) as the 'provocateurs' who were responsible for fomenting and prolonging the religious strife in Maluku.[54] The court proceedings were postponed, perhaps because Tomagola threatened 'to use the trial as a venue for enumerating the full details of the military's involvement in the Ambon conflict'.[55]

Meanwhile, another court case was attracting much wider publicity: Eurico Guterres was finally going on trial. Human rights advocates had hoped that Guterres would be held accountable for any one of the myriad abuses committed during 1999 by his Aitarak militia; instead, Guterres was charged with preventing his followers from surrendering their arms at a ceremony presided over by Megawati in October 2000, in response to the Atambua attack.

Guterres was sentenced to a mere six months in house arrest.[56] Because he had purportedly served several months in house arrest already, the decision meant that his term would end in just a few weeks. Moreover, he was allowed to serve the sentence at his family home in South Jakarta.

During the time that Guterres was supposedly under house arrest, he was linked to yet another intimidation campaign perpetrated by militia groups. Some 50 Islamist and right-wing groups founded what they called the Anti-Communist Alliance (AAK). The AAK began a 'sweeping' operation in May in which gangs would rob certain books from bookstores and publicly burn them. The AAK gangs claimed to be targeting pro-communist publications, but they were also attacking books that were simply anti-Soeharto or, especially, anti-military. In fact, the entire operation was not a genuine religious affair but rather a deliberate military operation.

Most (if not all) groups in AAK, such as FPI and Front Hizbullah, had close ties to the military. Another was Ikhwutan Sunnah Waljamaah, a group headed by Habib Al-Habsyi. A blind, militant cleric, Al-Habsyi was imprisoned in 1980 for bombing the world's largest Buddhist monument, the Borobudur temple. He was released before the end of his sentence in 1999—reputedly at the behest of Gen. Wiranto.[57] Other groups in AAK were military-backed *preman* organisations: Pemuda Pancasila and Laskar Merah Putih. And the latter was headed by none other than Eurico Guterres.[58]

In addition to book-burning, AAK staged a number of street rallies in downtown Jakarta, followed by efforts to harass and intimidate a variety of non-governmental organisations involved in legal aid and human rights. Another target was the Democratic People's Party (PRD)—the tiny party headed by Boediman Soedjatmiko, who had been blamed for instigating the rioting in July 1996. The pro-military news weekly, *Garda*, explicitly defended AAK's actions.[59]

Apparently the military was joining forces with political Islamists to begin rolling back the tide of free speech, while intimidating traditional opponents of the New Order. The episode was a stark warning of what might lie ahead in Indonesia's political future: a return to military-backed authoritarianism, but under the guise of Islamic politics.

On 30 May—the day parliament resolved to demand an accountability speech in a special MPR session, to be held on 1 August—several thousand NU demonstrators marched down the length of Jalan Sudirman and forced their way on to a portion of the parliament grounds. The thuggish-looking men had been transported to Jakarta from NU strong-holds in East Java, and it was widely believed that many had been paid to attend. The action only further besmirched Wahid's image. Rather than trying to generate genuine public sympathy, the president had resorted to manufacturing mass support.

Ironically, 30 May was also the day on which Jakarta hosted an assembly of G-15, an association of fifteen major developing countries. This was the first such meeting since May 1998, when Soeharto chaired the event in Cairo, Egypt. Attendees joked that every time the G-15 convened, an Indonesian president was toppled.

When Wahid rose to welcome the conference members, who included six foreign heads of state (plus a large array of vice-presidents and ministers), the blind president explained that his formal speech would be read aloud by his vice-president, Megawati. He then waited for Megawati to rise to the podium—but the PDI Perjuangan leader remained seated. She refused to assist Wahid. It was yet another humiliation for the president. The president of Zimbabwe, Robert Mugabe, rose to speak instead.

Before the G-15 conference had even concluded, Wahid was preparing his next manoeuvre. He had only two months, at most, to salvage his presidency. On 1 June, two days after parliament called for an extraordinary MPR session, Wahid sacked four ministers whose loyalties were suspect. These included the co-ordinating minister for politics and security, Bambang Yudhoyono, and Attorney General Marzuki Darusman. Many regarded their dismissals as long overdue. Only a few years before,

Yudhoyono had been regarded as the military's rising star: some had even compared him to *Satrio Piningit*, the just and longed-for leader who appeared in Javanese legends. But Yudhoyono's star was rapidly fading: he had failed to make an impact in the cabinet and he had been siding too closely with Gen. Sutarto. Wahid replaced him with Lt Gen. (ret.) Agum Gumelar, but little was expected from the former Special Forces commander. Meanwhile, Wahid announced another key change: he tried, in effect, to sack Gen. Bimantoro, the national police chief.

Wahid's authority to change the chiefs of the military or the police was questionable following the August 2000 MPR guideline that called for parliamentary review of such appointments. Parliament, however, had never turned the guideline into formal law. Moreover, Wahid tried to skirt the issue by declaring that Bimantoro was not fired but merely 'deactivated'. The president re-established the position of deputy national police chief and appointed Gen. Chaeruddin Ismail to the post; Wahid then declared that the new deputy chief would be in charge while Bimantoro was non-active.

The move triggered a sharp response. A host of parliamentary leaders denounced it as illegal and threatened to accelerate the start of the special MPR session. Bimantoro, for his part, continued to claim that he was the active police chief, and virtually every member of the police command, including Chaeruddin himself, signed a petition acknowledging him as such. The military, despite its rifts with the police, circulated a similar petition, which was signed by no fewer than 102 senior officers from all three services.[60]

Wahid renewed controversy by threatening yet again to fire the armed forces chief, Widodo. In response, PDI Perjuangan spokesman Sutjipto declared that, if Wahid did so, PDI Perjuangan would support a move to bring the special MPR session forward to 1 July. The irony was clear. During the final years of Soeharto's rule, Megawati had achieved fame for her stoic opposition to military-backed authoritarianism. Now some of the same generals who had perpetrated the PDI Headquarters raid, and others like them, were her allies. Even the military's growing proximity to militant Islam failed to alienate the staunchly nationalist Megawati—in fact, it seemed only to encourage her to curry favour with the military that much more energetically.

Perhaps the crowning irony, however, was that Megawati was arrayed against her lifelong friend, Abdurrahman Wahid. But she was not alone in opposing Wahid—and the president himself was largely to blame for his growing predicament.

Despite Indonesia's worsening political crisis, it is a tribute to the Indonesian public that so few people advocate a return to Soeharto-style authoritarianism. There is still a widespread recognition that the reimposition of military rule would almost certainly exacerbate Indonesia's condition. Apart from the political, social and cultural costs exacted by Soeharto's authoritarianism, the New Order seemed to demonstrate that an economy based on Ruler's Law cannot sustain growth over the long term. In any event, the elements that fed the Soeharto-era boom—such as donor goodwill, investor confidence and (misplaced) faith in a pegged exchange rate—would all be absent in the event of a military takeover. A military regime might live off the sale of non-renewable natural resources, but Indonesia, and Indonesians, would suffer. Nonetheless, Indonesia's predicament makes a return to military rule—or military-backed rule—seem practically inevitable.

Throughout Indonesia's history as an independent nation, civilian leaders have struggled to contain or check the military. In the revolutionary era, civilians never fully controlled Gen. Sudirman's military, while Soekarno ended Indonesia's unstable parliamentary system with the military's backing. Eight years later he himself fell victim to a takeover by Soeharto—a general who then ruled for more than three decades. Even Soeharto, however, frequently had difficulty controlling the generals beneath him. Shuffling commands and purging non-loyalists were a constant preoccupation. Eventually Soeharto's generals proved unreliable and Habibie took over—but neither he nor Wahid ever exerted firm control over the military. In fact, the Wahid era demonstrated that conservative military elements possess both the ability and the ruthlessness to sabotage—literally—specific efforts to impose democratic accountability or to move toward the rule-of-law.

If Indonesia is to break free from its centuries-old legacy of Ruler's Law, a strong popular leader is needed. With a clear popular mandate to govern, a dynamic president could work with the military's own internal reformers (of which there are a few) to begin instituting change. Only such a leader would be able to overcome the nexus of conservative generals, corrupt conglomerates and other remnants of the New Order. At present, only Megawati has the potential to muster such mass support—but, judging from her track record over the past five years, she seems unlikely to make use of it.

In the meantime, the military and other conservative elements can continue exploiting the divisive issue of religion to keep their opponents at bay. Both Wiranto and Sutarto were adept at eliciting support both from Islamist parties, such as PBB, and from secular-nationalist parties, such as PDI Perjuangan. This suggests that, if the military's leaders grow dissatisfied with a Megawati administration, they would willingly back a government led by Islamic parties. An alliance with Islamic parties would help the military stave off resistance from its most formidable foe: student demonstrators. Indonesia's student movement is only effective when it is galvanised, but a large portion of the country's student population is partial to Islamic politics—and might therefore be co-opted into supporting a military–Islamic alliance in the future.

It is often said that the military prefers secular-nationalist ideals, but the current leadership's active or tacit support of Islamic militias casts serious doubt on that adage. A large number of generals and Islamists have demonstrated that they are motivated not by specific ideals or philosophies but rather by a base urge to attain power. Although some of Indonesia's best leaders are Islamic politicians who are genuinely inspired by religious values, most Islamists seem willing to exploit religion as little more than a political vehicle.

In fact, the likelihood of an Islamic government taking power seems stronger now than ever before. It matters little that Islamic political parties attracted relatively weak support in the June 1999 election: Indonesia's power struggles take place at the elite level. Rather than a grassroots movement, an Islamic government would be a construction imposed from above, with the help of the military and, probably, Golkar. This would generally represent the same alliance that defended Habibie and (with the exception of the PKB) elected Wahid. After Wahid leaves office, President Megawati might soon find herself confronted by such an alliance—which would probably command a slim majority in the MPR.

Indonesia's political future may therefore hinge on whether Megawati can prevail, once and for all, over the nexus of entrenched interests that block reform. To do so, she would need to divide her opponents by sharing power generously with Islamic politicians who are moderate and genuine about pursuing reform. More importantly, she would need to generate active popular support for her presidency; although the electoral system lacks accountability, the party bosses would think twice about attacking Megawati if she clearly had the weight of public opinion on her side.

Overcoming Indonesia's entrenched interests will be a daunting task, but if Megawati simply began making progress towards implementing the rule-of-law she might soon generate momentum. Donors and friendly governments would enthusiastically pledge support. Investors might once again express interest in the resources, markets and labour supply that drew them to Indonesia in the past. With capable policy-making, a virtuous economic cycle might finally ensue. Asset restructuring and privatisation could then start redressing the mountain of debt bequeathed by the New Order. Prospects for a brighter and more democratic future might help dissuade separatists and reduce communal friction.

In short, there is no reason why Indonesia must sink inexorably into poverty and strife. Just as the pre-crisis euphoria was overdone, so too, perhaps, is the post-crisis gloom. Ordinary Indonesians are perfectly capable of governing themselves well—but they are prevented from doing so by a tiny elite that committed grievous excesses during four decades of authoritarian rule. A corrupt regime has no alternative other than to remain in power; Soeharto's regime, which was egregiously corrupt, has proven masterful at clinging to power. Despite its infighting, Jakarta's tiny political elite jealously protects its interests from outside incursions. Change, therefore, must be instigated from within—and hopes for change rest, at present, with Megawati.

Soekarno's daughter has shown few reformist instincts thus far: she has allied with conservative generals, delegated authority to her husband and quashed proposals for electoral reform. Most seriously, she has failed to reach out to the Indonesian people to engage them in politics. Thus, before a battle with entrenched interests can even begin, Megawati must first find the ability, at age 54, to undergo her own process of personal change. It is no exaggeration to say that Indonesia's future largely depends on the outcome of this process.

Hopefully, Megawati will realise that she has no alternative but to challenge the entrenched interests that have blocked democratisation and the rule-of-law thus far. To do otherwise would be to admit defeat. If Megawati shrinks from this challenge, she will either be driven out of office by lawlessness and recession—or be overthrown by the same people who toppled Soeharto, Habibie and Wahid.

EPILOGUE

At 1 am on Monday, 23 July, a haggard President Wahid appeared on television. His nervous facial twitch had grown more pronounced. First, he reaffirmed that he would not deliver an accountability speech before the MPR, despite receiving a formal summons two days previously. Next, he declared that he was disbanding the MPR, the parliament and, for good measure, Golkar (pending the outcome of a money politics case against the party in the Supreme Court). Lastly, he promised fresh elections within one year. He ignored the fact the constitution provided him with no authority to perform any of these acts.

Wahid seemed committed to a course of brinksmanship—he apparently hoped to call the MPR's bluff and intimidate its leaders into backing down. The bulk of his advisors and supporters warned him that this course of action would not only fail—but would actually accelerate his removal from office. But Wahid seemed desperate, and he defied the advice. When the MPR convened on Monday morning to hear his speech of accountability, he failed to appear.

Wahid's absence simplified the MPR's task. In the afternoon, the assembly convened to vote on a measure that would reject the undelivered accountability speech; revoke Wahid's mandate; and install Vice-President Megawati as president, effective at once. Wahid's PKB and one small faction, PDKB, boycotted the assembly, but with 591 members in attendance a quorum was easily attained. When asked who supported the measure, all 591 rose to their feet. Megawati had finally attained the presidency.

There were few qualms about the constitutionality of the process, and Megawati's ascension to the presidency had been generally expected for several months. And although there had been apprehension about whether Wahid would be willing to physically vacate the palace, this was laid to rest two days later when he announced that he would depart for the US for medical treatment.[1] But one critical unknown factor remained: who would become vice-president?

Some of Megawati's advisors had hoped that the post might remain vacant until the next parliamentary elections in 2004, but the leaders of other parties issued stern warnings not to repeat the mistakes of Wahid—meaning his lack of adequate power-sharing with those who elected him. Therefore, amid the typical flurry of political manoeuvring, the MPR prepared to elect a new vice-president.

The vote was crucial, considering that two successive vice-presidents had obtained the presidency within the past three years. If Megawati faltered—as Soeharto, Habibie and Wahid had done—the presidency would probably go to whomever won this vote. Moreover, the winner of this vote would be particularly well positioned in the approach to the 2004 elections: the new vice-president would have the national profile required to make his own run for the presidency.

Wahid's removal from office meant that, in effect, power was being further rotated among the party bosses. With Wahid sidelined and Megawati promoted, the other party bosses each moved one notch closer to the summit. Thus the vice-presidential front-runners were the heads of the second- and third-largest parties: Golkar's Akbar Tandjung and PPP's Hamzah Haz. The functional-groups faction nominated a 'dark horse' candidate, Siswono Yudohusodo, the former Golkar progressive whom Tandjung ousted from the party in 1998. Meanwhile, the military faction portrayed neutrality by nominating no candidate of its own; instead, as had been the case with Wiranto's vice-presidential candidacy in 1999, a small Islamist faction (FPDU) acted on the military's behalf. Although Wiranto and Agum Gumelar were considered, FPDU ultimately nominated Susilo Bambang Yudhoyono.

The picture became clearer when Pan's Amien Rais and PBB's Yusril Ihza Mahendra ruled themselves out of the running. This suggested that their factions would back the only other Islamic party candidate, Hamzah Haz. The Central Axis was once again demonstrating considerable unity and power. Moreover, certain Golkar delegates from the Iramasuka Caucus were deemed more sympathetic to Haz than to their own candidate, Tandjung. Still, Haz lacked an outright majority. The voting therefore took place in three rounds: the first two rounds to narrow the field from four candidates to two, after which the third round would determine the winner.

A potentially pivotal bloc of swing votes was held by PDI Perjuangan. Ironically, Megawati's faction would have the power to determine the vice-president—and thereby determine Megawati's likely opponent in 2004. But PDI Perjuangan was in a quandary. Siswono was the preferred choice of most faction members, but his candidacy lacked support and was largely symbolic. This left only three viable options—Haz, Tandjung and Yudhoyono—all of whom had been integral members of the New Order regime.

For weeks, Hamzah Haz had been touted as the front-runner. His supporters maintained that because he was from Kalimantan, he provided a balanced ticket to Megawati, who was viewed as being Javanese (even though she is only one-quarter Javanese). Haz's followers also argued that because his religious background stems from the broad NU fold, his appointment would help assuage the NU population that might feel slighted by Wahid's dismissal from office.

These arguments were unconvincing to many of the ardent secular-nationalists in Megawati's party. Moreover, Haz was steeped in the ways of the Soeharto-era: for a full 30 years he had occupied a PPP seat in the national parliament—a body renowned throughout most of that time as a weak, rubber-stamp institution. And through seniority, Haz had become a key figure in parliament's state budget review—a process perennially criticised for generating KKN. Finally, many PDI Perjuangan members remembered the days prior the June 1999 elections, when Haz cast aspersions on Megawati's 'Islamic credentials'.

Nonetheless, PDI Perjuangan had few alternatives. To back Tandjung risked alienating the powerful Central Axis—as well as some of the Iramasuka Caucus within Golkar. Meanwhile, to back Yudhoyono, a retired four-star general, would be unseemly. Worse, it might back-fire: backing Yudhoyono would eliminate Tandjung in the first round of voting, after which the Golkar faction would likely ally with the Central Axis to elect Haz—defeating Yudhoyono, embarrassing PDI Perjuangan and casting Megawati as the adversary of Islam.

After a fractious debate, PDI Perjuangan leaders finally determined that for the sake of unity—within the government as well as within the nation as a whole—Megawati's party must back Haz. Since the mid-1950s, the Islamic camp had been continuously prevented from attaining high office; under the circumstances, Megawati could ill afford to prolong its exclusion. After the first two rounds of voting eliminated Siswono and Yudhoyono, Tanjung was defeated in a landslide by Hamzah Haz.

On the surface, Megawati's ascension to the presidency could be viewed as the culmination of *reformasi*—but few Indonesians seemed to see it this way. The event stood in stark contrast to the jubilation that marked the public campaigning for PDI Perjuangan two years before. In May 1999, Megawati's supporters flooded the streets of Jakarta wearing the party's colours, rendering the city a veritable sea of red; but in July 2001, Megawati's inauguration received remarkably little fanfare. After months of sordid politicking, lacklustre leadership and economic malaise, the mood of the nation had unmistakably soured—and Megawati's aura had unmistakably diminished.

Early on the morning of 27 July, a shiny new Honda jeep wound through the narrow, dusty streets of Sunter, an affluent neighborhood in northern Jakarta. The jeep was driven by Syafiuddin Kartasasmita, one of Indonesia's 51 Supreme Court justices.[2] Nine months earlier, Syafiuddin had headed the three-member panel of justices who, to the surprise of all, sentenced Tommy Soeharto to 18 months in prison for corruption in the Goro land swap. And more recently, Syafiuddin had been tapped to head the committee to select the membership of a special human rights court that would be empowered to try the East Timor and Tanjung Priok cases.[3] The committee's initial meeting was only days away.

But that meeting would not take place as scheduled. As Syafiuddin steered towards a main road, Jalan Letjen Suprapto, two men on a black motorcycle pulled abreast of his vehicle. One of the men drew a handgun and fired two shots at the jeep, puncturing a tyre. Syafiuddin lost control, careening through two foodstalls and severely injuring a bystander before coming to a stop. The motorcycle also stopped and the gunman dismounted. He strode toward Syafiuddin, who was screaming, and emptied his pistol into his body and head from less than one metre away.[4] There was no doubt that this was a political assassination—and it occurred just four days into a new presidency that, it had been hoped, would bring Indonesia's political turmoil to an end.

Just eight weeks later, a panel of three Supreme Court justices voted to overturn the jail sentence of Tommy Soeharto—even though Tommy was still a fugitive. For the credibility of the Indonesian justice system, the decision marked a new low.

Meanwhile, the nation waited impatiently for Megawati to name a new cabinet. After nearly three weeks, she finally announced a roster that included a host of eminent figures in all key economic posts, including the re-instatement of Laksamana Sukardi as minister for state-owned enterprises. This economic team impressed Indonesia's donors, but it would make little headway on economic reforms without corresponding progress on legal system reform—and Megawati's choice for minister of justice was none other than Yusril Ihza Mahendra. Six months before, Wahid had sacked Mahendra from this same post (which was then called minister of laws). Through this appointment, Megawati was apparently appeasing both the Central Axis and, perhaps more importantly, the military—which Mahendra had consistently defended as minister.

Next, another week passed before Megawati finally announced her appointment for attorney general. The delay was believed to be due to behind-the-scenes wrangling over who should fill the pivotal post. Again, Megawati chose a figure who was deemed to be a military ally, Muhammad Abdur Rachman. An obscure bureaucratic insider, Rachman had been the state prosecutor who headed the anaemic effort to try the East Timor human rights cases.[5]

The overall cabinet roster suggested that the military was, in effect,

PDI Perjuangan's junior partner in a governing alliance. No changes were made to the military leadership. Meanwhile, Susilo Bambang Yudhoyono was restored as co-ordinating minister for politics and security, while Agum Gumelar returned to the communications portfolio. Perhaps most notably, a hard-line three-star general who had long chaired the military's MPR faction, Hari Sabarno, attained the powerful home affairs portfolio—an appointment with ominous implications for Jakarta's tense relations with provincial governments.

Finally, a key non-cabinet economic post, chair of Ibra, remained occupied by I Putu Gede Ary Suta, an appointee installed during the final days of the Wahid administration. The controversial head of the Capital Markets Regulatory Agency during the waning years of the New Order, Ary Suta was also known for his longstanding ties to Cendana and the military.[6] During his first weeks in office, Laksamana Sukardi raised the possibility of replacing Ary Suta, but the idea was quickly muted. Already, the economic team was encountering stiff resistance from entrenched interests.

Meanwhile, in late August 2001, the reform effort suffered a blow when Lt Gen. Agus Wirahadikusumah, the military's most ardent progressive, died suddenly of a heart attack at age 50. The square-jawed general was famed for having criticised military abuses, exposing corruption and sparring openly with Wiranto. It was often argued that military reform required a champion to spearhead change from within—and Wirahadikusumah had been widely viewed as the only senior officer with sufficient gumption for the task.

The 11 September attack on the World Trade Center resonated widely in Indonesia. There was an initial outpouring of sympathy and grief throughout Indonesia, but this quickly turned to dismay at the prospect of US-led attacks on an impoverished Muslim country, Afghanistan. A general outpouring of religious sentiment was unmistakable in Jakarta. And when bombing raids commenced in October, a segment of opportunistic Islamist leaders seized the moment. Vice President Haz publicly regretted the terrorist attacks, but he noted that the US should also 'perform introspection' regarding its shortcomings. 'Hopefully,' he said before a large audience, 'this tragedy will cleanse the US of its sins.'[7]

Harsher denunciations emanated from others, including Laskar Jihad leader Jaffar Siddiq and FPI leader Habib Muhammad Riziq Shihab. On an almost daily basis, various militant Islamic groups mustered crowds of protesters in front of the US embassy. Though small in number, the crowds were colourful, vocal and animated—characteristics that, by obvious design, conveyed powerful images when televised. As protesters threatened to 'sweep' the city to attack US citizens, Indonesia was being viewed as a place of dangerous, radical fervour.

The image was exaggerated. Although many Indonesians disagreed with bombings, and religious tensions had mounted, the radical protests were almost undoubtedly engineered for political ends. By inflaming sentiments, political Islamists exerted intense pressure on Megawati, who derived considerable domestic political strength from the resources and support of the international community. Trapped between US demands for support and protesters' demands to sever ties with Washington, Megawati risked alienating both camps.

But within days, the new president demonstrated surprisingly deft diplomacy. She responded to the Islamist pressure by backing down from her initial support for the US bombing campaign; at the same time, her ministers appeared to use back-channel means to smooth over relations with the US and others. The situation was helped by the arrival of a new US ambassador to replace the controversial Robert Gelbard. Megawati had averted the immediate crisis with relatively light political damage. However, the episode demonstrated that militant Islamist groups had become a powerful and well organised political force. There was ample reason to believe that they would eventually be heard from again.

During its first five months in office, the Megawati administration was regarded as being more effective than Wahid's, but progress on reform remained lacking. No significant efforts were made on trying human rights abuses; on the contrary, abuses and unexplained assassinations occurred at an alarming rate in Aceh, where the separatist war claimed around 100 lives per month. The judicial system continued to protect not only the military, but its surrogates as well: for instance, when state prosecutors sought harsher sentences for the six East Timorese militia members who had murdered three UN aid workers in Atambua, West Timor, the Jakarta High Court rejected the appeal.

Without military reform and legal system reform, asset restructuring remained stalled. The government had committed in 1998 to selling majority control of a state-owned cement producer, Semen Gresik, to a multi-national, Cemex. The sale would have netted around $500 million for the government—thereby achieving the privatisation revenue target that had been set for 2001, and helping to alleviate pressure on a sizeable fiscal deficit. But at the eleventh hour, the deal was scuttled—by vested interests that were profiting from corruption in the huge state-owned firm.[8]

Megawati did, however, make progress in one area where Wahid had failed: in late November she affirmed that the national police chief, Suryo Bimantoro, would retire at month-end. In just over a year in the post, Bimantoro had been a lightning rod for allegations of corruption. And just one day before he resigned, there was a news report that shocked the nation: police finally arrested Indonesia's most wanted man, Tommy Soeharto.

Tommy had been a fugitive for over a year, but it was apparent that police had known of his whereabouts for much of that time.[9] Upon Tommy's arrival at police headquarters, Bimantoro's trusted subordinate, Jakarta Police Chief Sofjan Jacoeb, greeted the unkempt prisoner with a warm embrace—perhaps not realising that the television cameras were already live, broadcasting the scene nationwide.

In addition to evading arrest and possessing illegal weapons, Tommy also faced charges for complicity in terrorist bombings and, most notably, the murder of Justice Syafiuddin Kartasasmita. There seemed little chance that Tommy would avoid jail this time. He would be only the third prominent Soeharto-era figure to undergo punishment—the others being Bob Hasan and a former head of Bulog, Beddu Amang, who was sentenced to two years in prison for colluding with Tommy in the Goro scandal. Tommy's case stood out for garnering massive media attention. For the credibility of Indonesian justice, the stakes were precipitously high.

As 2001 drew to a close, the stakes were also high for civil–military relations. The military abolished the post of kaster, but its staff functions were simply transferred to a different command. Meanwhile, armed clashes between soldiers and members of the police continued to take place.

The police had been subordinate to the military commander during the Soeharto-era, but under Wahid they were separated from the armed forces and made independent. In effect, this ended the military's monopoly over illicit activities—and caused at least 90 armed clashes between the two forces in locales across the country. Typically these were 'turf wars' over protection rackets.[10] Army leaders argued strenuously that the national police should be disarmed.

A key question for the future will be whether Megawati, who accommodated military interests in her cabinet, can exert her authority over the military. Soekarno, Habibie and Wahid had all failed to do this. Even Soeharto—himself a five-star general—eventually lost the military's loyalty. As 2001 came to a close, Megawati faced a potentially crucial test case in the country's most remote province, Papua (the new name for Irian Jaya).

In November 2001, Papua's most well-known independence leader, Theys Eluay, was kidnapped and murdered by asphyxiation. Eluay's driver had had time to register two phone calls before he himself disappeared; he reported that the kidnappers were non-Papuans. The timing of the assassination was suspicious: it occurred just three weeks after the national parliament had granted special autonomy to Papua—a landmark measure that represented a major step forward for the troubled relations between Jakarta and the province. Suspicions immediately focused on the military—specifically, the Special Forces. Both the new national police chief,

Dai Bachtiar, and the provincial police chief intimated as much in a parliamentary hearing in early December.[11]

Later, after protests in Papua forced Megawati to cancel a planned visit to the province, Papuan governor Jaap Salossa also steered blame for the murder to the Special Forces.[12] Yet the police remained inert. The army was apparently above the law—and stridently opposed to a crucial area of reform: decentralisation and special autonomy. Some suspected that the military was deliberately attempting to destabilise Papua. If autonomy succeeded, the military's heavy presence in Papua would lack justification—but for the military, Papua was a lucrative region. Military units were criticised for involvement in protection rackets, illegal logging and even the species trade. Unrest was needed to justify a continued military presence.

A further reason for suspicion was the fact that Papua's regional military command was headed by Maj. Gen. Mahidin Simbolon, a career intelligence officer in the Special Forces. Simbolon had played a key role in organising East Timor's pro-integration militias: for instance, the Mahidi militia, which was implicated in the notorious Suai Church Massacre, was apparently named after Simbolon. One of Simbolon's colleagues in Papua was a Special Forces intelligence official, Yaya Sudradjat, who was among the 14 military and police officers who had been named by the attorney general a year before as suspects in connection with human rights abuses in East Timor.

Soon after the Theys Eluay murder, human rights organisations obtained a central government document—which government officials admitted was authentic—that called for covert operations and terror to repress secessionism in Papua.[13] The document resembled the Garnadi document that had been uncovered in East Timor. The document reportedly included a blacklist of separatists, with Theys Eluay's murder, three of the 20 or so names on this list had now been murdered under mysterious circumstances. Apparently, Simbolon, Sudradjat and the Special Forces were re-applying some of the tactics from East Timor, such as the training of undercover operatives, the formation of para-militaries and the use of intimidation and terror.

As 2001 drew to a close, the Theys Eluay murder was becoming increasingly embarrassing for the government—and tension between Megawati and the army chief-of-staff, Sutarto, were beginning to show. But the military was not Megawati's only source of worry: another was the gradual ascent of political Islam.

The next major juncture in the post-Soeharto power struggle will be the 2004 elections. Although virtually anything is possible in Indonesian politics, there is ample reason to expect that these elections will produce an Islamic government. In 1999 the Islamic parties of the Central Axis garnered a combined 34 per cent of parliament's seats; in 2004, their appeal is likely to be considerably stronger.

Indonesia has experienced the socialism of Soekarno, the nationalist authoritarianism of Soeharto, and the nationalist democracy of Wahid and Megawati. But with the exception of an eight-month period during the parliamentary democracy period of the 1950s, the government has never been led by an Islamic party. At the same time, most would agree that Indonesia's Islamic identity has been growing steadily stronger ever since independence. Assuming that Megawati makes little headway on improving the economy or enforcing the rule of law, political Islamists will have a strong basis for arguing that Islamic government should finally be given a chance to perform where others have failed.

PPP will be particularly well-positioned to compete in 2004. As the only one of the top four parties that has not yet held the presidency, PPP is relatively less tainted by the disappointments of recent years. Meanwhile, the party has received a double boon from Haz's election to vice-president: in 2004, PPP will have a nationally recognised presidential candidate, but until then, Haz's lack of real power as vice-president means that PPP can continue to attract support by functioning, in effect, as an opposition party.

In contrast to PPP, the other three large parties are likely to ebb in strength. PDI Perjuangan was carried in 1999 by Megawati's popular appeal, which has since declined and appears unlikely to return. Golkar still has an image problem—but it now lacks the incumbency that conferred crucial advantages in 1999. And as for PKB, the party has been thrown into disarray since Wahid's downfall. Some conservative NU leaders have already indicated that they may abandon PKB in 2004 and support PPP, thereby reinforcing the Central Axis.

In another indication that Haz's party is accruing power, twelve prominent retired generals officially joined PPP in December 2001. These include the former information minister Yunus Yosfiah and the former attorney general Andi Ghalib. This suggests that the ties between political Islam and the military are growing stronger: both sides are keen to hold power, and neither seems sincere about reform. Although military leaders in the late 1980s and early 1990s were ideologically opposed to political Islam, the current generation seems guided almost entirely by pragmatism. If it is deemed likely to safeguard their interests, Sutarto's army leadership would willingly partner with political Islam. Such a strategy would provide an important advantage: it would be likely to divide and thereby neutralise the military's most formidable potential adversary—university students—many of whom are sympathetic to Islamic parties.

In the event than an Islamic government does emerge in 2004 or 2009, there will be a great deal of apprehension on the part of Indonesia's neighbours and foreign investors. There will be hopes that Indonesia can

draw on its distinctive attributes to produce a new type of Islamic government—one that genuinely draws upon religious values to govern with
integrity. However, the legacy of the Soeharto-era runs deep within
political Islam in Indonesia. Corruption, abuse of power and poverty are
likely to prevail. And if the military is a partner, an Islamic government
might also jeopardise Indonesia's fledgling democratic structures—
although this could happen regardless of who is in power, including
Megawati.

Looking to the future, the stakes are also high for Indonesia as a
whole. Can the world's fourth-largest country overcome poverty? Can the
world's third-largest democracy uphold human rights? Can the world's
most biodiverse country conserve its environment? And can the world's
largest Muslim nation avoid the political manipulation of religion? Some
three years after it began in earnest, Indonesia's post-Soeharto power
struggle is far from over. The saga will no doubt include more surprising
twists—some encouraging, some less so. Despite the political turmoil and
episodes of violence, the Indonesian people have proven remarkably stoic,
principled and tolerant of each other—and perhaps this is the best reason
for optimism for the future.

Following the arrest of Tommy Soeharto, the health of the elder
Soeharto took a turn for the worse. His robust, beaming face had
become hollow, gaunt and vacant. The police allowed Tommy to visit his
78-year-old father, and Megawati discussed granting 'absolution' for
Soeharto, meaning full immunity from prosecution. Everyone wondered
when he would finally pass away, but there was a more difficult question
that went unsaid: how much longer would his legacy live on?

APPENDICES

Appendix I

RUPIAH EXCHANGE RATE

Bank Indonesia middle rate at end of period

Period	RP/US$
June 1996	2353
Dec 1996	2383
June 1997	2450
Dec 1997	4650
June 1998	14 900
Dec 1998	8025
June 1999	6726
Dec 1999	7100
June 2000	8735
Dec 2000	9595
June 2001	11 400
Dec 2001	10 400

Appendix II

SHORT BIOGRAPHIES

ABENG, TANRI South Sulawesi native and former Bakrie & Brothers executive who served as minister of state enterprises in 1998–99; member of Tim Sukses; longstanding business partner of a major recipient of funds from the Bank Bali scandal.

ADISUTJIPTO, WIDODO navy admiral installed by Wiranto as armed forces chief in 1999.

ALATAS, ALI foreign minister under Soeharto.

ANWAR, DEWI FORTUNA influential advisor to President Habibie; proponent of East Timor's popular consultation.

ATMADJAYA, USMAN owner of Bank Danamon, the third largest recipient of BLBI liquidity credits.

BARAMULI, ARNOLD President Habibie's chief advisor and chair of the supreme advisory council; South Sulawesi native and longstanding Golkar campaigner; named by a parliamentary investigation as the chief mastermind of the Bank Bali scandal.

BAWAZIER, FUAD director-general of taxation until 1998; finance minister in Soeharto's seventh cabinet; financier of the Central Axis. Well connected to Cendana, the military and political Islam.

DAMIRI, ADAM assistant to Jakarta Garrison commander Syafrie Syamsoeddin during the May 1998 riots; commander of the Udayana Garrison, which encompassed East Timor, during the pro-integration militia campaign in 1999; promoted in 2000 to a strategic operations post at military headquarters. Named by both the Human Rights Commission and the attorney general's office as a suspected perpetrator of crimes against humanity.

DARUSMAN, MARZUKI chair of the Human Rights Commission until 2000; member of Golkar's executive board; instrumental in agitating against Golkar's pro-Habibie faction. Served as attorney general under Wahid; sacked in June 2001.

DJALIL, MATORI ABDUL chair of the NU's National Awakening Party

420

(PKB), the party founded by Abdurrahman Wahid.

DJIWANDONO, SOEDRADJAD   governor of Bank Indonesia from 1993 to February 1998, when he was abruptly dismissed by Soeharto; brother-in-law of Prabowo Subianto.

DJOJOHADIKUSUMO, HASHIM   brother of Prabowo Subianto; owner of the Tirtamas Group; business partner of Titiek Soeharto.

GARNADI   retired two-star general who served as an assistant both to Feisal Tanjung and Zacky Makarim in East Timor in 1999; author of a document outlining plans for a campaign of destruction following East Timor's ballot.

GHALIB, ANDI   two-star general, South Sulawesi native and Habibie ally who served as attorney general in 1998–99. Caught on tape discussing plans to fake an interrogation of Soeharto; subsequently dismissed following corruption revelations.

GIE, KWIK KIAN   ethnic-Chinese newspaper columnist who penned trenchant critiques of New Order economic policies for nearly two decades. Joined PDI Perjuangan and briefly served as the top economics official in President Wahid's first cabinet.

GUMELAR, AGUM   Special Forces commander in 1994–95; Sulawesi Garrison commander in 1998; minister of transportation and communications during 1999–2001; appointed co-ordinating minister for politics and security in June 2001.

GUSMAO, XANANA   East Timorese independence leader and Fretilin guerilla commander; jailed by the Indonesian military in 1992; released in 1999.

GUTERRES, EURICO   commander of East Timor's most well-known military-backed militia, Aitarak; named by both the Human Rights Commission and the attorney general's office as a suspected perpetrator of crimes against humanity; protected by the Indonesian military and sentenced to only a short period of house arrest in 2001.

HABIBIE, BACHARUDIN JUSUF   South Sulawesi native and German-trained aeronautical engineer; minister for research and technology from 1976 to 1998; criticised for wasting billions of dollars on ill-fated strategic industries; chair of the Association of Islamic Intellectuals (Icmi) from 1990 to 1998; tapped as vice-president in March 1998 and assumed the presidency two months later.

HABIBIE, TIMMY   brother of President B.J. Habibie; member of Tim Sukses.

HADISISWOYO, SUBAGYO   former presidential bodyguard; army chief-of-staff from February 1998 through November 1999; father of Agus Isrok, a Special Forces lieutenant convicted of possessing narcotics in 2000.

HALID, NURDIN   South Sulawesi native and former head of Tommy Soeharto's clove monopoly; member of President Habibie's Tim Sukses.

HAMENGKUBUWONO X   sultan of Yogyakarta and son of a former vice-president; revered by millions on Java; repeatedly cited in 1999 as a possible vice-presidential or presidential candidate.

HAMID, SYARWAN   Riau native and hardline general under Soeharto; as kaster in 1996, helped Feisal Tanjung convene the illegal PDI congress in Medan, followed by the raid on PDI Headquarters. As Deputy Speaker of parliament in 1998, was among the first generals to openly turn against Soeharto. Appointed home affairs minister under Habibie and oversaw the drafting of sound electoral laws that were later changed by parliament. Helped ensure a largely free and fair election in June 1999.

HARMOKO   minister of information throughout most of the New Order; owner of extensive shareholdings in the print media; famed for his sycophantic relationship with Soeharto; elected chair of Golkar in 1993; appointed Speaker of parliament and the MPR in 1997; called on Soeharto to resign in May 1998.

HARTONO   Army officer and Madura native who befriended Tutut Soeharto; became army chief-of-staff under Feisal Tanjung during the 'Islamisation' of the armed forces; enthusiastically promoted Golkar in the 1997 campaign while still an active general; staunchly defended Soeharto through the end of his rule; later accused by President Wahid of harbouring the fugitive Tommy Soeharto.

HASAN, MOHAMMAD (BOB)   also known as The Kian Seng. Central Java native who met Soeharto in the early 1950s, as the adopted son of Soeharto's superior, Maj. Gen. Gatot Subroto. Served as Soeharto's financier, golf partner and confidant. Became Indonesia's foremost timber baron, as chair of the Indonesian Plywood Association (Apkindo) and chair of the Indonesian Foresters Association (APHI). Part-owner, with Soeharto, of the Nusamba Group, with holdings in forestry, pulp and paper, banking and automobile manufacturing. Part-owner of Bank Umum Nasional, the fourth largest recipient of BLBI liquidity credits. Appointed minister of industry and trade in Soeharto's seventh cabinet; convicted of corruption in 2001 and incarcerated on a remote prison island.

HAZ, HAMZAH   chair of the United Development Party (PPP); member of parliament from 1971 until July 2001, when he was elected vice-president.

JOEDONO, SATRIO BUDIHARDJO (BILLY)   Habibie protégé and head of the financial inspection agency (BPK) during the Bank Bali scandal.

KALLA, JUSUF   South Sulawesi native, tycoon and Habibie supporter who obtained a ministerial position in President Wahid's first cabinet; later dismissed amid corruption allegations.

KARTASASMITA, GINANDJAR   long-serving New Order cabinet minister and top economic official in Soeharto's seventh cabinet and the Habibie administration. West Java native, retired air force marshal, deputy MPR Speaker and influential power broker within Golkar. Briefly detained on corruption charges in 2001, but released on the orders of Admiral Widodo.

KIEMAS, TAUFIK husband of Megawati Soekarnoputri and PDI Perjuangan legislator; closely associated with Marimutu Sinivasan and Syamsul Nursalim.

KUSUMAATMADJA, SARWONO progressive Golkar official; first cabinet minister to call on Soeharto to resign in 1998; abandoned Golkar following Akbar Tandjung's election to party chair; appointed minister for maritime affairs under Wahid.

LOPA, BAHARUDDIN Wahid ally and legal system reformer, appointed minister of law in February 2001; incarcerated Bob Hasan on Pulau Nusakambangan; appointed attorney general in June 2001; died weeks later of heart failure.

LUBIS, PANDE deputy director of Ibra who was jailed for his role in facilitating the Bank Bali scandal but was later released.

MA'ARIF, SYAFIE Muhammadiyah chair since 1998.

MADJID, NURCHOLISH renowned Islamic scholar and political moderate; played central role in negotiating with Soeharto in May 1998; helped prepare for the 1999 elections by chairing 'Team Eleven'; proposed as a compromise candidate for president in the October 1999 MPR assembly.

MAHENDRA, YUSRIL IHZA political Islamist who served as speechwriter for Soeharto and for Habibie; founded the Crescent and Star Party in 1998; appointed minister of law in October 1999; sacked in 2001; reappointed by President Megawati.

MAKARIM, ZACKY career Special Forces intelligence officer who helped perpetrate the PDI Headquarters raid in 1996 as head of Directorate A of the intelligence agency, Bais; subsequently promoted to majorgeneral and given command of Bais, which he commanded during the riots of May 1998; entrusted by Wiranto in 1999 with paramount authority over military operations in East Timor, as commander of the Taskforce on the East Timor Consultation (P3TT); named by both the Human Rights Commission and the attorney general's office as a suspected perpetrator of crimes against humanity.

MALLARANGENG, ANDI young political scientist who helped draft sound electoral laws, which were later diluted by parliament in late 1998; briefly served as a director-general under the state minister for regional autonomy in 2000; well-known commentator and insightful proponent of reform.

MARASABESSY, SUAIDI Wiranto loyalist tapped to head the Taskforce on the Restoration of Peace in Maluku in 1999; subsequently promoted to lieutenant-general and chief-of-staff for general affairs (kasum);

sidelined after Wiranto's dismissal.

MARDJONO, HARTONO   former PPP parliamentarian and member of the Indonesian Islamic Proselytising Board (Dewan Dakwah Islamiyah Indonesia); vice-chair of the Crescent and Star Party (PBB) and legal advisor to Wiranto during the East Timor investigation.

MARIMUTU MANIMAREN   deputy treasurer of Golkar; member of Tim Sukses and major recipient of funds in the Bank Bali scandal; brother of Texmaco owner Sinivasan.

MARIMUTU SINIVASAN   owner of the Texmaco Group and perpetrator of the Texmaco scandal, whereby the group used Soeharto's personal intervention to illicitly obtain nearly $1 billion from the central bank during the height of the economic crisis. Charged with corruption by Laksamana Sukardi in late 1998, but protected by President Wahid.

MOERDANI, BENNY   career Special Forces officer and intelligence specialist who served as armed forces chief from 1983 to 1988 and defence minister from 1988 to 1993. Protégé of Ali Murtopo.

MOERDIONO   state secretary from 1993 to 1998, conduit for presidential instructions to Bank Indonesia in the Texmaco and BLBI scandals.

MUHAMMAD, MAR'IE   technocratic finance minister in Soeharto's sixth cabinet; known as 'Mr Clean'; later chaired an official Ibra watchdog agency; joined Nurcholish Madjid in founding the Forum for a Peaceful Indonesia.

MULADI   Habibie's justice minister; unsuccessful candidate for chief justice of the Supreme Court.

MURTOPO, ALI   intelligence officer who worked directly beneath Soeharto from the 1950s until his death in 1984.

NASUTION, ABDUL HARIS   founder of the military, revolutionary hero and conceiver of the 'dual-function' doctrine; escaped assassination in September 1965; passed away in 2001.

NASUTION, ADNAN BUYUNG   founder of the Legal Aid Institute; noted human rights lawyer and ardent pro-democracy activist; supporter of the student movement and repeatedly cited as a candidate for attorney general; vice-chair of the General Election Commission (KPU) in 1999; later defended both Marimutu Sinivasan and Wiranto.

NOORSY, ICHSANUDDIN   outgoing Golkar legislator who aggressively investigated the Bank Bali scandal.

NOVANTO, SETYA   deputy treasurer of Golkar; president-director of PT EGP; key perpetrator of the Bank Bali scandal.

NURSALIM, SYAMSUL   owner of the Gadjah Tunggal Group whose bank, BDNI, was the second largest recipient of BLBI liquidity credits before it collapsed in 1998.

PRABOWO, TITIEK   also known as Siti Hediyati Haryadi. Soeharto's second daughter; wife of Lt Gen. (ret.) Prabowo Subianto; chair of the Capital Markets Society in 1997.

RAIS, AMIEN Muhammadiyah chair from 1995 to 1998; member of Icmi until 1997; supporter of the student movement in 1998; founder of the National Mandate Party (Pan); Speaker of the MPR since October 1999.

RAMLI, RIZAL media consultant hired by Marimutu Sinivasan in 1999; co-ordinating minister for the economy from August 2000 to June 2001, when he was demoted to minister of finance.

RAMLI, RUDY owner of Bank Bali.

RAWEYAI, YORRYS operational chair of Pemuda Pancasila; *preman* boss seen at Soeharto's side in 1999 and early 2000; repeatedly accused of fomenting riots and violence in Maluku and his native Irian Jaya.

RIADY, JAMES owner of the Lippo Group.

RUDINI former army chief-of-staff who served as chair of the General Election Commission (KPU) in 1999.

SABARIN, SYAHRIL appointed governor of Bank Indonesia by Soeharto in February 1998; implicated in Bank Bali scandal; detained for nearly a year on corruption allegations by the Wahid administration; returned to duty in 2001.

SAEFUDDIN, A.M. PPP official and Habibie minister who spearheaded Islamist criticism of Megawati.

SALIM, ANTHONY son of Sudono Salim and heir to the Salim business empire. Owner of Bank Central Asia (BCA), the largest recipient of BLBI liquidity credits in 1998.

SALIM, EMIL former technocratic environment minister and son of Muhammadiyah founder Haji Agus Salim (no relation to Anthony or Sudono); announced candidacy for vice-president in December 1997.

SALIM, SUDONO also known as Liem Sioe Liong. Longstanding financier of Soeharto and founder of the Salim Group, Indonesia's largest conglomerate prior to the crisis.

SAROSA, YAKOB army major from Battalion 745 whose soldiers are believed to have murdered Dutch journalist Sander Thoenes; named by the Human Rights Commission as a suspected perpetrator of crimes against humanity.

SARWATA former three-star air force marshal who served as chief justice of the Supreme Court until his retirement in August 2000; consistently obstructed judicial reforms.

SHIHAB, ALWI PKB official who was instrumental in securing Abdurrahman Wahid's election as president in October 1999; thereafter appointed foreign minister; travelled with Wahid to more than 50 foreign countries.

SIGIT, ARI grandson of Soeharto.

SILALAHI, SUDI assistant to Jakarta Garrison commander Syafrie Syamsoeddin during the May 1998 riots; promoted to major-general and handed command of the East Java Garrison; allowed several thousand Laskar Jihad forces to be shipped through the East Java port of Surabaya to Maluku in 2000; later became special assistant to Susilo Bambang Yudhoyono.

SITOMPUL, RUHUT   Pemuda Pancasila official who served as Wiranto's legal advisor in the East Timor investigations.

SOEHARTO   veteran of the revolutionary war; seized power from Soekarno in 1966; promoted to five-star general; appointed by MPR as Indonesia's second president in 1967; forced to resign on 21 May 1998.

SOEHARTO, BAMBANG   also known as Bambang Trihatmodjo. Soeharto's second son; owner of the Bimantara Group with holdings in media, communications, banking and energy.

SOEHARTO, SIGIT   also known as Sigit Haryoyudanto. Soeharto's eldest son and father of Ari Sigit; part-owner of the Nusamba Group and Salim's BCA, among others; assumed low profile in early 1990s following rumours of massive gambling debts.

SOEHARTO, TOMMY   also known as Hutomo Mandala Putra. Soeharto's third son; owner of the Humpuss Group with holdings in shipping, manufacturing and energy. Embroiled in controversy over rent-seeking facilities such as the clove monopoly and the Timor national car program. Accused by President Wahid of fomenting violence in retaliation for efforts to prosecute his father. Sentenced to jail in October 2000 but escaped custody and became a fugitive; finally captured in November 2001.

SOEHARTO, TUTUT   also known as Siti Hardiyanti Rukmana. Soeharto's eldest daughter, owner of the Citra Lamtoro Gung Group, with holdings in toll road construction, banking, media and forestry. Also owned a 15 per cent stake in Salim's BCA.

SOEKARNOPUTRI, MEGAWATI   daughter of Indonesia's founder and first president, Soekarno; entered politics in 1987; elected PDI chair in 1993 and deposed by the military in the illegal Medan party congress in 1996. Later founded PDI Perjuangan, which won a plurality of the national vote in the June 1999 parliamentary elections; elected vice-president by the MPR in October 1999; elected president in July 2001.

SUBIANTO, BAMBANG   finance minister under Habibie; implicated in the Bank Bali scandal.

SUBIANTO, PRABOWO   aristocrat and son-in-law of Soeharto; Special Forces commander responsible for abducting pro-democracy activists in 1998; promoted to lieutenant-general and Kostrad commander in March 1998; blamed by Wiranto for masterminding the May 1998 riots; discharged in August 1998.

SUDARSONO, JUWONO   longstanding civilian supporter of Soeharto and the military; appointed minister of defence in the Wahid cabinet, with

Wiranto's endorsement; broke ranks in July 2000 and disclosed that Soeharto family allies and former cabinet ministers had deliberately provoked Indonesia's wave of violence; sacked one month later.

SUDARTO, TYASNO head of the military intelligence agency, Bais, in 1999; promoted to four-star general and army chief-of-staff at Wahid's behest in late 1999; sidelined by military conservatives in late 2000.

SUDIBYO, BAMBANG former business professor who, at Amien Rais's behest, was appointed finance minister under Wahid; dismissed in August 2000.

SUDIRMAN military's first commander; acclaimed for sustaining the independence struggle in Java when certain politicians in Jakarta were prepared to compromise with the Dutch.

SUDRAJAT two-star general and Wiranto loyalist who defied President Wahid's authority as military spokesman in January 2000; eventually dismissed, but rehabilitated one year later.

SUDRADJAT, EDI former minister of defence and armed forces commander; among the few ministers who criticised Soeharto in cabinet meetings in 1997 to 1998; voiced mild encouragement for the student movement before being dismissed in March 1998; lost race for Golkar chair in July 1998.

SUKARDI, LAKSAMANA former Citibank executive and prominent advisor to Megawati; appointed state enterprise minister in October 1999; attempted to prosecute Marimutu Sinivasan for the Texmaco scandal, but was stopped by Wahid; brusquely dismissed in April 2000; reappointed to cabinet by President Megawati.

SUMARGONO, ACHMAD chair of the Indonesian Committee for World Muslim Solidarity (Kisdi), a militant Islamist organisation with close ties to Prabowo and other military figures; parliamentary faction leader of the Crescent and Star Party (PBB); advocate of *jihad* in Maluku; consistent supporter of Wiranto.

SUPARMAN, DJAJA commander of the Jakarta Garrison in late 1998, when he recruited Islamist para-militaries to defend the November MPR session; alleged to have close links to the Islamic Defence Front (FPI); promoted to three-star general and Kostrad commander in late 1999; replaced in April 2000 by Lt Gen. Agus Wirahadikusumah, who implicated Suparman in the Yayasan Kostrad corruption scandal.

SURATMAN, TONO colonel who commanded the East Timor military district in 1998 to 1999; acknowledged in December 1998 that his forces were forming civilian militias to support integration; promoted to brigadier-general in late 1999.

SURYADI reform-minded PDI chair until 1993, when he was deposed by the military; rehabilitated in 1996 to usurp Megawati through the illegal Medan congress; reviled thereafter by PDI's erstwhile supporters.

SUTARTO, ENDRIARTONO   Central Java native and commander of Paspampres, the Soeharto's family's private security force, in 1996–98;
promoted to three-star general in 1999; promoted to four-star general
and army chief-of-staff in 2000, where he functioned as the military's
most powerful figure; tacitly supported parliament's censure of Wahid
in February 2001; defied President Wahid's repeated attempts to sack
him.

SUTIYOSO   Jakarta Garrison commander during 1996 PDI Headquarters
raid; later promoted to lieutenant-general and appointed governor of
Jakarta.

SUTJIPTO, ADI ANDOJO   former Supreme Court justice; dean of Trisakti
University and member of the General Election Commission (KPU);
outspoken advocate of legal system reform.

SUTRISNO, TRY   Jakarta Garrison commander at the time of the 1984
Tanjung Priok massacre; armed forces commander from 1988 to 1993;
vice-president from 1993 to 1998.

SYAMSOEDDIN, SYAFRIE   career Special Forces officer and presidential
adjutant in mid-1990s; Jakarta Garrison commander during the May
1998 riots; thereafter served alongside Zacky Makarim as a key aide to
Wiranto; cited as candidate for kaster in 1999.

TANDJUNG, AKBAR   cabinet minister from 1988 to 1999; elected Golkar
chair in July 1998; elected Speaker of parliament in October 1999.
Played central role in agitating against presidents Soeharto, Habibie
and Wahid.

TANJUNG, FEISAL   armed forces commander from 1993 to 1998; oversaw
the 'Islamisation' of the armed forces; co-ordinating minister for
politics and security in both Soeharto's last cabinet and Habibie's
cabinet.

TJANDRA, DJOKO   owner of the Mulia Group and major recipient of funds
in the Bank Bali scandal.

WAHID, ABDURRAHMAN   also known as 'Gus Dur'. Grandson of Hashim
Ashari, who founded Indonesia's largest traditional Islamic organisation, Nahdlatul Ulama (NU). After studying in the Middle East,
elected NU chair in 1984. A lifelong proponent of religious pluralism
and, during the early 1990s, a high-profile opponent of President
Soeharto. Elected president in October 1999; removed in July 2001.

WIJOYO, AGUS   conservative lieutenant-general who served as kaster from
1999–2001, and later as speaker of the military's MPR faction.

WINATA, TOMMY   owner of the Artha Graha Group and financier of the
military.

WIRAHADIKUSUMAH, AGUS   nephew of Vice-President Umar Wirahadikusumah; graduate of Harvard's Kennedy School of Government;
leading military intellectual and reformer; while an active two-star
general in late 1999, conducted a media blitz to denounce military

abuses; promoted by Wahid to Kostrad commander in April 2000; sidelined by Gen. Sutarto four months later; succumbed to heart failure in August 2001.

WIRAHADIKUSUMAH, UMAR   Jakarta Garrison commander during the 30 September movement in 1965; later promoted to four-star general; vice-president from 1983 to 1988; uncle of Lt Gen. Agus Wirahadikusumah.

WIRANTO   Central Java native who pursued a lacklustre army career before being noticed by senior generals in the 1980s; brought to Jakarta and became presidential adjutant from 1989 to 1993; revolved through most of the army's most strategic posts, in rapid succession, from 1994 to 1998; appointed armed forces commander in February 1998. Touted as Soeharto's anointed successor, but acquiesced to the president's overthrow in May 1998; vowed to protect Soeharto and his family. While he served as armed forces commander in 1998–99 various elements of the military perpetrated the Trisakti shootings, the Semanggi I killings, the Bantiqiyah massacre, clashes with police in Maluku, the East Timor scorched-earth campaign, the Semanggi II killings and assorted other abuses. Promoted to co-ordinating minister for politics and security in October 1999; after a tense standoff with President Wahid, sacked in January 2000. Named by both the Human Rights Commission and the attorney general's office as a suspected perpetrator of crimes against humanity.

YOSFIAH, YUNUS   retired hardline kaster who, as minister of information under Habibie, dramatically liberalised the press; in 2001 joined PPP.

YUDHOYONO, SUSILO BAMBANG   assistant to the Jakarta Garrison commander during the 1996 PDI Headquarters raid; thereafter received two promotions in eighteen months; as kaster from February 1998 through October 1999, served as the military's key policy-maker while the security forces perpetrated a series of human rights abuses. Appointed minister for mines and energy in November 1999 and co-ordinating minister for politics and security in August 2000; retroactively promoted to honorary four-star general; dismissed in June 2001; re-appointed as co-ordinating minister by President Megawati.

YUDOHUSODO, SISWONO   former Golkar progressive and transmigration minister allied to Sarwono Kusumaatmadja.

YUSUF, GLENN   director of the Indonesian Bank Restructuring Agency (Ibra) from 1998 to 1999.

NOTES

CHAPTER 1   LOOMINGS

1. Soekarno referred to these three elements by an Indonesian acronym that he devised: Nasakon (*nasional, agama, Komunis*—or nationalist, religious and communist). See, for example, Howard Palfrey Jones, *Indonesia: The Possible Dream*, p. 260.
2. Jones, *Indonesia: The Possible Dream*, pp. 371–84.
3. For example, see: Jones, *Indonesia: the Possible Dream*, pp. 371–84; William H. Frederick and Robert L. Worden (eds), *Indonesia: A Country Study*, pp. 54–7; Col. Abdul Latief, *Pledoi Kol. A. Latief: Soeharto Terlibat G 30 S*; *Tempo*, 12 October 1998, p. 41; and Berpolitik.com, 'Hasan Raid: Soeharto Dalang Gerakan 30 September', 14 July 2000.
4. See, for instance, *Sydney Morning Herald*, 'Indonesia: The Secret Slaughter', 9 July 1999; and *Tempo*, 'Soal G30S', 2 October 2000.
5. Frederick and Worden (eds), *Indonesia: A Country Study*, p. 57.
6. Michael R.J. Vatikiotis, *Indonesian Politics Under Suharto: Order, Development and Pressure for Change*, p. 200.
7. John Bresnan, *Managing Indonesia*, pp. 1 and 286. See also: Adam Schwarz, *A Nation in Waiting*, pp. 58–9.
8. Hal Hill, *The Indonesian Economy in Crisis*, p. 5.
9. *Los Angeles Times*, 'Megawati Rises Above Stormy Clouds of Soeharto Era', 23 October 1999.
10. Schwarz, *A Nation in Waiting*, p. 265.
11. Officers of the navy and air force often claim that their services should not be blamed for the political proclivities of the army; however, given the political involvement of numerous navy and air force officers during the Soeharto era, these claims are dubious.
12. Robert Lowry, *The Armed Forces of Indonesia*, p. 188.
13. For purposes of simplicity and clarity, the term 'garrison' is used to denote regional military commands (or kodam).
14. Until 1998 the kaster position was called chief-of-staff for socio-political affairs (or kassospol), but for purposes of consistency, 'kaster' is used throughout.
15. Until 1998 the military's intelligence agency was known as the Armed Forces Intelligence Agency (or Bia), but for purposes of consistency, 'Bais' is used throughout.
16. Schwarz, *A Nation in Waiting*, p. 266.
17. *Asiaweek*, 'Suharto's Tough Guy: A Hardliner Takes Over a Powerful Post', 23 February 1996.
18. Schwarz, *A Nation in Waiting*, p. 322.
19. Loren Ryter, 'A Tale of Two Cities', *Inside Indonesia*, No. 63, July–September 2000.
20. Laksamana.net, 'Thugs for Hire: A Brief History of Premanism', 30 April 2001.

21. Schwarz, *A Nation in Waiting*, p. 322.
22. *Panji Masyrakyat*, 'Giliran Feisal Kena Gebuk', 23 February 2000.
23. Fittingly, the boulevard was named after Pangeran Diponegoro—the prince of Yogyakarta who waged the Java war of 1825–1830, the bloodiest insurrection in Dutch colonial history.
24. *Gamma*, 'Peradilan Jenderal, Nanti Dulu', 18 July 2000.
25. *Gamma*, 'Peradilan Jenderal . . .', op. cit.
26. See, for example: *Tempo*, 'Soeyono: Ada Duplikasi Komando Antara Feisal dan Hartono', 20 February 2000, p. 34.
27. See, for example: Ahmad Suaedy (ed.), *Premanisme Politik.*
28. *Wall Street Journal*, 'Thriving Papua Joins National Trend, Calling for Secession, Worrying Jakarta', 29 November 2000.
29. See, for example: *Far Eastern Economic Review*, 'Youth Leader Backs Irian Separatists', 22 June 2000.
30. Satunet, 'Liku-Liku Peristiwa 27 Juli 1996', 22 July 2000.
31. The other generals included Army Chief-of-Staff Gen. Hartono, Chief-of-Staff for General Affairs Lt Gen. Soeyono, Bais Director Maj. Gen. Syamsir Siregar, Jakarta Garrison Commander Maj. Gen. Sutiyoso, Assistant Kaster Maj. Gen. Suwarno and the director-general for socio-political affairs in the Ministry of Home Affairs, Maj. Gen. Sutoyo (*Gamma*, 'Peradilan Jenderal, Nanti Dulu', 18 July 2000).
32. Sutiyoso, then the two-star general commanding the Jakarta Garrison, testified that Soeharto gave the order to attack. Former PDI official Budi Hardjono and former Bais Chief Lt Gen. Moetojib concurred. See: *Jakarta Post*, 'Dibyo Denies Attending Meeting at Cendana', 20 September 2000; *Bali Post*, 'Semuanya Bermula Dari Pak Harto', 9 May 2000; and *Indonesian Observer*, 'July 27 Attack Ordered by Feisal Tanjung', 15 November 2000.
33. *Gamma*, 'Peradilan Jenderal . . .', op. cit. See also: Satunet, 'Liku-Liku Peristiwa . . .', op. cit.
34. *Jurnal Indonesia*, 'Yorris Akui PP Terima Undangan Mabes ABRI', 13 June 2000, p. 12.
35. *Kontan*, 'Bandar-Bandar Tragedi Sabtu Kelabu', 13 March 2000. See also: *Gamma*, 'Peradilan Jenderal . . .', op. cit.; *Kompas*, 'SB Yudhoyono Mengaku Tak Tahu Soal Penyerbuan', 20 May 2000, p. 8; *Kompas*, 'Pengerahan Massa Atas Perintah Aparat Kodam Jaya', 20 April 2000; and Satunet, 'Aparat Kembali Dituduh Terlibat 27 Juli', 10 June 2000.
36. *Jurnal Indonesia*, 'Yorris Akui . . .', op. cit., p. 12. See also: *Kompas*, 'Feisal Ttandjung Pernah Tegur Syamsir Siregar', 13 June 2000.
37. *Gamma*, 'Peradilan Jenderal . . .', op. cit.
38. *Gamma*, 'Peradilan Jenderal . . .', op. cit.
39. Schwarz, *A Nation in Waiting*, p. 322. See also: *Indonesian Observer*, 'July 27 Attack Ordered by Feisal Tanjung', 15 November 2000.
40. *Gamma*, 'Dulu Prestasi, Kini Dosa', 18 July 2000.
41. See, for example: Satunet, 'Aparat Kembali . . .', op. cit.
42. Howard M. Federspiel, *A Dictionary of Indonesian Islam*, p. 24.
43. Robert W. Hefner, 'Islam and Nation in the Post-Suharto Era', in Schwarz and Paris (eds), *The Politics of Post-Suharto Indonesia*, p. 46.
44. *Jakarta Post*, 'NU Sets Up New Political Party', 22 July 1998, p. 1.
45. Federspiel, *A Dictionary of Indonesian Islam*, p. 124.
46. Hefner, 'Islam and Nation . . .', op. cit., p. 50.
47. For example, see: Al-Chaidar and Amnesty International, *Bencana Muslimin di Indonesia, 1980–2000.*
48. Vatikiotis, *Indonesian Politics Under Suharto*, pp. 133–4.
49. Thanks to John McBeth for making this point.
50. Hefner, 'Islam and Nation . . .', op. cit., p. 60.

51. See, for example: Vatikiotis, *Indonesian Politics Under Suharto*, pp. 134–5.
52. Hefner, 'Islam and Nation . . .', op. cit., p. 50.
53. Schwarz, *A Nation in Waiting*, p. 191.
54. Hefner, 'Islam and Nation . . .', op. cit., pp. 58–9.

CHAPTER 2   LEGACY

1. For Indonesia's pre-crisis economic indicators, see: Hill, *The Indonesian Economy in Crisis*, pp. 5–10.
2. Hill, *The Indonesian Economy in Crisis*, pp. 31, 36.
3. Callum Henderson, *Asia Falling?*, pp. 18–19.
4. Henderson, *Asia Falling?*, p. 20.
5. See, for example: Hill, *The Indonesian Economy in Crisis*, pp. 49–50.
6. Hill, *The Indonesian Economy in Crisis*, p. 64; Liliana Halim, 'Reviving the Indonesian Banking Sector?', in ISEAS Working Papers, February 2000, p. 57.
7. The overvaluation of these currencies was not easy to discern, however. Measurement techniques based on 'purchasing power parity' produced varied findings depending on the basket of goods being compared.
8. Thanks to Christopher Lingle for making this point.
9. This term was brought into usage by economist Yoshihara Kunio in *The Rise of Ersatz Capitalism in Southeast Asia*.
10. See, for example: Adi Andojo Soetjipto, 'Legal Reform and Challenges', in Chris Manning and Pieter van Diermen (eds), *Indonesia in Transition: Social Aspects of Reformasi and Crisis*, p. 272.
11. For example, see the comments of a progressive-minded public official and business-man, Siswono Yudohusodo, who describes the practice and complains about its wide-spread use in *Suara Pembaruan*, 'Mark Up: Sumber Utama Kredit Macet', 18 November 1997.
12. Hamish McDonald, *Soeharto's Indonesia*, p. 31.
13. McDonald, *Suharto's Indonesia*, p. 32.
14. Bresnan, *Managing Indonesia*, p. 182.
15. In rare high-profile critique of Indonesia's 'high-cost economy', the Economist Sumitro Djojohadikusumo claimed in 1995 that corruption inflated the average cost structure of an Indonesian business by 30 per cent (Sumitro Djojohadikusumo, *Jejak Perlawanan Begawan Pejuang*, pp. 365–7),
16. *Asian Wall Street Journal*, 'The Suharto Regime Bungled Many Chances to Amass Wealth', 30 December 1998.
17. Soeharto family members themselves routinely used this term (which is pronounced 'Chen-dana' and literally means 'sandalwood') to refer to their own family. Soeharto's legal defence team, for instance, was officially called the Cendana Consultation Team.
18. Frank Taira Supit, comments made during the proceedings of the Indonesia Next Conference, 21–23 November 1999. For examples, see: Petromindo.com, 'Bob Hasan's Shares in Tugu Pratama Turn Out to be Empty', 22 February 2001.
19. World Bank, Indonesia: 'Improving Efficiency and Equity Changes in the Public Sector's Role', 9 June 1995, p. 19.
20. *Bisnis Indonesia*, 'Kredit Lancar Bank BUMN 88.9 Persen', 10 February 1998. As an example of how BI's official data strained credulity, Djiwandono testified to parliament on 9 February 1998 that state bank NPLs were lower in December 1997—four months into the crisis—than they had been a year earlier (*Bisnis Indonesia*, 10 February 1998).
21. See, for example: David C. Cole and Betty F. Slade, *Building A Modern Financial System: The Indonesian Experience*, p. 120.
22. World Bank, Indonesia: 'Improving Efficiency and Equity . . .', op. cit., pp. 15–17.
23. *Infobank*, 'Air Mata Endang Teteskan Rp2.2 Triliun', No. 229, September 1998, pp. 24–7.
24. Prevailing economic orthodoxy stipulated that major economic sectors (such as energy,

power, transport and telecommunications) should be deregulated and privatised first, and only then should the banking system be liberalised. Instead, Indonesia's economic managers lifted controls on banking in the landmark deregulation package of October 1988.

25. Binhadi, *Financial Sector Deregulation, Banking Development and Monetary Policy*, p. 172.
26. See, for example: Lisa Cameron, 'Survey of Recent Developments', *Bulletin of Indonesian Economic Studies*, Vol. 35, No. 1, April 1999, p. 23.
27. The weakness of BI's supervisory functions were the object of many criticisms. See, for instance, those of the BI governor himself, Soedradjad Djiwandono, in 'Bank Indonesia and the Recent Crisis', *Bulletin of Indonesian Economic Studies*, Vol. 36, No. 1, April 2000, pp. 50, 54. See also: *Infobank*, 'Soedradjad Djiwandono: Seharusnya BI Dulu Yang Disehatkan', July 1998; Anwar Nasution, 'Lessons From the Recent Financial Crisis in Indonesia', paper presented at the 1997 Economics Conference entitled, 'Sustaining Economic Growth in Indonesia: A Framework for the Twenty-First Century', Jakarta, 17–18 December 1997; World Bank, *Sustaining High Growth With Equity*, 1997, Abstract; and Cole and Slade, op. cit., p. 120.
28. Schwarz, *A Nation in Waiting*, pp. 66–70.
29. Based on audited accounts posted on Indoexchange.com.
30. Thanks to Richard Eary for making this point. See also: HG Asia Research, 'Kalbe Farma: Downgrade to Sell', December 1995; Deutsche Morgan Grenfell Research, 'Indonesian Pharmaceutical Sector', March 1996; *Asiaweek*, 'What the Doctor Ordered: Will Indonesia's Medicine-Makers Get Better?', 6 June 1997; and *Asiaweek*, 'Recommended: Kalbe Farma', 15 November 1996.
31. *Kontan*, 'Genjot Terus Iklan, Lupakanlah Soal Paten', 20 March 2000.
32. Confidential communication.
33. For a view on the ethics of the company's management, see: *Tajuk*, 'Antara Harga Obat Dan Etika Doktor', 27 May 1999. For the company's links to the Bank Artha Prima scandal, see: *Infobank*, 'Finding the Scapegoat of Artha Prima's Scandal', June 1997.
34. Waterfront Securities Research, 'Putra Surya Multidana', May 1997.
35. *Wall Street Journal*, 'IBRA to Take Over Chandra Asri', 6 October 1999.
36. *Gatra*, 'Uang Kembali Atau Masuk Bui', 18 December 1999.
37. Halim, 'Reviving the Indonesian Banking Sector?', op. cit., p. 46.
38. Halim, 'Reviving the Indonesian . . .', op. cit., p. 46.
39. Thanks to Fred Thomas for making this point.
40. *Jakarta Post*, 'Greed Consumes the Former First Family', 2 June 1999.

CHAPTER 3   CRISIS OF CONFIDENCE

1. Hill, *The Indonesian Economy in Crisis*, pp. 14–15.
2. Hill, *The Indonesian Economy in Crisis*, p. 15.
3. Soedradjad Djiwandono, 'The Rupiah—One Year After Its Float', in Forrester (ed.), *Post-Soeharto Indonesia: Renewal or Chaos?*, p. 145.
4. See, for example, the rationalisations of central bank officials quoted in Henderson, *Asia Falling?*, p. 122.
5. Henderson, *Asia Falling?*, p. 122.
6. See: Henderson, *Asia Falling?*, p. 122; and speech by Soedradjad Djiwandono to the 1997 Capital Markets Conference (he mentioned $500 million).
7. Some expected a devaluation to be less costly than the cost of hedging. For example, they believed that if the currency did devalue it would probably only do so by 15–30 per cent. Meanwhile, the annual cost of hedging was about 5 per cent. Thus the loss associated with a devaluation would be roughly comparable to the cost of hedging a five-year loan.
8. The six companies were: Hasan's giant paper-plant, Kiani Kertas; Sinivasan's textile and engineering concerns, Polysindo and Texmaco Engineering; Freeport's PT Smelting

Copper; PT Trans Pacific Petrochemical; and Indonesia's first major high-tech investor, Seagate Technology Sumatera.

9. The technocrat minister with the most seniority—and the best rapport with Soeharto—was the co-ordinating minister for the economy, Saleh Afiff. Afiff, however, had fallen critically ill during the pivotal month of September, effectively removing him from government service.

10. The funds that were readily available were $10.5 billion from the IMF and $7.5 billion from the World Bank and the Asian Development Bank. The 'second line of defence' initially included pledges from Singapore ($10 billion), Japan ($5 billion), the US ($3 billion), Brunei ($1.2 billion) and Malaysia ($1 billion).

11. McDonald, *Suharto's Indonesia*, p. 120.

12. Schwarz, *A Nation in Waiting*, pp. 156–7.

13. Anwar Nasution, 'Lessons From the Recent Financial Crisis in Indonesia', paper presented to the 1997 Economics Conference on Sustaining Growth in Indonesia, December 1997.

14. *The Economist*, 'Survey Indonesia: Engineering the Future', 17 April 1993, p. 12. See also: *Financial Times*, 'Survey: Indonesia', 13 May 1993, p. 5.

15. See: 'World Competitiveness Yearbook', Institutional Institute for Management Development (IIMD)/AP (as cited in *Kompas*, 20 April 2000, p. 13). Also: *Kompas*, 7 May 2001. Among major economies, Indonesia generally ranked second after Nigeria in terms of its susceptibility to the influence of corruption, both from internal sources and from foreign bribes.

16. *Infobank*, 'Inilah Keluarga Bergen Pengisap Bank', No. 229, September 1998, p. 21; Schwarz, *A Nation in Waiting*, p. 313.

17. *Infobank*, 'Inilah Keluarga...', op. cit. See also *Gantra* (English edition), 'Knocked Down and Yet Still Facing Imprisonment', 26 September 1998; *Sydney Morning Herald*, 'Bank Closures a Good Sign', 4 November 1997; and *Suara Pembaruan*, 'NCB Yakin Hendra Rahardja Bisa Diekstradisi', 14 June 1999.

18. See: McDonald, *Suharto's Indonesia*, pp. 143–65; and Frederick and Worden (eds), *Indonesia: A Country Study*, pp. 50, 61, 300.

19. A third of this debt was used, in a thinly veiled embezzlement scheme, to make Pertamina a force in the world market for supertankers: Sutowo rented entire fleets at egregiously marked-up prices. The technocrats eventually pared down Pertamina's total debt through project cancellations and litigation, but Sutowo's mismanagement nonetheless burdened government finances for years. Sutowo was also responsible for nearly $1 billion in bad debt to state-owned Bank Bumi Daya, which he secured in the mid-1970s for a conglomerate he backed, the Astra Group.

20. *Infobank*, 'Air Mata Endang Teteskan Rp2.2 Triliun', No. 229, September 1998, pp. 24–7.

21. *Asiaweek*, 'Now the Hard Part', 14 November 1997.

22. *Bisnis Indonesia*, 'Bambang Tri Minta Izin Bank Baru', 13 November 1997.

23. Hadi Soesastro and M. Chatib Basri, 'Survey of Recent Developments', *Bulletin of Indonesian Economic Studies*, Vol. 34, No. 1, p. 27.

24. *Harian Ekonomi Neraca*, 20 November 1997, p. 3.

25. Soedradjad Djiwandono, 'Sekitar Permasalahan BLBI', located at: <www.pacific.net.id/pakar/sj/sekitar_masalah_blbi1.html>.

26. Soesastro and Basri, op. cit., p. 21.

27. Julius Pour, *Jakarta Semasa Lengser Keprabon*, p. 176.

28. Badan Pusat Statistik, 'Indikator Ekonomi', September 1998, p. 100.

29. World Bank, 'Accelerating Recovery in Uncertain Times', Brief for the Consultative Group on Indonesia, October 2000. See also: Ann Booth, 'Survey of Recent Developments', *Bulletin of Indonesian Economic Studies*, Vol. 35, No. 3, December 1999, p. 20.

CHAPTER 4   PREDATORY STATE

1. The technocrats were now being led by Widjojo Nitisastro, the esteemed but elderly technocrat whom Soeharto had brought back into public service. At 80 years of age, Nitisastro was able to relate well with Soeharto, and he was infuriated that the IMF was broadcasting its displeasure through the foreign press, rather than communicating to Soeharto through him.

2. *Financial Times*, 'Asean Steps In', 14 September 1999.

3. *Bisnis Indonesia*, 'Djamaloedin Soerjohadikoesoemo: Apkindo Dipertahankan, Meski IMF Minta Kartel Dihapus', 17 January 1998.

4. See, for example: *Bisnis Indonesia*, 10 February 1998; and *Indonesian Observer*, 10 February 1998, p. 1.

5. While Tutut was unveiling this latest scheme to mobilise rents, Hong Kong's largest investment bank, Peregrine Securities, was preparing to declare bankruptcy the following day, due primarily to its involvement in another of Tutut's schemes—the Steady Safe deal.

6. *Suara Pembaruan*, 'Pembangunan PLTU Cirenti Terbentuk', 23 January 1998. See also: *Jakarta Post*, 'PLN Seeking Approval for Rate Increase', 19 October 2000.

7. *Asiaweek*, 'Past vs. Future', 24 December 1999.

8. *Republika*, 'Sinivasan Itu Pustakaan Jalan', 14 December 1999, pp. 1, 11.

9. See: *Asiaweek*, 'Past vs. Future', 24 December 1999; and *Gatra*, 'Uang Kembali Atau Masuk Bui', 18 December 1999.

10. For example, when Soeharto visited the Capital Markets Conference he was accompanied by Sinivasan and he lingered over the Texmaco display case—while studiously ignoring that of the ethnic-Chinese-owned Makindo, his family's investment bank of choice.

11. Having earned group-wide export revenues of around $500 million in 1997, Sinivasan projected this figure would reach $616 million in 1998. In fact, it fell to around $200 million.

12. Detik.com: 'Sinivasan Soal Skandal Texmaco: Saya Surati Soeharto, Tak Ketemu', 1 December 1999.

13. In his request to BI, Sinivasan promised to repay the facilities from the proceeds of a $750 million Yankee bond that, he claimed, was close to being launched in New York. In his letter to the president, however, Sinivasan said that the bond issuance had been scuttled as a result of the financial crisis.

14. Detik.com, 'Skandal Texmaco: Sinivasan Bantah Berkolusi', 4 December 1999.

15. *Gatra*, 'Uang Kembali Atau Masuk Bui', 18 December 1999.

16. Soedradjad Djiwandono, 'Bank Indonesia and the Recent Crisis', *Bulletin of Indonesian Economic Studies*, Vol. 36, No. 1, April 2000, p. 71.

17. Detik.com, 'Skandal Texmaco . . .', op. cit.

18. Yet another reason why the lending should not have taken place is that Sinivasan asserted that the funds would be used to finance expansion, whereas BI stipulated that pre-shipment export facilities were to be used exclusively for financing exports.

19. George Fane, 'Survey of Recent Developments', *Bulletin of Indonesian Economic Studies*, Vol. 36, No. 1, April 2000, p. 29.

20. Fane, op. cit., p. 29.

21. *Asiaweek*, 'Past vs. Future', op. cit.

22. Detik.com, 'Pengakuan Djiwandono: Texmaco Ada Intervensi Soeharto'.

23. *BusinessWeek Online* (international edition), 'Where Did the Billions Go?', 28 February 2000.

24. Detik.com, 'Karena 2 Disposisi HMS, Kredit Texmaco Naik 84%', 7 December 1999.

25. Confidential communication.

26. See, for example: *BusinessWeek Online*, op. cit.; *Kompas*, 'NV Bank Indover Hong Kong Lakukan Penyimpangan Kredit', 22 March 2000; *Kompas*, 'Indover Tak Terlibat

Pendanaan Illegal', 4 March 2000; and *Kompas*, 'BPK Soroti Deposito Valas BI di Indover', 14 February 2000.

27. *Kompas*, 'Indover Tak Terlibat', op. cit.; *Kompas*, 'BI Akan Tutup Indover', 5 April 2000; *Kompas*, 'Tiga Mantan Direktur BI Dicegah Ke Luar Negeri', 6 September 2000.
28. *Gatra*, 'Panitia Penghasil Misteri', 19 February 2000. See also: Detik.com, 25 February 2000.
29. Soedradjad Djiwandono, 'Sekitar Permasalahan BLBI', located at: <www.pacific.net.id/pakar/sj/sekitar_masalah_bibi1.html>.
30. *Gatra*, 'Panitia Penghasil . . .', op. cit.
31. Badan Pemeriksa Keuangan, 'Siaran Pers BPK-RI Tentang Hasil Audit Investigasi Atas Penyaluran Dan Pengunaan Dana BLBI', 4 August 2000.
32. Bank Indonesia, 'Statistik Ekonomi Keuangan Indonesia', p. 8.
33. Bank Indonesia, 'Statistik Ekonomi . . .', op. cit., p. 8.
34. Bank Indonesia, 'Statistik Ekonomi . . .', op. cit., p. 21. The figure of Rp50 trillion is obtained by applying prevailing exchange rates to the monthly data for foreign exchange deposits. It is conceivable that BLBI funds were recirculated through other private banks, thereby explaining the relatively small aggregate decline in private bank deposits. But few, if any, private banks received massive amounts of fresh deposits—and if they had, BI would presumably have reabsorbed the liquidity that had been injected into the troubled banks.
35. David Cole, 'Rebuilding the Indonesian Financial System: Lessons from the Past and Suggestions for the Future', paper presented at the Eleventh Annual ISEI-USIS Economic Seminar on 'Emerging from the Economic Crisis: Restructuring, Privatisation and Transparency', Jakarta, 23 September 1999.
36. Badan Pemeriksa Keuangan, 'Siaran Pers BPK-RI Tentang Hasil Audit . . .', op. cit. See also: Cole, 'Rebuilding the Indonesian . . .', op. cit.; and Detik.com, 'BPK Benarkan Ada Dana BLBI Untuk Main Valas', 8 June 2001.
37. *Media Indonesia*, 'BLBI: Bencana Luar Biasa Indonesia', 14 January 2000.
38. *Suara Pembaruan*, 'Keputusan Pemerintah Mengenai Bank "Sakit"', 22 August 1998; Warta Ekonomi, 'Was-Was Menjelang Tanggal 21', 14 September 1998; and *Infobank*, September 1998.
39. Of the total BLBI lending of Rp144.5 trillion, Rp6 trillion went to depositors of the 16 banks closed in November 1997, and Rp9.1 trillion went to repay offshore trade finance obligations of banks taken over by the government. The remainder, Rp129.4 trillion, was the amount disbursed to overcome liquidity shortages in private banks. The breakdown of this sum per bank is commonly cited as follows: BCA, Rp30 trillion; BDNI, Rp28 trillion; Bank Danamon, Rp26 trillion; and Bank Umum Nasional, Rp10.7 trillion. However, these figures differ marginally in various reports, and it seems that no official breakdown has been made public.
40. *Infobank*, 'Gajah Sjamsul Sedot Habis Uang Bank', No. 229, September 1998, p. 31. See also: *Suara Pembaruan*, 'Keputusan Pemerintah Mengenai Bank "Sakit"', 22 August 1998.
41. *Warta Ekonomi*, 'Was-Was Menjelang Tanggal 21', 14 September 1998.
42. Based on audited accounts posted on Indoexchange.com.
43. Detik.com, 'Laporan Khusus: MSAA Dan Penggelapan Dana BLBI (5): Si Lebah Penyedot Uang Negara'.
44. Djiwandono, 'Sekitar Permasalahan BLBI', op. cit.
45. BDNI's honorary president commissioner was the sultan of Yogyakarta, Hamengkubuwono X. The bank's president commissioner was a retired four-star general and former army chief-of-staff, Makmun Murod.
46. *Tempo*, 'Fuad Bawazier, Pencetak Raja, Penjaga Raja', 14 November 1999.
47. Djiwandono, 'Bank Indonesia and the Recent Crisis', op. cit., p. 65.
48. Djiwandono, 'Bank Indonesia and the Recent Crisis', op. cit., p. 70.

President Soeharto flanked in a 1990 appearance by four successive military chiefs: (from left) Feisal Tanjung, Edi Sudradjat, Soeharto, Benny Moerdani and Try Sutrisno. (Tempo/Dedi Asondi)

Soeharto's eldest daughter, Siti Hardiyanti Rukmana ('Mbak Tutut'), poses while donating gold during her 'Love the Rupiah' campaign in January 1998. With her are the economic 'technocrats' Central Bank governor Soedradjad Djiwandono (left) and finance minister Mar'ie Muhammad. (AFP)

Texmaco Group owner Marimutu Sinivasan, the Soeharto confidante who borrowed around $1 billion from the central bank during the height of the currency crisis. (Tempo/Fernandez Hutagalung)

Prominent members of Soeharto's short-lived Sixth Development Cabinet: (from left) Coordinating minister for the economy Ginandjar Kartasasmita, finance minister Fuad Bawazier, industry and trade minister Mohammad 'Bob' Hasan, and Central Bank governor Syahril Sabirin. (AFP)

As the commander of the Special Forces (Kopassus), Prabowo Subianto used his unit against political opponents of his father-in-law, Soeharto. (Tempo/Rully Kesuma)

Maj. Gen. Zacky Anwar Makarim, a career Kopassus intelligence officer and the military's leading expert in covert operations throughout the late 1990s. (Gamma/Mustaf a Kamal)

A water cannon and armoured personnel carrier face students rallying on Jalan Sudirman during the first week of May 1998. (Tempo/Rully Kesuma)

Later in the day, the rally turns violent. (Tempo/Rully Kesuma)

A typical street scene during the 1998 riots, Central Jakarta, 14 May. (Tempo/Rully Kesuma)

Looting during the May riots.
(Kees Metselaar)

High profile generals from Kopassus share a light moment during the tension of early 1998: (from left) Maj. Gen. Syafrie Syamsoeddin, Maj. Gen. Agum Gumelar, Maj. Gen. Prabowo Subianto and Lt Gen. Yunus Yosfiah. (Tempo/Hidayat SG)

Bachruddin Jusuf Habibie, the eccentric Soeharto protégé who ascended to the presidency on 22 May 1998. (Tempo/Rully Kesuma)

Democracy activist Reza Patria testifies about his abduction and torture by Prabowo's 'Rose Team' as members of the secret Kopassus unit look on in the background. (AFP)

Human rights advocate Adnan Buyung Nasution (left) confers with the longstanding Soeharto critic, Marine Maj. Gen. (ret.) Ali Sadikin. (Tempo/Gatot Sri Widodo)

At a critical junction in October 1998, Muslim cleric Abdurrahman Wahid initiates an alliance with the military by inviting top generals to a political rally: (from left) Gen. (ret.) Edi Sudradjat, Lt Gen. Susilo Bambang Yudhoyono, Jakarta governor Lt Gen. Sutiyoso, Army chief-of-staff Gen. Subagyo, Military chief Gen. Wiranto and Wahid. (Tempo/Rini PWI)

A local mob beats a man to death during North Jakarta's Ketapang religious riot on 22 November 1998 in which 16 lives were claimed. Like other episodes of violence, the riot appeared deliberately instigated with the complicity of military elements. (AFP)

In December 1998, Wahid (right) implored Soeharto (centre) to halt an apparent campaign of political violence. The embattled former president sent an ominous signal by attending the meeting with Yorrys Raweyai (left), a notorious underworld figure. (Tempo/Ardi Bramantyo)

Former Muhammadiyah Chair Amien Rais delivers a fiery oration to mark the declaration of his National Mandate Party (Pan). (AFP)

Three pillars of the Soeharto regime observe a Golkar party rally during the approach to parliamentary elections: (from left) Harmoko, Arnold Baramuli and Feisal Tanjung. (Tempo/Iben Zein)

PDI Perjuangan Chair Megawati Soekarnoputri addresses a typically large throng of supporters on the third anniversary of the PDI headquarters raid. (Tempo/Gatot Sri Widodo)

Soeharto's favourite son, Tommy, wears a confident grin in court just prior to being acquitted on corruption charges. (Tempo)

In August 1999, Megawati made a dramatic public appearance with Golkar Chair Akbar Tandjung, signalling a reconciliation with her erstwhile foe. (Tempo/Robin Ong)

A cameraman in East Timor ducks as military-backed Aitarak militiamen open fire on pro-independence supporters on 26 August 1999, four days before the ballot for self-determination. (AFP)

Dili burns on 9 September 1999 as militias force mass evacuations from the East Timorese capital. (AFP)

Sander Thoenes, the 30-year-old Financial Times *journalist who disappeared after encountering Indonesian Army regulars in East Timor on 21 September 1999. The next day he was found shot dead.*

In a clash near parliament in October 1999, an anti-military protestor hurls a Molotov cocktail at troops. (AFP)

Moments after narrowly winning election as Indonesia's fourth president, Abdurrahman Wahid clasps hands with a visibly shaken Megawati Soekarnoputri. (AFP)

Wiranto (right) and his trusted subordinate, Lt Gen. Djaja Suparman (centre). (Gamma/Moriza Prananda)

The Late Lt Gen. Agus Wirahadikusumah, a determined reformer who lacked civilian political support. (Gamma/Moriza Prananda)

Vice-president Megawati distances herself from President Wahid by making a high-profile visit to Kopassus headquarters in September 2000, days after two soldiers were implicated in the Jakarta Stock Exchange bombing. On her right is Army chief-of-staff Gen. Tyasno Sudarto and on her left, Susilo Bambang Yudhoyono. (AFP)

The military's 'new conservatives', Army chief-of-staff and former Soeharto bodyguard Gen. Endriartono Sutarto (left) and the military's chief political strategist, Lt Gen. Agus Wijoyo. (Gamma/Moriza Prananda)

While conferring with Icmi Chair Achmad Tirtosudiro (centre left), PPP Chair Hamzah Haz (centre) anxiously awaits the results of the 2001 vice-presidential election in the MPR. (Gamma/Mustaf a Kamal)

49. Colin Johnson, 'Survey of Recent Developments', *Bulletin of Indonesian Economic Studies*, Vol. 34, No. 2, August 1998, p. 28.
50. Benedict Anderson, *Language and Power: Exploring Political Cultures in Indonesia*, pp. 17–78. See also: McDonald, *Suharto's Indonesia*, pp. 1–6; and Vatikiotis, *Indonesian Politics Under Suharto*, p. 29.
51. The International Commission of Jurists Mission to Indonesia, 'Ruler's Law', April 1999, p. 58.
52. Thanks to John Haseman for making this point.
53. *Tapol Bulletin*, 'The Kopassus-Militia Alliance', No. 154/5, November 1999.
54. *Asian Wall Street Journal*, 'Hashim Emerges in Corporate Indonesia: Family and Political Connections Bolster Tough Expansionary Style', 2 February 1992.
55. See, for example: Schwarz, *A Nation in Waiting*, p. 367.
56. McDonald, *Suharto's Indonesia*, p. 55.
57. *Tapol Bulletin*, 'The Kopassus-Militia Alliance', op. cit.
58. *Suara Pembaruan*, 'Evaluas Akhir Tahun 1998: Titik Balik Penting Dalam Peran ABRI', 28 December 1998.
59. *Jakarta Post*, 29 April 1998, p. 1.
60. *Wall Street Journal*, 'Wiranto-led Armed Forces Could Seal Habibie's Fate', 9 June 1999.
61. Thanks to James Van Zorge for making this point, in early 1997.
62. *Tempo*, 'Di antara Stik Golf, Soeharto, dan Tongkat Komando', 26 December 1999.
63. The four key commands were the armed forces chief, the Kostrad commander, the Jakarta Garrison commander and the Special Forces commander.
64. *Jakarta Post*, 13 February 1998, p. 1.
65. *Media Indonesia*, 3 March 1998, p. 1.

CHAPTER 5   FORCING REFORM

1. Mietzner, 'From Soeharto to Habibie: The Armed Forces and Political Islam', in Schwarz and Paris (eds), *Post-Soeharto Indonesia: Renewal or Chaos?*, p. 74.
2. Presidential Decree #90/1995 only made the contribution voluntary; a subsequent decree, #92/1996, made it mandatory.
3. See: *Tempo*, 'Fuad Bawazier, Pencetak Raja, Penjaga Raja', 14 November 1999; *Forum Keadilan*, 'Menjaring Keppres, Menjerat Soeharto', 16 November 1998, p. 83; *Kompas*, 'Semua Digunakan Untuk Sejahteraan Sosial', 10 August 1998; *Kompas*, 'Tidak Ada Dana Yayasan Ke Golkar', 30 December 1998; and *Kompas*, 'Berawal Dan Berakhir Di Titik Start', 25 April 2000.
4. See, for example: Schwarz, *A Nation in Waiting*, p. 315.
5. *Gatra*, 'Kabinet Krisis Kini Dirombak', 23 May 1998, p. 39.
6. John Haseman, 'National Security', in Frederick and Worden (eds), *Indonesia: A Country Study*, p. 335.
7. *Bisnis Indonesia*, 19 March 1998, p. 1.
8. *Gatra*, 'Kabinet Krisis Kini . . .', op. cit., p. 39.
9. Harian Neraca, 17 March 1998, p. 1.
10. *Jakarta Post*, 17 March 1998, p. 1.
11. See, for example: *Bisnis Indonesia*, 15 April 1998, p. 1.
12. *Bisnis Indonesia*, 'President Soeharto: Kita Akan Konsisten Terapkan Reformasi', 14 April 1998.
13. *Jawa Pos*, 'President Risaukan Media', 17 April 1998.
14. *Suara Pembaruan*, 'Presiden: Kampus Dibangun Untuk Mendidik', 18 April 1998.
15. *Kompas*, 'Masyarakat Diharapkan Pelihara Keamanan dan Ketertiban', 17 April 1998.
16. *Kompas*, 'Andi Arief Ditanya Penculik Bagaimana Selamatkan Soeharto', 22 July 1998.
17. *Kompas*, 'Andi Arief Ditanya . . .', op. cit.
18. *Jakarta Post*, 29 April 1998, p. 1.

19. See, for example: *Suara Pembaruan*, 'Prabowo Subianto: "Saya Prajurit Sampai Ke Liang Kubur" ', 19 October 1999.
20. Richard Mann, *Plots and Schemes that Brought Down Soeharto*, p. 133.
21. *Jawa Pos*, 'Tersenyum Saat Diinterupsi', 26 April 1998.
22. *Suara Pembaruan*, 'Kassospol ABRI: Tidak Ada Perintah Pangab Untuk Menculik Aktivis', 26 April 1998.
23. *Suara Pembaruan*, 'Kassospol ABRI . . .', op. cit.
24. *Suara Pembaruan*, 'Wirabuana: Aspirasi Mahasiswa Benar dan Mewakili Rakyat', 25 April 1998.
25. These leaders included Subagyo, Makarim, Yudhoyono and Hamid. The latter had recently been made a Deputy Speaker of parliament.
26. *Jakarta Post*, 9 April 1998, p. 2.

CHAPTER 6 'CLOSER TO GOD'

1. *Suara Merdeka*, 'Peluru Karet Berseliwaran di UNS, 400 Mahasiswa Luka', 9 May 1998.
2. *Suara Merdeka*, 'Syarwan Hamid Tentang Kinerja DPR', 9 May 1998.
3. *Suara Pembaruan*, 'Presiden Soeharto: Saya Mengerti Penderitaan Rakyat', 9 May 1998.
4. *Kompas*, 'Mengikuti Perjalanan Terakhir Soeharto Selaku Presiden RI', 12 May 2000.
5. *Forum Keadilan*, 'Di Ujung Aksi Damai', 1 June 1998, p. 11.
6. *Kompas*, 'Kapten (Pol.) Agustri Heryanto: Banyak Kejanggalan dalam Kasus Trisakti', 12 May 2000, p. 22.
7. *Suara Pembaruan*, 'Kronologi Tragedi 12 Mei', 13 May 1998.
8. *Gatra*, 'Mereka Ingin Reformasi', 23 May 1998, p. 33.
9. *Forum Keadilan*, 'Di Ujung Aksi . . .', op. cit., p. 12.
10. *Asiaweek*, 'Ten Days That Shook Indonesia', 24 July 1998.
11. *Kompas*, 'Mengikuti Perjalanan Terakhir . . .', op. cit., p. 22; Detik.com, 'Jejak Trisakti, Jejak Prabowo (3): Kok, Wiranto tak Diutak-atik', May 2000.
12. Detik.com, 'Jejak Trisakti, Jejak . . .', op. cit.
13. *Forum Keadilan*, 'Di Ujung Aksi . . .', op. cit., p. 12.
14. *Forum Keadilan*, 'Di Ujung Aksi . . .', op. cit., p. 12.
15. *Suara Pembaruan*, 'Irsan: Perlu Rekonstruksi Dalam Kasus Penembakan 4 Mahasiswa Trisakti', 8 June 1998.
16. *Kompas*, 'Perjalanan Mengungkap Tiga Proyektil', 12 May, 2000, p. 20. Also see: Detik.com, 'Jejak Trisakti, Jejak Prabowo (2)', May 2000.
17. *Tempo*, 'Menegakkan Benang Basah', 25 February 2001, p. 32.
18. The account of Soeharto's visit to Cairo is taken from *Kompas*, 'Mengikuti Perjalanan Terakhir . . .', op. cit., pp. 7, 22.
19. *Kompas*, 'Mengikuti Perjalanan . . .', op. cit.
20. *Kompas*, 'Mengikuti Perjalanan . . .', op. cit.
21. *Kompas*, 'Mengikuti Perjalanan . . .', op. cit.

CHAPTER 7 IMPECCABLY AMOK

1. *Suara Pembaruan*, 'Kronologis Aksi Massa 13 Mei', 14 May 1998.
2. Danyel Urgen, eyewitness account. Also: *Forum Keadilan*, 'Di Ujung Aksi Damai', 1 June 1998; and *Gatra*, 'Mereka Ingin Reformasi', 23 May 1998, p. 2.
3. *Forum Keadilan*, 'Di Ujung Aksi . . .', op. cit.
4. *Forum Keadilan*, 'Di Ujung Aksi . . .', op. cit.; *Gatra*, 'Mereka Ingin . . .', op. cit., p. 2.
5. *Suara Pembaruan*, 'Kawasan Kota Lumpuh, 448 Bangunan Rusak', 14 May 1998.
6. Thanks to Brian Corbin for telling me this, in a telephone conversation that took place at that very time.
7. *Tajuk*, 'Pengakuan Para Jenderal', 15 October 1998, p. 20.
8. Witnessed by the author.

9. Witnessed by the author.
10. Witnessed by the author.
11. Geoff Forrester, 'Chronology of Events', in Forrester and May (eds), *The Fall of Soeharto*, p. 243.
12. Colin Johnson, 'Survey of Recent Developments', *Bulletin of Indonesian Economic Studies*, Vol. 34, No. 2, 2 August 1998, p. 51.
13. Tim Relawan Untuk Kemanusiaan, 'Perkosaan Massal Dalam Rentetan Kerusuhan: Puncak Kebiadaban Dalam Kehidupan Bangsa', in *Temuan Tim Gabungan Pencari Fakta Peristiwa Kerusuhan Mei 1998*, pp. 87–8. For the account of an attempted gang rape reported in the press, see: *Suara Pembaruan*, 'Kota Lumpuh, 448 Bangunan Rusak', 14 May 1998.
14. Tim Relawan Untuk Kemanusiaan, 'Perkosaan Massal Dalam . . .', op. cit., p. 89.
15. See, for example: *Jakarta Post*, 'Emil Calls on Govt to Set Up Independent Commission', 29 June 1998, p. 2.
16. *Tajuk*, 'Ita Pergi Di Tengah Kontroversi', 15 October 1998, p. 22.
17. *Tempo*, 'Jalan Panjang Tragedi Itu', 12 October 1998, p. 56.
18. *Wall Street Journal*, 'Some Indonesian Rape Photos on the Internet Are Frauds', 20 August 1998.
19. *Forum Keadilan*, 'Laporan Akhir Para Seteru', 30 November 1998, pp. 88–9.
20. *Reuters*, 'UN Official Confirms Indonesian Mass Rapes', 18 December 1998.
21. Tim Relawan Untuk Kemanusiaan, 'Pola Kerusuhan di Jakarta dan Sekitarnya', in *Temuan Tim Gabungan Pencari Fakta Peristiwa Kerusuhan Mei 1998*, p. 47.
22. *Suara Pembaruan*, 'Kronoligis Aksi Massa 13 Mei', 14 May 1998. See also: *Jakarta Post*, 15 May 1998, p. 2; and *Forum Keadilan*, 'Di Ujung Aksi . . .', op. cit.
23. *Forum Keadilan*, 'Di Ujung Aksi . . .', op. cit., p. 16.
24. *Jakarta Post*, 15 May 1998, p. 1.
25. Tim Relawan Untuk Kemanusiaan, 'Laporan Akhir Tim Gabungan Pencari Fakta', in *Temuan Tim Gabungan Pencari Fakta Peristiwa Kerusuhan Mei 1998*, pp. 17–18.
26. Tim Relawan Untuk Kemanusiaan, 'Laporan Akhir Tim . . .', op. cit., p. 18.
27. *Forum Keadilan*, 'Di Ujung Aksi . . .', op. cit., p. 15.
28. Tim Relawan Untuk Kemanusiaan, 'Pola Kerusuhan di Jakarta dan Sekitarnya', in *Temuan Tim Gabungan Pencari Fakta Peristiwa Kerusuhan Mei 1998*, pp. 50–3.
29. Tim Relawan Untuk Kemanusiaan, 'Pola Kerusuhan di . . .', op. cit., pp. 55–8.
30. *Asiaweek*, 'Ten Days That Shook Jakarta', 24 July 1998.
31. See, for example: *Forum Keadilan*, 'Di Ujung Aksi . . .', op. cit., p. 16.
32. *Jakarta Post*, 15 May 1998, p. 1.
33. Pour, *Jakarta Semasa Lengser Keprabon*, p. 69.
34. *Asiaweek*, 'Ten Days . . .', op. cit., 24 July 1998.
35. *Asiaweek*, 'Ten Days . . .', op. cit., 24 July 1998.
36. *Tajuk*, 'Menanti Akhir Misteri Kerusuhan Mei', 15 October 1998, p. 14.
37. *Tajuk*, 15 October 1998, p. 25.
38. *Tajuk*, 15 October 1998, p. 25.
39. *Panji Masyrakyat*, 'Menanti Pengadilan Bicara', 6 January 1999, p. 27.
40. *Tajuk*, 'Saksi-Saksi Setelah 100 Hari', 16 September 1998.
41. *Suara Pembaruan*, 'Kodam Jaya Akan Mengugat Majalah "*Tajuk*"', 9 September 1998.
42. See, for example: Suaedy (ed.), *Premanisme Politik*; *Tapol Bulletin*, 'The Kopassus-Militia Alliance', No. 154/5, November 1999; and *Kompas*, 'Merebaknya Paramiliter Bisa Dorong Perang Milisia', 30 January 2001.
43. See, for example: *Kompas*, 'Puluhan Ribu Mahasiswa "Duduki" DPR', 20 May 1998; *Kompas*, 'Merebaknya Paramiliter Bisa Dorong Perang Milisia', 30 January 2001; and *Jakarta Post*, 'Youth Organisations Committed to End Rivalry', 23 October 2000.
44. Suaedy (ed.), *Premanisme Politik*, p. 71.
45. Some have asserted that in fomenting the May riots Prabowo was acting not against

Soeharto but against Wiranto. This explanation speculates that Prabowo hoped to create instability which would reflect poorly on the armed forces commander, thereby prompting Soeharto to sack Wiranto and promote Prabowo. But apart from being a convoluted means of seeking a promotion, this course of action would have been self-defeating. By creating riots Prabowo would have been jeopardising the already precarious position of the only man empowered to give him that promotion—Soeharto.

46. *Jakarta Post,* 16 May 1998, p. 2.
47. *Jawa Pos,* 'Mayjen Muchdi Masuk Elite Circle', 13 February 1998.
48. See, for example: *Suara Merdeka,* 'Soeripto Klarifikasi Kepada Kapolri', 24 March 2001.
49. *Forum Keadilan,* 'Suatu Malam di Makostrad', 30 November 1998, p. 85.
50. *Forum Keadilan,* 'Suatu Malam . . .', op. cit., p. 85.
51. Detik.com, 'Jejak Trisakti, Jejak Prabowo (3)', May 2000.
52. *Tajuk,* 'Menanti Akhir Misteri Kerusuhan Mei', 15 October 1998, p. 14.
53. *Forum Keadilan,* 'Laporan Akhir Para Seteru', 30 November 1998, p. 89.
54. *Forum Keadilan,* 'Mengapa Para Jenderal Pergi?', 30 November 1998, p. 87.
55. Majalah Berita Populer Totalitas, *Buku Putih Prabowo: Kesaksian Tragedi Mei 1998,* p. 18.
56. Thanks to Michael Chambers for this information.
57. See, for example: *Tapol Bulletin,* 'The Kopassus-Military Alliance', No. 154/5, November 1999.
58. Mietzner, 'From Soeharto to Habibie: The Armed Forces and Political Islam', in Schwarz and Paris (eds), *Post-Soeharto Indonesia: Renewal or Chaos?,* p. 80.
59. *Jawa Pos,* 'Karier Pangab Jenderal TNI Wiranto', 13 February 1998.
60. Mietzner, 'From Soeharto to Habibie . . .', op. cit. p. 70.

CHAPTER 8   COUP À LA JAVA

1. Pour, *Jakarta Semasa Lengser Keprabon,* p. 99.
2. Abdul Gafur, *Hari-Hari Terakhir Seorang Presiden,* p. 17.
3. Gafur, *Hari-Hari Terakhir,* p. 17.
4. Gafur, *Hari-Hari Terakhir,* p. 17.
5. The description of the parliament leaders' meeting with Soeharto is adapted from Gafur, *Hari-Hari Terakhir,* pp. 77–80.
6. *Van Zorge Report,* 'Interview with Sarwono Kusumaatmadja', 18 June 1999.
7. Mietzner, 'From Soeharto to Habibie: The Armed Forces and Political Islam', in Schwarz and Paris (eds), *Post Soeharto Indonesia: Renewal or Chaos?,* p. 80.
8. Mietzner, 'From Soeharto to Habibie . . .', op. cit., p. 80.
9. Majalah Berita Populer Totalitas, *Buku Putih Prabowo,* p. 18.
10. *Tajuk,* 'Habibie, Prabowo, Dan Hari-Hari Dramatis Itu', 4 March 1999.
11. Mietzner, 'From Soeharto to Habibie . . .', op. cit., p. 81. Some reports claim that Subagyo agreed on one condition: that Amien Rais's long march planned for 20 May be allowed to take place first, after which a stern security response would be easier to justify (*Tajuk,* 'Habibie, Prabowo, Dan Hari-Hari Dramatis Itu', 4 March 1999).
12. *Gatra,* 'Kabinet Krisis Kini Dirombak', 23 May 1998, p. 38.
13. Majalah Berita Populer Totalitas, *Buku Putih Prabowo,* p. 18.
14. *Tajuk,* 'Habibie, Prabowo, Dan . . .', op. cit.
15. *Tajuk,* 'Habibie, Prabowo, Dan . . .', op. cit.
16. *Jakarta Post,* 'Wiranto Says He Already Passed Up Chance For Power', 5 March 1999, p. 2. See also: *Republika,* 'Wiranto Tentang Isu Kudeta: Saya Punya Kesempatan', 22 January 2000, p. 3.
17. For Mokodongan's version, see: *Tajuk,* 'Habibie, Prabowo, Dan . . .', op. cit. For the other version, see: *Asiaweek,* 'The Scapegoat?', 3 March 2000.
18. The meeting with Mursjid is taken from Nurcholish's account of events, as described in Schwarz, *A Nation in Waiting,* p. 360.
19. The following account is from Schwarz, *A Nation in Waiting,* p. 360.

20. Majalah Berita Populer Totalitas, *Buku Putih Prabowo*, p. 21.
21. See, for example: Pour, *Jakarta Semasa Lengser Keprabon*, p. 105, and *Asiaweek*, 'The Scapegoat?', op. cit.
22. Gafur, *Hari-Hari Terakhir*, pp. 85–6.
23. Gafur, *Hari-Hari Terakhir*, pp. 85–6.
24. Gafur, *Hari-Hari Terakhir*, p. 87.
25. Pour, *Jakarta Semasa Lengser Keprabon*, p. 114.
26. *Gatra*, 'Detik-detik yang Menegangkan', 30 May 1998, p. 28.
27. Gafur, *Hari-Hari Terakhir*, p. 88.
28. Mietzner, 'From Soeharto to Habibie . . .', op. cit., p. 81.
29. Schwarz, *A Nation in Waiting*, p. 361.
30. Mietzner, 'From Soeharto to Habibie . . .', op. cit., p. 82.
31. *Gatra*, 'Detik-detik yang Menegangkan', op. cit., p. 28.
32. *Gatra*, 'Detik-detik yang Menegangkan', op. cit., p. 28.
33. Mietzner, 'From Soeharto to Habibie . . .', op. cit., p. 83.
34. The following description of the meeting between Soeharto and the Muslim leaders is taken from both Mietzner, 'From Soeharto to Habibie . . .', op. cit., pp. 82–3, and Schwarz, *A Nation in Waiting*, pp. 361–2.
35. Schwarz, *A Nation in Waiting*, p. 361.
36. Gafur, *Hari-Hari Terakhir*, pp. 128–30.
37. *Gatra*, 'Bayang-Bayang Kelam Di Depan Habibie', 30 May 1998, p. 27.
38. Schwarz, *A Nation in Waiting*, p. 365.
39. Gafur, *Hari-Hari Terakhir*, p. 122.
40. Pour, *Jakarta Semasa Lengser Keprabon*, p. 112.
41. Pour, *Jakarta Semasa Lengser Keprabon*, p. 150.
42. Gafur, *Hari-Hari Terakhir*, p. 131.
43. Pour, *Jakarta Semasa Lengser Keprabon*, p. 143.
44. Pour, *Jakarta Semasa Lengser Keprabon*, p. 106.
45. Schwarz, *A Nation in Waiting*, p. 363.
46. Gafur, *Hari-Hari Terakhir*, p. 137.
47. See, for instance, the views of one of the nine Islamic figures who visited Soeharto on Tuesday morning: *Panji Masyrakyat*, 'Emha Ainun Nadjib: Saya Khawatir Muncul Taliban Seperti Di Afghanistan', 11 November 1998, p. 13.
48. Schwarz, *A Nation in Waiting*, p. 364.
49. *Kompas*, 'Cerita Dibalik Mundurnya Soeharto', 27 May 1998.
50. *Gatra*, 'Detik-detik yang Menegangkan', op. cit., p. 28.
51. *Kompas*, 'Cerita Dibalik . . .', op. cit.
52. Gafur, *Hari-Hari Terakhir*, p. 156.
53. Gafur, *Hari-Hari Terakhir*, pp. 155–6.
54. Gafur, *Hari-Hari Terakhir*, p. 158.
55. Gafur, *Hari-Hari Terakhir*, p. 158.

CHAPTER 9   ZING-A-BUST

1. A. Makmur Makka, *Bacharuddin Jusuf Habibie: His Life and Career*, pp. 12–13.
2. *Suara Pembaruan*, 'Si Pemilik Sepatu Bolong Itu Kini Menjadi Wapres', 11 March 1998.
3. Makka, *Bacharuddin Jusuf Habibie*, p. 8.
4. See: Schwarz, *A Nation in Waiting*, p. 86.
5. Schwarz, *A Nation in Waiting*, p. 87; also Colin Johnson, 'Survey of Recent Developments', *Bulletin of Indonesian Economic Studies*, Vol. 34, No. 2, August 1998, p. 33.
6. *The Economist*, 'Indonesia Survey: Engineering the Future', 17 April 1993, p. 12.
7. Schwarz, *A Nation in Waiting*, p. 313.
8. Schwarz, *A Nation in Waiting*, p. 313.
9. *Financial Times*, 'Survey Indonesia', 13 May 1993, p. 2.

10. Majalah Berita Populer Totalitas, *Buku Putih Prabowo*, p. 23.
11. Mietzner, 'From Soeharto to Habibie . . .', op. cit., p. 89.
12. Mietzner, 'From Soeharto to Habibie . . .', op. cit., footnote p. 233.
13. Majalah Berita Populer Totalitas, *Buku Putih Prabowo*, p. 23.
14. Ironically, Sintong, like Prabowo, was an anti-terror specialist. He was famed for his rescue of a hijacked Garuda jet in Bangkok in 1981, performed with the same Special Forces unit, Detachment 81, that Prabowo revived to kidnap pro-democracy activists. A rising star in the military, Sintong's career was suddenly cut short when he was held responsible for the 1991 Santa Cruz massacre in East Timor. Ironically, Prabowo would soon join Sintong as the only other senior officer summarily discharged without honour.
15. Takashi Shiraishi, 'The Indonesian Military in Politics', in Schwarz and Paris (eds), *The Politics of Post-Suharto Indonesia*, p. 85. See also: Mietzner, 'From Soeharto to Habibie . . .', op. cit., p. 89. Mietzner acknowledges that other accounts maintain that Prabowo did meet with Habibie (footnote, p. 233).
16. Majalah Berita Populer Totalitas, *Buku Putih Prabowo*, p. 24.
17. Majalah Berita Populer Totalitas, *Buku Putih Prabowo*, p. 24.
18. Gafur, *Hari-Hari Terakhir*, p. 147.
19. Mann, *Plots and Schemes*, p. 277.
20. *Suara Pembaruan*, 'Kassospol: ABRI Akan Dukung Pelaksanaan Pemilu', 25 May 1998.
21. *Jakarta Post*, 'Habibie Says He Won't Contest Next Election', 10 June 1998, p. 2.
22. *Sydney Morning Herald*, 'Former General Admits He Led Attack on Balibo', 5 June 1999. See also: the *Independent* (UK), 'Indonesians Planned to Kill Newsmen, Says Ex-Police Chief', 30 August 1998; Tapol Press Release, 'Ex-Police Officer Says Five Newsman Were Intentionally Killed', 27 August 1998; and *D&R*, 'Balibo: Kerikil di Sepatu M. Yunus Yosfiah', 31 October 1998, p. 27.
23. *Bisnis Indonesia*, 'Menpen: Deppen Bisa Dihapus', 24 June 1998.
24. *Van Zorge Report*, 'Interview with Lt Gen. (ret.) Muhammad Yunus Yosfiah', 3 September 1999, p. 20.
25. *Suara Pembaruan*, 'Gugatan Syarwan Hamid Diajukan Secara Resmi Ke Mabes Polri', 4 August 1998.
26. *Jakarta Post*, 'God Engineered My Appointment: Habibie', 13 June 1998, p. 1.
27. *Jakarta Post*, 'Habibie Yet to Decide on His Re-election', 30 June 1998, p. 2.
28. World Bank, *Indonesia In Crisis: A Macroeconomic Update*, 1998.
29. Bank Indonesia data at: <www.bi.go.id>.
30. *Straits Times*, 'Laid-up Buses and Cars Stripped for Spare Parts', 4 September 1998.
31. World Bank, *Indonesia: From Crisis to Opportunity*, p. 14.
32. *Van Zorge Report*, 'Seeing Through a Glass, Darkly: Observations on the Indonesian Economy', by Vikram Nehru, Lead Economist, World Bank, 18 July 2000, p. 21.
33. Colin Johnson, 'Survey of Recent Developments', *Bulletin of Indonesian Economic Studies*, Vol. 34, No. 2, August 1998, p. 39.
34. World Bank, *Indonesia: From Crisis to Opportunity*, p. 25.
35. World Bank, *Indonesia: From Crisis to Opportunity*, p. 57.
36. *Jakarta Post*, 'Habibie Checks Food Prices in Markets', 13 June 1998, p. 1.
37. *Jakarta Post*, 'Habibie Calls for Fasting to Save Rice', 7 July 1998, p. 1.
38. *Surabaya Post*, 'Wawancara Dengan Menkop/PKM, Zarkasih Noer: Masih Jadi Alat Politik', 11 July 2000. See also: *Tempo*, 'Siapa Yang Diuntungkan?', 25 February 2001, p. 108.
39. *Kontan*, 'Tertembak Di Politik Suap', 31 May 1999. See also: *Suara Pembaruan*, 'Mengenai Bantuan $1.4 Milyar: Bank Dunia Tidak Lupa Dengan Komitmen Awal', 18 May 1999; and *Gamma*, 'Eh, Sunat Di Sana-Sini', 20 February 2001.
40. Thanks to Gary Goodpaster for his work on this subject, and Michael Horn for his insights.

41. *Van Zorge Report*, 'Interview with Paulus Lotulung, Supreme Court Justice', 17 December 1999, p. 15.

CHAPTER 10 PHOTOCOPYING SOEHARTO
1. *Suara Pembaruan*, 'Tak Ada Niat ABRI Merakayasa Politik', 12 June 1998.
2. Mietzner, 'From Soeharto to Habibie . . .', op. cit., p. 90.
3. Mietzner, 'From Soeharto to Habibie . . .', op. cit., footnote p. 234.
4. *Suara Pembaruan*, 'Akbar: Habibie Calon Tunggal President Dari Partai Golkar', 11 April 1999.
5. Vatikiotis, *Indonesian Politics Under Suharto*, p. 87. See also: Schwarz, *A Nation in Waiting*, p. 273; and Frederick and Worden (eds), *Indonesia: A Country Study*, p. 242.
6. See: Schwarz, *A Nation in Waiting*, p. 275.
7. Mietzner, 'From Soeharto to Habibie . . .', op. cit., p. 94.
8. *Kompas*, 'DPR Usul Pembentukan Pengadilan HAM "Ad Hoc" ', 22 March 2001, p. 11.
9. Vatikiotis, *Indonesian Politics Under Suharto*, p. 185.
10. Michael Vatikiotis, 'Romancing the Dual Function: Indonesia's Armed Forces and the Fall of Soeharto', in Geoff Forrester and R.J. May (eds), *The Fall of Soeharto*, p. 154.
11. *Jakarta Post*, 'Golkar Chair Still a Coveted Post', 8 July 1998, p. 2.
12. *Bisnis Indonesia*, 'Akbar: B.J. Habibie Tak Langgar Aturan Golkar', 2 July 1998.
13. *Jakarta Post*, 'Golkar Meeting Cancelled', 30 June 1998, p. 1.
14. *Jakarta Post*, 'Observers Look for New Faces in Golkar Race', 9 July 1998, p. 2.
15. *Tempo*, 'Komisi Dibentuk, Soeharto Melempar Truf', 7 December 1998.
16. *Tempo*, 'Komisi Dibentuk, Soeharto . . .', op. cit. See also: *Suara Pembaruan*, 'Pergantian Jaksa Agung Dinilai Tidak Normal', 16 June 1998; and *Jakarta Post*, 'Soeharto Hires Lawyers', 12 June 1998.
17. Adi Andojo Soetjipto, 'Legal Reforms and Challenges in Indonesia', in Manning and van Diermen (eds), *Indonesia in Transition: Social Aspects of Reformasi and Crisis*, p. 275.
18. *Suara Karya*, 'Pangab: Munaslub Jangan Sampai Ganggu Stabilitas', 8 July 1998.
19. Six weeks later, Hamid rewarded Mardiyanto by appointing him to the coveted post of Central Java governor (*Kompas*, 'Mendagri Lantik Gubernor Jateng', 25 August 1998).
20. Mietzner, 'From Soeharto to Habibie . . .', op. cit., p. 96. See also: *Jakarta Post*, 'Veterans Slam ABRI for Meddling in Golkar', 14 July 1998, p. 2.
21. *Jakarta Post*, 'Veterans Slam ABRI . . .', op. cit.
22. *Jakarta Post*, 'Golkar Changes Its Vision, Image Under New Chairman', 13 July 1998, p. 1.
23. *Bisnis Indonesia*, 'Intervensi Kekuatan Eksternal Golkar Disesalkan', 11 July 1998. See also: *Jakarta Post*, 'Golkar Changes Its Vision . . .', op. cit.
24. *Jakarta Post*, 'Golkar Meeting Cancelled', 30 June 1998, p. 1. See also: *Jakarta Post*, 'Golkar to End Chief Patron's Veto Right', 8 July 1998, p. 1.
25. *Jakarta Post*, 'Veterans Slam ABRI . . .', op. cit.
26. *Jakarta Post*, 'Planned Meeting of Golkar Improper: Try', 1 July 1998, p. 2.
27. See, for instance, Howard Palfrey Jones, *Indonesia: The Possible Dream*, Epilogue.
28. Vatikiotis, *Indonesian Politics Under Suharto*, p. 141.
29. Vatikiotis, *Indonesian Politics Under Suharto*, p. 22.
30. McDonald, *Suharto's Indonesia*, pp. 245–7.
31. *Van Zorge Report*, 'Feature Interview: Prof. Dr. Subroto', Vol. 1, Issue 4, 27 November 1998, pp. 14–15.
32. *Jakarta Post*, 'President B.J. Habibie Names New MPR Members', 1 July 1998, p. 2. See also: *Jakarta Post*, 'Cronyism Not a Factor in New MPR Appointments: Akbar', 2 July 1998, p. 3; and *Jakarta Post*, 'Harmoko Installs New Assembly Members', 9 July 1998, p. 1.
33. *Jakarta Post*, 'Habibie Calls Trisakti Students "Reform Heroes" ', 23 June 1998, p. 2.
34. *Asiaweek*, 'The People Are My Boss', 4 September 1998.

35. *Bisnis Indonesia*, 'Habibie Tegaskan Bukan Fotokopi Soeharto', 29 August 1998.
36. *Jakarta Post*, 'Rights Activists Blast Bill on Street Protests', 3 July 1998, p. 1.
37. *Jakarta Post*, 'Djaja Becomes New City Military Chief', 13 July 1998, p. 3. In addition to ties to Wiranto, Suparman also had ties to Kassospol Bambang Yudhoyono: he had served as Yudhoyono's chief-of-staff in the Southern Sumateran Garrison in 1996.
38. Subagyo had initially indicated that Prabowo would be brought before a court-martial, but Wiranto preferred a less-public tribunal, perhaps fearing that Prabowo would divulge embarrassing facts in an open court-martial.
39. *Agence France Presse*, 'Military Recommends Court Martial for Suharto's Son-in-law', 15 August 1998.
40. *Sydney Morning Herald*, 'Rights Watchdog Says 781 People Killed in Aceh', 25 August 1998.
41. See: *Suara Pembaruan*, 'Sepuluh Kuburan Massal Ditemukan Di Aceh', 6 August 1998; and *Waspada*, '12 Lokasi Kuburan Massal Terdapat Di Aceh Utara', 30 August 1998.
42. *Agence France Presse*, 'Shots Fired as Students Protest Habibie in East Java', 9 September 1998.

CHAPTER 11   'CRUELISM VERSUS CRUELISM'

1. Peter Turner, *Java: A Lonely Planet Travel Survival Kit*, pp. 362–3.
2. *Forum Keadilan*, 'Darah Mengalir di Tapal Kuda', 2 November 1998, p. 12.
3. *Reuters*, 'Toll Mounts in Mystery Indonesia Murder Spree', 9 October 1998.
4. *Forum Keadilan*, 'Darah Mengalir . . .', op. cit., p. 12; *Panji Masyrakyat*, 'Geger Gantung di Banyuwangi', 14 October 1998, p. 28.
5. *Forum Keadilan*, 'Darah Mengalir . . .', op. cit., p. 12.
6. *Panji Masyrakyat*, 'Jihad Melawan Ninja', 28 October 1998.
7. *Gatra*, 'Gerakan Politik Membantai Dukun Santet', 17 October 1998, p. 37.
8. *D&R*, 'Ninja Palsu Pun Dibantai', 31 October 1998, p. 20.
9. *Forum Keadilan*, 'Misteri Para Ninja Sinting', 16 November 1998, p. 22.
10. *D&R*, 'Ninja Palsu Pun . . .', op. cit., p. 20.
11. *D&R*, 'Ninja Itu Berubah Jadi Orang Tua', 31 October 1998, p. 16.
12. *Straits Times*, 'Eight Charged Over Bizarre Java Killings', 28 November 1998.
13. See, for example: *Wall Street Journal*, 'Mysterious Killings Strike Fear in Poor Villages of East Java', 16 October 1998.
14. *D&R*, 'Ninja Itu Berubah   ' op. cit., p. 16.
15. *Gatra*, 'Gerakan Politik . . .', op. cit., p. 39.
16. Frederik and Worden (eds), *Indonesia: A Country Study*, pp. 56–7.
17. *Tajuk*, 'Operasi Intelijen Di Banyuwangi?', February 1998.
18. *Gatra*, 'Teror Santet: ABRI Sampai Menteri Kabinet Kena Tuduh', 31 October 1998, p. 26.
19. On the forced resignation of Banyuwangi's *bupati*, Col. Purnomo Sidik, see: *Forum Keadilan*, 'Bupati Tersandung Dukun Santet', 22 February 1999, p. 76.
20. See: *D&R*, 'Ninja Itu Berubah . . .', op. cit., p. 17; *Gatra*, 'Teror Santet: ABRI . . .', op. cit., p. 27; and *Forum Keadilan*, 'Misteri Para Ninja . . .', op. cit., p. 22.
21. *Gatra*, 'Teror Santet: ABRI . . .', op. cit., p. 28.
22. See, for example: *Agence France Presse*, 'Mob Lynches Three Travelling Businessmen Amid Java Killing Spree', 8 November 1998.
23. *Gatra*, 'Operasi Ninja, Operasi Intelijen', 31 October 1998, p. 32. See also: *D&R*, 'Ninja Itu Berubah . . .', p. 18.
24. *Gatra*, 'Operasi Ninja, Operasi . . .', op. cit., p. 33.
25. *Gatra*, 'Operasi Ninja, Operasi . . .', op. cit., pp. 32–3.
26. *Tajuk*, 'Operasi Intelijen Di . . .', op. cit.
27. *Straits Times*, 'Indonesian Probe Finds 182 Murders But No Murderer', 10 December 1998.

28. *Forum Keadilan*, 'ABRI Punya Batas Kesabaran', 16 November 1998, p. 78.
29. *Forum Keadilan*, 'ABRI Punya Batas . . .', op. cit., p. 78.
30. See, for example, *Panji Masyrakyat*, 'Menyeret Ketapang Ke Kupang', 9 December 1998, pp. 78–9.
31. *Reuters*, 'Toll Mounts . . .', op. cit. Roesmanhadi cited a much publicised case in which police discovered a 'cell' of ninja killers led by a former PKI member. Others suspected that the cell was contrived.
32. See: *Van Zorge Report*, 'Preparing for the Elections: Megawati Soekarnoputri's PDI Congress and After', 9 October 1998, p. 5.
33. *Panji Masyrakyat*, 'Jika Habibie Menuding', 14 October 1998, p. 30.
34. *Reuters*, 'Mystery Murder Spree Takes New Twist in Indonesia', 2 October 1998.
35. See: *Sydney Morning Herald*, 'Indonesia's Black Death', 11 July 1998.
36. The following quotations from Wahid are taken from an interview conducted by the author and Dennis Heffernan with Abdurrahman Wahid on 13 October. See: *Van Zorge Report*, 'Feature Interview: Fair Elections? Or "Cruelism Versus Cruelism"?', 30 October 1998.

Chapter 12   'Stay Indoors'

1. McDonald, *Suharto's Indonesia*, p. 128. See also: Schwarz, *A Nation in Waiting*, p. 171.
2. See, for example: McDonald, *Suharto's Indonesia*, p. 103.
3. Schwarz, *A Nation in Waiting*, p. 172. See also: McDonald, *Suharto's Indonesia*, p. 239.
4. *Reuters*, 'Details of Indonesia's Special Assembly Meeting', 8 November 1998.
5. *Forum Keadilan*, 'Sidang Untuk Reformasi Pro Status Quo', 16 November 1998, p. 16.
6. *Forum Keadilan*, 'Mengusik Sidang, Mengharap Habibie Terbenam', 16 November 1998, p. 15.
7. Thanks to Gordon Bishop for making this point.
8. Thanks to Pan secretary-general Faisal Basri for making this point.
9. Confidential communication.
10. *Forum Keadilan*, 'Setelah Skenario Presidium Macet', 30 November 1998, p. 17.
11. A fifth figure, Bishop Belo of East Timor, declined an invitation because of illness.
12. *Forum Keadilan*, 'Sejumlah Ketatapan Di Tengah Kegamangan', 30 November 1998, p. 21 (translation by the author).
13. The November MPR session produced twelve resolutions; among these were measures requiring the government to: conduct parliamentary elections by May or June 1999; grant greater regional autonomy to the provinces; and strengthen the Human Rights Commission. Another resolution prohibited a president from serving more than two terms in office. None of these met significant opposition.
14. *Forum Keadilan*, 'Sejumlah Ketetapan Di . . .', op. cit., p. 22 (translation by the author).
15. *Forum Keadilan*, 'Sidang Untuk Reformasi . . .', op. cit., p. 17.
16. *Forum Keadilan*, 'Sidang Untuk Reformasi . . .', op. cit., p. 17.
17. *Forum Keadilan*, 'Sejumlah Ketatapan Di . . .', op. cit., pp. 21–2.
18. The military used a great many names to refer to various para-military units. In general, para-militaries were referred to as Ratih (Rakyat Terlatih, or Trained Civilians). These included: Hansip (Pertahanan Sipil, or Civil Defence) under the Home Affairs Ministry; Wanra (Perlawanan Rakyat, or People's Resistance) under the police; and Kamra (Keamanan Rakyat, or People's Security) under either the police or the military. The units recruited directly by the military in late 1998 were termed Pam Swakarsa (Pasukan Pengamanan Swakarsa, or Volunteer Security Forces).
19. Suaedy (ed.), *Premanisme Politik*, pp. 59, 93. See also: *Tempo*, 'Pam Swakarsa: Aktor Atau Korban?', 30 November 1998; and *Tempo*, 'Pasukan 240 Milyar Yang Kontroversial', 21 December 1998.
20. Suaedy (ed.), *Premanisme Politik*, p. 71.
21. See, for example: Schwarz, *A Nation in Waiting*, p. 367.

22. *Bali Post*, 'Perjalanan FPI Membasmi Tempat Maksiat', 19 December 2000.

23. *Forum Keadilan*, 'Mereka Bertarung Lagi Di Luar Gelanggang', 30 November 1998, p. 19. Several reports in the international press cited a figure of 125 000 civilian auxiliaries, mostly from Islamic groups.

24. *Agence France Presse*, 'Criticism Mounts Against Use of Civilian Vigilantes', 11 November 1998.

25. *Tempo*, 'Pam Swakarsa: Aktor . . .', op. cit. See also: Suaedy (ed.), *Premanisme Politik*, p. 98.

26. *Agence France Presse*, 'Criticism Mounts Against . . .', op. cit.

27. *Forum Keadilan*, 'Hari Dan Detik-Detik Mencekam Di Ibu Kota', 30 November 1998, p. 15. See also: *Kompas*, 'Pangab Soal Penembakan Di Semanggi', 23 November 1998.

28. *Forum Keadilan*, 'Hari Dan Detik-Detik . . .', op. cit.

29. *Forum Keadilan*, 'Sidang Berakhir, Darah Beralir', 30 November 1998, pp. 14–15.

30. *Dow Jones Newswires*, 'Indonesian Armed Forces Chief Warns Indonesians to Stay at Home', 12 November 1998.

31. *Dow Jones Newswires*, 'Indonesian Armed Forces . . .', op. cit.

32. *Tempo*, 'Pam Swakarsa: Aktor . . .', op. cit. See also: *Forum Keadilan*, 'Sidang Berakhir, Darah . . .', op. cit., p. 15.

33. *Reuters*, 'Fighting Turns Jakarta into War Zone', 13 November 1998. See also: *Washington Post*, 'Indonesian Troops Fire on Students, Killing 5', 14 November 1998.

34. *Forum Keadilan*, 'Sidang Berakhir, Darah . . .', op. cit., p. 13.

35. *Agence France Presse*, 'Indonesian Soldiers Fire Warning Shots, Tear Gas at Protesters', 13 November 1998.

36. *Agence France Presse*, 'One Killed as Indonesian Soldiers Open Fire on Demonstrators', 13 November 1998.

37. *Agence France Presse*, 'Three Killed as Soldiers Open Fire on Protesters', 13 November 1998. See also: *Forum Keadilan*, 'Sidang Berakhir, Darah . . .', op. cit., p. 13.

38. *Forum Keadilan*, 'Sidang Berakhir, Darah . . .', op. cit., p. 13.

39. *Reuters*, 'Fighting Turns Jakarta . . .', op. cit.

40. BBC, 'No Respite on the Streets of Jakarta', 14 November 1998.

41. *Jakarta Post*, 'Black Friday', 14 November 1998. See also: *SiaR*, 'Mysterious Armed Bands Discovered Behind Atmadjaya University Campus', 18 November 1998.

42. *Suara Pembaruan*, 'Komnas HAM Punya Bukti Baru Berupa Rekaman', 1 December 1998.

43. BBC, 'Five Students Killed; Jakarta Resembles Battle Zone', 13 November 1998.

44. BBC, 'Five Students Killed . . .', op. cit.

45. *Forum Keadilan*, 'Sidang Berakhir, Darah . . .', op. cit., p. 13.

46. *Forum Keadilan*, 'Sidang Berakhir, Darah . . .', op. cit., p. 14.

47. *Forum Keadilan*, 'Sidang Berakhir, Darah . . .', op. cit., p. 14.

48. *Washington Post*, 'Indonesian Troops Fire on Students, Killing 5', 14 November 1998.

49. *Agence France Presse*, 'Marine Wounded as Indonesian Troops Open Fire', 14 November 1998.

50. *Agence France Presse*, '1500 Students, Accompanied by Marines, Reach Parliament', 14 November 1998.

51. *Forum Keadilan*, 'Sidang Berakhir, Darah . . .', op. cit., p. 14. See also: *Forum Keadilan*, 'Jumat Berdarah Di Semanggi', 11 January 1999, p. 74.

52. *Kompas*, 'Pangab Soal Penembakan Di Semanggi', 23 November 1998.

53. *Kompas*, 'Agum Ajak Rembuk Nasional', 24 November 1998. See also: *Kompas*, 'Pangab Soal Penembakan . . .', op. cit.

54. *Forum Keadilan*, 'Sidang Berakhir, Darah . . .', op. cit., p. 15.

55. *Agence France Presse*, 'Forensic Experts Find Metal Bullet Fragments in Most Indonesian Shooting Victims', 20 November 1998.

56. *Suara Pembaruan*, 'Mahasiswa Dipaksa Menjadi Informan', 22 November 1998. For the

full transcript of Pratiwo's account, see: www.unfilteredonline.com, 'Orato Webzine'.

57. *Kompas*, 'Pengakuan Informan Di Komnas HAM', 22 November 1998.

58. www.unfilteredonline.com, 'Orato Webzine'.

59. *Kompas*, 'Wiwid Dan Prada Budi Adu Keterangan Di Puspom', 4 December 1998.

60. *Kompas*, 'Prada Budi Leksono Di Komnas Ham', 12 December 1998.

61. *Kompas*, 'Info Jabotabek', 8 December 1998.

62. *Suara Pembaruan*, 'Wiwid Dipertemukan Dengan Prada Budi', 4 December 1998.

63. *Agence France Presse*, 'Suharto Criticizes Habibie Government Over Inability to Prevent Clashes', 14 November 1998.

64. See, for example: *Tajuk*, 'Habibie, Prabowo Dan Hari-Hari Dramatis Itu', 4 March 1999; and the *Van Zorge Report*, 'Soldiers and Statesmen', 11 February 1999, p. 16.

65. See, for example: www.dephan.go.id, 'Peristiwa Ketapang', located at: <www.dephan. go.id/news/takah_puspen/fakta/PERIS_KETAPANG.html>.

66. *Panji Masyrakyat*, 'Lagi Massa Tersulut', 2 December 1998, p. 75.

67. Some witnesses claim that the window was broken by stones thrown by local residents trying to defend themselves; others say the Ambonese *preman* deliberately attacked the mosque. For the former view, see: *Panji Masyrakyat*, 'Lagi Massa Tersulut', op. cit., p. 76. For the latter view, see: *Sabili*, 9 December 1998, pp. 31–2.

68. www.dephan.go.id, 'Peristiwa Ketapang', op. cit.; also: *Panji Masyrakyat*, 'Lagi Massa Tersulut', op. cit., p. 76.

69. www.dephan.go.id, 'Peristiwa Ketapang', op. cit.

70. Suaedy (ed.), *Premanisme Politik*, pp. 113–15.

71. Suaedy (ed.), *Premanisme Politik*, pp. 117.

72. Personal interview with Muhammad Sidik, intelligence chief of the Islamic Defence Front (Ketua Badan Intelijen FPI).

73. *Panji Masyrakyat*, 'Lagi Massa Tersulut', op. cit., p. 76.

74. www.dephan.go.id, 'Peristiwa Ketapang', op. cit. See also: *Far Eastern Economic Review*, 'Ambon Violence May Have Had Its Origins in Jakarta', 25 March 1999.

75. Pemuda Pancasila was founded and built up by Yapto Soerjosoemarno, the son of a general who was related to the royal court of Solo. The Solo court also included, as one of its distant members, Soeharto's wife, Ibu Tien. Soeharto's children were very close to Yapto. By the late 1990s, Yapto had receded somewhat to allow Yorrys to oversee Pemuda Pancasila's routine operations.

76. *Forum Keadilan*, 'Provokator Menjahili Negeri', 8 February 1999, p. 25.

77. *Straits Times*, 'Wiranto Seeks Opposition's Help on Unrest', 26 January 2000. See also: *Forum Keadilan*, 'Provokator Menjahili Negeri', op. cit.; and *Asiaweek*, 'Suharto: Part II', 19 February 1999.

78. Thanks to John McBeth for making this point. See also: *Far Eastern Economic Review*, 'Ambon Violence . . .', op. cit.

CHAPTER 13 NAIL OF THE UNIVERSE

1. *Panji Masyrakyat*, 'Seluas Pulau Jawa Untuk Pandito', 2 December 1998, pp. 28–9. See also: *Agence France Presse*, 'Suharto's Family Has Huge Land Holdings in West Java, North Sumatra', 25 November 1998.

2. *Agence France Presse*, 'Suharto's Family . . .' op. cit.

3. *Agence France Presse*, 'Suharto Hands Over Seven Charity Foundations to Indonesian Government', 25 November 1998.

4. The former figure was conservatively estimated by *Forbes* in its July 1998 issue: *Jakarta Post*, '*Forbes* Lists Soeharto as Billionaire with US$4b', 22 June 1998. The latter figure was often mentioned by commentators and academics, such as George J. Aditjondro. For example, see: *Panji Masyrakyat*, 'Seluas Pulau Jawa . . .', op. cit., p. 28; and *Asian Wall Street Journal*, 'The Suharto Regime Bungled Many Chances to Amass Wealth', 30 December 1998.

5. *Jakarta Post*, 'Forbes Lists Soeharto as Billionaire with US$4b', 22 June 1998.

6. *Jakarta Post*, 'Tommy's Remarks Give Students New Spirit', 29 November 1998.

7. *Agence France Presse*, 'Son Backs Suharto's Denial of Wealth Abroad', 12 September 1998.

8. *Agence France Presse*, 'Chronology of the Faltering Search for Soeharto's Wealth', 9 December 1998.

9. Habibie's encounter with Buyung is taken from an account, which itself is based on interviews with Buyung and others directly involved, in *Van Zorge Report*, 'In Pursuit of Soeharto', 11 December 1998, pp. 4–7.

10. *Agence France Presse*, 'Chronology of the Faltering Search . . .', op. cit.

11. *Tempo*, 'Komisi Dibentuk, Soeharto Melempar Truf', 7 December 1998.

12. *D&R*, 'Yohanes Yacob: "Kami Sudah Pegang Kartu Truf"', 12 December 1998, p. 20.

13. *D&R*, 'Malaikat Pun Tahu, Kami Sudah Kerja Sungguh-Sungguh', 12 December 1998, p. 16.

14. *Indonesian Observer*, 'Wiranto Blocked Soeharto Trial', 17 January 2001.

15. See, for instance: *Tajuk*, 'Siapa Mau Presiden Wiranto?', 20 May 1999.

16. *Forum Keadilan*, 'Saat Angin Tak Sejuk Lagi', 28 December 1998, p. 15.

17. www.dephan.go.id, 'Berita Penerangan: Peristiwa Kupang'. See also: *Agence France Presse*, 'Mosques, Buildings Burned in Anti-Muslim Backlash in Eastern Indonesia', 30 November 1998.

18. *Forum Keadilan*, 'Siapa Pengembus Badai SARA?', 28 December 1998, p. 14. See also: *Panji Masyrakyat*, 'Menyeret Ketapang Ke Kupang', 9 December 1998, p. 79.

19. *Forum Keadilan*, 'Siapa Pengembus Badai . . .', op. cit., p. 15.

20. *Asian Wall Street Journal*, 'Indonesian Mobs Burn Mosques in Rampage Targeting Muslims', 1 December 1998. See also: *Dow Jones Newswires*, 'Indonesian Troops Guard Troubled Kupang, Food Scarcity Seen', 2 December 1998.

21. *Forum Keadilan*, 'Saat Angin Tak . . .', op. cit., p. 15.

22. *Panji Masyrakyat*, 'Menyeret Ketapang Ke Kupang', 9 December 1998, p. 79.

23. *Jakarta Post*, 'Third Party Behind Bloody Kupang Riots', 21 December 1998.

24. *Forum Keadilan*, 'Siapa Pengembus Badai . . .', op. cit., p. 15.

25. *Forum Keadilan*, 'Dentuman Bom Menjelang Fajar', 25 January 1999, p. 73.

26. *Forum Keadilan*, 'Dentuman Bom Menjelang . . .', op. cit., pp. 72–3.

27. *Forum Keadilan*, 'Dentuman Bom Menjelang . . .', op. cit., pp. 72–3.

28. *Forum Keadilan*, 'Gara-Gara Tilang, Karawang Berkobar', 25 January 1999, p. 26. See also: *Tajuk*, 'Fokus: Kerusuhan Di Karawang', January 1999.

29. *Forum Keadilan*, 'Provokator Menjahili Negeri', op. cit., p. 25. See also: *Straits Times*, 'Proof Emerges Violence Instigated by Pemuda Pancasila', 26 January 1999; and *Panji Masyrakyat*, 'Skenario Darurat Perang Provokator Agung', 10 February 1999, p. 23.

30. *Forum Keadilan*, 'Provokator Menjahili Negeri', op. cit., p. 25. See also: *Panji Masyrakyat*, 'Skenario Darurat . . .', op. cit., p. 23.

31. *New York Times*, 'As Troops Face Protesters, Suharto is Queried About Wealth', 10 December 1998. See also: *Forum Keadilan*, 'Menggelar Lakon . . .', op. cit., p. 75.

32. *Forum Keadilan*, 'Menggelar Lakon Soeharto Terperiksa', 11 January 1999, p. 75. See also: *Forum Keadilan*, 'Tiada Kata Jera Dalam Demo', 11 January 1999, p. 23.

33. *Tempo*, 'Pasukan Rp240 Milyar Yang Kontroversial', 21 December 1998.

34. *Forum Keadilan*, 'Gus Dur Datang, Yang Lain Senang', 11 January 1999, p. 14.

35. *Forum Keadilan*, 'Provokator Menjahili Negeri . . .', op. cit., p. 25. See also: *Asiaweek*, 'Suharto: Part II', 19 February 1999.

36. *Forum Keadilan*, 'Misteri Pertemuan Tanjung', 11 January 1999, p. 14.

37. *Forum Keadilan*, 'Gus Dur Datang . . .', op. cit., p. 14.

38. *D&R*, 'Mencermati Manuver Politik Gus Dur', 26 December 1998, p. 23.

39. *Forum Keadilan*, 'Provokator Menjahili Negeri . . .', op. cit., p. 25.

40. See, for example: *Forum Keadilan*, 'Ketua Ketoprak Yang . . .', op. cit., p. 17.

41. *Forum Keadilan*, 'Berkah Politik Saat Lebaran', 8 February 1999, p. 26.

42. *Forum Keadilan*, 'Berkah Politik Saat . . .', op. cit., p. 26.
43. *Forum Keadilan*, 'Berkah Politik Saat . . .', op. cit., p. 26.
44. The businessman was Setiawan Djody, who was also a performing artist and close friend of Tommy Soeharto.
45. *Forum Keadilan*, 'Berkah Politik Saat . . .', op. cit., p. 26.
46. Confidential communication.
47. See, for instance, *Panji Masyrakyat*, 'Setelah Ambon, Mana Lagi?', 3 February 1999, p. 75. See also: *SiaR*, 'Cendana Group's Revenge', 2 December 1998.

CHAPTER 14   OLIGARCHY OF THE PARTY BOSSES

1. This system is usually called the 'district system' (or, more vaguely, the 'first past the post' system), but to avoid confusion the term 'direct system' has been adopted and used throughout. Confusion could arise because Indonesia's regencies, or *kabupaten*, are also called districts, and there was a debate about variants of the proportional system—one was a provincial-level proportional system and the other, confusingly, was a district-level proportional system.
2. The two exceptions—i.e. the parties preferring a direct system—were PBB and PDKB (a small Catholic party).
3. *Van Zorge Report*, 'Interview with Team Seven's Andi Mallarangeng', 27 January 1999, p. 15.
4. *Van Zorge Report*, 'Interview with Team Seven's . . .', op. cit., p. 17.
5. *Jakarta Post*, 'Golkar Sticks to Guns on Civil Servants in Politics', 5 January 1999.
6. *Van Zorge Report*, 'Interview with Team Seven's . . .', op. cit., p. 17.
7. *Suara Pembaruan*, 'Golkar Bersedia Menarik Diri, Tapi Minta RUU Kepegawaian', 9 January 1999.
8. *Reuters*, 'Indon Poll Team Sees Agreement by Deadline', 15 January 1999.
9. *Jakarta Post*, 'ABRI Seats Still Being Disputed', 25 January 1999. See also: *Van Zorge Report*, 'Interview with Team Seven's . . .', op. cit., p. 14.
10. Lowry, *The Armed Forces of Indonesia*, p. 188.
11. See, for example: Lowry, *The Armed Forces of Indonesia*, pp. 120–1 and 91–4.
12. For example, a lieutenant colonel commanding a *kabupaten*-level military district (or kodim) would typically wield more authority among local residents than the *bupati*, the civilian administrator ostensibly in charge. The same would hold for a captain commanding a *kecamatan*-level military sub-district (or koramil) vis-à-vis the civilian *camat*. And in any event, the *bupati* and *camat* themselves would often be retired officers.
13. The functional group concept is an anachronism from the era of Soekarno, who ostensibly sought to model a distinctly Indonesian style of democracy on the lines of an archetypal Javanese village council. In theory, such 'deliberative' councils incorporate input from all groups performing meaningful 'functions' in village society—i.e. religious leaders, cultural figures, educators, farmers, fishermen and so on. MPR seats were therefore reserved for representatives of major religious organisations, ethnic groups, farming associations, artists and so on.
14. The 700-member MPR would consist of 462 elected parliamentarians, 38 military appointed parliamentarians, 135 regional representatives and 65 functional group representatives.
15. *Van Zorge Report*, 'Feature Interview: Fair Elections? Or "Cruelism vs Cruelism"?', 30 October 1998, p. 11.
16. *Van Zorge Report*, 'Feature Interview: Fair Elections? . . .', op. cit., p. 9.
17. *Van Zorge Report*, 'Feature Interview: Fair Elections? . . .', op. cit., p. 8.
18. *Bisnis Indonesia*, 'Siapa Mengapa', 14 October 1998.
19. *Bisnis Indonesia*, 'A.M. Saefuddin Minta Maaf', 21 October 1998.
20. Syafie's reformist credentials stemmed from his controversial stance as a military parliamentarian prior to the 1997 elections. He famously told voters that abstaining was a

valid option. In fact, the practice was illegal because it was interpreted as tacit support for the ousted PDI leader Megawati. After that declaration, Syafie was recalled from parliament and retired from the military.

21. Confidential communication.
22. These included PKU, PNU and Suni.
23. The balance of 15 per cent would include 'regionally neutral' seats—i.e. 38 from the military and 65 from functional groups. Thus the MPR breakdown was as follows: 500 parliamentary seats (234 from Java, 228 from the Outer Islands, and 38 reserved for the military); 135 regional representatives (25 from Java and 110 from the Outer Islands); and 65 functional group representatives. For more detail (including a breakdown by province), see: *Van Zorge Report*, 'Shifting Alliances and the Electoral Imbalance: Who Needs What to Win', 4 June 1999, p. 16.
24. For example, see the objections of Laksamana Sukardi in *Van Zorge Report*, 'Interview with Laksamana Sukardi', 24 February 1999, p. 24.
25. In late November, for instance, a rumour emerged that Sasono had met secretly with Icmi chair Achmad Tirtosudiro and Tommy Soeharto. No longer trusting Habibie, Cendana wanted to back Sasono for the presidency, according to the widely reported rumour. Regardless of its veracity, the story showed the sort of consternation that Sasono was creating among Jakarta's political elite.
26. Personal communication, Sarwono Kusumaatmadja.
27. Vatikiotis, *Indonesian Politics Under Suharto*, p. 188.
28. *Jakarta Post*, 'Troops "To Be Reduced Gradually in E. Timor"', 25 June 1998, p. 1.
29. *Suara Pembaruan*, 'Timtim Dilepas Bila Status Khusus Otonomi Ditolak', 28 January 1999.
30. *Straits Times*, 'East Timor is Nothing but Rocks: Habibie', 25 February 1999.
31. Lisa Cameron, 'Survey of Recent Developments', *Bulletin of Indonesian Economic Studies*, Vol. 35, No. 1, April 1999, p. 37.

CHAPTER 15   UNDER-DEMOCRACY

1. *Van Zorge Report*, 'Political Briefs', 11 February 1999, p. 22.
2. Criticism of Hamid and Team Eleven tended to come only from staunch radicals or headline-seekers. For example, Agus Miftach of the Indonesian People's Party (Pari) and Sri Bintang Pamungkas of the United Democracy Party (Pudi) accused Team Eleven of being a neo-Kopkamtib—even though both of their parties passed the screening process and both men sat on the KPU themselves.
3. *Jakarta Post*, 'Mulyana Kusumah: Entering the Multi-Party System', 25 January 1999.
4. The following account of Megawati's rally in Magelang is taken from: *Van Zorge Report*, 'Megawati Power', 23 April 1999, pp. 4–5.
5. This was a key post through which the ministry administered the appointment of governing officials at provincial and district levels.
6. The two other government representatives had also been on the leaked slate: Gadjah Mada University academic Affan Gaffar and Expert Staff to the Minister of Justice Oka Mahendra.
7. The party was Partai Musyawarah Kekeluargaan Gotong Royong (Partai MKGR). This might translate to English as the Co-operative Familial Consensus-forming Party, or the Family Self-help and Consensus Party.
8. *Suara Pembaruan*, 'Mobil Dinas BMW di Kejaksaan Dipertanyakan', 31 December 1998. See also: *Panji Masyrakyat*, 'Wow, Parcel Untuk Jaksa', 13 January 1999, p. 79.
9. The conversation between Habibie and Ghalib is taken from *Panji Masyrakyat*, 'Transkip Rekaman Itu', 24 February 1999, p. 76. Translation by the author. The Indonesian transcript is also posted as a downloadable audio file at: <www.geocities.com/CapitalHill/4120/ghalibgate.html>.
10. On Wahid's connections with Sofyan Wanandi and Yusuf Wanandi of the Centre for

Strategic and International Studies, see: *Tempo*, 'Peristiwa: Kursi Direktur Untuk', 17 May 1999.

11. *Panji Masyrakyat*, 'Mengaku Juga, Akhirnya', 20 May 1999. See also: *Suara Merdeka*, 'BIA Menilai Telepon Habibie Dan Ghalib Bukan Penyadapan', 20 March 1999; and *Van Zorge Report*, 'Interview with Sarwono Kusumaatmadja', Issue Ten, 10 March 1999.

12. *Panji Masyrakyat*, 'Yang Untung Karena Sadapan', 3 March 1999, p. 24. See also: *Dow Jones Newswires*, 'President Says Phone Tap Violated His Human Rights', 23 February 1999.

13. *Tempo*, 'Mirip-Mirip Untuk Kepentingan Umum', 23 February 1999.

14. *Suara Pembaruan*, 'Jagung Menangkis Kontroversi Soal Penggantian Jamintel', 18 February 1999.

15. Ghalib's office had recently reported that official queries by more than 17 Indonesian embassies around the world had failed to produce any trace of personal wealth stashed abroad by Soeharto.

16. *Agence France Presse*, 'Tapped Habibie Phone Conversation May Be Authentic', 23 February 1999. See also: *Suara Pembaruan*, 'Hukum Diperalat Untuk Kepentingan Politik', 23 February 1999.

17. *Suara Pembaruan*, 'Dan Puspom: Masyrakyat Jangan Main Hakim Sendiri', 22 January 1998.

18. *Suara Merdeka*, 'BIA Menilai Telepon . . .', op. cit.

19. For a comment by a general on the importance of the Central Java Garrison command, see: *Republika*, 'Kapuspen: Presiden Bukan Pangti TNI', 28 December 1999, p. 2. For Kertanegara's presence on Subagyo's honour council, see: *Gatra* (English edition), 'Recommendation Ends Here', 22 August 1998.

20. *Suara Merdeka*, 'PPP-PDI Bentrok, 1 Tewas, 15 Luka', 22 March 1999.

21. *Suara Pembaruan*, 'Golkar Protes Keras Insiden Purbalingga', 2 April 1999.

22. *Suara Merdeka*, 'Korban Tewas Di Maluku 159 Jiwa', 4 March 1999.

23. *Dow Jones Newswires*, 'Death Toll from Violence in Indonesia's Borneo Reaches 260', 27 March 1999.

24. *Suara Merdeka*, 'Mega: Diam Bagian Strategi Politik Saya', 22 March 1999.

25. *Tempo*, 'Calon Presiden Sebelum Sampai Senayan', 10 May 1999.

26. *Business Times*, 'Interview with Abdurrahman Wahid', 23 March 1999.

27. *Agence France Presse*, 'Indonesia Can't Have a Woman President: Moslem Leader', 24 March 1999.

28. For example, see: *Business Times*, 'Interview with Abdurrahman Wahid', op. cit.

29. Soeharto had confined Soekarno to house arrest despite his serious illnesses in the late 1960s, and it was popularly believed that the confinement had hastened Soekarno's death.

30. Ghalib later told parliament that his staff had promptly cooked the chicken, which 'tasted delicious because it had been presented by a beautiful girl'.

31. *The Independent*, 'Suhartos Sell Boltholes in UK for £11m', 16 March 1999.

32. See, for example: *Jakarta Post*, 'Ghalib Ignores Impending Sale of Suhartos' Homes', 19 March 1999.

33. *Australian Financial Review*, 'Indonesian Elite Scale the Heights of Privilege', 3 June 1999.

34. *Australian Financial Review*, 'Indonesian Elite . . .', op. cit.

35. *Tempo*, 'Buang Duit Gaya Dinasti Cendana', 23 March 1999.

36. *Tempo*, 'Buang Duit Gaya . . .', op. cit.

37. *Tempo*, 'Setelah "*The Independent*" Menggebar Harta Cendana', 19 March 1999.

38. The following description of the Goro transaction was taken from: *Suara Pembaruan*, 'Tommy Soeharto Diadili', 12 April 1999; *Agence France Presse*, 'Suharto's Son Faces Trial Over Land Scam', 24 March 1999; *Tempo*, 'Rahardi Membela, Tommy Bebas?', 13 April 1999; *Tempo*, 'Ini Pengadilan Atau Sandiwarna?', 11 May 1999; and *Tajuk*, 'Menjerat

Tommy Dengan Rasa Keadilan', 6 May 1999.

39. *Kontan*, 'Menggorok Koruptor di Bulog', 28 February 2000.

40. *Jakarta Post*, 'Bambang Denies Misusing Funds', 30 December 1998, p. 2.

41. *Suara Pembaruan*, 'Pemboman Istiqlal, Perbuatan Keji', 20 April 1999.

42. *Suara Pembaruan*, 'Polda Metro Jaya Dituduh Main Tangkap', 25 April 1999.

43. See, for example: *Media Indonesia*, 'Derita Kampung Maseng', 15 March 2000; and *Suara Hidayatullah*, 'AMIN, Pola Orba Pojokkan Islam', May 1999.

44. *Media Indonesia*, 'Derita Kampung Maseng', 15 March 2000.

45. *Far Eastern Economic Review*, 'Bombings Leave Southeast Asia Puzzled', 24 January 2001.

46. See, for example: *Fokus Akhir Pekan Radio Nederland*, 'Benarkah Seorang Mantan Menteri Terlibat Dalam Pemboman Mesjid Raya Istiqlal?', at: <www.isnet.org/archive-milis/archive99/apr99/0979.html>.

47. For Tasmara's background, see: *Suara Hidayatullah*, 'Toto Tasmara, Profesor Dajal', at: <www.hidayatullah.com/sahid/9908/siapa.htm>.

48. *Tempo*, 'Mencari Sang Provokator', 20 April 1999.

49. *Agence France Presse*, 'Suharto Does Not Believe in Democracy', 15 April 1999.

50. See, for example: *The Australian*, 'Violent End Feared for Timor Vote', 22 May 1999.

51. *Gatra*, 'Habibie Lolos Dengan Rapor Jeblok', 22 May 1999, p. 26.

52. *Gatra*, 'Habibie Lolos . . .', op. cit., p. 26. See also: *Van Zorge Report*, 'Candidate Habibie: Indonesian Engineering At Its Best?', 11 May 1999.

53. *Tempo*, 'Dana Politik Calon Tunggal', 24 May 1999.

54. *Tempo*, 'Dana Politik Calon . . .', op. cit.

55. *Far Eastern Economic Review*, 'Habibie Feels the Heat', 9 September 1999.

56. *Tempo*, 'Satu Nol Buat Rudy', 24 May 1999.

57. *Tempo*, 'Satu Nol Buat . . .', op. cit.

58. *Tempo*, 'Satu Nol Buat . . .', op. cit.

CHAPTER 16   'SLANDER IS WORSE THAN MURDER'

1. *Tempo*, 'Peristiwa: PPP-PKB Bentrok, Enam Tewas', 10 May 1999.

2. *Time*, 'Suharto Inc.', 24 May 1999.

3. *Jakarta Post*, 'Time Magazine Report "Cruel Slander": Soeharto', 22 May 1999.

4. *Suara Pembaruan*, 'Pak Harto: "Laporan *Time* Fitnah"', 22 May 1999.

5. *Agence France Presse*, 'Attorney General to Quiz *Time* Staff over Suharto', 19 May 1999.

6. *Jakarta Post*, 'The Soehartos Should be More Frank: Muladi; Titiek's Holdings', 5 June 1999.

7. Since the recovery of Jewish assets stolen by the Nazis during the holocaust, Austrian banks were viewed as more secure than those in Switzerland.

8. *Suara Pembaruan*, 'Menurut Habibie, Soeharto Tidak Pernah Bohong', 24 May 1999.

9. *Kompas*, 'Swiss Dan Austria Memerlukan Putusan Pengadilan', 7 June 1999.

10. *South China Morning Post*, 'Muslim Voters Presented with Religious Drawcard and Double Dilemma', 7 June 1999.

11. Carter Center, 'Results Trickle In', located at: <www.cartercenter.org/INDONESIA/07indo.html>.

12. *Van Zorge Report*, 'Political Briefs', 23 July 1999, pp. 32–3.

13. Moreover, several sub-districts in Aceh had been unable to conduct their voting on 7 June because of security concerns; although re-votes were scheduled, they were never carried out.

14. *Tempo*, 'Menteri Rahardi dan Isu "Ghalib Syndrome"', 27 June 1999. See also: *Suara Pembaruan*, 'Rahardi Bantah Istrinya Tertangkap Karena Bawa Uang $600 Ribu', 20 June 1999.

15. *Siar*, 'Golkar Harus Bubar?', 30 April 2001.

16. *Van Zorge Report*, 'Political Briefs', 23 July 1999, p. 33.

17. *Suara Pembaruan*, 'Syamsu Djalil: Ghalib Jangan Cari Kambing Hitam', 22 January 2001.
18. *Suara Pembaruan*, 'Proses "Due Diligence" Lewati Batas Waktu', 26 July 1999.
19. *Suara Pembaruan*, 'Bank Bali Korban "Money Politics" ', 31 July 1999.
20. *Suara Pembaruan*, 'Kronologi Skandal Bank Bali', 5 August 1999.
21. *Suara Pembaruan*, 'Baramuli Sarankan DPP Golkar Tuntut Pradjoto', 3 August 1999.
22. *Suara Pembaruan*, 'Baramuli Sarankan DPP . . .', op. cit.
23. Gauzali Saydam, *Skandal Bank Bali: Tragedi Perpolitikan Indonesia*, p. 195.
24. *Suara Pembaruan*, 'PT EGP Dan BPPN Beda Pendapat', 4 August 1999.
25. *Suara Pembaruan*, 'Delapan Pejabat BPPN Diperiksa', 13 August 1999.
26. Anne Booth, 'Survey of Recent Developments', *Bulletin of Indonesian Economic Studies*, Vol. 35, No. 3, December 1999, p. 5.
27. *Suara Pembaruan*, 'IMF: Segera Tuntaskan Skandal BB', 14 August 1999.
28. Since the start of the crisis, the IMF had disbursed just over $10 billion of its $12.3 billion Extended Funds Facility (EFF). In addition to funds from other lenders, Indonesia risked losing $2.7 billion in loans before year-end.
29. The following quotations are from *Gamma*, 'Saya Ngeri Aja Novanto Ini', 15 August 1999. Translation by the author.
30. When a creditor doubts a debtor's ability to repay a debt in full, the creditor might sell its claim on the debtor to a third party. Because the claim is unlikely to be paid in full, it is sold at a discount—i.e. the third party pays only a fraction of the debt's face value, to reflect the risk associated with taking over the claim.
31. *Suara Pembaruan*, 'Pertemuan Mega-Akbar: Jangan Tersusupi "Golkar Hitam" ', 13 August 1999.
32. *Suara Pembaruan*, 'Ginandjar Somasi Joko Chandra', 16 August 1999.
33. *Van Zorge Report*, 'Interview with Muchyar Yara', 17 September 1999, p. 23.
34. The exact size of the military's MPR faction was still unknown at this point. In addition to its 38 parliamentary seats, it was expected to obtain a significant portion of the 135 MPR seats reserved for regional representatives. These representatives were appointed by provincial assemblies, in each of which the military controlled 10 per cent of the seats.
35. See, for example: *Van Zorge Report*, 'Interview with Hartono Mardjono', 6 August 1999, p. 16.
36. In the course of his myriad press interviews of the previous few days, Novanto had referred to Pemuda Pancasila chair Yapto Soerjosoemarno as a 'debt collector'. Pemuda Pancasila immediately launched a defamation suit and, according to Novanto, terrorised his home. Novanto therefore sought police protection (Saydam, *Skandal Bank Bali*, pp. 39–40).
37. *Suara Pembaruan*, 'BB Buka "Extra Account" Untuk Tampung Pengembalian Uang', 16 August 1999.
38. Saydam, *Skandal Bank Bali*, p. 29.
39. *Suara Pembaruan*, 'Gubernur BI: Rp 546 Miliar Dikembalikan', 18 August 1999.
40. *Suara Pembaruan*, 'Akbar Bisa Duga Identitas Peneror Dalam Tubuh Partai Golkar', 19 August 1999.
41. *Suara Pembaruan*, 'DPP Golkar Periksa Mereka Yang Gerilya Politik', 21 August 1999.
42. *Suara Pembaruan*, 'DPP Golkar Periksa . . .', op. cit.
43. The following account of Ramli's chronicle is taken from the chronicle itself, which is reproduced in Saydam, *Skandal Bank Bali*, p. 101. Translations by the author.
44. See, for example: *Tempo*, 'Tanri Abeng: Apa Saya Bisa Memerintah Menteri Keuangan?', 12 March 1999, p. 32.
45. Saydam, *Skandal Bank Bali*, p. 39.
46. Saydam, *Skandal Bank Bali*, p. 39.
47. *Suara Pembaruan*, 'Hasil Pemeriksaan Auditor Asing Akan Diumumkan', 26 August 1999.

454 REFORMASI

CHAPTER 17 HEROES OF INTEGRATION

1. In fact, fears of 'falling dominoes' were overblown: important distinctions between Indonesia's three most troubled provinces meant that the independence movements of Aceh and Irian Jaya had weaker rationales and dimmer prospects than the movement in East Timor had. Unlike Aceh and Irian Jaya, which had been part of the Dutch empire and which used Bahasa Indonesia as their *lingua franca*, East Timor had been a Portuguese colony until 1974. And whereas the UN recognised Indonesia's 1965 annexation of Irian Jaya, it never endorsed the 1975 takeover of East Timor. But perhaps most importantly, these provinces' prospects for independence were also driven by international prejudices: Catholic, Portuguese-speaking East Timorese engendered strong empathy in certain first-world states—in marked contrast to the Papuans of Irian Jaya and the fervent Muslims of Aceh.

2. Badan Pusat Statistik, *Statistik Indonesia 1998*, p. 554.

3. Badan Pusat Statistik, *Statistik Indonesia 1998*, p. 430.

4. *Sydney Morning Herald*, 'ABRI Inc.: Unmasking the Interests Behind the Pro-Jakarta Militias', 5 May 1999.

5. Prior to the formation of this taskforce, the senior officer in the territory was the commander of the East Timor military district (Korem 164), Col. Tono Suratman. Korem 164 was part of the Bali-based Udayana Garrison, which encompassed southeastern Indonesia. At the time, the Udayana commander was Maj. Gen. Adam Damiri, who had been serving the previous year as an aide to Syafrie Syamsoeddin in the Jakarta Garrison. Damiri's assistant was Brig. Gen. Mahidin Simbolon, a Special Forces intelligence officer and himself a former Korem 164 commander. Simbolon was reputed to be Makarim's understudy in covert operations.

6. Robert Lowry, 'East Timor: An Overview of Political Developments', in Manning and van Diermen (eds), *Indonesia in Transition: Social Aspects of Reformasi and Crisis*, p. 96.

7. *Far Eastern Economic Review*, 'East Timor is About to Vote: So is Indonesia's Military Letting Go?', 2 September 1999.

8. Damien Kingsbury, 'TNI and the Militias', in Kingsbury (ed.), *Guns and Ballot Boxes*, p. 70.

9. *Sydney Morning Herald*, 'Army Plan to Divide and Rule', 8 December 1998.

10. See, for example: *Far Eastern Economic Review*, 'Indonesian Military Looks Set to Sour Independence Plans', 18 February 1999; *The Economist*, 'Crossbows and Guns in East Timor', 13 February 1999; and *Washington Post*, 'Residents of East Timor Weigh Independence, Autonomy', 14 February 1999.

11. See, for example, the findings of the Human Rights Commission, Subcommission on East Timor (KPP-Ham) in Suaedy (ed.), *Premanisme Politik*, p. 159.

12. *Far Eastern Economic Review*, 'Indonesian Military . . .', op. cit.

13. Suaedy (ed.), *Premanisme Politik*, op. cit., pp. 128–9. See also: *Kyodo Newswires*, 'Indonesian Military Trained, Armed Us: East Timor Militias', 8 October 2000.

14. Kingsbury, 'TNI and the Militias', op. cit., p. 71. Also see, for example: The Carter Center, 'Weekly Report on East Timor, No. 3', 4 August 1999.

15. Kingsbury, 'TNI and the Militias', op. cit., p. 71.

16. *Far Eastern Economic Review*, 'East Timor . . .', op. cit. See also: *Tapol Bulletin*, 'The Kopassus–Militia Alliance', No. 154/5, November 1999.

17. Peter Bartu, 'The Militia, the Military and the People', in Kingsbury (ed.), *Guns and Ballot Boxes*, p. 89.

18. Bartu, 'The Militia, the Military and the People', op. cit., p. 89.

19. Australian Broadcasting Corporation, 'East Timor: A Licence to Kill', 15 March 1999.

20. *Agence France Presse*, 'Hundreds of Pro-Indonesia Militia Launch Attack in East Timor', 5 April 1999. See also: MoJo Wire, 'Who Are the Militias?', August 1999; and Suaedy (ed.), *Premanisme Politik*, p. 135.

21. *BBC Summary of World Broadcasts*, 'Compelling Evidence Indonesian Military Involved in Liquisa Killing', 12 April 1999.

22. Komisi Penyelidikan Pelanggaran Hak Asasi Manusia (KPP Ham), 'Ringkasan Eksekutif Laporan Penyelidikan Pelanggaran Hak Asasi Manusia Di Timor Timur'. See also: *Sydney Morning Herald*, 'Indonesian Riot Squad "Took Part in Massacre" ', 9 April 1999; and Dow Jones, 'East Timor Bishop Says Indonesian Military Harms Peace Talks', 10 April 1999.

23. Lowry, 'East Timor: An Overview . . .', op. cit., p. 94.

24. *The Guardian*, 'Killings Bleed East Timor of Hope', 12 April 1999. See also: *South China Morning Post*, 'Evidence of East Timor Massacre Wiped Away by Military', 12 April 1999.

25. *Agence France Presse*, 'Jailed East Timorese Leader Declares Resumption of War', 5 April 1999.

26. *Reuters*, 'Analysis: East Timor Battle Cry Aims to Force UN Hand', 6 April 1999.

27. *The Age*, 'The Criminal History of an East Timorese Militia Leader', 17 April 1999.

28. *Far Eastern Economic Review*, 'Second Thoughts on East Timor Independence', 29 April 1999.

29. *Agence France Presse*, 'At Least 30 Feared Dead in Killing Spree by Pro-Indonesia Militia in East Timor', 17 April 1999. See also: *Asian Wall Street Journal*, 'Vigilantes Kill at least 14 in East Timor', 18 April 1999.

30. Lowry, 'East Timor: An Overview . . .', op. cit., p. 95.

31. *Reuters*, 'East Timor Militia Leader Vows Fight to the Death', 25 April 1999.

32. Bartu, 'The Militia . . .', op. cit., p. 90. See also: *The Guardian*, 'Killings Bleed East Timor . . .', op. cit.; and *International Herald Tribune*, 'Jakarta Hears Chorus of Criticism on Timor', 10 April 1999.

33. See, for example: *Van Zorge Report*, 'Interview with US Army Col. (ret.) John Haseman', 1 October 1999, p. 18.

34. Australian Broadcasting Corporation, 'The Ties That Bind', 14 February 2000.

35. *Sydney Morning Herald*, 'UN Steps Up Timor Pressure', 26 May 1999.

36. See, for example: Australian Broadcasting Corporation, 'Video Footage Shows Militia Incited to Violence in East Timor', 17 August 1999.

37. Suaedy (ed.), *Premanisme Politik*, p. 154.

38. The full document is exhibited in Suaedy (ed.), *Premanisme Politik*, pp. 162–8. See also: East Timor Action Network, 'English Translation of the Garnadi Document', 29 July 1999; and *International Herald Tribune*, 'Document Details an Exit Plan from East Timor', 20 July 1999.

39. *Kompas*, 'Giliran Mantan Wakasad Diperiksa', 4 May 2000.

40. *The Age*, 'Australia Troops Set to Go to Timor', 29 July 1999.

41. The Carter Center, 'Weekly Report on East Timor, No. 3', 4 August 1999.

42. Helene Van Klinken, 'Taking the Risk, Paying the Price', in Kingsbury (ed.), *Guns and Ballot Boxes*, pp. 56–7.

43. *Agence France Presse*, 'Close to 450 000 East Timorese Register to Vote', 7 August 1999.

44. Lowry, 'East Timor: An Overview . . .', op. cit., p. 98.

45. *Agence France Presse*, 'Registration for Timor Vote to Go Ahead, But Poll Date in Doubt', 27 July 1999.

46. See, for example: *Reuters*, 'Indonesian Military Helping East Timor Militias—Carter', 3 August 1999; *Reuters*, 'Carter Says Indonesia Trying to Derail Timor Vote', 11 August 1999.

47. *The Australian*, 'How We Dishonoured a Debt', 30 August 1999. See also: Schwarz, *A Nation in Waiting*, p. 199.

48. Scott Burchill, 'East Timor, Australia and Indonesia', in Kingsbury (ed.), *Guns and Ballot Boxes*, p. 170.

49. *Asia Pulse*, 'Indonesia Protests at Australia's Nagging on East Timor', 29 July 1999. See also: *Jakarta Post*, 'Australia Under Fire for Document Leakage', 21 July 1999.

50. See, for example: *Agence France Presse*, 'Two East Timorese Students Reported Dead, Two Abducted in Attack', 11 August 1999.
51. Regarding Suratman, Makarim and Noer Muis, see: *Far Eastern Economic Review*, 'East Timor . . .', op. cit.; and Lowry, 'East Timor: An Overview . . .', op. cit., p. 94. For the Aitarak attack, see: *New York Times*, 'Foes of Independence Run Amok', 27 August 1999; and *Australian Financial Review*, 'Dili Violence Threatens Independence Vote', 26 August 1999.
52. See: *Sydney Morning Herald*, 'World Pressure Brought Indonesian Military Shake-up', 30 August 1999; and Komisi Penyelidikan Pelanggaran Hak Asasi Manusia (KPP Ham), 'Ringkasan Eksekutif . . .', op. cit.
53. *The Age*, 'UN Finds High-level Army Terror Role', 6 September 1999.
54. *Reuters*, 'Indonesian Army Says it Can't Guarantee East Timor Security', 29 August 1999.
55. Kingsbury, 'TNI and the Militias', op. cit., p. 76.
56. Helene Van Klinken, 'Taking the Risk, Paying the Price', op. cit., p. 64.
57. Helene Van Klinken, 'Taking the Risk, Paying the Price', op. cit., p. 64.
58. See, for example: *New York Times*, 'Anti-Independence Thugs Terrorize East Timor', 1 September 1999; *Guardian*, 'A Nation on the Edge of Anarchy', 1 September 1999.
59. See, for example: Kingsbury (ed.), *Guns and Ballot Boxes*; and *Jakarta Post*, 'East Timor Vote Count Begins Amid Heavy Security', 2 September 1999.
60. *Suara Pembaruan*, 'Gubernor Tim Tim Tak Sependapat Dengan Menlu Alatas', 2 September 1999.
61. *Associated Press*, 'UN Workers Evacuated from Parts of East Timor, Violence Grows', 3 September 1999.
62. The ballot result also strengthens doubts about the fairness of the 7 June parliamentary vote: in that ballot, just 11 weeks prior to the self-determination vote, Golkar won 45 per cent of the vote. If both votes were fair, this discrepancy would be difficult to explain. It could be argued that many East Timorese were grateful to Habibie and therefore chose Golkar, but this seems unlikely.
63. *The Independent*, 'Timor Votes for Freedom But Terror Holds Sway', 5 September 1999.
64. *The Independent*, 'Panic as UN Flees Lawless Timor', 5 September 1999.
65. *Far Eastern Economic Review*, 'Indonesia: No Way Out', 23 September 1999.
66. East Timor International Support Centre, 'Update from Becora', 5 September 1999.
67. *Reuters*, 'Australian Ambassador Shot at in Dili', 6 September 1999.
68. *Reuters*, 'Grenade Explodes Near UN Compound in East Timor', 5 September 1999.
69. Komisi Penyelidikan Pelanggaran Hak Asasi Manusia (KPP Ham), 'Ringkasan Eksekutif . . .', op. cit.
70. Australian Broadcasting Corporation, 'UN Pull-out Puts Refugees in Peril', 6 September 1999.
71. Australian Broadcasting Corporation, 'East Timor News Summary', 7 September 1999.
72. Lowry, 'East Timor: An Overview . . .', op. cit., p. 101.
73. Australian Broadcasting Corporation, 'Reports of Unspeakable Horrors', 6 September 1999.
74. Lowry, 'East Timor: An Overview . . .', op. cit., p. 117. See also: *Sydney Morning Herald*, 'Crimes Against Humanity in East Timor: Report by James Dunn', 27 April 2001; US State Department, 1999 Country Report on Human Rights Practices, 25 February 2000; *Washington Post*, 'A Killing Ground Without Corpses', 22 October 1999; and Komisi Penyelidikan Pelanggaran Hak Asasi Manusia (KPP Ham), 'Ringkasan Eksekutif . . .', op. cit.
75. Komisi Penyelidikan Pelanggaran Hak Asasi Manusia (KPP Ham), 'Ringkasan Eksekutif . . .', op. cit.
76. See: Lowry, 'East Timor: An Overview . . .', op. cit., p. 101; and *Straits Times*, 'Inside Story: The Silent "Coup" ', 12 September 1999.
77. *Financial Times*, 'Military Manoeuvres', 13 September 1999.

78. *Tempo*, 'Tim-Tim Membara, Habibie Rontok?', 19 September 1999.
79. *Straits Times*, 'Inside Story . . .', op. cit. See also: *Tempo*, 'Tim-Tim Membara . . .', op. cit.
80. In the event that both the president and the vice-president are incapacitated, the Constitution stipulates that power will pass to a triumvirate comprising the defence, home affairs and foreign ministers. The triumvirate allegedly proposed by Wiranto, therefore, would have been unconstitutional on at least two grounds: Habibie was not incapacitated and the role of the foreign minister would have been usurped by that of the co-ordinating minister for politics and security.
81. *Straits Times*, 'Inside Story . . .', op. cit.
82. The following account of the meeting is taken from the *Independent*, 'A Chilling Audience with Dr Strangelove of Jakarta', 11 September 1999.
83. *Far Eastern Economic Review*, 'Indonesia: No Way Out', op. cit.
84. *Time*, 'East Timor: Marching into Trouble', 27 September 1999.
85. *South China Morning Post*, 'Jakarta in Dark on Scale of Destruction, Says UN', 15 September 1999.
86. *South China Morning Post*, 'Jakarta in Dark . . .', op. cit.
87. *Financial Times*, 'Military Manoeuvres', op. cit.
88. *Jakarta Post*, 'Military Ready to Evacuate up to 250 000 from East Timor', 3 September 1999.
89. *Financial Times*, 'Habibie Sanctions UN Peace-keeping Force', 13 September 1999.
90. *New York Times*, 'Indonesian Troops Loot UN Compound', 15 September 1999.
91. *Jakarta Post*, 'Military Ready to Evacuate . . .', op. cit.
92. *Agence France Presse*, 'Clinton Tells Indonesia to Stop Violence Now', 15 September 1999.
93. *Christian Science Monitor*, 'Indonesian Unit Suspected in Thoenes Murder', 8 November 1999.
94. See, for example: US State Department, 1999 Country Report on Human Rights Practices, 25 February 2000.
95. Lowry, 'East Timor: An Overview . . .', op. cit. p. 100. See also: Human Rights Watch World Report 2001: Indonesia.
96. *The Independent*, 'A Cynical Bandit and Vicious Murderer', 31 January 2000.
97. Lowry, 'East Timor: An Overview . . .', op. cit. p. 105.
98. *The Australian*, 'East Timor Independence Toll Put At 2000', 22 December 2000. See also: *Sydney Morning Herald*, 'UN Legal Code Abysmal: Lawyers', 7 June 2000.
99. See, for example: *Jakarta Post*, 'Military Ready to Evacuate . . .', op. cit.
100. *Tempo*, 'Titik Bidik Sang Jenderal', 23 January 2000.
101. *Associated Press*, 'The Feelings of Indonesia's Leader', 12 September 1999.
102. *Tapol Bulletin*, 'Major General Syafrie Syamsuddin Now in East Timor', 29 August 1999.
103. *Tapol Bulletin*, 'Major General Syafrie . . .', op. cit.
104. *Tapol Bulletin*, 'The Military–Kopassus Alliance', No. 154/5, November 1999. For Damiri's role as an aide to Syamsoeddin at the Jakarta Garrison, see: *Suara Pembaruan*, 'Pangdam Jaya Mayjen TNI Syafrie Syamsoeddin: Selama Bersatu Tak Ada Ancaman Yang Bersifat Politik', 31 December 1997.
105. The one exception, as will be discussed later, was Maj. Gen. Agus Wirahadikusumah.

CHAPTER 18   ACRIMONY AND LARCENY

1. Saydam, *Skandal Bank Bali*, p. 105.
2. *Suara Pembaruan*, 'Muladi Patut Diduga Terlibat Skandal BB', 10 September 1999.
3. *Tajuk*, 'Habibie Menghitung Hari', 16 September 1999.
4. Saydam, *Skandal Bank Bali*, p. 117.
5. Saydam, *Skandal Bank Bali*, p. 128.

6. *Tajuk*, 'Habibie Menghitung Hari', 16 September 1999.
7. Like many others involved in the Bank Bali scandal, Kim Yohannes had ties to Bank Bapindo: his companies had perpetrated the fictitious export scam of 1994. At the time, exporters who imported their raw materials enjoyed a tax loophole: they could collect rebates on import duties paid for their imported raw materials. Kim Yohannes falsified export records in vast quantities and then claimed the import duty rebates from Bapindo. (See, for example: Saydam, *Skandal Bank Bali*, p. 119; and *Tempo*, 'Jurus Bobol Kas Negara ala Kim', p. 44.)
8. Saydam, *Skandal Bank Bali*, pp. 119–20.
9. Saydam, *Skandal Bank Bali*, pp. 183–4.
10. Saydam, *Skandal Bank Bali*, p. 106.
11. The subsequent account of the testimony of Yusuf, Subianto, Abeng and Novanto is taken from: Saydam, *Skandal Bank Bali*, pp. 39, 186–9.
12. Saydam, *Skandal Bank Bali*, p. 195.
13. Saydam, *Skandal Bank Bali*, p. 196.
14. Joedono became minister of trade in 1993, but Soeharto sacked him unceremoniously in 1995. Thereafter he was despatched to an ambassadorship in Europe.
15. Saydam, *Skandal Bank Bali*, pp. 133, 138.
16. *Far Eastern Economic Review*, 'How PwC Sleuths Cracked the Bank Bali Case', 16 December 1999.
17. Saydam, *Skandal Bank Bali*, pp. 139, 143.
18. Saydam, *Skandal Bank Bali*, p. 146.
19. Saydam, *Skandal Bank Bali*, p. 141.
20. *Van Zorge Report*, 'From the Editor', 3 September 1999, p. 3.
21. Saydam, *Skandal Bank Bali*, p. 138.
22. *Tempo*, 'Bocoran Pricewaterhouse dan Jejak Sang Menteri', 19 September 1999.
23. *Far Eastern Economic Review*, 'How PwC Sleuths Cracked the Bank Bali Case', 16 December 1999.
24. Jarre and Abeng hailed from the same remote island, Selayar, off the coast of South Sulawesi. They worked together for several years as executives at the Indonesian affiliate of Heineken, Multi Bintang. Jarre also served as a director of Mondialindo Graha, a company jointly owned by Setya Novanto and a son of Abeng (*Tempo*, 'Tanri Abeng: "Apa Saya Bisa Memerintah Menteri Keuangan?" ', 12 March 2000, p. 32).
25. The subsequent details on the flow of funds are taken from Saydam, *Skandal Bank Bali*, pp. 281–7.
26. Manimaren later testified that Abeng was the prime mover behind the scandal and that his gross take reached Rp200 billion (*Tempo*, 'Tanri Abeng', op. cit., p. 32). It is conceivable that this sum was passed on to Timmy Habibie, as it matches what Timmy claimed to have received—according to Rudy Ramli's chronicle. A host of witnesses confirmed that Abeng took part in planning sessions at the Mulia Hotel with Lubis, Baramuli, Tjandra and Novanto (*Republika*, 15 December 1999, p. 3). Nonetheless, Manimaren may have been exaggerating Abeng's role to divert blame from himself. Abeng, whose political clout was relatively weak, would have been the most natural 'fall guy' for the group.
27. *Van Zorge Report*, 'Political Briefs', 17 September 1999.
28. *Van Zorge Report*, 'A Serpentine Path to Democracy', 3 September 1999, p. 4.
29. *Duta Masyrakyat*, 31 August 1999, p. 1. See also: *Tempo*, 'Fuad Bawazier, Pencetak Raja, Penjaga Raja', 14 November 1999.
30. *Tempo*, 'Siapa Kakap, Siapa Ditangkap', 16 July 2000. See also: Suaedy (ed.), *Premanisme Politik*, p. 59.
31. *Van Zorge Report*, 'A Serpentine Path to Democracy', 3 September 1999, p. 8.
32. *Van Zorge Report*, 'Political Briefs', 3 September 1999, p. 23. Also: *Van Zorge Report*, 'Political Briefs', 17 September 1999, p. 30.

33. *Tempo*, 'Profil Agus Isrok: Dari Cijantung Ke Hotel Travel', 7 April 2000. See also: *Asia Times* Online, 'From Ecstasy to Agony: Indonesia's War on Drugs', 26 November 1999, at: <www.atimes.com/se-asia/AK26Ae01.html>.
34. *Suara Pembaruan*, '5 Oknum Bawa 60 Kg Ganja', 18 September 1999.
35. Interview with Abdul Garuda Nusantara, 20 September 1999.
36. *Van Zorge Report*, 'Political Briefs', 1 October 1999.
37. *Gatra*, 'Belum Ada Jurus Mundur', 23 October 1999, p. 31.

CHAPTER 19 GUERILLA POLITICS

1. In addition to the 462 elected members of parliament, the MPR comprised 38 appointed military seats, 65 functional group seats and 135 regional representative seats.
2. *Tajuk*, 'Kartu Golkar di Tangan Akbar', 21 October 1999. See also: *Jakarta Post*, 'Regional Representatives Threaten to Walk Out', 9 June 2001. Five of the 135 regional representative seats remained unfilled due to the situation in the 27th province, East Timor, which was granted independence by the MPR in October. Golkar therefore obtained 62 of the remaining 130 seats; PDI Perjuangan obtained 40.
3. *Van Zorge Report*, 'The Presidential Race: The MPR in Disarray', 18 October 1999, p. 4.
4. *Far Eastern Economic Review*, 'Habibie Feels the Heat', 9 September 1999.
5. The five ministers were Agung Laksono, Theo Sambuaga, Fahmi Idris, A.M. Saefuddin and Marzuki Usman. The latter served as a functional group representative. Syarwan Hamid and Ginandjar Kartasasmita also obtained seats as regional representatives. All ministers serving in the MPR were required to vacate their cabinet positions.
6. *Van Zorge Report*, 'The Presidential Race . . .', op. cit.
7. *Tempo*, 'Bermula Dari Tata Tertib', 10 October 1999.
8. To rationalise the choice of a secret ballot some MPR members argued that, because the 7 June elections provided for voter secrecy, so too should the presidential election. The argument, which obscured the difference between a sovereign electorate and its representative assembly, illustrated how some MPR members paid little heed to the task of representing their constituents.
9. *Van Zorge Report*, 'The Final Stretch for the General Election Commission', 20 August 1999.
10. See, for example: *Van Zorge Report*, 'Feature Interview with Andi Malaranggeng', 20 August 1999.
11. *Gatra*, 'Belum Ada Jerus Mundur', 23 October 1999, p. 33.
12. *Kompas*, 'Amien Ketua MPR', 4 October 1999.
13. *Kompas*, 'Amien Ketua MPR', op. cit.
14. Wahid had appointed Matori to serve as party chair the previous year, but in recent months Matori and a number of others in the party leadership had broken ranks with Wahid: they adamantly supported Megawati, eschewing the political Islamists of the Central Axis.
15. The hotel was owned by military financier Tommy Winata, and the meeting was attended by Lt Gen. (ret.) Hendropriyono, such that the event may have been arranged at the military's behest.
16. *Kompas*, 'Akbar Ketua DPR', 6 October 1999.
17. Ironically, the bulk of those not voting for Tandjung were from the party that had originally counted on his support from the outset: PDI Perjuangan. Some 65 PDI Perjuangan legislators ignored Megawati's orders to back Tandjung, apparently because they refused to vote for a Golkar politician on principle.
18. *Tempo*, 'Salam Tempel Dari Tim Sukses', 24 October 1999, p. 27.
19. See, for example: *D&R*, 'Wawancara Dengan Gus Dur', 30 December 1998.
20. *Tajuk*, 'Bila Kingmaker Ingin Menjadi King', 21 October 1999.
21. *Van Zorge Report*, 'Political Briefs', 17 September 1999, p. 26.

22. *Van Zorge Report,* 'Political Briefs', 17 September 1999, p. 26.
23. *Kompas,* 'Penyidikan Kasus Yayasan Soeharto Dihentikan', 12 October 1999, p. 1.
24. *Tempo,* 'Antiklimaks Penyidikan Soeharto', 24 October 1999, p. 34.
25. *Kompas,* 'Manuver Golkar Disesuaikan Keadaan', 12 October 1999, p. 11.
26. *Gatra,* 'Massa Mencencang, Habibie Memikul', 23 October 1999, p. 25.
27. *Gatra,* 'Massa Mencencang, Habibie . . .', op. cit., p. 25.
28. *Tajuk,* 'Bila Kingmaker Ingin . . .', op. cit.
29. *Gatra,* 'Massa Mencencang, Habibie . . .', op. cit., p. 25.
30. *Tajuk,* 'Bila Kingmaker Ingin . . .', op. cit.
31. *Kompas,* 'Habibie Berpidato, Massa Mendemo', 15 October 1999, p. 1.
32. *Kompas,* 'Pisah Dari RI, Persoalan Timtim Selesai', 15 October 1999, p. 1.
33. Reinforcing this impression was the move to form a special subcommission to decide whether to call for a full vote; the chair of the subcommission was the leader of a tiny Islamic party, Yusuf Hasyim. Although Yusuf was the uncle of Abdurrahman Wahid, he was an unabashed Habibie supporter.
34. *Kompas,* 'Bentrokan Aparat dengan Massa: Makin Kasar dan Brutal', 16 October 1999, p. 1.
35. *Panji Masyrakyat,* 'Apa Boleh Buat, Gus Dur', 27 October 1999.
36. *Gatra,* 'Calon Tak Berkeringat', 23 October 1999, p. 34.
37. This faction included Zarkasih Noer and Tosari Widjaya.
38. *Kompas,* 'Nurcholish Madjid: Pemerintah Terpilih Adalah Pemerintahan Transisi', 16 October 1999, p. 13.
39. *Kompas,* 'Poros Tengah Dukung Pencalonan Cak Nur', 18 October 1999, p. 13.
40. *Kompas,* 'Diajak Duet dengan Habibie: Wiranto Menolak', 19 October 1999, p. 1.
41. *Far Eastern Economic Review,* 'Unlikely Victor', 28 October 1999.
42. *Kompas,* 'Diajak Duet dengan Habibie . . .', op. cit., p. 11.
43. *Panji Masyrakyat,* 'Apa Boleh Buat . . .', op. cit.
44. Some of Megawati's advisors were urging her to accept Habibie's speech, which would prompt a two-phase presidential election the following day. The first phase would eliminate the weakest candidate and the second phase would be a run-off between the two finalists. These advisors maintained that Megawati could defeat Habibie but not Wahid, therefore Megawati would be better served by keeping Habibie in the race: this could potentially split the anti-Megawati vote in the first phase and, hopefully, eliminate Wahid. The path would then be clear for Megawati to defeat Habibie in the second phase. In the meetings prior to the accountability vote, Wahid may have been trying to forestall this strategy.
45. *Panji Masyrakyat,* 'Apa Boleh Buat . . .', op. cit.
46. Mietzner, 'The 1999 General Session', in Manning and van Diermen (eds), *Indonesia in Transition,* p. 55.
47. *Panji Masyrakyat,* 'Apa Boleh Buat . . .', op. cit.
48. *Asian Wall Street Journal,* 'Dark Before Dawn: How Elite Made a Deal Before Indonesia Woke Up', 2 November 1999.
49. *Tajuk,* 'Segi Banyak Menuju Puncak', 4 November 1999.
50. *Tempo,* 'Selawat Gedung Rakyat Untuk President Gus Dur', 31 October 1999, p. 18.
51. *Tempo,* 'Selawat Gedung Rakyat . . .', op. cit., p. 18.
52. *Tempo,* 'Selawat Gedung Rakyat . . .', op. cit., p. 18.
53. *Forum Keadilan,* 'Gus Dur Pilihan Terbaik Bagi Bangsa', 31 October 1999, p. 17.
54. *Straits Times,* 'Habibie Aide Pulls Gun on Akbar', 21 October 1999.
55. *Forum Keadilan,* 'Gus Dur Pilihan Terbaik . . .', op. cit., p. 17. See also: *Asian Wall Street Journal,* 'Dark Before Dawn . . .', op. cit.; and *Tajuk,* 'Segi Banyak Menuju . . .', op. cit.
56. *Forum Keadilan,* 'Manuver Dalam Detik-Detik Menegangkan', 31 October 1999, p. 23.
57. *Forum Keadilan,* 'Gus Dur Pilihan Terbaik . . .', op. cit., p. 17.
58. *Tempo,* 'Selawat Gedung Rakyat . . .', op. cit., p. 19.

59. *Forum Keadilan*, 'Manuver Dalam Detik-Detik . . .', op. cit., p. 23.
60. *Asian Wall Street Journal*, 'Dark Before Dawn . . .', op. cit.
61. *Forum Keadilan*, 'Manuver Dalam Detik-Detik . . .', op. cit., p. 23.
62. *Asian Wall Street Journal*, 'Dark Before Dawn . . .', op. cit.
63. *Kompas*, '15 Menit Di Ruang Mawar', 21 October 1999, p. 1.
64. *Asian Wall Street Journal*, 'Dark Before Dawn . . .', op. cit.
65. *Asian Wall Street Journal*, 'Dark Before Dawn . . .', op. cit.
66. Mietzner, 'The 1999 General Session', op. cit., p. 53.
67. *South China Morning Post*, 'Indonesia Vote: Flaws Surface in Day of Political Scheming', 22 October 1999.
68. *Tempo*, 'Sebilah Tongkat Untuk Megawati', 31 October 1999, p. 20.
69. Mietzner, 'The 1999 General Session', op. cit., p. 51.
70. *Kompas*, 'Presiden Harapkan Bimbingan MPR' , 21 October 1999, p. 11.
71. Mietzner, 'The 1999 General Session', op. cit., p. 47.
72. *Tajuk*, 'Segi Banyak Menuju Puncak', 4 November 1999.
73. *Tempo*, 'Sebilah Tongkat Untuk . . .', op. cit., p. 20.
74. *Tempo*, 'Sebilah Tongkat Untuk . . .', op. cit., p. 21.
75. *Tempo*, 'Sebilah Tongkat Untuk . . .', op. cit., p. 21.
76. *Tempo*, 'Sebilah Tongkat Untuk . . .', op. cit., p. 21.

CHAPTER 20 SHOCK THERAPY

1. Ross McLeod, 'Survey of Recent Developments', *Bulletin of Indonesian Economic Studies*, August 1999, Vol. 35, No. 2, p. 13.
2. Anne Booth, 'Survey of Recent Developments', *Bulletin of Indonesian Economic Studies*, December 1999, Vol. 35, No. 3, p. 12.
3. Eric D. Ramstetter, 'Survey of Recent Developments', *Bulletin of Indonesian Economic Studies*, December 2000, Vol. 36, No. 3, p. 20.
4. Eric D. Ramstetter, 'Survey of Recent Developments', op. cit., p. 8.
5. This was Rear Admiral Freddy Numberi, state minister for administrative reforms.
6. *Tajuk*, 'Intrik di Kabinet Pelangi', 4 November 1999.
7. *Van Zorge Report*, 'Wiranto's Balancing Act', 12 November 1999, p. 30.
8. Those promoted to garrison commands included Sudi Silalahi, the former Yudhoyono aide who had served as the second-in-command of the Jakarta Garrison under Syafrie Syamsoeddin in May 1998.
9. Mietzner, 'The 1999 General Session', op. cit., p. 53.
10. *Wall Street Journal*, 'Indonesian Minister Vows Public Corruption Battle', 13 December 1999.
11. *Van Zorge Report*, 'The Texmaco Case: A Frontal Attack on Entrenched Interests', 17 December 1999, p. 20.
12. See, for example: *Gatra*, 'Uang Kembali Atau Masuk Bui', 18 December 1999; *Suara Pembaruan*, 'Kasus Texmaco dan Pemulihan Ekonomi Indonesia', 11 December 1999; and *Kontan*, 'Kroni Baru Penebar Putaw', 19 October 2000.
13. *Gatra*, 'Uang Kembali Atau Masuk Bui', 18 December 1999.
14. Data from the Indonesian Bank Restructuring Agency (Ibra), as of 30 March 2001.
15. *Republika*, 'Seluruh Tapol dan Napol Dibebaskan', 24 December 1999, p. 1.
16. This was the National Economics Council (DEN), which included the highly able Sri Mulyani Indrawati in the council's number-two post.
17. *Agence France Presse*, 'Indonesian President Says Acehnese have Right to Referendum', 4 November 1999.
18. *Agence France Presse*, 'Indonesian President . . .', op. cit.
19. Dow Jones, 'Indonesia Wahid: Wants to Hold Referendum on Aceh in 7 Months', 16 November 1999.
20. Note that Maj. Gen. Sudradjat (one name) has no relation to Gen. (ret.) Edi Sudradjat.

21. *Agence France Presse*, 'Wahid's Statement on Aceh Vote Only Personal Opinion: Army Spokesman', 17 November 1999.
22. *Jakarta Post*, 'President Rules Out Martial Law in Aceh', 25 November 1999.
23. *Kompas*, 'Dr Bambang Sudibyo MBA', 16 January 2000, p. 2.
24. *Van Zorge Report*, 'The Texmaco Case: A Frontal Attack on Entrenched Interests', 17 December 1999, p. 21.
25. *Gatra*, 'Safari Mayjen Agus', 25 December 1999.
26. Ironically, although Sudrajat and Wirahadikusumah were arch-rivals, they were the only generals with graduate degrees from Harvard University. Sudrajat had attended Harvard Business School, while Wirahadikusumah studied at the Kennedy School of Government.
27. The following quotes from Wirahadikusumah are taken from various media interviews that were translated and reproduced in: *Van Zorge Report*, 'I'm Just Anticipating Change Earlier than the Others', 7 January 2000.
28. *Kompas*, 'Marzuki Harus Lakukan Reformasi Struktural', 9 February 2000, p. 8.

CHAPTER 21   EAST TIMOR WRIT LARGE

1. *Van Zorge Report*, 'Interview with Siswono Yudohusodo', 3 September 1999, p. 16.
2. *Van Zorge Report*, 'Civil–Military Relations: Gus Dur Versus Wiranto', 7 January 2000.
3. *Suara Pembaruan*, 'Guterres Datang Pakai Seragam Loreng ke KPP HAM', 31 December 1999. See also: *Van Zorge Report*, 'Civil–Military Relations', op. cit.
4. *Kompas*, 'Mayjen Zacky Makarim Akui Ada "Contingency Plan"', 5 January 2000, pp. 1, 11.
5. *Kompas*, 'Mayjen Zacky . . .', op. cit.
6. *Gatra*, 'Roda Nasib Wiranto Bergerak', 12 February 2000.
7. *Republika*, 'Kapuspen: Presiden Bukan Pangti TNI', 28 December 1999, p. 2.
8. *Washington Post*, 'Indonesia's Leader Makes It Up As He Goes', 1 January 2000.
9. *Republika*, 'Marzuki Siap Mundur Dari Komnas Ham', 21 December 1999, p. 1.
10. *Tempo*, 'Wisma Doulos: Serangan Malam', 26 December 1999.
11. Khatulistiwamgz.com, 'Interview with Tamrin Amal Tomagola', September 2000, at: <www.khatulistiwamgz.com/Sep/Wawancara.htm>. See also: George Aditjondro, 'Financing Human Rights Abuses', 20 November 2000, at: <www.koteka.net/part1.htm>.
12. *Bali Post*, 'Perjalanan FPI Membasmi Tempat Maksiat', 19 December 2000.
13. *Bali Post*, 'Perjalanan FPI Membasmi . . .', op. cit.
14. Berpolitik.com, 'FPI Pertanyakan Profesionalisme KPP HAM Dan Marzuki Darusman', 27 December 1999, located at: www.berpolitik.com/articles/99/12/27/1948200.shtml>.
15. *Bali Post*, 'FPI Ngamuk, Kantor Komnas Ham Dirusak', 24 June 2000. See also: *Bali Post*, 'GAM Masuk Jakarta, Ingin Kacaukan ST MPR', 5 August 2000.
16. *Tempo*, 'Wisma Doulos: Serangan Malam', op. cit.
17. *The Manila Times*, 'Security Tightened in South', 2 January 2001, at: <www.manilatimes.net/2001/jan/02/top_stories/20010102top2.html>.
18. *Republika*, 'Selesaikan Sendiri Pertikaian di Maluku', 13 December 2000, p. 1.
19. International Crisis Group, 'Overcoming Murder and Chaos in Maluku', 19 December 2000. See also: *Republika*, 'Korban Jiwa Kerusuhan Maluku Selama Desember 1999', p. 1; and *Republika*, 'Kerusuhan Maluku Makin Meluas', 23 December 2000, p. 1.
20. George Aditjondro, 'Financing Human Rights Abuses in Indonesia', op. cit.
21. Interview with Eggi Sudjana, 18 January 1999.
22. *Jakarta Post*, 'Calls for Calm, Jihad over Maluku Mayhem', 10 January 2000.
23. *Tempo*, 'Gertakan Jihad Lewat Posko', 17 January 2000.
24. International Crisis Group, 'Overcoming Murder and Chaos in Maluku', op. cit.
25. *Tempo*, 'Mengapa TNI Tak Berdaya', 17 January 2000.
26. *The Age*, 'Wiranto: I Could Have Taken Power', 23 January 2000.
27. Lowry, 'East Timor: An Overview of Political Developments', in Manning and van

Diermen (eds), *Indonesia in Transition: Social Aspects of Reformasi in Crisis*, p. 104. See also: *The Age*, 'Wiranto . . .', op. cit.; and *Tapol Bulletin*, 'The Kopassus–Militia Alliance', November 1999.

28. *Republika*, 'Pembantaian Kambuh Lagi di Malang', 24 December 1999, p. 12.
29. *Republika*, 'Pelaku Pembunuhan "Dukun Santet" di Malang Dibayar Rp 3 Juta', 27 December 2000, p. 1. See also: *Van Zorge Report*, 'Political Briefs', 4 February 2000.
30. *Sydney Morning Herald*, 'Soeharto Forces "Building Militias"', 21 January 2000.
31. Such a paradigm was also said to have been used in Aceh, where army-backed double-agents had reputedly infiltrated the Free Aceh Movement (Gam).
32. Interview with Eggi Sudjana, 18 January 1999.
33. *Van Zorge Report*, 'Political Briefs', 18 February 2000.
34. John M. MacDougall Jr., 'Lombok Unrest: Description and Analysis', 22 January 1999, located at: <www.groups.yahoo.com/group/berita-bhinneka/message/14813>.
35. *The Independent*, 'Dark Forces Strike Lombok', 23 January 2000.
36. Interview with eyewitness photo-journalist.
37. John M. MacDougall Jr., 'Lombok Unrest . . .', op. cit. See also: *Far Eastern Economic Review*, 'Reports Highlight Army's Role in Lombok Riots', 27 January 2000.
38. *Far Eastern Economic Review*, 'Reports Highlight Army's Role', op. cit.
39. *The Independent*, 'Dark Forces Strike . . .', op. cit.
40. *Tempo*, 'Titik Bidik Sang Jenderal', 23 January 2000.
41. *Tempo*, 'Palu Komisi Untuk Menteri Wiranto', 23 January 2000.
42. *Far Eastern Economic Review*, 'Indonesia's Wahid Close to Confronting Wiranto', 26 January 2000.
43. *Far Eastern Economic Review*, 'Indonesia's Wahid . . .', op. cit.
44. See, for example: *Media Indonesia*, 'Tidak Ada "Reshuffle" Kabinet, Gus Dur Bantah Spekulasi Mengenai Wiranto', 18 January 2000.
45. The following quotes from Wiranto are from: *Republika*, 'Wiranto Tentang Isu Kudeta: Saya Punya Kesempatan', 22 January 2000, p. 3.
46. Wahid portrayed the decision as something over which he had no control: he pointed out that the military's official policy required officers serving in civilian posts to either retire or return to a military job. Ironically, the author of this policy had been the former kaster, Yudhoyono—who was now among those to fall victim to it. However, upon taking office in the cabinet, Yudhoyono had pointed out that exceptions to the rule could be made for ministerial-level posts; in fact, such exceptions had been made in the past.
47. *Associated Press*, 'Indonesia's Wahid Rejects Coup Rumors', 27 January 2000.
48. *Associated Press*, 'Indonesia's Wahid . . .', op. cit.
49. *Kompas*, 'Rekomendasi Komnas HAM Soal Timtim', 1 February 2000, p. 11.
50. *Kompas*, 'Rekomendasi Komnas . . .', op. cit., p. 1.
51. *Kompas*, 'Surjadi Soediradja Gantikan Wiranto', 14 February 2000, p. 1.
52. *Kompas*, 'Surjadi Soediradja', op. cit.
53. *Kompas*, 'Saya Dan TNI Siap Bertanggung Jawab', 2 February 2000, p. 11.
54. *Kompas*, 'Saya Dan TNI . . .', op. cit., p. 1.
55. *Kompas*, 'Saya Dan TNI . . .', op. cit., p. 1.
56. *Gatra*, 'Jenderal Kancil di Lautze', 12 February 2000.
57. *Kompas*, 'PM Italia Peringatkan Militer Indonesia', 6 February 2000, p. 1.
58. *Gatra*, 'Menghitung Suara Tokek', 19 February 2000.
59. *Kompas*, 'President Abdurrahman Wahid: Kabinet Bisa Tanpa Wiranto', 13 February 2000, p. 1.
60. *Kompas*, 'Surjadi Soediradja', op. cit., p. 1.
61. *Kompas*, 'Surjadi Soediradja', op. cit., p. 1.
62. *New York Times*, 'Jakarta General Fired in a Day of Zigzags', 14 February 2000.
63. *Gatra*, 'Ad Interim di Telepon', 26 February 2000.

CHAPTER 22 'RAID CENDANA'

1. *Gatra*, 'Ad Interim di Telepon', 26 February 2000.
2. *Garda*, 'Tokoh: TNI Tolak Dekrit', 23 May 2001, pp. 4–5.
3. *South China Morning Post*, 'Political Adultery', 27 June 2000.
4. *South China Morning Post*, 'Political Adultery', op. cit.
5. The post vacated by Kalla was filled by Luhut Pandjaitan, a three-star general and career Special Forces officer with negligible qualifications to serve as minister of industry and trade. This brought the number of underqualified generals serving in key economic ministries to three.
6. See, for example: Satunet.com, 'Pemerintah Gagal Lantik Hakim Ad Hoc', 11 April 2000, at: <www.satunet.com/artikel/isi/00/04/11/12132.html>.
7. *Gamma*, 'Ketika Hukum Seharga Rupiah', 9 May 2000.
8. *Kompas*, 'Beberapa Keputusan Kontroversial Hakim', 19 February 2001, p. 8.
9. Thanks to Tom Shreve for his research on this point.
10. *Bloomberg*, 'IBRA Chairman Tries to Clean Up Indonesia's Financial Debris', 3 March 2001.
11. *Kompas*, 'Gus Dur Dan Kabinetnya', 8 January 2001, p. 10.
12. *Agence France Presse*, 'Verdicts for Sale Tape Embarrasses Indonesian Supreme Court', 13 April 2000.
13. *Australian Financial Review*, 'Tackling Indonesian Corruption Head On', 13 April 2000.
14. *Kontan*, 'Siapa Bohir Proyek Pembunuhan Matori', 13 March 2000. See also: *SiaR*, 'Penganiayaan Matori: Kelompok Radikal Dan Djaja Terlibat?', 13 March 2000.
15. *Kompas*, 'Terdakwa Perkara Matori Dituntut 12 Tahun', 28 September 2000.
16. Thanks to Air Marshal (ret.) Saleh Basarah for making this point. See also: *Wall Street Journal*, 'Soeharto Regime Blew Many Chances to Amass Wealth', 30 December 1998.
17. *The Economist*, 'Dear Daddy', 31 December 1997. See also: *Wall Street Journal*, 'Soeharto Regime Blew . . .', op. cit.
18. Schwarz, *A Nation in Waiting*, p. 156.
19. *Tempo*, 'Bayangan Teror Sepanjang Hukum', 5 July 2000, at: <http://www.*Tempo*.co.id/harian/fokus/30/2,1,7,id.html>. See also: *Kompas*, 'Gedung DPR Ditembak Saat Tommy Diperiksa', 14 March 2000.
20. *Tempo*, 'Juwono Sudarsono: Kroni Soeharto Mendanai Kerusuhan', 19 July 2000.
21. *Tempo*, 'Juwono Sudarsono . . .', op. cit.
22. Detik.com, ' "Bomb" Gus Dur Buat Tommy: Menyorot Kinerja Buruk Polisi', 18 September 2000, at: <www.detik.com/peristiwa/2000/09/18/2000918-150151.shtml>.
23. *Media Indonesia*, 'Pelaku "Bom Kejaksaan" Eks Paspampres, Sebuah "Hard Top" Putih Diamankan', 13 July 2000. See also: *Suara Pembaruan*, 'Peledakan Bom, Ada Isyarat Akan Berlanjut (1)', 6 January 2001.
24. *Suara Pembaruan*, 'Bom Di Kajagung: Dua Pria Dalam Hardtop Diperiksa', 14 July 2000, pp. 1, 4.
25. *Media Indonesia*, 'Sudah 27 Saksi Diperiksa Dalam Kasus Kejaksaan', 18 July 2000.
26. Satunet.com, 'Senin Ini, Berkas Perkara Suwondo Diserahkan ke Kejati Jakarta', 30 October 2000, at: <www.satunet.com/artikel/isi/00/10/30/32262.html>.
27. *Far Eastern Economic Review*, 'Bombings Leave Southeast Asia Puzzled', 24 January 2001.
28. *Indonesian Observer*, 'Tommy and Habib Ali Baaqil', 18 September 2000.
29. *Tempo*, 'Lubang Kebocoran Di "Kapal Keruk" Kostrad', 13 August 2000.
30. *Tempo*, 'Lubang Kebocoran . . .', op. cit.
31. *Dow Jones Newswires*, 'Indonesian Police Admit 2 Soldiers Arrested for Bombings', 25 September 2000.
32. *Tempo*, 'Pati Geni Jenderal Wirahadikusumah', 6 August 2000.
33. It remains unclear whether the military's position in the MPR was the deciding factor that allowed Wahid to remain in power. Other factors were that Megawati was uneasy about being seen as power-hungry, and the other party bosses were apparently unable

to agree on how to share power among themselves after removing Wahid.

34. Ironically, both Agus Wirahadikusumah and Ryamizard Ryacudu were related to former vice-presidents: Agus was the nephew of Gen. (ret.) Umar Wirahadikusumah, while Ryacudu was the son-in-law of Gen. (ret.) Try Sutrisno.
35. Detik.com, 19 July 2000.
36. *Tempo*, 'Darurat Sipil Di Maluku, Lalu Apa?', 9 July 2000.
37. *Tempo*, 'Darurat Sipil Di Maluku . . .', op. cit.
38. *Kompas*, 28 July 2000.
39. Detikworld, 'Human Rights Commission Releases Report on Maluku Conflict', 6 February 2001.
40. *Reuters*, 'Verdicts in West Timor UN Trials Delayed', 27 April 2001.
41. *Far Eastern Economic Review*, 'Timor: Jakarta's Shame', 21 September 2000.
42. See: Berpolitik.com, 'Irman Sediono, Mantan Bupati Cova Lima, Hari Ini Tandatangani BAP', 12 September 2000; *Sydney Morning Herald*, 'Crimes Against Humanity in East Timor: Report by James Dunn', 27 April 2001; Lowry, 'East Timor: An Overview . . .', op. cit., p. 117; US State Department, 1999 Country Report on Human Rights Practices, 25 February 2000; *Washington Post*, 'A Killing Ground Without Corpses', 22 October 1999; and Komisi Penyelidikan Pelanggaran Hak Asasi Manusia (KPP Ham), 'Ringkasan Eksekutifc Laporan Penyelidikan Hak Asasi Manusia Di Timor Timur'.
43. Berpolitik.com, 'Pakai Topeng Marzuki, Sommak Unjuk Rasa Dukung Soeharto', 12 September 2000.
44. *Dow Jones Newswires*, 'Jakarta Police Spokesman: Will Arrest Tommy Friday or Saturday', 15 September 2000.
45. *Reuters*, 'Drop Suharto Trial to Avoid More Violence—Minister', 15 September 2000.
46. *Reuters*, 'Drop Suharto Trial . . .', op. cit.
47. *Dow Jones Newswires*, 'Jakarta Police Spokesman . . .', op. cit.
48. *Dow Jones Newswires*, 'Jakarta Police Spokesman . . .', op. cit.
49. *Wall Street Journal*, 'Suharto's Son Talks with Police after Wahid Issues Arrest Order', 16 September 2000.
50. Detik.com, 'Komplotan Bom Ciganjur: "Gank" Aceh di Kampung Gus Dur', 28 September 2000.
51. *Van Zorge Report*, 'Political Briefs', 2 February 2001, p. 49.
52. *Bali Post*, 'Menjelang Masuknya Tommy Ke LP Cipinang (2): Jika Main Suap, Tommy Bisa Dinusakambangkan', 1 October 2000.
53. *Asiaweek*, 'Battle of Wills', 6 October 2000.
54. *Jakarta Post*, 'Gus Dur Tells Students to March to Cendana', 30 September 2000.
55. *Jakarta Post*, 'Gus Dur Tells Students . . .', op. cit.
56. *Tempo*, 'Gus Dur Temui Tommy Demi Uang Negara', 17 October 2000.
57. *Riau Post*, 'Titiek Minta Gus Dur Diperiksa', 25 November 2000.

CHAPTER 23   STATE OF EMERGENCY

1. *Far Eastern Economic Review*, 'Undercut', 13 July 2000. See also: *Australian Financial Review*, 'Mystery Creditors, Law of the Jungle Claim ANZ', 21 February 2001; and *The Age*, 'Corruption Fears Endanger Indonesia's Autonomy Plans', 2 January 2001.
2. Data from Indonesian Bank Restructuring Agency, as of 30 March 2001.
3. See, for example: *Van Zorge Report*, 'Reflections on Corruption in Indonesia (Part II)', 2 April 2001, pp. 27–8. Gary Goodpaster discusses Mancur Olsen's distinctions between 'stationary bandits' (such as Soeharto) who provide security so that they may steal from one territory over the long term, versus 'roving bandits' who are in competition with others and therefore devastate territories as they pass through.
4. *The Age*, 'The Criminal History of an East Timorese Militia Leader', 16 April 1999.
5. The following data is from *Tempo*, 'Sekelumit Fakta Seputar Bom Natal', 25 February 2001, pp. 62–3.

6. *Tempo*, 'Cerita Dari Mosaik Bom Natal', 25 February 2001, p. 60.
7. *Tempo*, 'Cerita Dari Mosaik . . .', op. cit., p. 61.
8. *Tempo*, 'Tamu Misterius di Biara Fransiskan', 25 February 2001, p. 76.
9. *Tempo*, 'Bom di Jalur Kontak GAM-TNI', 25 February 2001, p. 69.
10. *Kompas*, 'Menhan: Orang Kuat Orde Baru Dibalik Teror Bom', 28 December 2000.
11. *Kompas*, 'Menhan: Orang Kuat . . .', op. cit.
12. *Van Zorge Report*, 'Political Briefs', 22 January 2001, p. 38.
13. *Gatra*, 27 January 2001, p. 27.
14. Saurip Kadi, *TNI-AD: Dahulu, Sekarang dan Masa Depan*.
15. *Indonesian Observer*, 'Indonesian Army Chief Chides Attorney General', 8 January 2001.
16. *Far Eastern Economic Review*, 'Indonesian Military Treading Softly, Carefully', 22 February 2001.
17. *Tempo*, 'Segitiga Presiden-Aris-Farika', 10 December 2000, p. 24.
18. *Kompas*, 'Lika-Liku Dana Yanatera Bulog', 29 January 2001.
19. *Kompas*, 'Konsistensi Presiden Abdurrahman Wahid', 2 April 2001.
20. *Tempo*, 'Rusdihardjo: Presiden Adalah Tersangka', 10 December 2000.
21. See, for example: *Gatra*, 'Nada Konspirasi di Balik Nyanyian Aryanti', 2 September 2000, p. 23; and *Tempo*, 'Segitiga Presiden-Aris-Farika', op. cit.
22. *Kompas*, 'RUU Politik Versi Koalisi Ornop: Menawarkan Sistem Pemilu "Jalan Tengah" ', 1 March 2001.
23. *Kompas*, 'Mayjen Sudrajat Siap Pimpin Ditjen Strategi Pertahanan', 22 January 2001.
24. *Kompas*, 'KSAD Tentang Penggantian Pangdam Jaya: Untuk Antisipasi Perkembangan di Jakarta', 19 January 2001. The Wahid loyalist was Maj. Gen. Slamet Kirbiantoro, who became the military's deputy inspector-general (Wakil Irjen TNI).
25. *Kompas*, 'Ulah DPR Mengundang Kontroversi', 14 May 2001. See also: *Van Zorge Report*, 'Political Briefs', 2 February 2001, p. 47.
26. *Kompas*, 'Konsistensi Presiden Abdurrahman Wahid', 2 April 2001.
27. *Van Zorge Report*, 'Political Briefs', 22 January 2001, p. 44.
28. *Van Zorge Report*, 'Political Briefs', 19 February 2001, p. 43.
29. *Tempo*, 'Baharuddin Lopa: Maklumat Itu Tidak Berarti Jika Menterinya Melanggar', 25 February 2001, p. 40.
30. See, for example: Pramoedya Ananta Toer, *The Mute's Soliloquy: A Memoir*, pp. 8–11.
31. *Tempo*, 'Raja Hutan Kembali Ke Hutan', 8 April 2001. In Indonesian, the phrase reads: '*Kemarin aku melanggar hukum, hari ini aku belajar, agar esok dapat turut membangun.*'
32. *Panji Masyrakat*, 'Suaranya Asli, Lo!', 7 March 2001, p. 74.
33. *Tempo*, 'Lopa, "The Untouchable" ', op. cit. See also: *Jakarta Post*, 'Opinion: Focusing on Brunei, Bulog Scams', by George Aditjondro, 10 January 2001.
34. See, for example, the allegations by a former Opec chair and energy minister, Dr Subroto, in: Satunet.com, 'Subroto: Ada Markup Dalam Kasus Balongan', 8 March 2001.
35. *Van Zorge Report*, 'Political Briefs', 19 March 2001, p. 41.
36. *Agence France Presse*, 'Borneo Under Control: Violence Exaggerated: Wahid', 27 February 2001.
37. *Time*, 12 March 2001, front cover.
38. *Suara Merdeka*, 'Akbar Dampingi Mega Ke Sampit', 1 March 2001.
39. *Banjarmasin Post*, 'Salah Paham, Aparat Bentrok', 28 February 2001.
40. *Kompas*, 'Di Tengah Evakuasi Pengungsi Sampit: TNI Dan Brimob Baku Tembak', 28 February 2001. See also: *Banjarmasin Post*, 'Salah Paham, Aparat . . .', op. cit.
41. *Suara Merdeka*, 'Akbar Dampingi Mega . . .', op. cit.
42. *Deutsche Presse-Agentur*, 'Ethnic Leaders Reject Madurese Return to Central Kalimantan', 6 March 2001. See also: BBC Worldwide Monitoring, 'Indonesia: Missionary Agency Says Borneo Massacre Death Toll 3000, Not 400', 6 March 2001.
43. *Tempo*, 'Terusir Dari Sampit, Merana Di Madura', 18 March 2001, p. 28.

44. See, for example: *Agence France Presse*, 'Troops in Borneo Incompetent or Deliberately Passive: Analysts', 1 March 2001.
45. *The Economist*, 'Descent Into Darkest Borneo', 1 March 2001.
46. *Jakarta Post*, 'TNI Should be Given More Authority to Maintain Security', 2 March 2001. See also: *Kompas*, 'Di Tengah Evakuasi . . .', op. cit.; and *Kompas*, 'Perlu Ada Aturan Kapan TNI Bisa Bertindak Proaktif', 13 March 2001.
47. *Jakarta Post*, 'TNI Should be Given . . .', op. cit.
48. *Jakarta Post*, 'TNI Should be Given . . .', op. cit.
49. *Van Zorge Report*, 'Political Briefs', 2 April 2001, p. 34.
50. *Van Zorge Report*, 'Political Briefs', 16 May 2001, p. 34.
51. *Jakarta Post*, 'TNI Chiefs Say No to Dissolving DPR', 17 May 2001.
52. See, for example: National Democratic Institute, 'States of Emergency: Some Thoughts on the Legal Issues', 3 June 2001.
53. *Reuters*, 'UN Refugee Body Blasts Timor Verdicts As "Mockery"', 4 May 2001.
54. *Jakarta Post*, 'Wiranto Sues UI Sociologist', 1 May 2001.
55. *Tempo*, 'Peristiwa', 13 May 2001, p. 38.
56. *Reuters*, 'Court Sentences Timor Militia Boss to 6 Months in Jail', 30 April 2001. See also: *Jakarta Post*, 'Eurico Trial Adjourned', 2 May 2001.
57. Confidential communication.
58. *Adil*, 'Hantu Lama Bernama Komunisme', 26 April 2001.
59. *Garda*, 23 May 2001.
60. Detik.com, '102 Jenderal Teken Sikap Polri', 3 June 2001.

EPILOGUE

1. *The Age*, 'With Wahid at the End', 28 July 2001.
2. Syafiuddin was no relation to Golkar's Ginandjar Kartasasmita.
3. *Suara Pembaruan*, 'Empat Kemungkinan Pembunuhan Hakim Agung Syafiuddin', 27 July 2001.
4. *Gamma*, 'Teror Terhadap Jubah Hakim', 7 August 2001.
5. See, for example, *Suara Merdeka*, 'Rahman Diragukan Mampu Tuntaskan Kasus HAM', 19 August 2001.
6. See, for example, *Tempo*, 'Putu Ary Suta: Penghuni Baru Kursi Panas', 8 July 2001.
7. Suara Pembaruan, 'Wapres Hamzah Minta AS Introspeksi', 15 September 2001.
8. *Far Eastern Economic Review*, 'Indonesia's President Megawati Tested Over Cement Co Sale', 15 November 2001.
9. See, for example, *Forum*, 'Agenda Tersembunyi Dibalik Penangkapan Tommy', 9 December 2001.
10. *Straits Times*, 'Sulawesi Strife Highlights Acute Police–Army Rivalry', 16 December 2001.
11. *Koran Tempo*, 'Panglima TNI: Jangan Berspekulasi Soal Pembunuhan Theys', 6 December 2001. See also, *Straits Times*, 'Police Chief Says Soldiers Killed Theys', 1 January 2002.
12. AFP, 'Papua Governor Sees "Opportunity for Change" in New Autonomy', 3 January 2002.
13. See: *Tempo* (English edition), 'The Deepening Mystery of Theys' Death', 27 November 2001; *Gamma*, 'Masih Seperti Yang Dulu', 11 December 2001; *Tempo* (English edition), 'Under an Increasingly Terrorized Thumb?', 10 December 2001; and *Kompas*, 'Depdagri Tidak Pernah Miliki Konsep Operasi Khusus Hilangkan Orang', 27 November 2001.

BIBLIOGRAPHY

NEWSPAPERS AND WIRE SERVICES

Agence France Presse
Asia Pulse
Asia Times
Asian Wall Street Journal
Associated Press
Australian Financial Review
Bali Post
Bisnis Indonesia
Bloomberg
Business Times
Christian Science Monitor
Deutsche Presse-Agentur
Dow Jones Newswires
Duta Masyrakyat
Financial Times
Harian Ekonomi Neraca
Indonesian Observer
International Herald Tribune
Jakarta Post
Jawa Pos
Jurnal Indonesia
Kompas
Kyodo Newswires
Los Angeles Times
Manila Times
Media Indonesia
New York Times
Republika
Reuters
SiaR
South China Morning Post
Straits Times
Suara Karya
Suara Merdeka
Suara Pembaruan
Surabaya Post
Sydney Morning Herald
The Age
The Australian
The Guardian
The Independent
Wall Street Journal
Washington Post
Waspada

PERIODICALS

Adil
Asiaweek
Bulletin of Indonesian Economic Studies
D&R
Far Eastern Economic Review
Forum Keadilan
Gamma
Garda
Gatra
Inside Indonesia
Kontan
Panji Masyrakyat
Sabili
Statistik Ekonomi Keuangan Indonesia
Tajuk
Tempo
The Economist
Time
Van Zorge Report

WEBSITES

www.berpolitik.com
www.bi.go.id
www.dephan.go.id
www.detik.com

www.groups.yahoo.com/group/berita-
   bhinneka
www.hidayatullah.com
www.indoexchange.com
www.isnet.org
www.khatulistiwamgz.com
www.koteka.net
www.laksamana.net
www.pacific.net.id
www.petromindo.com
www.satunet.com
www.unfilteredonline.com

OTHER SOURCES

Amnesty International
Australian Broadcasting Corporation

Badan Pusat Statistik
British Broadcasting Corporation
Carter Center
East Timor Action Network
East Timor International Support Centre
Human Rights Watch
International Crisis Group
Komisi Penyelidikan Pelanggaran Hak Asasi
   Manusia (KPP Ham)
Mojo Wire
National Democratic Institute
Tapol
US State Department
Waterfront Securities Research
World Bank

BOOKS AND PAPERS

Aditjondro, George J. 'Chopping the Global Tentacles of the Suharto Oligarchy', Keynote address at the conference on Seizing Suharto's Assets, organized by the Indonesian Human Rights Committee (IHRC) and the Campaign Against Foreign Control of Aotearoa (CAFCA) in Auckland, New Zealand, April 2000.

Anderson, Benedict R. O'G. *Language and Power: Exploring Political Cultures in Indonesia*, Cornell University Press, Ithaca, 1990

Backman, Michael. *Asian Eclipse: Exposing the Dark Side of Business in Asia*, John Wiley & Sons, Singapore, 1999

Bartu, Peter. 'The Militia, the Military and the People of Bobonaro District', in *Guns and Ballot Boxes*, ed. Damien Kingsbury, Monash Asia Institute, Victoria, 2000

Baumol, William J. and Alan S. Blinder. *Economics: Principles and Policy*, Harcourt Brace Jovanovich, San Diego, 1991

Binhadi, *Financial Sector Deregulation, Banking Development and Monetary Policy: The Indonesian Experience, 1983–93*, Institut Bankir Indonesia, Jakarta, 1995

Biro Pusat Statistik. *Statistik Indonesia 1998*, Biro Pusat Statistik, Jakarta, 1998

Bourchier, David. 'Habibie's Interregnum: *Reformasi*, Elections, Regionalism and the Struggle for Power', in *Indonesia in Transition: Social Aspects of Reformasi and Crisis*, eds Chris Manning and Peter van Diermen, Institute of Southeast Asian Studies, Singapore, 2000

Bresnan, John. *Managing Indonesia: The Modern Political Economy*, Columbia University Press, New York, 1993

Bresnan, John. 'The United States, the IMF, and the Indonesian Financial Crisis', in *The Politics of Post-Suharto Indonesia*, eds Adam Schwarz and Jonathan Paris, Council on Foreign Relations Press, New York, 1999

Buku Putih Prabowo: Kesaksian Tragedi Mei 1998, Majalah Berita Populer Totalitas, Tangerang, 2000

Burchill, Scott. 'East Timor, Australia and Indonesia', in *Guns and Ballot Boxes*, ed. Damien Kingsbury, Monash Asia Institute, Victoria, 2000

Business International Asia/Pacific Ltd. *Indonesia to 1982: Economic and Political Outlook for Business Planners*, Business International Asia/Pacific Ltd, Hong Kong, 1978

Cole, David C. and Betty F. Slade, *Building a Modern Financial System: The Indonesian Experience*, Cambridge University Press, Cambridge, 1996

Cribb, Robert and Colin Brown. *Modern Indonesia: A History Since 1945*, Longman, Singapore, 1995

DBS Investment Research. 'Family Values: A Guide to Indonesian Business Groups', Unpublished paper, November 1997

Djiwandono, Soedradjad. 'The Rupiah—One Year After Its Float', in *Post-Soeharto Indonesia: Renewal or Chaos?*, ed. Geoff Forrester, Institute for Southeast Asian Studies, Singapore, 1999

Djojohadikusumo, Sumitro. *Jejak Perlawanan Begawan Pejuang*, Pustaka Sinar Harapan, Jakarta, 2000

Evans, Kevin. 'Economic Update', in *Post-Soeharto Indonesia: Renewal or Chaos?*, ed. Geoff Forrester, Institute for Southeast Asian Studies, Singapore, 1999

Federspiel, Howard M. *A Dictionary of Indonesian Islam*, Centre for International Studies, Athens, Ohio, 1995

Forrester, Geoff, ed. *Post-Soeharto Indonesia: Renewal or Chaos?*, Institute for Southeast Asian Studies, Singapore, 1999

Forrester, Geoff and R.J. May, eds. *The Fall of Soeharto*, Crawford House, Bathurst, Australia, 1998

Fox, James. 'The UN Popular Consultation and Its Aftermath in East Timor: An Account by One International Observer', in *Indonesia in Transition: Social Aspects of Reformasi and Crisis*, eds Chris Manning and Peter van Diermen, Institute of Southeast Asian Studies, Singapore, 2000

Frederick, William H. and Robert L. Worden, eds. *Indonesia: A Country Study*, Federal Research Division, Library of Congress, Washington, DC, 1993

Gafur, Abdul. *Hari-Hari Terakhir Seorang Presiden*, Pustaka Sinar Harapan, Jakarta, 2000

Halim, Liliana. 'Reviving the Indonesian Banking Sector? Indonesia's Economic Crisis: Impact on Finance and Corporate Sectors 1997–1999', ISEAS Working Papers, Visiting Researchers Series No. 7, 2000

Hanna, Donald P. 'Indonesia's Experience with Financial Sector Reforms', World Bank Discussion Papers, 1994

Hefner, Robert W. 'Islam and Nation in the Post-Suharto Era', in *The Politics of Post-Suharto Indonesia*, eds Adam Schwarz and Jonathan Paris, Council on Foreign Relations Press, New York, 1999

Henderson, Callum. *Asia Falling? Making Sense of the Asian Currency Crisis and Its Aftermath*, McGraw-Hill, Singapore, 1998

Hill, Hal. *The Indonesian Economy in Crisis: Causes, Consequences and Lessons*, Institute of Southeast Asian Studies, Singapore, 1999

Human Rights Watch, *Human Rights World Report 2001*, New York, 2001

International Commission of Jurists Mission to Indonesia, 'Ruler's Law', April 1999

Johnson, Colin. 'The Indonesian Economy in 1999: Some Comments', in *Indonesia in Transition: Social Aspects of Reformasi and Crisis*, eds Chris Manning and Peter van Diermen, Institute of Southeast Asian Studies, Singapore, 2000

Jones, Howard Palfrey. *Indonesia: The Possible Dream*, Gunung Agung (S) Pte Ltd, Singapore, 1971

Kadi, Suarip. *TNI-AD: Dahulu, Sekarang dan Masa Depan*, Pustaka Utama Grafiti, Jakarta, 2000

Kingsbury, Damien. 'The TNI and the Militias', in *Guns and Ballot Boxes*, ed. Damien Kingsbury, Monash Asia Institute, Victoria, 2000

Kingsbury, Damien, ed. *Guns and Ballot Boxes*, Monash Asia Institute, Victoria, 2000

Kunio, Yoshihara, *The Rise of Ersatz Capitalism in Southeast Asia*, Oxford University Press, Singapore, 1988

Kusumaatmadja, Sarwono, ed. *Kesan dan Kenangan dari Teman 70 Tahun H. Sudharmono, S.H.*, Gramedia Widiasarana Indonesia, Jakarta, 1997

Latief, Col. Abdul. *Pledoi Kol. A. Latief: Soeharto Terlibat G 30 S*, Institut Studi Arus Informasi, Jakarta, 2000

Liddle, William R. *Leadership and Culture in Indonesian Politics*, Allen & Unwin, Sydney, 1996

Liddle, William R. 'Indonesia's Unexpected Failure of Leadership', in *The Politics of Post-Suharto Indonesia*, eds Adam Schwarz and Jonathan Paris, Council on Foreign Relations Press, New York, 1999

Lowry, Robert. *The Armed Forces of Indonesia*, Allen & Unwin, Sydney, 1996

Lowry, Robert. 'East Timor: An Overview of Political Developments', in *Indonesia in Transition: Social Aspects of Reformasi and Crisis*, eds Chris Manning and Peter van Diermen, Institute of Southeast Asian Studies, Singapore, 2000

McBeth, John. 'Political Update', in *Post-Soeharto Indonesia: Renewal or Chaos?*, ed. Geoff Forrester, Institute for Southeast Asian Studies, Singapore, 1999

McDonald, Hamish. *Suharto's Indonesia*, Fontana Books, Blackburn, Victoria, 1980

Magnis-Suseno, Franz. '*Langsir Keprabon*: New Order Leadership, Javanese Culture, and the Prospects for Democracy in Indonesia', in *Post-Soeharto Indonesia: Renewal or Chaos?*, ed. Geoff Forrester, Institute for Southeast Asian Studies, Singapore, 1999

Makka, A. Makmur. *Bacharuddin Jusuf Habibie: His Life and Career*, Pustaka CIDESINDO, Jakarta, 1996

Mann, Richard. *Economic Crisis in Indonesia: The Full Story*, Gateway Books, Jakarta, 1998

Mann, Richard. *Plots and Schemes That Brought Down Soeharto*, Gateway Books, Jakarta, 1998

Manning, Chris and Peter van Diermen, eds. *Indonesia in Transition: Social Aspects of Reformasi and Crisis*, Institute of Southeast Asian Studies, Singapore, 2000

Mietzner, Marcus. 'The 1999 General Session: Wahid, Megawati and the Fight for the Presidency', in *Indonesia in Transition: Social Aspects of Reformasi and Crisis*, eds Chris Manning and Peter van Diermen, Institute of Southeast Asian Studies, Singapore, 2000

Mietzner, Marcus. 'From Soeharto to Habibie: The Indonesian Armed Forces and Political Islam During the Transition', in *Post-Soeharto Indonesia: Renewal or Chaos?*, ed. Geoff Forrester, Institute for Southeast Asian Studies, Singapore, 1999

Mietzner, Marcus. 'Between Pesantren and Palace: Nahdlatul Ulama and Its Role in the Transition', in *The Fall of Soeharto*, eds Geoff Forrester and R.J. May, Crawford House, Bathurst, Australia, 1998

National Democratic Institute for International Affairs and the Carter Center, 'Post-Election Developments in Indonesia: The Formation of the DPR and the MPR', Jakarta, 26 August 1999

National Democratic Institute for International Affairs, 'A Commentary on Selected Aspects of Indonesia's Draft Electoral Legislation', Jakarta, 7 December 1998

Pour, Julius. *Jakarta Semasa Lengser Keprabon*, Elex Media Komputindo, Jakarta, 1998

Rencana Strategis 1999–2004, Badan Penyehatan Perbankan Nasional, 1999

Ricklefs, M.C. *A History of Modern Indonesia: c. 1300 to the Present*, Indiana University Press, Bloomington, Indiana, 1981

Robison, Richard. *Indonesia: The Rise of Capital*, Allen & Unwin, Sydney, 1986

Samego, Indria, ed. *Bila ABRI Berbisnis*, Mizan, Jakarta, 1998

Saydam, Gauzali. *Skandal Bank Bali: Tragedi Perpolitikan Indonesia*, Raja Grafindo Persada, Jakarta, 1999

Schwarz, Adam. *A Nation in Waiting*, Allen & Unwin, Singapore, 1999

Schwarz, Adam. 'Introduction: The Politics of Post-Suharto Indonesia', in *The Politics of Post-Suharto Indonesia*, eds Adam Schwarz and Jonathan Paris, Council on Foreign Relations Press, New York, 1999

Schwarz, Adam and Jonathan Paris, eds. *The Politics of Post-Suharto Indonesia*, Council on Foreign Relations Press, New York, 1999

Shiraishi, Takashi. 'The Indonesian Military in Politics', in *The Politics of Post-Suharto Indonesia*, eds Adam Schwarz and Jonathan Paris, Council on Foreign Relations Press, New York, 1999

Smith, Anthony. 'The Popular Consultation in Ermera District: Free, Fair and Secret?', in *Guns and Ballot Boxes*, ed. Damien Kingsbury, Monash Asia Institute, Victoria, 2000

Soesilo. *Monopoli Bisnis Keluarga Cendana*, Permata, Jakarta, 1998

Soetjipto, Adi Andojo. 'Legal Reform and Challenges in Indonesia', in *Indonesia in Transition: Social Aspects of Reformasi and Crisis*, eds Chris Manning and Peter van Diermen, Institute of Southeast Asian Studies, Singapore, 2000

Suaedy, Ahmad, ed. *Premanisme Politik*, Institut Studi Arus Informasi, Jakarta, 2000

Tim Relawan Untuk Kemanusiaan, *Temuan Tim Gabungan Pencari Fakta Peristiwa Kerusuhan Mei 1998*, Publikasi Komnas Perempuan, Jakarta, 1999

Toer, Pramoedya Ananta. *Anak Semua Bangsa [Child of All Nations]*, Hasta Mitra, Jakarta, 1980

Toer, Pramoedya Ananta. *The Mute's Soliloquy: A Memoir*, Hasta Mitra, Jakarta, 1999

Turner, Peter, ed. *Java: A Lonely Planet Travel Survival Kit*, Lonely Planet Publications, Hawthorn, Australia, 1995

Van Klinken, Helen. 'Taking the Risk, Paying the Price', in *Guns and Ballot Boxes*, ed. Damien Kingsbury, Monash Asia Institute, Victoria, 2000

Van Zorge, James. *Indonesia Into the Twenty-First Century: Setting the Stage for the Post-Suharto Era*, Economist Intelligence Unit, Hong Kong, 1997

Vatikiotis, Michael R.J. *Indonesian Politics Under Suharto: Order, Development and Pressure for Change*, Routledge, London, 1993

Vatikiotis, Michael R.J. 'Romancing the Duel Function: Indonesia's Armed Forces and the Fall of Soeharto', in *The Fall of Soeharto*, eds Geoff Forrester and R.J. May, Crawford House, Bathurst, Australia, 1998

World Bank, 'Indonesia: From Crisis to Opportunity', Jakarta, 21 July 1999

World Bank, 'Indonesia in Crisis: A Macroeconomic Update', Jakarta, 16 July 1998

World Bank, 'Indonesia: Improving Efficiency and Equity Changes in the Public Sector's Role', Jakarta, 9 June 1995

GLOSSARY

ABANGAN	Nominal Muslims who adhere to *kebatinan* (q.v.), or Javanese mysticism; often contrasted with *santri* (q.v.).
ABRI	Armed Forces of the Republic of Indonesia; *Angkatan Bersenjata Republik Indonesia*. Now called TNI (q.v.).
AITARAK	Pro-Indonesia militia in Dili, East Timor.
AMIN	Indonesian Mujahidin.
APHI	Indonesian Foresters Association; *Assosiasi Pengusaha Hutan Indonesia*.
APKINDO	Indonesian Plywood Association; *Assosiasi Panel Kayu Indonesia*.
BAIS	Armed Forces Strategic Intelligence Agency; *Badan Intelijens Stratejis*. Nationwide intelligence network that reports to the armed forces commander; focused on identifying and repressing internal security threats; often works closely with para-military forces.
BAKIN	State Intelligence Co-ordinating Agency; *Badan Koordinasi Intelijen Negara*.
BATIK	Type of traditional Indonesian cloth.
BI	Bank Indonesia.
BLBI	Bank Indonesia Liquidity Support; *Bantuan Likuiditas Bank Indonesia*.
BPK	Financial Inspection Board.
BPS	Central Statistics Bureau; *Biro Pusat Statistik*.
BRIMOB	Mobile Police Brigade; *Brigade Mobil Polisi*. A police unit armed similarly to light mobile infantry.
BULOG	State Logistics Agency; *Badan Urusan Logistik Nasional*.
BUPATI	Head of *kabupaten* or district.
CBS	Currency board system, an economically orthodox way to fix an exchange rate.
CENTRAL AXIS	Alliance of Islamic parties.
CNRT	National Council of Timorese Resistance; *Concelho Nacional da Resistencia Timor*.
CONSUMER PRICE INDEX	Benchmark measure of inflation.
CP	Commercial paper.
DPR	People's Representative Assembly; *Dewan Perwakilan Rakyat*.
DUKUN SANTET	Practitioner of sorcery.
DUKUN TENUNG	Practitioner of 'black magic'.

EGP	Era Giat Prime, the privately owned company that perpetrated the Bank Bali Scandal.
FALINTIL	Armed Forces of East Timor; *Forcas Armadas in Timor Leste*. East Timorese pro-independence guerillas—the military wing of the CNRT (q.v.); formerly known as Fretelin.
FDI	Foreign direct investment.
FKPPI	Communication Forum for the Sons and Daughters of Armed Forces Personnel and Retirees; *Forum Komunikasi Putra-Putri Purnawirawan dan ABRI*.
FORKOT	City Forum; *Forum Kota*.
FPDU	Sovereign Islamic Community Faction; *Fraksi Perserikatan Daulatul Ummah*.
FPI	Islamic Defence Front; *Front Pembela Islam*.
GAM	Free Aceh Movement; *Gerakan Aceh Merdeka*.
GDP	Gross domestic product.
GMNI	Indonesian National Students Movement; *Gerakan Mahasiswa Nasional Indonesia*.
GOLKAR	Functional Groups; *Golongan Karya*. Soeharto's political party.
HAJ	Pilgrimage to Mecca.
HMI	Islamic Students Association; *Himpunan Mahasiswa Islam*.
IBRA	Indonesian Bank Restructuring Agency. The country's most important economic entity in the *reformasi* era, controlling most banking sector assets as well as a large portfolio of corporate assets; charged with recovering bad debts and auctioning nationalised assets.
ICMI	Indonesian Association of Muslim Intellectuals; *Ikatan Cendekiawan Muslim Indonesia*. Political vehicle created jointly by supporters of Soeharto and Islamic leaders; rivalled Golkar in influence in the mid-1990s.
IMF	International Monetary Fund.
INKUD	Association of Village-level Government Co-operatives; *Induk Koperasi Unit Desa*.
IPB	Bogor Agricultural Institute; *Institute Pertanian Bogor*.
IPK	Association of Offspring of Military Personnel Posted to the Civilian Bureaucracy; *Ikatan Pemuda Kekaryaan*.
IPO	Initial public offering.
IPTN	Archipelago Aircraft Industry; *Industri Pesawat Terbang Nusantara*.
IRAMASUKA	Irian Jaya, Maluku, Sulawesi, Kalimantan and Nusa Tenggara.
ISLAMIC MODERNISM	A twentieth-century movement to reconcile modern lifestyles and economics with the teachings of the Prophet; seeks to align Indonesian Islam more closely with Middle Eastern 'orthodoxy'; championed by Muhammadiyah (q.v.).
ISLAMIC TRADITIONALISM	A syncretic form of Islam that features elements of Javanese mysticism; reluctant to review or reform religious teachings; championed by Nahdlatul Ulama (q.v.).
ITB	Bandung Institute of Technology; *Institut Teknologi Bandung*.
JCI	Jakarta Composite Index.
JIHAD	Righteous struggle or 'holy war'.
JSE	Jakarta Stock Exchange.
KABUPATEN	District level administrative unit—below the provincial level, but above the sub-district or kecamatan level.

KAHMI	Alumni of the Islamic Students Association; *Korps Alumni Himpunan Mahasiswa Islam.*
KAMMI	Indonesian Muslim Students Action Group; *Kesatuan Aksi Mahasiswa Muslimin Indonesia.*
KAMPUNG	Village or low-income urban neighbourhood.
KASTER	Chief-of-staff for territorial affairs; *kepala staf teritorial.* The military's key policy-making post; previously called 'chief-of-staff for socio-political affairs'.
KEBATINAN	An amalgam of animist, Hindu–Buddhist and mystical Islamic beliefs; also known as *kejawen, agama Jawa,* or Javanism.
KEKARYAANISASI	The military program whereby active military officers were placed in civilian posts within the bureaucracy and state-owned enterprises.
KETERBUKAAN	Literally, 'openness'—the liberalisation of political discourse.
KISDI	Indonesian Committee for Solidarity with the Islamic World; *Komite Indonesia Untuk Solidaritas Dunia Islam.*
KKN	Corruption, collusion and nepotism; *Korupsi, kolusi dan nepotisme.*
KNPI	Indonesian National Youth Organisation; *Komite Nasional Pemuda Indonesia.*
KODAM	Military region or 'garrison'; *Komando Daerah Militer.*
KONTRAS	Commission on Victims of Violence and Missing Persons; *Komisi Untuk Orang Hilang Dan Korban Tindakan Kekerasan.*
KOPASSUS	Special Forces Command; *Komando Pasukan Khusus.*
KOPKAMTIB	Operational Command for the Restoration of Law and Order; *Komando Operasi Pemulihan Keamanan dan Ketertiban.*
KOSTRAD	Army Strategic Reserve; *Komando Cadangan Stratejis Angkatan Darat.* Army's main combat force, consisting of around 40 000 well-equipped, mobile troops.
KPU	General Election Commission; *Komisi Pemilihan Umum.*
LEBARAN	The Muslim feast period after the fasting month of Ramadhan (q.v.)
M1	Base money supply.
MILF	Moro Islamic Liberation Front.
MNC	Multinational corporation.
MPR	People's Consultative Assembly; *Majelis Permusyawaratan Rakyat.* Seven-hundred member body that represents the highest constitutional authority and that elects the president every five years. Since 1999, consists of 462 elected parliamentarians; 38 appointed parliamentarians from the military and police; 135 regional representatives and 65 functional group representatives.
MUHAMMADIYAH	Organisation representing Islamic modernism (q.v.) in Indonesia.
MUI	Religious Scholars Council of Indonesia; *Majelis Ulama Indonesia.*
NAHDLATUL ULAMA	Literally, 'Revival of the Religious Scholars'; organisation representing Islamic traditionalism (q.v.) in Indonesia.
NEW ORDER	The period of Soeharto's rule (1966–98).
NGO	Non-governmental organization.
NU	Nahdlatul Ulama (q.v.).
OPEC	Organisation of the Petroleum Exporting Countries.
OUTER ISLANDS	Islands of Indonesia, excluding Java, Madura and Bali.
P3TT	Task Force for Carrying Out Popular Consultation in East Timor; *Satuan Tugas Panitia Pelaksanaan Penentuan Pendapat di Timor Timur.*

Pam Swakarsa	Volunteer Security Forces; *Pasukan Pengamanan Swakarsa.*
Pan	National Mandate Party; *Partai Amanat Nasional.*
Pansus	Special Parliamentary Committee; *Panitia Khusus.*
Panwaslak	Committee to Oversee the Conduct of the Election; *Panitia Pengawas Pelaksanaan Pemilu.*
Paspampres	Presidential Security Force; *Pasukan Pengamanan Presiden.*
PBB	Crescent and Star Party; *Partai Bulan Bintang.*
PDI	Indonesian Democratic Party; *Partai Demokrat Indonesia.*
PDI Perjuangan	Indonesian Democratic Party of Struggle; *Partai Demokrat Indonesia Perjuangan.*
Pepabri	Retired Armed Forces Officers Association; *Perikatan Purnawiraan Angkatan Bersenjata Republik Indonesia.*
Pertamina	National Oil and Gas Mining Company; *Perusahaan Tambang Minyak dan Gas Bumi Nasional.*
Pesantren	Islamic boarding schools of the NU (q.v.) tradition.
PK	Justice Party; *Partai Keadilan.*
PKB	National Awakening Party; *Partai Kebangkitan Bangsa.*
PKI	Indonesian Communist Party; *Partai Komunis Indonesia.*
PLN	National Electric Company; *Perusahaan Listrik Nasional.*
PNI	Indonesian National Party; *Partai Nasional Indonesia.*
PPP	United Development Party; *Partai Persatuan Pembangunan.*
Preman	Thug, hoodlum or mercenary; often recruited into para-military forces.
Pribumi	Indigenous Indonesian—persons who share the racial features of the Javanese, Sundanese, Malay and other similarly featured ethnic groups. With the exception of Arabs, excludes Indonesians of 'foreign' descent—namely ethnic-Chinese, but also Indians.
Priyayi	Javanese aristocratic class.
PwC	PricewaterhouseCoopers.
Ramadhan	The Muslim fasting month.
Rapim	Leadership meeting; *rapat pimpinan.*
Reformasi	Literally, 'reform'; generally meaning political liberalisation and economic transparency, but sometimes misused as a bland, catch-all term. Also used to refer to the period following Soeharto's fall.
Rose Team	Eleven-member team of Special Forces personnel who were responsible for the abduction of pro-democracy activists in early 1998.
Ruler's Law	Legal system whereby instruments of the state are used to uphold the authority of the ruler, rather than uphold justice.
Rupiah	Basic unit of Indonesia's currency. Fixed at Rp415/US$ from 1971 to 1978, when it devalued to Rp625/US$. Two subsequent devaluations occurred in 1983 and 1986 and the currency was allowed to depreciate by about 3–5 per cent per annum thereafter. The currency suffered devaluations of 48 per cent in 1997, 42 per cent in 1998 and 2 per cent in 2000.
RUU KKN	Draft Law on State Safety and Security; *Racangan Undang-Undang Keselamatan dan Keamanan Negara.*
RUU PKB	Draft Law on Imposing a State of Emergency; *Racangan Undang-Undang Penyelenggarakan Keadaan Bahaya.*
Santri	Orthodox Muslims; often contrasted with *abangan* (q.v.).
SBPU	Money Market Certificates; *Surat Berharga Pasar Uang.*
Siaga	Solidarity for Mega and Amien; *Solidaritas Mega dan Amien.*

TEAM ELEVEN	The group of civic leaders and pro-democracy activists who screened prospective political parties in early 1999.
TEAM SEVEN	The group of political scientists who produced the draft electoral laws in 1998.
TERRITORIAL STRUCTURE	Organisational structure of the army whereby troops are stationed throughout the country, with commands paralleling the civilian administrative system.
TGPF	Joint Fact-finding Team set up by the Indonesian government to investigate the events of the May 1998 riots.
TIM BULDOSER	The New Order troika that consistently produced electoral victories for Soeharto; consisted of the military, Golkar and the civil service.
TIM SUKSES	President Habibie's informal committee of campaign advisors and lobbyists. Most were natives of South Sulawesi, and several were implicated in the Bank Bali scandal.
TNI	Indonesian National Military; *Tentara Nasional Indonesia*. Formerly called Abri (q.v.); referred to herein as 'the military'.
UGM	Gadjah Mada University.
UI	University of Indonesia; *Universitas Indonesia*.
ULAMA	Islamic scholar or cleric.
UN	United Nations.
UNAMET	United Nations Assistance Mission in East Timor.
UNHCR	United Nations High Commissioner for Refugees.
WAYANG	Javanese play, typically involving leather puppets, that dramatises themes from Hindu epics.

Notes on the Text

Indonesian names have certain characteristics that are worthy of note. Some Indonesians have only one name, and many names have valid alternative spellings. An Indonesian's last name is not necessarily the family surname; moreover, it is relatively common for the main-stream Indonesian press to refer to public figures using only their given (that is, first) names.

In this text I have tried to adhere to standard spellings and mainstream conventions, but in certain instances I have taken small liberties when doing so would clearly aid reader comprehension. For instance, when two characters have the same or a similar surname, I have differentiated the two by consistently referring to one using the given name. Most notably, for ease of reference I have applied 'Soeharto' as the surname for all of Soeharto's children, even though not all of them are commonly referred to in this way. I have provided full names, alternative names and aliases in the short biographies that appear in an appendix.

Similarly, there are certain posts or military commands whose names have changed over time. In some of these cases, I have simplified by using one name consistently throughout (for instance, the post of 'kaster', which was known prior to 1998 as 'kassospol'). These instances are also noted in the footnotes.

Note that the province of Papua is referred to throughout this book by its former name, Irian Jaya (the official name change took place after preparation of this manuscript). Finally, references to dollars refer to the US currency, unless otherwise noted.

INDEX

11 March Letter *see* Supersemar
20 May rallies 132
30 September Movement 5
5 May Accord 263–4

Aachen 140
AAK *see* Anti-Communist Alliance
Abangan see cultural streams
Abeng, Tanri
    background 75, 144, 273, 420
    Bank Bali Scandal 246–9, 252–3, 285–7,
        289–90, 364
    fall of Soeharto 129
    Tim Sukses 273
Abu Sayyaf rebels 347
Aceh
    autonomy law 372
    background 235, 332–3
    Bantiqiyah massacre 293, 307
    comparisons to East Timor 211, 257,
        260, 280, 333–4
    drug trade 294
    human rights 164–5, 368, 412
    JSE bombing allegations 378
    referendum demands 333–4, 343
    Syafrie Syamsoeddin 110
Adi Andojo *see* Sutjipto, Adi Andojo
Adil 186
Adisutjipto, Widodo 328–9, 335, 349, 375,
    380, 393, 399, 402, 420
Afghanistan 411
Afri, Yanni 80
Ahmad, Fatimah 125
air force 9, 133, 363, 393; *see also* military
Air Wagon International 388

Aitarak 262, 268, 272, 397, 400; *see also*
    Guterres, Eurico
al Baaqil, Habib Alwi 377
Alatas, Ali 95–6, 272, 420
Albright, Madeleine 133, 267, 268, 316
Al-Habsyi, Habib 400
Amang, Beddu 231–2, 413
Amin *see* Indonesian Mujahidin
Andjaba, Martin 274
Andrews, David 262
Annan, Koffi 264, 266–7, 269, 275, 358, 376
Ansor 169, 296, 397
Antara 95
Anti-Communist Alliance (AAK) 400–1
anti-terror *see* Special Forces
Anugerah Bintang 163, 251
Anwar, Dewi Fortuna 212, 268, 420
ANZ Bank 245
Apkindo *see* Indonesian Plywood
    Association
Ariawest 381
Arief, Andi 79–81
Arifin, Bustanil 230
Aritonang, Edward 370
Ariwibowo, Tunky 56–7
armed forces *see* military
armed forces academy 215
Armed Forces of East Timor (Falintil) 257,
    259–63 *passim*, 266, 269, 274, 278–9,
    351
armed forces staff college 108, 143
army 4, 18–19, 329, 371–2; *see also* military
Artha Graha 13, 156, 223
Arthur Andersen Prasetio Utomo 34
Arun 332–3

Arung Gauk Jarre 289–90
Ashari, Hasyim 15, 204
Asian Development Bank 148–9
Asian Wall Street Journal 101
ASIS *see* Australian Secret Intelligence
 Service
asset restructuring 150–1, 323–26 *passim*,
 364–6, 382–5 *passim*, 394–5, 412;
 see also Indonesian Bank
 Restructuring Agency
Association of Islamic Intellectuals (Icmi)
 alleged military collaboration 357
 Amien Rais connections 63, 292, 313
 fall of Soeharto 127
 founding of 18–19
 Ghalibie tape scandal 220
 support for Habibie 63–4, 141, 144,
  154, 180, 186, 205, 228, 305, 312
Association of Offspring of Military
 Personnel Posted to the Civilian
 Bureaucracy (IPK) 107
Atambua UNHCR attack 375–6, 378, 385,
 400, 412
Atmadjaya University 91, 180, 181–2, 184
Atmadjaya, Usman 61–2, 364–5, 420
Atmonegoro, Soedjono 158, 222
Australia 66, 230, 238, 245, 263–8, 271,
 275–7, 280
Australian Secret Intelligence Service
 (ASIS) 263
Austria 240
AW International *see* Airwagon
 International
Aziz, Captain Andi 139

Bachtiar, Dai 413–4
Bahamas 384
Bais *see* Strategic Intelligence Agency
Bakin *see* National Intelligence Coordi-
 nating Agency
Bakrie & Brothers 75, 249
Bali 166, 172, 205, 238, 317, 321
Balibo affair 146, 267
Balongan refinery scandal 393
Bandung Institute of Technology (ITB) 90,
 139
Bank Andromeda 48, 50
Bank Bali 245, 381; *see also* scandals
Bank Bukopin 231–2
Bank Central Asia (BCA) 61–2, 364
Bank closures 47–51
Bank Danamon 61–2
Bank Duta 234

Bank Harapan Sentosa (BHS) 47
Bank Indonesia (BI)
 interference with 50–1
 policies of 24, 39–3, 49, 53, 381
 scandals 47, 57–62, 208, 246–9, 252–3,
  287, 289, 330
Bank Indover 59; *see also* scandals
Bank Lippo 290
Bank Negara Indonesia (BNI) 57, 330
Bank of Thailand 28, 39–42
Bank Pacific 32, 47
Bank Panin 245; *see also* Panin Overseas
 Finance
Bank Secrecy Law 287
Bank Umum Nasional 61–2
Bankers Trust 382
banking system 41, 43, 46–50, 245, 248, 323;
 see also state banks; Bank Indonesia;
  scandals
Bankruptcy Law 383
Bantiqiyah massacre *see* strife
Banyuwangi killings 166–73 *passim*, 235,
 350, 371
Bapindo 32, 57, 285–6
Baramuli, Arnold
 background 222, 420
 Bank Bali scandal 246–9, 251–4, 284–7,
  289–90, 364, 391
 political manoeuvring 222, 236, 316,
  273, 298, 362
Baringbing, Rudolf 170
Bawazier, Fuad
 background 420
 Central Axis role 292, 327–8, 335, 361
 fall of Soeharto 130
 role in finance portfolio 64, 66, 75, 77
BBC *see* British Broadcasting Corporation
BCA *see* Bank Central Asia
BDNI 61–2, 208, 246, 393
Belo, Carlos 272
Bentoel 34
Berita Keadilan 221
Besa Merah Putih 261
BHS *see* Bank Harapan Sentosa
BI *see* Bank Indonesia
Bimantoro, Suroyo 377–8, 383–5, 402,
 412–3
Bisnis Indonesia 95
BLBI *see* liquidity credits
BNI *see* Bank Negara Indonesia
Boedisantoso, Asman 119–20
Bogor 69
Bogosari Flour Mills 45, 47

bombings
  attorney general's office 369–71
  Bank Indonesia 50
  campaign related 317
  Christmas Eve church 385–7
  effect on economy 381, 385
  Istiqlal mosque 233–4, 366
  Jakarta Stock Exchange 376–8
  Kelapa Gading Mall 233
  Philippine embassy 374–5
  Plaza Atrium 233–4
  Plaza Hayam Wuruk 233
  Ramayana Jalan Subang 193, 233–4
Borneo 36
Borobudur temple 400
BPK see Financial Inspection Board
BPN see National Land Agency
BPPC see clove monopoly
Bre-X 36–7
Brimob see police
British Broadcasting Corporation (BBC)
      270, 374
British Virgin Islands 240, 382
Brunei 388
Bugis 139
Bulog see National Logistics Agency
Buloggate and Bruneigate scandals 373,
      379, 388–91
Busang see scandals
Buyung Nasution see Nasution, Adnan
      Buyung

Calgary Stock Exchange 36
Cambodia 240
Camdessus, Michel 53
Canada 93, 240
Canadian embassy 383
Capital Markets Regulatory Agency
      (Bapepam) 33, 383–4, 411
Capital Markets Society 39
Carrascalao, Manuel 262
Carter Center 267
Carter, Jimmy 267
CBS see currency board
Cemex 381, 412
Cendana raid 379
Cendana see Soeharto family
Center for Strategic and International
      Studies (CSIS) 194
Central Axis
  cabinet representation 327–8, 335, 361,
      410
  formation of 251, 292–3

political alliances 297, 301–5, 308,
      310–11, 314–17, 321, 408, 414–5
  stance on Wahid 387, 394
  support for Wiranto 345
central bank see Bank Indonesia
Central Java Garrison 5, 223, 335, 390
Chamsyah, Bachtiar 389, 393
Chandra Asri Petrochemicals 35
Chaniago, Djamari 111, 335–6
charitable foundations 30–1, 306, 338
China 23
China see People's Republic of China
Chretien, Jean 383–4
Christmas Eve church bombings 385–7
Ciamis killings 235
Ciganjur Declaration 177–8
cigarette industry 34, 46, 368
Ciputra 97
Cirenti power plant 54
Citra Lamtoro Gung 54
civil service 200–2, 209, 217, 265, 326, 354
Clinton, Bill 53, 65, 276, 288, 334
clove cigarettes see cigarette industry
Clove Marketing and Bufferstock Agency
      (BPPC) see clove monopoly
clove monopoly 45–7, 66, 75, 85, 367–8
CNRT see National Council of East
      Timorese Resistance
Cohen, William 269
Cole, David 61
commercial paper (CP) 32, 47
Commission on Investigating Human
      Rights Abuses in East Timor (KPP
      Ham Timtim) 340–4, 351–4
communal conflict see strife
Communication Forum for the Sons and
      Daughters of Armed Forces
      Personnel and Retirees (FKPPI)
      107
Communist Party (PKI) 4–5, 8, 169, 171–3,
      204, 362–3, 400; see also pogrom,
      anti-communist
Constitution
  bearing on elections 144, 153, 160,
      407
  founding of 4, 67
  respect for 115, 126, 133–4
  vagaries in 75, 128, 131
co-operatives
  ministry of 66, 75–6, 144, 328
  political patronage 150, 210–11, 368
co-ordinating ministry for politics and
      security 265, 342

corruption
 crony tycoons 332
 effects on economy 6, 22–37 *passim*,
  327, 365–6, 381, 403–4
 in the legal system 150, 309, 324–6,
  363–5 *passim*, 382–5 *passim*, 391–4
  passim, 410, 416
 Liquidity Credits scandal 59–62
 mega-projects 54, 365
 Soeharto investigations 189–92 *passim*,
  355–6, 376–8, 392
 state banks 361
 Texmaco scandal 50–9, 330–2
 see also KKN; rents; cronyism; reform
coup d'état 5, 72, 112, 116, 143–4, 273–4,
 307, 343, 353–8 *passim*
court system 29–30, 151, 158, 200, 202, 242,
 355–6, 363–6 *passim*, 378–9, 382–5
 passim, 400, 410, 412
CP *see* commercial paper
Crescent and Star Party (PBB)
 electoral strength of 177, 204–5
 political alliances 211, 305, 313, 316,
  320, 327, 408
 support for military 345, 353, 387,
  403
 see also Central Axis
crisis *see* financial crisis
cronyism 29, 42, 48, 51–73 *passim*, 323–6
 passim, 330, 365–6, 381
CSIS *see* Center for Strategic and
 International Studies
cultural streams 204
currency board (CBS) 24, 64–6, 75–6
currency speculators *see* currency traders
currency traders 27, 40–1, 77

Da Costa, Willem 399
Dahlan, Alwi 84
Damiri, Adam 110, 279, 350, 341–2, 375,
 420
Danutirto, Haryanto 75–6, 129
Darmawan, Hariadi 124
Darul Islam 106
Darusman, Marzuki
 background 420
 Bank Bali scandal 247–8, 252
 East Timor investigations 340, 345, 355,
  357, 375–6, 385, 387
 political alliances 159, 229, 236, 310,
  315
 role as attorney general 330–2, 340,
  355–6, 364–5, 370, 392–3, 401

 role in human rights commission 111,
  183
 Soeharto family investigations 339,
  376–8
 stance on advocacy 163, 178, 201
De Javasche Bank 59
debt levels
 private sector 42, 53, 151
 public 135, 324–5
decentralisation *see* reform
Delta Force 68–9
democracy campaigners *see* student
 movement
Democracy Forum 20–1, 83
Deutsche Telkom 31
development 6
Dharmala Group 382–5 *passim*
Dharmala Sakti Sejahtera *see* Dharmala
 Group
Dharsono, H.R. 161
Diaz, Agus 370
Diaz, Boli 370
Dipasena 365
Diponegoro University 151
direct voting *see* electoral system
Discipline Enforcement Cadres 113
Djadjoesman, Noegroho 101, 187
Djaelani, Abdul Qaedir 387
Djalil, Matori Abdul 292–3, 302–4, 308–9,
 320, 366–7, 420–1
Djaluluddin, Syamsu 222–3
Djamari *see* Chaniago, Djamari
Djiwandono, Soedradjad
 background 44, 421
 economic policies 39, 47–51, 65
 scandals 57–9, 60, 62
Djojohadikusumo, Hashim 35, 67–8, 240,
 421
Djojohadikusumo, Sumitro 67, 90, 109, 140
Downer, Alexander 269
DPA *see* supreme advisory council
DPR *see* parliament
DSS *see* Dharmala Sakti Sejahtera
Dunija 217–18

East Timor
 autonomy ballot 212, 256–80 *passim*,
  266–7, 270–1, 293
 brutality 261, 262, 268, 276–8, 307
 comparisons to Aceh 211, 257, 260,
  280, 333–4
 Garnadi document 265, 275, 342, 414
 history 101, 107–8, 211–12, 257

investigations 229–44 *passim*, 351–4,
    364, 385, 391, 410, 414
military activity in 107–10, 116, 236,
    257, 336
see also East Timorese militias
East Timorese militias
    alleged role in May riots 105, 107–8
    attacks by 261–2, 266–7, 268, 270–1,
        349–50, 375–6
    investigations of 341–3, 355, 400, 412
    military backing for 192, 236, 257–9,
        264, 342
economic growth 22, 51, 135, 147–8, 323,
    327, 365–6, 381
Edhy, Sarwo 81
Effendi, Ari 383
EGP *see* Era Giat Prima
Egypt 89, 117–18, 401
El Nino weather phenomenon 44, 148
Election Law *see* political laws
Election Oversight Committee (Panwaslak)
    242
elections
    1997: 10, 15, 20–1, 127, 238
    1998: 74–5
    1999: 147, 176, 203–5, 213–14, 224,
        238–9, 241–3, 295–6, 297–322
        passim, 394, 408
    pre-1997: 4, 7–8, 330
electoral laws *see* political laws
electoral system
    candidate selection debate 299–300
    proportional versus direct 198–9, 390
    regional imbalance 209–10, 243
Eluay, Theys 413–4
emergency powers 76, 115, 120
Era Giat Prima (EGP) 246–9, 251–4, 286–90
ersatz capitalism 29
ethnic-Chinese
    cronyism 31, 247
    discrimination and persecution 52, 55,
        85, 98–102, 150, 169, 179, 186, 238,
        332
EU *see* European Union
European Union (EU) 262
exchange rate 24, 26, 39, 42, 147, 323, 364,
    366, 394, 419
exports 42–3, 147

Falintil *see* Armed Forces of East Timor
Famred 179
Far Eastern Economic Review (FEER) 188, 234
Farika, Siti 388–9

FEER *see Far Eastern Economic Review*
financial crisis 28–30, 38–51 *passim*, 62
Financial Inspection Board (BPK) 287–9
Financial Times 277, 355
Firdaus, Lukman 181
Fischer, Stanley 288
FKPPI *see* Communication Forum for the
    Sons and Daughters of Armed
    Forces Personnel and Retirees
food prices *see* inflation
Forbes 190
forest fires 44
Forkot *see* Forum Kota
Fort Benning 67
Fort Bragg 67
Forum Democracy *see* Democracy Forum
Forum for a Peaceful Indonesia 386–7
Forum Kota (Forkot) 165, 179
FPDU *see* Sovereignty of the Islamic
    Community Faction
Free Aceh Movement (Gam) 258, 280, 333,
    386
Freedom of Expression Bill 163
Front for a United Islamic Ulama (FUIB)
    180
Front Hizbullah 400
fuel subsidies 87–8
FUIB *see* Front for a United Islamic Ulama
functional groups *see* People's Consultative
    Assembly

G-15 *see* Group of 15
Gadjah Mada University (UGM) 78–9, 223,
    328
Gadjah Tunggal Group 35; *see also*
    Nursalim, Syamsul
Gafur, Abdul 125–6, 159, 236, 286, 298
Gam *see* Free Aceh Movement
Gamma 248
Garda 401
Garnadi document *see* East Timor
Garnadi 265, 342, 421; *see also* East Timor
Garuda Matraman Brigade 139
GDP growth *see* economic growth
Gelael, Ricardo 230–1, 233
Gelbard, Robert 310–11 *passim*, 358, 412
General Election Commission (KPU)
    213–15, 217, 242–3, 299–300, 346
Germany 66–7, 112, 140, 141, 205
Ghalib, Andi
    background 158, 421
    political orientation 273, 415
    scandals 218-24 *passim*, 244–5

Soeharto investigations 189–92, 229–30, 239–40

Ghalibie tape *see* scandals

Ghurkas 275

Gie, Kwik Kian 308, 319, 328, 421

Ginandjar *see* Kartasasmita, Ginandjar

GMNI *see* Indonesian National Students Movement

Goh, Chok Tong 53

Golden Key Group 57; *see also* Tansil, Eddy

Golkar
  Bank Bali Scandal 236–7
  cabinet representation 144, 291, 297, 301–5, 314, 318–21
  campaigning 224, 238–9, 226
  congresses and rapims 154–60, 210, 228, 240, 244, 309, 315–16
  co-operatives 150, 368
  divisions over presidential nominee 226, 345
  electoral strength of 154, 203–5, 209–10, 227, 242–3, 286, 415
  fall of Soeharto 119
  Iramasuka caucus 228, 236, 306–7, 408
  political alliances 246–9, 251–2, 290, 408–9
  political laws debate 197–202 *passim*, 213
  preman links 104, 180
  relations with military 9, 154, 159, 179, 345, 359
  relations with political Islam 226, 404
  stance on reforms 362–4, 372, 391
  stance on Wahid 327, 344–5, 360, 387, 397–8

Gondokusumo family 382–5

Goro 77, 104, 230–3 *passim*, 236, 378, 410, 413

Government Watch 388

Group of 15 89, 401

guerilla warfare *see* para-militaries

Guided Democracy *see* Soekarno

Gumelar, Agum 82, 132, 172, 329, 402, 408, 411, 421

Gunadarma University 91

Gus Dur *see* Wahid, Abdurrahman

Gusmao, Xanana 256, 259–62, 272, 421

Guterres, Eurico 262–3, 268, 342, 385, 397, 400–1, 421

Habibie, Bacharuddin Jusuf
  background 139–40, 421
  fall of Soeharto 128–31, 134–5, 397

presidential campaign 300, 304–6, 308–14, 320, 330

presidential candidacy 145, 154–63, 172, 210, 228, 225–6, 236–7, 244, 271, 295, 297–8

relations with military 109, 123–4, 140–4, 158–60, 163, 171, 271, 273–4, 328, 403

relations with political Islam 18–19, 63, 174–5, 177, 180, 205

relations with students 165, 175–6, 179–80, 308

scandals 53, 141, 148–50, 163, 218–24 *passim*, 237, 248, 251, 254, 284–6

stance on East Timor 211–12, 237, 256–7, 264–5, 268–9, 275, 308, 340

stance on reforms 145–7, 150–2, 197–8

stance on Soeharto 158, 185, 189, 228–30, 237, 239–40, 306–7, 365

technology ministry and IPTN 46, 140–2, 287

vice-presidency 63–4, 75

Habibie, Hasrie Ainun 290

Habibie, Timmy 254, 286, 304, 421

Hadisiswoyo, Subagyo 72, 111, 115, 133, 164, 173, 294, 329, 335, 421

Hakim, Arif Rachman 94

Halid, Nurdin 236, 298, 421

Hamdi, Al-Hilal 313

Hamdun, Deddy 80

Hamengkubuwono IX 208

Hamengkubuwono X 131, 178, 208, 225, 227–8, 306–7, 422

Hamid, Syarwan
  background 10, 422
  fall of Soeharto 115, 120–1, 125–6
  political manoeuvring 158–9, 273, 320
  stance on reforms 146–7, 197–8, 213–14
  stance toward activists 67, 79, 81, 88–9, 214

Hanke, Stephen 64–5

Harijanto, Farid 253, 286

Harmoko
  1998 Golkar congress 154–60
  background 63, 146, 422
  Bank Bali scandal 286
  currency board proposal 65
  fall of Soeharto 88, 109, 114, 119–21, 124–6, 130, 132–3
  role as MPR Speaker 74, 162, 175, 179, 183, 295

Hartanto, Hery 93

Hartono 21, 75, 84, 131, 379, 422
Hartono, Dimyati 295
Harvard University 336
Haryadi, Siti Hediyati Titiek *see* Prabowo,
    Titiek
Haryoyudanto, Sigit *see* Soeharto, Sigit
Hasan, Mohammad Bob
    alleged links to political violence 187,
        234
    background 31, 422
    corruption scandals 37, 43, 45, 54,
        61–2, 221, 332, 392, 413
    relations with Soeharto ties 45, 76–7,
        130
Hasbi, Mohammed 237
Hashim *see* Djojohadikusumo, Hashim
Hashimoto, Ryutaro 53
Hasyim, Wahid 15, 305
Hasyim, Yusuf 208
Hatta, Mohammad 4
Haz, Hamzah
    background 422
    Bank Bali hearings 286
    candidacy for high office 251, 320–21,
        328, 394, 408–9, 415
    political alliances 241, 302, 313–14,
        344–5, 360
    relations with US 411
Head, Jonathan 270
Hendrawan, Herman 80
Hendropriyono 130, 143, 158, 185
Heryanto, Agustri 93
Hokiarto 232
Holbrooke, Richard 353, 378
home affairs ministry 197, 199, 217–18
Hong Kong 22, 36, 240
Howard, Paul 268
Human Rights Commission *see* National
    Commission on Human Rights
human rights 6, 68, 211, 332, 345, 355–6,
    372, 374, 391, 397, 401, 410, 412,
    414, 416; *see also* National
    Commission on Human Rights
Humpuss 230, 367

Ibra *see* Indonesian Bank Restructuring
    Agency
Ibrahim, Marwah Daud 328
Icmi *see* Association of Islamic Intellectuals
ICRC *see* International Committee of the
    Red Cross
ICW *see* Indonesian Corruption Watch
Idris, Fahmi 123–4, 236, 316, 318–9

Idris, Kemal 161, 162
IFC *see* International Finance Corporation
Ifes *see* International Foundation for
    Election Systems
Ikhwutan Sunnah Waljamaah 400
IMF *see* International Monetary Fund
Independent 229
India 240
Indonesian Bank Restructuring Agency
    (Ibra)
    asset restructuring 150–1, 324–6, 332,
        365, 381
    Bank Bali scandal 246–9, 252, 287–9,
        364, 391
    Manulife case 382–5 *passim*
Indonesian Committee for World Muslim
    Solidarity (Kisdi) 68, 180, 349
Indonesian Corruption Watch (ICW) 244,
    252, 284–5, 298, 389
Indonesian Council of Ulama (MUI) 241
Indonesian Democratic Party (PDI) 3, 7–9,
    11, 20, 74, 154, 174, 176, 200, 330
Indonesian Democratic Party of Struggle
    (PDI Perjuangan)
    cabinet representation 327, 361
    campaigning 203–7 *passim*, 215–17, 224,
        226, 238–9, 317, 319
    candidate lists 240–1
    electoral strength of 217, 243, 415
    founding of 172, 174, 205
    Lippo scandal 288
    political alliances 291–3, 296–7, 300–1,
        304–5, 308–9, 408–9
    stance on reforms 389, 391
    stance on Wahid 362, 387, 397, 402
    see also Soekarnoputri, Megawati
Indonesian Mujahidin (Amin) 233–4, 366
Indonesian Muslim Students' Action Group
    (Kammi) 176
Indonesian National Students Movement
    (GMNI) 249
Indonesian National Youth Organization
    (KNPI) 119
Indonesian Nationalist Party (PNI) 7
Indonesian Plywood Association (Apkindo)
    45, 47, 53–4, 77
Indonesian Solidarity for Amien and Mega
    (Siaga) 69
Indrawati, Sri Mulyani 332
inflation 4, 22, 24–6, 52, 60, 62, 65, 147–8,
    323; *see also* financial crisis
integrationist militias *see* East Timorese
    militias

intelligence *see* Strategic Intelligence
    Agency
Interfet *see* International Force on East
    Timor
International Commission of Jurists 146
International Committee of the Red Cross
    (ICRC) 272
International Finance Corporation (IFC)
    382–5 *passim*
International Force on East Timor
    (Interfet) 276–7
International Foundation for Election
    Systems (Ifes) 225–6
International Monetary Fund (IMF)
    assistance package 44–7, 324
    attention to corruption 59, 231, 366,
        384
    Bank Bali audit 248, 283, 287–9
    November 1997 bank closures 47–51
    political relations 52–4, 64, 76–7
    stance on currency board 66, 75
    structural reform 53, 85, 87, 372
investment 23, 28, 38–42, 323, 326–7, 366
IPK *see* Association of Offspring of Military
    Personnel Posted to the Civilian
    Bureaucracy
IPTN *see* Nusantara Aircraft Industry
Iramasuka caucus *see* Golkar
Iran 18, 173
Iraq 15, 173
Irian Jaya
    autonomy 333, 372–3
    cabinet representation 327
    comparisons to East Timor 211, 257,
        260, 280
    conflict 235, 350–1, 395
    military role 110, 390, 413
Iskandar, Muhaiman 292
Islamic Clerics Conference 206–7
Islamic Defense Front (FPI)
    alleged political violence 187–8, 192,
        346–7, 377
    November 1998 MPR session 180
    political stance 400, 411
Islamic militants 188, 233–4, 350, 357,
    374–5, 385, 412
Islamic Students Alumni Association
    (Kahmi) 155, 220, 249
Islamists
    origins 16
    relations with military 348–9, 400–1,
        403–4
    stance on Amien Rais 177

stance on Megawati 205, 412
stance on Wahid 251, 305, 362, 394
Ismail, Chaeruddin 402
Ismail, Nur Mahmudi 292, 397
Ismudjoko 245, 306–9, 339
Israel 363
Isrok, Agus 294
ITB *see* Bandung Institute of Technology
Istiqlal Mosque 233; *see also* bombings

Jacoeb, Sofjan 413
Jakarta Garrison
    former officers of 72, 110, 164, 217–18,
        336, 375, 390
    May riots and aftermath 99, 105–6, 110,
        124, 143
    use of para-militaries 13, 163, 183, 188,
        346–7
Jakarta Post 95
Jakarta Stock Exchange (JSE) 23, 38–40,
    42–4, 50
Jakarta Stock Exchange bombing 376–8
Japan 66, 267
Javanese culture
    consensus 179, 195, 201
    influence on presidents 66, 176–7, 179,
        204, 327, 367
    mysticism 15, 166–7, 402
    power 66, 108, 113, 116
    wayang operas 113, 196
Jiwa Asuransi Manulife Indonesia *see*
    Manulife
JSE *see* Jakarta Stock Exchange
judiciary *see* court system
Justice Party *see* Partai Keadilan
Justice and Unity Party (PKP) 219, 223
Joedono, Satrio Budihardjo 'Billy' 287–8,
    422
Joint Fact-Finding Team (TGPF) 101–4
Jordan 240

Kadi, Suarip 373, 387, 399
Kahmi *see* Islamic Students Alumni
    Association
Kalbe Farma 35
Kalimantan strife 224–5, 395-6
Kalla, Jusuf 344–5, 362, 422
Kammi *see* Indonesian Muslim Students'
    Action Group
Karawang riot 193
Kartasasmita, Ginandjar
    background 422–3
    candidacy for high office 63, 228, 306–7

economy portfolio 76–7
political alliances 129, 144, 250–51, 303,
   313, 315
scandals 288–9, 393
Kartasasmita, Syafiuddin 410, 413
kekaryaanisasi 202
Kelapa Gading Mall 231, 233; *see also*
   bombings
Kertanegara, Yusuf 223
Ketapang riot 186-8, 193, 346, 348, 375
keterbukaan 146
Kia Motors *see also* Timor Putra Nasional 46
kidnappings *see* student movement
Kiemas, Taufik 7, 293, 321, 362, 394, 405,
   423
Kisdi *see* Indonesian Committee for World
   Muslim Solidarity
KKN 29–31, 44, 72, 365, 409;
   see also corruption
KKN Bill *see* State of Emergency Bill
KNPI *see* Indonesian National Youth
   Organization
Kohl, Helmut 53
Komite Reformasi 128, 132, 134
Komnas Ham *see* National Commission on
   Human Rights
Kompas 95–6, 365, 391
Kopassus *see* Special Forces
Kopkamtib *see* Operational Command for
   the Restoration of Security and
   Order
Korpri *see* civil service
Kosgoro 104, 119
Kostrad *see* Strategic Army Reserve
KPP Ham Timtim *see* Commission on
   Investigating Human Rights Abuses
   in East Timor
KPU *see* General Election Commission
krismon *see* financial crisis
Kristiono, Bambang 69
Kupang riots 192, 207
Kusumaatmadja, Sarwono 94, 121, 154, 156,
   162, 183, 328, 423

Laksono, Agung 236
Lamborghini SpA 230, 367
Laskar Jihad
   anti-US protests 411
   Kostrad scandal 371–2
   Maluku violence 347, 349, 374
   November 1998 MPR session 180, 292
Laskar Merah Putih 401
Latief, Abdul 75

Latief, Col. Abdul 5
Latumahina, Freddy 290
Law on Sharing Natural Resource Revenues
   333
Lebaran *see* Ramadhan
Legal Aid Foundation 69, 70, 80, 106, 185,
   233–4, 242, 342, 378
legal formalism 119, 126, 247, 288
legal system reform *see* reform
Lehman Brothers 365
Leksono, Budi 184–5, 371
Liquica massacre 261
liquidity credits (BLBI) 42, 49, 64, 324, 365;
   see also scandals
Litaay, Alex 206
Lombok riot 350, 357
Lopa, Baharuddin 392, 423
Lotulung, Paulus 151
Lubis, Pande 253, 285–6, 364, 391, 423
Lubis, Todung Mulya 242
Lucas 384–5
Lukita, Enggartiasto 290
Lustrilanang, Pius 69–70, 79–81

M/V *Doulos* 347
Ma'arif, Syafii 313–14, 423
Ma'arif, Syamsul 184
Madagascar 240
Madjid, Nurcholish
   background 392, 423
   election preparations 145, 213–14
   fall of Soeharto 90, 121–4, 126–30, 134
   presidential candidacy 310–11
   stance on violence 192, 195, 207, 386–7
Mahathir *see* Mohamad, Mahathir
Mahendra, Yusril Ihza
   background 132–4, 423
   consideration for high office 251, 314,
     316, 408
   justice portfolio 328, 356, 410
   political alliances 211, 292, 313, 362
   stance on reforms 363–6, 391–2
   support for military 345, 387
Mahesa, Desmond 70, 80
Mahfud, Mohammad 377, 386, 390, 396
Mahidi militia 259, 272–3, 413
Makarim, Zacky Anwar
   background 12, 423
   East Timor investigations 341–3, 351,
     375
   East Timor role 257–61, 268–9, 279,
     335, 348, 390
   May riots and aftermath 108–10, 115–16

Makassar 139
Makro 230
Malaysia 22, 36, 44, 85
Maliana massacres 270, 273
Mallarangeng, Andi 197, 201, 213, 218, 423
Maluku
    conflict 193, 395
    links to Ketapang riot 186, 188, 348
    military role 224, 234–5, 293, 347–51,
        368, 371, 374–5
Manan, Bagir 363, 398
Mandala Airlines 371
Mangkoedilaga, Benjamin 363
Mangkusubroto, Kuntoro 129
Manulife 382–5
Marasabessy, Suaidi 235, 348, 359, 400,
    423–4
Mardiyanto 159
Mardjono, Hartono 316, 345
Marimutu Manimaren 59, 236–7, 252–4,
    286, 287, 289–90, 424
Marimutu Sinivasan
    background 424
    Texmaco Scandal 55–9, 247, 330–32,
        335, 337, 342, 361, 372, 387–8
    Tim Sukses 236, 289–90
    see also Texmaco
Marin, Djasri 185
marines 90, 97, 105, 165, 183–4, 193, 350
Marthadinata 100–1
martial law 4, 115, 133
Martin, Ian 271, 274
Mastamu, Sadrakh 187–8
Masud 92, 94
Matraman riot 14–15, 67, 214
Maulani, Zen 172
May riots 97–117 *passim*, 142, 164, 223, 341
Mbak Tutut *see* Soeharto, Tutut
McBeth, John 188, 234
McCarthy, John 272
Mecca 206
Medan Congress of 1996 *see* Indonesian
    Democratic Party
Medan riots 85, 87–8, 98
Medco 391
Media Indonesia 95
Megawati *see* Soekarnoputri, Megawati
Merpati 142
Messerschmitt 140
Metareum, Ismail Hasan 121, 125
military (TNI)
    backing vice 223, 293–4, 332, 338,
        413–4

Banyuwangi killings 169–71
business interests 62, 82, 97, 107, 219,
    257, 338, 371–2, 386, 414
cabinet representation 144, 327, 374
civilian supremacy over 330, 334, 341,
    360, 380, 387, 389–90, 403
clashes with police 395–7, 413
criticism of 82, 171, 336–9
dual-function doctrine 8–9, 200, 202,
    326, 393
East Timor investigations 341–4, 355–6,
    385, 397
historic role 4, 8, 106, 113, 153, 280,
    403
links to Islamic militants 348–9, 350–1,
    371, 374–5, 385, 400–1
links to political violence 234, 370–71,
    374–5, 377–8, 380, 385–7
May riots 99–101, 104–8, 164
parliamentary representation 86, 89,
    178–9, 195, 202–3, 374, 410–11
political alliances 250–1, 291, 301–3,
    307–8, 311–12, 315, 317, 318–21,
    408
political manoeuvring of 162, 200, 218,
    307, 310–11, 373–4, 390, 398–9
preman and para-military links 12,
    106–8, 180–6, 235, 342, 346–7, 350
proposed legislation 163, 293–5 *passim*
relations with Amien Rais 82, 251, 313
relations with Habibie and Golkar 142,
    144, 154, 159
relations with political Islam 18, 174,
    180, 345, 349, 387, 402, 404, 410,
    415
relations with Soeharto 81–2, 113–17,
    126, 130, 195
reshuffles 70–1, 257, 328–30, 359, 367,
    390, 398
role in Aceh 164–5, 332–4
role in East Timor 211–12, 235, 256–61,
    263, 267, 271, 352, 412
stance on Wahid 387, 398, 402
student movement 78–9, 96, 114,
    131–2, 309, 379, 403–4
territorial system 9, 107, 202, 337–8;
    see also army; navy; air force;
    marines; military police; police;
    ministry of defence; Strategic Army
    Reserve; Wiranto; Strategic
    Intelligence Agency; Special Forces;
    Sutarto, Endriartono
military police 82, 185, 223, 386

militias *see* para-militaries
ministerial triumvirate *see* triumvirate
ministry of defence 122, 133, 264, 329
ministry of finance 245, 247–8, 328, 384
ministry of forestry 54, 189, 370, 397
ministry of information 328, 360
ministry of research and technology 141,
    144, 287, 312
Moerdani, Benny 18, 79, 194, 195, 234, 424
Moerdiono 57–8, 60, 424
Mohamad, Mahathir 36
Mokodompit, Endang 47
Mokodongan 122–3
money politics
    attorney general's office 244–5
    Bank Bali scandal 251–4, 280, 283–91
        passim
    in Sulawesi 236, 242–3
    ministry of co-operatives 210–11
    political laws 203, 209
    poverty alleviation fund 75
    regional representatives 244, 297–8
    see also scandals
Mongid, A. 290
Morgan Stanley 24
Moscow *see* Russia
MPR *see* People's Consultative Assembly
MSCI *see* Morgan Stanley
Muchdi *see* Purwopranjono, Muchdi
Mugabe, Robert 401
Muhammad, Mar'ie 42–4, 47–51, 65, 287,
    386, 424
Muhammad, Yusuf 169
Muhammadiyah 16–7, 19, 81–2, 127–9, 169,
    177, 207–9, 221, 313–14
MUI *see* Indonesian Council of Ulama
Muis, Noer 268, 275–6
Muladi
    background 151, 424
    Bank Bali scandal 254, 283–4
    consideration for high office 316,
        318–9, 327, 372
    Soeharto investigations 191, 230, 240
    Tim Sukses 236–7, 250
Mulia Group 290
Mulya, Elang 93
Muni, Rozy 362
Murphy, Dan 258–9
Mursjid, Saadillah 123–4, 126–7, 130, 132–4
Murtopo, Ali 5, 174, 424
Myanmar 173, 240

N-2130 142

N-250 Gatotkaca 142
Nahdlatul Ulama (NU)
    anti-Communist pogrom 204, 362
    Banyuwangi killings 168–73 *passim*
    fall of Soeharto 118–19, 122, 127–9
    functional group representation 243
    origins 15–16, 17
    political counselling 304, 309, 311, 319,
        327
    political role 153, 176, 204, 208, 215,
        221, 409, 415
    stance on Megawati 208–9, 292–3
    use of para-militaries 194, 296, 397–8,
        401
    see also Wahid, Abdurrahman; Ansor
Nasution, Abdul Haris 31, 106, 220, 424
Nasution, Adnan Buyung
    background 69, 424
    defence of alleged corruptors 284, 331
    defence of Wiranto 342, 345
    election preparations 145, 213, 218
    May riots 110–11
    pro-democracy activism 90, 94, 195
    Soeharto investigations 190–92
National Awakening Party (PKB)
    cabinet representation 327, 335
    campaigning 207–8, 215, 226, 238
    chairmanship 366
    defence of Wahid 393, 407
    electoral strength of 205, 243, 415
    founding of 176
    political alliances 250–1, 292–3, 301–5,
        308–9, 311, 313–14, 317, 319, 321,
        404
    stance on Megawati 196, 208–9, 227
national car program *see* Timor Putra
    Nasional
National Commission on Human Rights
    (Komnas Ham)
    Banyuwangi killings 169
    East Timor investigations 258, 336, 340,
        345, 355-6, 375–6, 397
    Islamist protests against 347–9
    Kupang riots 192
    Maluku conflict 375
    mass rapes 100–2
    Semanggi shootings 184–5
    see also Commission on Investigating
        Human Rights Abuses in East
        Timor; Darusman, Marzuki
National Council of East Timorese
    Resistance (CNRT) 259, 269
National Discipline Campaign 113

National Front 160–2, 178
National Intelligence Coordinating Agency
    (Bakin) 172, 222
National Land Agency (BPN) 189
National Leadership Meeting (Rapim)
    see Golkar
National Logistics Agency (Bulog) 45, 53,
    231–3, 239, 364, 378, 388–90, 413
National Mandate Party (Pan)
    campaigning 207–9, 215, 226
    electoral strength of 205, 243
    founding of 177
    political alliances 305, 313–14, 362, 408
    see also Central Axis
National Unity Cabinet 327–30 passim
navy 9, 328–9, 380; see also military
Neiss, Hubert 76
Netherlands, the 59, 80, 240, 341
New Zealand 230, 264–6, 275
NGOs see non-government organizations
Nigeria 395
Ninja killings see Banyuwangi killings
Nobel Peace Prize 256, 272
Noer, Zarkasih 328, 344
non-government organizations (NGOs)
    101, 211, 233, 265, 401
Noorsy, Ichsanuddin 283–4, 288–9, 424
Northern Ireland 93
Notre Dame 15
Novanto, Setya 246–9, 251–2, 286, 289–91,
    364, 424
NU see Nahdlatul Ulama
Nurcholish see Madjid, Nurcholish
Nursalim, Syamsul 35, 61–2, 208, 246,
    304–5, 393, 424
Nusamba Group 37, 43, 53–4
Nusantara Aircraft Industry (IPTN) 46,
    140–2

Obuchi, Kiezo 268
OECD see Organisation for Economic
    Co-operation and Development
Officers Honour Council 111
Opec see Organization of Petroleum
    Exporting Countries
Operational Command for the Restoration
    of Security and Order (Kopkamtib)
    76, 107, 121–3
Organisation for Economic Co-operation
    and Development (OECD) 212
Organization of Petroleum Exporting
    Countries (Opec) 161

P3TT see Taskforce on the East Timor
    Consultation
Pakubuwono 196
Pan see National Mandate Party
Pancasila Youth see Pemuda Pancasila
Pangestu, Prajogo 35, 332, 393
Panigoro, Arifin 219–20, 391
Panin Overseas Finance 384
Panjaitan, Luhut 335
Panjaitan, Sintong 143
Panji 219–21, 248
Panwaslak see Election Oversight Committee
Papua see Irian Jaya
para-militaries
    Anti-Communist Alliance 400
    army doctrine 106, 258
    controversy over 178, 346–7
    May riots 104–5
    November 1998 MPR session 180–6
    Wiranto 113, 163–4, 194
    see also East Timorese militias; preman,
        FPI; Laskar Jihad
parliament (DPR)
    composition of 9, 89, 179, 209
    hearings on scandals 49, 60, 283–9
        passim, 330, 388–91, 397–8
    political influence of 265, 354, 360, 402
    political laws 197–203 passim
    relations with Soeharto 88, 119–21, 124,
        125–6, 130, 132–4, 368, 409
    stance on reforms 337, 356, 368, 372,
        389
Partai Keadilan 292, 327
PBB see Crescent and Star Party
PDI see Indonesian Democratic Party
PDI Headquarters raid
    military involvement 9–15, 20, 107, 223
    political significance of 3, 67, 174, 402
    student movement 67, 69
PDI Perjuangan see Indonesian Democratic
    Party of Struggle
PDKB 407
Pemuda Panca Marga 107, 180
Pemuda Pancasila
    Anti-Communist Alliance 401
    involvement in strife 13, 104–7, 187–8,
        193, 348, 350
    PDI Headquarters raid 180, 194–5, 238,
        342, 346, 352
Pentagon 67, 112, 263, 274–5; see also US
    military
People's Consultative Assembly (MPR)
    alliances within 285, 293

appointed members 203, 210, 243–4
August 2000 session 373
composition of 145, 175, 203, 209–10, 243
constitutional authority 86, 115, 120, 153, 160, 361
emergency powers 76, 86, 115
July 2001 session 398, 401–2, 407
jurisdiction over East Timor 256
November 1998 extraordinary session 160–5 *passim*, 171–3, 178–9, 258
October 1999 session 295–6
Soeharto-era elections 6–8, 21, 73–5
see also Harmoko
People's Democratic Party (PRD) 67, 79–80, 214, 401
People's Economy concept 148, 149
People's Mandate Council 89–90, 109
people's power movement *see* student movement
People's Republic of China (PRC) 101
Pepabri *see* Retired Armed Forces Officers Association
Peregrine Securities 36
Pertamina 31, 47, 140, 232, 239, 367, 393
Petition of 50 161
Petrus, Bimo 80
Philippine embassy bombing 374–5; *see also* bombings
Philippines 22, 44
PKB *see* National Awakening Party
PKI *see* Communist Party
PKP *see* Justice and Unity Party
PKU 208, 215
Plaza Atrium 233; *see also* bombings
Plaza Hayam Wuruk 233; *see also* bombings
plywood industry 45, 53–4, 55; *see also* Indonesian Plywood Association
PNI *see* Indonesian Nationalist Party
pogrom, anti-communist 5, 169, 171–2, 362
police (Polri)
    alleged corruption 363, 383–5, 412
    clashes with military 395–7, 413
    East Timor role 256, 263–4, 267, 271, 355, 376, 396
    Liquica massacre 261
    Lombok riot 350
    Maluku role 293, 374, 396
    May riots 97, 105
    organization of 9, 91, 93–4, 264, 329
    Semanggi shootings 183
    stalled investigations 233–4, 287–8, 366, 370–1, 374, 385, 413
    student demonstrations 165, 308–9
    Tommy Soeharto case 377–80
political laws 197–203 *passim*, 213, 217, 360–1
Polri *see* police
population 3, 10, 17
Portugal 211
Poso strife 196
poverty 6, 51, 142, 148, 209, 416
PPP *see* United Development Party
Prabowo *see* Subianto, Prabowo
Prabowo, Titiek 39, 67, 229, 239–40, 424
Pradjoto 245–6
Pradopo, Timur 92
Pratama, Rama 176
Pratiwo, Wiwid 184–5
Prawiro, Radius 230
PRC *see* People's Republic of China
PRD *see* People's Democratic Party
preman
    origins 11–15
    May riots 97, 99–100, 105–8
    Ketapang riot 186–8
    FPI 346–7
    alleged political attacks 350, 366–7
    see also para-militaries; East Timorese militias
presidential security guards (Paspampres) 184–6, 192, 360, 370–1, 380
PricewaterhouseCoopers (PwC) 283, 287–91, 305, 364
privatisation *see* state-owned enterprises
Probosutedjo 46, 47, 127, 185, 349
pro-democracy activism
    demands for elections 144–5, 176, 178
    protests 291, 308–9, 317, 319, 379
    see also student movement
pro-integration militias *see* East Timorese militias
proportional voting *see* electoral system
PSM *see* Putra Surya Multidana
Purwopranjono, Muchdi 109–10, 115–16, 126
Puspowardojo, Tuti Marini 139
Putra, Hutomo Tommy Mandala *see* Soeharto, Tommy
Putra Surya Multidana (PSM) 35
Putra Surya Perkasa Group 382
PwC *see* PricewaterhouseCoopers

Queen Beatrix 357

Rachman, Muhammad Abdur 410

Radjasa, Hatta 313
Raffles, Stamford 55
Rahardja, Hendra 47
Rais, Amien
    as MPR Speaker 302, 321
    background 15, 19, 425
    calls for *jihad* 349
    campaigning 195, 207–9, 215, 225–6
    consideration for high office 63, 251,
        313, 394, 408
    fall of Soeharto 115, 124, 127, 130–2
    military relations 82, 251
    November 1998 MPR session 162,
        176–8
    political alliances 301–5, 310, 312–14,
        317, 320, 327–8
    pro-democracy activism 73, 74, 79, 82,
        84, 89–90, 94, 109, 114, 308
    relations with Wahid 227, 251, 292
    stance on reforms 142, 144–5, 229,
        372
rallies *see* student movement
Ralston, Joseph 269
Ramadhan 52, 201
Ramayana department store 193, 233–4;
        see also bombings
Ramelan, Rahardi 144, 232–2, 244–5
Ramli, Rizal 331, 335, 373, 383, 425
Ramli, Rudy 245–9 *passim*, 252–4, 283–5,
        364, 425
rape 85, 100–2
Rapim *see* National Leadership Meeting
Rasyid, Ryaas 197, 199, 328
Raweyai, Yorrys 13–15, 187–8, 194–5, 342,
        350; *see also* Pemuda Pancasila
Razi, Fachrul 329, 335, 356, 360
recapitalisation *see* banking system
Rector's Forum 242
reforestation funds 53, 141; *see also* scandals
reform
    anti-corruption efforts 330, 391–4
    decentralisation 332–3, 395, 413
    deregulation 42, 45–7, 53
    of electoral system 146, 198–9, 390, 405
    of state-owned enterprises 361-3
    of the legal system 44, 150, 158, 309,
        324–7, 335, 363-6 *passim*, 393–4,
        398, 410
    of the military 335–9 *passim*, 354,
        359–60
    of the press 146, 308
    prospects for 404–5, 416
Reform Cabinet 128–9, 134

reformasi 10, 95, 179, 197, 199, 202, 222;
        see also reform
refugees 266, 270–1, 277, 343, 375–6, 395–6
Regional Autonomy Law 333
rents (economic) 29, 45–6, 75, 77, 367
Republican Party 214
Republika 95
Retired Armed Forces Officers Association
        (Pepabri) 156
Riady, James 288, 290, 425
riots *see* student movement; May riots
riots *see* strife
Roesmanhadi 172
Roman Gold Assets International 382–4,
        385
Rose Team 69–70, 79–81, 115; *see also*
        Special Forces
Roy, Stapleton 269
Royan, Hafidin 93
Rubin, Robert 65
Rudini 145, 147, 218, 300, 425
Rukmana, Siti Hardiyanti *see* Soeharto,
        Tutut
rule-of-law
    contrast with Ruler's Law 150, 151, 191,
        221–2, 264, 322, 326, 385, 403
    deficiencies under Soeharto 29, 44,
        101, 135
    pledges to enforce 216, 245, 330–2
    prospects for 404–5, 416
    Wahid-era resistance to 358–9, 365,
        392–3, 398
Ruler's Law *see* rule-of-law
Rusdihardjo 377, 389
Russia 240
Ryacudu, Ryamizard 373–4

Saad, Hasballah 328
Saadillah *see* Mursjid, Saadillah
Sabarno, Hari 411
Sabirin, Syahril 59, 65, 252, 254, 285–6,
        425
Sadikin, Ali 160–1
Saefuddin, A.M. 205–6, 241, 425
Salim Group 45–6, 48, 254, 327, 365;
        see also Salim, Sudono; Salim,
        Anthony; Bank Central Asia
Salim, Anthony 51, 254, 425
Salim, Emil 63, 90, 94, 145, 147, 386–7, 425
Salim, Haji Agus 63
Salim, Sudono 31, 45, 51, 61, 254, 332,
        364–5, 425; *see also* Salim Group
Salossa, Jaap 414

Sambas *see* Kalimantan strife
Samoa 382, 384
Sampit *see* Kalimantan strife
Sandstrom, Sven 288
Sandyawan, Romo 104
Santa Cruz massacre 155–6, 211
santri see cultural streams
Sapuan 388–9
Sarosa, Yakob 276–7, 425
Sarwata 133–4, 151, 363–5, 425
Sasono, Adi 144, 149–50, 196, 210–11, 244
Sastrowardoyo, Sanyoto 75
Satelindo 31, 239
Satrio Piningit 402
scandals
    Balongan refinery 393
    Bank Bali 245–9, 251–4, 280, 283–91
        passim, 293, 324, 339, 355–6, 364,
        388, 391
    Bank Indover 59
    Buloggate and Bruneigate 373, 388–91
    Bulog-related 244
    Busang Gold 36–7
    forestry helicopters 370
    Ghalib graft 244–5
    Ghalibie tape 218–24 *passim*
    Goro-Bulog 230–3, 364, 378, 410, 413
    Kostrad 371–3
    Lippo 288
    Liquidity Credits 59–62, 208, 364–5
    reforestation funds 53, 141
    social safety net 149–50, 244
    Special Forces narcotics 293–4
    Texmaco 55–9, 330–2, 334, 339, 355–6,
        361, 364
    Ustraindo Petro Gas 393
    see also money politics
Sediono, Herman 376
Semanggi I 181–6 *passim*, 193, 294, 353–4,
    371
Semanggi II 295, 307
Semanggi interchange 180, 181
Semen Gresik 381, 412
Sempati 367
Seventh Development Cabinet 75–6, 303
Shelton, Hugh 274–5
Shihab, Alwi 304, 313–14, 316, 320, 425
Shihab, Habib Muhammad Riziq 411
Shihab, Quraish 134
Siaga 288
Siaga *see* Indonesian Solidarity for Amien
    and Mega
Siagian, Burhanudin 269

Siddiq, Jaffar 411
Sie, Hendriawan 93
Sigit, Ari 230, 239, 425
Sigit, Eno 229
Sihaloho, Aberson Marle 295
Silaen, Timbul 341
Silalahi, Sudi 217–18, 110, 370, 375, 400,
    425–6
Simbolon, Mahidin 259, 390, 414
Simbolon, Romulo 373
Sinambela, Mahadi 244
Singapore 22, 44, 66, 240, 253–4, 384
Siregar, Hariman 252–4, 286
Sitompul, Ruhut 342, 350, 352–3, 426
Soares, Abilio 265, 270
social safety net *see* World Bank
Soedirdja, Surjadi 358
Soedjatmiko, Boediman 67, 214, 401
Soegianto, Djoko 355
Soeharto
    background 3–5, 8, 30, 139, 426
    corruption investigations 189–92 *passim*,
        219, 228–30, 306, 355–6, 364–5,
        376–8, 391
    corruption scandals 49, 51, 55–62, 85,
        239–40, 330
    demands for prosecution of 158, 171,
        175, 178, 193, 239, 379, 416
    economic management 6, 42, 44, 47,
        51–4, 64–6, 74–5, 77
    emergency powers 76, 115, 120, 354
    fall from power 95–6, 109, 114–16,
        118–35 *passim*, 394
    loyalists of 188, 329, 335, 350, 360, 380,
        388, 400
    military management 71–2, 109, 114,
        328, 403, 413
    opposition to elections 235
    PDI HQ raid 3, 13, 15, 20
    political management 18–9, 63–4, 115,
        155–7, 161, 211–2, 218, 363, 366
    political violence 369, 376–7
    relations with Bob Hasan 31, 45, 54, 77,
        392
    relations with Habibie 18, 46, 128–9,
        139–41, 185, 397
    student protests 66–7, 72, 79, 84, 88,
        94–5
    traditional worldview 66, 179, 367
Soeharto family
    banks 48, 50
    corruption scandals 31–2, 36, 44, 62,
        327, 393

links to Islamic militants 234
political associates 76, 187, 214, 231,
    292
relations with military 71, 185, 223, 335,
    351
wealth 189–90, 229–30, 239, 309
Soeharto, Bambang
    alleged corruption 31, 48, 50, 75, 157,
        233
    alleged political violence 50, 233–4
    background 426
    defence of Soeharto 123, 190, 194
    role in FKPPI 107
Soeharto, Maj. Gen. 112
Soeharto, Sigit 37, 62, 229, 239–40, 426
Soeharto, Titiek see Prabowo, Titiek
Soeharto, Tommy
    alleged Islamic-militant links 234, 377
    alleged political violence 233–4,
        368–71, 377
    background 426
    evasion of justice 377–81, 385, 410,
        412–3, 416
    Goro-Bulog scandal 230–3 passim, 236,
        364, 378
    monopolies 46, 75, 77, 367
    Soeharto investigations 190
    wealth 229–30, 239–40
Soeharto, Tutut
    alleged preman ties 348
    background 426
    corruption scandals 36–7, 44, 50, 54,
        75, 62, 73, 157
    currency board system 64
    fall of Soeharto 134
    political allies of 75–6, 120, 335
    relations with Wahid 21, 83, 309
    wealth 229–30, 239–40, 257
Soekarno
    background 4, 5, 7
    Constitution 115
    Guided Democracy 214–15, 403
    leadership style 179, 203–4, 332
    political demise 94, 161, 162
    tributes to 305
Soekarnoputra, Guntur 10
Soekarnoputri, Megawati
    attention to strife 347, 396
    background 5, 20, 426
    campaigning 203–4, 215–17, 225, 239
    November 1998 MPR session 162, 171,
        172, 176–8
    PDI Headquarters raid 3, 10–15, 63

political alliance-forming 249–51, 285,
    291–3, 295, 300–1, 308–11, 313–14
presidential administration 407, 410–12
presidential campaign 304–5, 315–17,
    393
relations with political Islam 82, 204–7,
    226–7, 240–1, 313, 404, 409, 415
relations with student movement 79, 83,
    85, 94
relations with the military 216, 294, 308,
    357, 372–3, 402, 413
stance on East Timor 212, 400
stance on reforms 198–9, 389, 404–5
stance on Soeharto 130, 228–9
stance on Wahid 394, 397, 401
vice-presidential election 318–21, 328
see also Indonesian Democratic Party of
    Struggle
Soekarnoputri, Rachmawati 10
Soenarto 364
Soewondo 388–9
Sonny 80
South Africa 240
South Korea 22, 32, 46, 142, 147
Sovereignty of the Islamic Community
    Faction (FPDU) 320, 345, 408
Spain 240
Special Forces
    activist kidnappings 68–70, 79–81
    alleged political violence 172–3, 234,
        350, 378, 386, 413–4
    covert operations 107–8, 234, 258
    East Timor role 146, 258–60, 268, 272
    May riots and aftermath 105–6, 143–4
    narcotics scandal 293–4
    Trisakti shootings 93–4
speculators see currency traders
Sriwijaya Garrison 386
Standard Chartered 245–6, 364, 381
state banks 29, 31, 32, 361, 49, 56–7, 330;
    see also banking system; state-owned
    enterprises
State of Emergency (KKN) Bill 293–5 passim
state-owned enterprises 9, 140–2, 202, 325,
    327, 330, 361–3, 372; see also state
    banks
Steady Safe 36
Strategic Army Reserve (Kostrad)
    bombing links 378
    corruption scandal 371–2
    former commanders of 5, 9, 71, 143
    May riots and aftermath 106, 108–11,
        143–4

role in Maluku 293, 371
strategic industries *see* state-owned
  enterprises
Strategic Intelligence Agency (Bais)
  alleged political violence 170–3 *passim*,
    386
  command changes 257, 269, 335–6
  East Timor role 274
  Ghalibie tape scandal 223
  political manoeuvring of 279, 318, 336,
    357
  role 9, 222
  use of para-militaries 107, 258
strife, episodes of
  Aceh 164–5, 333–4, 349, 395
  anti-Chinese 85, 98–100
  Bantiqiyah massacre 293
  Banyuwangi killings 166–73 *passim*,
    350–1, 371
  Carrascalao house massacre 262
  Cendana raid 379
  Ciamis killings 235
  election-related 224, 238, 317, 319
  food riots 52
  Kalimantan 224–5, 395-6
  Karawang riot 193
  Ketapang riot 186–8, 193, 346, 348, 375
  Kupang riots 192
  Liquica massacre 261
  Lombok riot 350, 357
  Maliana massacres 270, 273
  Maluku 193, 195, 234–5, 347–50, 371,
    374–5
  Matraman riot 14–15, 67, 214, 401
  May riots 97–117 *passim*, 142, 164, 341
  Medan riots 85, 87–8, 98
  Poso 196
  Santa Cruz Cemetery massacre 211
  Semanggi I and II 181–6 *passim*, 294–5,
    353–4
  Suai church massacre 272–3, 376, 414
  Tanjung Priok massacre 155, 410
  Trisakti shootings 90–4, 103, 106, 108–9,
    116–17
  UNHCR attack 375–6, 378
  Wisma *Doulos* attack 345–6, 351
student activists *see* student movement
student movement
  anti-Soeharto rallies 72–3, 77–9, 83–6,
    90, 95, 114, 120–1, 124–5, 130–2,
    229, 306, 379
  clashes 88–90, 103, 180–6, 193
  kidnappings 69–70, 79–81, 164, 223

PDI Headquarters raid 13–14
pro-democracy activism 74–96 *passim*
stance on Habibie 142, 161–5 *passim*,
  175–7, 179–80, 308–9
stance on military 294–5, 353, 403–4,
  415
Trisakti shootings 90–4 *passim*
Suai church massacre 272–3, 376, 414
Suara Pembaruan 96
Subagyo *see* Hadisiswoyo, Subagyo
Subandrio 161
Subianto, Bambang 252–4, 285–6, 426
Subianto, Prabowo
  activist kidnappings 69–70, 79–81
  alleged aid to Tommy Soeharto 379
  background 67–8, 426
  fall of Soeharto 122–4, 126, 132
  May riots 108–12, 116
  military tribunal 164, 223
  relations with political Islam 180, 349
  relationship with Habibie 140, 141,
    142–4
  rivalry with Wiranto 71–2, 164
Subroto 161
Subroto, Djoko 169, 371–2
Sudan 240, 395
Sudarsono, Juwono 329, 390, 368–9, 371,
  427
Sudarto, Tyasno
  background 223, 427
  East Timor role 269, 274
  political manoeuvring 279, 308, 318,
    357
  promotion to Army chief-of-staff
    335–6
Sudharmono 131, 154
Sudibyo, Bambang 328, 335–6, 361, 372,
  427
Sudirman 220, 403
Sudjana, Eggy 350, 357
Sudono, Agus 290
Sudradjat, Edi 63, 71, 81, 155–9, 162, 219,
  223, 427
Sudradjat, Yaya 414
Sudrajat 334, 337, 343–4, 390, 427
Sugiono 329
Sukardi, Laksamana 330, 331–2, 335–6,
  360–1, 410–11, 427
Sulawesi Garrison 82, 132
Sultan of Brunei 388
Sultan of Yogyakarta *see* Hamengkubuwono X
Sumargono, Achmad 345, 349, 353, 427
Sumitro *see* Djojohadikusumo, Sumitro

Suparman, Djaja
    background 163, 329, 427
    links to Islamic militants 163, 180, 187,
        188, 346–7, 350, 371–2, 400
    October 1999 MPR session 295
    rivalry with Wirahadikusumah 336–7,
        359–60, 371–2
Supersemar 161
supreme advisory council (DPA) 222, 236,
    248, 284
Supreme Court 133, 151, 202, 289, 363,
    372, 378, 382–4, 391, 398, 407, 410
Surabaya protest 165
Suratman, Tono 258, 261, 268, 341–2, 427
Suryadi 7, 10–15, 174, 427
Suryo, Roy 223
Suta, I Putu Gede Ary 411
Sutarto, Endriartono
    background 360, 428
    relations with political Islam 403
    stance on reforms 371–2, 380, 387, 390,
        396, 399, 402
Sutiyoso 15, 163, 188, 295, 428
Sutjipto 402
Sutjipto, Adi Andojo 91–3, 213, 218, 428
Sutowo, Ibnu 47, 140
Sutrisno, Try 63, 76, 131, 155–9, 219, 223,
    374, 428
Suyat 80
Swain, Jon 276
Switzerland 191, 240, 309, 356
Syachrudin, Eky 286, 288
Syafie, Theo 207
Syahnakri, Kiki 279
Syamsoeddin, Syafrie
    background 72, 164, 218, 375, 428
    East Timor investigations 341
    fall of Soeharto 115, 124, 131–2
    May riots 99, 105–6, 258

Taiwan 22, 101
Tajuk 106
Tamaela, Max 348, 374–5, 398
Tamin, Feisal 217–18
Tandjung, Akbar
    1998 Golkar congress 155–9, 162
    background 155, 428
    Bank Bali Scandal 246, 248, 283, 285,
        288, 290
    campaigning 224–5
    consideration for high office 303, 315,
        317–21, 394, 408–9
    fall of Soeharto 119, 129–30

fall of Wahid 393, 397
Ghalibie tape scandal 221
    political alliances 249–51, 291, 293,
        301–6, 310–12, 314, 317, 327
    political loyalties 210, 228–9, 237, 240,
        244
    stance on East Timor 212
    stance on reforms 189, 197–8, 200–1,
        372, 389, 391
    see also Golkar
Tanjung Priok massacre 155, 410
Tanjung, Feisal
    alleged political violence 369
    background 71, 428
    East Timor investigations 351
    Garnadi document 265, 279, 342
    Ghalibie tape scandal 221
    political manoeuvring 207, 273
    politics and security portfolio 144, 245,
        276
Semanggi I 183
slander suit 146–7
Tansil, Eddy 47, 57
Taskforce on Restoration of Peace in
    Maluku 348
Taskforce on the East Timor Consultation
    (P3TT) 257–8, 279, 348
Taslam, Haryanto 70, 80
Tasmara, Toto 234
Team Eleven 213–14
Team Seven 197–200, 203
Telkom 381
Tempo 141, 146, 230, 351, 363, 369, 386
territorial system see military
Texmaco 43, 236–7, 289–90, 331–2, 361;
    see also scandals
TGPF see Joint Fact-Finding Team
Thailand 22, 27, 29, 39–41, 44, 147
Thoenes, Sander 276–7, 355
Thukul, Wiji 80
Tiananmen Square 132
Tim Buldoser 200, 209, 217
Tim Sukses Habibie
    Bank Bali Scandal 246–9, 251–4 passim,
        283–91
    May 1999 Rapim 236–7
    MPR strength 298, 305
    political alliance-forming 250, 293,
        312–13, 316, 328
Time 239–40, 395
Timor Gap Treaty 267
Timor Putra Nasional 46–7, 53, 66, 75, 142,
    367

Tirtamas Group 35, 67
Tirtosudiro, Achmad 220
Tjakrawerdaya, Subiakto 75, 129
Tjandra, Djoko 247, 249, 252–3, 286,
    289–90, 364, 428
TNI *see* military
Tomagola, Thamrin Amal 400
Tose, Philip 36
Tragedy at Semanggi *see* Semanggi I
Trihatmodjo, Bambang *see* Soeharto,
    Bambang
Trikora Garrison 390
Trisakti shootings
    description of 90–4
    explanations for 103, 106, 108–9, 116–7
    stalled investigation of 163, 164, 223,
    294
Trisakti University 90, 97; *see also* Trisakti
    shootings
triumvirate 133, 273
Truk *see* Volunteer Team for Humanity
Tutut, Mbak *see* Rukmana, Siti Hardiyanti;
    Soeharto, Tutut

Udayana Garrison 110, 259, 279, 341, 390
UGM *see* Gadjah Mada University
UI *see* University of Indonesia
UK *see* United Kingdom
Ummat 186
UN *see* United Nations
Unamet *see* United Nations Assistance
    Mission in East Timor
Ungaren Sari Garment 286
UNHCR *see* United Nations High
    Commissioner for Refugees
United Development Party (PPP)
    cabinet representation 327, 344–5
    campaigning 154, 209, 224, 238–9, 226
    electoral strength of 204–5, 243, 415
    fall of Soeharto 121
    history 20, 74, 80, 174
    November 1998 MPR session 175,
        178–9, 180
    political alliances 302, 305, 310, 320,
        408–9
    political laws 198, 200
    relations with Habibie 221, 286
    relations with Wahid 292, 344, 360, 262,
        389, 392
    see also Central Axis
United Kingdom (UK) 229, 267
United Nations (UN)
    contemplation of tribunal 341, 358

demands for justice 400
East Timor ballot 256–80 *passim*, 280
Millennium Summit 376
pressure for peace-keeping force
    262–4, 269, 288
recognition of East Timor 211–12,
    260
statement on mass rapes 101
see also United Nations Assistance
    Mission in East Timor
United Nations Assistance Mission in East
    Timor (Unamet) 256, 271, 266–7,
    270, 272, 274–5
United Nations High Commissioner for
    Refugees (UNHCR) 266, 375–6,
    378, 400; *see also* Atambua UNHCR
    attack
United Nations Security Council 271,
    274–5
United States (US)
    finance 23, 26, 32
    mass rapes 100–1
    stance on Aceh 280, 333
    views on presidential election 310–11,
    316
University of Indonesia (UI) 69, 119, 124,
    176, 180, 181, 400
university students *see* student movement
Untung 5
US *see* United States
US Congress 263
US military 67
US State Department 145; *see also* Albright,
    Madeleine; Holbrooke, Richard
US Treasury 240
Usborne, David 274
Usman, Marzuki 397
Ustraindo Petro Gas 393
Uzbekistan 240

Vietnam 240
Virgin Islands *see* British Virgin Islands
Volunteer Team for Humanity (Truk) 100–2

Wacano, Anneke 93
Wahid, Abdurrahman
    background 15–17, 20–1, 83, 219, 428
    Buloggate and Bruneigate 373, 379,
        388–91, 398
    cabinet formation 322, 326–30 *passim*
    campaigning 205, 207–9, 225–7, 243,
        296
    emergency decree 398–9, 407

erosion of support 344–5, 360–62, 365,
372–3, 376–7, 387–91, 397–8,
401–2, 407–8
November 1998 MPR session 162,
172–3, 176–8
political alliances 250–1, 292–3, 298,
301–2, 317–18
presidential campaign 305, 309–11,
313–17
relations with Amien Rais 82, 128, 227,
302
relations with Soeharto 21, 63, 83, 118,
127–8, 130, 194–6, 229, 309
relations with the military 172–3, 294,
335–9, 343–4, 353–8 *passim*, 359–60,
376, 380, 387, 413
stance on autonomy 212, 333
stance on corruption 332, 335, 362–3,
383, 387–8, 392–4
stance on student movement 79, 83, 85,
128, 379
Tommy Soeharto case 378–80
views on strife 340, 346–7, 349, 351,
387, 395–6
see also Nahdlatul Ulama; National
Awakening Party
Winata, Tommy 156, 219, 223, 428; *see also*
Artha Graha
Wahono 154
Wall Street 52
Waluyo, Bibit 390
Wanandi, Sofyan 79, 219
Washington Post 52
wayang see Javanese culture
Wayne, John 289
Widjaya, Yopie 36
Widjojanto, Bambang 106
Widodo *see* Adisutjipto, Widodo
Wijaya, Adi Purnomo 383
Wijoyo, Agus 360, 428
Wirahadikusumah, Agus
background 428–9
demise 411
Islamist attacks on 387
Kostrad role 359–60
military reform efforts 336–9, 341, 343,
368, 371–2, 399
Wiranto confrontation 356–7, 359,
372–4
Wirahadikusumah, Umar 5, 131, 336,
429
Wiranto
1998 Golkar congress 156, 158–9

alliance with political Islam 345, 350,
400, 403, 408
background 71, 82, 112–13, 429
candidacy for high office 225–6, 228,
293, 306–11, 317–21, 408
duplicity on East Timor 257–9, 262–3,
272, 274–5, 278–9, 288
East Timor investigations 341–4, 351–6,
365, 375
explanations for violence 171–3, 184,
195
fall of Soeharto 109, 114–16, 123–4,
126, 130–1, 133–5, 354
handling of Maluku strife 224, 348, 400
links to political violence 369, 371
November 1998 MPR session 162–5,
171–3, 176, 179, 345
para-militaries 113, 178, 180, 188, 194,
263, 279
political alliances 250–1, 292, 301,
313–14, 317, 327
political manoeuvring of 145, 153, 293
politics and security portfolio 328–30
protection of Soeharto 191–2, 220–1,
228–9
rift with Habibie 221–2, 271, 273–4
rivalry with Prabowo 72, 108, 142–4,
164, 185–6
role in May riots 108–14
Ruhut Sitompul link 342, 350
stance on Aceh 333–4
stance on East Timor ballot 212, 256–7,
266, 268–9
stance on military reform 294, 335–9
passim, 359–60, 372, 390
stance on political laws 200, 202, 218
student movement 73, 78, 81
Wahid confrontation 343–4, 353–8
passim
see also military
Wisma *Doulos* attack 345–6, 351
Witoelar, Erna 328
World Bank
attention to legal system 366, 382–5
passim
Bank Bali audit 252, 288–9
East Timor warnings 267
social safety net 148–50, 244
structural reform 45-6, 53–4, 87
World Trade Center attack 411

Yacob, Yohanes 191
Yafie, Ali 128, 241, 273

Yakmi 348
Yara, Muchyar 250
yayasan see charitable foundations
Yemen 240
Yohannes, Kim 284, 286
Yosfiah, Yunus 146–7, 158, 273, 415, 429;
    see also Balibo affair
Yudhoyono, Susilo Bambang
    background 81, 429
    cabinet portfolios 329, 373–4, 401–2,
        411
    May riots and Soeharto fall 112, 115,
        122, 124

PDI Headquarters raid 12–13, 15
political manoeuvring 195, 217
stance on East Timor brutality 280
stance on reforms 81–2, 145, 294, 336
vice-presidential candidacy 408–9
Yudohusodo, Siswono 94, 154, 156, 162,
    342, 408–9, 429
Yusril *see* Mahendra, Yusril Ihza
Yusuf, Glenn 246–7, 253, 285–6, 429
Yusuf, Muhammad 71

Zein, Kivlan 132
Zimbabwe 401